Linda McIntire.

Dawn

THE POLITICS OF MILITARY RULE
IN BRAZIL, 1964–85

THE POLITICS OF MILITARY RULE IN BRAZIL, 1964–85

THOMAS E. SKIDMORE

New York   Oxford   OXFORD UNIVERSITY PRESS   1988

Oxford University Press

Oxford   New York   Toronto
Delhi   Bombay   Calcutta   Madras   Karachi
Petaling Jaya   Singapore   Hong Kong   Tokyo
Nairobi   Dar es Salaam   Cape Town
Melbourne   Auckland
and associated companies in
Beirut   Berlin   Ibadan   Nicosia

Published by Oxford University Press, Inc.,
200 Madison Avenue, New York, New York 10016

Oxford is a registered trademark of Oxford University Press

Library of Congress Cataloging-in-Publication Data

Skidmore, Thomas E.
   The politics of military rule in Brazil 1964–85.
   Includes index.
   1. Brazil—Politics and government—1964–1985.
2. Military government—Brazil—History—20th century.
3. Brazil—Economic conditions—1964–   . I. Title.
F2538.25.S58 1988   981qr178.063   87-11147
ISBN 0-19-503898-3

for
Francis M. Rogers

9 8 7 6 5 4 3 2 1

Printed in the United States of America
on acid-free paper

PREFACE

Readers of my *Politics in Brazil, 1930–64: An Experiment in Democracy* (1967) may ask how it relates to this book. In the earlier work I was drawn into analyzing politics and economic policy making as far back as 1930 because the existing secondary literature was so thin. But my principal purpose was to explain the overthrow of the Goulart government in 1964. I saw that constitutional rupture as ending the era of democratic politics that had begun in 1945. Seen from the perspective of two decades later, that judgment seems confirmed. In analyzing the historical process that led to 1964, I looked closely at how the political elite had dealt with the difficult choices in economic policy, focusing on the party system and the constitutional structure, as well as the nationalistic economic views and vote-getting strengths of the populist politicians. Finally, I looked at the decisive actors of 1964—the military, especially the army officer corps.

The *raison d'être* for my new book can also be traced to 1964. But here I seek to describe and explain the political process created by the military's determination *not* to return power promptly to the civilian politicians, as they had done after all their other interventions since 1945. What kind of regime did they create as they successively tightened their grip in 1965, 1968, and 1969? And what kind of opposition emerged? To answer these questions I have treated at length the presidency of General Médici (1969–74), which saw the "national security state" in its purest form. Those years have repelled many scholars, both because of the government's unapologetic repression and because of its superficial success (1970 World Cup victory, 11 percent economic growth, etc.). Yet we can only understand the democracy of the New Republic if we understand in depth the authoritarian era—both the repression and the armed opposition—out of which it grew.

It is obviously more difficult to study an authoritarian political system than an open one. Censorship and repression have distorted the record, and much of the most important political bargaining was done offstage. The written sources therefore do not fully reflect the clash of interests, whether regional, sectoral, class, or institutional. We must infer much more than was the case for the 1945–64 era. That means any interpretation will be uncommonly subject to extensive revision as more official sources and key personal accounts become available.

During their rule the military were notoriously close-mouthed to outsiders. Yet even some prominent officers have told their story (and more revelations will undoubtedly appear). Brazil's journalists have also furnished a wealth of first-class reporting and commentary, despite difficult working conditions. In short, the printed sources on Brazil's authoritarian years are richer than an outsider might guess. Brazil, in comparison with military governments in Argentina, Uruguay, and Chile, has been far more accessible. This is partly because the repression was less severe in Brazil than in the other three countries. But it is also because post-1945 Brazilian political culture in general has proved more open that that of, for example, Argentina, with which Brazil is most often compared. That relative openness has been a great asset for researchers, both Brazilian and foreign.

One result has been the rapid maturation of Brazilian social science research. If there ever was a time when Brazilians needed to know English to follow scholarship about their country, those days are long past. In the story that follows I have tried to tap as much of that rich and rapidly growing Brazilian literature as possible. But in many cases I was only able to draw on selected findings. I hope my footnotes will guide readers wanting to consult this literature in depth.

One set of historical actors about which much is already being said is the group of "grass-roots" organizations, such as the Church's ecclesiastical base communities, the neighborhood associations, and the shop-floor union organizations. Alongside them have been active such established elite groups as the Bar Association, the national conference of bishops, and the industrial and commercial associations. All have wielded political weight, albeit at differing times and to differing effect. Continuing research on their role will be essential, not only to reveal how Brazil emerged from authoritarian rule but also to illuminate the dynamics and democratic potential of the New Republic. Just as the political polarization of the 1945–64 era determined much of the shape of military rule, so the political dialectics of the authoritarian years will continue to be played out as democratic habits are reinforced. Brazilian politics have long been famous for their continuity. The New Republic has proved no exception. It is no coincidence that President José Sarney and Congress President Ulysses Guimarães are both politicians whose careers extend back well beyond 1964.

Yet Brazil's hopes are understandably fixed on what has changed. My final chapter is devoted to an analysis of the first fifteen months (with a postscript to June 1987) of the New Republic. It is already clear that Brazil's new democracy will be severely tested by the need to deal with hard economic choices and with the insistent demands for greater social justice. Those of us who study Brazil from afar and who have come to love the country and its people can only add our fervent hope that Brazil will be able to realize the democracy, prosperity, and peace that its finest minds have articulated so often and so eloquently.

ACKNOWLEDGMENTS

In the course of writing this book I have received help from many friends who facilitated my research and made invaluable suggestions and comments. Those in the U.S. were Barry Ames, Werner Baer, Thomas Bruneau, John Cash, Joan Dassin, Peter Evans, Albert Fishlow, David Fleischer, Stanley Hilton, Samuel Huntington, Peter Knight, Joseph Love, Abraham Lowenthal, Dennis Mahar, Frank McCann, Samuel Morley, Robert Packenham, Carlos Peláez, Riordan Roett, Keith Rosenn, Alfred Stepan, David Trubek, Brady Tyson, and John Wirth.

There were many Brazilian friends who guided me to sources and offered invaluable advice: Neuma Aguiar, Márcio Moreira Alves, Fernando Henrique Cardoso, Luiz Orlando Carneiro, Claudio de Moura Castro, Roberto Cavalcanti, Celso Lafer, Bolivar Lamounier, Pedro Malan, Carlos Guilherme da Mota, Vanilda Paiva, José Pastore, Paulo Sergio Pinheiro, Wanderley Guilherme dos Santos, Glaucio Soares, Amaury de Souza, and Sandra Valle.

Two veteran interpreters of Brazilian reality, Alberto Dines and General Golbery do Couto e Silva, were kind enough to read an early draft. So was Jim Bumpus. All made invaluable comments but none saw the final version. Over the years I have profitted greatly from conversations with Carlos Chagas, Oliveiros Ferreira, and Fernando Pedreira, three eminent journalists always willing to share their insights into Brazilian politics. Other Brazilian friends of many years who have been especially generous with their support and knowledge of Brazil are Francisco de Assis Barbosa, Fernando Gasparian, Francisco Iglesias, Helio Jaguaribe, Isaac Kerstenetzky, Roberto da Matta, José Honório Rodrigues, and Alberto Venancio Filho. Among those who have served in U.S. government positions in Brazil and have helped me greatly are Myles Frechette, Lincoln Gordon, John Griffiths, Robert Sayre, and Alexander Watson. John Crimmins kindly gave me detailed comments on a draft of Chapter VI.

The Ford Foundation office in Rio de Janeiro has been most generous in allowing me to use their facilities, for which I am indebted to Eduardo

Venezian, David Goodman, James Gardner, and Bruce Bushey. Michael
Turner and Steve Sanderson, Ford Foundation program officers in Rio,
were both generous with their time. A special word of thanks goes to
Prescilla Kritz, who handled myriad tasks with an efficiency that multiplied
by many score the value of my time in Brazil. I am indebted also to the
staffs of the *Biblioteca da Camara dos Deputados* (Brasília) and of *O
Estado de São Paulo* for their efficiency in providing Xerox copies of
clippings.

Over the years I benefited from the able research assistance of Judith
Allen, Megan Ballard, Peter De Shazo, Thomas Holloway, Steve Miller,
Ernie Olin, Carlos Baesse de Souza, Anne True, and Helio Zylberstajn.
Kate Hibbard handled the entry onto the word processor with admirable
patience and disconcerting accuracy. Robert Skidmore did the index.

For financial support at successive stages of this book I am indebted to
the John Simon Guggenheim Foundation, the Woodrow Wilson International Center for Scholars, the Fulbright Faculty Research Abroad program and, at the University of Wisconsin, the Graduate School Research
Committee and the Nave Fund.

Sheldon Meyer has been my editor for my entire scholarly career. His
support and shrewd advice have meant much. Although a number of
friends gave valuable comments on portions of the manuscript, none saw it
in final form. Unfortunately, any errors that remain are mine. I thank my
wife for reasons that people who know her well or work with her will
understand.

Madison, Wisconsin   T.E.S.
July 1987

CONTENTS

THE POLITICS OF MILITARY RULE
IN BRAZIL, 1964–85

I

THE ORIGINS OF THE 1964 REVOLUTION

It was an early April 1 morning in Rio de Janeiro. Brazilian President João Goulart had spent the previous night at Palacio Laranjeiras, the Rio presidential residence. His trip to Rio had come at a critical time in 1964. His advisers warned that dissident army units from the inland state of Minas Gerais were marching on Rio to overthrow his government. A few die-hard advisers tried to convince Goulart that the military were loyal and would soon take this rebel faction into custody.

As the hours passed, however, the reports grew more alarming. A contingent of the Rio-based First Army had been sent to interdict the rebel army column approaching from Minas Gerais. But the loyalist commander and troops from Rio joined the rebel side as the two forces met. In Rio the marines had been alerted for action against Carlos Lacerda, the passionately anti-Goulart governor of Guanabara (greater Rio de Janeiro city). As tension at the marine base grew, a tank suddenly left, without orders, for Lacerda's palace. On arrival the tank drivers declared their support for the revolt and were greeted with jubilation by Lacerda and his aides. The ranks of loyalist troops were shrinking by the hour.

By late morning Goulart could see the military balance tipping against him. He had one last hope. No military coup could succeed without São Paulo's Second Army. It was commanded by General Amaury Kruel, who had not joined the revolt, in part because of his enmity toward General Castelo Branco, a key leader of the military revolt. The president called General Kruel and appealed for his continued loyalty. Kruel replied that his support depended on the president's breaking with the communist-led CGT (General Labor Command), whose influence the military rebels decried. Goulart demurred, arguing that his labor support was indispensable. "Then, Mr. President," Kruel replied, "there is nothing we can do."[1]

Goulart now knew his rule had effectively ended. From the U.S. Embassy and contacts at the airport, U.S. Ambassador Lincoln Gordon and his staff had been monitoring the traffic between Palacio Laranjeiras and Santos Dumont, the downtown airport. In the morning the presidential

3

limousine had set out for the airport but then returned to the palace. Did the president have second thoughts? Meanwhile, in Washington, National Security Adviser McGeorge Bundy was personally monitoring the cable traffic from Brazil, a sure sign of White House worry that Brazil might lurch to the left.[2] In the late morning the U.S. embassy again spotted the presidential limousine heading toward Santos Dumont. This time Goulart went straight to his plane and took off for Brasília.

Was he planning a last-ditch defense there, as his top civilian staff adviser Darcy Ribeiro was urging? But resistance without military support would be suicidal. It rapidly became apparent that Goulart's military support had vanished. From Brasília, Goulart flew to his home state of Rio Grande do Sul. There the Third Army commander had not yet joined the coup, so federal Deputy Leonel Brizola, Goulart's brother-in-law and the most visible radical nationalist spokesman, was calling for popular resistance. Goulart refused to join in. By April 2 the Third Army had joined the rebellion, precluding any chance of repeating the 1961 Third Army revolt that had won Goulart his succession to the presidency over the attempted veto of the military ministers. Two days later Goulart reluctantly crossed into Uruguay, a long-time refuge for South American political exiles.[3]

How had the Brazilian president's enemies been able to drive him from his office and his country? The most immediate explanation was that his die-hard civilian enemies had won over the military, essential for a successful coup. Some military needed no convincing. By 1963 they had decided Goulart was leading Brazil toward a socialist state which would liquidate the country's traditional values and institutions. They propounded their views in anti-Goulart memoranda circulated in military barracks throughout Brazil. They argued that the president must be deposed before his actions (military appointments, financial decisions, etc.) could undermine the military itself. The coordinator of the military conspirators was army chief of staff General Castelo Branco, a quiet, reserved soldier who had served with Brazil's army combat division in Italy in 1944–45. He was known as a highly correct and apolitical officer, a good reason to make him the coordinator.[4]

These conspirators shared a strongly anticommunist view developed in the military's *Escola Superior de Guerra* (Higher War College), modeled on the U.S. National War College. In Brazil it became a highly influential center of political thought through its one-year classes composed of equal numbers of senior-level civilians and military. The Cuban Revolution stimulated the Brazilian military to apply the theory of "internal war" to Brazil. Now the primary threat was defined as coming not from external invasion, but from leftist labor unions, intellectuals, peasant unions, clerics, and university students and faculty. They all threatened the country, and would all have to be neutralized or rooted out by decisive action.[5]

This anticommunist view was not new to Brazilian politics. In 1954 President Getúlio Vargas had been driven to suicide by a military conspiracy similar to that against Goulart. Vargas, who had earlier been Brazil's president from 1930 to 1945 (the last eight years in an authoritarian regime), had returned to the presidency by popular vote in 1951.[6] Given the many parallels between the fall of Vargas in 1954 and the overthrow of Goulart a decade later, the 1950s need a closer look.

Vargas's troubled 1951–54 presidency was marked by a deepening political polarization. The president's main party support came from the PTB (*Partido Trabalhista Brasileiro,* or Brazilian Labor Party), founded under Vargas's aegis in 1945. It was modeled on the European democratic socialist parties, and it became the major party on the left. But it was marked by personalism, and its ideological hue varied by state. The president launched an ambitious public investment program, only to see the economy founder, pulled down by plummeting coffee prices abroad and surging inflation at home. Determined to carry out his nationalist economic program (such as creation of a national oil monopoly) and at the same time improve workers' wages, Vargas, now a populist, found himself in 1953 forced to adopt a highly unpopular anti-inflation program. As if the economic crisis were not enough, he also faced a military conspiracy. His nationalist and populist policies had provoked an angry reaction among anticommunist officers, who by 1953 had captured the military leadership. The latter were especially upset in early 1954 over a large proposed minimum wage increase, while officers' take-home pay continued to shrink. The Labor Minister who recommended the wage increase was João Goulart, a young PTB politician and Vargas protégé from the same Rio Grande do Sul locale as his president.[7]

The anti-Vargas politicians and press dubbed Goulart "the chief of Brazilian Perónism."[8] Under intense political pressure, Vargas in late February 1954 fired Goulart, an early casualty in Vargas's battle with the antipopulists. The latter were led by the UDN (*União Democrático Nacional*), founded to fight the Vargas dictatorship in 1945 but soon to be the leading conservative party. By 1954 it was the anti-getulista force par excellence. Its most visible spokesman was Carlos Lacerda, a talented journalist who used his Rio daily, *Tribuna da Imprensa,* to blast Vargas with vicious personal and political attacks of every description.[9]

Firing Goulart proved no solution. Vargas's problems only got worse. Coffee sales abroad fell drastically, due in part to Brazil's misguided marketing policies. Vargas's ex-foreign minister accused Getúlio of plotting with Argentina's Juan Perón to form an anti-U.S. bloc in Latin America. The press was filled with exposés of government financial scandals. Faced with this onslaught, Vargas cast about for political allies. In May he decreed a 100 percent increase in the minimum wage, more even than Goulart had recommended. But it came too late to help mobilize working-class support.

By August, Vargas had been isolated by his enemies, whose ranks were growing daily. The president's head bodyguard, moved by his chief's plight, decided to arrange the elimination of Carlos Lacerda, Vargas's greatest tormentor. The assassin hired to kill Lacerda only wounded him but did kill an air force officer accompanying Lacerda. Vargas had known nothing of the assassination plot but was now even more vulnerable to his enemies. The air force mounted its own investigation, quickly tracing the assassin to the presidential palace. This inquiry also turned up more financial scandals, and thus more ammunition for Lacerda and the UDN.

The decisive voice now came from the army, always the ultimate arbiter in Brazilian politics. Twenty-seven generals, including both anti-getulistas and centrists, issued a manifesto demanding Vargas's resignation. "Criminal corruption" was a prime charge. The "politico-military crisis" threatened "irreparable damage to the country's economic situation." Finally, there was a threat of "grave internal disturbances."[10]

Vargas defied his accusers. He warned them he would never resign. After receiving another military ultimatum endorsed by the war minister, and after a somber cabinet meeting on November 24, Vargas exercised his last option. He retired to his quarters and fired a bullet through his heart. He left a suicide note blaming his defeat on "a subterranean campaign of international and national groups." Vargas was aiming at the international oil companies which had fought his successful creation of Petrobrás, the national oil monopoly. He denounced the "violent pressure upon our economy to the point of having to surrender," referring to the U.S. reaction to Brazil's attempt to keep coffee prices up. The now-dead Vargas concluded: "I gave you my life. Now I offer my death. Nothing remains. Serenely I take the first step on the road to eternity as I leave life to enter history."[11]

With his suicide Vargas turned the tables on his enemies. They had been moving into the vacuum created by the moral and political discrediting of the Vargas government. But with the president now a martyr, the anti-getulistas were suddenly on the defensive. Carlos Lacerda, once the wounded hero, ducked into hiding and then exile. Angry crowds stoned the U.S. embassy windows and burned delivery trucks of *O Globo,* a leading anti-getulista daily. Those targets fit the description of Vargas's tormentors given in his suicide letter.

The denouement of Vargas's 1951–54 presidency set the political context and agenda for the next decade. There was first the question of economic nationalism. How should Brazil treat its foreign investors? What areas (such as oil, minerals, etc.) should be reserved for national capital, either public or private? How could Brazil maximize its gains from foreign trade?

A second key area was economic equity within Brazil, reflected in the public debate by the minimum wage adjustment. No economic issue of 1954 had bedevilled Vargas more than the minimum wage adjustment. What was a "fair" wage rate? To what extent should workers be able to bargain collectively? The corporatist labor law (dating from the 1937–45 authoritarian regime) virtually proscribed such bargaining. Nonetheless, independent São Paulo labor organizers—i.e., beholden neither to the government nor to the previously established elements on the left such as the Communist Party—were making headway. In the short run that was likely to create even more political headaches for Vargas.[12]

Agricultural labor relations also claimed the spotlight during Vargas's presidency. In early 1954 the president authorized Labor Minister Goulart to begin organizing agricultural workers in the state of São Paulo.[13] Brazil's greatest poverty lay in the countryside, where income and public services lagged far behind the urban scene. Yet Vargas lacked any mobilizable political support for this initiative. Landholders, on the other hand, were well represented at every government level. The result was to increase the number of Vargas's active enemies without achieving any reform.

Finally, Vargas's presidency and his tragic departure raised crucial political questions. First was the future of the political party system. The UDN had accomplished its immediate goal: to drive Vargas from power. But it had also made him a martyr, thereby helping the PTB, which now carried high Vargas's flag of economic nationalism. As elections strengthened the PTB, the UDN found itself fighting the anti-getulista battles all over again. Meanwhile, the PSD was caught in the UDN–PTB cross fire. The third of the three major parties created in 1945 was the PSD. Its original leaders were the top-level administrators and political oligarchs favored by the Vargas dictatorship of 1937–45. By its ideology and practice the PSD was centrist, straddling the UDN on the right and the PTB on the left. The PSD leaders were the would-be pragmatists and natural peacemakers. But the inflamed political tempers of 1954 did not lend themselves to conciliation.

Tempers eventually cooled, and a PSD president, Juscelino Kubitschek, was elected to a five-year term in 1955. He made his government known for rapid economic growth and imaginative innovations, such as building the new capital city of Brasília and creating SUDENE, the regional development authority of Brazil's Northeast. Kubitschek was the prototype of a centrist PSD politician. He downplayed ideology and concentrated on attracting maximum support for his "developmentalist" industrialization. He solicited foreign investment in sectors such as vehicle manufacture. He also broke with the IMF (International Monetary Fund) in 1959 over its demand for an orthodox stabilization program, thus unleashing strong nationalist feelings. The UDN and anti-getulista military attacked Kubitschek's PSD government, but the president's ebullient political style and imaginative development program reduced the effectiveness of the attacks.

The UDN thought their chance had finally come in 1960. They had never elected a president, but Jânio Quadros, a charismatic former São Paulo schoolteacher, looked like a winner. He had been elected São Paulo mayor and then governor of São Paulo state. Jânio was not a conventional politician. He regarded party identification as a mere convenience and had often switched parties. The UDN wanted Jânio because he shared many UDN positions, such as a crusading attitude toward corruption, a suspicion of grandiose reforms, a preference for free enterprise, and an emphasis on the values of home and family. Quadros also promised to eradicate inflation and rationalize the state's role in the economy. Most important, the UDN wanted Jânio because he was a phenomenal vote-getter.

Winning the presidential election of 1960, Quadros did not disappoint the UDN, on whose ticket (along with others) he ran. Yet it was a highly personal victory. That was confirmed by the fact that his UDN running mate, Milton Campos, lost to João Goulart, the vice presidential candidate on the opposing slate (the electoral law permitted ticket-splitting).

Quadros took office in January 1961, enjoying enormous political prestige. His campaign (its symbol was a broom) had convinced both friends and enemies that he meant business. Hope was especially high among the military, who longed for a moral crusade against what they saw as the unprincipled and opportunistic politicians. Rumors of political payoffs (from contractors in Brasília, land-sellers in Minas Gerais, and agents for multinational firms) had been rife for years. Quadros gave a sense of control as he settled into the Planalto, the presidential palace in Brasília. His famous broom was now aimed at dishonest politicians and slothful bureaucrats.

Quadros's political magic did not take long to be tested. Always known as an eccentric, he took some surprising zags to the left. He presented Che Guevara with the order of the Cruzeiro do Sul, Brazil's highest decoration for a non-citizen. Why should he be honoring an Argentine-cum-Cuban guerrilla? the UDN asked. On a more important issue, Quadros hesitated over an IMF-style economic stabilization program, which he had promised would stop inflation. Was he stepping back from economic austerity? Quadros also complained that the Congress was obstructing his legislative program, although he had submitted few proposals.

The president's pro-Cuban gestures were enough to rouse the ire of Carlos Lacerda, still the UDN's most powerful and strident voice. He hurled insults at Quadros, himself a formidable polemicist. But the president did not try to slug it out. Instead, to everyone's complete surprise, Quadros sent a written resignation to Congress in August 1961. The president's action came as a bombshell. His millions of supporters were bewildered, their high hopes dashed. Although Quadros may have thought the Congress would summon him back and give him DeGaulle-style powers (what he apparently wanted), he left Brasília the same day and went incognito.

Congressional leaders quickly removed the uncertainty by taking the resignation at face value. Quadros had suddenly made Vice President João Goulart his legal successor. Thus had fate (and Jânio) elevated to the presidency the same PTB politician whom the UDN had helped drive from office in 1954. As if to underscore his ideological leanings, Goulart was then on a goodwill tour of the People's Republic of China.

Before Goulart could arrive back, the three military ministers, led by Army Minister Marshal Odílio Denys, announced he would not be allowed to succeed to the presidency. They accused Goulart as Vargas's labor minister, of having awarded key union positions to "agents of international Communism." The ministers' manifesto ended by charging that once in the presidency Goulart might promote infiltration of the armed forces, thus transforming them into "simple Communist militias." The specter of a worker–soldier conflict could not have been better described.[14]

The military ministers assumed they could enforce their veto of Goulart's succession. In fact, that assumption soon proved unfounded. Their manifesto stimulated creation of a nationwide "legality" movement, whose members demanded that the military honor Goulart's legal right to succeed. The backbone of the movement came from the PTB and allied groups on the left, but it also included centrist politicians and military officers who believed that honoring the constitution was the only way to strengthen Brazilian democracy. In other words, Goulart should be given a chance to prove or disprove the accusations from the right.

The weakest link in the ministers' forces was the Third Army in Rio Grande do Sul. The commander, General Machado Lopes, rejected the veto. He was enthusiastically encouraged by the young governor, Leonel Brizola, Goulart's brother-in-law and a PTB firebrand leader in the "legality" campaign. Brizola and Machado Lopes had devised a strategy to force the ministers' hand. Goulart would re-enter Brazil via Rio Grande do Sul. If the navy moved against Rio Grande do Sul, Brizola threatened to sink enough ships to block the entrance to the port of Pôrto Alegre. This move checkmated the ministers, who now had to negotiate a compromise.

The solution was to allow Goulart to succeed to the presidency, but with reduced powers. A hastily passed constitutional amendment transformed Brazil into a parliamentary republic. Executive power was effectively transferred to the parliamentary cabinet, which would govern subject to retaining a congressional majority. Goulart reluctantly accepted this compromise, but immediately began planning to regain full presidential powers. He got them in January 1963 when a national plebiscite restored the presidential system. But only a little more than half of the original five-year presidential term now remained.

What kind of Brazil did Goulart face? The first matter was economic. Since 1940 Brazilian GNP had grown at 6 percent a year, a record few Third World countries could match. Both Brazilians and foreign observers, noting the abundant resources of almost every kind, predicted a bright future for Latin America's largest country. Kubitschek's industrialization drive and construction of Brasília seemed to signal Brazil's "takeoff."

But further development would not be easy. Basic infrastructure was woefully inadequate. Electric power production, for example, could not meet basic demand in Rio and São Paulo. São Paulo factory managers often maintained their own diesel-powered generators to keep production lines going. Rio de Janeiro suffered frequent water and electricity rationing. Paved highway in a country larger than the continental United States totaled only 5,518 miles.[15] The overburdened railway system ran on different gauge track in different regions, and most of its rolling stock was antiquated.

The educational system was little better. Primary and secondary education was a local and state responsibility, but fewer than 10 percent of the children enrolled in first grade finished primary school, and only 15 percent of secondary school students managed to finish.[16] The causes included inadequate funding to staff and house schools, parental unconcern, lack of family funds to pay for school uniforms, parental pressure on children to work, and many others. In most cities the best secondary schools were private. They served the children of the wealthy, who then had a head start on competitive entrance exams to the tuition-free federal universities. Not surprisingly, the federal universities were filled with the children of the well-to-do. With more than half of the federal education appropriations going to federal universities, the government was stacking the cards against upward mobility via education.

This educational system not only failed to meet minimal literacy goals for the general population, it also failed to train the skilled work force demanded by industrialization. Brazil depended almost entirely on imported technology, most of which was owned by foreign firms. The roll call was international: Brown Boveri (generators), Bayer (drugs), Bosch (electrical equipment), Coca-Cola (soft drinks), and Volkswagen (vehicles). The Brazilian government did not even print its own currency (except for the rapidly disappearing one-cruzeiro note). That was a job for American Bank Note Company or Thomas Larue, Ltd. (British), whichever more lavishly lobbied the Brazilian authorities.

Health care was another neglected area in Brazil. In health, as in education, the greatest contrasts were between city and country. City dwellers, even in the slums, generally received more social services than their counterparts in the countryside. To what extent did this rural poverty result from the pattern of landholding? Although patterns varied by region, almost everywhere there were large amounts of cultivable land not in use. The owners were both private individuals and government bodies. Not far from such idle lands were millions of rural landless. Why did they not invade those lands? Because police power in the countryside was controlled by the large landholders or their allies among the city elites. But it was not only coercion that deterred the landless and the marginal landowners. It was also the web of socio-economic and moral relations that linked the powerful to those below. It included the *compadre* (co-godfather) system. The godchild looked to the (powerful) godfather for protection and benefits. This system channeled aspirations of the inferior to the one figure who was expected to reach down and help his moral charge. It was the very opposite of the collectivist impulse, by which inferiors would use their collective strength to extract concessions. The result was that Brazil's twentieth-century peasant movements had never demanded the scale of agrarian reform achieved in Mexico or Bolivia. Nor was agrarian reform a high priority for the political left, which clung to the traditional Marxist dogma that only the urban proletariat could launch a revolution.

In the cities the newly inaugurated President Goulart would find a surging population of in-migrants who left the countryside looking for a better life. What they found were burgeoning slums (often known by the Rio term of *favelas*). However foul these shack settlements may have looked to the outsider—Brazilian or foreign—many residents saw them as their stepping stone to economic betterment. These new city dwellers worked at whatever they could get. Women found jobs as domestics or shop clerks, men found jobs as bus conductors, janitors, or runners for the numbers racket (*jôgo do bicho*). The lucky ones got jobs in the formal sector, covered by the minimum wage and therefore by the social security system.

These latter workers formed the natural basis for an urban labor movement. But were they good material for unionization? President Vargas preempted that question during his semi-corporatist dictatorship of the Estado Nôvo (1937–45) by producing a labor code that gave the state vast power over labor relations. Union membership was made compulsory, as was dues payment (payroll deduction sent to the Labor Ministry and then distributed to the union, the federation, or the confederation). There was no room for collective bargaining, and strikes were virtually illegal. Disputes, if adjudged legal, went to an elaborate network of labor courts. In short, it was a structure designed to prevent the emergence of any independent union leaders. Its continued successful operation depended on the existence of a huge labor surplus. It also depended on the government to raise the minimum wage often enough to satisfy the few militant urban unions (dock workers, bank workers, metalworkers). Such increases usually did little more than compensate for past inflation, although those by President Vargas in 1954 and by President Kubitschek in 1956 and 1959 did, if only briefly, set new highs for the minimum wage's buying power. Yet Brazil, like Mexico, had a large labor surplus which inevitably undercut labor's bargaining strength.[17]

Turning from these basic features of the economy in the early 1960s, any observer would have been struck by two urgent short-run economic problems. Both had long dogged Brazilian policymakers. The first was the chronic deficit in the balance of payments. Brazil's deficit in the early 1960s could be attributed to several factors. First, its export earnings depended on a single crop, coffee, for which the world price varied greatly. In the Vargas presidency of 1951–54, for example, Brazil got caught in a coffee price war with the U.S. and lost. Brazil, the world's leading coffee producer, sought to keep the coffee price high on the New York market. The U.S., as the principal consumer of Brazilian coffee, wanted a low price. Brazil then withheld coffee from the market, in hopes of forcing a higher price. That gambit failed when other producers took up the slack and U.S. coffee retailers slowed their buying. To make matters worse, several U.S. Congressmen accused Brazil of having tried to blackmail the U.S. housewife. Unless Brazil could diversify its exports it would remain vulnerable to fluctuations such as these of a single market.

On the import side, Brazil had huge needs: capital goods to industrialize, oil to power its vehicles, raw materials such as copper and potash, to name only a few. The level of imports was closely linked to industrial growth: the faster the growth the higher the import demand.

Besides imports there were other negative items on the balance of payments. Profit remittances, loan repayments, and capital repatriation were the principal ones. They were balanced by new foreign investment, along with loans and grants (as from international agencies).

When the foreign accounts were added up, Brazil found that a steadily increasing share of its export earnings had to go for debt service. In 1960 it was 36.6 percent, up from only 11.6 percent five years earlier.[18] Few observers doubted Brazil's long-run development potential. In the short run, however, it lacked the hard currency to finance the imports required for continued rapid industrialization. The options were stark. It could slash imports, thereby crippling industry and transport (because of reduced imports of capital goods and oil). Or, it could suspend payment on loans or stop profit remissions on foreign investment in Brazil. Either of the latter actions would frighten foreign lenders and investors (a closed community of like-minded capitalists) into blacklisting Brazil. In sum, Brazil had to produce an economic plan that would satisfy her creditors and thereby keep trade flowing under the prevailing rules of international capitalism.

Quadros had faced this problem and had decided to turn to the IMF. The IMF was crucial because most other creditors waited for it to signal when a debtor country had undertaken a sufficiently orthodox adjustment program. Quadros had presented an orthodox stabilization program, which won IMF approval. He had only begun to feel its effects—inevitably recessionary—when he resigned.

Goulart reached the presidency with truncated powers, to find Brazil's creditors highly skeptical.[19] The new government had to start the debt negotiations anew. And the creditors had taken due notice of the ugly political fight surrounding Goulart's succession. They also noted his leftist politics—a severe liability in the eyes of foreign bankers.

The second urgent short-run economic problem facing Goulart was inflation. From 1949 to 1959 Brazil had suffered inflation rates ranging from 12 to 26 percent. Brazilians, like many Latin Americans, took a more relaxed attitude toward inflation than do North Americans or Western Europeans; they knew from experience they could not expect the same monetary stability the North Atlantic economies took for granted. In 1960, however, inflation shocked even the Brazilians when it hit 39.5 percent. Savers found their accounts depreciating more rapidly, while major lenders simply refused to make long-term commitments. The premium was on finding a loan at a high negative interest rate. Distortions riddled the economy. The state enterprises, especially public utilities, let their prices, often set by elected politicians, lag far behind inflation. This swelled the public sector deficit, as did inflation's effect on revenues collected with a lag.

But no postwar Brazilian government had been willing to carry out an orthodox anti-inflation program. Both Vargas and Kubitschek, for example, had development goals they were unwilling to sacrifice to orthodoxy. Both managed to keep the economy going without acquiescing in an IMF-style stabilization program. For Goulart, however, time was short because the economy he inherited gave less room for maneuver.

By late 1962 the problems on both the balance of payments front and the inflation front had become acute. Goulart's response was to summon the best minds on the moderate left, San Thiago Dantas and Celso Furtado, to draw up a stabilization program. In early 1963 they produced a plan that won the approval of both the IMF and the Kennedy White House. But Brazil's creditors were suspicious, so they demanded a short leash, with each credit to Brazil dependent on demonstrated progress in implementing the stabilization program.

The Dantas-Furtado plan called for devaluation (to cure the overvalued cruzeiro), which would raise the cost of such imports as oil and wheat, in turn raising the cost of bread and bus fares—two basics in the urban worker's budget. The plan also called for holding the line on wages, another unpopular move, since inflation was now over 50 percent. In order to cut the public sector deficit the government would have to lay off workers, yet another blow to the urban work force. Goulart, long a politician of the left, found himself saddled with a stabilization program that might appeal to the UDN but never to his PTB. Furthermore, Dantas and Furtado could give no assurances on how long it would take to work, although Goulart's term had only a little more than two years to go.

Goulart stuck with the Dantas-Furtado plan for six months. By June 1963, however, he had decided its political costs were too high, so he switched to another option, the radical nationalist strategy. The radical nationalists argued that the economy's foreign sector was the *cause* of much of its current economic ills. Most foreign investors, they argued, entered Brazil only to gain monopolistic market power and then remit maximum profits to their home firms. In pharmaceuticals and heavy electrical equipment, for example, they manipulated the market in order to block Brazilian firms. Whatever technology they brought in, argued the radical nationalists, remained corporation property and had little spillover effect in the economy at large. The solution? Tighter controls on foreign firms, such as the tougher profit remittances law passed by the Congress (radical nationalist Congressmen had taken the lead) in 1962.

The radical nationalists also attacked the terms under which Brazil's foreign trade took place. They argued that Brazil's export prices were manipulated by major traders, such as the U.S., thereby reducing Brazil's export earnings. At the same time the prices of industrial imports, also allegedly manipulated by the major traders, increased steadily. The resulting negative trend in Brazil's terms of trade (the ratio of the prices of Brazil's exports to the prices of her imports) contributed greatly to Brazil's chronic balance of payments deficit.

Finally, the radical nationalists blamed the IMF and the World Bank for their role in allegedly keeping developing countries, such as Brazil, in economic subordination. It was true that the World Bank, for example, had suspended all lending to Brazil because it disapproved of Brazil's policies (exchange rate, fiscal, etc.) surrounding the industrialization drive. For its part, the IMF's orthodox approach included tough monetary and fiscal policies which Brazil, like other developing countries, had rejected as not appropriate for its economy. Yet Brazil could not get help from its creditors without acceding to the IMF's orthodox strategy.

Underlying this radical nationalist analysis lay the assumption that the industrial countries, especially the U.S., would block any Third World economic development that might threaten their control of world trade and finance. And it was true that in the 1950s the U.S. had generally refused to aid state-owned industrial ventures. Goulart had not totally embraced this radical nationalist diagnosis of the economy's foreign sector, but he was clearly moving toward it after mid-1963.

The other aspect of his turn to the left was domestic policy, where Goulart felt on more familiar ground. The Dantas-Furtado plan had aroused the anger of Goulart's original constituency, the unions. From mid-1963 Goulart pushed with increasing enthusiasm a set of "structural reforms" that included landholding, education, taxes, and housing. He now argued that Brazil's economic crisis—of which the balance of payments impasse and inflation were the most immediate symptoms—could *only* be solved by enacting his package of reforms. By linking them, Goulart had raised the stakes.

Goulart's most determined opponents—centered in the UDN and the military—now began to argue that the president had no intention of carrying out these reforms. Instead, they charged, he was seeking to polarize opinion and thereby pave the way for a radical nationalist takeover of his government. The radical nationalists would then subvert the constitutional order from within. In effect, his enemies were accusing Goulart of having already violated the 1946 Constitution and therefore having lost his presidential legitimacy.

The legal recourse for these militant anti-Goulart forces was impeachment. Because they claimed that the president's unconstitutional conduct was blatant, they needed only to mount a congressional trial.[20] But impeachment required a majority vote of the Chamber of Deputies, which the anti-Goulart forces lacked. The PTB deputies would certainly support their president, and most of the PSD would vote against an impeachment that could help only the UDN.

The anti-Goulart military were therefore in a quandary. They sought Goulart's ouster for his alleged illegalities, yet they would find no legal way to remove him. This was by no means unprecedented. They had found a way to remove Vargas in 1945 and again in 1954. So the military conspirators were not overly worried by their lack of a congressional majority. In fact, they had important civilian allies, such as Governor Carlos Lacerda of Guanabara (greater Rio de Janeiro), Governor Adhemar de Barros of São Paulo, and Governor Magalhães Pinto of Minas Gerais. The anti-Goulart forces could also now count on such leading newspapers as *Jornal do Brasil, O Globo, Estado de São Paulo,* and *Correio da Manhã.* There was, in addition, a network of civilian oppositionists in IPES, an organization founded in the early 1960s by a group of businessmen, lawyers, technocrats, and military officers. They created a "shadow government," publishing statistics on the economy (they did not trust the government figures) and spawning study groups on such policy issues as educational funding, population control, labor law reform, and minerals development. IPES had a clear conservative bent, standing well to the right of the current congressional majority and far to the right of Goulart's late 1963 position. Paralleling the IPES organizing was a women's movement, CAMDE, which was to specialize in organizing protest marches on such issues as inflation and alleged communist influence in government. In a country where mass mobilization of women for political purposes was still rare, a CAMDE march could have a significant impact on middle-class opinion.[21]

By the beginning of 1964 Goulart found himself stymied on every front. He had little hope of winning congressional approval for any of his major reforms—above all, land reform. (The same PSD Congressmen who would oppose his land reform were not ready, paradoxically, to vote for his impeachment.) Time was running out on his presidency, but Goulart had no desire to withdraw into a merely ceremonial role. He wanted to fight for his reforms. But how? The radical nationalists around Goulart argued that he must go over the heads of the politicians and take his fight to the people.[22]

Goulart accepted their advice and scheduled a series of rallies around the country. He held the first on Friday, March 13, in Rio. Thousands of placard-waving spectators (many bused in at government expense) cheered the president as he decreed the nationalization of land lying within six miles of federal highways, railways, or national borders. The elated Goulart promised more rallies and more presidential decrees.

It was clear the president had made a momentous decision. He was now determined to turn up the heat on Congress and on the opponents of his reforms. The radical nationalists told him his enemies were on the run. Top labor union leaders assured him that union power was growing daily and furnished an ideal base for his upcoming rallies. His top military advisers knew that dissident officers were organizing, but discounted them as an insignificant minority.

When Goulart turned to the left, he found there was no unity. The Moscow-line Communist Party (PCB), with its bitter experience of repression under the Estado Nôvo (1937–45), counseled caution. The Peking-line Communist Party (PC do B), demanded radical action, but its numbers were few. Two national political figures also called for radical action. One was Pernambuco governor Miguel Arraes, who favored a direct, if patient approach toward a drastic redistribution of income and wealth, especially land. The second figure was Leonel Brizola, Goulart's brother-in-law and a PTB Congressman from Guanabara (greater Rio de Janeiro city) elected in 1962 with a record-breaking vote. Brizola had designs on higher power, and was organizing his "groups of eleven" around Brazil to answer the call to battle when his signal came. The most significant force on the left, both in numbers and in depth of passion, were the so-called Jacobins, the militant nationalists who accepted the discipline of neither the PCB nor the PC do B and who came from the Catholic left or the National Union of Stu-

dents (*União Nacional de Estudantes,* or UNE), The Jacobins were political amateurs, pushing for stronger measures by the indecisive Goulart
government. When added up, this patchwork on the left was hardly the
base for a serious attack on Brazil's established order.

There was the further question of Goulart's intentions; by early 1964
everyone had his suspicions, for which there were ample grounds. Goulart
had asked Congress in October 1963 for state-of-siege powers, to last 30
days. The request supposedly originated with the military ministers disturbed by the wave of strikes and politically motivated violence across the
country. Three days later, however, Goulart withdrew the request. It had
alarmed even the labor leaders, who feared they would be jailed under the
state of siege. By these moves Goulart had aroused widespread fears about
his plans.[23]

On one point there could be no doubt: his new strategy was certain to
mobilize the opposition. By going over the head of Congress he was helping to convince centrist opinion that he was threatening the constitutional
order. Furthermore, he had chosen to support an ancillary move sure to
infuriate military officers: the unionization of enlisted men. Officers saw
this as an obvious threat to military discipline, immobilizing the ultimate
line of defense for conservatives. This threat to military hierarchy alarmed
even centrist officers who had hesitated to conspire against a legally elected
president.

By late March 1964 political tensions had reached an unprecedented
pitch. Goulart was locked into a series of rallies at each of which he would
announce new decrees. Meanwhile, the military-civilian conspiracy had
picked up steam. General Castelo Branco, the army chief of staff who was
coordinating the recruitment of officers for the conspiracy, found that
Goulart's move to the left since late December had simplified his task.
Nonetheless, the conspirators faced formidable obstacles. Most officers did
not want to be among the first to join a conspiracy, for fear it might fail, nor
among the last, for fear it might succeed.

The last days of March proved decisive, as we have seen. The higher
military across the country, only some of whom were active conspirators,
rapidly endorsed the coup. There was virtually no fighting, despite calls to
battle from Justice Minister Abelardo Jurema in Rio and head of the
Civilian Presidential Staff Darcy Ribeiro in Brasília. Calls for a general
strike from CGT leaders went similarly unanswered. The president and his
radical nationalists discovered that their popular mobilization had not gone
very deep. Once again, as in 1954, a populist government had been ended
by the men in uniform.

Now began the struggle over who would run the new government. The
military—primarily the army but also the navy—quickly stepped into the
vacuum and arrested activists on the left, such as student leaders, labor
union leaders, organizers of Catholic groups such as JUC (*Juventude
Universitária Católica*) and AP (*Acão Popular*), and rural union and peasant league organizers. Hundreds were jailed in Rio, with many confined to

a makeshift prison ship in the harbor. The repression was most severe in the Northeast, where the Fourth Army and state and local police cracked down on the peasant leagues and the recently legitimized rural labor unions. Some peasant organizers simply disappeared, the victims of summary execution. Others suffered torture, usually at the hands of the Fourth Army.

The repression was also carried out by the Lacerda government in Rio and the Adhemar de Barros government in São Paulo. In both cases the political police (DOPS, or *Departamento de Ordem Política e Social*) went after leftist activists whom they had long been watching. The press overwhelmingly endorsed the coup, playing up the civilian role. They were aided by the pro-coup governors and Congressmen who basked in the welcome publicity.

But Goulart's ouster was first and foremost a military operation. The civilian anti-Goulart forces had not been able to stop the president's swing toward a radical nationalist strategy. At best they might have fomented increasing confrontation on such fronts as land reform and labor union militancy. In fact, a proto civil war was already underway, with São Paulo anticommunist paramilitary groups (MAC, CCC) terrorizing leftist student leaders, and with landowners paying gunmen to kill peasant organizers. Still, that would not have stopped a national government with the powers that Goulart was consolidating. Indeed, it was the relative weakness of the civilian anti-Goulart forces that led top-level officers to conclude that only their intervention could save Brazil from a prolonged civil war.

II

CASTELO BRANCO: CLEANING HOUSE—
APRIL 1964–MARCH 1965

The military-civilian conspirators who overthrew João Goulart in March 1964 had two objectives. The first was to "forestall the communist plan for seizing power and to defend miltary institutions"; the second was to "reestablish order so that legal reforms [could] be carried out."[1] The first turned out to be easy. The second proved far more difficult.

The Military Take Control

The rebels' first task after their military victory was to take over the presidency and the vast executive machinery it controlled. But the Constitution of 1946 (articles 66, 88, and 89) provided only three legal ways a living President could leave office before the end of his term: by resignation, by congressional impeachment, or by leaving the country without congressional approval.

Goulart's congressional opponents had not even attempted to impeach him because they knew they lacked the votes to win, just as Getúlio Vargas's enemies (who came from the same ideological and party origins as Goulart's enemies) had lacked when they sought to oust Vargas in 1954. Although most Congressmen suspected Goulart's intentions, no centrist congressional leader was prepared to lead an impeachment campaign, nor to support the UDN militants (such as Bilac Pinto) in such an effort— primarily because they were apprehensive that Goulart's ouster might set off a general purge of the "ins." As for the other two ways to vacate the presidency, Goulart was certainly not going to resign, and he had not yet left the country. How, then, to fill the presidency? Senate president Auro Moura Andrade solved the short-run problem. The military were demanding that he smooth the way for a new president whom they would indicate—undoubtedly a general. In the early morning hours of April 2, Moura Andrade simply declared the presidency vacant, an act without any legal basis and one that provoked furious protests from the PTB deputies. The Constitution specified that if the presidency were vacant the next in line would be the president of the Chamber of Deputies (Ranieri Mazzilli) for a maximum 30-day period, while the Congress elected a new president. The Constitution was honored in this step: Mazzilli became acting president. The Revolution's assumption of power, born in an arbitrary act, was now following strict constitutionality. This would not be the last example of such schizophrenia.

The next hurdle was the mandatory election, for which there was no precedent. It was unlike 1954 when the army, after Getúlio Vargas's suicide, endorsed Vice President Café Filho's succession. It was also unlike 1961, when the legality advocates got Vice President Goulart into the presidency (albeit with reduced powers). Now there was no vice president in line to succeed, since Goulart had done that in 1961. A new president would have to be found, and the politicians started their soundings. Would it be an experienced center-left PSD leader, such as Tancredo Neves, or an older politician, such as Gustavo Capanema? Perhaps a centrist general such as Second Army Commander Amaury Kruel? Or a military-civilian patriarch such as Marshal (and former president) Eurico Dutra?[2]

Such speculation was far wide of the mark. The succession belonged to the military, and it was being decided behind the scenes. A large majority of military, among whom the most outspoken were known as the "hardline" (linha dura), was adamant. They wanted to stop the merry-go-round in which recurrent military interventions since 1945 had been followed by the rapid return to civilian rule.[3] As the hardliners believed this strategy had solved nothing, they wanted no more direct presidential elections until they had changed the political rules. They especially wanted the more dangerous actors removed.

The hardliner spokesman was General Artur Costa e Silva, who had appointed himself (as the senior general on active duty in Rio on April 1) war minister in the new government. He then announced that he had organized a Comando Supremo Revolucionário (Supreme Revolutionary Command), which included Admiral Rademaker and Air Force Brigadier Francisco de Assis Correio de Melo. The latter two had assumed the other military ministries because they were senior conspirators with legitimacy in the eyes of their anti-Goulart fellow officers. This extra-legal Command was their defense against a possible counter-coup effort by those top military still loyal to Goulart.

Acting President Mazzilli confirmed the Command's de facto power by dutifully naming the three as the military ministers in his new cabinet. On April 7 the new military ministers publicly demanded emergency legislation, suspending normal legal procedures in order to purge the civil service, the military, and elected officeholders at every level. But the old-line congressional leaders were not yet ready to surrender their powers. They drafted their own "Constitutional Act," which would have delegated to the Revolutionary Command (only after a two-thirds vote of the Congress) limited powers to purge the Congress and the federal bureaucracy.

The three military ministers ignored the politicians' draft. On April 9 they issued their own "Institutional Act"—the first, it later turned out, of many.[4] The drafters were Francisco Campos, the durable jurist who had authored the authoritarian Constitution of 1937, and Carlos Medeiros da Silva, a highly conservative lawyer. The Act made ambitious claims for the Revolution, which "distinguishes itself from all other armed movements by the fact that it represents not the interests and will of a group, but the interests and will of a nation." No less important, the "victorious revolution legitimizes itself." The Congress, they announced, received its legitimacy "from the Institutional Act," and not vice versa. The Act included such major provisions to break the political deadlock as these:

(1) The President could now submit constitutional amendments to the Congress, which would have only 30 days to consider the proposals, and need only approve them by a majority vote (rather than the two-thirds vote required in the existing 1946 Constitution).

(2) The President was given exclusive power to propose expenditure bills to Congress, which could not increase any spending item.

(3) The President was given the power to declare a state of siege for up to 30 days, or to prolong such a state of siege once declared for a maximum period of 30 days (with the requirement of a report to the Congress within 48 hours).

(4) The President, "in the interests of peace and national honor," was given sweeping powers to suspend for 10 years the political rights of any citizen and to cancel the mandates of federal, state, and municipal legislators.

(5) Suspension of job security in the civil service for six months.

These expanded powers for the Executive were needed, according to the Act, to carry out "the economic, financial, political, and moral reconstruction of Brazil." The objective was "the restoration of internal order and the international prestige of our country." The new powers were needed because the existing constitutional powers had not been enough to stop a government that "was deliberately attempting to Bolshevize the country."

This Institutional Act was not a total surprise. It was only the latest in a series of responses to a crisis of political authority evident in Brazil since the mid-1950s. President Jânio Quadros, for example, had complained that he lacked sufficient powers to deal with Congress. He cited the irresponsibility of the "politicians" as the reason for his abrupt departure after only six months in office in 1961. Goulart, who had repeated the complaint of insufficient presidential power, had even proposed a state of siege in October of 1963, and in early 1964 had made specific proposals for strengthening the hand of the Executive. The Supreme Revolutionary Command of 1964 had taken a new tack, however. It did not attempt to work through the rules of democratic politics as its predecessors had done. It unilaterally changed the rules.

The most immediate impact was on the presidency itself. By voiding the

1946 Constitution's clause making military officers ineligible for elective office, and by requiring that an election for president and vice president be held within two days of its publication (rather than the 23 days that remained under the constitutional provision of 30 days), it made inevitable the election of the consensus candidate of the military and the anti-Goulart governors. That candidate was General Castelo Branco, the coordinator of the anti-Goulart military conspiracy and the overwhelming choice of both military and civilian revolutionaries. On April 11 the Congress duly elected Castelo Branco by 361 votes against 72 abstentions and 5 votes split for other conservative military heroes.

The New Government: A UDN–Military Alliance

Castelo Branco was an interesting product of both Brazilian and foreign influences.[5] He was born the son of an army officer in the Northeastern state of Ceará. The family moved often, as the father rotated among posts. They were in Rio Grande do Sul when the son entered the Pôrto Alegre military academy. Subsequently Castelo followed a military career in the infantry, progressing up through the most important training school. He later took the two-year course at France's Ecole Supérieure de Guerre and the staff and general command course at Fort Leavenworth in the United States. He gained combat experience in the Brazilian Expeditionary Force that fought alongside the U.S. Fifth Army in Italy in 1944–45. Castelo had thus had extensive first-hand experience with the two foreign countries that most deeply influenced twentieth-century Brazil: France and the U.S.[6]

Castelo was known as a cautious and introspective officer. He was short, bull-necked, and accustomed to derogatory comments on his appearance (his future father-in-law had demanded Castelo undergo a physical exam before he would approve the marriage). He had always preferred reading and study to feats of physical endurance. A quiet and reflective man, Castelo was determined to return dignity to the presidency.

Castelo was also the acknowledged leader of the "Sorbonne" group—officers closely associated with the *Escola Superior de Guerra* (Higher War College), a military-sponsored institute whose one-year course attracted equal numbers of the military and civilian elite. Other Sorbonne officers included Generals Golbery do Couto e Silva, Cordeiro de Farias, Ernesto Geisel, and Jurandir da Bizarria. This group, more moderate than the hard line, was for free enterprise (though also seeing the need for a strong government), anticommunist in foreign policy, preferring technical solutions and committed to democracy but believing that in the short run arbitrary government was necessary. These Sorbonne officers had been molded into a self-aware group by their common experiences in FEB (*Fôrça Expedicionária Brasileira,* or Brazilian Expeditionary Force), which fought alongside the U.S. Fifth Army in Italy in 1944–45; in the *Escola Superior da Guerra* (either as students but especially as faculty); and in attending military schools abroad, especially in the U.S. This Sorbonne group was later to be known as the *castelistas* and would play a key role in subsequent military governments.[7]

As vice-president the Congress elected Minas Gerais's PSD leader José Maria Alkmin, whose party had been promised the vice presidency in negotiations earlier that month between representatives of Castelo Branco and former President Kubitschek, the titular head of the PSD. Many in the UDN were furious at that deal, which smacked of a compromise with the "old, corrupt politics." They were upset because it benefitted the PSD, a bitter rival which they thought the Revolution should have eliminated from any role in the new government. They remembered too well the 1954 crisis, when President Vargas's suicide threw them off balance and helped prevent them from taking full political control.[8] But the UDN now had reason to be pleased with their spoils in the Congress. Daniel Krieger, a veteran UDN politician-lawyer from Rio Grande do Sul, assumed the Senate presidency, while Bilac Pinto, a UDN firebrand in the anti-Goulart mobilization, became president of the Chamber of Deputies.

The new cabinet consisted in part of Costa e Silva's picks immediately after the coup and Castelo Branco's choices during the following week.[9] They were a combination of political conservatives and technocrats. The navy and air force ministers, only in power since April 2, left the cabinet. Rademaker, known for his strongly right-wing views, was replaced by Admiral Ernesto de Melo Batista, and Correia de Melo was replaced by Brigadier Lavanère-Wanderley. Because the army exercised the overwhelming political weight, the role of the navy and air force ministers was relatively minor.

Among the more prominent members of Castelo's cabinet were Senator Milton Campos (Minas Gerais), a distinguished constitutional lawyer and twice unsuccessful UDN candidate for vice president, now Minister of Justice; Marshal Juarez Távora, an unsuccessful UDN candidate for president in 1955, now Minister of Transportation and Public Works; Flávio Suplicy de Lacerda, Rector of the University of Paraná and an outspoken UDN partisan, now Minister of Education; Raimundo de Brito, also of the UDN, now Minister of Health; career diplomat (but known to be sympathetic to the Revolution) Vasco Leitão da Cunha, now Minister of Foreign Relations; PSD Congressman Daniel Faraco (Rio Grande do Sul), now Minister of Commerce and Industry. Another prominent UDN political figure, Luiz Viana Filho (Bahia), was named head of the Civilian Presidential Staff (*chefe da casa civil*) with ministerial status. Viana's counterpart as head of Military Presidential Staff (*chefe da casa militar*) was General Ernesto Geisel, a notably self-confident officer and key anti-Goulart conspirator.

The all-important Finance Ministry went to Economics Professor Octávio Gouveia Bulhões of the Getúlio Vargas Foundation, a leading government-financed teaching and research center in economics. A respected monetarist, he was outspoken on the need to reorganize the entire financial structure and to "sanitize" Brazil's public finances. Despite the strength of his views, Bulhões was a professional figure, little given to partisan rhetoric or bureaucratic intrigue.[10]

The other key economic position, Planning and Economic Coordination, went to Roberto de Oliveira Campos, a more colorful and controversial figure. Campos was an economist who had chosen a career in Brazil's prestigious diplomatic corps. By the 1950s he was a rising technocrat who served on the U.S.–Brazil Joint Economic Commission (1951–53), which drew up investment priorities for Brazil. In the later 1950s he was Director of the National Development Bank (BNDE, or *Banco Nacional do Desenvilvimento*) and then a key figure in President Juscelino Kubitschek's aborted economic stabilization program of 1958–59. In order to gain IMF approval—crucial to the foreign debt renegotiation then underway—the Kubitschek government would have had to adopt very restrictive wage, credit, and fiscal policies. That prospect provoked a wave of nationalist opposition. During the political battles over the government's highly un-popular anti-inflation measures, Campos revealed a penchant for rough and tumble debate. He especially liked to ridicule the nationalist attacks on foreign capital. The nationalists returned the compliment by branding him "Bobby Fields," an unsubtle play on his name.[11]

The new cabinet had several interesting features. First, it was heavily UDN. Second, outside the service ministries and the head of the military presidential staff (which had always been occupied by an officer) it contained only one military officer with recent active service: General Cordeiro de Farias, now heading a new Ministry for the Coordination of Regional Agencies.[12] Did the victorious consider their goal accomplished? Or did they plan to exercise influence through extraministerial channels? And what would be the role of such organizations as IPES (*Instituto de Pesquisas e Estudos Sociais*), the well-financed research and action group that had since 1961 brought together key military and moderate-to-conservative politicians, professionals (especially economists) and businessmen? They had created a "shadow government," with plans of action in such fields as educational reform, foreign investment and labor. IPES and IBAD (*Instituto Brasileiro de Ação Democrática*) had contributed significantly to mobilizing the opposition to the Goulart government. Would IPES ideas and blueprints now take over the Castelo Branco government?[13]

The Purges and the Torture

The military plotters against Goulart had expected to meet armed resistance. They assumed that loyalist officers would defend the President and his government, perhaps plunging Brazil into a civil war. They therefore wanted to strike before the loyalists could mobilize.

To virtually everyone's surprise, the loyalist resistance never materialized. The rebels were "pushing on an open door," in the classic Brazilian phrase. But it was not only armed opponents the rebels were after. They also wanted to seize those "subversive" leaders allegedly leading Brazil to communism. Thousands were arrested across Brazil in "Operation Clean-Up" (*Operação Limpeza*). Targets included the Catholic Church organizations MEB (*Movimento de Educação de Base,* or Basic Education Movement), JUC (*Juventude Universitária Catholica,* or Catholic University Youth), and others whose organizing or charitable activities aroused the suspicion of military intelligence or DOPS, the political police. Hit also were political parties on the left, such as the Moscow-line Communist Party (*Partido Comunista Brasileiro,* or PCB), the Maoist Communist Party (*Partido Comunista do Brasil,* or PC do B) and the Trotskyists, such as the ORM-POLOP (*Organização Revolucionária Marxista–Política Operária,* or the Revolutionary Marxist Organization/Workers' Politics). Other targets were military officers and enlisted men whom the rebels' intelligence had branded as pro-leftist. And there were the labor organizers, both urban and rural.[14]

The Northeast saw especially sharp repression. That was hardly surprising, for the area harbored so many leaders deemed dangerous, such as Pernambuco Governor Miguel Arraes, SUDENE Superintendent Celso Furtado, literacy specialist Paulo Freire, peasant league lawyer Francisco Julião, and long-time Communist Party activist Gregorio Bezerra. Indeed, coastal Pernambuco had long been home to one of the strongest centers of Communist Party activity in Brazil, although it was modest in absolute numbers.

The Fourth Army G-2 (intelligence) had been closely watching peasant league organizers and left-wing political activists. The military arrested hundreds in the Northeast and brought many to Recife, Fourth Army headquarters. Some were picked out for tortures, such as the "telephone" (slapping open palms against the victim's ears, often bursting the eardrums), the "parrot's perch" (the victim suspended by the bound ankles and wrists from a pole supported by wooden stands at either end, and subjected to beatings or electric shocks), and the "Chinese bath" (plunging the victim's head into a vat of sewer water or oil until virtually suffocated).

The torturers believed their prisoners held vital secrets, such as the names of their Russian contacts or of the Brazilian military officers to be liquidated. The ill-fated prisoners were therefore divided into two groups: those who had confessed and those who needed more "interrogation."

Word of these tortures soon reached Rio, where the *Correio da Manhã,* once an enthusiastic coup supporter, printed detailed accounts. Márcio Moreira Alves, an enterprising young *Correio* reporter, went to the Northeast to cover the story. He reported that 39 prisoners had been tortured, with at least ten officers directly involved. Alves described the tortures as well as giving accounts by medical personnel who treated the victims. Veteran police reporters noted that many of these tortures were of the kind long used on ordinary criminal suspects. Now, however, the victims were political suspects.

Violence against political detainees was not limited to the Northeast. Rio had two centers of torture. The first was CENIMAR (*Centro de Informações da Marinha,* or Naval Intelligence). The other was the DOPS (the political police of the state of Guanabara). CENIMAR tapered off its torturing soon after the coup, but the DOPS continued. The latter, an arm of volatile anticommunist Governor Carlos Lacerda's state government, had been primed to go after the left. Lacerda's police were delighted to round up union, church, and student organizers. There was torture scattered elsewhere in Brazil, although the published record is highly incomplete. The state of Goiás, for example, saw violence toward political prisoners as the military and UDN politicians moved in to depose incumbent PSD Governor Mauro Borges.

What were the overall dimensions of this repression? Much, probably most, occurred in the ten days between Goulart's overthrow and Castelo Branco's election, although torture in the Northeast continued into June. The number arrested in the coup's aftermath can only be estimated, since there was no official tally; it probably totalled between 10,000 and 50,000. Many were released within days and most within weeks. Those subjected to prolonged torture (more than a day or two) were probably several hundred. Apologists for the repression argued that any excesses paled in comparison with what the left would have perpetrated had it won power. Yet the fact remained that duly authorized police and military officers had resorted to torture.[15]

In politics the new government planned to rely not on torture but on the power to revoke legislative mandates and suspend political rights. That power (granted under Article X of the Institutional Act) was to expire on June 15, 1964, giving the Castelo Branco government two months to complete the purge.

The hard-line military had a list of some 5,000 "enemies" whose political rights they intended to suspend. A witch-hunt atmosphere engulfed government offices as ideology mixed with personal vendettas. The accused had no right of self-defense, nor were any charges ever published.[16] The new government argued (off the record) that, being revolutionary, it could set its own rules in punishing the subversive and the corrupt. Accountability was not one of the rules.

Some military wanted to extend the June 15 expiration date of the article (Article 10) authorizing suspension of political rights and cancelling mandates until November 9, so it would coincide with the cutoff date for the civil service purges. Indeed, Marshal Taurino de Rezende, who headed the general investigating commission, publicly asked Castelo Branco to extend the life of Article 10. The "moderates" won out, however, and the article lapsed on June 15, as scheduled.

The purge proved narrower than many had feared.[17] The revolutionary government had, over the 60 days, suspended the political rights and/or revoked the electoral mandates of 441 Brazilians. They included three former presidents; six state governors; fifty-five members of the federal Congress; and assorted diplomats, labor leaders, military officers, intellectuals, and public officials.

The list of purged politicians held few surprises. Goulart's place on it was a foregone conclusion. So was that of Jânio Quadros, who had triggered Brazil's current political crisis with his unusual resignation in August 1961. The list of 45 Congressmen hit hard the Nationalist Parliamentary Front (*Frente Nacionalista Parlamentar,* or FNP), a leftist coalition working to shift Brazil from its traditional pro-U.S. stance toward more nationalist economic and political policies. The best represented party in the FNP was the PTB, with such Congressmen (now purged) as Leonel Brizola, Sergio Magalhães, and Rubens Paiva.[18]

Another presidential name on the list, however, was a surprise: former President Juscelino Kubitschek. Castelo Branco had been reluctant to include Kubitschek, now a senator from Goiás. Not the least of Castelo Branco's reasons was Kubitschek's position as titular PSD leader, whose help Castelo would need in Congress. Kubitschek was also a frontrunner for the 1965 presidential election, having campaigned for a new term (election to a second successive term was prohibited) from the moment he left the presidency in 1961. He was undeniably a formidable candidate for an election now less than 19 months away. His extensive political network, sustained through the PSD (which had furnished Castelo's vice president), was aided by his image as the dynamic leader who had created the auto industry and built Brasília.

The American embassy, an enthusiastic backer of the Revolution, was now warning Castelo Branco and key military that purging Kubitschek would be taken badly by U.S. and European public opinion. Kubitschek, they explained, was seen favorably both for his record of economic development and his commitment to the democratic process.[19]

Kubitschek knew his enemies were closing in on him.[20] The hard-line military had long had him on their lists. They bombarded Castelo via War Minister Costa e Silva, accusing Kubitschek of corruption and collaboration with subversives. These charges were a stock-in-trade among UDN politicians, such as presidential aspirant Carlos Lacerda, who wanted to drive Kubitschek from the field.

Most of Kubitschek's political advisers urged him to keep a low profile, thereby minimizing possible pretexts for purging him. As the hard-line pressure mounted in early June, Kubitschek even offered to renounce his presidential candidacy. It was too late. Hard-line military pressure overwhelmed any recalcitrance in the Planalto. On June 6 Castelo signed the decree suspending for ten years Kubitschek's political rights and those of 39 other, mostly minor, figures.[21]

Kubitschek's cassation marked a watershed. Unlike Quadros or Goulart, Kubitschek had shown that he could weave conflicting interests and competing aspirations into an effective government. His 1956–61 presidency had been the last triumph of old-style politics. The hard-line military wanted to pronounce those politics a thing of the past. Turning Kubitschek into a political non-person certainly sent that message.[22]

The political purge was not restricted to civilians; an equally important one hit the military. Between April 1 and June 15, some 122 officers were forced to retire (though with full pension). Many of the targeted officers had opposed the coup, while others were known to regard the new government as constitutionally illegitimate. Still others were regarded as so far left politically, or so identified with Goulart, that they could not be trusted. Such a military purge was of course nothing new in Brazil—earlier upheavals such as the Revolution of 1930 and the Communist revolt of 1935 were followed by similar forced retirements.[23]

Supporters and Critics

The Revolution of 1964 was enthusiastically celebrated by most of the Brazilian media. Such key dailies as *Jornal do Brasil, Correio de Manhã, O Globo, Folha de São Paulo,* and *O Estado de São Paulo* had openly called for the Goulart government's removal. So had the magazine, newspaper, and radio-TV empire of "Diários Associados." The only major paper to oppose the coup was *Ultima Hora,* whose director and founder, Samuel Wainer, had to flee.[24]

The lawyers had been another oppositionist force. The Bar Association's Federal Council, for example, hailed Goulart's overthrow.[25] This stance was risky, given the irregularity of the transition from Goulart to Mazzilli. Still, in early 1964 the leaders of the bar were so alarmed about the threat to constitutionalism from the left that they were ready to overlook the legal defects in the succession.

The Church hierarchy was another source of elite opinion supporting the military intervention. In a May 26 manifesto a group of key bishops welcomed the coup, noting "the armed forces came to the rescue in time to avoid the implementation of a Bolshevik regime in our country." Although the statement defended progressive lay activists from the charge of being communist, the statement's net effect was to reinforce middle-class fears that the battle over the Goulart government was a battle for their future. On the other hand, the hierarchy's stand bewildered and deeply angered younger Catholics who were active in such groups as *Ação Católica Brasileira* (Brazilian Catholic Action) and *Ação Popular* (Popular Action). The arrest and mistreatment of many of them led some in the hierarchy to rethink their support of the coup.[26]

As for the politicians, the coup of 1964 caught most by surprise. The prominent civilians involved in the conspiracy lost little time, however, in trying to use the military intervention for their own purposes. Virtually the entire UDN and half the PSD quickly endorsed the Revolution, adding their denunciations of the Goulart regime.

A military-led movement had forced the legal President into exile and installed a government that could never have reached power via the ballot box. How far would this reversion to arbitrary power go? Everyone knew the hard-line military were looking for an excuse to silence more politicians. Much of the PTB and the left wing of the PSD, nonetheless, zeroed in on the dubious legality of Goulart's removal, and denounced the cassations of such distinguished figures as the nutritionist and public health specialist Josué de Castro, the economist Celso Furtado, and the educational reformer Anísio Teixeira. It was "cultural terrorism," charged a new magazine on the left, *Revista Civilização Brasileira,* which published a 60-page inventory of the arrest, harassment, and intimidation of leading figures in the arts, science, and education.[27]

The attack on the government was led by publisher Ênio Silveira, novelist and political commentator Carlos Heitor Cony, Austrian-born literary critic Otto Maria Carpeaux, and journalist Márcio Moreira Alves. The latter three appeared in *Correio da Manhã,* a Rio daily that had strongly endorsed Goulart's overthrow but was now disillusioned with its new military rulers.[28] Another noted critic was Alceu Amoroso Lima, a long-time lay Catholic leader. He saw Brazil now swinging to the right and warned in April 1964 that "the far right is just as antidemocratic as the far left. . . ." A month later he had an even more ominous warning: "until today I have never feared communism in Brazil. Now I'm beginning to fear it."[29]

Other opponents on the left likened Brazil's "Revolution" to a Central American *pronunciamiento*—a serious charge for Brazilian officers who fancied themselves a cut above their Spanish-American counterparts. The left dismissed the military as nothing more than agents of imperialism and of the wealthy and privileged at home, desperately acting to prevent Brazil from undertaking fundamental social change.[30]

The U.S. government was another enthusiastic supporter of the coup. President Lyndon Johnson, under prodding from Ambassador Lincoln Gordon in Rio, had sent a congratulatory message to Ranieri Mazzilli only hours after he took the oath as Acting President. Johnson was pleased the Brazilians were resolving their difficulties "within a framework of constitutional democracy," which was not, of course, entirely accurate. Johnson also anticipated "intensified cooperation in the interests of economic progress and social justice for all."[31]

Further U.S. support for the coup came rapidly. In early April Adolf Berle, former U.S. Ambassador to Brazil and a father of the Alliance for Progress, declared that Goulart had been leading Brazil toward the ranks of Communist Cuba and thus had to be removed. Berle was an authentic voice of the liberal establishment that had urged the carrot and the stick in Latin America—the carrot for the U.S.-endorsed reformers and the stick for revolutionaries threatening radical change. He was joined in early May by Ambassador Gordon, who described Brazil's 1964 Revolution as an event that "can indeed be included along with the Marshall Plan proposal, the Berlin Blockade, the defeat of Communist aggression in Korea, and the resolution of the missile crisis in Cuba as one of the major turning points in world history in the middle of the twentieth century.[32]

But the Embassy was already nervous over the witch hunt under way.

Ambassador Gordon admonished the Brazilians to distinguish between subversion and political dissent while also reiterating that a communist coup was likely if Goulart had remained in office. The effect was to express U.S. nervousness and therefore put distance between the U.S. government and possible revolutionary excesses.[33]

During his initial months as President, Castelo Branco attempted to dissociate his regime from the extreme right-wing revolutionaries. "We shall move forward with the certainty that the cure for the ills of extreme leftism is not to be found in the creation of a reactionary right but in the reforms which have become necessary," Castelo announced in his inaugural address.[34] But the government's heavy emphasis on anticommunism, coupled with the cassation of a figure so widely popular as Kubitschek, showed that the influence of the hard line was great.

It was also true that the new government's economic and political program, which included both anti-inflation and reform measures, was certain to provoke strong opposition. Were the extremists posed to demand resumption of emergency powers if the new government's monopoly of power were threatened? And, if so, what kind of regime would they produce? And would the U.S. government then be identified with a highly unpopular regime?

Economic Stabilization: A Quasi-Orthodox Approach

Having consolidated the takeover and centralized authority in the executive, Castelo Branco and his fellow revolutionaries turned to Brazil's economic ills.[35] Because they frequently argued they needed arbitrary powers to be able to carry out an effective economic policy, the latter bears detailed examination. By any calculation the Brazilian economy was in deep trouble by early 1964. The Goulart government, refused further credit abroad, was headed for unilateral default on its $3 billion foreign debt. Foreign suppliers, such as the international oil companies, were no longer honoring Brazil's credit. Sales were for (hard currency) cash only, and that was just about gone. Inflation had hit an annual rate of 100 percent. The endless patchwork of government subsidies and controls was distorting resource allocation throughout the economy. Businessmen, bankers, and even ordinary Brazilians found the scene so chaotic that they were postponing all but the most immediate economic decisions.

The new government's economic team, led by Roberto Campos and Octávio Gouveia de Bulhões, seemed well suited for their politically thankless task. Both Campos and Bulhões enjoyed wide contacts in the business and financial community, and both had highly relevant previous experience as key officials in the controversial stabilization program that former President Kubitschek had adopted in 1958 and then jettisoned in 1959. The new government's economic diagnosis was contained in a 240-page "Government Economic Action Program: 1964–1966," (*Programa de Ação Econômica do Govêrno,* or PAEG),[36] written by Campos and

Bulhões. Like many other economic diagnoses of Brazil in the early 1960s, it identified accelerating inflation as the prime obstacle to healthy economic development. The authors argued that the inflation was caused primarily by excess demand, which, in turn, had three sources: public sector deficits, excessive credit to the private sector, and excessive wage increases. When the money supply was increased to meet the demand, it stimulated a "chronic and violent inflationary process." A host of economic distortions were the result: wild swings in real wage rates, disorganization of the credit market, distortion of the foreign exchange market, and an incentive to use capital to manipulate inventories or speculate in foreign currencies. The resulting chaos precluded the long-term investment Brazil so badly needed.

Faced with this anemic patient, Bulhões and Campos prescribed a "gradualist" approach—in contrast to the IMF-favored "shock treatment" of a freeze on all wages and prices. They proposed to concentrate on gradually reducing (therefore the label "quasi-orthodox") the public sector deficit, contracting private credit, and stabilizing wage rates. By these and other measures, the government planned, on good monetarist principles, to reduce the growth rate of the means of payment in the economy (which had been 64 percent in 1963 and was to reach 86 percent in 1964) to 30 percent in 1965 and 15 percent in 1966. Assuming a constant velocity of circulation of money, that would reduce the annual inflation rate from 100 percent in early 1964 to 25 percent in 1965 and 10 percent in 1966.[37]

The government thought the deficit most needed immediate action. In 1963 the federal government's deficit had been 4.2 percent of GDP.[38] Such a deficit, if not reduced through fiscal measures or compensated for by an absorption of private savings, was inevitably inflationary. The new policy makers proposed to cut the public sector deficit by slashing all "nonessential" expenditures, running the state enterprises in the black, and increasing tax revenues.

Formulating policies was only a first step. Putting them into action would be far harder. No perceptive observer could have failed to note that Brazil in the early 1960s lacked the administrative capacity to implement complex economic policies. The ad hoc governing style of the 1950s was more suited to a time of easy economic expansion than to an era of economic trouble. No government taking power in early 1964, whether of the right or left, could have avoided the need for institutional overhaul.[39]

A major institutional gap was the lack of a true central bank. The *Banco do Brasil,* long the lender of last resort to the public sector, was also the principal commercial bank. There was, in addition, the Commission on Currency and Credit (*Superintendência da Moeda e do Crédito,* or SUMOC), which had been created in 1947 as the agency to coordinate monetary policy. But it had not escaped the Banco do Brasil's control and therefore failed to develop into a central bank. The new government was not able to create such a bank until April 1965, when it converted SUMOC into the *Banco Central do Brasil,* and it took several years for this new institution to function effectively. Yet the Campos-Bulhões team did swiftly establish a National Monetary Council which after mid-1964 acted as the forecaster and coordinator of the fiscal and monetary accounts.[40]

Reorganization of fiscal policy instruments was done more rapidly, partly with the help of the first Institutional Act, which gave the President exclusive authority to initiate spending bills. Castelo Branco delegated this authority to Roberto Campos's Planning Ministry. The new government then pushed through a law that prohibited state governments from offering new bond issues without federal permission. This was a major step in getting control of public sector finance, because state governments in the past had on their own issued bonds to cover budget deficits.

The Campos-Bulhões team immediately used its authority in managing public enterprises. The PAEG diagnosis correctly assumed that inflation had been fed by federal government deficits. Failure both to increase prices and to control expenditure in the public enterprises had resulted in large deficits financed by monetary issues. The Castelo Branco government moved quickly to end the huge deficits in the state-owned railroad, shipping, and oil industries. In every case it meant increasing the price of services, a step that directly increased the cost of living in the short run. But covering costs meant that long-deferred investment could be made in these public enterprises, thus increasing productivity and thereby lowering costs for the future. The government also boosted the cruzeiro price of key imports, such as oil and wheat, by using a realistic exchange rate instead of the previous artifically low exchange rate. The latter had been used by the Goulart government (and others before it) as a means of keeping down the cost of bus fares (highly dependent on imported oil) and white bread (made from imported wheat). Many of the Castelo Branco government's "corrective" price hikes increased inflation in the short run. Policymakers described them, however, as one-time adjustments needed to eliminate previous (inflationary) subsidies whose effects had simply been repressed under previous policies. Yet these price increases were intensely unpopular. The general public was riled over higher prices for bus fares, train fares, electricity, and bread. Could any elected government have carried out such measures and survived? The odds were low.[41]

The new government also attacked the other side of fiscal policy: taxes. Brazil, like most developing countries, was notoriously inefficient at tax collection except for sales and turnover taxes. Part of the inefficiency was due to the hideously complex tax structure, fragmented among federal, state, and local government authority. Bulhões and Campos attempted to simplify the system. The inefficiency was also due to lack of enforcement and to the incentive to delay tax payments because they were not adjusted for inflation. The gains from inflation-induced depreciation of a taxpayer's liability far outweighed the penalties for late payment.

The new government attacked the problem in two ways. First, it cracked down on tax enforcement. Second, it made all unpaid taxes, including social security payroll deductions, subject to adjustment (or indexation—*correção monetária* was the Brazilian term) for inflation. The delinquent taxpayer was henceforth denied any financial advantage from late payment.[42]

The Campos-Bulhões team had not announced indexation as a general policy instrument. It was mentioned only in passing in the PAEG, for example. The first use of indexation was in a law (4357) passed by the Congress in July 1964, which established obligatory indexing for all fixed assets, applied indexation to overdue tax bills, and authorized a new indexed government bond (*Obrigações Reajustáveis do Tesouro Nacional,* or ORTNs) whose principal was adjusted monthly according to a moving average of the wholesale price index.[43] In August there followed a law (4380) creating the National Housing Bank (*Banco Nacional de Habitação* or BNH) and giving it authority to index both the bonds it issued and the mortgage loans it granted. The PAEG noted all these uses of indexation without describing it as a major innovation. In July 1965 Law No. 4728 extended indexing to virtually the entire capital market (the indexation rate was the same as for the government ORTNs).[44] Without ever being announced as such, indexation was becoming an indispensable instrument in post-1964 economic policy.

The government chose indexing as a "transitional" measure to induce more efficient resource allocation *while reducing inflation.* The objective was to induce all the economic actors to think in real terms, rather than in terms of how to benefit by playing off inflation-adjusted credits against inflation-depreciated debits. Brazil's use of indexation raised eyebrows in such orthodox financial circles as the IMF.[45] But Brazil did not need to heed orthodox opinion unless it needed IMF help.

The tough tax collection measures resulted in a significant increase in federal revenues. They went from 7.8 percent of GNP in 1963 to 8.3 percent in 1964, then 8.9 percent in 1965 and 11.1 percent in 1966.[46] The combination of expenditure cuts and tax increases reduced the annual federal deficit from 4.2 percent of the GDP in 1963, to 3.2 percent in 1964, and 1.6 percent in 1965.[47] The declining deficit was financed through treasury bonds (ORTNs), the value of which was indexed, and which paid an interest rate of six percent.[48]

The second major instrument in the Campos-Bulhões stabilization policy was control of private sector credit. Such control had proved unachievable in the stabilization efforts of the 1950s and 1960s. Often the Finance Ministry had been at such odds with the Banco do Brasil that the orthodox monetarist stabilization efforts of the former had been thwarted by the pro-private business policies of the latter. Campos and Bulhões had little trouble achieving coordination, given their sweeping authority.

But the problem was more than coordination. Brazilians were understandably skeptical about any new attempt at economic stabilization, given the failed efforts of 1953–54, 1955–56, 1958–59, 1961, and 1962–63.[49] Those experiences had trained both debtors and creditors in the habits of economic survival during inflation—habits they were loath to break. Inflation that outpaces expectations favors the debtor who can pay off the loan and the interest in depreciated currency. The Brazilian inflation was no exception. Under such conditions lenders run the danger of business failure and become unwilling or unable to lend except on the shortest term, meaning weeks or at most months. Lenders had survived the 1950s and 1960s because of heavy government subsidy funnelled toward priority areas such as agriculture, capital goods, and infrastructure. Campos and Bulhões knew this precarious credit structure badly needed an overhaul. In the meantime, they had to leave private sector interest rates to the market.[50]

The reaction of the private ssector would obviously be crucial to the success of stabilization. The objective was to induce businessmen to think in terms of real resources, thereby helping funnel credit to the businesses where the real rate of return was highest.[51] Businessmen, bankers, and merchants could be expected, even if they endorsed government action in principle, to feel threatened whether they were debtors (likely to lose if lower inflation left the real value of their debts higher than expected) or creditors (upset over cuts in long-standing credit subsidies). Campos and Bulhões knew this, and that is why they preached to businessmen that they would pursue their policies no matter what. It was a key skirmish in the battle of expectations.

Wage Policy

The third main instrument of the anti-inflation program, after public deficit reduction and tighter control of credit, was wage policy. To understand the Castelo Branco government's wage policy requires a brief look at the structure of labor relations in the urban sector as of 1964. The legal framework (the *Consolidação das Leis do Trabalho,* or CLT) codified during President Getúlio Vargas's Estado Nôvo (1937–45) created a semi-corporatist structure in which unions were closely tied to federal control. First, all employees covered by the CLT had a compulsory union contribution (of one day's pay per year) deducted from their paychecks. The money went directly to the Labor Ministry and was then distributed to the unions, with expenditures under Ministry supervision. Second, all union elections were monitored by the Ministry, which had to validate all election results. It could even disqualify candidates from running for office. Furthermore, all union officers were subject to removal by the Ministry, under guidelines which were purposely vague. Third, the law made strikes virtually illegal, as almost all possible disputes had to be referred to the Labor Court system for decision. Fourth, unions could only be formed to represent a single *categoria* (trade) within a single *município* (a unit of local government approximating a U.S. county or township). There could then be a federation (on the state level) and a confederation (on the national level) of such unions. But bargaining on either of those two levels was extralegal. Equally important, the code gave no legal status to any horizontal alliance of unions, i.e., from different trades. Any attempt at a CGT on French or Argentine lines was therefore extralegal. Finally, the law had heavily discouraged, if not impeded, direct bargaining. One of the most vital issues, the minimum wage, was controlled by the government. Almost all other issues went to the labor courts for compulsory settlement.[52]

Brazil's "redemocratization" in 1945–46 had left this corporatist labor relations structure intact. The 1946 Constitution recognized the right to strike (Article 158), with its practice to be spelled out in subsequent legislation that was never enacted. Employer–union disputes in the years since 1945 had generally gone to the labor courts. But since the labor court judges were federal appointees, they tended to follow government signals.

It should by now be obvious why successive governments had found the CLT structure easy to live with. In the late 1940s the government of President Dutra used the law to purge the union leadership of all leftists. In his 1951–54 presidency Getúlio Vargas used the law, via his young Labor Minister João Goulart, to encourage labor mobilization in São Paulo. In the early 1960s President Goulart used the official union structure to generate political support for his ill-fated reforms.[53] Despite differing political ideologies, successive governments happily exploited the corporatist structure for their own purposes.

How had that structure functioned when it came to stabilization programs? The Goulart experience was instructive. In mid-1963, when the Goulart government faced raging inflation, it created a National Wage Policy Board (*Conselho Nacional de Política Salarial*) with wage-setting authority for the entire public (and mixed public–private) sector, plus all private firms licensed to provide public services.[54] Goulart hoped that this new mechanism might better control wages and thereby hold down price increases by these firms, whose output weighed heavily in the cost of living. In fact, however, wage settlements in these firms for the rest of 1963 were no lower than in uncontrolled firms. Goulart fell before he could experiment further with new forms of wage control.

The Revolution of 1964 promised to change the framework of economic policymaking. The First Institutional Act strengthened the president's hand at the expense of the Congress. Nowhere was the new government more anxious to demonstrate its powers than in labor policy. The Castelo Branco government was determined to get control of wages. It began with a housecleaning of union officers. During the initial two-month purge the government removed such prominent union leaders as Clodsmith Riani, Hercules Correia dos Reis, Dante Pelacani, and Oswaldo Pacheco da Silva, and suspended their political rights; a few were even tried on charges of subversion.[55] Even after its purge authority lapsed, the government used its normal labor law powers to intervene unions and remove their leaders. A total of 428 unions had been intervened by the end of 1965, including many of the largest industrial unions.[56]

Having eliminated any possible opposition in the unions, the new government turned to defining its wage policy in June and July of 1964. The goal was to keep wages from rising faster than the declining inflation rate. The Campos-Bulhões team first concentrated on public-sector wage policy. They reorganized Goulart's National Wage Policy Board and established a complex formula for calculating future public-sector wage increases. First, wages would be adjusted no more frequently than every 12 months. Second, the adjusted wage would be based on: (1) the average real wage paid over the last 24 months; (2) compensation for the preceding year's productivity increase; and (3) an adjustment for the residual inflation expected over the next year, as forecast by the government. This formula, although modified slightly in succeeding months and years, remained the basis for government wage policy until 1979. What mattered most, of course, were the numbers fed into the formula.[57]

As for private sector wages, the 1963 law had left it free to determine its own wages, subject to the labor courts' ultimate authority over disputes. The new government maintained that law, hoping that private firms and the labor courts would take their cue from public-sector wage settlements.

The optimism was unwarranted. Private sector wages rose much faster than the target levels set in the PAEG. In August 1965 the government asked Congress to extend federal wage-setting authority to the private sector. Campos and colleagues argued that adjusting wages by "simply applying indices for cost of living increases is incompatible with anti-inflation policy." Labor union leaders fought the proposed law, but to no avail. The bill was passed by Congress (now purged of the leading spokesmen for labor), and when union leaders appealed to the labor courts, the latter ruled for the government in September 1965.[58] The new law also extended the government's comprehensive wage-setting authority for three years. The implication was that by mid-1968 stabilization would be achieved and collective bargaining could "return" to the free conditions which the PAEG implicitly endorsed.

Convincing the Foreign Lenders and Investors

The fight against inflation was vital not only in itself but also for reestablishing creditworthiness abroad. Brazil's lurch toward a unilateral debt moratorium under Goulart had left foreign creditors highly suspicious. Now the Castelo Branco government faced the difficult task of laying those suspicions to rest.

The first phase was psychological: to convince all that the new government meant what it said and had the power to last the race. Brazil's post-1945 history was littered with abandoned stabilization programs. In every case the government had found the political costs too high and scuttled the program. The Castelo Branco government had to prove that *it* was different. One of its first moves was to repudiate the radical nationalism ("romantic nationalism," as Campos called it) that had won growing support in Brazil since the mid-1950s.[59] In July 1964 the Castelo Branco government moved to repeal the 1962 profit remittances law, which had clapped a ceiling on remittances (10 percent per year of the original investment, excluding reinvested profits).[60] Many foreign firms and governments, especially the U.S., had protested the law as unfair. As on the wage law, congressional agreement was assured by the government's earlier purge of the major radical nationalist congressmen. In revoking the 1962 law (and by other steps explained below), the government hoped for a rapid increase in private foreign investment that would bring technology as well as improving the balance of payments. In addition, such investment might also help take up the slack resulting from the deflationary squeeze on Brazilian businessmen.[61] The Castelo Branco government also thought a rapprochement with foreign investors would help convince the United States government and the international agencies—IMF, World Bank (IBRD), and Inter-American Development Bank (IADB)—that Brazil was once again committed to the "free world" economy.

Although the Castelo Branco government fervently preached its case, doubts lingered abroad. Almost three months after the Revolution, Brazil had not gotten a single commitment from any foreign creditor, public or private, despite having written its stabilization plan largely to please the IMF, the toughest judge.[62] The log jam finally broke in late June when the United States announced a $50 million "program loan" giving the Brazilian government great flexibility in its use.

As for the foreign debt, Brazil desperately needed to renegotiate the repayment schedule. Brazil had, since the late 1950s, increasingly used short-term foreign credits to finance trade deficits. The Goulart government had opened debt negotiations in 1963 but had gotten nowhere. Goulart's advisers had estimated that debt service for 1964 would run to 40 percent of export earnings, a disturbingly high figure by historical standards. In the short run Brazil had no choice but to ask for renegotiation. In the meantime, foreign suppliers were refusing to extend further credit.

Brazil's creditors had been awaiting a more cooperative government in Brasília. They warmly welcomed (mostly off the record) the overthrow of Goulart and the appointment of an economic team of orthodox views. The Castelo Branco government wanted to capitalize on this receptivity and so moved quickly on debt scheduling. In July 1964 the Brazilians agreed on a new payment schedule with all major creditors, including those in the U.S., Japan, and Western Europe. For example, 70 percent of the payments on medium-term commercial credits scheduled for 1964 and 1965 were refinanced with the U.S. Treasury, the IMF, the Eximbank, and a consortium of European creditors. This reduced Brazil's 1964–65 balance of payments burden by $153 million and greatly improved Brazil's import capacity, always crucial in an economic recovery.

The next renegotiation came in early 1965. Brazil now focused on her heavy commercial arrears, mostly for oil, which by January 1965 totalled

$109 million. In February 1965 the Brazilian government agreed with U.S. and European commercial banks and suppliers to regularize repayment at a level realistic for Brazil. The Campos-Bulhões team was pleased though far from euphoric. They expected to face further rescheduling in 1966, at which time Brazil would have to present proof of a genuine turnaround in the domestic economy.[63]

Although debt renegotiation was more urgent, attracting new foreign capital was also vital. Success here, however, proved much more difficult. The initial $50 million U.S. loan did not trigger a capital influx. The international agencies remained cautious through mid-1964. Only in early October did encouraging signs appear. The World Bank favorably evaluated the new policies and announced it would resumme lending to Brazil (after a 14-year hiatus). But other multilateral agencies did not follow suit, and by late 1964 the World Bank had still not formalized any loans. In mid-November Castelo Branco was so frustrated that he seriously considered suspending the negotiations then under way with a visiting IMF team.[64]

In these difficult months the Castelo Branco regime's most reliable ally continued to be the U.S. government. In early November 1964 Ambassador Lincoln Gordon announced that in the seven months since April the U.S. government had committed $228 million for Brazil. In mid-December, USAID (U.S. Agency for International Development) Director David Bell, after touring U.S.-funded projects in Brazil, announced further aid of $650 million. Uncle Sam was upping his bet on the revolution he had so lavishly praised.

In February 1965 the commitments finally began to multiply. The World Bank announced a series of new loans. The IMF authorized a $126 million "standby" agreement and a "line of credit" Brazil could tap at any time. This was significant because it was the highest credit rating the IMF offered. It also meant the IMF was endorsing (despite some staff skepticism) the PAEG (and other policies) as sufficiently orthodox by the Fund's standards.

Was the Castelo Branco government's creditworthiness greater than that of any government of the past 15 years? Evidently the World Bank thought so, since its 1965 loans were the first to Brazil since 1950. Or had the Bank relaxed its standards? Perhaps some of both. Roberto Campos was highly respected in U.S. and European financial circles, and he was very effective in arguing Brazil's case there. It was also true that the relatively orthodox Campos-Bulhões plan, if carried out, would sharply improve Brazil's balance of payments. The latter was, after all, the IMF's principal concern.

The Campos-Bulhões program called for a devaluation policy aggressive enough to keep the cruzeiro at a realistic value. The year 1964 had brought five successive Brazilian devaluations, reducing the cruzeiro's value by 204 percent against the U.S. dollar. Two of those devaluations came before Goulart's fall, but three (accounting for 57 percent of the total) came afterwards. By early 1965 the new Brazilian government had already devalued to the degree the IMF had wanted before granting standby status. The prevailing exchange rate at the end of 1964—1,825 cruzeiros to the U.S.

dollar—was maintained until November 1965, when the cruzeiro was devalued another 21 percent.[65]

In awarding Brazil standby status, the IMF was finally giving the green light to creditors and investors considering commitments there. Renewed approval came also from the U.S. In August 1965 a mission led by Senator William Fulbright, Chairman of the Senate Foreign Relations Committee, and consisting of three other Senators, along with the president of the U.S. Eximbank and Assistant Secretary of State Thomas Mann, visited Brazil. Fulbright announced in Rio that his official mission was "evidence of the approval" in the U.S. for events since April 1964.[66]

Enthusiasm from international agencies and the United States government were not enough, however, to satisfy the private foreign investors. Nor were legal guarantees, such as the February 1965 U.S.–Brazil agreement protecting U.S. investors against expropriation. What, then, was missing? Business was looking for the prospect of economic growth, which alone could generate profits. In mid-1965 it was by no means clear the Castelo Branco government's program could achieve growth soon, so foreign private investors remained cautious. In 1964 new net direct foreign private investment in Brazil actually declined to $28 million from $30 million in 1963. And the total for 1965 reached only $70 million. Net foreign investment did not resume on a significant level until after 1967, and even then it was primarily short term.

If we consider for a moment net capital flow to Brazil, then the reluctant private investor was not the only problem. Equally troublesome were the transactions with the U.S. Eximbank and the multilateral agencies. They contributed a net capital inflow of only $82 million in 1964, and a net capital *outflow* of $6 million in 1965.

Two factors explained this trend. First, in order to obtain loans from such sources as the World Bank and the IADB, Brazil had to prepare requests for project loans (for roads, schools, hydro-electric sites, etc.), which then had to be processed. Even new loans from the World Bank, for example, totalled less than Brazil's repayments on old loans. From 1964 to 1967, the World Bank took more money out of Brazil (in loan repayments) than it put in. Second, the U.S. Eximbank, which had lent heavily to Brazil, now wanted to reduce its very large share (20 percent) of Brazil's outstanding foreign debt. For the *six* years after 1964 Brazil's repayments to the Eximbank exceeded new credit by $200 million. Thus, for the Castelo Branco presidency (1964–67), both the World Bank and the Eximbank took more capital out of Brazil than they put in.

Fortunately for Brazil, other creditors saved the day. One was the Inter-American Development Bank, which contributed a net capital inflow of $172 million between 1964 and 1967. The major savior, however, was the U.S. government, especially USAID, the principal U.S. government arm of the Alliance for Progress. In 1965 Brazil's net inflow from USAID was $147 million, and from 1964 to 1967 the total was $488 million. This aid was especially welcome to the Brazilian government for two reasons. First, USAID had the flexibility to disburse money quickly. Second, much of it came in the form of "program loans." As noted earlier, such loans were not earmarked for specific projects, unlike USAID's own "project loans" and loans from the World Bank and the IADB. One well-informed economist has estimated that USAID provided over 80 percent of the net inflow of long-term capital to Brazil between 1964 and 1967.[67]

Not surprisingly, this help was not free. USAID program loans, for example, required the Brazilian government to present USAID officials with quarterly reports on macroeconomic performance, whereas for project loans USAID was entitled only to reports on the projects themselves. As each quarterly report came in, the U.S. embassy closely inspected the government's total economic performance. This process turned the U.S. into a kind of unilateral IMF, overseeing *every* aspect of Brazilian economic policy.

Whatever the legal obligations to the U.S. taxpayer, the political effect was to dramatize the closeness of the Castelo Branco and U.S. governments. There was a rapid proliferation of contracts with USAID in such fields as agricultural education, agrarian reform, fish production, malaria eradication, textbook production, training of labor union leaders, and expansion of capital markets.[68] They contributed to the image of the U.S. as the omnipresent power ready to supply money, technology, and advisers for Brazil's every development need. When a new U.S. ambassador arrived in Brazil in 1966, he was dismayed to find that "in almost every Brazilian office involved in administering unpopular tax, wage, or price decisions, there was the ubiquitous American adviser.[69]

The UDN: A Viable Political Base?

From the beginning of their rule the revolutionaries disagreed about how profoundly they needed to change Brazil's political structure. The three military ministers resolved that argument initially by issuing the (first) Institutional Act on April 9, 1964. There they limited themselves to a relatively short timetable. The political purges of April–June 1964 would be all that was needed. The country would then presumably return to a constitutional regime. But the Castelo Branco government found its task much more difficult than expected. It turned out to be not simply a matter of removing "subversives" from public life. It would also require, as the new president had said in April 1964, "reforms that would open new pathways and new horizons so that each person can rise according to his ability."[70] What reforms: In land holding? In education? In labor relations? In housing? The revolutionaries were unlikely to show a consensus when it came to formulating and implementing significant reforms in these areas.

In their first weeks in power the revolutionaries realized that the 18 months left on Goulart's presidential term were too few to achieve their ambitious goals. Castelo Branco's economic team knew by mid-1964 that they could not conquer inflation by January 20, 1966, when a new President was scheduled to take office. Furthermore, the stabilization measures were certain to anger much of the public. If the presidential election were to take place as scheduled in November 1965, the revolutionaries might well lose. They needed more time.

Castelo Branco had refused even to discuss extending his mandate.[71] He was committed to the principles of legal, constitutional, democratic government, contending that to extend his mandate would be the essence of illegality. As he once confided, "I'm not cut out to be a dictator." Back in 1963 he had been reluctant to conspire against the legal President. Ironically, it was his belief in legality and his conviction that Goulart was undermining it that turned Castelo Branco into a conspirator. In his inaugural address Castelo had declared, "Our call is a call to democratic liberty—a government of the majority with the collaboration and respect of the minorities."[72] Although he had ambition (no officer could have risen to general without it) he gave no sign of coveting long-term power.

In July 1964 Castelo finally gave in. He approved a constitutional amendment (which had easily passed the Congress) lengthening his term by 14 months (to March 1967) and postponing the next presidential election until November 1966. The revolutionaries defended the extension as needed to give time to clean out the subversives and the corrupt and to implement needed reforms. Accomplishing these tasks was in turn the necessary prelude to a return to constitutional government.

Although Castelo had striven to avoid the impression of political partisanship, it was clear when he talked about "normal" politics he meant power in UDN hands. Not only did the President espouse the UDN's political philosophy, he was personally close to such UDN leaders as Juracy Magalhães, Milton Campos, and Bilac Pinto. Indeed, archconservative Bilac Pinto's 1963–64 campaign against Goulart helped convince Castelo that only a conspiracy against the President could save Brazilian democracy. The new President therefore thought it natural that the UDN would play a central role in a "restored" democracy.

The first step he took in this direction was adding a provision to the July 1964 constitutional amendment postponing the presidential election, henceforth requiring an absolute majority of the popular vote to elect the president. The UDN had long fought for this change.[73] Back in 1951 the UDN leaders had tried to prevent Getúlio Vargas's inauguration by arguing (unsuccessfully) that his plurality victory did not meet the constitution's implicit requirement of an absolute majority. They had presented similar arguments in 1955 when Kubitschek also won by only a plurality. Now the UDN politicians, installed in power by a military coup, got their chance. As Castelo told them: "We must transform this proposition of our party into a constitutional precept."[74] It was done.

Castelo Branco next set out to consolidate the UDN by unifying it. This was difficult, in large part because the party's loudest voice belonged to the volatile Carlos Lacerda, hardly known as a team player. Lacerda had his sights set on the presidency, and he had fiercely opposed lengthening the presidential mandate.[75] Lacerda feared that the generals would soon close the door on his only hope for the presidency: direct election.

Castelo Branco and his political advisers knew how dangerous an opponent Lacerda could be. He had a deserved reputation as the destroyer of presidents. In 1954 he was the catalyst in arousing public opinion (and, more important, military opinion) against Getúlio Vargas, who committed suicide rather than resign. In 1961 Lacerda helped goad Jânio Quadros to resign, and in 1964 Lacerda's strident voice was instrumental in mobilizing opinion against João Goulart. Castelo Branco tried hard to maintain communicaton with his renegade governor. In July of 1964 he offered Lacerda a cabinet post, inviting him to help lead the fight against inflation. Lacerda not only refused; he launched a full-scale attack on the government's entire anti-inflation program. Castelo Branco, worried about his shrinking civilian political base, remained low-key.

There was now another threat on Lacerda's presidential horizon. The Planalto wanted to postpone the UDN's November 1964 presidential nominating convention. It failed, and Lacerda won a huge convention victory, with 309 out of 318 votes. The party on whose support Castelo's political strategy was based had nominated an intemperate opponent of his policies. Lacerda was also soliciting support among the hard-line military, as he had throughout his political career. This made him doubly dangerous.

Despite this setback, the President continued his attempt to strengthen the UDN. Throughout November 1964, for example, he worked to promote the UDN's fortunes in the western state of Goiás. Incumbent Governor Mauro Borges was a member of the powerful Ludovico clan which had long controlled Goiás politics in the name of the PSD. But he had accumulated many enemies, both local and national, not least among *linha-dura* military. Rumors linked Borges to a guerrilla flareup against the Castelo Branco regime. Such news delighted the state's UDN leaders, who hoped to reach power via a purge of the Ludovicos by the federal government. Since the first Institutional Act had expired, Castelo Branco lacked the arbitrary power used in earlier political purges. Instead, he tried to persuade the state legislature to request federal intervention. The federal Congress made such a request unnecessary by voting to "intervene" in Goiás. Borges was ousted, and an aged army marshal, hand-picked by Castelo, was made governor. This purge of a governor months after the Institutional Act had expired indicated that the "negative phase" of revolutionary politics was not over.[76]

Castelo Branco's pro-UDN bent surfaced again when the long-time PSD president of the Chamber of Deputies, Ranieri Mazzilli, sought re-election to the presidency in February 1965. Most Congressmen expected a routine re-election. Castelo Branco had different ideas. His candidate was Bilac Pinto, and after strenuous effort by presidential go-betweens, Bilac Pinto won.[77] The UDN rise, via arbitrary intervention, continued apace.

Defeat at the Polls and the Hard-Line Reaction

Castelo Branco's political strategists knew that the political purges and the economic stabilization program would alienate many voters. The question was, How much of the pro-revolution opinion could be retained until the economic program began to pay off? The government's first electoral setback came with the election for mayor of São Paulo in March of 1965. It was a setback because the winner, Brigadier Faria Lima, had been supported by Jânio Quadros, already stripped of his political rights. Although the Castelo Branco government had no direct stake in the election, the result provoked rumblings from the military hardliners, who were growing nervous over the eleven gubernatorial elections scheduled for October 1965. (The other nine were on a different electoral cycle.) Many military officers wanted to suspend direct elections in order to forestall defeat.

Two states were of major importance, Guanabara and Minas Gerais.[78] Both incumbent governors (legally ineligible for re-election) were prominent UDN leaders—Carlos Lacerda in Guanabara and Magalhães Pinto in Minas Gerais. Both had been leading supporters of the anti-Goulart conspiracy, but both were now outspoken critics of the stabilization program. Naturally, the opposition candidates also strongly attacked the Campos-Bulhões policies. A victory for either candidate in either state, therefore, could be interpreted as a protest against the federal government.

Hoping to increase the UDN's electoral chances, the Castelo Branco government tightened its control over the electoral system.[79] First, it got Congress to approve a constitutional amendment, supposedly to reduce "electoral corruption," which required that candidates prove four years of voting residence in the state where they ran. The second measure was an "ineligibility law," passed by the Congress under great government pressure in July 1965, which, inter alia, barred from candidacy anyone who had served as a minister in the Goulart government after January 1963. This measure, like the preceding one, was aimed at opposition politicians the Planalto thought might be hard to beat in the upcoming elections.

The UDN gubernatorial candidates in the two key states where Roberto Resende in Minas Gerais and Flexa Ribeiro in Guanabara. Both were vigorously endorsed by the incumbent UDN governors, who tried to help put distance between their candidates and Castelo Branco's unpopular stabilization policies. In August the opposition parties in both Guanabara and Minas Gerais looked for electable anti-government candidates. The opposition had been kept off-balance by the government's manipulation of the rules. Not surprisingly, many political candidates could not pass muster with the hard-line military. In Guanabara the PTB's early favorite was Hélio de Almeida, a well-known and respected engineer, who was quickly disqualified under the ineligibility act. The government's real concern about Almeida was his electoral appeal. The PTB's second choice was Marshall Henrique Lott, Kubitschek's "nationalist" war minister (1956–61) and later unsuccessful presidential candidate in 1960. The hardliners hated Lott for his alleged acceptance of communist support in 1960, as well as for his supposed fraternization with "subversives." Lott's candidacy was quashed on residency grounds by the Electoral Tribunal, deliberating under intense government pressure. The PTB and PSD then jointly nominated Negrão de Lima, a PSD scion and a former foreign minister in the Kubitschek government.

In Minas Gerais, the PSD (the PTB lacked a large following) nominated Sebastião Pais de Almeida, a leading PSD politician and Kubitschek's last finance minister. He was also a *bête noire* to the hard-line military because of his reputation for buying votes. After the Electoral Tribunal ruled Pais de Almeida ineligible on the grounds that he had won an earlier election through improper influence, the PSD nominated another long-term Kubitschek protegé, Israel Pinheiro. The nominations of Negrão de Lima and Israel Pinheiro were allowed to stand, perhaps because the Planalto and the UDN leaders thought they could beat them. These two elections shaped up as UDN-PSD contests, with the PSD candidates soon picking up wide opposition support.

Both the government and the opposition saw these two elections as the first major electoral test since the coup. Interest in the campaigns intensified when former President Kubitschek, after a dramatic return from his European exile, endorsed both PSD candidates.

Election day brought bad news for the Planalto. Negrão de Lima defeated Flexa Ribeiro in Guanabara and Israel Pinheiro outpolled Roberto Rezende in Minas Gerais. The UDN candidates had lost decisively, and in both cases to Kubitschek protégés.[80] Pro-government (or at least non-opposition) candidates won in the other nine states. Yet attention was fixed on the big two, which the Planalto and the press had pictured as the real test for the government.

First Army officers in Rio were furious at the election results and even more furious at Castelo Branco for having promised to abide by the ballot box. Rumors flew that military hotheads were about to depose Castelo Branco and install a "genuine" revolutionary government. Even the moderate officers were highly upset. Two officer groups were plotting action. One was the pro-Lacerda entourage. They wanted a coup that would land their man in power. More threatening was a second group, led by General Albuquerque Lima. Their more radical members wanted to march to the ballot-counting center at Maracanã soccer stadium and burn the ballots, then march on Palácio Laranjeiras, the president's Rio residence. All these plots had a common element: repudiation of the election results and installation of an open dictatorship.[81]

Castelo Branco suddenly faced the biggest crisis of his short presidency. How could he maintain his commitment to democracy and also fend off the hardliners threatening to depose him? Radical political measures had failed to prevent the return of PSD politicians of the kind which had made the Revolution necessary.

This political challenge was occurring within the context of a stabilization progrm that was alienating voters. The technocrats, led by Roberto

Campos, feared their program might now be endangered because it had become a political albatross for the UDN candidates. Was it possible that the economic policies necessary for Brazil's long-term economic development might fall victim to future elections?[82]

The worry was well founded. By mid-1965 the government's anti-inflation strategy was just beginning to show results. There was a sharp drop in the rate of growth of the money supply and in the level of public spending, which fell from 12.1 percent of GNP in 1963 to 10.5 percent in 1965.[83] But the orthodox measures had also produced a recession in the industrial heartland of São Paulo by late 1964, although GDP growth rose by 2.9 percent for the year. For 1965 industrial output declined 5 percent, an ominous sign for a society burdened with so much un- and underemployment.[84] While industry was in decline, GDP for the country was up 2.7 percent in 1965. Yet the opinion-makers lived in the Southeastern Triangle (bounded by Minas Gerais, Rio de Janeiro, and São Paulo). They trained their guns on the industrial distress in their region and thereby largely dominated the opposition critique of economic policy. They also argued that, in view of Brazil's 2.8 percent population growth rate, the per capita GDP growth was effectively zero in 1964 and 1965. The political opposition aroused by the industrial decline was, ironically, evidence that the technocrats' medicine was working.

Yet their tough monetary policy was soon undermined by two factors having nothing to do with public opinion. The first was coffee, long the key export crop. The 1964–65 coffee harvest proved to be one of the largest ever. The government, following traditional policy, had guaranteed a minimum price at which it would buy all coffee offered for sale. When the huge harvest arrived, the government was stuck with buying a large surplus. These purchases had to be financed by government recourse to the printing press, a move that added greatly to the federal deficit and thus to the inflationary pressure.[85]

The second unexpected factor was the surplus on current account in the balance of payments. The constrictive fiscal and monetary policies had produced a domestic slowdown, in turn reducing the demand for imports. Since export earnings remained fairly constant, as did the capital account, the balance of the payments showed an immediate surplus. The government was unprepared for this surprise. Uncertain that the trade surplus—so rare for post-1945 Brazil—would persist, the policymakers took no steps to neutralize ("sterilize," in economic jargon) the resulting inflow of foreign exchange. The latter was immediately converted into cruzeiros, thereby expanding the monetary base and creating further inflationary pressure.

Nor were the reactions to the huge coffee harvest and the unexpecteed trade surplus the only steps backward in the fight against inflation. The government aggravated the problem by announcing in early 1965 a schedule of tax reductions on consumer durables. The expressed purpose was to stimulate demand and thereby boost industrial production. It was also undoubtedly aimed at strengthening pro-government candidates for the

October 1965 gubernatorial elections. In any case, the combination of events led to a 75 percent increase in the money supply in 1965, more than double the target level of 30 percent laid down in the PAEG.[86]

In the wake of the November election results, the hard-line military presented the President with an ultimatum. He could remain President only if he vetoed inauguration of the two PSD winners. There was even pressure to have the winners investigated by military tribunals. Castelo Branco strongly believed, however, that the Revolution's legitimacy depended on honoring the outcome of legal elections.[87] After strenuous argument a compromise was reached. Negrão de Lima and Israel Pinheiro could take office in Rio and Minas Gerais, but only if the government assumed powers to prevent any such political reverses in the future. Under this hardliner pressure Castelo first tried to convince the Congress to pass a law granting the government such powers. He probably had enough votes in the Senate, but not in the Chamber. He lobbied the PSD leaders, including especially Amaral Peixoto and Gustavo Capanema, to join in the legal and political steps essential to returning Brazil to constitutional normality. But the PSD leadership, which had refused to vote such powers in the wake of Goulart's overthrow, once again balked.

Just as the earlier PSD refusal had led to the first Institutional Act, so the second led to the president's issuing on October 27 a Second Institutional Act. It empowered the government to abolish the existing parties and to make all future elections of president, vice president, and governor indirect.[88] This new Act was a compromise between the demands of the hardline and the moderates. It was also government recognition that in seeking a political base it would have to manipulate the political actors more fully than the moderates had anticipated. The implication was disturbing. How long must the electorate be deprived of its right to choose directly its governors and President? And who would benefit from the manipulation? Might this coup prove "revolutionary" by devouring many of its own children?

III

CASTELO BRANCO:
THE ATTEMPT TO INSTITUTIONALIZE

With the Second Institutional Act (AI–2) in force, Castelo Branco ended his hopes that Brazil's political and economic ills could be cured in the short term. But the castelistas, as the moderate military came to be called, did not abandon their belief that they had the cure for turning Brazil into a stable, capitalist democracy. It might just take a little longer. Castelo Branco's remaining tenure as president is the story of ever stronger doses of the same medicine. Meanwhile, the President defended his increasing political manipulation as short-term actions that would strengthen democracy in the long run.[1]

The Second Institutional Act and Its Political Aftermath

The main purpose of AI–2, scheduled to last until March 15, 1967 (the end of Castelo's term), was to make more difficult any opposition election victories. President, vice president, and all governors were now to be elected indirectly—president and vice president by the Congress and the governors by the state legislatures. The latter were readily controllable from Brasília because much state patronage and finance were federally determined.

In a second major provision, the president was again, as in the first Institutional Act, empowered to cancel the mandates of all other elected officeholders, including Congressmen. Third, the president regained the right to suspend any citizen's political rights for ten years. Fourth, the Federal Supreme Court was increased from 11 to 16 judges. This court-packing had been forced on Castelo by hard-line military furious over the Court's repeated rulings against government prosecutors in key "subversion" cases. Supreme Court Chief Justice Ribeiro da Costa denounced the move, but to no avail.[2] Lastly, AI–2 abolished all existing political parties.[3]

AI–2's most damaging side effect, from the government's standpoint, was that it further alienated many moderate and conservative politicians (mainly UDN), on whom Castelo Branco relied for his civilian political base. Milton Campos, the UDN Justice Minister and a widely respected exemplar of the legal tradition of Minas Gerais, had refused to draft AI-2. He resigned and was promptly replaced by Juracy Magahães, a veteran UDN politician from Bahia who was prepared to enforce AI-2.[4]

For Castelo AI-2 was a painful compromise between his liberal democratic principles and his need to maintain hard-line military support. He had sent AI-2 to the Congress, but his supporters could not muster the votes, even in the purged Congress. Defeat was ensured by the pro-Lacerda UDN faction, which saw the new powers as a threat to Lacerda's presidential prospects. Castelo had to proclaim AI-2 unilaterally, just as the military junta had done with the first Institutional Act in April 1964. He did so in his capacity as "Chief of the Revolutionary Government and Supreme Commander of the Armed Forces."[5]

Castelo tried to save face for the UDN by nominating Milton Campos and Adauto Lúcio Cardoso, pillars of UDN respectability, to Supreme Court seats. Both refused to serve. At the same time, Castelo had greatly reduced his own political power by insisting, over the vehement pleas of his closest advisers, that AI-2 include a clause making him ineligible for the 1966 presidential election.[6]

Carlos Lacerda responded to AI-2 dramatically by renouncing his presidential candidacy. Even though he had split the UDN by his fight for the party's nomination, and by his blistering criticism of the government, Lacerda's withdrawal further weakened the UDN. It also underlined the dwindling prospects for any politican who challenged the government through the civilian political process.

Castelo Branco knew the politicians thought he was embracing the right. To demonstrate his continuing commitment to moderation, he immediately used his new AI-2 powers against right-wing military extremists. Most visible was an officer group known as LIDER (*Liga Democratica Radical,* or Radical Democratic League). They had gained control over many military-cum-police inquiry panels (*Inquérito Polícia Militar,* or IPM), an ideal vantage point from which to promote greater repression. In June 1965, Colonel Osnelli Martinelli, a key figure in LIDER, publicly criticized the government's failure to punish all the subversive and corrupt. LIDER raised the heat by announcing that the President was merely a representative of the Supreme Command of the Revolution. Castelo had had enough. Martinelli was given 30 days house arrest. Castelo wrote War Minister Costa e Silva, urging him to ride herd on the hardliners, who needed "to be properly enlightened, restrained, and, if necessary, repressed."[7]

Justice Minister Juracy Magalhães then used the AI-2 powers to dissolve LIDER. Castelo followed by warning of a "creeping conspiracy" among military radicals. He repeated that warning over the succeeding months. In February 1966 he told his military ministers that he feared a military dictatorship might emerge. In May the question of the role of the military arose in different form. General Alves Bastos, Third Army commander, wanted to run for Governor of Rio Grande do Sul but would not be eligible unless the

1965 electoral code residence requirement were waived. General Amaury Kruel, Second Army commander, had similar ambitions (Governor of São Paulo in this case) and faced the same obstacle. Upon learning that Castelo was opposed to a waiver, Bastos denounced the residence requirement and, by implication, the President. Castelo promptly fired Bastos, appointing in his place General Orlando Geisel, brother of the head of Castelo's Military Presidential Staff. Kruel, who had been more discreet than Bastos, was allowed to retain his command.[8]

Castelo had taken another important step not widely noted at the time, a revision in the law governing military promotions and retirements. Before 1964 there had been no limit on active duty service of four-star generals. In December 1965 the Planalto guided through a law which specified promotion or forced retirement at each of four steps after an individual had reached the rank of general (admiral in the navy and brigadier in the air force). Further, no rank at that level could be held for longer than 12 years or beyond age 62. Castelo wanted to reduce the opportunity for senior officers to build up personal followings that could be mobilized for political purposes. In other words, he wanted to prevent some future general from doing what he himself had done in the anti-Goulart conspiracy. Two other provisions were probably the most significant. The first limited four-star generals to four years of active duty at that rank. The second limited all officers to a maximum of two years off duty before they had either to retire or return to active duty.[9]

While he was pulling the teeth of the military rightists, Castelo was also overhauling the electoral system. The objective was to resume open politics, but in a "more responsible" vein. Many military thought Brazil's political crisis could be traced to its multi-party system. By frequently shifting alliances, it was alleged, politicians had maneuvered for their personal advantage but at the cost of the public interest. The response in AI–2 was to abolish all existing political parties. Supplementary Act No. 4 (November 1965) laid down the rules for forming new parties. Organizers would need a minimum of 120 deputies and 20 senators. Although the total congressional seats (409 deputies and 66 senators) would have made possible the creation of three parties, the organizers of the pro-government party quickly picked up 250 deputies and 40 senators. That left room for only one other party, which would now harbor all the congressional opposition. The pro-government party was ARENA (*Aliança Nacional Renovadora*), and the opposition was MDB (*Movimento Democrático Brasileiro*). The authors of the party regulations forbade the use of any previous party names. Nonetheless, that background was bound to be important. The largest single previous party affiliation among ARENA was UDN, with almost as many from the PSD, whereas in the MDB the largest was PTB and the next largest PSD.[10]

Given the government's unpopular economic policies, the creation of a two-party system was likely to hasten polarization. The prestige of the Anglo-Saxon democracies' two-party systems undoubtedly influenced Planalto policymakers.[11] Yet they had now steered Brazil into a two-party system more rigid than either the U.S. or the British had experienced in recent years. Castelo Branco's fierce belief in maintaining his political neutrality led him to delay implementation of the new parties until March 1967, when he would leave office.

In a further effort to show a democratic face, Castelo reshuffled his cabinet between November 1965 and January 1966, with most of the new appointees having previously succeeded in electoral politics. Taking over Agriculture was Governor Nei Braga of Paraná; Labor was Federal Deputy Peracchi Barcelos of Rio Grande do Sul; Justice was Senator Mem de Sá, also of Rio Grande do Sul; Foreign Relations was Juracy Magalhães, the Bahian UDN leader moving over from Justice; and Education and Culture was Pedro Aleixo, the emininent UDN leader from Minas Gerais, who took over from Flavio Suplicy de Lacerda. The latter had become a prime opposition target because of his heavy-handed campaign to stamp out oppostion political activity at universities. Castelo was trying to give his government a more politically conciliatory image. But the hard truth was that he had been pushed sharply to the right. The most important politics now was the politics of the army officer corps.[12]

More Acts were yet to come. It took only until February 1966 for the Planalto to decide it needed a Third Institutional Act to protect itself in the upcoming elections. Mayors of state capitals and other designated "national security" cities were henceforth to be appointed by the state governors (now elected by state legislatures). The government was acknowledging that it could no longer afford to risk open and direct elections at any level that mattered. Another AI–3 provision moved up the timetable for implementing the new party system. In order to fend off the hard line the Planalto had to show quick electoral results.

Sources of Opposition

Despite the three institutional acts, the supplementary acts, and other arbitrary measures, the Castelo Branco government had failed to reshape Brazilian politics to its liking. In 1966 anti-government sentiment grew among the public. A few opponents had opted for violence in 1965. In March a contingent of 30 men crossed into Rio Grande do Sul from Uruguay, overcame *Brigada Militar* soldiers at Tres Passos, then took over a local radio station and transmitted an anti-government manifesto. Subsequently they clashed with local police and were finally captured in Paraná, two states north of Rio Grande do Sul. This unsuccessful rebel column was linked to Leonel Brizola, exiled in Uruguay. Its commander was Colonel Jefferson Cardim, who had been involuntarily retired after the 1964 coup.

Further armed opposition emerged in 1966, as minor terrorist attacks (carried out by differing groups) occurred around Brazil.[13] In February the U.S. consul's home in Pôrto Alegre was bombed; in June bombers hit the

USIS library building in Brasilia. In late July there was a far more serious incident at the Recife airport. Guerrillas planted a bomb intended to kill War Minister Costa e Silva as he passed through the airport. At the last minute engine trouble with his plane forced him to change his travel plans. He did not appear at the airport at the appointed hour, but the assassins' bomb exploded, killing three people and injuring nine. In early October bombs went off at the War Ministry, at the Finance Ministry, and at the home of the foreign minister. Although worrisome and dangerous, these attacks did not signal a serious guerrilla offensive.

The year 1966 also saw a series of protest statements and marches. University students led most of them, though, ironically, it was the Castelo Branco government's attempt to reorganize the university system that helped mobilize the students. One reform under discussion was charging tuition at the (then and still tuition-free) federal universities. Starting in July 1966, UNE, the outlawed but nonetheless active university student organization, mounted protest marches and demonstrations. Their target was the government's outlawing of UNE and its state affiliates. In July 1966 UNE leaders defied the ban by holding their national congress in Belo Horizonte. Police stopped the meeting before it even started. More than 20 students were arrested, and over 100 more took refuge in Dominican and Franciscan monasteries, where the police were loath to pursue. The willingness of the monks to shelter the students showed that some within the Church had become active opponents.

The student protest demonstrations continued into August and September, student leaders increasingly attacking the "dictatorship." And new elections for student government officerships either reinstalled the former officers or produced new ones of similar views. Clashes between students and police, although seldom involving more than a few hundred protestors, spread across Brazil in late September. Every clash strengthened the hand of the military hardliners. Indeed, some in the opposition began asking if *agents provocateurs* might not be behind these demonstrations.

Opposition now arose also from a sector whose leaders had at first welcomed the 1964 Revolution: the Church. The key figure was Dom Helder Camara, who had been appointed archbishop of Olinda and Recife shortly after the 1964 coup. In his previous position as auxiliary bishop of Rio de Janeiro, Dom Helder had spoken eloquently for social justice, winning a large following in Brazil and abroad. He was an early critic of the Castelo Branco government, thereby arousing the ire of the President. In July 1966 Dom Helder led 15 bishops from the Northeastern states of Pernambuco, Paraíba, Rio Grande do Norte, and Alagoas in formally supporting a March manifesto of three Catholic activist groups attacking Brazil's unjust social structure, its worker exploitation, and its police persecution. Military officers in Fortaleza were incensed, and they distributed a "clandestine" pamphlet attacking Dom Helder.

Castelo hoped he could defuse the conflict. He replaced the army commander who had given his blessing to the pamphlet distribution and in July he used a trip to Recife to meet with Dom Helder. But the talk (and Castelo's subsequent speech at the Federal University of Pernambuco) only underlined their radically different conceptions of the Church's proper role.[14]

Dealing with the Succession

The hardliners' strong influence contributed to Castelo Branco's major political problem of 1966: how to handle the presidential succession. The castelistas knew that the President's lame-duck status during his last year would reduce his effectiveness. They hoped to minimize the problem by getting the official candidate, once chosen, to commit himself to continuing castelista policies. The front-runner by a mile was General Arthur Costa e Silva, who had named himself War Minister on April 1, 1964, and thereafter had become a hardliner spokesman. In the tumultuous aftermath of the October 1965 election, for example, Costa e Silva spoke for those in the military who demanded that the two opposition governors-elect be barred from taking office. His role in that crisis clinched Costa e Silva's support among a decisive faction of the military.

Costa e Silva was a barracks-room officer with a jovial manner that endeared him to junior officers.[15] His style could not have been more different from Castelo Branco and his "Sorbonne" officers, such as Generals Golbery and Ernesto Geisel. They thought Costa e Silva incapable of understanding the profound political reorganization which the Revolution had begun. Campos and Bulhões feared that Costa e Silva might scrap their economic policy for some ill-considered nationalism or for a "premature" redistribution of income.

Castelo had a further objection to Costa e Silva. It was a visceral antipathy to any government minister who would campaign while still serving in the government. Castelo thought this abused the privileges of high office, thereby capitalizing on an advantage denied other candidates. For Castelo this was especially distressing if the candidate were the war minister, whose supreme duty, in his view, was to preserve the professional integrity of the army. Castelo's view here was more than a little ironic, since he himself, while holding a high administrative position, had coordinated a military conspiracy that overthrew a president.

In late 1965 and early 1966 Castelo had tried to head off Costa e Silva's candidacy by coming up with his own candidate. In 1964 it would have been Carlos Lacerda, but he had taken himself out of the race. In 1965 names such as Marshal Cordeiro de Farias, General Jurandir Mamede, Juracy Magalhães, Senator Daniel Krieger, Ambassador Bilac Pinto, and Governor Nei Braga were discussed in the Planalto. But it was very late. Costa e Silva had been soliciting officer support since 1964, and his stand in the October 1965 crisis had consolidated his hardliner following.[16]

Costa e Silva's backers claimed that he alone could preserve military unity. This was a powerful argument for Castelo, who knew all too well the dangers of divisions within the army. Without army unity, nothing else could be done—certainly not the complex reforms the castelistas thought essential to the 1964 Revolution.

After elaborate soundings and a face-to-face meeting in late February 1966, Castelo and Costa e Silva moved toward a modus vivendi. Castelo, along with key advisers such as Generals Golbery and Geisel, pressed for a commitment to continuing the Campos-Bulhões economic policy. Castelo also wanted an explicit commitment to democracy. His own government, he argued, "had had to opt for the legal path, instead of sliding toward a dictatorship."[17]

Castelo got no guarantees from Costa e Silva, but that was hardly surprising. Castelo had been so against Costa e Silva's candidacy from the outset that he had no personal leverage with his successor-to-be. But the war minister's supporters muted their campaign propaganda, thereby assuaging the castelista fear that they might undercut the governmental drive for reform in 1966.[18] Meanwhile, Castelo had decided to make a virtue out of necessity. Having lost his bid to control the nomination, he argued in an April press conference that for him to indicate his preference would be "a personalistic and ill-timed act" and perhaps even "disrespectful and disparaging of the revolutionary political structure."[19]

In May the ARENA presidential convention rubber-stamped the army officers' choice of Costa e Silva for President. His running mate was Pedro Aleixo, another wily veteran politician from Minas Gerais. He shared with his predecessor, José Maria Alkmin, a common political background. Both had risen through their respective parties (Aleixo was UDN and Alkmin was PSD) in Minas Gerais, both were highly experienced party politicians, although they were also bitter rivals in state and national politics. In July Costa e Silva began his national campaign as the official candidate. In the same month Castelo Branco finally decided to become "partisan" by joining ARENA, in order to demonstrate that the moderate wing was closing ranks behind Costa e Silva. It was yet another sign that the quick "housecleaning" Castelo and other moderates had hoped for in 1964 had failed. That would take at least another full presidential term, presided over by another general.

The campaign hardly seemed necessary. The MDB had already announced it would boycott Costa e Silva's election as a protest against the government's electoral manipulation. But campaign he did, across the country, in a journey that resembled the travels of a Mexican presidential candidate of the official party, PRI. The Mexican election is decided when a handful of PRI leaders choose a nominee, who then wins by a popular landslide. But the official candidate nevertheless tours the country for months, listening to carefully staged debates and colloquies from interest groups and local officials. The Brazilian campaign now resembled Mexico's, except that the deciding body was the higher military, not the party chieftains.

The election schedule for 1966 began in September with the election of governors. All the government-backed candidates won, although in Rio Grande do Sul Castelo Branco had to purge some state legislators to guarantee the election of his candidate, Walter Peracchi Barcellos. On October 3 the federal Congress duly elected General Costa e Silva the new President by 295 to 41. The nays were primarily MDB abstentions.

The UDN and Lacerda Again

Despite this apparent success, the government feared the congressional elections scheduled for November 15. In mid-October Castelo Branco used AI–2 to purge six federal deputies, including MDB deputy leader Doutel de Andrade and Sebastião Paes de Almeida. The government considered all guilty of one or more of the sins of subversion, corruption, or direct involvement in a new opposition movement, allegedly supported by Kubitschek and Goulart. As usual, no public explanation was given. These *cassações* were meant to intimidate the opposition in the congressional election. Castelo had to keep his MDB critics under control to preserve his credibility with the military.

In this case one of Castelo's closest civilian collaborators proved troublesome. Chamber of Deputies president Adauto Lúcio Cardoso was furious at the cassations. He announced that the cassation order would have no effect in the Congress and invited the cassated members to move into the Congress building. This was all the more significant because Cardoso was a long-time UDN stalwart and a personal friend of Castelo. Castelo answered with Supplementary Act No. 23, which recessed the Congress until a week after the elections. News of recess was brought to the Congress by a contingent of well-armed military police, who took the precaution of cutting off electricity to the building. Once shown the new Supplementary Act, the Congressmen dispersed. When Castelo reconvened the Chamber of Deputies a month later to consider a new constitution, the Chamber overruled Cardoso's continuing protest and declared that the six deputies had been unseated. Cardoso immediately resigned his presidency.

In the November elections for federal and state legislatures and for municipal offices, ARENA scored an impressive triumph, at least in national terms. It won 277 seats to 132 for the MDB in the Chamber of Deputies (thus giving ARENA 68 percent), and in the Senate it won 47 seats to 19 for the MDB (thus giving ARENA 71 percent). Only in Guanabara did the MDB outpoll ARENA in statewide voting for both the Senate and the Chamber of Deputies. As Rio had long been an opposition stronghold (whatever the government), those results were hardly a new trend. More encouraging for the opposition was the fact that in the principal cities of the developed Center-South the MDB consistently outpolled

ARENA. The MDB could therefore hope to benefit from Brazil's rapid urbanization. Finally, spoiled ballots and blank ballots (*nulos e em branco*) in these 1966 elections totalled 21 percent, as compared to 7 percent in 1954, 9 percent in 1958, and 18 percent in 1962. This new high reflected both the confusing nature of the voting procedure and the effectiveness of anti-government activists, who urged blank ballots as a sign of protest.[20]

As the government's political manipulation increased in 1966, one politician continued to act as if open politics mattered. Carlos Lacerda, who had renounced his UDN presidential candidacy in 1965, now decided to create a new vehicle for his political ambitions. Because there were only two legal parties, the ploy required some skillful circumlocution. He called his new movement the *frente ampla* (broad front). And as Lacerda himself had never generated a broad-based national following, he needed to ally with politicians who could. The obvious choices were Kubitschek and Goulart, notwithstanding Lacerda's long-standing hostility to both. Through emissaries in mid-1966 he contacted Kubitschek in Portugal and Goulart in Uruguay, asking for their preliminary support. He drew up a manifesto in September and published it in late October in Brazil, without the signatures of either Kubitschek or Goulart. It called for a new popular movement to be launched on January 1, 1967. Its goals: a return to democracy at home, and a return to nationalism and independence in foreign relations. Economic policy must no longer be hostage to the IMF. Higher wages would build stronger internal demand, reduce unemployment, and thereby increase Brazil's control over its economic destiny. In short, the aim was to pressure the President-elect, Costa e Silva, into economic concessions of exactly the kind the castelistas feared.

Although the manifesto was far closer to the past positions of Kubitschek and Goulart than of Lacerda, only the last had signed. Kubitschek, after making suggestions on the manifesto's wording, had turned cautious, evidently because of Brazilian government pressure (backed by the implicit threat of harassment whenever he might return to Brazil). Goulart's reasons for not signing were less clear, but probably had to do with a fundamental distrust of Lacerda, one of the major architects of Goulart's overthrow. Lacerda eventually persuaded Kubitschek to sign in November a "Declaration of Lisbon," similar in content to the earlier manifesto. Goulart's signature was still missing, largely because Kubitschek had convinced Lacerda that at this stage Goulart's name would be a political liabilty. The Declaration called for a new (third) political party favoring a resumption of economic development along nationalist lines. In press interviews Lacerda argued that such a party could, through its support, legitimize Costa e Silva's upcoming government. Not surprisingly, the Costa e Silva team ignored Lacerda. He aroused only skepticism from most of the public and the political elite who could not forget that this nationalist rhetoric contradicted his views of the last 15 years. The failure of Lacerda's desperate lunge toward nationalism was a sure sign that the day for his political style had passed.[21]

The Economic Scene in 1966

The castelistas enjoyed better luck on the economic front than in politics. The Brazilian economic stabilization program continued to enjoy praise (and dollars) from the U.S. government and the Washington-based multilateral agencies. In December 1965 the U.S. announced another $150 million loan,[22] and in February 1966 the IMF and the U.S. reiterated their confidence with new financial commitments. As of late 1965 and early 1966 her foreign creditors believed Brazil was on the eve of a resurgence of growth. Even the Russians joined in, announcing a $100 million trade credit in early August 1966.

Such foreign support was merited if a reduction in inflation was the prime criterion. From 1965 to 1966 Brazilian inflation fell by a third—from 61 percent to 41 percent. Three factors were responsible for the drop.

The first was the government's coffee purchase policy. Still smarting from the surplus coffee debacle of 1965, Roberto Campos froze the government-guaranteed purchase price for the 1966 crop at the 1965 level. Because inflation had been 66 percent in 1965, the coffee growers now faced a government buying price less than half of last year's, in real terms. It also enabled Campos to avoid any further drain on the Treasury caused by government coffee purchases. In fact, the federal coffee account showed a handsome surplus in 1966, at the coffee growers' expense.[23] Second, a close eye was kept on the trade balance. Although 1966 brought another trade surplus, it was much lower than in 1965, and its potentially inflationary effect was therefore smaller. Thus two of the prime sources of inflationary pressure in 1965 were largely neutralized in 1966.

Meanwhile, with the 1965 elections past, and given the expanded executive powers of AI–2, Campos and Bulhões could embrace more orthodox monetarist policies with little fear of the political consequences.[24] The rate of increase in bank credit to the private sector was reduced to 36 percent in 1966 from 55 percent in 1965. Increase in the minimum wage rate in 1966 was held to 31 percent, as against 54 percent in 1965. With the cost of living up 41 percent in 1966, the purchasing power of the minimum wage obviously dropped. Finally, the money supply increase for 1966 was held to the startlingly low figure of 15 percent. Equally important, the cash deficit of the federal government as a percentage of GDP was reduced to 1.1 in 1966, down from 1.6 in 1965 and 3.2 in 1964.

By the criteria of the monetarist approach, the Brazilian government was doing everything right in 1966. It had drastically curtailed the money supply, reduced the real minimum wage rate, and significantly cut the public sector deficit. Yet inflation still registered 41 percent for 1966. The persistently high inflation (that 41-percent rate did not look much better than 1965's rate of 46 percent) seemed to mock the once-confident predictions of Campos and Bulhões.

In fact, the inflation picture was to look better at the end of 1967—too late to help the Castelo Branco government. On one point the latter could draw some satisfaction: GDP growth was 5.1 percent in 1966, greatly aided by the stimulus to industry adopted in late 1965.

National Security and a New Legal Structure

Although the castelistas managed to get Costa e Silva's vague commitment to policy continuity, the likelihood of its being fulfilled was far from high.[25] The castelistas therefore devoted their last months in office to limiting the next government's freedom of action on both political and economic fronts. They tried to create a new legal structure that would protect Brazil against excesses from either right or left. This structure had three major components.

The first was a new Constitution, which a presidentially appointed team of four constitutional lawyers (Levy Carneiro, Temistocles Cavalcanti, Orozimbo Nonato, and Miguel Seabra Fagundes, though he resigned before their draft was presented) had drawn up during 1966. This draft was then thoroughly revised along more authoritarian lines by Justice Minister Carlos Medeiros da Silva. The new version was formally presented to the reopened Congress on December 17, 1966, and the first vote, largely along party lines, came on December 21. Neither the debate, led by such distinguished constitutional lawyers as Afonso Arinos de Melo Franco, nor the flood of proposed amendments made any difference to the final text. The new constitution was approved on January 24, 1967, by 223 to 110 in Chamber and by 37 to 17 (with 7 abstentions) in the Senate. Castelo and his advisers had gotten their way.

How did this new constitution differ from the Constitution of 1946? A key change was indirect election of the president. A second was the federal government's strengthened control over public expenditure (the Congress henceforth could neither originate a spending bill nor increase one proposed by the government), a change vigorously advocated by Roberto Campos. A third was the sweeping powers given the federal government to combat "criminal infractions against national security, the political and social order, or to the detriment of the property, services, and interests of the federal government" (Article 8). In essence, the new constitution was a synthesis of the three Institutional Acts and related laws.[26]

Changes were not limited to the new constitution. There were also new laws and executive decrees. Significant among them was a decree-law of late February 1967 which subjected the entire federal executive to military-style planning. Multi-year plans were to be reviewed annually and all changes coordinated through a complex network connecting every ministry. At the top of this administrative pyramid stood the President, with ultimate responsibility for the formulation and control of national policy. Helping him were the High Command of the Armed Forces (*Alto Comando das Forças Armadas*), the General Staff of the Armed Forces (*Estado Maior das Forças Armadas*), and the National Intelligence Service (*Servico Nacional de*

Informações, or SNI). This law directed the SNI to establish itself within every ministry. SNI officers would now have continuous access to every executive office and could easily monitor policy, as well as screen all appointments and promotions.

Another new law was aimed at the media, which had been a thorn in Castelo's side. The new grounds for government intervention, censorship, or prosecution were broad-ranging, from divulging state secrets to arousing distrust in the banking system. When Castelo's draft law became known in September, a storm of protest arose from such leading papers as *Jornal do Brasil, Correio da Manhã,* and *O Estado de São Paulo.* In its final version (after presidential approval of several key amendments), the law proved largely acceptable to the press. But Castelo *could* have imposed his original (tougher) version simply by issuing it as a decree-law (over which the Congress had no control). It was one of the rare instances in late 1966 and early 1967 when Castelo decided to allow the public and the Congress real input in writing the new laws that were to institutionalize the Revolution.

Castelo showed no such generosity with the National Security Law (*Lei de Segurança Nacional,* or LSN), which he signed as a decree-law only four days before he left office. The law was designed to defend against the kind of "internal war" which had allegedly threatened Brazil under Goulart. Perpetrators of psychological warfare or strikers threatening the federal government now faced penalties. The language and concepts came from the doctrines developed in the Higher War College (*Escola Superior de Guerra*), where Castelo had been a key participant. Castelo and his fellow officers were obligating every Brazilian to embrace the doctrines they thought had saved Brazil in 1964. Article 1 gave the flavor: "Every individual or juridical entity is responsible for national security, within the limits defined by the law." The law's provisions detailed the many ways national security could be infringed. In the hands of an aggressive government this law could be devasting to civil liberties. The implications for every citizen's political vulnerability were not lost on MDB politicians and the opposition press. But their angry protests had no effect.[27]

This frenzy of law was intended to shape definitively post-1967 Brazil. But the attempt was shot through with irony. By codifying the arbitrary powers they considered necessary, for example, Castelo thought he could forestall future recourse to even more arbitrary measures. By formulating a 10-year economic plan, Castelo and Campos thought they could prevent haphazard, shortsighted, and inefficient economic policymaking. By writing a new Constitution and a new National Security Law, Castelo and colleagues hoped to create a political system that would reconcile the military and constitutionalist ideas of the nation, the society, and the individual. Most important and most paradoxical, the castelistas believed these laws—almost all in conflict with pre-1964 constitutional principles—were the only way to preserve democracy. In fact, the castelistas had fallen victim to the long dominant Portuguese and Brazilian elitist assumption that the solution to any problem was a new law. The UDN, Castelo's party, had been a prime example of this mentality. His government was acting within a very old Brazilian political tradition.

The Economic Record of the Castelo Branco Years

The castelistas believed that the politically most vulnerable elements in their economic policy were the encouragement of foreign capital and the fight against inflation.[28] Government fears about possible subsequent policy shifts under Costa e Silva came in part from knowing that many hard-line military held strongly nationalist economic ideas. General Albuquerque Lima and his circle, for example, were outspoken economic nationalists and were known to have contacts with Costa e Silva.

In order to head off such apostasy, Roberto Campos's staff drew up a seven-volume Ten-Year Plan for Economic and Social Development (*Plano Decenal de Desenvolvimento Econômico e Social*), published in March 1967.[29] Its laboriously outlined targets for an entire decade would obviously limit any new economic team's freedom of maneuver. In fact, the plan was a dead letter from the start. By early 1967 Costa e Silva's economic brain trusters (headed by Finance Minister-designate Delfim Neto) were already hard at work on their own ideas even before the *Plano Decanal* was released.

What was the economic legacy of the Castelo Branco government? All would agree it had faced high economic stakes and limited room for maneuver, despite the government's arbitrary powers. Three of Castelo Branco's major economic goals had been: (1) reduce inflation, (2) improve the balance of payments by expanding exports, and (3) lay the foundations for long-term growth. Let us review the record in these areas, each of which involved far-reaching implications for social welfare in Brazilian society.

It was hardly surprising that the government fell short of its goal of reducing inflation to 10 percent by 1966. Nonetheless, they did reduce it from the March 1964 annual rate of approximately 100 percent to a 1966 rate of 38 percent. In 1967 it declined further, to 25 percent.

The fall was largely due to government fiscal, monetary, and wage policies. The real value of the minimum wage, for example, declined by 25 percent in the three years following Castelo's assumption of power in 1964.[30] Although no *public* statement explicitly stated the wage goal in terms of *reduced* real wages, this trend was no accident. It is obvious the policymakers had decided to reduce the minimum wage, as can be seen from the manner in which the wage adjustment formulae were calculated and applied. In applying the formula for the annual minimum wage adjustment, the government consistently underestimated the residual inflation for the succeeding year. Furthermore, there was no effort in subsequent years to compensate the minimum wage earner for the loss of past earnings caused by this underestimate. With the labor union leadership purged, with the Congress brought to heel, the Campos-Bulhões team could bear down on wages, thereby improving, they hoped, Brazil's competitiveness in the world market. Undoubtedly another function of the 1964–67 wage policy was symbolic. It signalled to Brazilian business and the outside world that Brazil was ready to take a tough line toward labor, with all the obvious implications for production costs.[31] Could any directly elected government have carried out such a wage policy in the mid-1960s? The unsuccessful stabilization attempts of the 1950s and early 1960s had amply demonstrated its unlikelihood. It was now easy, however, under the "cover" of an authoritarian government, installed by military coup.

Foreign trade was another crucial area for Brazil's economic development. Four kinds of imports were vital: (1) capital goods for industrialization; (2) petroleum, indispensable because oil-poor Brazil (importing 80 percent of its oil needs in 1964) had opted for transportation by the internal-combustion engine; (3) raw materials that Brazil lacked in readily exploitable form, such as copper and bauxite; and (4) technology and services.

Paying for these imports required either trade surpluses or capital inflow in the form of foreign loans, credits, grants, or direct foreign investment. Since the 1950s most Brazilian politicians and economists, like their Latin American counterparts, had grown pessimistic about greatly increasing their export earnings.[32] Because the prices of these exports—mostly primary products—were highly unstable, and because finished goods, which Latin America imported, enjoyed constantly rising prices, the terms of trade were often stacked against Latin America. According to this reasoning, most clearly enunciated by Raul Prebisch and the Economic Commission for Latin America (which he founded and long headed), Latin American economies could not expect to gain from their participation in the world economy and should, therefore, adapt to this unfavorable international climate by industrializing.[33]

The Campos-Bulhões team rejected this approach. They thought Brazil's export potential had been greatly underestimated. They launched an export drive to exploit not only Brazil's enormous natural resources (iron ore, timber, and food products, for example) but also the finished goods in which Brazil had recently developed export capacity. Campos and Bulhões further hoped that the market "discipline" now being promoted would increase industrial efficiency. Finally and very importantly, they openly welcomed more foreign capital in the export sector.[34]

The Campos-Bulhões attempt to use foreign investment in export promotion provoked fierce criticism at home. A good example was iron ore mining. Early on the Castelo Branco government approved concessions to the U.S.-owned Hanna Corporation to mine and export iron ore. This move touched a raw nerve among nationalists and some military. The latter protested directly to the President. After intense debate within the government, a compromise was reached. The Hanna concession would be balanced by sharply increased government investment in the Rio Doce Valley Corporation, the state-owned iron ore company. Not even an authoritarian government could completely flout nationalist opinion.[35]

Export diversification came too slowly to help the balance of payments significantly during Castelo Branco's presidency. The scant results of export promotion did not matter in the short run, because the balance of payments improved more rapidly than expected. By late 1965 there was enough foreign exchange to meet all foreign debt obligations on schedule, so the debt reschedulings of July 1964 and February-April 1965 did not have to be repeated. This was a result, quite unintended, of a reduced demand for imports, stemming from the constrictive fiscal and monetary policy of 1964 and early 1965. There was a surplus of $85 million on the trade balance (goods and services) for 1964, and 1965 showed a startling surplus of $293 million. For 1966 the balance of trade was in deficit only $25 million, a low figure for Brazil at its stage of economic development. The next years trade deficit was $314 million, but by then the government had enough foreign exchange reserves to last until heavier foreign financing began to arrive.

Improving Brazil's foreign debt profile was also one of the government's major successes. Castelo Branco was able to leave his successor with far more room to maneuver on the foreign debt than he had enjoyed when taking office in 1964. The U.S. had helped the Castelo Branco regime on this score with its flexible program loans. These were used largely to pay foreign creditors rather than finance imports when the latter had dropped sharply in the slow growth of 1964–65.

The political fallout from such policies was predictable. Brazilian critics attacked the U.S. for financing a policy of payments to foreign bankers ahead of jobs in Brazil. By 1966 some USAID officials wondered whether from the U.S. political standpoint it would have done better to stick to project loans—for schools, construction, health programs, literacy campaigns, etc. President-elect Costa e Silva, mindful of the importance of U.S. support, visited Washington in January 1967 for a talk with Secretary of State Dean Rusk. The President won a ringing endorsement from New York's Cardinal Francis Spellman, the most powerful Catholic cleric in the U.S. In March, only days before Costa e Silva was to take office, U.S. Ambassador Tuthill and Castelo Branco signed an agreement for another $100 million loan. Castelo Branco's presidency ended as it had begun, with a conspicuous *placet* from the U.S. government.[36]

Strengthening the Market Economy

Campos and Bulhões believed healthy economic growth required an effectively functioning private sector. As Roberto Campos was fond of observing, capitalism hadn't failed in Brazil; it had never been tried.

Everywhere the Campos-Bulhões team looked they saw obstacles to efficient Brazilian capitalism. A brief discussion of labor turnover will illustrate the problem. Businessmen had long complained that Brazilian labor laws locked them into an inefficient use of labor. They especially criticized the job security (*estabilidade*) law, which levied a high severance payment on an employer who dismissed, without "due cause," a worker with 10 years or more on the job. The fine was so severe and so certain (the labor courts rarely found "due cause") that employers protected themselves by routinely dismissing employees in their ninth year, often rehiring them on a new nine-year track. The result was to disrupt production and undermine rational personnel policies.

The Campos-Bulhões team drafted a new law, creating a trust fund (the FGTS, or *Fundo de Garantia do Tempo do Serviço*) to be financed by compulsory contributions from both employer and employee. The employee's claim on the new fund represented the equivalent of severance pay, although the worker could only collect in the case of, inter alia, marriage, home purchase, retirement, or unemployment. The longer the employment, the larger the compensation. By eliminating the "artificial" 10-year cutoff point, the new law was supposed to remove a labor market distortion. It was part of the drive to improve factor mobility and thus promote an efficient market.

Under the new law, job applicants could opt for either the FGTS or the *estabilidade* coverage. In practice, however, employers routinely refused to hire applicants opting for *estabilidade*. With the passage of time, FGTS replaced *estabilidade* in most of the economy. This de facto change was bitterly denounced by union leaders and by opposition spokesmen, especially on the left. They argued that workers were losing their chance at job security (workers already enjoying it were allowed to continue) in return for a dubious forced savings plan that could easily be manipulated by the government.[37]

Brazil's lack of investment capital was another barrier to development, in the view of the Castelo Branco policymakers. They sought to increase the capital available by promoting domestic saving. The first step was to create a financial instrument that would protect the principal against inflation by indexing while offering an attractive rate of interest. The first such instrument was the indexed Treasury bond (ORTN) issued in mid-1964 as part of the effort to finance the federal deficit. The government followed by creating a network of new savings banks (*caderetas de poupança*) that soon became important in capturing private savings, primarily for investment in housing.

The government also attempted to strengthen and enlarge the small stock market, but here the results were disappointing. The failure was in part due to the strong Brazilian preference for maintaining businesses under family control, rather than face the risks of going public. Despite incentives for privately held firms to issue common stocks, and despite generous tax write-offs (12 percent off the personal income tax) for stock purchasers, the stock market had not become a major new financing source by 1967, although there was a stock market boom.[38]

Another vital component for long-term growth was technology. In the mid-1960s Brazil's educational and scientific infrastructure was, by universal agreement, sorely inadequate for its economic needs. There was an urgent need to restructure Brazil's schools, universities, and research institutions, and to greatly increase their funding. The stabilization policy, however, brought sharp cuts in public expenditures, with education budgets as prime victims. For enterprises needing technology the short-run alternative was to turn to foreign firms or foreign technical missions. Yet foreign firms could never substitute for the long-run modernization of Brazil's educational system.

There was a final—and crucial—capitalist trait the Castelo Branco regime sought to strengthen: the entrepreneurial mentality. A generation of Brazilian businessmen had been shielded from foreign competition by virtually total protection from competing imports and by loans at negative interest rates, below-cost transportation, etc. When business howled over the impact of stabilization, Campos lectured them on the need for "a profound change in the way our businessmen think. They need to stop thinking in terms of small volume and high prices, they need to stop counting on excessive loans via government-subsidized credit, and they need to give up their morbid fear of competition."[39] Businessmen were warned they could no longer expect to make money through favoritism; now they could only make it by sound business practices. The Castelo Branco policymakers delivered on their message by selectively reducing tariffs, arguing that the increased competition would free Brazilian producers to become more efficient.

Did Campos and Bulhões succeed in building Brazilian capitalism? The answer as of 1967 was ambiguous at best.[40] For one thing, the anti-inflationary measures had provoked a severe industrial recession. The combination of slack demand and tight monetary policy, especially after late 1965, plus the reduced protection against foreign imports, drove many Brazilian businesses to the verge of bankruptcy and beyond. And it cannot be denied that the heavy reliance on credit control made it easy for foreign firms (because they had access to credit from their home offices) to buy up financially distressed local firms. The private sector suffered badly, and many businessmen were bitterly critical of the government.[41]

The Brazilian counterweight to expanding foreign ownership proved to be the public sector. This was ironic, for the revolutionaries of 1964 had repudiated the earlier pro-public sector policies that had allegedly stifled the private sector. Interestingly enough, however, few of the major state corporations was dismantled under Castelo Branco. Instead, most were reorganized, to strengthen both output and productivity.[42]

One further economic feature of the 1964–67 period deserves mention: the government's unwillingness to rethink Brazil's industrial structure. Castelo's policymakers said they wanted to strengthen "rationality" in the economy. But they never asked whether Brazil's industrial structure as of 1964 was an optimal base for future development. Kubitschek's industrialization (1956–61) had emphasized consumer durables, such as motor vehicles, refrigerators, air conditioners, etc. Yet the demand for these products had declined after 1962. The *quickest* way to boost the economy was to stimulate demand for consumer durables, thus activating the idle capacity. But to follow that path was to raise the purchasing power of a relatively affluent segment of Brazilian society.

This point was demonstrated when Campos and Bulhões sought to reverse the economic slide of early 1965. They eased restrictions on installment-buying, which was most important in consumer durables. This action, logical in a short-run macroeconomic context, reinforced the existing industrial structure. What rural worker in the Northeastern interior, after all, could afford a refrigerator, much less a Volkswagen? Consumer products within the reach of lower income buyers—such as inexpensive clothes, bicycles, and cheap stoves—experienced no spurt in demand, because the wage policy had reduced the purchasing power of those potential buyers. The pattern was thus self-reinforcing: increased consumer demand for durables, expansion of productive capacity for those products, then the need again to augment demand in the top 10 percent of the income scale. The industrial structure of the 1950s become an iron maiden for perpetuating a highly skewed income distribution.[43]

Was there an alternative? Not without a fundamental shift in Brazilian industrialization. And how could that come from the Castelo Branco government? Campos and Bulhões had thrown themselves into the formidable task of stabilization. Although they were committed to reforms, especially in the administrative and financial spheres, they had neither the mandate nor the time to rethink the consumption patterns they had inherited. They wanted to unleash the forces of the market. Few participants in the March 1964 pro-Revolution "March of the Family for God and Country" would have expected the new government to tell them that henceforth domestic appliances would be harder to buy. The Revolution of 1964, after all, was aimed at removing the populist politicians who were the leading spokesmen for greater social equality.

Castelo Branco's Political Legacy

What had Castelo and the revolutionaries wrought by March 1967? In the political sphere, they had codified arbitrary powers for the executive, sharply reduced the legislative and judicial powers, and resorted to direct manipulation of elections and parties, while banishing from public life much of the left, plus some of the center.

One feature of the 1964–67 period was unmistakably clear. The general elected President by Congress in 1964 was fiercely determined not to become a caudillo. Castelo Branco's austere personality and ferocious sense of duty combined with an antipathy toward anything resembling the military strongman role so familiar in modern Spanish America.[44]

Castelo held fast to this belief even as in 1964 he exercised his arbitrary power to purge politicians, military officers, and civil servants, and despite a powerful force pushing Brazil away from civilian democracy. That force was military officer outrage against the politicians they thought subversive or corrupt or both. After the 1965 state elections Castelo desperately sought a constitutionally respectable way to satisfy military pressure for renewed powers to cassate and suspend political rights. His failure set the political tone for the Revolution for years to come.

Yet even then he resisted the temptation to assume greater power himself. That was clearest in his insistence (against unanimous advice from his civilian advisers) on a clause in the Second Institutional Act making him ineligible for another presidential term. By this clause and by his eventual willingness to accept the military consensus in favor of Costa e Silva's candidacy, Castelo set the pattern for succeeding military governments: no caudillos, only succession by officer consensus.

In practical terms, decision-making in the army officer corps remained as hierarchical as it had always been. That procedure worked against the emergence of a caudillo because it was based on strict rules about promotion and retirement. Those rules created relatively rapid turnover at the highest levels of the Brazilian army command. Even though he continued his presidential term by one year by refusing to accept the possibility of a second term, Castelo Branco made clear his conviction that military presidents should not have prolonged tenures.

The most important result was to maintain military promotion procedure and therefore military unity. If that unity were shattered, the results for the military could be incalculable. If it were maintained, then the decision-making procedure, for better or worse, was clear. To analyze officer opinion required a close knowledge of the pattern of army officer promotions. Journalists made the effort to find out, but found that almost all officers refused to go on the record with any political views. Schooled in the Brazilian military tradition, they wanted to protect their service by denying the outsider information about internal divisions. Lacking information, the outsiders, i.e., the civilian politicians, could not attempt to recruit a military faction to serve their ambition.

What of the political parties and their part in Castelo's political legacy? Castelo steadfastly believed in the UDN. It was the party that had fought the populists. It was the party that thought it had won power with Goulart's overthrow. Again and again Castelo relied on UDN leaders to carry the day, but too often they failed. Nor should that have been surprising. After all, the UDN had been a minority party in pre-1964 national politics. Never able to win the presidency under its own banner, the UDN had in 1960 turned to the maverick Jânio Quadros, whose quixotic resignation in 1961 dashed their hopes for a normal turn in power.

Why was the UDN unable to win (under the normal rules) the electoral victories Castelo and the military expected of it? The fault must have lain either with the UDN politicians or with the electorate. Castelo chose to believe it was the latter. So to save the voters from the temptation of voting for the wrong candidates, the political rights of any such candidates were suspended (that UDN nemesis Jânio Quadros was at the top of the first list) and election for the higher offices was made indirect. Thus was born the revolutionary electoral logic: Brazil would need a tutelary democracy until the body politic was fully purged of its subversive and/or corrupt elements. How long would it take? The Second Institutional Act was scheduled to expire the day the Castelo Branco government left office.

Castelo's estimate of ARENA's vote-getting potential contributed strongly to his belief (and that of his political advisers) that both the Revolution and the Brazilian public could return to a relatively open democracy by March 1967. A more realistic assessment of ARENA's prospects might have led to greater government efforts to favor and strengthen it. Here again Castelo's scruples (which undoubtedly reflected one strain of military thinking) were crucial. He thought it would be "unfair" for the government to favor ARENA over other parties. That inhibition, combined with the fact that government regulations had created a de facto two-party system, simplified the MDB's task of consolidating the opposition. Should the latter become a threat, the government could always change the rules again. Castelo, however, believed that would not be necessary. In August 1966, for example, he explained that "on March 15, 1967, the Revolution will have completed its basic institutionalization so that in the next phase it can reinvigorate Brazilian democracy and the economic development of the country."[45]

As he approached his final days in the Planalto, Castelo believed that his three years (minus a few weeks) in the presidency had done the job. The subversives and populists had been defeated, discredited, and purged. The economy had been stabilized, the financial system reorganized, and the foreign debt renegotiated. Brazil could now rejoin the ranks of the democracies, albeit with a constitution that sharply increased executive (and military) power at the expense of the legislature and judiciary.

IV

Costa e Silva: The Military Tighten Their Grip

It was a tense moment when Marshal Costa e Silva received the presidential sash on March 15, 1967. Castelo Branco and his allies had stubbornly fought Costa e Silva's nomination. Having lost that battle, they pushed through a welter of new laws and a new constitution, ostensibly to consolidate the Revolution, but also to box in the new government.

When Costa e Silva put on the sash, Brazil said goodbye to a troubled presidential term. It had begun with Jânio Quadros's election in 1960, followed by his resignation in 1961, João Goulart's tumultuous succession in 1961, the military-imposed parliamentary system from 1961 to 1963, Goulart's overthrow in 1964, and, finally, Castelo Branco's presidency, which the military extended one year beyond the original 1961–66 mandate. Costa e Silva was now starting on the first full presidential term since the Revolution.[1]

The questions about the new government were legion. Would Costa e Silva, as promised, "humanize the Revolution"? Would that mean easier wage and credit policies? Or more nationalist policies toward foreign capital? Castelo's camp feared both. And how would any policy changes affect army officer opinion, now the crucible of Brazilian politics?

A New Cast

The new President fit the stereotype of the Latin American military officer. He was jovial, more at home at the horse races than studying tomes on military strategy.[2] The apparent contrast with the austere, intellectual Castelo Branco could hardly have been greater, but that contrast in images was not entirely accurate. Costa e Silva had graduated top of his class at his Colegio Militar and at the junior officers school (*Escola de Aperfeiçoamento de Oficiais*). He had done a six-month training course at Fort Knox in 1944, he had spent two years as a military aide in the Brazilian embassy in Buenos Aires, and he had commanded the Fourth Army in the politically volatile Northeast in 1961–62. The new President was a more talented and more complex figure than his popluar image suggested.

The new cabinet included not a single carry-over from the previous government. The lack of continuity that Castelo and Roberto Campos had feared was now evident, at least in personnel. Of the three military ministers (navy, army, air force), two went to hardliners: Admiral Augusto Hamann Rademaker Grunewald at navy and Air Marshal Marcio de Souza e Melo for the air force. The new minister of the army was General Aurelio de Lyra Tavares, a former commandant of the Higher War College (ESG) and clearly identified with the "Sorbonne" group. The fourth important military position, head of the Military Presidential Staff, went to General Jayme Portella de Mello, Costa e Silva's close collaborator in the anti-Goulart plot.

Two other key cabinet positions went to army officers. The Transportation Minister was Colonel (reserve) Mario David Andreazza, right-hand man to Costa e Silva when the new president was war minister. Interior went to General (reserve) Afonso Augusto de Albuquerque Lima, a noted engineer and outspoken economic nationalist. Finally, the sensitive post of Chief of the National Intelligence Service (SNI) was assumed by General Emílio Garrastazú Médici, a relative unknown who had been military attaché in Washington and, more important, a close friend of Costa e Silva. Médici's March 17 swearing-in ceremony was boycotted by General Golbery, the SNI's founder and outgoing director. It was a powerful insult to the victorious Costa e Silva team from one of Castelo's chief collaborators.

Reinforcing the cabinet's military tone were three reserve army officers: Jarbas Gonçalves Passarinho became Minister of Labor and Social Security, Colonel José Costa Cavalcanti became Minister of Mines and Energy, and General Edmundo de Macedo Soares became Minister of Trade and Industry.

Among the civilian ministers, the key figures for the economy were Antonio Delfim Neto in Finance and Helio Beltrão in Planning. Delfim Neto was a brilliant 38-year-old São Paulo economist on his way up; Beltrão was a respected figure from private business who was chief planner for Carlos Lacerda's governorship of Guanabara. The remaining civilian ministers were respectable, if politically lightweight, with two exceptions. One was José de Magalhães Pinto, the new Foreign Minister. He was a former Governor of Minas Gerais and a leading conspirator against Goulart. He had become an outspoken critic of the austerity policies of Castelo Branco. He was now the most politically visible civilian cabinet minister. The other exception was Professor Luis Antonio da Gama e Silva, the new Minister of Justice, who was the Rector of the University of São Paulo, Brazil's leading university and home of a famous law faculty which Gama e Silva had headed. Yet the new Justice Minister was no liberal. In the October 1965 crisis, Gama e Silva had proposed that the Castelo Branco government become a full-blown dictatorship.[3]

The new Vice President was Pedro Aleixo, a political veteran from

Minas Gerais, long a pivotal state in Brazilian politics. Aleixo was a veteran UDN Congressman who became parliamentary majority leader during the Quadros presidency (1961) and again during the Castelo Branco presidency. He was then appointed Education Minister in January 1966. The military had made a similar choice for Vice President in 1964 when they selected José Maria Alkmin, another well-known political leader from Minas Gerais. In both cases it was a limp gesture to gain legitimacy from the political class.

The strongly military makeup of the cabinet was inevitable. After all, the politicians had long enjoyed the fruits of power. Why shouldn't military officers, who had (by their reasoning) saved Brazil from chaos and communism, enjoy control over the government—for the benefits it could bring to compatriots and favored civilian sectors, if for no other reason? But that the cabinet was predominantly military did not mean it resembled its predecessor. A close look at Costa e Silva's cabinet makes it clear that few of these ministers were cut from the same austere cloth as Castelo Branco and his closest collaborators.

In fact, these officers represented a political position very different from the castelistas.[4] They were not from, nor heavily influenced by, the "Sorbonne" or the FEB, and few had close links to the U.S. The new profile suggested possibly a more nationalist stance. Would Brazil move away from the Castelo Branco government's instinctive reliance on the U.S.?

The New Economic Strategy

The new government's most urgent task was the economy, still sluggish due to Campos's deflationary policies of 1966. Critics on the left, as well as many spokesmen for commerce and industry, had denounced Castelo Branco and Campos for having turned Brazil over to the orthodox formulae of the IMF. The well-known economist Celso Furtado, for example, accused the Castelo Branco government of subjecting Brazil to a "pastoralization" plan such as the U.S. had allegedly tried to impose on Germany in 1945. Industrial investment would be "reduced to zero," while government expenditure would be concentrated on the countryside.[5] Such critics predicted the ruin of Brazilian industry in the face of generous concessions to foreign capital. No less important, they charged, was the pauperization of the Brazilian worker, hit by a government-induced decline in real wage rates. Campos and Castelo had treated these charges with contempt. They had argued that Brazil was returning to financial sanity—something only the inefficient (or worse) had reason to fear.

That the economy (and Brazilian business) had suffered under stabilization was irrefutable. That foreign firms did buy up some Brazilian firms was also fact. Real wage rates did decline; some households in the city of São Paulo, for example, maintained their real income levels but only because more family members got jobs. Every economic sector had losses. The issue was the allocation of those losses, and that was an acutely political question.

There was another truth: the Castelo Branco government's unpopular policies had left a favorable macroeconomic legacy for the new regime. First, they had sharply reduced inflation and dramatically improved the balance of payments. They had reduced the government sector deficit, both by cutting expenditures and raising revenues. They had rationalized the public sector, including better management of public corporations. They had skillfully used tax and credit incentives in key areas such as export promotion.[6] Finally, the renegotiation of the large short term foreign debt and the increase of capital inflows (primarily public) helped to strengthen Brazil's balance of payments, thus giving policymakers more room for maneuver.

The Castelo Branco government had worried that nationalists might engineer a resurgence of inflation or economic nationalism under Costa e Silva.[7] Their fears were not realized. Economic policy passed into the hands of technocrats ideologically indistinct from the Castelo team. The dominant figure now was the outstanding economist Antonio Delfim Neto, as noted earlier.[8] Short, stout, and voluble, from an Italian immigrant family, he had studied economics at the University of São Paulo, one of Brazil's few graduate economics faculties of international standing. He specialized in econometrics, and in 1958 he won the chair of economic theory at his university, supplementing his teaching with outside consulting. In 1966, when Delfim Neto was 37, Castelo Branco named him Economic Secretary for the State of São Paulo, in the wake of the federal intervention that deposed Governor Adhemar de Barros. In less than a year Delfim had straightened out the chaotic state finances, largely wiping out the state budget deficit. In the process he had developed close ties to São Paulo commerce and industry. On Roberto Campos's recommendation he had been brought into two high-level planning councils in the Castelo Branco government. He was now looking for new worlds to conquer. And he was an enthusiastic supporter of "the Revolution of March 31," which he described as a "huge demonstration by society" and "the product of a collective consensus."[9]

Anyone looking at the Brazilian economy in early 1967 might have concluded that it had excess capacity which could accommodate increased output with little pressure on prices. If so, an easier monetary policy was the obvious option. Yet the Campos team had believed Brazil's only choice was to continue the orthodox medicine of tight monetary and fiscal policy. Why? Because inflation was still too high (38 percent in 1966) and domestic industry still too inefficient for healthy long-term growth to be resumed.

Delfim Neto took a very different view. He and his team (mostly his former students and economists of IPEA, a government research institute) had developed a new analysis of Brazilian inflation. They argued that it was no longer demand-induced, but cost-induced. The most important cost was credit, further tightened in 1966–67. They therefore proposed turning the

Campos-Bulhões credit policy on its head: stimulate demand by easing credit. Delfim Neto argued they could achieve "rapid development without increasing inflation," because of excess capacity.[10] The new government's economic goal, explained Delfim, was "rapid development without inflationary pressures." That meant "increasing per capita growth, rapidly expanding employment, reducing inequalities among individuals and regions, and maintaining a relative monetary equilibrium," to which Delfim added, "without major problems in the balance of payments."[11] A tall order, as even Delfim's admirers would have admitted.

When he assumed office in March 1967, Delfim went full speed ahead by pumping credit into the economy. His team's diagnosis proved correct. In 1967 bank credit to the private sector was expanded 57 percent and the economy grew at 4.8 percent, while inflation reached only 24 percent.[12]

Full speed ahead did not mean ignoring rising prices, which Delfim's team took seriously. To constrain inflationary expectations they resorted to a distinctly un-free enterprise solution: price control.[13] The Castelo Branco government had tried a voluntary price-control system (begun in February 1965) which gave firms tax and credit rewards if they followed government-endorsed price guidelines. Since the latter applied only to the Campos-Bulhões inflation targets, and since those were greatly exceeded each year, few firms followed the guidelines.

Delfim took a different line. A December 1967 decree required all price increases to have prior government approval. The system was given an administrative apparatus in August 1968 with the creation of the Interministerial Price Council (*Conselho Interministerial de Preços,* or CIP). The new government now committed itself to all-out price control. Tough penalities were specified for violators. The CIP became a central policymaking organ, with most businesses needing its approval to raise prices. This resort to price control, interestingly enough, was hardly what businessmen had envisaged when they supported the 1964 revolution.[14]

The new government also became even more interventionist in wage policy. At first Campos and Bulhões had limited their authority to public sector wages, but in 1965 they extended it to the private sector. Compliance became mandatory, although the 1965 law had only a three-year life. That law's impending expiration in 1968 gave the Costa e Silva policymakers the opportunity to decide on continuation.

It did not take long. In 1968 the government asked the Congress to make the 1965 law permanent. The Congress readily agreed. The Brazilian revolutionaries, product of a revolt against an alleged statist threat from the left, were now embracing their own *dirigisme:* indefinite wage control.

Everyone agreed that workers had suffered a sharp loss in real wage rates during the 1964–67 stabilization effort. The Castelo Branco government claimed that correcting harmful past policies required sacrifice by all in the short run. But the application of the wage formula reduced the real minimum wage rate by repeatedly underestimating expected inflation. By 1967 this underestimate had cost workers at least 25 percent of their buying power at the minimum wage rate. Delfim therefore proposed to add a new element in the formula—a "correction for the inflationary residual"—to make up for previous losses caused by inflation underestimates. He publicized this change widely, hoping thereby to popularize the Costa e Silva government.[15]

The change had minimal impact. In 1968 and 1969 the real value of the minimum wage increased slightly. In 1970, however, the decline resumed. Meanwhile, the Costa e Silva government had indefinitely extended its power to set the minimum wage. Further, the government-controlled corporatist structure of labor relations remained intact, and worker protests, up to now infrequent and small, were handily suppressed. As the Costa e Silva government loosened credit to accelerate growth, labor appeared to present no problem.

By making permanent in 1968 its economy-wide control over the minimum wage, the Costa e Silva government opened a new stage in economic policy. Whereas the Castelo Branco government talked of temporary measures—wage control, indexation—to achieve stabilization, Delfim was now adapting those instruments for long-term use. It was clear that Brazil was moving beyond stabilization toward a new economic development strategy.

In staking out that path, Delfim made extraordinary claims about his government's total lack of self-interest. Seldom has Brazilian history ever seen, he argued, "a government such as this, with absolutely no commitments to any social classes or economic groups, and without the least interest in the defense or preservation of social institutions that hamper economic activity." Here was the technocrat par excellence, disclaiming involvement in the social and moral questions that were inherent in economic policymaking.[16]

Politics: Back to "Normal"?

President Costa e Silva had worked hard to project a conciliatory image. He began his term by promising to humanize the Revolution. And the country was alive with jokes about the President, always a sign that the public breathed easier. He talked with a wide range of groups, from clergy to businessmen to politicians, assuring them his government would listen to their legitimate demands for change. He also created a new public relations office (*Assessoria Especial de Relações Públicas,* or AERP) in the presidency, a body intended to help shape the opinion to which the government would respond.

But the opposition (and some pro-government) politicians would not settle for a polite dialogue. Castelo Branco's mass of new laws, decrees, and institutional acts drastically reduced public participation—at least through their elected representatives—in government. Opposition politicians were angry at the military regime's steady usurpation of power. But any thoughts of trying to regain power ran up against the new rules of the political game. Was Costa e Silva ready to loosen the legal straitjacket Castelo had fashioned?

The new government looked lethargic and ill-coordinated during its early months. Ministers promised major new projects without considering the cost. The President, though conciliatory in tone, seemed hesitant and tentative. The new government's indecision was mirrored in the legal opposition's hesitation. Lacerda's Broad Front had still not materialized. Lacerda's friends in the new cabinet (Magalhães Pinto and Helio Beltrão) were urging him to give Costa e Silva a chance. Meanwhile, the MDB's left was maneuvering to make sure their weight would be felt if the Broad Front should appear.

In April Costa e Silva made a gesture to demonstrate his moderation. He announced that there would be no further IPMs, the investigatory military tribunals that had often turned into kangaroo courts under Castelo Branco. But even this gesture was tempered by the warning that political exiles—again, Kubitschek was the most obvious target—would have to cooperate by shunning any political role.

While the president courted the legal opposition, there were also signs of the emergence of an illegal opposition. In April the army came upon a guerrilla training camp in Minas Gerais. In June the Second Army headquarters in São Paulo was attacked by guerrillas. Both incidents were minor, and the legal opposition continued to hold the spotlight.

The atmosphere for politics was, however, badly overheated. Indicative was the ugly incident following Castelo Branco's death in the collision of two small aircraft in July 1967. Rio's *Tribuna da Imprensa,* once controlled by Lacerda and still often reflecting his views, published a vicious obituary, saying "humanity has lost little or nothing by the death of Castelo Branco," who was branded "a cold, insensitive, vindictive, implacable, inhuman, calculating, cruel, frustrated man . . . with a heart like the Sahara Desert."[17] Castelo's army colleagues were incensed; Costa e Silva answered by jailing the author (and owner of the paper), Helio Fernandes. That incident convinced Lacerda it was time to make his move. He announced his candidacy for the 1971 presidential election. Shortly therafter, in August, he announced that Kubitschek was supporting the Broad Front, whose goals included redemocratization and faster economic development.[18]

Lacerda now returned to his favorite role: the reckless orator. He heaped abuse on Costa e Silva and his ministers. In late August (the fateful month of Getúlio Vargas's 1954 suicide and Jânio Quadros's 1960 resignation) the government banned Lacerda from television. Humanization was proving far from simple.

In September politicians from both ARENA and MDB debated at length their relations with the Broad Front, which was monopolizing the political spotlight. Late in the month Lacerda visited Montevideo and won Goulart's endorsement for the Broad Front. Leonel Brizola, however, remained aloof from Lacerda's effort. He had decided to back no opposition political movement within Brazil. Jânio Quadros, the other cassated former President, hesitated and then declined to join.

In subsequent months the Front languished, partly because Lacerda had to concentrate on cultivating his contacts on the right. His former hard-line military supporters were angered by his pact with Goulart, and denounced his "return to the past." Interior Minister Albuquerque Lima's "Military Circle of Fortaleza," an important indicator of hardliner opinion, also hurled that charge.

During the interregnum, the left, especially former PTB leaders, called for decisive action to change the wage policy and to restore democracy. In addition, by October 1967 Costa e Silva had begun to sound more decisive. He told ARENA Congressmen he had no intention of modifying the Constitution or changing the wage policy. In his message to the closing session of Congress the President warned that he had the weapons needed to fight any possible subversion.

In December Lacerda took off the gloves. In a series of university commencement addresses he called the government a corrupt dictatorship which had compromised Brazilian sovereignty by its deals with foreign economic interests. His invective was beginning to sound like that of the nationalist congressmen the military had purged.[19]

In February and part of March the drama of the Broad Front continued to play itself out. Lacerda was now maneuvering over the entire political landscape. He had two meetings with U.S. Ambassador John Tuthill. Press leaks sensationalized these contacts, suggesting the U.S. might be hedging its bets on Costa e Silva.[20] The hard-line military grew angrier, accusing the ARENA politicians of ineptitude in replying to the aggressive opposition. By mid-March Lacerda had zeroed in on General Jaime Portella, head of Costa e Silva's Military Presidential Staff. Echoing earlier attacks by Broad Front spokesmen, Lacerda denounced Portella as a Svengali who had usurped the presidential powers of an ineffectual Costa e Silva. Some hard-line military, identified with Albuquerque Lima, thought the government should be tougher on Lacerda. Their real worry was that the Broad Front might become little more than a Trojan horse for the return of Kubitschek and Goulart. But Costa e Silva's advisers knew that when in a dogfight with Lacerda it was a mistake to let his invective set the pace. They bided time for a showdown of their choosing.

From the Broad Front to a Challenge by Students and Workers

The Broad Front was not the government's only political problem. More important, at least in the short run, was student opposition. A brief look at the post-1964 history of students in politics is needed in order to understand their role in 1968.[21] Before the 1964 coup student radicals had been a vociferous element pushing the Goulart government to the left. They were thus a prime target for post-coup repression. Prominent student leaders were arrested, some tortured, and the student government structures at the national, state, and university level (the best known was the *União Nacional de Estudantes,* UNE) were abolished. The Castelo Branco government successfully pressured the Congress to pass a November 1964 law (soon dubbed the "Suplicy de Lacerda law" after the Education and Culture Minister), creating a new structure of student associations forbidden to engage in politics.

The more militant students refused to be intimidated during 1965 and 1966. On many campuses they sabotaged the compulsory student government elections and organized protests over such issues as faculty purges at the University of Brasília, the repression of national meetings of the outlawed UNE, and government-proposed tuition fees at federal universities.

By late 1966 the student militants were finding the going much harder. A combination of disunity (the ideological battles among PCB, Maoist, Trotskyist, and independent factions were nonstop) and police pressure weakened them, forcing them into clandestine operations. The repressive atmosphere of the universities continued to radicalize many of the politically oriented students, especially in the social sciences and humanities faculties. But when Costa e Silva took office the student radicals seemed under control, unable to mobilize on a national scale, as they had in 1965 and 1966.

In early 1968 that scene changed. A series of student protests erupted in Rio in March. Student political action—completely dominated by the left—was directed at rising university fees, inadequate classroom facilities, and cuts in the government's education budget. Downtown, near the Federal University, there was another complaint: a partially constructed canteen ("Calabouço") where the students were demanding better food and completion of construction on the building.

On March 28 the students mounted a demonstration, and the Military Police arrived in force. Soon there was gunfire. One student, Edson Luis de Lima Souto, lay dead from a police bullet. Now the militants had a martyr, a death that could mobilize anti-government sentiment. The students carried Edson's body to the (MDB-controlled) state assembly, where they mounted a vigil. An experienced anti-government lawyer warned them to make sure the body did not "disappear," as had happened to other casualties of police violence since 1964. The next day's funeral procession turned into a huge downtown march. On April 4 a memorial noon mass for the slain student was held in Rio's Candelaria Cathedral, located downtown. Thousands appeared, including *cariocas* using their lunch hour to register their grief and anti-government feelings. Upon leaving the cathedral the crowds were attacked by saber-wielding cavalry. Such a reaction only fed the growing protest movement. Sympathy marches erupted as far away as Salvador and Pôrto Alegre. Brasília was the next flashpoint, where a student strike ignited conflict in early April.

The Costa e Silva government now decided to move against Lacerda. On

April 5 Justice Minister Gama e Silva prohibited further political activities by the Broad Front. The press was forbidden to publish any statement linked to the Front or to any of its members or other *cassados*. The government was using the student unrest as a pretext to liquidate Lacerda's Front. It was also responding to pressure from the hardliners, who were still angry that ARENA had been so ineffectual against Lacerda.

That took care of the Front, but it did not address the student demands. In fact, they and their families had one legitimate protest. Brazil's higher education system was anachronistic, even by Latin American standards. Economic growth had not been accompanied by an equivalent expansion in the federal university system. Candidates for university had to pass a national *vestibular* exam. Because the number of candidates was two and a half times the number of university places, the exam and its grading became harder and harder, in order to keep the number of "passing" students low. In 1967, for example, 183,150 applied for entrance, but only 38 percent, or 70, 915, passed. The number of applicants had increased at 12 percent a year for 1964–66. In 1967, however, the increase was 48 percent, a jump that undoubtedly contributed to the growing tension among middle-class families.[22]

Pressure to enter the tuition-free federal universities was especially great because the private universities (to which the unsuccessful *vestibular* takers usually turned) charged high tuition fees. The frustrated university applicants and their families were a ready reservoir of discontent, especially because a university degree was the indispensable passport into the elite. The student marchers' cry in 1968 was "vagas! vagas!" (more places! more places!) Some of those voices were from high schoolers about to take the university entrance exam.

Virtually everyone agreed on the need for university reform, including an overhaul of the admissions system. But there were sharp disagreements over the exact changes needed.[23] The Castelo Branco government had proposed ambitious reforms (for all educational levels) to be designed and carried out by the Ministry of Education (MEC) in conjunction with USAID (thus the label MEC–USAID). The program was immediately attacked by Brazilian nationalists, especially among the students, who denounced it as an "imperalist infiltration in Brazilian education."[24]

The Costa e Silva governnment was less than happy with some of MEC–USAID's joint projects, especially those in higher education, due to expire at the end of June 1968. In late December 1967 the president appointed General Meira Mattos to chair a commission to inquire into the university system and make their recommendations. Their report, although confidential, was known to recommend institutional reforms along with stern measures to prevent any recurrence of pre-1964 style student politics.[25]

But the student demonstrations did not stop. In late June both the Federal University and the school system in Rio were closed because of student demonstrations. Days later a group of at least 100,000 marchers protested police violence, in the largest political demonstration since 1964. The government, seeking to defuse the situation, had allowed the march to take place. But for the military that appeared to be government weakness.[26]

Having learned his lesson, Justice Minister Gama e Silva in early July prohibited any further marches in Brazil. Days later the National Security Council, heavily influenced by the military hardliners, endorsed the ban, which Costa e Silva reiterated.

In July, with the MEC–USAID higher education project having expired, Costa e Silva announced his own preparations for university reform. A major reform was badly needed, he argued, notwithstanding the recent politicization of the issue. To prepare the plan he appointed a 12-person working group, which was to start from the Meira Mattos report. The 12 included two students, who were appointed but refused to serve.

The students were not appeased by the President's efforts. In late August student demonstrators at the Federal University of Minas Gerais forced suspension of classes. At the University of Brasília on August 30, student demonstrations led to police occupation of the campus, with arrests of students and faculty. Police violence was visible enough for Costa e Silva to order an immediate investigation of police behavior by General Garrastazú Médici, the SNI chief. His report in early October remained secret—always the means for hiding internal criticisms of the security forces.

After police excesses in the August demonstrations in Brasília, the Congress had taken up the cry against police violence. The mere fact the events occurred in the federal capital increased their importance. Some of the students involved were children of Congressmen and government (even army!) officials. In late September a Commission of Inquiry of the Chamber of Deputies accused the Federal Police in Brasília of premeditated violence. That same month the President sent his university reform proposals to Congress. Among the many provisions was a regularization of status for about 7,000 professors, making them eligible for full-time salary. This was aimed at correcting the practice of paying faculty such low salaries that they had to find other jobs (often other teaching posts) to survive. Another provision was to expand the federal university system, which had been a constant demand of student demonstrators and their families.[27]

But the damage had already been done. The demonstrations and police violence had exacerbated the tension between the executive and the Congress (including many ARENA Congressmen), and damaged Costa e Silva's attempt to accommodate the opposition. Most serious for the government was the fact that most of the demonstrators came from the middle class, the backbone of the Revolution of 1964.

While the student demonstrations were intensifying tensions, the government faced militant opposition from another, less expected and potentially more dangerous quarter. In April 1968 metalworkers in Contagem, an industrial town in Minas Gerais, staged a wildcat action and occupied their factory. It was Brazil's first major industrial strike since 1964. They were protesting the steady decline of real wage rates during those years, and they demanded an immediate 25 percent pay raise. The strikers elected their own commission, completely independent of the union, whose officers disclaimed any role in the strike. The commission then negotiated with the factory management, which offered a 10 percent raise (to be deducted from the next annual wage increase). The offer was rejected.

Meanwhile, other industrial workers from the area joined the strike, bringing to 15,000 the number of workers defying the Labor Ministry's back-to-work order. Labor Minister Jarbas Passarinho, seeking to apply Costa e Silva's liberalization policy, entered the negotiations. He convinced the employers to make the 10 percent wage bonus not deductible from the annual increase. The strikers, showing remarkable solidarity, rejected this also. Passarinho now decided to crack down. Contagem was occupied by police, meetings were prohibited (thus undercutting the workers' assembly which had guided the commission) and the employers threatened to fire those who did not return to work. The strike collapsed, both because of government repression and because the workers lacked organization and experience.

Nonetheless, the 10 percent wage bonus was granted in Contagem, and, by Labor Ministry decision, throughout Brazil. The strike had given the government the opportunity to do what it had already decided to do, i.e., break with the Castelo Branco wage policy.

The chain of command in the Contagem strike had bypassed the official union leaders. Indeed, they were not even involved in the negotiations. By negotiating with it, management recognized the legitimacy of the wildcat commission. This recognition was underlined when Passarinho took charge of the negotiations that led to the 10 percent bonus. Had the government softened its attitude toward worker militancy?

In May there was an ugly incident in São Paulo that suggested further labor trouble in store. A contingent of 800 militant São Paulo workers (out of crowd of 20,000) erupted at a May Day rally run by government-appointed union leaders (*pelegos*). The protestors chased the speakers and government figures (including São Paulo Governor Abreu Sodré) from the platform, gave their own speeches attacking government economic policy, and ended with a march that culminated in a protest at the local branch of Citibank. The riot police, which had anticipated no problems, arrived too late.[28] Two months later a strike similar to Contagem—or so it seemed—broke out in Osasco, an industrial suburb of São Paulo. Here again it was metalworkers, but this time they had more ambitious demands: a 35 percent wage increase, two-year work contracts, and quarterly wage adjustments. Their strike literature also attacked the government's "anti-strike law" and the FGTS law.

In fact, this strike was much more political than that in Contagem. The Osasco union president, José Ibraim, was not only a metalworker but also a university student from the ranks of the Catholic student activists. This union's anti-government militants were emboldened by the student mobilization in Rio, achieved despite (and in the end because of) army and police repression.

For Labor Minister Passarinho this industrial strike was especially threat-ening. First, the union took responsibility for the strike, as had not hap-pened at Contagem. This might set an example for other unions. Second, its demands and its leadership were explicitly anti-government. Third, the locale was São Paulo, Brazil's industrial heartland.

Although Passarinho had negotiated at Contagem, the Costa e Silva government's commitment to liberalization was now showing signs of wear. On the strike's second day the Labor Minister intervened the union. The student-worker president, knowing what was in store, fled. Police and military saturated the area and workers were arrested en masse. Some were headed straight for torture.[29] Costa e Silva's "humanizing" face had begun to slip. It was clear to all that the government was not prepared to alter significantly its wage policy or to allow negotiation with representative shop floor leaders. Once again it was repression that met worker protest.

This labor activism was part of a growing confrontation between the sec-ond military government and its bolder opponents. The Church constituted another important battlefield. Most of the bishops had moved away from their enthusiastically pro-military government stance of 1964 to a more criti-cal position. Dom Helder Camara, Archbishop of Olinda, had emerged as a leader of the Church "progressives," who attacked government policies they believed reinforced or deepened the existing social injustices. By 1968 the Church was caught up in the same currents that were radicalizing university students and industrial workers. Meanwhile, the Church was experiencing its own process of intense self-examination and inner renewal, whose even-tual outcome was uncertain.

One trend was unmistakable, however. The Church had no choice but to confront the government's national security doctrine, with its attempt to control every social institution, including the Church.[30] In July 1968 the National Conference of Brazilian Bishops issued a working paper which denounced that doctrine as "fascist."

In October Cardinal Rossi of São Paulo refused to celebrate a birthday mass for President Costa e Silva at the headquarters of the Second Army. In Catholic Brazil this gesture was inevitably seen as a personal insult to the President. The Church was being drawn, like it or not, into the growing political storm. (Greater detail on this topic will be given in the next chapter).[31]

There was also mobilization on the right. Most prominent were the Anti-Communist Command (*Comando da Caça aos Comunistas,* or CCC) and the Anti-Communist Movement (*Movimento anti-Comunista*). A favorite tactic of both in 1968 was to invade a theater during the performance of a play they labelled as "subversive," physically attacking the cast and some-times even the audience. In September 1968 the CCC, along with students from the nearby private and highly conservative Mackenzie University laid siege to the Faculdade de Filosofia of the University of São Paulo, home of faculty and students they branded as "communist agents." The CCC attack-ers destroyed the main building's interior while the police looked on.[32]

Politics had taken to the streets, raising the question of whether the Costa e Silva government had lost control of the process of "humanization." No group was more interested in that question than the military.

Arousing the Hardliners

Since 1964 the hard-line military had battled with the military moderates over how repressive their government needed to be. Costa e Silva had been trying hard to work within the legal system. The 1967 Constitution and accompanying laws were designed to create a "strong government" along with a residual of representative democracy and the rule of law. But the protest movements had put the government on the defensive. Behind the scenes the hard line was attacking the moderates for having underestimated the opposition. Officers at every level were becoming radicalized, more distrustful of all politicians. Their political unrest was also fueled by anger over an erosion in their status and pay.[33]

An additional factor complicated the Brazilian scene. A worldwide wave of student protest was under way, engulfing Berlin, Paris, Berkeley, Tokyo. Throughout the industrial world students took to the streets in the hundreds of thousands. In Paris, always influential with the Brazilian elite, students joined workers to extract major concessions from the French government—higher pay for the workers and a promise to reorganize France's antiquated university structure. In the U.S. the public support for the war in Vietnam was threatened by the protest movement, with students playing a key role. These events alarmed Brazilian hardliners, who feared that protest in Brazil might get out of hand. If the government did not crack down quickly, the argument went, it might face larger numbers controllable only with greater force, perhaps involving army troops. The latter was anathema to army officers, who feared for the army's future if thrown into combat against the people.

Into this volatile atmosphere came a completely unexpected challenge. It started as a little noticed congressional speech, but it soon became a life and death issue for the Costa e Silva government. In late August and early September 1968 Márcio Moreira Alves, the former journalist who was now a Congressman and a militant critic of the government, delivered a series of congressional speeches denouncing police brutality (as in the recent repression of students in Brasília) and torture of political prisoners. He suggested that parents protest against military rule by keeping their children away from the patriotic ceremonies on Brazil's Independence Day, September 7.[34] Alves also proposed "Operation Lysistrata," whereby Brazilian women, like their forebears in Greek drama, should withhold their favors from men in uniform until the government ceased its repression. Those newspaper readers who noticed the story had a laugh and left it at that. Alves himself later said he had meant it as a "wild volley," assuming that the real critique of the government would come from hard-hitting speeches on torture and foreign economic penetration.

But the military fixed on Alves's "wild volley."[35] His "Lysistrata speech" was duplicated and sent to all military posts. Officers read it and were livid. Their honor had been impugned and their manhood threatened. The three military ministers demanded that the Congress lift Alves's parliamentary immunity so he could be prosecuted for insulting the armed forces (an infringement of the National Security Law). The request went to the congressional Judiciary Committee, which had an ARENA majority. Surprisingly, the first soundings in the committee showed sentiment running against the President's request. Even pro-government Congressmen had gotten their backs up. As the angry military grew impatient, the stakes rose. The generals had taken a publicity stunt (which they correctly saw had a highly serious message) and elevated it into a struggle over not only freedom of speech, but also the powers of the Congress.

It happened that the hard-line military had their own agenda before this crisis arose. They were so anxious to remove from politics a group of militantly anti-government Congressmen (dubbed the *auténticos*), of whom Márcio Alves had suddenly become the most notorious.[36] His speech, so unimportant in itself, and its hesitant handling by the Planalto, gave the hard-line military an opportunity to radicalize officer opinion against the castelistas' fragile constitutional structure. To make matters worse, the country was in a nasty mood. As Carlos Castello Branco put it, "business is apprehensive, the students are insubordinate, the clergy rebellious, the politicians demoralized, and the military frustrated. They all think something has to change or the ambigious scenario will degenerate into a much larger drama."[37]

Although September 7 had long since passed and the Congress had adjourned, the military refused to let the issue die. The President's prestige was now at stake, much as Castelo Branco's had been in the October 1965 crisis. Responding to military pressure, Costa e Silva called Congress into special session in early December. He had already ordered ARENA congressional leaders to stack the Judiciary Committee, which had jurisdiction in the case. Committee members known to oppose suspension of Alves's immunity were replaced by deputies whose lack of expertise in constitutional law was exceeded only by their eagerness to follow presidential orders. The reconstituted Judiciary Committee, now stacked in the government's favor, duly voted to remove Alves's congressional immunity. Their recommendation went to the full chamber on December 10, 1968.

Márcio Moreira Alves and Hermano Alves (no relation), a deputy of similar views whose immunity the President also wanted to lift, lobbied their colleagues hard. Voting to lift immunity, they argued, would make Congress no longer even a respectable debating society. The two deputies also played on Congressmen's guilt over their failure to fight the growing authoritarianism at crucial moments since 1964.

A factor here was the conscience of the ARENA liberals, virtually all from the UDN. Faced with such a direct vote, they rediscovered their democratic principles. One example was Senator Daniel Krieger, the

ARENA National President, who had spoken out against the presidential request. Another was ARENA Federal Deputy Djalma Marinho, chairman of the Chamber Judiciary Committee, who also opposed the presidential request.[38] ARENA's periodic reversion to principle had not escaped the military's attention. By early 1968 they were angered over the political vacuum created, in their view, by ARENA's failure to act like a government party. There had been several cases in point. In September 1968, for example, 70 ARENA deputies protested police repression at the University of Brasília. In October the ARENA steering committee advocated a return to direct election of the president, although Costa e Silva emphatically opposed it. It was clear that, despite all the pressure and purges, ARENA was falling short of the "revolutionary" party the military had expected and were now demanding.[39]

The vote on Márcio Moreira Alves and Hermano Alves shaped up as the most important since 1964. On December 10–11, the hard-line military saw new cause for alarm: the Supreme Court ordered the release of 81 students, including the key leaders of the Rio marches, who had been detained since July. Every journalist in Brasília knew that Justice Minister Gama e Silva had a new Institutional Act in his desk drawer. Would the Congress call his bluff?

The Chamber voted on December 12. To the surprise of many, and to the fury of the hardliners, the Chamber rejected the government request by 216 to 141 (with 15 abstentions). Of the 216 votes against the government, 94 came from ARENA. Pandemonium reigned on the floor of the Chamber. Someone started singing the national anthem, and all joined in. Deputies congratulated each other on their courage. The thrill of having defied the military was contagious. But Márcio Alves knew that he was now public enemy number one. He quickly exited the Chamber and disappeared onto a clandestine route to exile.

The Authoritarian Crackdown

The President's reaction was swift—as it had to be if he were to remain in power. His chief military aide was already being bombarded with generals' demands for immediate action. On the morning of December 13 he convened the 23-member National Security Council (the cabinet ministers, the vice president, the chiefs of staff of each of the three services, the chief of staff of the armed forces, the heads of the military and civilian presidential staff, and the director of the SNI) to advise on the new Institutional Act about to be proclaimed. Justice Minister Gama e Silva began to read a draft even more draconian than expected. Army Minister Lyra Tavares angrily stopped him: "That way you'll bring the whole house down." Gama e Silva, whose verbosity and poor judgment were a constant trial to the Planalto, then pulled out a second draft, this along the lines Costa e Silva and other military had expected. An extended discussion showed all in favor, except Vice President Pedro Aleixo, who vainly argued for the constitutional alternative of invoking a state of siege. The higher military were angered at Aleixo's dissent, which he refused to withdraw. That night the President issued Institutional Act No. 5 and Supplementary Act No. 38. With the latter he suspended Congress indefinitely.[40]

Under the new legal umbrella military censorship hit the media. Not even the most prestigious journalists were exempt. Carlos Castello Branco, Brazil's best-known political columnist, was arrested, along with the director of his paper, *Jornal do Brasil*. Later the paper's editor, Alberto Dines, was also arrested. The hardliners, led by Interior Minister Albuquerque Lima, let it be known that Brazil might need 20 years of authoritarian rule. They talked also of the need for a new, reliable government party, should the legislature ever reconvene. Costa e Silva summed up military opinion in his first public speech after AI–5, when he asked, "How many times will we have to reiterate and demonstrate that the Revolution is irreversible?"[41]

For the next six months the government issued a steady stream of Institutional Acts, Supplementary Acts, and decrees. All were aimed at increasing executive and military control over government and its citizens.[42] The Congress was purged, first of 37 ARENA deputies, then of another 51 Congressmen, beginning with Márcio Moreira Alves and Hermano Alves. Carlos Lacerda, a key supporter of the 1964 Revolution, was finally deprived of his political rights. Many state legislatures, including those of São Paulo and Rio de Janeiro, were suspended. In early 1969 Costa e Silva issued a decree placing all state military and police forces under the control of the war minister, further stipulating that state forces must always be commanded by an armed forces officer on active duty. In addition, all police were henceforth subordinated to the state agency responsible for public order and internal security. More and more power over security was shifting to the federal government, eroding the federal structure to which even the military paid lip service.[43]

The judiciary was another target of the government offensive. In January 1969 three Supreme Court justices were forcibly retired: Victor Nunes Leal, Hermes Lima, and Evandro Lins e Silva. Supreme Court president Gonçalves de Oliveira then resigned in protest. Using the Sixth Institutional Act of February 1, 1969, Costa e Silva then reduced the Supreme Court from 16 judges to 11 and put all offenses against national security or the armed forces within the jurisdiction of the Supreme Military Tribunal and the lower military tribunals. He also forceably retired General Pery Bevilácqua, a Supreme Military Tribunal justice the hardliners thought too sympathetic to defendants.

The censorship that had emerged in an ill-coordinated, ad hoc manner in December 1968 was regularized in March 1969 by a decree that outlawed any criticism of the Institutional Acts, government authorities, or the armed forces. As if to indicate where they thought the opposition would originate, the architects of censorship also forbade the publication of any news of workers' or student movements. All media were placed under the supervision of military courts.[44]

Seventy professors at the University of São Paulo (USP) and several other universities were involuntarily retired in May 1969. Included were such internationally known scholars in São Paulo as anthropologists Florestan Fernandes and his former students (then professors) Fernando Henrique Cardoso and Octavio Ianni. Others included Isias Raw, chairman of the USP Biochemistry Department, and José Leite Lopes, professor of physics, along with Abelardo Zaluar, professor of fine arts at the Federal University in Rio. Motivation for many of the firings seemed a mystery, although some victims were outspoken leftists and many others had advocated modernization of the antiquated university structure. As always, personal grudges and crude ambition played a role in compiling the victim lists.[45]

Along with these purges, the government launched what it considered a positive measure, a new curricular device for promoting patriotism. In early 1969 a decree-law established a compulsory curriculum in *Educação Moral e Cívica* (Moral and Civic Education). Henceforth every student would have to take, every year, a course—with approved instructor and approved course material—designed to promote support for the Brazilian version of the National Security Doctrine. The plan had been developed by a working group at the *Escola Superior de Guerra* as their answer to the need to reshape the mentality of the upcoming generations in line with the new realities of the Revolution of 1964.[46]

Launched in early 1971, the plan required every registered student—from first grade to post-graduate—to take a course in this subject every year. The law defined the program's purpose as to "defend the democratic principle by preserving the religious spirit, the dignity of the human being, and the love of liberty, with responsibility under God's inspiration." It was also intended to promote "obedience to the law, commitment to work, and integration into the community." All teaching materials needed government approval, which stimulated the production of a mound of uninspired volumes filled with tales of heroes and discussion of such problems (certainly genuine but, more important, safe) as the need for more hydroelectric projects and more technology. Many schoolchildren and university students considered the courses a joke, but their content did offer a clue to how the military government wanted to define Brazil's future.[47]

Finally, the government lashed out at what it saw as wealth and property "illicitly" gained by politicians or government officials at all levels (presumably excluding the military). A new Special Commission of Inquiry (*Comissão Geral de Investigações*) was created to investigate and judge all corruption cases. Its jurisdiction was soon extended to include anyone suspected of gaining riches "illicitly."

The Costa e Silva government was reverting to the use of arbitrary powers that characterized the early months of the Revolution. The rationale, however, had to be different. In the days and weeks after the Congress had been suspended and Institutional Act No. 6 issued, the President defended the new authoritarian measures as necessary to "reactivate the

Revolution." He noted bitterly that his government's tolerance had been answered with intolerance, and its magnanimity seen as weakness. He could not stand by and see democracy destroy itself, supposedly in the name of democracy, he argued.[48] The rationale given for the crackdown was the National Security Doctrine, which argued that the nation, and ultimately the military, had as great a duty to protect itself from internal enemies as from external enemies. That doctrine was now invoked to the limit as Brazil descended deeper into authoritarianism.

The first six months of 1969 saw a steady retreat from the elections that Costa e Silva had hoped to carry out. The government wanted neither the upheaval of a campaign nor the chance of a defeat. The Eighth Institutional Act of February 1969 suspended all the upcoming elections, down to the municipal level. By June the President's political strategists had devised an interesting ad hoc solution to the problems of political party organization. They issued electoral regulations allowing candidates of the two officially recognized parties, ARENA, and MDB, to be identified by a "sublabel" (*sublegenda*) indicating affiliation with one of the old parties, such as UDN or PSD. The government thought the sublabels, which would attract voters still identifying with the old parties, would help ARENA more than MDB. It was to be a short-run measure, not intended to compromise the eventual goal of a strictly two-party system.

Given this rapidly changing political scene, and given the Brazilian military's penchant for formal legitimacy, a new constitution was inevitable. Throughout the first half of 1969 the President himself labored on a preliminary version, much of its drafted by Vice President Pedro Aleixo. By late August the draft proposal was virtually finished.[49]

Why this mania for yet another constitution? It reflected the continuing desire of the revolutionaries, even the military hardliners, to have a legal rationale for their assertion of arbitrary authority. Now, however, there was a blatant contradiction between the commitment to constitutionalism and their will to rule. Their most important legal self-justification, the Fifth Institutional Act, had no expiration date. And the Act gave the President the power to suspend *habeas corpus* indefinitely. For the first time since the coup of 1964, there was no date scheduled for a return to the rule of law.[50]

The Guerrilla Emerges

As the new authoritarian order took shape, Costa e Silva faced a problem that had dogged Castelo Branco: how to regain control of the government after hardliner pressure had forced an authoritarian turn. Just after issuing the Second Institutional Act in late 1965, Castelo Branco had to fight hard to stay in power. Now Costa e Silva and his senior officers had to convince the hardliners that these newest acts and laws would keep the opposition far from power; indeed, would prevent the opposition from even propagating its ideas.

That strategy had its drawbacks, however. Muzzling the legal opposition created a vacuum, into which an armed opposition now tried to move.[51] Guerrillas were no novelty in Latin America. Fidel Castro's stunning triumph over Cuban dictator Fulgencio Batista's ill-trained and ineptly led army had helped give birth to the "foco" theory. Its proponents argued that by careful choice of a rebel base in the countryside a small contingent of well-disciplined guerrillas could—by armed action and propaganda aimed to arouse mass action—destabilize an oppressor government and eventually bring it down. It had worked in Cuba but nowhere else in Latin America.[52] Che Guevara's attempt to duplicate the feat in Bolivia brought him only death and martyrdom. Yet the aspiring revolutionaries elsewhere in Latin America did not give up. Faced with repressive military regimes such as post-1964 Brazil and post-1966 Argentina, a few militants, mostly young and from the middle class, refused to abandon their revolutionary commitment.

The guerrilla theory and strategy in Brazil emerged slowly and was closely related to the Brazilian left's fortunes after 1964.[53] The 1964 coup had hit much of the left as a nasty surprise. In the final months of Goulart's presidency the radical nationalists had convinced themselves that they were taking control of the government. They believed the rightist military had been neutralized and that Goulart's popular support was growing daily. Among those least surprised were the Moscow-line Communists (PCB). Their elders remembered well their failed 1935 military revolt and the years of prison that followed. Even as the coup struck, PCB leaders were going underground.

In the aftermath of the coup bitter debates broke out within the left. How could they have so misdiagnosed the political scene? Why was there so little resistance to the coup? What should the left do now?[54] The PCB continued to be highly cautious. It hid PCB leaders in its clandestine network, while routinely denouncing the "fascist" government and its "imperalist" sponsors. The party did *not* call for armed resistance. This caution meshed with the Moscow line, to which the PCB was still loyal.[55]

The non-PCB left was a different matter. Most had been new to politics. Few had practical experience in evading or outwitting the police. They were overwhelmingly young—many were in their 20s—and often activists in student politics. Their social background was predominantly middle-class, which in Brazil meant the wealthiest five to ten percent of the population.

These militants had come to radical activism from two major groups: the revolutionary left parties (such as the Maoist PC do B or POLOP, one of several Trotskyist groups) or the radical Catholic movement (such as *Ação Popular* [AP], *Movimento de Educação de Base* [MEB], or *Juventude Universitária Católica* [JUC]).

With the coup, many of these militants withdrew quickly from the political scene, some out of fear, others out of prudence. Not a few had been arrested in "Operation Cleanup" in 1964. As the months passed, however, a few radicals on the left, both civilian and military, began organizing an armed opposition.

Who joined (or supported) the guerrillas, and why? It was not the PCB, whose position alienated—often infuriated—militants on the left. Some PCB members could stand it no longer and deserted. They, along with veterans of the Trotskyist and Church groups, were to form the backbone of the armed resistance to the military government.

These dissidents were few between 1964 and 1967. Yet they were able to carry off a series of terrorist actions, especially the bombing of U.S. government installations and the bombing at the Recife airport.[56] Through 1966 the attacks worried high officials but the security forces considered them little more than a nuisance. Early 1967, however, brought the first serious attempt at a rural guerrilla front. The action, closely linked to Leonel Brizola (exiled in Uruguay), was in the Caparaó mountains between Minas Gerais and Espírito Santo. The guerrillas, mostly former military men purged from their services early in the Castelo Branco government, were detected by the army before they could establish contact with the local population. Some were captured, but a number got away. Brizola later said this venture convinced him the guerrilla was not viable in Brazil.[57] The year 1967 also saw bombings of the U.S. Peace Corps office in Rio and the home of the U.S. Air Force attaché in Rio.[58] Bombings were a crude form of protest—perhaps effective in arousing opinion but hardly threatening to the government. If the leftist militants were to transform Brazilian politics, they needed a longer-term strategy.

A key event in the growth of the guerrillas was the defection of Carlos Marighela from the PCB. Marighela, a tall, muscular Bahian, had been a PCB member since his youth in the mid-1930s. In 1939 he was jailed for six years by Felinto Muller's police. In 1946 Marighela, along with his fellow Bahian and PCB member Jorge Amado, was elected to the Constituent Assembly. In 1953–54 he visited the People's Republic of China. Back in Brazil he continued to demonstrate the courage and energy that had earned him a place on the party's executive committee. In May 1964 Marighela was arrested and imprisoned for two months. He then returned to party work but became increasingly frustrated at the party's caution after 1964. In December 1966 he resigned from the executive committee. In August 1967 he attended the first Organization of Latin American Solidarity (OLAS) conference in Havana. Because the PCB, following the Soviet line, was boycotting the meeting, Marighela's presence dramatized his alienation from the PCB. On his return from Havana he resigned from the party. Later that year he founded a new movement, the *Ação Libertadora Nacional* (ALN), and became the leading theoretician of the armed resistance in Brazil. His key ally in the ALN was Joaquim Câmara Ferreira, another renegade from the PCB.[59]

Yet the guerrillas were far from united. There were at least a half dozen armed groups in the Rio–São Paulo–Minas Gerais area. For security reasons they had to operate in small cells, to minimize the damage if any cell or individual were captured. Ideological and personal rivalries divided these groups, so that guerrilla actions were often uncoordinated. Nonetheless, there were early successes. Needing money, they learned how to rob banks in early 1968. Soon they were looting poorly guarded banks of hundreds of thousands of dollars. The raids became "a kind of entrance exam for apprenticeship in the techniques of revolutionary war," in Marighela's words.[60] For trainning in guerrilla tactics and for arms and logistical support, the Brazilians turned to Cuba and North Korea, among others.[61]

The guerrillas' objectives were several. First, they hoped to arouse sympathy from the urban poor, who could readily identify with an attack on an obvious symbol of capitalist power. Here they were imitating the even more epic successes of the Tupamaro guerrillas in Uruguay. Second, they wanted to show that resistance to military rule was possible. What better way than bank robberies carried out with military precision? Third, the guerrillas needed money, and lots of it. Most of the comrades in the clandestine networks could not hold jobs and had to be supported with cash. Finally, attacking banks would force the bank directors and the police to increase the armed guards, thereby revealing, in the guerrillas' logic, this capitalist society's foundation of naked force.

The sudden return of worker and mass protest in early 1968, especially in Rio and São Paulo, had greatly encouraged the guerrillas. The strikes in Contagem and Osasco, along with the student rallies and marches in Rio, later spreading to other cities, showed that some social sectors were prepared, for the first time since 1964, to take to the streets. This evidence of activism strengthened the hand of those on the left who favored armed action.

Just before these events, Marighela's ALN, with fattened coffers from a series of bank and payroll robberies in early 1968, had called for armed struggle in the cities. In June another group, the VPR (*Vanguarda Popular Revolucionária*), which included non-PCB Marxists from São Paulo, attacked a São Paulo Army hospital and escaped with captured arms. The Second Army commander, General Manoel Lisboa, was furious and called a press conference, where he shouted "They attacked a hospital! Let's see them attack my barracks!" Four days later VPR guerrillas launched a truck loaded with dynamite into the Second Army headquarters, killing a sentry. Rising to the general's bait was a good example of how the guerrillas could be distracted from their long-term goal, thereby running the risk of identification, capture, or death.[62]

In October 1968 the VPR raised the stakes when they assassinated U.S. Army Captain Charles Chandler as he stepped outside his house in São Paulo. Chandler was taking university courses (at the highly conservative Mackenzie University) as part of his training to teach Portuguese at West Point. The guerrillas pointed to his previous tours of duty in Vietnam and Bolivia as proof that he was in Brazil to help train rightist paramilitary groups, such as the Anti-Communist Command (CCC). The VPR and ALN held a secret tribunal, where they sentenced Chandler to death for his alleged war crimes in Vietnam and his alleged CIA role in Brazil. His assassins hoped by "executing" (their term) Chandler they would dramatize the U.S. role as the indispensable prop to the military regime. The leaflets scattered at the scene ended with Che Guevara's famous cry: "Two, three, many Vietnams." By now it was clear that Brazil's military government faced a serious guerrilla opponent. Washington was alarmed, and assigned its deputy chief Public Safety Officer in Brazil to work full-time with Brazilian authorities in investigating Chandler's assassination.[63]

In January 1969 the guerrillas got a highly welcome convert. Army Captain Carlos Lamarca defected to the VPR with three sergeants and a truckload of weapons. Lamarca was a major catch for the guerrillas. A champion marksman, he had been assigned to teach bank guards how to shoot. Indeed, the public knew Lamarca's face from the posters showing him giving lessons. His defection infuriated the military.[64]

Six months later the VPR scored a different kind of triumph in Rio. They went after the safe (*caixinha*) of legendarily corrupt Adhemar de Barros, former Governor of São Paulo and staunch supporter of the 1964 coup. The safe was kept in the Rio home of Adhemar's long-time mistress. The guerrillas knew the site and had a carefully fomulated plan. Lamarca commanded a squad of 13 guerrillas, who disguised themselves as federal agents. They descended on the house, conducting a whirlwind search and interrogation, looking for "subversives." Meanwhile, a subgroup located the 500-pound safe and maneuvered it out a second-story window. As the "federal agents" ended their blitz, the safe was on its way to a VPR hideout. Once cracked, it proved to contain $2.5 million in U.S. currency. The guerrillas' money worries were over for the moment.[65]

Yet the dangers were growing, in part because every foray exposed them to possible detection and capture. In early 1969 the security forces discovered a major VPR action in the making and arrested many of those involved. Police and military efficiency had increased over the past year because of information they were now routinely getting by torturing guerrilla suspects (or anyone possibly connected with them).[66] Brutal interrogation methods, such as the "parrot's perch", the "dragon's chair," and the "refrigerator" made many suspects talk. Despite the guerrillas' best efforts to guard their secrets, there was almost always some clue—a nickname, an address, a code word—the interrogators could extract.[67] With the scrap (and sometimes more) the police and military would leap into action, dragging in new suspects to be beaten and given electric shocks in the hunt for clues. Clandestine groups on the right were also at work. In May 1969 such a group assassinated Father Antônio Henrique Pereira Neto, who worked closely with Dom Helder Camara in Recife. Given the government's obsession with silencing Dom Helder, the meaning of this murder could not be lost.

In June 1969 the São Paulo police and military introduced a new repressive technique: the massive dragnet, which detained thousands, all of whose identity papers were checked. The innocent were intimidated, while the guerrillas now had to be much more cautious when moving about. The São Paulo dragnet, soon duplicted in other cities, was part of "Operation Bandeirantes," a new police–army joint action.[68]

In short, the Brazilian government was now, in mid-1969, using any and every means (torture of small children in front of their parents and gang rape of a wife before her husband have both been documented) to get the information needed to exterminate the guerrilla threat. The interrogators now often tortured suspects for as long as two months—far beyond any hope of extracting information. Torture had become a grisly ritual, a calculated onslaught against body and soul.

It became a stark warning to other Brazilians who might contemplate active opposition. Carrying out this orgy of torture was also made to order for the sadists who can be found in every police force and penal institution, whatever the country.

Yet torture became something more. It became an instrument for social control. Nothing travelled faster, especially among the younger generation, than the news that your friend, or a friend of your friend, had fallen into the hands of the torturers. The latter warned their victims not to talk about their torture, knowing full well that many would. In short, torture was a powerful instrument, if degrading to its users, for subduing a society. By mid-1969 the torture machine (discussed in the next chapter) was running smoothly.

The Economy: Pragmatism Pays Off

Although it was a politico-military crisis that led to increased executive power, the latter was quickly put to use in economic policy-making.[69] Speaking to the Higher War College in December 1968, Costa e Silva confessed that his new power to legislate by decree was making it easier to carry out the Strategic Program (*Programa Estratégico*).[70] The President soon demonstrated the point by using his new power to revise tax policy. Most important was a January constitutional amendment, masterminded by Delfim Neto, which reduced from 20 percent to 12 percent the constitutionally designated share of the principal federally collected taxes distributed to state and municipal governments. This hit the Northeast hard, since the old distribution formula favored the poorer states. Delfim was also eyeing the budget of SUDENE (*Superintendência do Desenvolvimento do Nordeste,* or Superintendency for the Development of the Northeast), hoping to increase his control over it.[71]

These measures provoked a strong reaction from two key administrators. In January 1969 Minister of the Interior General Albuquerque Lima, regarded as a likely presidential candidate in 1970, resigned his post in protest over Delfim's policies. He had been a threat to Delfim Neto because he wanted more federal spending to correct regional inequalities in Brazil. He was also more nationalist on foreign capital. Both positions contradicted Delfim's strategy of rapid growth, which maximized investment (foreign included) regardless of the regional effects. Instead of retiring, however, Albuquerque Lima returned to active military duty, thereby hoping to consolidate his officer following. Only days later, he was joined in resignation by General Euler Bentes Monteiro, the director of SUDENE. Euler was also angered over the cut in federal funds for SUDENE. Both he and Albuquerque had argued forcefully for more resources for the poorer states, but to no effect. This was early proof that the authoritarian turn in December 1968 had made it even easier for Delfim and his technocrats to avoid public debate over fundamental economic and social priorities.

While Brazil slid deeper into authoritarian rule, its economy responded well to the government's strategy. In 1967, a transition year, the GDP grew 4.7 percent, slightly less than the previous year's mark of 5.4 percent. The disappointing growth could be traced to the anemic industrial performance, only 2.4 percent. Agriculture, in contrast, grew by 7.1 percent. In 1968, however, the Costa e Silva government's first full year in office, there were excellent results. GDP growth surged to 11 percent, with inflation continuing at 25 percent, the same as 1967. Industrial growth came in at 13.3 percent, vindicating the new policy of easier credit. Agricultural growth was 4.4. percent, comfortably ahead of the population growth rate of 2.8 percent. Exports grew at the healthy rate of 14 percent. This was the result of efforts in both 1967 and 1968 to extend export incentives, especially for manufacturers. They included special credit to finance production and reduced taxes on export profits. The goal was to end Brazil's long-term dependence on coffee export earnings. There was encouragment on that score in 1968, as non-coffee exports rose by 17.6 percent.[72]

The strong industrial recovery in 1968 was led by transportation equipment (especially passenger vehicles), chemicals, and electrical equipment. Construction boomed, rising 19 percent—growth that was fueled by the large funds from compulsory payroll deductions earmarked for the *Banco Nacional de Habitação* (National Housing Bank). Some 170,000 low-cost housing units were built with these funds. The only potential danger sign was the 28 percent increase in imports, suggesting that a high-growth strategy would create continuing problems for the balance of payments. The resulting trade deficit was covered by a heavy net inflow of capital. The appearance of the latter was highly important, because it enabled the Costa e Silva government to avoid a return to the IMF. Delfim Neto's unorthodox policies would hardly have appealed to the keepers of the IMF's rigid formulae.

The President was euphoric over the economy's favorable turn. In March 1968 Costa e Silva told the Higher War College: "We are building a great civilization in the southern hemisphere because we refuse to bow to geographical determinism."[73]

This government's philosophy was more pragmatic than that of Campos and Bulhões. There were fewer sermons about the free market (although many about the need for hard work) and more emphasis on solving immediate problems, such as prices and minimum wages (discussed earlier in this chapter). Another key area was exchange rate policy. Campos and Bulhões had assumed that inflation could be reduced to zero, or at least no higher than the U.S. and Western European rates by 1967 (the average U.S. rate up to 1967 was less than 2 percent). That would have made exchange rate policy simple. With Brazil's inflation rate no higher than that of the U.S. and Western Europe, there would have been no need to devalue, other things being equal. But such was not the case. Even if Brazilian inflation had stabilized in the 10–20 percent range (which Delfim often implied as a de facto goal), there would still be a growing disequilibrium between the cruzeiro and the dollar. Even under Delfim's most optimistic projections, the cruzeiro was bound to become overvalued.

The Campos-Bulhões team had at first stuck to a fixed exchange rate. When the cruzeiro began to drop, the Brazilian government bought enough cruzeiros for dollars (or other hard currencies) to restore the cruzeiro to its fixed value. Obviously, this could continue only as long as Brazil had the dollars to keep buying. And those dollars could disappear quickly if businessmen and bankers tried to protect themselves by speculating against the cruzeiro. The game was over in 1968.[74] A flight from the cruzeiro had disrupted the Brazilian capital market, leading to a January 1968 devaluation of the cruzeiro by 18.6 percent against the dollar. Over the next six months the pressure built for another devaluation. In late August, the government devalued another 13.4 percent. Delfim had had enough of these devaluations. The speculative swings surrounding them were making coherent monetary policy impossible. The government decided to move to a "flexible" exchange rate system. Henceforth there would be frequent small devaluations (1–2 percent). Thus was born Brazil's "crawling peg," or flexible rate.[75]

Though the impetus for this innovation came from the need to eliminate the disruptive capital flows provoked by speculation, the flexible rate soon became famous as a powerful tool in stimulating exports. The reason was simple. One of the exporter's greatest uncertainties was the exchange rate at which he would be paid for his exports. With infrequent, large devaluations, an exporter could easily lose 15–25 percent on his transaction if caught between devaluations. The loss had nothing to do with product quality or competitive pricing. This uncertainty discouraged Brazilian firms from entering the export market. Delfim's new crawling peg, if maintained, removed that risk.[76]

In retrospect, most observers have regarded the flexible rate as the indispensable counterpart to indexation—both "automatic" devices that allowed Brazil to live with inflation. In fact, neither was automatic or neutral in their application. Both were under the continuous and discretionary control of the policymakers.

Two examples of indexation ("monetary correction") from the Castelo Branco period serve to illustrate the point. In order to fight inflation the Castelo Branco government had set the total return (interest and indexation) on government bonds (ORTNs) at 54 percent for 1965 and 46 percent for 1966. Since inflation for 1965 was 55 percent and for 1966 was 38 percent, holders of these bonds enjoyed relative protection of their capital in 1965 and a significant real interest rate (8 percent) in 1966. Let us compare this with the effects of monetary correction, as applied in the same years to the minimum wage. In 1965 workers in the private sector, not yet entirely under federal wage control, received an average wage increase of 40–45 percent, while those in the public sector had their wages frozen. With inflation running at 54 percent, private sector workers suffered a setback, while public sector workers were pushed to the wall. In 1966 private sector wage increases averaged 30–35 percent, while the public sector workers got 35 percent. The inflation rate of 38 percent was *still* outrunning nominal wage hikes. These two examples show how in the same years the application of indexation could produce highly different results. It might be objected that these outcomes simply reflect different government priorities: the need to reduce "artificially" high wage rates and the need to attract private savings in order to finance the public deficit. But that explanation, close to Campos's logic, only underlines the point.[77]

A third key area of economic policy was agriculture.[78] Delfim's team had given high priority to agriculture for several reasons. First, food prices weighed heavily in the cost of living. The fight against inflation would be lost if agricultural production did not at least keep pace with growing demand generated by higher urban real incomes and by the growing population. Second, Brazil had to increase exports rapidly, and agricultural exports would be easiest in the short run. Third, improving rural income might slow the exodus to the overburdened cities.

Whatever his reputation as an orthodox economist, Delfim was not hesitant to compromise those principles in stimulating the agricultural sector. First, he got the National Monetary Council to waive taxes on farm products. Then he got the tax advantage extended, by stages, to all key farm inputs—fertilizer, tractors, processing equipment, etc. Second, Delfim convinced the National Monetary Council to approve special interest rates for agriculture. In effect, these were to be low—or even negative—real rates.[79] Finally, the minimum-price program was expanded. It was aimed at a key problem for farmers: uncertainty over prices on harvest day. Because storage facilities were poor or nonexistent, the farmers had no bargaining power when their crops or cattle were ready for market. Now, with assurance of government-guaranteed minimum prices, farmers had an incentive to maintain or increase their investment.

As these examples show, Delfim preached the virtues of the free market while building in a bevy of specific incentives. All involved a cost to the public, usually not as appropriated funds, but rather as a tax or credit concessions.[80]

The Costa e Silva government also enjoyed success in the balance of payments. The current account balance had been positive in 1964, 1965, and 1966 largely because of low import levels due to the recessionary effects of stabilization. The current account balance turned negative in 1967 and thereafter, because of a shrinking trade surplus and a growing net outflow for services and dividend payments. How, then, was Brazil able to finance these current account deficits? Largely through capital inflows. For

1968, for example, the net inflow was $541 million, more than double any year since 1961. In 1969 there occurred a further jump, to $871 million. In October 1968 the World Bank announced it was lending Brazil a billion dollars for development projects. The capital inflow was in part the result of the Castelo Branco government's vigorous effort to attract both private and public capital. It was also a reaction to that government's success in reducing inflation and in strengthening government finances. No less important, Brazil's resumption of high economic growth also made it again attractive to private foreign investors. The economy was humming, at least by conventional macroeconomic indicators, and Delfim Neto's team was well positioned to exploit the favorable trends.[81]

A Paralyzed President and a Succession Crisis

The sharp authoritarian turn in December 1968 had taken the Costa e Silva government far from its promise to humanize the Revolution. How much further would it go? A brief comparison of the authoritarian turns of October 1965 and December 1968 will help put the rest of Costa e Silva's presidency in perspective.

Despite the goods news on the economy, the Costa e Silva government found 1968 to be a difficult year. There was hardly time to enjoy the economic successes before the workers of Contagem and Osasco erupted in strikes. Then came the tumultuous student protest marches that spilled over into violence in Rio and Brasília. Where was Costa e Silva's hoped-for base of civilian support? ARENA, the government party, could not even handle an MDB crippled by purges. Even worse, Carlos Lacerda, once a pillar of the Revolution, was now trying to forge an alliance with officially proscribed ex-Presidents Goulart and Kubitschek. With November came heightened tension, and the military mood grew more ugly over their failure to win "satisfaction" in the Márcio Alves case.

Costa e Silva was at the center of these cross pressures just as Castelo Branco had been in October 1965. Both faced military backlash after progovernment politicians failed to achieve the result they had promised and the military had demanded—winning key elections in 1965 and winning a congressional vote on immunity in 1968. Both presidents were forced to make a radical change of course, swinging toward more arbitrary government. It was a shift both had hoped to avoid.

Although their moments of truth were similar, the two men reacted very differently. In October 1965 Castelo Branco was performing as expected, stubbornly commited to accepting the electoral results. When he saw the inevitable, however, he jumped in time to stay on top of the military backlash, and to be the President who proclaimed AI–2. Having made his decision, Castelo felt supremely confident in carrying it out. In December 1968, on the other hand, the emotional Costa e Silva was all too ready to believe the pro-government Congressmen who were predicting a government victory in the Márcio Moreira Alves affair. The truth was that the well informed considered that prospect less and less likely. But the Planalto had gone too far to turn back.

In the midst of the crisis leading up to the adverse congressional vote, the presidential physician watched Costa e Silva closely, mindful of his chronic high blood pressure. As the vote neared, the presidential blood pressure soared. When his doctor suggested he take his medication, Costa e Silva refused, saying, "Today I need it really high!"[82] His stated reason was the upcoming meeting of the National Security Council, where he would face enormous military pressures. Like Castelo, he would have had to master them or be run over by them. He did preside over the issuing of AI–5. But he never made the emotional transition from the role of the "humanizing" President to the role of the South American dictator. After issuing AI–5 he was still at the helm of state, but its direction was in the hands of the hard-faced security men, telephone tappers, and torturers.[83] Brazil now had the dubious distinction of qualifying for major attention from Amnesty International, the human rights watchdog for "prisoners of conscience."

As we saw earlier, Costa e Silva reacted to his government's descent into authoritarianism by throwing himself into drafting a new constitution. Somehow, he reasoned, there must be a way to reconcile the new arbitrary power (AI–5) with the eventual redemocratization constantly promised since 1964. This was, given the differing contexts, exactly what Castelo Branco had hoped to accomplish with the Constitution of 1967 and its many legal corollaries.

Vice President Pedro Aleixo had done the initial drafting of the new constitution, which was ready on August 26. It was then presented to a panel of eminent constitutional lawyers who were all implicitly willing to accept, at least in the short run, a constitution overshadowed by gross military restrictions on civil liberties. The suggested revisions, including a number from Costa e Silva and cabinet members, were studied by Vice President Aleixo, who produced a final draft. The President was delighted with it and planned to promulgate the new constitution (as a constitutional amendment to the 1967 Constitution, not via AI–5) on September 2. It would take force on Independence Day, September 7. The Congress would then reopen on September 8. But the government was not agreed on this timing. On August 27 the three military ministers warned Costa e Silva that a majority of the military commanders were against reopening Congress so soon and equally against surrendering any powers given them in the institutional acts. It was the same message the President had heard in May from the commanding generals of the First Army (Syzeno Sarmento), the Second Army (José Canvarro Pereira), and the Third Army (Emílio Garrastazú Médici).[84]

Costa e Silva became even more determined to go ahead with issuing the constitution. But his potential opposition from within the army was growing. His army minister was under attack from ambitious officers seeking to exploit the military desire for a more repressive regime. Costa e Silva knew that reopening the Congress and promulgating a new constitution would fly in the face of this radical military opinion.

On August 27, while speaking with the governor of Goiás, the President became momentarily disoriented, unable to follow the conversation. The next day Costa e Silva's doctor warned him: "Mr. President, you must rest immediately. You can't survive this pace." The patient replied: ". . . Only after September 8. That will be the most important week of my government. On the 8th I shall give the nation a great present."[85]

But time ran out. On August 29 Costa e Silva suffered a stroke that left his right side paralyzed, including the right side of his face. Although able to hear and understand, he could not speak. Suddenly the highly centralized military government had a mute, immobile commander.[86]

The first move of the stricken President's staff, led by General Portella de Mello, was to go ahead with his scheduled flight to Rio. Trying to hide Costa e Silva's true condition, his aides wrapped his face in a scarf, covering the paralyzed side. At Rio's Galeão airport there was a welcoming party—government ministers and a lineup of air force cadets to be reviewed, none of whom knew of the President's condition, although rumors were already flying. The ministers each got a firm (left) handshake from the silent President, and the cadets saw only a weak wave from behind the limousine's back window. The car headed straight for Laranjeiras Palace, where the military ministers would gather to decide how to handle this newest crisis.

The three military ministers immediately agreed to reject Article 78 of the Constitution of 1967, which stipulated: "If the President is incapacitated the Vice President substitutes for him, if the office is vacant the Vice President succeeds to it." The reason was simple: they deeply distrusted Vice President Pedro Aleixo. They were still angered over his refusal to support the issuing of AI–5 in December 1968; they regarded him as just another politician who clung to his legal niceties in the face of vile insults to the armed forces. The presidential staff deliberately failed to inform Aleixo of the President's stroke until after the military ministers had agreed on their strategy.

They did not take long to rule out all the other constitutionally stipulated successors: president of the Chamber of Deputies, president of the Senate, and president of the Supreme Court. The first two were out because their succession would have required reopening Congress—which the military opposed—and the third was out because Supreme Court justices were still suspect for their excessive independence in the Castelo Branco presidency.

The military ministers next had to decide who would exercise the presidency now. General Portella suggested a "Triple Regency" of the three military ministers governing in the name of the President (while continuing in their ministerial positions). The precedent, argued Portella, was the 1830s Regency, which ruled for the underage Emperor Dom Pedro II until he assumed the throne in 1840. The military ministers refused to make a decision on their own, instead turning to the armed forces High Command as the body to decide how Costa e Silva would be replaced for the short run. That group included the three service ministers, the chief of General Staff of the armed forces, and head of the Presidential Military Staff. The High Command then said it would designate three military ministers to govern for the interim but noted it "needed some kind of decree" to legalize the action.[87] Since three of the High Command's five members made up the body to whom power would be delegated, the High Command's concern showed how, even at moments of arbitrary action, the Brazilian military persisted in believing a respectable legal rationale for their actions could be found.

Vice President Aleixo, still in Brasília, soon realized the President had more than a cold. Congressmen were now pressing Aleixo, suggesting how he might become president despite military opposition. An air force plane was sent to bring Aleixo to Rio. He then met with the military ministers, who bluntly informed him they were going to govern in the President's name "so that the peace enjoyed by the country would not be disrupted, thereby endangering the political program the President wanted to carry out."[88] The Vice President, greatly upset, firmly defended his constitutional right to succeed. He had been summoned to Rio, he complained, "not to examine the situation, nor for consultation or a joint decision." Rather, he had been "summoned to be informed of a fait accompli . . ." He warned, "I deplore it, not for the harm it causes me, but for the harm it will cause the nation."[89] The ministers finally laid it on the line, informing Aleixo that "various armed forces commands around the country" had registered their opposition to his succession, and that "the armed forces High Command had to heed the will of such military units since they are the basis of the government."[90] Aleixo was unconvinced and considered returning to Brasília, presumably to put up a fight. That option disappeared when the military ordered that he not be allowed to leave Rio.

Pedro Aleixo was only the most recent of a generation of distinguished UDN politicians (Milton Campos, Adauto Lúcio Cardoso, and Daniel Krieger) who had assumed pro-government leadership in the Congress and then found they could not reconcile a liberal conscience with the military demands for more and more arbitrary power.[91]

That night the cabinet, minus the Vice President, met and approved Institutional Act No. 12. It had been drafted only hours earlier by veteran lawyer Carlos Medeiros. It authorized the temporary replacement of the President by the military ministers.[92] Events had moved swiftly. It had been only two days since Costa e Silva's stroke on Friday, August 29. Brazil now had a stricken President, a Vice President incommunicado, and a military triumvirate giving orders.

The arragement was obviously unstable. As for the President's health, the doctors' reports were highly guarded. Many inside and outside the government seriously doubted that he could recover. The higher military were deeply worried, for any government instability would arouse political ambitions in the officer corps and thereby threaten army unity. Nonetheless, they had to start the process of choosing a new president. It was to be a kind of election from within the services, under rules not always explicit. September was punctuated with politicking by generals, admirals, air force brigadiers, and their junior colleagues. Up to now the Brazilian military had, despite the crises of October 1965 and December 1968, avoided serious splits within or among the services. What effect would this succession struggle have?

It was a foregone conclusion that Costa e Silva's successor would be another army general. The army had a strong claim in that it had furnished the President whose unfulfilled term was now in question. Even more important, the army was by far the largest service and had the largest number of officers serving in government posts. Perhaps most important, it had the greatest stake in a successful military government, because in the last analysis it was the army that would have to maintain civil order.

Notwithstanding the army's senior role, each service was to participate in the selection process by indicating its top three or four choices. The procedure for sounding out the officer ranks was never specified (enlisted men were to have no role). The kind of consultation varied, but for all three services the final order of preference was to be decided by that service's most senior officers.[93]

The most conspicuous candidate from the army was General Afonso Albuquerque Lima, an outspoken critic of the post-1964 economic policies. His nationalist views appealed to many politicians and intellectuals, including former PTB militants. But they also disturbed some businessmen and military. In mid-September Albuquerque Lima took the unusual step (for that era) of publicly defending his nationalist views, a move that alienated some officers who thought the contest should be kept strictly within military ranks.[94]

As September wore on, Albuquerque Lima picked up strong support in the navy and air force to add to his strength in the army. He was especially popular among younger officers, many of whom thought their commanders incapable of dynamic leadership. Senior officers replied that Brazil was fortunate to have escaped having any "charismatic military figures" who might well have led their men and their nation to disaster. Such comments, often delivered in a paternalistic tone, only emboldened the Albuquerque Lima forces. Their man was clearly the front-runner.[95]

There was, however, no lack of other army candidates. An obvious one was Army Minister Lyra Tavares. Exhausted from struggling to contain the indiscipline within his own service, he forbade any mention of his name for President. There was virtually none. A stronger candidate was General Antonio Carlos Muricy, the Army Chief of Staff, who had developed contacts with army installations throughout Brazil. Yet his image had never recovered from an inept bid (quashed by Castelo Branco) to become governor of Pernambuco in 1965. General Orlando Geisel, Chief of Staff of the Armed Forces, was yet another candidate. He was closely identified with the castelistas and considered an enemy by the Costa e Silva camp. General Syzeno Sarmento, Commander of the First Army and a candidate, was also unpopular with the Costa e Silva government. The cause of his unpopularity was his continuing attempt to grab police and censorship power in the wake of AI–5. Syzeno was soon to ally with Albuquerque Lima, broadening the latter's following in the all-important First Army (Rio) area. Finally, there was General Emílio Garrastazú Médici, commander of the Third Army and former director of the SNI. Médici was a close friend of the President and would probably have been Costa e Silva's choice for successor. That fact influenced some higher officers who felt the stricken President did not deserve a replacement opposed to his key policies. Médici was the least visible candidate, and he repeatedly announced he would not accept nomination.

As October neared, it was clear that Albuquerque Lima was still running very strong in the army. His supporters were issuing manifestos and negotiating with prominent civilian candidates for positions in his government. It was beginning to look as if the pro-Albuquerque Lima younger officers would prevail over their seniors, should a head count be taken.

In early October the military ministers met to evaluate the situation. Albuquerque Lima and Médici were running neck and neck in the army. The ministers were distressed, since they had decided that Albquerque Lima had to be ruled out. Why? First, it would be disrespectful to Costa e Silva—whose term was to be filled out—because Albuquerque Lima's nationalist and populist ideas contradicted those of the stricken President. Even more important, the military ministers and virtually all the senior army generals opposed Albuquerque Lima's ideas. They disapproved of him also because he had campaigned outside military ranks, thus opening the military to manipulation from without. Finally, the ministers pointed to Albuquerque Lima's links with Carlos Lacerda as proof of his bad judgment. Although these were the real reasons for ruling out Albuquerque Lima, the ministers avoided stating them publicly. Happily for them, they had another out.

No one could have failed to notice that of the six army candidates all but one had four stars. The exception was Albuquerque Lima, with only three. Until now there had been no explicit agreement on a minimum rank for candidates. Faced with the threat of Albquerque Lima's candidacy, however, the military ministers announced that only four-star generals were eligible. The ministers were applying to the presidency the military rule that no commander could hold lower rank than those he commanded. Since the President could give orders to four-star generals, he could not be outranked by them.

This decision prompted a furious protest letter from Albuquerque Lima to the army minister. It warned of the dangers ahead if his "new message for the Brazilian people" were now lost. Equally serious was the danger of "new and deep divisions in the army caused by top decisions which ignore the true feelings of those under your command." He claimed to represent "the majority of the armed forces," who soon might turn to "other leaders perhaps more reckless and less cautious." The tone of the letter suggested that Albuquerque Lima was laying the groundwork for a later campaign. Lyra Tavares replied (unwisely, thought his military colleagues), announcing, "What we haven't had and couldn't have, without compromising the army's democratic traditions, was an election among all levels of the military hierarchy, because our institution is not a political party."[96] The army minister's argument that his service's democratic traditions did not incude elections highlighted the military's problem: how to achieve a military consensus that included all ranks without creating divisions and without producing a result the top officers could not accept?

The army High Command now had to agree on their candidate. With Albuquerque Lima out, Médici had the broadest support. The main obstacle to choosing him was his adamant refusal to accept. The generals solved that problem by calling him (from his Third Army command in Rio Grande do Sul) to Rio. There they convinced him he was the only candidate who could hold together the army and the military. It was a "mission" only he could fulfill. By presenting the issue in military terms, the generals got Médici to accept.

The pro-Médici forces were not yet home free. Because army officer opinion had been so split, it was important that the other two services strongly support the army's choice. The air force had done so, but the navy officers still strongly supported Albuquerque Lima. The only solution was for Navy Minister Rademaker to intervene. He urgently appealed to his fellow admirals, on the grounds of inter-service solidarity, to switch to Médici. He succeeded, but by only a narrow margin. Now the ministers called for the "official" poll from each service. Interestingly, all three now reported the same order of preference: (1) Médici; (2) Orlando Geisel; (3) Muricy; and (4) Syzeno. Lyra Tavares was right—it was no simple election from the lower ranks up.

Médici now announced Admiral Rademaker as his choice for Vice President. The admiral at first refused, as aware as anyone that the three military ministers had pledged not to become candidates for the office they were temporarily filling. But the admiral soon succumbed to the same argument (a "mission" to carry out) he had used on Médici. Rademaker's success in converting his colleagues to the Médici camp had not gone unnoticed by the President-designate.

The key question at the end of September was the President's health. He had failed to regain his speech, and the chances of a recovery seemed remote. A statement from the doctors made clear that, even if he recovered, the President could never again endure the rigors of the office. That was all the armed forces High Command needed to hear. On October 8–9 the Command met and chose Médici for President and Admiral Rademaker for Vice President. Both men had vigorously opposed their own selection, a stance which was becoming a *sine qua non* for success in the politics of the higher military.

The High Command had also decided that it must recall Congress, suspended since December 1968, to vote for president and vice president. Not having Congress vote, it was agreed, "might give the impression of a dictatorship and create a bad image at home and abroad."[97] So much for the higher military's political sensitivity. On October 14 the High Command issued Institutional Act No. 16, which declared the presidency vacant, specified that the new presidential term would run until March 15, 1974, thus creating a full new term, and set the rules for the election of the next president and vice president. The Congress was to reconvene and the parties were to present their candidates. The congressional election occurred as specified, on October 25. The ARENA Congressmen, thoroughly purged of any hint of independence, duly elected Médici and Rademaker. The MDB astained, as extreme a gesture as they could afford.

The military also gave Brazil a new constitution. Médici promulgated it on October 17, eight days before the Congress met to elect him. That timing dramatized the Congress's lack of a role in revising the country's most fundamental law. The new constitution consisted of large unrevised chunks of the 1967 constitution, along with key changes (it became known as the 1967 Constitution with the Amendment of October 17, 1969). The changes further increased the power of the executive. Some new features were aimed at the guerrilla threat, such as a strengthened National Security Law and an increased maximum length for a state of siege. The legislatures were another target. The number of seats in the federal Chamber of Deputies was reduced from 409 to 310, and the total number of seats in all state assemblies reduced from 1,076 to 701. Especially important was the change in the method of allocating federal deputies by state. The new basis was to be the number of registered voters per state, instead of, as previously, the population per state. The change was bound to favor the more developed states, whose higher literacy rates produced a higher rate of registered voters. The scope of congressional immunity was reduced—no more cases like Márcio Moreira Alves. Finally, there was a new device to prevent ARENA legislators from voting against the government. "Party fidelity" would now require all legislators (federal and state) to vote with the party leadership if the latter classified an upcoming vote as of prime importance to the party. This measure was also aimed at preventing any recurrence of independent voting as in the Márcio Moreira Alves case.[98]

The crisis of 1968 was still playing itself out. The higher military now had all the powers their lawyers could conceivably codify. The Congress, having performed the required election ritual, was sent back into recess. The legal opposition, the MDB, had been riddled by purges and rendered ineffective by intimidation and censorship. The guerrillas were troublesome, but they were also useful because they helped justify the repression.

The real threat to the government came not from the left but from within the military. Choosing Médici had been a bruising process. Generals such as Syzeno Sarmento and Albuquerque Lima had hurled ominous threats. Not surprising then, that Institutional Act No. 16, setting up Médici's election, was accompanied by Institutional Act No. 17, strengthening the president's hand in dealing with military indiscipline. The president could now transfer to the reserve any officer "who commits or plans to commit a crime against the unity of the Armed Forces . . ."[99] This stern penalty was tempered by a subsequent article that assured the victims their full salary and emoluments.

In his first address to the country in October President Médici said he hoped "to leave democracy definitively established in our country at the end of my administration."[100] In the meantime, he called for a closer dialogue with students, clerics, the press, etc. It was the Janus face of the Revolution—assuming more authoritarian powers while promising that, if the public were cooperative, Brazil would someday return to the rule of law.

The U.S.: A Missing Ambassador and Some Second Thoughts

We must now look back to early September, when a kidnapping suddenly thrust the U.S. into the center of the succession crisis. The U.S. government's rapid embrace of the post-1964 military governments, along with its traditional position as Brazil's principal investor and trading partner, made it a natural target for the nationalist opposition. Radical students and Catholic activists zeroed in on U.S. imperialism as a (some said *the*) prime cause of Brazil's ills. Those who had become guerrillas had staged small actions, as we have seen, and some were now gathering their forces for a major action. They chose to strike in Rio by kidnapping U.S. Ambassador Charles Burke Elbrick on September 4.[101] The kidnappers were from the ALN and the MR–8, the revolutionary movement named for October 8th, the date of Che Guevara's death. The kidnappers hid Elbrick in a rented house in Santa Teresa, in the Rio hills, and made two demands on the military triumvirate now ruling the country.

First, their revolutionary manifesto had to be broadcast within 48 hours over all Brazilian radio stations. Second, the government had to release 15 specified political prisoners. The guerrillas' list was drawn up to appeal to as wide a spectrum of the opposition as possible. It included student leaders Luis Travassos and Vladimir Palmeira, union leader José Ibraim, guerrilla Onofre Pinto, who was a former air force sergeant, and long-time PCB activist Gregório Bezerra from Recife. By naming the prisoners to be ransomed, the guerrillas forced the government either to release them (and thereby reveal their physical condition) or admit they were dead. The government was henceforth on notice that in the future any prisoner's name might suddenly appear on a ransom list. It was, to quote one criminal lawyer, a de facto *habeas corpus*.[102]

In their manifesto the kidnappers announced "that it is possible to defeat the dictatorship and the exploitation if we arm and organize ourselves." They accused the military government of "creating a false happiness in

order to hide the misery, exploitation and repression in which we live."
They ended on an ominous note: "Finally, we would like to warn all those
who torture, beat, and kill our comrades, that we will no longer allow this
to continue," concluding "now it is an eye for an eye and a tooth for a
tooth."[103]

The kidnappers' ploy turned out to be well conceived for the short run.
They had taken prisoner the ambassador of Brazil's most powerful ally.
The Brazilian government was now forced to make apparent concessions
where the military were most sensitive: the war against the armed left.

The kidnappers' demands also provoked a fierce debate among the military. One faction (centered especially in the First Army installation at the
Vila Militar outside Rio) wanted to leave the ambassador to his fate,
arguing that the price of his safe return would be the humiliation of the
military. As could be expected, the U.S. government was applying intense
pressure on the military junta to get Elbrick back. The strains created by
that pressure might lead to a rejection of the kidnappers' demands. The
government could have chosen to assault Elbrick's prison, a private house
in a hilly section of Rio de Janeiro. Naval intelligence had the house under
24-hour surveillance.[104]

Moderate voices prevailed, however, and the demands were met. The
revolutionary manifesto was sent out over all the media and the prisoners
were assembled. On September 7, Independence Day, the ransomed prisoners left Rio on an airliner bound for Mexico, as instructed by the guerrillas. When word of the airliner's safe arrival in Mexico reached the kidnappers, Elbrick was released; he was immediately recalled to Washington by
the State Department.

This acquiescence to the kidnappers' demands had provoked bitter opposition within the ranks, just as the guerrillas had hoped it would. On
September 6 paratroop officers had invaded a radio station near Rio de
Janeiro and announced they were seizing power in Brazil. They soon left
the studio, however, and did not resurface. A more serious incident occurred when the plane holding the ransomed prisoners was on the runway
ready to leave Rio for Mexico. Two hundred marines (hardliners in the
navy) surrounded the aircraft, refusing to let it take off. They were finally
persuaded (or ordered) to desist by higher authorities, who feared delay
would endanger the U.S. ambassador's life. The last incident occurred
soon after the prisoners arrived in Mexico. A group of colonels publicly
attacked the government's decision. But it was too late. The precedent had
been set: the Brazilian government would trade Brazilian prisoners for
abducted foreign diplomats.[105]

In the wake of the kidnapping the Junta quickly showed its toughness.
On September 5, it issued two Institutional Acts, as we saw earlier. AI–13
gave the government the power to ban permanently from the country any
Brazilian deemed dangerous to national security (the law was immediately
applied to the 15 hostages flown to Mexico). AI–14 restored the death
penalty (non-existent in peacetime Brazil since 1891) for cases of "Foreign

War, or Psychological Revolutionary or Subversive War." The military government had given itself the right to do virtually anything in the name of national security. By mid-September the security forces had arrested 1,800 suspects. Many underwent torture.[106]

Among those arrested were guerrillas from Carlos Marighela's ANL. Evidently the interrogators extracted enough information to mount a trap for Marighela himself. On November 4 he was ambushed and shot to death on a São Paulo city street. The government trumpeted the news (and the unforgettable picture of the dead Marighela sprawled halfway into a Volks-wagen backseat), claiming their information on Marighela's movements had come from several Dominican monks alledgedly collaborating with the ANL. Given the power of censorship, the government found it easy to impose its version on the public.[107] The authorities had scored a double coup: the liquidation of the best-known (and most able) guerrilla leader and the discrediting for many of one element in the Church, now a prime focus of opposition. As one of Elbrick's kidnappers later put it, "Marighela's death was the government's spectacular answer to the kidnapping of the American ambassador."[108]

Yet the government's new crackdown only reinforced U.S. doubts, grow-ing since the authoritarian turn in 1968.[109] In 1964 the U.S. had embraced the Revolution, lending heavy support to Castelo Branco's stabilization and reform policies. In U.S. government eyes the Fifth Institutional Act (1968) was a giant step backward in what the U.S. had thought was prog-ress toward constitutional rule. In mid-December the State Department made its concern known by "nonattributable comments" to the press.

The press didn't have to be discreet. The *New York Times* editorialized thus: "The military leaders have behaved like spoiled children and put even further into the future the day Brazilians dream of when this giant of a country will assume a position of respected leadership in the Americas and the world."[110] Once again Washington listened to a re-run of the long-standing debate over proper U.S. policy toward Latin American dictatorships.

Brazil's December 1968 crisis caught Washington at a moment of transi-tion. The lame-duck Johnson administration, soon to be suceeded by Rich-ard Nixon's, had been shocked by the sharp authoritarian turn of AI–5. In response the Johnson White House delayed disbursement of $50 million in aid and $125 million in previously approved loans for Brazil. Once in office in January 1969, the Nixon administration continued the freeze. USAID officials made clear that it was part of a reconsideration of the U.S.'s strong identification with the Brazilian generals. The freeze continued until May, when administration "realists" prevailed and aid was resumed. Nonethe-less, U.S. bilateral assistance to Brazil for 1969 totalled only $27.3 million, a dramatic decline from the 1964–68 average of $303 million a year.[111] But such aid was also much less important to Brazil now, in view of her increas-ing capital inflow and rising export earnings.

From the U.S. vantage point, Brazil was only one instance of a trend toward authoritarianism in Latin America. In the midst of a fierce debate over how the U.S. should react to this trend, President Nixon resorted to a well-worn tactic: he appointed a commission to study the problem.[112] The chairman was Nelson Rockefeller, a prominent Republican politician and a long-time participant in U.S.–Latin American affairs (both in government posts and as a private investor). In June the commission set off on a tour of Latin America. The visit to Brazil was important because of the recently lifted freeze on U.S. aid.

The Costa e Silva government honored the Americans even before their arrival. It warned the Brazilian press not to print unfavorable news about the mission, nor any references to strikes, student demonstrations, suspension of political rights, nor any of a long list of other taboo topics.[113] Once in Brazil in mid-June, Rockefeller expressed concern over the suspension of the Brazilian Congress, now seven months old.[144] But the mission's final report, issued at the end of August, revealed a different concern. "Communist subversion," it noted, "is a reality today with alarming potential." A key recommendation was that "the United States should reverse the recent downward trend in grants for assisting the training of security forces for the other hemisphere countries."[115] This proposal spoke louder than incidental comments about Brazil's lack of democratic liberties. The U.S. had made at most a half-hearted attempt to pressure the Brazilian revolutionaries on the issues most on the minds of the Brazilian government's critics, both at home and abroad: When would Brazil return to the rule of law, and when would its economic policies begin to help the millions in abject poverty?

V

MÉDICI:
THE AUTHORITARIAN FACE

General Emílio Garrastazú Médici was virtually unknown to the public when he assumed the presidency in October 1969. By contrast, his two predecessors had been major figures in the Revolution of 1964. Both had a strong following among the military and the public by the time they became president. And both were eager for the job. Médici, by contrast, was a soldier's soldier. He was dead set against becoming president and gave in only on grounds of military duty. Médici became President, not because he or his military electors thought he had the vision or the knowledge a president needed, but because he was the only four-star general who could stop the army from tearing itself apart.[1]

The Personality, Cabinet,
and Governing Style of Médici

Médici was another native of Rio Grande do Sul, which was rapidly developing a monopoly on the presidency. He had been chief of staff for Costa e Silva in the late 1950s when the latter commanded the Third Military Region. The two became close friends during those years. Later he served as military attaché in Washington for the Castelo Branco government. Upon his return to Brazil, he was named chief of the SNI, a post which gave him a rapid education on his country. Congressional leaders who knew him as SNI director described him as easy to talk with and "always interested in a political dialogue."[2] He later said the SNI had introduced him to "the legal side and the underside of Brazil and its people."[3] In 1969, after winning his fourth star, Médici was named commander of the Third Army in Rio Grande do Sul, from whence he came to the presidency. An early convert to the conspiracy against Goulart, Médici favored the hard line, although he was not one of its better-known public spokesmen.

The new president appointed a largely new cabinet to help govern during the presidential term, which would last until March 1974. The two leading economic policymakers, however, were carryovers from Costa e Silva's cabinet. The more important was Finance Minister Delfim Neto, the technocrat nonpareil and architect of the economic boom. His retention meant there would be no break with the economic policies which were now so successful (in terms of growth) and were so controversial (in terms of social equity). The other major technocratic carryover was João Paulo dos Reis Veloso, who had headed the research arm of the Planning Ministry under Costa e Silva, and who now became Planning Minister. He worked easily with Delfim and was skillful with the growing state bureaucracy.

Other ministerial carryovers were Antonio Dias Leite as Minister of Mines and Energy; Mario Andreazza as Transportation Minister; José Costa Cavalcanti as Minister of the Interior; Marcio de Souza e Mello as Air Minister; and Jarbas Passarinho, who remained in the cabinet but moved from Labor to Education.

The new cabinet ministers were primarily administrators, as contrasted to other cabinets since 1964, which had more professional politicians and representatives of economic or social interests. The Médici government claimed it was a state rising "above" its society, with technocrats and military ruling in the best interests of the nominally unrepresented social sectors. As Médici explained in October 1969, he had chosen his ministers while "immune to pressures of any kind. . . . whether political, military, or economic." This "non-political" stance was a favorite one for the military. According to Médici, "the only commitments I have are to my conscience and the future of our country."[4] The Justice Minister was a São Paulo lawyer, Alfredo Buzaid; the Agriculture Ministry went to Luiz Fernando Cirne Lima, a gaucho agronomist, and the Labor Ministry to Júlio de Carvalho Barata, a former president of the Superior Labor Tribunal. The new Minister of Industry and Commerce was Fabio Riodi Yassuda, former head of a Paulista agricultural cooperative and the first Japanese-Brazilian ever to hold ministerial status. Health went to Francisco de Paula da Rocha Lagoa, a medical researcher. The new Foreign Minister was Mario Gibson Barbosa, a professional diplomat who had most recently been ambassador to the United States. The Ministry of Communications went to Colonel Higno Corsetti, a relative unknown. The two new military ministers were Orlando Geisel, the runner-up to Médici in the military's straw ballot for Costa e Silva's successor, who was made Army Minister,[5] and Admiral Adalberto de Barros Nunes, who was made Navy Minister.

Médici also chose new men for two other key cabinet posts. The new head of the Civilian Presidential Staff was João Leitão de Abreu, a lawyer from Rio Grande do Sul and a brother-in-law of General Lyra Tavares. The appointment to the comparable position in the Military Staff was General João Batista de Oliveira Figueiredo. The head of the SNI remained General Carlos Alberto Fontoura.

General Médici began his presidency in circumstances far different from those of his two predecessors. Castelo Branco had arrived confident that the 22 months remaining on Goulart's mandate would be enough to purge the subversives, restore economic order, and enact major reforms. Costa e

Silva took office promising to liberalize, now that a new constitution was in place. Both Castelo and Costa e Silva had taken power on an optimistic note.

Médici took over in a darker moment.[6] Ten months earlier a blanket of repression had settled over the country. Now the military consensus demanded that the repression continue. The hard line was in the saddle.[7]

Médici's presidency saw relative outward calm in Brazil. There were no student marches, no union pickets, and no rabble-rousing rallies. Or at least none the wider public could see.[8] Government repression and censorship were the principal reasons. Students, for example, a major source of opposition in 1968, had been silenced by heavy intervention in the universities. There were expulsions, arrests, and torture for some. Repression was also proving effective against guerrillas.

The legal opposition, the MDB, was rendered ineffectual. MDB politicians orated in Congress, but censorship emasculated their speeches before they could appear in the media. And the MDB faced an electoral system stacked against it. So complete was the government grip that President Médici didn't need to cassate anyone. The Catholic Church became, *faute de mieux,* the only institution able to confront the government and survive. But even the Church was divided and sometimes unable to protect its clergy from the horrors of torture.

Yet repression alone does not explain Médici's Brazil. Along with the stick came the carrot. Rapid economic growth paid off in dramatically increased salaries for the Brazilians at the top—the professionals, the technocrats, the managers. Indeed, their salaries rose above those for comparable professinals in the U. S. and Western Europe. Wage rates lower down the occupational scale may not have increased much, but the 10 percent annual rate of economic growth created new jobs at all levels. Many workers moved up the job ladder, increasing their wages on the way. Many previously unemployed workers found jobs under Médici.[9] Finally, the federal universities, although under strict political control, received record-high appropriations. The Médici government's bravado about Brazil's destiny to be a world power struck a responsive chord among Brazilians with rising incomes. Many of them actively favored the Médici regime.

At the same time, however, millions of Brazilians saw little improvement in their economic lot. Many were in the rural sector, where harsh control by landowners and the government discouraged any organizing. Those in the cities were cowed by governmental repression. Both the rural and the urban disadvantaged were inhibited because of the habits of deference so deeply ingrained by the traditional culture. As a result, there was no significant, sustained worker protest, either organized or unorganized.

All in all, the government came out ahead—on its terms. Rapid economic growth worked. Government propaganda worked. Repression worked. Censorship worked. The hard-line military, repeatedly frustrated since 1964, saw their vision about to be vindicated.

General Médici's presidential style differed sharply from that of his two predecessors. Castelo Branco had taken an intense personal interest in certain policy areas, especially the economy. Costa e Silva had shed his initial image of the jovial but unlettered general as he struggled to stabilize the runaway authoritarian regime. Both presidents had intervened directly whenever they thought an issue crucial.

Médici was far more detached. He divided his government into three areas: military, economic, and political. He put Army Minister Orlando Geisel in charge of all military affairs, the most sensitive area. Finance Minister Delfim Neto had responsibility for all economic affairs. Leitão de Abreu, chief of the president's civilian staff, supervised everything political. Each was a viceroy within his realm; the technocrats and even other ministers had to work through them.[10] The same procedure applied to those outside the government, such as businessmen and landowners. In the case of the economy, this broad delegation of power to Delfim Neto consolidated the rule of the technocrats, who were spread through the public banks, utilities, and state enterprises. Their rise had begun when Roberto Campos was given the key role in 1964 and was reinforced by Delfim's appointment in 1967. Now the technocrats were underwritten in power by the hardest-line government Brazil had seen. The focus for (non-economic) domestic policymaking within this structure soon proved to be the National Security Council (*Conselho Nacional de Segurança*).[11]

Médici's delegation of power allowed him to keep his distance from day-to-day decision-making. It was a style well suited to a repressive regime, one in which the President never had to face any direct questioning from the controlled press.

Within this structure the most important link was the military-technocratic alliance. How had it come about? Let us start with the hard-line military. These extreme authoritarians did not believe that Brazil could, over the short run, achieve economic growth under an open political system. As a militant minority they were determined to prevent any access to power by the rival minority which had made, they thought, near-fatal inroads before 1964—the subversive Left. They saw Brazil as plagued by weak-willed politicians and treasonous intellectuals. Because the hardliners never emerged into the public arena to defend their ideas, their power could only be assessed by looking at the policies they forced upon successive governments. And the tightening authoritarian rule was eloquent testimony to that power.

The principal reason for their failure to take a public stance could be found in the structure of the military. The essence of organization within any military officer corps is hierarchy and discipline. Yet in Brazil this structure has allowed room for an intricate process of participatory decision-making, as was demonstrated in the choice of Médici to succeed Costa e Silva.[12] The higher levels retain the final word, but they cannot diverge too far from the views of their junior officers. In each political crisis the officers heatedly debated the proper government policy. Manifestos occasionally leaked to the press, but the controversy was essentially private. The exact lineup of factions and arguments was known only to the higher-level participants and a few privileged outsiders (including some journalists who protected their sources by seldom giving details).

Thus the heart of decision-making in Brazilian politics after 1964—the formation of officer opinion—remained hidden from the public. In order to preserve discipline and the image of unity, the disagreements were submerged in the final position adopted by higher command. That policy may have been subject to subsequent attack and revision, but only within the closed world of barracks-room debate. With rare exceptions, the losers guarded their silence. This maintenance of unity, at least in public, contrasted sharply with the frequent divisions that had arisen among the officers in the political-military crises between 1945 and 1964. When divided, as in 1961, the military found it impossible to intervene effectively. After 1964 their power made the need for unity even greater, lest they fall into the pattern of the Argentine military, whose warring factions often proved unable to impose any consistent policy on the civilians.

Within this closed opinion-making context, the more authoritarian officers increasingly held the initiative. Castelo Branco had clearly been a moderate; but Costa e Silva had pushed for more arbitrary presidential power in 1964–65, codified first in AI–2 and then AI–5. Now Médici was unequivocally identified with the hardliners. The latter usually relegated the explanation of the government's authoritarian side to civilian apologists, such as successive Justice Ministers Gama e Silva, Carlos Medeiros, and Alfredo Buzaid.[13] The truly militant officers did not believe in the official commitment to the principle of liberal democracy, but they had thus far lacked either the will or the intellectual self-confidence to emerge *on their own* and drop the pretense of civilian government. So, unlike their counterparts in Peru's 1968 Revolution, they used stalking horses. A further explanation for this reticence to rule openly in the capacity of military leaders was a strong consensus among the higher officers that no caudillo should be allowed to establish himself as a Franco-style dictator.

In this absence of any explicit rationale by the hard line, the government lawyers had to continue revamping the old constitutional forms in order to "legalize" the executive's growing powers. Although it avoided repudiating the liberal ideal per se, the government used constitutional amendments, institutional acts, and executive decrees to reduce even further the roles of the legislatures and judiciary. The National Security Law of September 1969 was a prime example. It authorized the federal government to intervene on virtually any level of social activity if it deemed national security to have been violated. In October the Médici regime proclaimed (Congress was in forced recess) a lengthy amendment to the 1967 Constitution, which gave the executive vast powers to protect national security (it was issued in the wake of the kidnapping of the U.S. ambassador).[14] At the same time it circumscribed (and often suspended) civil liberties and rights of political organization.

The tightening authoritarian system made possible political "stability," which the hard-line military defined as the absence of any serious opposition or criticism, thus satisfying their desire to suppress the tension and overt conflict of an open system. They no longer had to tolerate Marxist rhetoric, student demonstrations, or wheeling and dealing politicians with their payoffs among states, regions, and social groups.

Yet the application of this reactionary political philosophy was hardly the exclusive function of the authoritarian system. On the contrary, for most middle-sector Brazilians it was probably not even the principal function. They shared neither a devotion to national security nor the polarization (torturers vs. terrorist-kidnappers) forced upon them. But they did quickly acknowledge the remarkable economic progress made since 1964 and appeared to accept tacitly the authoritarian system because it made possible a new continuity and coherence in economic policy-making.

The result was a working alliance between military extremists and technocrats. Each had their own reasons for wanting an authoritarian regime, and each needed the other. The hard-line military needed the technocrats to make the economy work. The technocrats needed the military to stay in power. The high growth rates in turn gave legitimacy to the authoritarian system.

Undoubtedly the technocrats were less happy about this growing authoritarianism than the extremist military who had never entertained any illusions about the virtues of liberal democracy. Whatever qualms the technocrats may have felt, however, they appreciated the extraordinary power base that they would enjoy if the military continued to grant them carte blanche in economic policymaking. De facto evidence of this mutual alliance could be found in the fact that the hardliners had usually spared economics faculties in their periodic purges of Brazilian universities.

PR in a New Vein

President Médici's face rapidly became familiar to Brazilians as the centerpiece in a shrewd public relations strategy. The new government drove home the message that Brazil was rapidly becoming a world power, thanks to its 10 percent economic growth rate and its strong government vigilance against the nay-sayers and the terrorists. Many Brazilians naturally concluded that increased national power and a rapidly growing economy were a *result* of going authoritarian.

The heart of the Planalto's public relations offensive was the *Assessoria Especial de Relações Públicas* (AERP, or Special Advisory Staff on Public Relations). Now headed by army Colonel Octavio Costa, it had been established in 1968 to create a single center of government propaganda. Previously every government agency had had its own such arm.[15]

Colonel Costa's men turned AERP, which had not gotten off the ground in Costa e Silva's presidency, into the most professional government PR operation Brazil had seen. Together this team of journalists, psychologists, and sociologists decided on the themes and general approach, then contracted advertising agencies to produce the TV and movie shorts, along with items for the print media. The catchphrases reflected AERP's tone: "You build Brazil!", "Nobody can hold this country back!", and "Brazil, count on me!". A study of 116 spots contracted with 24 ad agencies found that 80 percent were devoted to the importance of work, the value of education, and the constructive role of the armed forces.[16] The messages were reasonably subtle, with skillful use of images, voice-overs, and phrases taken from current popular language. They were designed, in Colonel Costa's words, to strengthen "a healthy mentality of National Security," which is "indispensable for the defense of democracy and for the guarantee of a collective effort toward development."[17]

This use of television was not surprising. Brazil had suddenly emerged as one of the Third World's most dynamic TV markets. Generous installment credit had been extended to purchases of TV sets in 1968, and the public responded with a buying surge. In 1960 only 9.5 percent of urban homes had TV, but by 1970 it was 40 percent.[18] When Médici took office Brazil had 45 licensed TV stations. His government issued 20 new licenses, and in the process greatly aided the growth of the *O Globo* network. A creation of Brazil's most successful conservative newspaper publishing empire, TV-Globo had earlier accepted partial financing from Time-Life. Its opponents—especially those connected with a rival TV network that was losing its licenses to TV-Globo—charged that the latter's financial link to Time-Life violated Brazil's Communications Law forbidding foreign ownership in the media. The government rejected this argument, and TV-Globo continued its climb to a dominant position in Brazilian TV. Its critics suggested this rise could be explained by TV-Globo's strongly pro-government programming during the Médici presidency.[19]

The AERP's theme was Brazil's emergence as a dynamic and original society. The backdrop was the rapid economic growth, now at 10 percent a year. The AERP added its own message about Brazil's national unity, its new purpose, its disciplined march toward the company of developed nations.

One of AERP's most effective techniques in this effort was to link soccer, popular music, President Médici, and Brazilian progress. Médici was good material for such a campaign. He loved playing the father figure, and he was a fanatical soccer fan. AERP exploited both.[20] Médici became so upset about the Brazilian team's training for the World Soccer Cup in Mexico in 1970 that he complained to the national commission supervising the coach. The latter was promptly replaced.[21] Médici predicted Brazil would win the cup, and they did, to the hysterical cheers of their countrymen. Brazil was now the first country to have won the Jules Rimet (world championship) soccer cup three times, thereby earning the right to retire it.

Brazil's team returned to a country in delirium. The country got an official holiday to acknowledge the carnival-style celebration already underway. Médici received the team at the presidential palace, gave each player a tax-free bonus of $18,500, and basked in the endless photos with the players and the huge silver cup. This was exactly the image the Planalto needed to counteract foreign criticism over the regime's repression at home.

The presidential PR staff lost no time in following up on the World Cup glory. The catchy marching tune "Pra Frente Brasil" ("Forward Brazil"), written for the Brazilian team, became the government's theme song and was played at all official events. A multitude of posters appeared showing Pelé leaping aloft after scoring a goal and next to him the government slogan *"ninguem segura mais este pais"* ("Nobody can stop this country now"). This bread-and-circuses strategy succeeded brilliantly, to the dismay of the demoralized and fragmented opposition.[22]

Médici and Electoral Politics, 1969–72

Médici and his technocratic-military team had little reason to fear electoral opposition. The phalanx of arbitrary powers assumed in AI–5 gave the executive unlimited authority to intimidate and silence its critics. The Planalto was determined, nonetheless, to produce a semblance of popular support within the electoral system.[23]

Given that goal, Médici's first task was to decide how to deal with ARENA. The military had long complained that ARENA was unreliable and, some said, disloyal. Its failure in 1968 to deliver the votes to lift the parliamentary immunity of Márcio Moreira Alves still rankled. Many hard-line officers thought ARENA's useful days were over. The President did not. He thought ARENA could be salvaged, and began with the party leadership. He and his advisers selected Rondón Pacheco, an experienced politician from Minas Gerais and the former head of Costa e Silva's Civilian Presidential Staff, as their candidate for party president. ARENA's November 1969 national convention, following Médici's instructions, elected Pacheco party president. Médici was equally aggressive in choosing the new governors to be elected indirectly by the state legislatures in early October of 1970.[24] The President simply laid down the law to the ARENA leadership in each state. It should be noted that Médici flatly opposed the candidacy of active-duty military officers, which he believed would undermine military hierarchy.[25] Here was a clear example of the military's consensus against allowing politically minded officers to assume civilian political positions, giving to some an authority that could then cause partisan political divisions among the officers.

The presidential hand was decisive in naming the candidate and therefore the winner in all except a few states such as Guanabara (greater Rio de Janeiro), where ARENA did not control the state legislature. But even the MDB winner in Guanabara, Chagas Freitas, was no left-wing (or even centrist) threat. His political power was built on ownership of Rio's most sensationalist daily newspaper, *O Dia,* and on a close alliance with the bosses of the numbers racket *(jôgo de bicho).* As could have been predicted, his governorship proved no problem for Brasília.[26]

Having stage-managed the election of almost all the new governors,

Médici was well positioned to orchestrate the November 1970 elections—the first at the national level since the authoritarian turn of 1968–69.[27] The military, it is important to remember, had not abolished the Congress, although they had kept it in recess since December 1968 (except for the brief convocation to ratify Médici's succession to the presidency).[28] Despite their successful public relations campaign, government strategists were nervous about the elections.

Their first response was to alter the electoral rules. Although ARENA already had large majorities in the federal congress, the Planalto (especially Leitão de Abreu, head of the Civilian Presidential Staff) feared possible election reverses and decided to overhaul the entire federal legislative system. Although these changes were mentioned in the previous chapter, they took effect only in the Médici presidency. The first measure reduced the number of seats in the Chamber of Deputies from 409 to 310. It also changed the basis for calculating each state's congressional delegation from population to registered voters. The government thought this reform would stimulate party organization at the *município* level by creating the need for local directorates and signing up of new voters. Government strategists further thought ARENA's enormous patronage and spending power would give it a decisive advantage under the new method of determining congressional delegations. In fact, the change in the method of computing the congressional seats favored the more developed states of the Center-South, whose higher literacy and life-expectancy rates meant a higher percentage of their population were registered voters than in the less developed states, especially in the North and Northeast.

The Planalto further changed the electoral system by setting the dates of upcoming *município* elections (1972, 1976, and 1980) so they would not coincide with the legislative elections (1974, 1978, and 1982). The idea was to prevent national issues from influencing local issues and vice versa. Government reasoning here was that the federal government's unpopularity (for its macroeconomic decisions) might swamp ARENA candidates running on the local level. Finally, "tied" voting (*voto vinculado*), akin to the "straight ticket" in U.S. parlance, was now required when voting for state and federal deputy. By forcing the voter to choose candidates of the same party for the two levels of legislature, the government thought it could eliminate the inter-party alliances ("*dobradinhas*") between government and opposition, often used by the politicians to divide the spoils on a local or state level. Such alliances especially irritated the military, who saw them as dishonest "deals." These officers wanted a party loyalty from ARENA more akin to military discipline.[29]

Why all this tinkering with the electoral system? Given its position and powers, why didn't the government abolish elections? Or simply resort to more indirect elections (as had already been done for governor and president)? The answer is the military (and their civilian collaborators) still saw elections as an important legitimizing process. They had to be maintained, and manipulated if necessary.

Equally relevant, why did the MDB continue to play the electoral game? After all, the president had the power, in AI–5, to eliminate from the scene any politician he and his advisers thought undesirable. This threat put the opposition constantly under the gun. It is therefore not surprising that some in the MDB thought their party should withdraw from the electoral scene. It was a farce, they argued, and participating in it only conferred legitimacy on the military regime. These dissidents did not prevail, however, in part because almost all radically left MDB politicians, who might have led a dissolution of the party, had lost their political rights and hence any influence in the party. So the MDB continued to run candidates and to keep alive its party structure, above all on the local level.

The local level gave it a major source of continuity. It had inherited members from the old parties—the PSD, the PTB, and the PDC—who had staying power on the state and local level. Local interests formerly represented through these parties were now accustomed to working through the MDB. And the room for political maneuver in many states and cities had remained large enough for opposition politicians to cooperate successfully.

The MDB also stayed in the electoral game because it was the only party refuge for any government opponent. By its exercise of arbitrary power, the government created a steady supply of enemies. Whatever their differences, they shared the need for an umbrella under which they could pursue their opposition. Thus the government, by allowing an opposition party to operate, created an ideal recruiting process for the MDB.

In 1970, however, the odds were stacked against the legal opposition. Up for election were the entire federal Chamber of Deputies, two thirds of the federal Senate, and all 22 state assemblies. Governorships were also up, but they were to be elected in early October by the lame-duck state assemblies, almost all of which followed President Médici's instructions, as we have seen. Médici himself was campaigning actively for ARENA candidates in the November elections.

Despite all its electoral weapons, the government (especially the security forces) grew nervous as the election neared. In early November the police and military laid down a dragnet over Brazil's largest cities. "Operation Birdcage" picked up at least 5,000 suspects arrested or detained in the first two weeks of November. The arrestees included politicians of both parties, party activists, and anyone who had aroused the suspicion of the security forces. The official explanation for the crackdown was the need to head off an alleged guerrilla "master plan" to use kidnappings and bombings to disrupt the elections. The guerrillas would purportedly be acting on the first anniversary of Carlos Marighela's death on November 4, 1969.[30]

This atmosphere, along with the memory of the government's 1968–69 purges that had hit so many of the radical MDB leaders, led most MDB politicians to take a low-key approach. They could see it was no time for an ostentatious challenge to the legitimacy of the military regime. Meanwhile, President Médici claimed the election campaign was proceeding in a "climate of great liberty." Médici thought this exemplary democratic exercise ought to silence all those critics, domestic and foreign, who claimed Brazil wasn't democratic.[31]

When the votes were counted, ARENA had won a smashing victory. In the Senate, the highest federal office still directly elected, ARENA won 40 seats, while MDB won only 6. Since only one of the incumbent Senators was MDB, that meant that the new Senate would have 59 ARENA Senators to only 7 for MDB. In the Chamber of Deputies ARENA came away with 220 seats, while MDB got 90. The latter was actually an increase because the MDB's 132 seats won in the 1966 election had been reduced by subsequent government purges to only 65 by 1970. Among the prominent MDB candidates defeated were party president Oscar Passos, party vice presidents Ulysses Guimarães and Nogueira da Gama, treasurer José Ermírio de Morais, as well as the Senate floor leader and the Chamber minority leader.[32] ARENA's victory was even more sweeping on the *município* level, where federal power could be brought to bear on voters whose only hope of gaining desperately needed funds for their community was to vote ARENA.M3[3]

Clearly the government had won by a landslide. Yet a closer look suggests that many voters had spoken against the government without ever voting MDB. In the valid ballots for Senate, ARENA won 44 percent to the MDB's 29 percent. For the Chamber of Deputies, ARENA had 48 percent against MDB's 21 percent. But the blank votes, i.e., ballots not filled out but cast, totalled 22 percent for the Senate and 21 percent for the Chamber. Let us look more closely at elections for the Senate, since it was the only statewide office still elected directly. Some blank balloting was normal. In 1966, for example, the blank ballots in the Senate elections had totalled 12 percent. In the 1970 election they ran almost double that figure.[34] Why?

First, there had been a campaign in the larger cities (especially the state capitals) urging voters to cast blank ballots. To vote for either ARENA or MDB, these militants argued, was to accept the legitimacy of the government-manipulated system. So the only meaningful action was to cast a blank ballot. There was another source of blank votes. In races where the MDB ran no candidate or where the MDB candidates had no chance, blank balloting was high. In most cases this was a protest against ARENA's de facto one-party status.[35]

None of these nuances mattered to the Planalto as it celebrated ARENA's victory. Yet abstentions and blank ballots were not the only pattern that should have given pause to the President's political strategists. Another was the rural–urban split. As we have seen, the government had earlier in 1970 switched the basis for calculating congressional representation from population to number of registered voters. In the 1970 elections ARENA ran very strong in the rural areas, hardly surprising since that was where it controlled the patronage and government spending so important in the interior. Furthermore, the MDB lacked any party organization in many rural *municípios*. Yet the opposition ran strongly in the urban areas, as might have been predicted, especially in the Center-South. That suggested the MDB vote might well grow as Brazil became steadily more urban.

What did the elections say about Brazil's political situation? First, the government would not hesitate to use force ("Operation Birdcage," for example) in order to intimidate the opposition. Second, ARENA's highest rate of electoral support was in the rural sector. Third, many voters were alienated from the election process itself, as evidenced in the high incidence of blank ballots. Finally, ARENA's victory in terms of candidates elected was so overwhelming that many observers asked whether Brazil was headed for a one-party regime, such as Mexico's. Discouraged MDB activists asked themselves whether their party still had any meaning.

Such thoughts about the future did not worry Médici and his men. They basked in the news of their landslide. U.S. embassy analysts, a bellwether of Brazilian government thinking, assured U.S. visitors that the election had demonstrated Médici's enormous popularity.

In the wake of the 1970 electoral landslide, the MDB leadership could only lie low and avoid the omnipresent repression. Ironically, one of the safer forums was the Congress. The minority could still speak there and enjoy the normal congressional prerogatives.[36] Yet it was a dark hour for the MDB. Hovering over its leaders was the threat of harassment, cassation, imprisonment, or worse. A few were still willing to mock the Planalto. MDB deputy Alencar Furtado, for example, in September 1971 contemptuously denounced the "pagan cult" of worshippers around the President.[37] That cult's high moment came in mid-November 1971, when the government gave itself the power to issue secret decrees.[38] Although secret, such decrees were to have the rule of law. One veteran politician journalist concluded that "to be in the opposition today is more difficult than in any period of our history."[39] Some within the MDB wanted to dissolve the party as a final protest against the executive's abuse of power.

The MDB declined to self-liquidate, but it did split deeply over strategy and tactics. The *auténticos* ("authentics") wanted an aggressive stance, protesting every illegality and arbitrary act of the military-dominated government. The *moderados* ("moderates"), on the other hand, urged a cautious line, so as to minimize possible pretexts for further government abuse of power. The "moderates" thought the "authentics" were hot-headed and immature. The latter returned the compliment, branding the "moderates" as unprincipled opportunists.[40]

Somehow the party hung together. In the end these politicians knew only *they* could keep alive the hope of a return to the rule of law and democracy. It was neither easy nor safe. In the words of one political journalist, politics for the MDB was like playing soccer without the ball.[41]

As might be expected of a party enjoying such power, ARENA indulged in some ill-advised maneuvers. In early 1972 President Médici named Senator Felinto Muller to the presidency of ARENA. This was an extraordinary choice for a government supposedly worried about its image. Muller had

never shaken his role as Rio de Janeiro's police chief during the dictatorship of Getúlio Vargas from 1937 to 1945, when police torture of political
suspects became routine. The MDB lost little time in dragging up Muller's
past.

Yet Muller's past was a nuance that passed by most Brazilians. The
President remained hugely popular (although government control of the
media made an objective estimate difficult), and his powers seemed to
grow daily. (Médici's popularity is discussed in greater detail in the last
section of this chapter.) Brazil's most authoritarian government in living
memory had all the momentum on its side. How could mere elections
derail it?

The Liquidation of the Guerrilla Threat

We saw earlier how the guerrillas had become troublesome, but were no
major threat to the government before the end of 1969. Indeed, by Latin
American standards, they were unimpressive. In numbers of guns and
adherents, they were notably inferior (if measured per capita) to the
Tupamaros of Uruguay or the *Montoneros* of Argentina. The Brazilian
guerrillas were best known for kidnapping the U.S. ambassador. Yet this
was a side act in which the kidnappers wanted to save some imprisoned
comrades from torture or death. The guerrillas had also hoped, by the
kidnapping, to divide the government (they came close) and to mobilize
popular opinion against the generals. The latter goal was beyond reach.
The public watched with fascination as the ambassador's life hung in the
balance. But few appeared to think *they* had any role in the drama. Would
the guerrillas have been better off if the government had refused the ransom deal? Then they would have had to kill Elbrick. *That* would have
poisoned U.S.–Brazilian relations, one of the guerrilla goals. It would also
probably have deepened polarization among Brazilians, another guerrilla
goal.[42]

The Brazilian military excluded this option by meeting all the guerrillas'
demands. They freed the indicated prisoners and published the guerrillas'
manifesto, thereby obligating them to free the ambassador. The contrast
with other political kidnappings in Latin America during 1970 was sharp. In
March West German Ambassador von Spreti had been killed by his Guatemalan guerrilla kidnappers when the Guatemalan government refused to
release 24 political prisoners. In July U.S. police adviser Daniel Mitrione
had been kidnapped and killled by the *Tupamaros* when the Uruguayan
government refused to negotiate for his release.[43] By comparison, the Brazilian government came across <u>as humanitarian, a</u> crucial factor in what was
above all a symbolic and psychological war.

Brazilian guerrillas repeated such abductions through the rest of 1970. In
March they kidnapped Nobuo Okuchi, the Japanese consul-general in São
Paulo. His possible fate worried the prominent Japanese-Brazilian commu-
nity and the Japanese government, an increasingly important trading part-

ner and source of investment capital for Brazil. The consul-general was ransomed for five specified political prisoners, who were flown to Mexico. Early the next month VPR kidnappers bungled an attempt on the U.S. consul in Pôrto Alegre, who, although wounded, raced his large American van through the guerrillas' Volkswagen barrier.[44] The Médici government now stepped up its security measures.

The reader might be forgiven for thinking that the guerrillas spent all their time kidnapping diplomats. In fact, kidnapping had begun as a way to save comrades in jail and to use the media to get across the guerrilla message. It helped force the government to impose odious security measures—constant identity checks, obtrusive surveillance, etc. And it was an embarassment for the government vis-à-vis the diplomatic community. But it could hardly contribute to what the guerrillas most needed: the recruitment of thousands of Brazilians to organize clandestinely against the military government. The latter could be done only by a patient, long-term effort. To be successful, many new recruits would have to avoid any public actions, such as the kidnappings, waiting for the right circumstances in which to surface. The more experienced guerrillas, such as Carlos Marighela, knew of the need for this long-term view. But the foot soldiers were less patient. These warriors, many in their early twenties and a few in their teens, were uninterested in a long-term strategy. They hated the military, and they wanted to demonstrate their bravery *now*. So the strategy of abducting diplomats fed on itself as the most ready outlet for action.

In June the VPR struck again in Rio de Janeiro. They kidnapped West German Ambassador Ehrenfried von Holleben, who greatly irritated his captors with his arrogant manner. They demanded in ransom 40 specified prisoners. The size of that number was a sign both of improving police efficiency and of the kidnappers' desperation. In fact, disagreement over who should go on the ransom list led to ugly fights among von Holleben's captors. The denouement of this kidnapping was rapid, much to the relief of the VPR militants. Von Holleben had been seized on June 11. On the 14th the government agreed to terms; on the 15th the 40 prisoners were flown to Algeria; and on the 17th the guerrillas released the German ambassador.[45]

What had the guerrillas accomplished with this kidnapping? They had again saved some comrades from torture and possible death. They had successfully pressured the government (as part of the deal to release von Holleben) to publish another grandiloquent manifesto, announcing that "popular discontent is growing," and warning that "only a guerrilla revolution . . . can lead the Brazilian people to liberate itself."[46]

Yet few Brazilians paid attention to the manifesto. Their eyes and ears were glued to the radio and TV sets as they followed their soccer team at the World Cup competition in Mexico City. They wanted to know whether Brazil could win the cup for an unprecedented third time. The team did win (shortly after von Holleben's kidnapping), and Brazil went berserk in the national celebration. There was no time for talk of missing ambassadors and guerrilla manifestoes.[47]

The guerrilla-kidnappers next struck in early December of 1970. The target was Swiss Ambassador Giovannia Enrico Bucher, whose bodyguard was killed in the abduction. It was the first fatality in a diplomatic kidnapping.[48] The guerrillas set three conditions for Bucher's release. First was the ransom of 70 specified prisoners, a new high.[49] Second was publishing every four hours a new manifesto in which the guerrillas declared "total war" on the Médici government. Third was giving free train service into Rio from the scattered suburbs. With each kidnapping the guerrillas had upped the ante.

The government, meanwhile, acted with new confidence. It ignored the demands to broadcast the manifesto and furnish free train rides.[50] As for supplying the 70 prisoners, Sergio Fleury and his São Paulo Death Squad (see next section) replied first. Later on the day of Bucher's kidnapping the security services announced that Eduardo Leite (with the *nom de guerre* of "Bacurí," he had defected from the army with Lamarca), one of the shrewdest and most courageous VPR guerrillas, had died in a shoot-out. Leite was dead, but not in a shoot-out. He had just gone through two months of gruesome torture (both eyes gouged out, both ears cut off, his teeth removed, his legs paralyzed). At word of Bucher's kidnappinng, Sergio Fleury knew Leite would be on the ransom list (he would have been the top name). The only certain way to avoid producing him was to execute him. The kidnappers got the Death Squad's message.[51]

The guerrillas sent their list (never published), and the government vetoed 18 names. Among the reasons were commission of capital crimes and prisoner unwillingness to accept the permanent banishment from Brazil (now imposed on any prisoners ransomed in guerrilla kidnappings). Carlos Lamarca, chief of the Bucher operation, grew worried. The government was pushing an all-out hunt to find their hideout and, presumably, to attack it. Such had not been true in Ambassador Elbrick's kidnapping. On the contrary, Naval Intelligence, which knew Elbrick's location soon after his seizure, made certain there was *no* move against the kidnappers. In the case of the German ambassador, the government soon called off its searches in order to facilitate the negotiations. Yet now the government was staging raids and traffic checks throughout greater Rio.

The guerrillas decided they had no choice but to honor the government's veto of 18 names. They sent a replacement list, some of which were also vetoed. Furthermore, the security forces had succeeded in intimidating several political prisoners on the previous list into declaring on TV their refusal to leave Brazil in ransom for kidnapped diplomats. The guerrillas now realized they were dealing with a more cunning regime. Could they be maneuvered into a position where they would *have* to execute Bucher?

The protracted negotiations took their toll on the guerrillas' nerves. As the weeks went by, the guerrillas stopped using their hoods around the prisoner. Those hoods had been their protection against later identification (many torturers also wore hoods, for the same reason). As the guerrillas were repeatedly forced to come up with new names, they became more frustrated. Finally their anger drove them to the conclusion the government's more cynical tacticians hoped for: their honor demanded they kill Bucher and be done with it. A vote was taken, and the majority favored execution. Bucher, who spoke excellent Portuguese, was terrified. Fortunately for him, the guerrilla command was not a democracy. Carlos Lamarca, who knew more about killing than his younger comrades, said no. They must keep trying to agree on names.[52]

Lamarca's patience was rewarded. The government approved 70 names, out of some 100 that had been sent. The 70 were flown to Chile in mid-January, where they got a hero's welcome from Brazilian exiles and Chilean sympathizers, still jubilant over Salvador Allende's recent accession to the presidency.

Bucher was released on January 14. He had been held for 40 days, far longer than any other kidnapped diplomat. But the guerrilla action had an interesting coda: just as Bucher was released, a team of guerrillas stole two huge delivery trucks from the depot of a supermarket chain, loaded them with food and canned goods, and headed for the *Rato Molhado* (the wet rat) *favela,* one of Rio's poorest slums. There they distributed their stolen cargo to disbelieving but soon-gleeful *favela* dwellers. The guerrillas had the pleasure of watching the police and military (with helicopters!) converge on the site too late to catch them.[53]

Despite the false starts, the Bucher kidnapping had in the end followed the pattern set by the Elbrick case. Both sides negotiated, a deal was reached, the prisoners were flown out, and the diplomat was freed. The Brazilian government continued to present a humane face to the world, showing a readiness to negotiate in order to save lives.

The government's other response to each diplomatic kidnapping was anything but humane.[54] As soon as the ransomed prisoners were flown abroad, the police and military went all out to capture the guerrillas. In the early days the interrogators had encountered a troublesome guerrilla tactic. The latter had a pact that, once captured, a prisoner must withhold vital information for 24 hours. Thereafter, his or her comrades would have abandoned all the prisoner's known addresses and contacts, thereby making a confession harmless. The tactic worked in the early days of the guerrillas, but the security men soon caught on. They then made the first day's interrogation relentless. It was an assault that few prisoners could withstand—electric shocks, beatings, near-drownings, mock executions, and forced viewing of the torture of friends or family.

Guerrilla courage was now pitted against lengthening odds. Each successive guerrilla action increased the risk of capture, as the security forces were becoming better and better informed. The suspected guerrillas' friends, relatives, and every known contact were put under surveillance, their mail opened and their telephones tapped. Legions of informers fed tips to the voracious security force. The torturers got their information, along with a flood of irrelevancy spilling out of innocent suspects. In this system the prisoner was presumed guilty until proven otherwise. The only proof was to show that, even under torture, he or she knew no secrets.

Greatly increased surveillance and the systematic torture of suspects furnished security men with ample leads. The cities were "turning into a cemetery for the revolutionaries . . ."[55] Recruiting new members became perilous, for fear of infiltration. In fact, one infiltrator was already working with CENIMAR and other security organs. He was José Anselmo dos Santos, who as a sailor (thus his nickname "Cabo Anselmo") had in early 1964 led a sailors revolt that helped frighten the higher military into deposing Goulart. When the armed resistance to the military government arose he joined the VPR and went to Cuba for guerrilla training. Back in Brazil he secretly made contact with Sergio Fleury and subsequently furnished information that led to (by his estimate) 100–200 arrests. He was directly responsible for the liquidation of the entire VPR unit in Recife. Anselmo had the personality for his role, repeatedly talking his way out of confrontations with suspicious comrades. He later claimed to have known "six or eight" other infiltrators.[56]

The repressive apparatus succeeded in hunting down the guerrilla leaders. Carlos Marighella had been ambushed in 1969 as a result of information obtained through torture. In late October 1970 Joaquim Camara Ferreira, a former Congressman and Marighella's designated successor as ALN leader, was captured and tortured to death in jail.

The capture of Carlos Lamarca took longer.[57] The Bucher kidnapping had convinced Lamarca that the VPR had to change course. They were now down to no more than 30 militants, who were in constant danger of arrest. In early 1971 the other VPR leaders urged Lamarca to go abroad, arguing that he was too valuable to risk capture in the difficult months (perhaps years) ahead.

To withdraw from battle contradicted Lamarca's character. Instead, he plunged into building a rural guerrilla base. In May he left the VPR, because it was too "vanguardista," and joined MR-8, the group responsible for the Elbrick kidnapping but now in a state of collapse. When its leader, Stuart Jones, was captured in mid-May, Lamarca and his mistress, fellow guerrilla Yara Iavelberg, fled northward.[58]

Thus began the chase which Sergio Fleury and military intelligence had so eagerly anticipated. They hated Lamarca because he was a military turncoat and an arrogant combatant. He had killed in cold blood (or ordered the killing of) an army lieutenant in an earlier action. Lamarca was the last living member of the "big three—Fleury had already taken care of Carlos Marighela and Joaquim Camara Ferreira. Lamarca and Yara split up; he headed for the interior of Bahia state and she for the capital city of Salvador. The police soon cornered her in an apartment house. She shot herself before she could be captured, taking with her Lamarca's unborn child.

Lamarca was on the run deep in the interior of Bahia. He had discovered that the territory selected for guerrilla operations was unsatisfactory because the land was too poor. Meanwhile, the entire repressive apparatus of Brazil was on his tracks. The intelligence arm of each military service (the army's CIEX, or *Central de Informações do Exército,* the air force's CISA, or *Centro de Informações da Aeronautica,* and the navy's CENIMAR, or *Centro de Informações da Marinha*), DOI-CODI from both Bahia and Rio, and DOPS were all ostensibly under the command of the Fourth Army. Each unit wanted the honor of finishing off the famous fugitive, and it was not to be hard. Lamarca and his companion, a peasant from the region, were an easy target. They were exhausted, having covered 300 kilometers in the last 20 days. When an army unit caught up with Lamarca in early September, he was barefoot and sick. José Carlos (the companion) reached for his gun and was immediately shot. Lamarca, the champion marksman, was asleep under a tree and never had a chance.

The government gave Lamarca's death maximum media coverage. The press was awash with documents on Lamarca's final days. There were the love letters to Yara Iavelberg, pictures of the death scene, detailed accounts of how the local population had informed on Lamarca and his companion. The net effect was to show Lamarca's death as inevitable and to convince any would-be terrorists (the government term) that they would suffer the same fate. This is how Brazil's leading conservative daily ended its story of Lamarca's rise and fall: "Like Guevara, he dreamed of seeing the continent transformed into a string of Vietnams. Now his dreams have been buried."[59]

In Rio and São Paulo the main urban guerrilla units were in collapse. Those militants still at large could not mount any significant operations. By the beginning of 1972 the urban guerrillas had been defeated; most were dead, the rest were in prison or in exile.

The city, however, was not the only front. All the guerrillas had paid at least lip service to the importance of opening a rural front, a *foco* in Régis Debray's term. Marighela had himself said in early 1969 the urban struggle must lead to the rural guerrilla war. With success on both those fronts, "we will go on to form the Revolutionary National Liberation Army" and "the military dictatorship will be liquidated."[60] Just before his death Marighela was working on plans for a rural guerrilla front.[61] Yet most guerrilla groups had failed to try such a task, in part because most members were city children who knew nothing about the countryside.

One group did turn away from the city, the PC do B, Maoist dissenters who had broken away from the PCB in 1962. Now they cast their lot in Araguaia, a tropical rain forest area in the Amazon basin. The site was located in the far east of Pará state, close to the border with northern Goiás. The region had huge gold deposits, as well as iron ore and other minerals. The nearby Carrajás region of Pará had already been selected as the site for a mammoth iron mine.[62]

This area was inhabited by Indians and peasants, the latter subsistence farmers. As the developers and speculators moved in, these peasants were on the defensive. In 1970 they were joined (a few at a time) by 69 PC do B militants. But the PC do B would remain the only group to gamble on a major rural guerrilla operation.

The PC do B militants had chosen Araguaia because it was remote enough to allow the guerrillas time to put down roots, and because it was strategically situated near the Carrajás iron ore mine and lands in dispute between peasants and speculators.[63]

The guerrillas had a well-thought-out plan of action.[64] Their initial objective was to build and settle into dwellings like those of the peasants. They would then slowly win the peasants' confidence by giving basic lessons in health care and farming. During this first phase the peasants would not know the real identity of the new settlers. During 1970 and 1971 the 69 militants settled in without their true identity or purpose becoming known. The first phase had gone smoothly.

In 1972 their luck changed. Military intelligence uncovered the guerrilla *foco* in gestation, but the army's initial action was inept in the extreme. It saturated the area with troops, though it had no detailed intelligence on the region or the guerrillas. The soldiers, ill-prepared for this terrain, immediately became disorganized, even firing at each other. The PC do B guerrillas were giving the army its first taste of a well-organized rural insurgency. The army command soon realized it could not mount a true counterinsurgency operation, and withdrew. It then created a jungle warfare force trained to operate in small units.

The army returned and went about its task methodically. The entire area was declared a national security zone, subject to special police and military powers. All residents had to carry identity cards at all times. A heliport, an airport, and five new barracks were built. The latter also housed an interrogation center.

Despite all these resources, it took the army more than two years to finish the job. By 1975 all the guerrillas were dead or in prison; their preparations and bravery, not withstanding, they were no match for the army's counterinsurgency teams, just as the military and police's use of torture had earlier eviscerated the urban guerrillas. Many innocent peasants were caught up in the dragnet and tortured, and those who had joined the guerrillas were hunted down relentlessly. The army was said to have decapitated guerrillas and displayed their heads to the local peasants and villagers. If so, it was a reversion to a tactic the Portuguese used in dealing with rebels in colonial Brazil two centuries earlier.[65]

Colonel Jarbas Passarinho, who had been a minister in the Médici government, called the Araguaia front "the only well prepared and important one." Perhaps this is why the Médici government kept all notice of it (except one story which inexplicably appeared in *O Estado de São Paulo,* September 24, 1972) from the public until 1978. The Araguaia experience showed the communications problems facing any rural guerrilla action in Brazil. The urban workers in São Paulo, who were the PC do B militants' eventual target, were thousands of miles from Araguaia, a place few could even locate on the map. The guerrillas sent out mimeographed bulletins (a special courier took them to São Paulo), but they were never cited in the press, which was under strict censorship on anything military.[66]

The guerrilla threat had now been met and liquidated both in the city and in the countryside. The most disciplined fighters had chosen to stand their ground in Brazil's most forbidding habitat, They followed the oft-praised strategy of opening a rural front. They had succeeded in gaining the peasants' confidence far better than had, for example, Che Guevara in Bolivia. Yet it was not enough. Skeptics had long said that Brazil was too big to be won over by urban combat or by any single *foro*. The defeat of the guerrillas between 1969 and 1975 seemed to confirm that belief.[67]

The liquidation of the Araguaia front ended the guerrilla challenge in Brazil. In neighboring Argentina and Uruguay, guerrilla movements had seriously threatened governments. In Cuba and Nicaragua the armed opposition had won. Yet in Brazil they fell far short of either outcome.[68] Why?

First, Brazil was not promising territory for guerrilla strategy. Modern guerrilla wars have succeeded only under special circumstances.[69] One is in a country under foreign rule, formal or informal. Then a native guerrilla movement can capitalize on nationalist sentiment against the colonial or imperial power. Cuba and Nicaragua fit the latter description. But Brazil did not.

Nor did Brazil suffer from the ethnic or religious cleavages which might have given the guerrillas a base of support. It lacked, for example, any significant non-Portuguese-speaking minority comparable to the Quechua- and Aymara-speaking Indians of the Andes. Nor was there an ethnic minority elite such as the Chinese in Malaysia. Brazil had racial tensions, but they did not furnish material for guerrilla recruitment.

Another national factor worked against the guerrillas. Brazil was a country of enormous economic extremes, the Northeast being the hemisphere's greatest concentration of economic misery. An economic determinist might well expect fertile ground here for political radicalization. Yet the economic growth of 10 percent a year, along with the skillful government propaganda, had generated popular optimism about individual economic chances, however improbable it might have been. As a disillusioned Carlos Lamarca confessed in 1970, "It was ridiculous during the world soccer tournament to argue that Brazilian capitalism was in a crisis of stagnation. For three years it's been growing at 10 percent a year and the left was the last to notice."[70]

Brazil was relatively invulnerable on another front. The most powerful element in the government, the military, did not doubt its own legitimacy or the morality of its actions. Any officers with doubts either hid them or found themselves forced to retire early. The military was therefore not a good target for splitting the government.

Finally, the guerrillas suffered from an inherent liability. They were predominantly middle-and upper-class youths from a few cities. Although they could be fearless and highly efficient, they did not have, as many of them later acknowledged, a profound knowledge of Brazilian society. Fresh from the university classrooms or church halls, they knew their Régis Debray bettter than their Brazilian geography. Their intense intellectualism could not be better seen than in their decision to kidnap foreign diplomats in the descending order of the size of the country's investment in Brazil (U.S., Japan, West Germany, and Switzerland). The point was utterly lost on the Brazilian public.

Several technical factors also worked against the guerrillas. First, the odds favor a modern state in any confrontation with an armed opposition, not least because of the powerful technology modern governments command. Brazil's security forces were far better able to monitor opposition activities than anyone would have predicted in 1964. The government's communications network had grown enormously: teletype, satellite-aided links, microwave-assisted long distance telephone, and so on. By using a computer bank of dossiers, the security authorities were able to maintain a highly effective nationwide watch for suspects.

Second, the federal government had centralized control over the security forces. The steady erosion of federalism after 1964 was nowhere more marked than in the fight against "subversion." All the state secretaries of security were subordinated to federal direction—meaning, in effect, to the army high command. Third, torture proved to be very effective for intelligence-gathering and for terrifying potential guerrilla recruits.

Taken together, these factors worked against Brazil's armed left. Despite the guerrillas' initial success in embarrassing the government via kidnappings, they never became a major political threat to the military regime. Yet their attacks, even when minor, confirmed the hardliners' prediction of an armed threat. In the end, the guerrillas' principal effect was to strengthen the hand of those arguing for greater repression.[71]

The Uses of Repression

The defeat of the guerrillas did not end government torture. That should not be surprising, since the torturers had not waited for an armed threat to begin their work. Government torture of political suspects in the Northeast, for example, had begun within days of the 1964 coup, well before any guerrillas appeared.[72] It recurred thereafter and intensified in 1968, again before any significant guerrillas had suffered. When the bank robberies and kidnappings did occur in 1969, they gave the hard-line military the evidence they needed to justify a crackdown. The Médici government argued it had to protect the public from conspirators who wanted to plunge Brazil into chaos. "War is war," army officers replied, when asked about their interrogation methods.

By late 1971 the urban guerrillas had been reduced to a minor nusiance. During early 1972 there appeared to be a concomitant decline in torture. But by May the security forces had reverted to frequent torture, and by

July President Médici had announced that the curbs on civil liberties would have to continue because of the subversive threat. Amnesty International announced in September, as we have noted, that it had confirmed 1,076 cases of torture in Brazil by no fewer than 472 torturers. Why did it continue?[73]

To answer that question we need to look at the institutional structure of the repression and at the psychological and political context in which it operated. An essential starting point is an understanding of the administration of criminal justice in Brazil.[74] Scholars of the history of police enforcement in Brazil agree that at least since the late nineteenth century physical torture has been routine in interrogating non-elite prisoners.[75] The pervasiveness of slavery must have played a large role. As in most slave societies, the dominant elite maintained slave discipline by brutal punishment. One of the most famous scholars of Brazilian slavery, Gilberto Freyre, published a book based on newspaper classified ads by masters whose slaves had escaped. The means of identification were the scars (described in detail in the ads) from past beatings.[76]

During the Old Republic (1889–1930) police used physical torture against both the rural and urban poor. But it seldom touched the elite. They were protected by the (usually unspoken) police understanding that they were immune from such treatment. Their immunity was eroded during the *Estado Nôvo* dictatorship of Getúlio Vargas (1937–45). Vargas's Rio police chief, Felinto Muller, introduced new techniques, such as electric shock, to pry information and confessions out of political suspects, who were often from the elite.[77]

The end of the *Estado Nôvo* allowed elite political activists to breathe easier. They regained their immunity from physical torture. But police measures against ordinary suspects took a new turn. In 1958 Rio Police Chief General Amaury Kruel organized a special police squad (*Grupo de Diligencias Especiais,* or GDE), which was soon accused of assassinating suspected thieves and murderers. This was said to be the origin of the Rio Death Squad of such notoriety in the 1960s.[78]

By the 1960s one could say that under "normal" police procedures suspects were treated according to their apparent social status. This status-oriented standard originates in the highly stratified society produced by the extremes of wealth and poverty occurring throughout Brazil's history. It was not merely a question of being able to hire a lawyer, pay bail, and collect favorable evidence. It was also the suspect's right to decent physical treatment. Brazilian lawyers, along with a long list of office-holders, for example, have traditionally had the right, if detained, to be quartered in a better-equipped jail cell than those for ordinary prisoners. Any apparently middle- or upper-class suspect would normally get preferential treatment because the police would assume that he or she might have relatives or friends with connections to those in power. If the booking policeman guessed wrong on that count, he could soon found himself in trouble with his superiors.

By the same token, the poor or low-status prisoner was never surprised at harsh treatment. In the words of one police chief to his suspect, "Do you want to talk with torture or without?" The suspect sensibily replied, "Without."[79] Interrogation about common crimes, such as robbery or assault, could include physical abuse of a kind that leaves few marks (beating with a rod wrapped in wet towels, electric shocks, near suffocation, etc.). The police might comment on such a prisoner's inferior social status, which they would regard as implying guilt, especially if the crime had been committed against a social superior.

Given this context of normal police methods, government treatment of political suspects after 1968 falls into perspective. The police and military began to treat detainees from the middle and upper social sectors (which produced most of the guerrilla leaders) as if they were ordinary suspects. These prisoners soon learned that their politically important friends or relatives counted for nothing in the interrogators' world. Now middle- and upper-class dissenters were being intimidated by the violence long used to control low-status prisoners.

At this point it is worth remembering that police or judicial use of torture is no stranger to human history. Governments that have foregone it are few and primarily of recent vintage. In medieval and early modern Europe, for example, torture was routinely used to gather evidence in ordinary criminal cases. In our own day a philosophy professor at the City College of New York announced that "there are situations in which torture is not merely permissible but morally mandatory." He posited the classic case of a captured terrorist who has set a bomb that will kill untold scores of innocent victims. "If the only way to save those lives is to subject the terrorist to the most excruciating possible pain, what grounds can there be for not doing so?" This was exactly the argument used by the Brazilian torturers of the 1960s and 1970s.[80]

Until mid-1968 the military had not become directly and systematically involved in interrogating political prisoners, except for the months right after the 1964 coup. Most officers had hoped that the bureaucratic and congressional purges would get Brazil back on the right track. That had also been President Costa e Silva's hope. But 1968 ended these hopes. The student protests and labor strikes seemed a throwback to the Goulart era. As we have seen, many officers became convinced that they would have to take a more direct hand in controlling the "subversives." The officers had a ready rationale. By the doctrine of national security, the military would have to assume direct responsibility for internal security. By this logic, a subversive threat from within was as great as, if not greater than, the threat from without.[81] A strong advocate of this view was General Jayme Portella, the head of Costa e Silva's Military Presidential Staff.[82] He pushed for a stronger role for the military in fighting the subversives.

A first sign of his strategy appeared in early 1969, as noted earlier, with the creation of OBAN (Operação Bandeirantes). It combined civilian police with military security officers and got financial backing from prominent

São Paulo businessmen, who loaned them equipment and provided cash. Prominent among them was Henning Albert Boilesen, a Danish-born naturalized Brazilian who headed Ultragaz, a highly successful liquid gas company. Boilesen was especially adept at raising funds from multinational firms or executives. Brazilian firms were also pressured to contribute money, cars, trucks, and other in-kind aid to OBAN and its successor unit, DOI-CODI. Some businessmen were enthusiastic, others responded only under duress. Several well-known merchants, for example, with sons in prison, had to be intimidated into contributing. Governor Abreu Sodré helped raise private funds for a bigger headquarters, and Mayor Paulo Maluf was also supportive, giving the OBAN project the tone of a civic project.[83]

Military support for OBAN was, however, far from unanimous. Second Army Commander General Carvalho Lisboa refused to cooperate in the creation of the unit.[84] He and other army skeptics argued that the military were not trained to carry out police functions. Other critics within the army argued that by assuming a police function the army would jeopardize its ability to carry out its traditional role in Brazilian society. Finally, the critics argued that participating in the repressive apparatus would expose officers to possible corruption. OBAN squads, for example, had access to cash or valuables seized in raids.

But the political momentum among the military buried such doubts. The President set the tone. In February 1970 Médici announced that there would be no rights for "pseudo-Brazilians," and a month later warned: "Yes, there will be repression—harsh and implacable. But only against crime and only against the criminals."[85] In the preceding November Senator Petrônio Portella, ARENA leader, explained that extra-legal measures would be used only against "those on the fringe of the law," who should expect "extra-legal remedies." The Senator wished the President well in "destroying, once and for all, the foci of subversion, and then building the future of Brazil."[86]

By July 1969 this sentiment had already resulted in the Second Army's acquiescence to OBAN's creation. Meanwhile, the military were busily creating their own repressive network.[87] Its locus was in the intelligence staff of each of the armed services: CIEX (for the army), CISA (for the air force) and CENIMAR (for the navy). All had authority to make arrests and initiate investigations.

The entry of the military into the repressive efforts soon created jurisdictional conflicts with the civilian police. The latter resented a supposedly superior power entering their territory. The civilian–military rivalry sometimes erupted into open warfare. This was especially true of aggressive units such as Sergio Fleury's São Paulo Death Squad (discussed below). The military met this problem by creating yet another bureaucratic level in the structure of the security forces. Each military region had a CODI (*Comando Operacional de Defesa Interna,* or Operational Command for Internal Defense), an interservice body under army command (in practice under the apposite regional armies). One level down was DOI (*Destaca-mento de Operações Internas*), the operational unit on the local level. It was a "strike force" of military and police, all operating in plain clothes. In São Paulo the DOI-CODI replaced OBAN. Meanwhile, the federal government reorganized the *Polícia Militar* (PM), the traffic and crowd control unit formerly under the command of each state government. They were now subordinated to the army minister through the army General Staff and the four regional army commands. Henceforth the army could use the PMs as an anti-guerrilla force, thereby avoiding use of army troops in what the higher military knew was a messy business.[88]

These new units had an immediate problem in that they lacked experienced interrogators. So they turned to police detectives who knew how to interrogate "common" prisoners. The most notorious was Sergio Fleury, the leader of the São Paulo Death Squad.[89] Like death squad leaders in the state of Rio de Janeiro, Fleury made his mark by the brutal execution of ordinary criminal suspects, especially drug dealers. He was said to be an addict, and his police work gave him easy access to narcotics. Fleury and his ilk were also linked to violent right-wing groups such as the CCC (*Comando de Caça aos Comunistas,* or Anti-Communist Command).[90] In 1969 Fleury and his team were transferred from the Criminal Investigation Division (DEIC, or *Departamento Estadual de Investigações Criminais*) to the Political Police (DEOPS, or *Departamento Estadual de Ordem Política e Social*) which was the state-level equivalent of DOPS, (*Departamento de Ordem Politica e Social*) the federal Political Police. He now had a hunting license to track the guerrillas.

Fleury had an ideal personality for the role of the brutal interrogator. He had an instinct for hunting down clues and suspects. He relished playing on the emotions of his prisoners. His mere appearance in the interrogation room could create panic among the prisoners—not surprising, for he had tortured many a prisoner. Fleury constantly feuded with the military and DOI-CODI. Often he kept them uninformed about his prisoners and sometimes hid them on his farm outside São Paulo. Early in 1970, when forced to turn a prisoner over to DOI-CODI, he broke the man's ribs, making him useless for further torture.[91] Fleury had one source of strong military support, however. Naval intelligence (CENIMAR) worked well with him and protected him from the other services. The navy showed its gratitude to Fleury by awarding him a medal (*Amigo da Marinha*).[92]

Within the Brazilian gulag there were three types of specialists: the torturers, who could apply electric shocks, beatings, and near drownings in the right combination to produce confessions; the analysts, who were fed information from the latest torture session and matched it (often via computer) with previous information to indicate what else the victim might know; and the doctors, who checked the physical condition of the victims to see how much more torture they could withstand yet still talk.[93]

News of the spreading torture in 1969 terrified anyone contemplating active opposition.[94] Word of the torture and sometimes death of middle-

and upper-class prisoners made an immediate impact. The more prominent the victim, the greater the shock. Rubens de Paiva was a perfect example.[95] From a socially prominent Rio background, he was a distinguished geological engineer. Paiva was seized by a DOI-CODI unit, who later claimed he had been kidnapped from them several days later while they were transferring him from one jail to another. The story was universally rejected because the details on the abduction were so implausible, including the claim that the portly Paiva had somehow leapt out of the back seat of a two-door Volkswagen and into an escape car while the plainclothesmen presumably watched. The security forces disclaimed any knowledge of Paiva's subsequent fate. It was widely believed that he had been killed (and his body dumped into the Atlantic) by PARA-SAR, the crack air-sea rescue team.[96] Striking with such impunity against a well-known figure demonstrated that every Brazilian was equally helpless before the security forces. As the public identified with the victims, their demoralization and sense of isolation made them into the frightened citizens the security forces preferred. Only thus could the internal enemy be identified and liquidated.

The government continued to use the repressive apparatus well after liquidation of the guerrillas. It was a powerful instrument, with the latest technology—microwave communication systems, computer-based suspect lists, and tape recorders for tapped telephones. Furthermore, it was relatively cheap, since police and military forces had to exist in any case. Finally, any Third World government struggling to stabilize its political base (measured by acquiescence, if not support) can find repression tempting. The mass arrests on the eve of the 1970 elections were a prime example of how repression could help produce an electoral victory.[97]

The repressive apparatus operated in part on its own momentum. Some military and police involved got monetary bonuses from civilian anti-subversive zealots or from property confiscated in raids. If the repression stopped, these rewards would stop. But there was another, more sinister factor at work. Once a detective or a military officer had tortured his first prisoner, he joined, like it or not, the brotherhood of the torturers. Their morality was upside down: to save Christian, democratic Brazil they had to violate its moral and legal foundations. Not that torture was new in Brazilian history. We have seen that it was not. Yet most of the torturers knew they were outlaws against the moral and constitutional traditions to which even the military presidents professed loyalty. This sense of guilt explained in part why the torturers tried so hard to conceal their identity. It also explained why they saw themselves as the courageous few involved in a dirty business in order to save their country.

One development did threaten the torturers' role, the new shortage of plausible suspects. So with the liquidation of the urban guerrilla threat by early 1972, the DOI-CODI cast about for new enemies. Their paucity only reinforced the fanatical security men's view that the subversives were lying low only for the moment. Indeed, the torturers argued that it was only because of their vigilance that Brazil was now spared bank raids and kidnap-

pings. Finally, torture under army command had become so widespread
and institutionalized that no higher military could claim non-involvement.
Virtually all had held a command where the torturers operated. As a result,
the generals and colonels were implicated, if only indirectly.

Could any government official have foreseen what this repression, especially torture, would do to Brazil? Along with the scraps of information
that might incriminate the dwindling guerrilla band, torture produced
mountains of unrelated facts. But for minds obsessed with security, no facts
were unrelated: all were clues to opposition plots. A huge security apparatus watched every source of possible opposition: university classrooms,
union headquarters, seminaries, lawyers' associations, high schools, newspaper offices, slum dwellers' associations, and church groups. Brazilians,
ordinarily a garrulous and spontaneous people, fell silent. Serious politics
were never discussed with strangers present. A Brazilian Big Brother had
been born.

This repressive apparatus did not, however, completely escape the framework of institutional limits. Legal authority for the security forces lay with
military justice. In the 1946 Constitution the jurisdiction of military justice
had been limited to military crimes, although it extended to civilians who
committed "crimes against external security or military institutions." The
Second Institutional Act of October 1965 substituted "national security"
for "external security," and the Constitution of 1967 (as amended in 1969)
maintained that change. Given the broad interpretation of these terms,
virtually everyone arrested by the security forces fell within the jurisdiction
of military justice. The latter included 21 lower tribunals (*auditorias*), each
staffed by four military officers and a civilian, with the next (and highest)
level being the Supreme Military Tribunal (*Superior Tribunal Militar*),
composed of ten military justices and five civilians. Appeal to the Federal
Supreme Court (*Superior Tribunal Federal*) was theoretically possible but
became rare after 1965.[98]

The fact that military justice had jurisdiction was important for the handful of criminal lawyers who worked desperately to locate their clients in the
police and military labyrinth. The latter was not easy, given the absence of
habeas corpus. So the lawyers badgered the military tribunals, trying every
gambit to find the prisoners. Through persistence and courage they were
sometimes able to extract bits of information. They received anonymous
phone calls telling them where a prisoner was being held. Were the callers
employees of the military justice system? Prisoners communicated by tapping through the light switches or the water outlets, sending news of new
internees via prisoners about to be released.[99]

Their greatest ally was the traditional nature of military justice. The
noted civil rights lawyer Sobral Pinto had long argued that in Brazil military
justice was more liberal than civil justice.[100] In the Médici presidency this
tradition was potentially reinforced because the regime appointed liberal
senior generals to judgeships to get them away from active commands. The
tribunal staffs and some justices often collaborated with the lawyers in

trying to locate prisoners. They usually met a stone wall. Nonetheless, military justice did sometimes serve as a buffer between the world of DOI-CODI and its frightened captives.

What was its record during the Médici presidency, the most repressive of all the military governments? The data available (which cover 1964–73, though most of these cases fall in 1969–73) show an acquittal rate of 45 percent—startlingly high for a repressive military regime, though many of the acquitted might well answer that their humiliation, degradation, and often torture before trial overshadowed the final verdict.[101] The most extensive study of military justice records for the entire repressive period focussed on 695 of 707 trials occurring between April 1964 and March 1979. There were 7,367 defendants, of whom 1,918 reported they had been tortured. Another 6,385 were accused in initial proceedings but never taken to trial. Of these, about two-thirds were imprisoned.[107] As for acquittals vs. convictions, the most comprehensive source reports (on the basis of a slightly different time period) that 6,196 defendants were tried, from October 1965 to November 1977, with 68 percent acquitted and only 32 percent convicted.[103] Again, an impressive acquittal rate.

One of the better-known acquittals was of Caio Prado Junior, who had been charged with "inciting to subversion" in a press interview. The distinguished historian and São Paulo intellectual was imprisoned (not tortured) for a year. In 1971 he found not guilty by the Supreme Military Tribunal and released (two others in the same case were found guilty).[104] In another São Paulo case those arrested in the wake of the apprehension of the Dominican friars in 1969 as part of the hunt for Carlos Marighela were two years later acquitted of all charges.[105]

The degree to which the workings of military justice mitigated the repression should not be overestimated. Torturers sometimes simply defied the tribunals, abusing and sometimes killing their prisoners with little concern for accountability to higher military authority. There were also prisoners who were "disappeared" before any lawyer could confirm their locale. Finally, there was the slowness of justice, which could be highly dangerous to the prisoner.[106]

Military justice did, nonetheless, make a difference. It provided a mechanism which for some prisoners increased the odds of survival or of shorter incarceration. (To say how many would require a thorough study of tribunal records and personal testimony.) Second, it was a legal arena in which cases could finally be discharged. In practical terms, that meant that defendants who were cleared of all charges escaped any subsequent legal limbo. In this respect there was a sharp difference between the lower military courts and the *Superior Tribunal Militar*. The latter was more liberal, and on appeal often reversed convictions or reduced harsh sentences passed by the lower courts.[107] Third, military justice served as a "safeguard for the nation's dignity," in the words of the newsmagazine *Veja*.[108] This function was important when the military regime later moved toward civilian government. It gave the military a symbolic rallying point, a proof that at least some officers had spoken out for the tradition of due process and decency in handling prisoners.

Finally, the operation of military justice meant much of the repression was registered—in its horrifying detail—in the records of military justice. This is the source the São Paulo archdiocese research team was able to tap for the extraordinary documentary *Brasil: Nunca Mais*. As a result, the principal exposé of the Brazilian military government's human rights violations is documented from official military archives, It also seems likely that access to those records must have been aided by someone inside. If so, that underlines again the role played by military justice both during and after the repression. In Argentina, on the other hand, the source has had to be the testimony of survivors, witnesses, or relatives, which can always be contested as second- or thirdhand accounts. In Brazil the military and their apologists can never impugn the sources for the chilling facts about the years of terror.

But there was never any question of military justice threatening the fundamental structure of repression. That could only come from the highest military command, or from whatever force might displace it.

An interesting example of the former occurred in late 1971. By that point the air force had developed its own interrogation and torture network, theoretically subordinated to the armed forces command. In fact, however, the air force teams operated increasingly on their own. The reponsible officer was Air Brigadier Burnier, a notoriously sadistic torturer. In late November 1971, Army Minister Orlando Geisel, the de facto viceroy of the armed forces, forced the resignation of Air Force Minister Sousa e Melo, long a braggard about his strong-arm squads. Those squads did not give up without a fight. Soon after assuming office, the new Air Force Minister, backed by Orlando Geisel, forced the retirement of ten more high-ranking air force officers, including Burnier.[109]

The significance of these dismissals is not that Orlando Geisel and the Planalto struck a blow against torture. Rather, they were asserting their control over the security operations. To speculate that such power might someday be used to eliminate torture was hardly comforting to those who were traversing the inferno infested by Sérgio Fleury and his ilk.

Could President Médici or the military ministers have stopped the torture, if they had wanted to? There were several institutional barriers. First, the torturers had a vested interest in continuing. Those in São Paulo, for example, received financial favors. Local businessmen rewarded them with large cash bonuses after successful operations. Sergio Fleury flaunted his winnings, which had been translated into a mansion and a yacht.[110] Yet this bonanza would continue only if the torturers could find a continuing supply of suspects to justify their system.

The hardliners argued that subversives had infiltrated every institution, so there should be plenty of suspects among church activists, university students and faculty, purged military, artists, and journalists. Because it took time for the higher military to acknowledge and to decide how to react

to the fact that the guerrillas were effectively eliminated, the security apparatus continued on its deadly path.

The torturers also had the asset of direct access to the higher military.
They could readily show the latest evidence of guerrilla activity (a clandestine publication, an incriminating confession, an intercepted letter or phone
conversation) to prove the danger was still alive. Finally, they could argue
that any decline in the guerrilla threat was directly due to their vigilance. To
let up would be to invite a return of the armed revolutionaries.

Furthermore, what high-level military officer had the moral and political
authority to end torture? By 1971 virtually every ranking officer had held a
command where torture had occurred. Any top-level officer trying to end
the horror ran the risk of being exposed as a hypocrite.[111] And there was
the futher worry that someday military officers might be tried for the
barbarities practiced under their command. Journalists called it the "Nuremberg syndrome."

Censorship was another government instrument of repression. It had
begun in mid-December 1968, under the authority of Institutional Act 5.
Until mid-January 1969 army officers enforced the censorship. Then began
a period of self-censorship negotiated between newspaper owners and the
military authorities. That arrangement broke down when the Federal Police assumed jurisdiction in September 1972, and the owners refused to
deal with the police. Subsquently the Federal Police sent its censorship
orders, by phone or in writing, to the editors. Topics most often forbidden
were student political activities, workers' movements, individuals deprived
of their political rights, and bad news about the economy. Most sensitive of
all was news about the military—anything that might cause dissention
among the military or tension between the military and the public.[112]

Censorship was simply the reverse side of the Planalto's propaganda
campaign run by AERP. The censors' job was to stop the media from
casting any doubt on AERP's picture of a dynamic and efficiently governed
country where the military led the way, avidly supported by the citizenry.
A good example of the censors in action was a letter they stopped from
being published in O Estado de São Paulo. The letter (written by Ruy
Mesquita of the family that owned the paper) attacked censorship as having
reduced Brazil to "the status of a banana republic." That metaphor was
bound to infuriate the military, who considered themselves several cuts
above the traditional Spanish-American dictators. The censors kept it out
of O Estado de São Paulo, but it appeared in Pôrto Alegre's Correio do
Povo, which was not under prior censorship. The local police were alerted;
they surrounded the printing plant and confiscated all copies before they
could go on sale.[113]

In September 1972 the military government decided to take a more
direct hand in controlling the press.[114] It now gave written orders specifying
what could not appear in print. Highest on the list were the activities of the
security apparatus and the struggle over the presidential succession.

Censorship excesses inevitably produced their own reaction. The most widely read challenge to censorship was *Pasquim,* a satirical humor weekly, which needled the generals mercilessly in cartoon and word. In 1970 the entire staff of *Pasquim* was jailed for more than a month (the news quickly spread by word of mouth). With the staff's release the circulation shot up to 200,000, a record for this kind of Brazilian periodical. Even when shorn of its most stinging cartoons and prose, *Pasquim* rallied spirits against the military government's edenic propaganda.[115]

Other prime targets for the censors were *Opinião,* a weekly of center-left views; *Movimento,* a militantly leftist weekly; *O Estado de Sño Paulo,* the conservative São Paulo daily owned by the pugnacious Mesquita family; *O São Paulo,* weekly organ of the archdiocese of São Paulo; and the centrist *Veja,* Brazil's leading weekly newsmagazine.

The print media were one battlefront for the censors. More important, from the standpoint of public impact, were television and radio. There the government made clear what could and couldn't be broadcast.[116] It monitored especially closely popular songs, often by such favorites as composersinger Chico Buarque de Holanda. Others were Gilberto Gil and Caetano Veloso, both of whom lived abroad in the Médici period.[117]

All these moves by Federal Police censors were supposed to bar from circulation the dangerous words, cartoons, and songs of the enemies of the national security state. By controlling the media the generals thought they could control behavior. In the short run they succeeded. The media knuckled under.

The Church: An Opposition Force

As the repression settled over Brazil, the Roman Catholic Church provided virtually the only center of institutional opposition.[118] We saw earlier how certain Church elements were drawn into battle with the Costa e Silva regime, especially after December 1968. The battles often arose from the Church's effort to protect their clergy or laity who fell foul of the security forces.[119] The Catholics most likely to suffer this fate were those who had been active in Catholic groups such as *Ação Popular* (AP), *Juventude Universitária* (JUC), *Juventude Operária Católica* (JOC), and other groups headed toward the political left.

These were the "popular" elements to have emerged out of the intellectual and institutional ferment within the Church in the 1950s and early 1960s. Many Catholics once active in "popular" groups stopped out of fear. But others (both lay and clerical) did not give up. They saw the deepening political repression and increasing economic inequality as confirming their radical leftist diagnosis of Brazilian capitalism.

That kind of radical thought had become increasingly common among Catholic clergy in three regions of the country. One was the Amazon region, where the building of the Transamazon Highway, the government-promoted development of large-scale cattle culture, and official promises of land distribution had led to open warfare (discussed later in this chapter) in key areas of the Amazon valley. The clergy—usually missionaries and often foreign—generally took the side of the squatters and the small farmers being crowded out, sometimes violently. Both federal and local government authorities—when present—almost invariably backed the big operators. Clergy who had never been political grew increasingly indignant and convinced the bishops of their region that grave social injustices were being committed. The bishops raised their voice in radical tones, influencing clergy elsewhere in Brazil. A parallel radicalization occurred among the clergy in the Northeast. There social injustice came from a centuries-old economic structure that perpetuated Brazil's grossest socio-economic inequalities. The Northeastern bishops, like the Amazonians, denounced the entire economic system as unjust. Another important center of radical opposition to the government was in São Paulo, where the newly appointed (1970) archbishop, Dom Paulo Evaristo Arns, was denouncing the repression which had hit Church activists, union organizers, students, and journalists harder than anywhere else.

The Brazilian Church in fact was sharply divided over its proper role in politics, in the broadest sense of that term. The bishops were split into roughly three groups, which reflected both clerical and lay opinion.[120] One was the "progressive" wing, whose most conspicuous figure was Dom Helder Camara, the internationally famous Archbishop of Olinda and Recife, in the heart of Brazil's poverty-stricken Northeast.[121] These bishops would speak out against government violence and, with equal vehemence, against social injustice. In discussing the latter, they assumed a more radical political position, since they necessarily had to attack the government policies that had increased economic inequality.

The second group of bishops were the "conservatives," of whom Dom Geraldo de Proença Sigaud, Archbishop of Diamantina, was the most outspoken.[122] They were the right-wing counterweight to the "progressives." They denounced the "subversive" threat to Brazil and unabashedly supported the military government.

The third group were the "moderates," those bishops hoping to avoid taking any public position on socio-economic justice or politics. They feared for the Church's survival in a battle with the government, notwithstanding urgent issues. The "moderates" swung over to join the "progressives," thereby providing a majority, when clergy themselves became victims of harassment and torture. When fighting to protect their own, the bishops extended their mantle over all the victims of repression. Their instrument was the Commission on Peace and Justice, vigorously supported by Archbishop Arns in São Paulo. It had a small but dedicated staff of clerics, lay volunteers, and lawyers who struggled to locate political prisoners, get them legal representation, and counsel their families. Often they could do little more than counsel.

The military took a dim view of this Church opposition. Hardliners had long accused clergy of aiding the armed revolutionaries. In 1969 they thought they saw an opportunity to prove their point. After guerrilla leader Carlos Marighela died in a police ambush in São Paulo in October, seven Dominicans were arrested on a charge of having aided Marighela. Government-inspired newspaper stories said the Dominicans, under torture, had helped lure Marighela to his death. The National Council of Brazilian Bishops (*Conferência Nacional de Bispos Brasileiros,* or CNBB) rejected the charge. Knowing how the military government would capitalize on public opposition to guerrilla violence, then Cardinal Rossi of São Paulo denounced all violence, thereby hoping to build credibility for subsequent criticism of the government.

The year 1969 had brought increased violence against the religious. In May, as we have seen, Father Pereira Neto, a young priest who worked closely with Dom Helder Camara in youth programs, was lynched in Recife. The killers were never identified, but few doubted that such a crime could only be carried out by someone closely linked to the security forces. Elsewhere the police were regularly raiding convents and schools. One arrest of 40 suspects included the mother superior of a convent. In mid-November the archbishop of Riberão Preto in the state of São Paulo excommunicated the local police chief and his deputy on the grounds that they had abused some religious. In mid-December the bishop of Volta Redonda (in the state of Rio de Janeiro) and 16 other clergy were indicted on the charge of distributing subversive literature. A day later 21 more suspects were arrested, including nine Dominican monks. Cardinal Rossi and 18 other members of the 32-member Central Committee of the CNBB strongly supported the accused bishop. Bitter clashes continued throughout 1970. Periodic arrests of clergy alternated with denunciations of government torture from the more progressive bishops. The latter often coupled their antigovernment statements with a denunciation of terrorism, whatever its source, hoping thereby to maintain credibility.

As a result, the Church became the most conspicuous opponent to the Brazilian authoritarian state. It was not only that the CNBB aggressively sought to protect its clergy and laity from torture (often without success). It was also that the Church activists mobilized their contacts abroad—through the Vatican, sympathetic clergy and laymen in Europe and the U.S., and other human rights activists outside Brazil, thereby generating protests in the U.S. and European press. Criticism from those quarters made the Brazilian military especially uneasy.[123]

In January 1970, for example, a Canadian cardinal and member of the Church's "Justice and Peace Commission" reported that the Pope was watching Brazilian events closely, and was especially concerned over human rights violations. Later in 1970 the Vatican's newspaper, *L'Osservatore Romano,* suggested that the Brazilian government should avoid repression. In October 1970 the Pope himself spoke out against torture, although without mentioning Brazil by name. The Médici government bitterly resented this international campaign, and planted anti-Church stories in the

Brazilian press. At the same time, the Brazilian opposition clung to the hope that such pressure from abroad might help end the nightmare of repression.

Through the remaining Médici years the Church continued to be a thorn in the side of the military regime. In March 1973, for example, the bishops spoke out against the continuing curbs on freedom. This merely confirmed, for the hard-line military, the Church's complicity in the armed subversion. But the Church held fast, despite its internal weaknesses and divisions. Indeed, it became a rallying point for Brazilian Catholics and non-Catholics who in normal times would probably have given little thought to the Church.

The Economic Boom and Its Critics

President Costa e Silva's stroke in September 1969 had raised the immediate question: Would Delfim's economic policies continue? Médici quickly made clear that he wanted no major changes in economic policy. Most important, Costa e Silva's chief policymakers, Delfim at the Treasury and Reis Velloso at the Planning Office, stayed on. Given the authoritarian government's hold over Brazil, no interest group or social sector could hope to gain by bringing pressure in the public arena (behind the scenes was obviously another matter). The technocrats were still at the helm and they had clear sailing.[124]

At Médici's first cabinet meeting in January 1970 Delfim Neto announced three economic targets: (1) 8–9 percent GDP growth; (2) inflation under 20 percent; and (3) adding at least $100 million to the foreign exchange reserves. Reis Velloso, now Minister of Planning and Coordination, wanted the ministers to think in a "triple perspective": Médici's term (until 1974), the entire 1970s, and until the end of the century, looking to "our entry into the developed world."[125]

This ambitious tone also surfaced when the Médici government published its first comprehensive planning document in September 1970. The spirit of *Metas e bases para a ação de govêrno* ("Targets and Foundationns for Government Action") was clear in the introduction.[126] The March 1964 Revolution had created "the basic conditions for true development, democracy, and sovereignty." Brazil needed, "above all, a government without commitments to the interests of any group, class, sector, or region."[127] Here again were the technocrats proclaiming their disinterested service to the nation.

If repression was the Médici government's gravest liability in international opinion, the economic boom was its greatest asset. Observers both in Brazil and abroad agreed that rapid growth was "legitimizing" the regime, especially in the eyes of the middle class.[128] Delfim's three targets were largely met. Economic growth under Médici was the highest sustained rate since the 1950s. GDP rose at an annual average of 10.9 percent from 1968 through 1974. The lead sector was industry, which grew at 12.6 percent a

year. Agricultural growth was more erratic, averaging 5.2 percent. Inflation averaged 17 percent (although the official figure of 15.7 percent for
1973 was later admitted to be a gross understatement)[129] As for Brazil's
foreign exchange reserves, they shot up from $656 million in 1969 to $6.417
billion in 1973.

Many critics had earlier predicted that high growth would be unlikely, if
not impossible. Economists such as Celso Furtado had presented an under-
consumptionist analysis, arguing that the mid-sixties stagnation was the
best that could be expected. For these economists growth could be
achieved only by carrying out structural reforms (such as land reform,
educational reform, etc.) to redistribute income and thereby broaden effective demand. But Delfim Neto and his technocrats were achieving rapid
growth through very different means, such as tax incentives, skillful manipulation of the financial system, and reducing labor costs. There did not
seem to be any shortage of demand, which Furtado and other leading
critics such as Maria Conceição Tavares now acknowledged.[130]

Economic performance in 1969 set the trend for the rest of Médici's
presidency. GDP grew at 10.2 percent led by industry at 12.1 percent. The
most dynamic industrial sector was motor vehicles, growing at an annual
rate of 34.5 percent. Of that production, which reached an annual output in
1969 of 354,000 units, 67 percent were passenger cars, the rest trucks and
buses. That ratio contrasted sharply with the 1957–69 period, when the
passenger car share was only 49 percent. Production was tilting toward the
least fuel-efficient form of transportation.

Several post-1964 economic policy decisions had contributed to this tilt.
One was the easier credit policy begun in 1967, with special terms for car
purchases. The post-1964 governments had also opened the Brazilian market to the three giant U.S. automakers—General Motors, Ford, and
Chrysler—which had not invested in Brazil (in passenger car production)
because they saw too little profit in building only the small, fuel-efficient
cars stipulated by the Brazilian government when Brazil's auto industry
was created in the late 1950s. After 1964 the regulations were revised,
allowing the production of medium-sized (by Detroit's definition) cars. The
gambit worked, as new car purchases boomed.

The reliance on motor vehicles as the leading industrial sector had significant social costs. First, the heavy emphasis on passenger cars encouraged a
relatively inefficient form of transportation. The fuel question was vital,
because Brazil then imported 80 percent of its petroleum.

Second, this concentration of demand in automobiles stimulated further
investment in that sector, to the detriment of other sectors where investment was badly needed, such as health and education, not to speak of
consumer nondurables, whose growth rate lagged badly in these years. It is
interesting that the argument for a policy mix favoring consumer durables,
especially cars, was never laid out, much less defended, in either of the
Médici government's two principal economic documents (1970 and 1971).
In its rhetoric the government emphasized social investments, vigorously

defending the private sector and avoiding discussion of the likely overall distributional effects of its policies.

The 1969 performance was also impressive for the public sector. The government demonstrated an ability to increase signficantly its tax collections. The largest increase in 1969 revenues was from income tax collection, which rose by 60 percent in real terms. This was impressive for a country where skeptics thought an income tax was unenforceable. Overall, the financial management of the public sector was non-inflationary, as the government sold enough bonds to finance its deficit. This neutralization of the public sector deficit helped to lower the 1969 price increase to 20.1 percent in comparison to 1968's rate of 26 percent. It appeared that Delfim's team had discovered the secret of rapid growth with falling inflation.

The other good news for 1969 was in the balance of payments, always crucial for Brazilian development strategy. Exports for 1969 rose 22.9 percent, creating a trade surplus, something unheard of since 1966, when an industrial recession cut import demands. The export surge resulted from the government's aggressive use of tax and credit incentives to favor exports. Important also was the continued use of mini-devaluations (or the "crawling peg"), thus assuring exporters of a realistic cruzeiro value for their sales.[131] The balance of payments was also strengthened by a foreign capital inflow of just over $1 billion, mostly in loans. This was almost double the inflow for 1968 and five times the total for 1967. All in all, 1969 was another excellent year, as measured by orthodox macroeconomic criteria. Brazil was fortunate to have this balance of payments bonanza, because its economic policies by no means pleased the IMF. In its 1971 annual report the Fund criticized Brazil's reliance on indexation and mini-devaluations, arguing that if they made it easier to live with inflation in the short run, "they make its eventual elimination more difficult."[132] Because Brazil had such a strong balance of payments, it had no need to go to the Fund for help and therefore no need to hew to IMF orthodoxy.

The rest of the Médici years (1970–73) saw 1969's pattern largely maintained. Growth continued at nearly 11 percent a year. The public sector continued to pay its non-inflationary way by covering any deficits (which were not large) by borrowing, rather than by printing money. This was a significant accomplishment, given the past public sector performance in Brazil and the rest of Latin America.

The years 1970–73 also saw Brazil's foreign trade continue to grow rapidly. Brazil increased its exports by 126 percent, going from $2.7 billion in 1970 to $6.2 billion in 1973. Imports increased slightly more, going from $2.8 billion in 1970 to $7.0 billion in 1973. As in the past, rapid growth proved to be import intensive.

Brazil's export success had several explanations. Her terms of trade improved dramatically from 1971 through 1973. Crucial in that trend was a 137 percent increase in the average international price of soybeans from 1972 to 1973, a product Brazil had only begun exporting in the late 1960s. Also,

Brazil significantly diversified among commodity exports, as well as between commodities and industrial products. Exports of the latter increased by 192 percent from 1970 through 1973, with their share of total exports rising from 24 to 31 percent. Contrary to what many critics had predicted, Brazil was finding markets for her industrial goods in both the developed countries and the Third World. In addition, government policies begun under Castelo Branco and Costa e Silva were crucial in stimulating Brazilian exports. Most obvious were tax and credit incentives, which helped convince the private sector that exports could be consistently profitable.[133]

Finally, Brazil continued to attract large inflows of foreign capital, which were vital in covering deficits on current account. The capital inflow was primarily in long- and medium-term loans. Two Brazilian policies were at work. One was high real interest rates, assured through regular indexation, and the other was the mini-devaluation policy that meant the foreign investor could get his money out at a realistic exchange rate.

In the short run this capital inflow was highly beneficial. It helped finance the trade deficit caused by the surge in imports Brazil needed to maintain rapid growth. There was also a deficit to be covered in the services category, which included shipping, insurance, profit remittances, and interest on loans. Brazilian industry, the economy's most dynamic sector, consumed a large share of the imports, especially in capital goods and petroleum products. Ironically, Brazil's successful import-substituting industrialization had produced an industrial structure that was, at least in the short run, import intensive. This was not surprising, since Brazil had attempted across-the-board industrialization, moving into areas where the technology was highly sophisticated and prone to rapid obsolescence. This high short-run need for imports, combined with the large deficit in services, outpaced the growth of exports and made Brazilian growth dependent on the inflow of foreign capital. Because the latter came primarily in the form of loans, Brazil was running up an ever greater bill for payment of interest and amortization. Ultimately, Brazil could only pay this bill from its export earnings. Every loan it incurred was therefore a further mortgage on Brazil's future.

Such a financing strategy was conventional. It had been followed by every industrializing country except Japan. The U.S., for example, was a net borrower of foreign capital until about 1900, when it reversed roles and became a net exporter until the 1980s. Brazil was not charting, in principle, an unknown path.

By 1973 the capital inflow had reached the record-breaking annual level of $4.3 billion, almost double the 1971 level and more than three times the figure for 1970. The Brazilian government grew worried over the increased cruzeiro buying power created by the inflow. To control it they began requiring a percentage (first set at 25 percent, then at 40 percent) of incoming loans to be put on deposit. They also established a minimum time period (first six years, then ten) for loans to remain in Brazil. The compulsory deposit was a means of reducing the inflow's impact on Brazil's money

supply, which otherwise would have suddenly expanded, accelerating inflation. The minimum time limit was to discourage the speculators and would
make more predictable the timing of capital outflows. For one of the few
times in its history, Brazil was forced to limit capital inflow.[134]

By the end of the Médici presidency, the size of the foreign debt had
begun to worry some observers, both Brazilian and foreign. At the beginning of 1974 the debt stood at $12.6 billion, a 32 percent increase over 1972
and a 90 percent increase over 1971. Delfim Neto downplayed the worries.
He pointed to the rapid rise in exports and the record-high foreign exchange reserves, which stood at $6.4 billion at the end of 1973. Judged by
these two variables, he argued, Brazil was in a good position to manage
prudently its foreign debt.

The economic boom also brought high salaries for professionals and
managers. The Médici government had increased the budget for higher
education, thereby creating more university places, as well as hiring more
faculty. The Brazilian government had largely succeeded in reversing the
brain drain which occurred in the 1964–70 period, in contrast to the continuing hemorrhages from authoritarian Chile, Uruguay, and Argentina. For
Brazilians willing to reconcile themselves to living in a dictatorship, the
rewards could be great, both for them and their institutions. The effect was
strongest among the young of the middle and upper social sectors—the
very strata from which the armed opposition had once successfully recruited. Thus the economic gains helped generate genuine middle-sector
support for the government. The 1970 congressional elections, when
ARENA won an overwhelming victory, seemed to confirm that support.
Even Brazilians disgusted by authoritarian government drew pride from
the evidence that Brazil was on the move. Whatever its political imperfec-
tions, Brazil was approaching international status at a faster pace than most
Brazilians had dared hope in the early 1960s. The signs were reassuring. By
1974 Brazil's foreign exchange reserves exceeded those of Britain, while
Volkswagen's German headquarters, experiencing low profits at home,
were congratulating themselves for their booming subsidiary in Brazil. Yet
the middle sectors remained ambivalent. While aware of their material
gains, they were angered and frightened when repression hit them, or,
more frequently, their children. This government brutality forced some to
ask troubling questions about their government.

In this picture the working classes counted for little in terms of collective
power. Labor unions were under rigid control, and attempts at spontaneous protest, as in 1968, were easily quashed. Protest was limited to occasional "work to rule" actions. The chance for collective action in the countryside was even dimmer, given the long-standing efficiency of repression
there. This does not mean that individual workers did not benefit from the
boom years. Someone had to fill the new positions created by rapid growth.
Workers benefitted from promotions and job definitions, above all in the
rapidly industrializing Center-South region. But these gains resulted from
economic growth and individual job mobility, not from collective action.

Brazil's growth strategy was not without its critics. MDB leaders Alencar Furtado, Franco Montoro, Ulysses Guimarães, and Freitas Nobre frequently arose in Congress to attack Médici and Delfim Neto (usually in guarded tones) for policies that allegedly deepened economic divisions at home while granting undue favors to the foreign investor.[135] Such criticisms gained credence with anyone who compared the latest São Paulo apartment house towers (with their three- and four-car garages) to the city's thousands of street urchins (immortalized in the film *Pixote*), who lived from purse-snatching and worse.

The critics got new ammunition from the 1970 census. Its income distribution data could now be compared with the 1960 data, making possible Brazil's first time series on this important indicator. The data showed that between 1960 and 1970 Brazil's distribution of income, as measured by its deviation from a perfectly equal distribution (the measure was the Gini coefficient), had grown more unequal.[136]

The publication of the data in 1972 caused a furor in Brazil. The Médici government was presiding over a boom, with production and exports leaping ahead. Euphoria was the order of the day for the government, as economists and planners from around the world arrived to learn Brazil's secret. But the image was disrupted in May 1972 when World Bank President Robert McNamara, at a U.N. conference on trade and development, singled out Brazil for having neglected the welfare of its poor in its drive for growth. MDB leader Alencar Furtado drew the lesson: "An anlaysis of demand profiles shows that the commercial-industrial process of recent years has aggravated the inequality of buying power among social sectors, as well as increasing regional inequalities of development." Furtado drove home his point: "We live in an economy that benefits the few while sacrificing the millions . . ."[137]

The Médici government, knowing that its legitimacy both at home and abroad turned on the economic "miracle," reacted heatedly to the charge that it had neglected the welfare of its least privileged citizens. Delfim Neto, never modest in such circumstances, defended his high-growth policies, saying, "I have absolutely no doubt that there is in this country a consensus in favor of accelerated development." Here Delfim was repeating the familiar argument that rapid growth was more important than improved distribution in the short run. Thus the immediate trade-off between growth and equity had to be resolved in favor of growth. He then argued, as did fellow neo-liberal economists Roberto Campos and Mario Henrique Simonsen, that rapid growth was bound to increase inequalities in the short run, even as it increased everyone's absolute income. For that reason Delfim rejected changes in relative income distribution (as opposed to absolute living standards) as the most appropriate measure of the progress of an economy such as Brazil's. He took the example of workers in the construction industry and the auto industry. Obviously, wages in the latter are more unequal than those in construction. "I would like to ask those who are preoccupied with income distribution," Delfim said, "whether they would rather work in construction or in the auto industry." And who would not agree that rapid growth must be the top priority? Perhaps, answered Delfim, "some intellectual who is rich enough and now thinks we ought to give preference to distribution."[138]

Other defenders of government policy were quick to argue that the census data had been misinterpreted by the critics. The defenders pointed out that the 1960–70 period had seen unusual unheaval, including the political instability of the mid-1960s and then the Castelo Branco stabilization program. Because only decennial data had been collected, it was impossible to see trends within the decade. Thus one could not isolate the record of the post-1964 governments, which is what the MDB and other critics wanted. Finally, ARENA and government spokesmen pointed out that even though inequality may have increased, every decile had gotten an absolute increase in income. Thus, the economic boom was lifting all Brazilians, if at a differential rate.

The Médici regime's counterattacks boiled down to two points. First, the government was already taking steps to improve the income distribution, through such measures as higher minimum wage adjustments, expanded social welfare programs (better health service, more subsidized housing, increased schools, extended profit sharing, pensions, etc.) and improved rural incomes. Second, the real answer to poverty and unequal income distribution was rapid economic growth, thereby increasing the total economic pie. Such, Roberto Campos and the government technocrats argued, had been the secret of prosperity in North America and Western Europe. Brazil could reach that goal also, if it did not succumb to the temptation now to divide up an inadequate pie. As Delfim argued: "You can't put [better] distribution ahead of production. If you do, you'll end up distributing what doesn't exist."[139]

Opening the Amazon: Solution for the Northeast?

Although Médici continued many of the economic policies he inherited, his government had its own policymaking style. Nowhere was it more evident than in a region which had long been an economic problem for Brazilian governments, the Northeast, and a region most governments had ignored, the Amazon.

The Northeast presented an economic problem whose solution was far beyond the resources committed by any previous Brazilian government.[140] No major region of Brazil could compare to the scale of misery in which most of the 30 million Northeasterners lived. In 1961 the federal government had established a 50 percent tax write-off for corporations that invested in the Northeast. This measure led to a surge of investment in the new industrial parks around Bahia and Recife. But the ultimate effect on the local economies was questioned by many critics, because the investment almost invariably was in capital-intensive rather than labor-intensive technology.[144] The Castelo Branco government, preoccupied with slashing government expenditures, had done little new for the Northeast. The Costa e Silva government began with the usual rhetoric about helping the Northeast in order to promote national integration. But such talk did not translate into significantly more funds. Delfim Neto and his team saw their mission as reinvigoration of the national economy, which meant primarily the developed Southeast. They saw no point in diverting large sums to an area where the return on investment was bound to be low.

When Médici replaced Costa e Silva there was again no alteration in Brasília's policy toward the Northeast. That changed quickly, however, when a devastating drought struck the Northeast in 1970. Hearing of the growing natural disaster, President Médici flew to Recife for a firsthand look.[142] He was shocked. Tens of thousands of drought victims were streaming into the coastal cities, only to find pathetically inadequate supplies of food and housing. No one knew how long the drought might last.

Médici called for the obvious action: increased federal funds for emergency relief. But the President soon discovered, as so many had before him, there was no magic solution for the misery of the Northeast. The drought had merely laid bare an agony long evident.

Forced to look hard at the Northeast's future, Médici concluded the obvious: the Northeast, given its resources, had too many people. Since bringing in enough resources was out of the question, he opted for the idea of moving Northeasterners out. But where? A SUDENE project of the early 1960s had attempted colonization in Maranhão. It failed; but was the experiment conclusive? Flying back from Recife, Médici decided that the Northeast and the Amazon must be attacked as a single problem. Brazil must build a Transamazon Highway that would open up the "underpopulated" Amazon valley. The Northeast's excess population could then flow to the Amazon, attracted by the cheap and fertile land to be provided by the National Integration Program (*Programa de Integração Nacional,* or PIN). Médici called it "the solution to two problems: men without land in the Northeast and land without men in Amazonia." The PIN was to include three elements: (1) the opening of the Amazon valley by a new highway which would facilitate the settlement of 70,000 families; (2) the irrigation of 40,000 hectares in the Northeast during 1972–74; and (3) the creation of export corridors in the Northeast.[143]

This process, according to the government's initial planning document, would be the "gradual occupying of the empty spaces," a phrase indicative of the Médici government's thinking.[144] Difficult social problems—such as the misery in which at least a third of Brazil lived—would be solved not by nationalizing or redistributing the wealth or income of anyone else, but by finding *new* resources. The huge population of the Northeast would be steered away from its normal migration path to the "overpopulated metropolitan centers of the Center-South" and channeled toward the semihumid regions of the Northeast and the Amazon and Central Plateau.[145] Constructing the Transamazon Highway and the Cuiabá-Santarém highway was to have "absolute priority."[146] Such an ambitious new program obviously required substantial new federal funding. Where was it to be found? Delfim informed the President there were no funds—"unless we take it out of the incentive funding." So the solution was to commandeer part of the federal funds already earmarked for the Northeast in the tax incentive programs. Médici later said he diverted "only 30 percent" of the incentive funding.[147]

Why did Médici and his policymakers find Amazon development such an attractive solution to the Northeast crisis? First, because a *direct* attack on the problems of the Northeast would have been prohibitively expensive, both economically and politically. It would have required a massive transfer of resources from the Center-South to raise the productivity of Northeastern agriculture, commerce, and industry. Private capital had never moved to the Northeast on this scale because the rate of return on investment was much higher in the Center-South and West. To help the Northeast would have required Brazilians elsewhere to forego economic benefits in order to subsidize (at least in the short run) Northeastern development.

The Médici government, like its post-1964 predecessors, had no mandate to carry out such radical regional redistribution. In fact, the groups that before 1964 had demanded restructuring of power in the Northeast, such as the peasant leagues and the coastal intellectuals, were the most heavily repressed by the military governments after 1964. Their voices had long been silenced when the 1970 drought hit.

Médici's forcus on the Amazon had another logic, apart from the need to help the Northeast by moving Northeasterners. The Brazilian elite, especially the military, had long worried that their country might lose the Amazon valley for want of settling it. Generations of Brazilian army cadets had been taught the Amazon's geopolitical significance; now as officers they feared possible Peruvian or Venezuelan incursions into Brazil's vast but thinly held territory upriver. This worry deepened as the Amazon's extraordinary mineral wealth—especially iron ore—became known. The issue of foreign exploitation of Amazonian resources was dramatized by the launching of Jarí, the huge tree farm project undertaken by American shipping billionaire Daniel Ludwig under a concession granted by the Castelo Branco government.[148] Thus the Northeastern drought offered a new stimulus to the historic Brazilian aspiration to develop the Amazon. In Médici's words, "we must start up the Amazon clock, which has been losing time for too long."[149]

The Transamazon Highway had a further attraction. It was an engineering challenge the army engineers could attack with relish. By focusing on the road, Médici set a formidable task but not an impossible one. It had a clear beginning and end. It could be visited, photographed, and described. Like the construction of Brasília and the Bélem-Brasília highway during Kubitschek's presidency, building the Transamazon had great symbolic value.[150] To cut through the jungle forest and build a pioneer highway appealed to those many Brazilians whose romanticized view of Amazonia did not differ from that of the average North America or Western European. It also appealed to the large construction firms whose government champion was Transportation Minister Andreazza. They stood to profit handsomely from huge contracts in the Amazon valley, and they could also furnish important support for Andreazza's presidential ambitions.

Delfim Neto was placed in a difficult position by Médici's decision to throw large-scale resources into the Amazon. There was no way it could be defended by normal investment criteria. In 1967, for example, the Castelo Branco government had drawn up a national road-building plan. The Transamazon did not even appear.[151] Before Médici's decision in 1970, the road had no strong backers. Once the President made his decision, however, Delfim quickly fell into line.

In July 1970 he explained that the PIN was "an attempt to move the center of gravity of the economy northward, trying to repeat in that region what had already been accomplished in the Center-South."[152] Several months later Delfim ridiculed those critics who questioned the Transamazon Highway's viability from a cost-benefit standpoint. "Nothing that has altered the face of the world would have ever passed a preliminary test on its rate of return," he scoffed. If Pedro Cabral (the discoverer of Brazil in 1500) had had to prove the profitability of his voyage, Delfim suggested, Brazil would still be undiscovered. He then argued the Transamazon would be as good an investment as the Belém-Brasília highway, a surprising comparison from a minister whose government constantly denigrated Kubitschek, the Belém-Brasília's builder. Finally, Delfim fell into a totally unnscientific enthusiasm about the Amazon's resources. He declared that the Amazon had "a strain of red soil comparable to that in any state of the Center-South."[153] Here Delfim was repeating the myth of the fertility of Amazon soils, which actually are primarily laterite and cannot sustain harvest agriculture because of the rapid leaching of the soil in the heavy rains.

This rhetoric presented interesting psychological overtones. The Transamazon Highway project, key to the PIN, for example, tapped Brazil's aspiration to reach out into the huge unoccupied distances within its borders. In October 1970 Médici exuberantly announced that "Amazonia, which covers more than half the national territory, could absorb much more than the entire population of Brazil."[154] In late 1972 Médici told his countrymen that "Brazil has not yet reached the era of a finite world, so we have the privilege of incorporating into our economy, step by step, new, immense, and practically empty regions."[155] In fact, the Amazon's ecosystem was and is extremely fragile and its agricultural potential sharply limited, as noted, by its soils. But in the heady atmosphere of the Médici presidency there was no time for doubt. As Médici had confidently announced in October 1970, "there are few examples of countries so blessed in natural and human resources and so slow to make use of them. It's this lost time that we have to make up for, thereby fulfilling a fundamental commitment of the Revolution."[156] The Amazon programs fit ideally into the government's high-powered public relations campaign that extolled Brazil's "grandeur" and its inexorable climb to world-power status.

Thus, policymaking for the Amazon was an interesting case of the Brazilian authoritarian regime at work. The President and his advisers could easily ignore the agronomists, geographers, and anthropologists who knew the development limitations of the Amazon valley. They could also ignore their elite opponents, such as the Northeastern political leaders, who saw their federal revenue being diverted to another region. The traditional source of opposition, the Congress, was still in forced recess (decreed by President Médici at the end of 1969) when the Amazonia program was approved.

Finally, the Médici government's attempt to solve the problem of the Northeast by developing Amazonia had its precedents. President Juscelino Kubitschek (1956–61), for example, uséd the construction of Brasília as a partial "solution" for such problems as endemic rural poverty in the Brazilian interior. He argued that building transportation links to Brasília would stimulate commercialization of agriculture and thereby raise incomes. Médici's Amazonian program resembled Kubitschek's creation of Brasília in another respect: both were monumental building projects in which they invested enormous prestige. In this sense Médici's grandiose scheme was in a mainstream political tradition having little to do with the 1964 coup.[157]

The military government's ambitious public-sector projects, such as in Amazonia, must be seen in the context of an economic strategy aimed at maximizing both private and public investment. In the private sector the capital was to come from rising profits—fattened by a wage policy that gave most of the productivity gains to the employers—and from tax incentives, especially in agriculture and the export sector. For state enterprises, capital was to come from their retained earnings—facilitated by full cost pricing policies—and loans from foreign sources such as the World Bank and the Inter-American Development Bank. Both these institutions became prime lenders for the Northeast and Amazonia.

Let us now take another look at the overall Médici economic record and its social implications. The basic policy aimed at maximizing growth from the given structure of production and income. That meant stimulation of the durable goods sector, since it had the skills and experience to produce efficiently and, when necessary, to expand capacity effectively. Automobile factories were booming while the clothing factories lagged. Why? Because income was continuing to be concentrated at the upper levels. The Médici strategy also called for heavy public-sector investment—energy, transportation, education, regional development, raw materials, etc.

The description resembles the economic strategy of the Kubitschek years. Then, the durable goods sector was also a leading private sector, while public sector investments were also large scale—in transportation, energy, and regional development (SUDENE), plus Brasília. Obviously, Kubitschek's policies were formulated and carried out in a very different context, a democratic system in which the government had to defend its policies against well-marhsalled opposition. And the Kubitschek government took pains to estimate the social effects of its policies. Nonetheless, a look at the record suggests that the Médici policies for the Amazon and the Northeast show surprising parallels with Kubitschek's policies.

Continued Electoral Manipulation and the Choice of Geisel

Despite its reliance on repression, the Médici government continued to hold elections, albeit subject to rapid changes in the rules of the game. After ARENA's overwhelming victory in the 1970 elections, the President continued his strong personal control over the party. His hand-picked Senate president, Petrônio Portella, and Chamber president, Pereira Lopes, proved unambiguously loyal to the Planalto. It is worth noting, however, that the leadership posts were evenly divided between ex-UDN and ex-PSD members, illustrating how even a powerful military government had to take careful note of pre-1964 political forces. Meanwhile, the Planalto had no trouble controlling the agenda and the outcomes in the national Congress. The same proved true in the ARENA-controlled state governments.

The presidential succession, always a delicate operation for any military regime, proved more troublesome. In 1972 the rumor mills began churning out names of possible successors to Médici, although the election was not until January 1974, for a term that would begin the following March. This speculation was beginning to undermine the President's effectiveness, threatening to turn him into an early lame duck. Médici reacted rapidly. In late March 1972 he prohibited any public discussion of the succession before mid-1973.[158] Thanks to government censorship, the presumption was that this edict could be readily enforced.[159] Médici and his advisers had been determined to head off the divisions within the military that had been generated by the choice of Castelo Branco's successor in 1965–66 and that of Costa e Silva's in 1969.

Despite the President's warning that public speculation about his successor must cease, *O Estado de São Paulo* continued printing stories on the subject. In late August the government imposed prior censorship (it had been spot censorship before) on the prestigious Paulista daily, because the *Estado* had violated a warning not to print a story about the conflict between Delfim Neto and Agriculture Minister Cirne Lima in which Delfim had been described as "amoral." *All* copy for *O Estado* now had to be screened by a censor, normally a military officer.

Even when under prior censorship, *O Estado de São Paulo* and *Jornal da Tarde,* its companion afternoon paper, were allowed (editors of other publications tried and failed) to fill the spaces left by censored material with conspicuous items, such as recipes (sometimes for inedible dishes) and verses from the Portuguese poet Camões. Upon seeing these "fillers," the reader knew a story had displeased the censors and knew how long it had been. This lapse from good authoritarian practice was typical of the Brazilian military governments. So often there was an incompleteness about their dictatorial practice. It seemed to signal a lack of total confidence in their ideology and a lack of total commitment in applying it. The operation of military justice, as we saw earlier, was a similiar example.

In April 1972 the Médici government became worried about another electoral front. Its problem was that the Constitution (as amended in 1969) called for state governors to be directly elected in 1974. Now, however, the government foresaw probable defeat in important states, so the Planalto pushed through a constitutional amendment making gubernatorial elections indirect in 1974 and postponing direct elections until 1978. MDB leaders attacked this latest manipulation of the electoral rules, but to no avail.

The Médici regime had now left itself only one test at the polls: the *município* elections of November 1972. ARENA won resoundingly, taking 88 percent of the mayoralties. It was a victory everyone expected, however, given the atmosphere of continuing intimidation against the MDB and given ARENA's advantage in controlling government patronage. Although gravely weakened, the opposition party had by no means given up. It preserved its organizational structure, especially in the major cities, where future national and state elections were likely to be decided.

Despite its overwhelming victory in the elections, the Médici government lacked any clear-cut political doctrine. It exemplified what sociologist Juan Linz has called an "authoritarian situation" rather than an institutionalized "authoritarian regime."[160] Into this vacuum had moved a group of right-wing theorists led by Justice Minister Alfredo Buzaid. They proposed a corporatist model for Brazil, harking back to the Integralist movement of the 1930s with which several of them had personal ties. The corporatist model would have replaced liberal representative institutions (which the military had retained, albeit in truncated form) with functionally defined bodies, with the executive power to take up where Getúlio Vargas's semi-corporatist dictatorship had left off in 1945.

The public debate over this corporatist offensive in 1971–72 was muted by censorship. But the Bar Association vigorously opposed the idea, as did a small segment of the press. What struck the death knell of the corporatists was the direction taken by the presidential succession, which dominated politics in 1973. Médici could outlaw public speculation over the identity of his likely successor, but he could hardly stop private speculation.

First came the rumors that 1974 would see no new president, because Médici's term was to be extended.[161] Few insiders believed that rumor, however, because the military abhorred the prospect of a possible *caudillo,* a military strong man ruling personally and indefinitely. Other rumors had it that the candidate would be a "military populist," a general committed to a massive attack on basic socio-economic needs, such as education, health, agrarian reform, and development of the interior (not just the Amazon valley). In short, it was the hope for another Albuquerque Lima, who had carried this standard in the losing fight to become Costa e Silva's successor.[162] Yet few believed the number of officers favoring that position had increased since Albuquerque Lima failed in 1969. If there had been a trend, it was against military populism, as suspect an idea to many officers as was the plan to extend Médici's term.

Who, then, would be the new general-president? Leitão de Abreu began a campaign to name a civilian candidate. Such a civilian, trusted by the military, was to launch a program to "demilitarize the Revolution." Leitão's tactic did not survive for long. Although few outside observers could have known, the leading castelistas had been marshalling their forces to take control of the succession. General Golbery, their most articulate spokesman (in private; he rarely spoke in public), helped direct a castelista campaign to regain power by designating the new president. Their candidate was General Ernesto Geisel, president of Petrobrás, former head of Castelo Branco's military staff, and former Supreme Military Court justice. Ernesto Geisel's brother, Orlando, was the army minister, a crucial fact because the holder of that post could control dissension in the officer corps, whose collective opinion weighed heavily in the selection process. Orlando was also in a position to neutralize SNI head General Carlos Alberto Fontoura, a powerful opponent of Ernesto's nomination. By May 1973 Ernesto Geisel had won a consensus within the military.[163] In June he was designated the ARENA candidate. His running mate was to be General Adalberto Pereira dos Santos, a justice of the Supreme Military Court and little known outside military circles. Geisel's selection, even when in gestation in 1972, brought to an abrupt end the attempt of Justice Minister Buzaid to convince the generals that a corporatist model would best fit Brazil's future. Thus the Médici government had lost any chance to institutionalize the Revolution by its own lights.[164]

Médici and the *duros* had now lost control of the succession. Geisel had never been their candidate, and they viewed a return of the castelistas as portending a dangerous relaxation of revolutionary fervor. But with Orlando Geisel in the Army Ministry, the castelistas held the command post. Orlando was aided by the fact that many younger hard-line officers who had pushed for radical measures in 1964, 1965, and 1968 were now worrying about their careers, since dissent over the succession could jeopardize their future promotions and assignments. Médici and his allies had been outmaneuvered.[165]

The MDB was under no illusions about challenging Geisel's candidacy in the Electoral College, set to meet in January 1974. Nonetheless, the party decided to play the presidential election game. They nominated São Paulo federal deputy Ulysses Guimarães for President and Barbosa Lima Sobrinho for Vice President. The latter was a distinguished nationalist intellectual from the Northeastern state of Pernambuco who was also president of the Brazilian Press Association. Ulysses Guimarães was a parliamentary veteran, having first been elected federal deputy in 1951 on the PSD ticket. After 1965 he had emerged as an energetic and fearless opposition leader, winning the MDB presidency in 1971. Ulysses had also become one of the

Médici government's most eloquent and savage critics. Indeed, to many military officers he was anathema. His nomination by the MDB in late September 1973 provoked tirades from such officers, who considered the MDB leaders as little more than apologists for terrorism and treason. The MDB leaders were well aware of this military opinion. Nominating Ulysses was in direct defiance of it.

In his September nomination acceptance speech Ulysses tore into the "pompous technocrats who curse and exorcise their opponents . . ."[166] An MDB president, he promised, would be committed to "an urgent break" with Brazil's "wretched structure of misery, disease, illiteracy, and backwardness, both technological and political."[167] Given the government's solid support for Geisel, the January 1974 vote seemed a foregone conclusion.

ARENA leaders made no secret of their confidence. In late October 1973 São Paulo MDB Senator Franco Montoro attacked government censorship, reading into the record a recent report on censorship in Brazil to the Inter-American Press Association by Júlio de Mesquita Neto, of the family who owned *O Estado de São Paulo*. Montoro knew that neither the report nor the stories about it would make it past the censors, any mention of censorship being strictly *verboten* in the press. So Montoro played upon this absurdity.

Senator Eurico Rezende, ARENA majority leader, replied aggressively, arguing that Brazil needed censorship "so they won't form a negative image of Brazil abroad." He threw down a challenge to Montoro. Why not have a plebiscite on whether to keep AI–5? "If Médici were to speak in São Paulo, Rio, and Belo Horizonte, you'd find out that in your state at least 70 percent of the public would favor retaining AI–5 for some time to come, and that would include some who have voted for you." It was an effective rhetorical device. It also posed no risk, since none of the leaders would ever contemplate such a plebiscite.[168]

In early December 1973 Senator Petrônio Portella, the ARENA leader, congratulated the government on the skill with which it had "defended the nation from terrorism." The government had successfully distinguished between the "necessary and useful work of the opposition" and the "surreptitious methods of subversive agents." Political conditions had been idyllic: "electoral campaigns have come and gone without any pressure or coercion, in a climate of mutual respect."[169] Speaking before the Electoral College in January 1974, Portella patronized the MDB, describing it as a "party shrinking with every election," and as "lacking both the political structure and the popular support to elect a President of the Republic."[170]

Some MDB leaders shared that conclusion, although not the arguments leading to it. They had argued for dissolving the party as a protest against continued collaboration with the military's sham democracy. But these party leaders had lost when the MDB nominated Ulysses Guimarães and Barbosa Lima Sobrinho in September 1973.

Now the question for the MDB was, How could they campaign within government rules and yet preserve any integrity? The MDB majority leaders answered with the idea of a "symbolical" campaign. They would declare themselves the "anti-candidates," denying the legitimacy of both the "anti-Constitution" and the "anti-elections." They would denounce torture, censorship, neglect of the workers, and favoritism to foreign economic interests. Not least important, this tactic would enable the MDB to continue its mobilization efforts among the wide range of Brazilians who were afraid to express any opposition to the military government.[171] The spirit of the MDB campaign was evident in its motto: *Navegar é preciso, viver não é preciso* (freely translated: "we must keep struggling, even in the face of death").[172] Ulysses and Barbosa Lima crisscrossed Brazil, attacking the government's record but never the military itself. They pressured the government censors to allow their speeches to reach the public. In fact, media coverage of the MDB increased. Yet the government's security forces continued their heavy-handed surveillance and police intimidation at opposition rallies.

The meeting of the Electoral College in January was an anticlimax. Geisel and Santos were elected by 400 to 76. Ulysses and Barbosa Lima did not even receive all the MDB votes. A dissident band (the *autênticos*) of 23 MDB deputies abstained. In their manifesto they announced they were "returning our votes to the great absentee: the Brazilian people, whose will, excluded from this process, should be the source of all power." They demanded the restoration of "democratic guarantees" (also demanded by Ulysses and Barbosa Lima), and appealed to Brazilians to support their protest.[173]

This split in the MDB was less serious than it may have appeared at the time. At issue was the MDB's proper role under a highly repressive regime. Both MDB factions wanted the end of that regime. Both sought to remain true to their moral and political principles. Neither thought there was any simple solution to their electoral plight. Both were working to guarantee their party a major role in a freer Brazil of the future.

The survival of the Congress offered one hint in that direction. True, the Congress had been humiliated at the end of 1968—suspended for almost two years, its powers largely shorn. MDB Congressmen were subjected to harassment and intimidation. Yet the thread of congressional legitimacy had not been broken. The Congress was never abolished, as were its counterparts in Argentina, Chile, and Uruguay during military governments in the 1960s and 1970s. Indeed, the Brazilian Congress was the scene of heated exchanges between ARENA and MDB orators in both houses.[174] Some sitting Congressmen and Senators were purged (none under Médici), and the threat of such arbitrary intervention hung over the head of every opposition (and some government!) deputy and senator; nonetheless, the congressional speeches were seldom censored. It is true that the most critical passages never saw light outside the pages of the *Diário de Congresso*. Yet ARENA Congressmen had to reply to the slashing MDB attacks on the government policies in every sphere from taxes to torture.

Even the Médici regime, Brazil's most repressive since 1964, thought it politic to reopen the Congress in 1970. The generals had left ajar a door that might open the way to democracy and the rule of law.

Human Rights and Brazil–U.S. Relations

We have seen in the preceding chapter how torture by the security forces of the Costa e Silva government drew worldwide attention. The Brazilian regime worried most about the reaction in the U.S. As Brazil's most important trading partner, investor, political ally, and mentor in anticommunism, the U.S. was crucial to Brazil's development. There had already been a strain on the alliance when the U.S. government grew worried over the authoritarian turn in December 1968 and then froze new U.S. aid commitments for the first five months of 1969. Aid commitments were resumed in mid-1969, not because Brazil's human rights record had improved but because "realists" in the U.S. government thought the freeze counterproductive. In fact, U.S. leverage was on the wane, because the dollar value of U.S. government assistance had become marginal in relation to Brazil's balance of payments and to its domestic public sector expenditures. In fiscal year 1974, for example, U.S. government aid totalled only $69.9 million, of which $52.7 million was military aid. The latter could easily be replaced if Brazil used its own dollars to buy arms elsewhere.[175]

Whatever U.S. "realists" thought about U.S. leverage, Brazil's record on human rights became steadily worse and more conspicuous during 1969. In December came a denunciation of Brazilian torture from a respected non-Brazilian source—Amnesty International, the international watchdog group that tracks "prisoners of conscience" around the world. Its report stimulated the first of many official Brazilian governmental "investigations," this time by the justice minister. In 1970 the charges were repeated by *Civiltà Cattolica,* a Jesuit publication, and by the International Commission of Jurists.[176] The U.S. government joined the chorus by issuing a statement in April confirming its expression of concern to the Brazilian government.[177] In August 1970 the Médici government created a Human Rights Council to hear alleged violations of human rights. Its subordination to the justice minister, who had denied all charges, doomed it to futility. In October President Médici flatly denied all charges of government torture. Two days later the Pope issued a statement condemning torture and alluding to Brazil. In early December Education Minister Jarbas Passarinho opened the first chink in the government armor. He admitted that torture had occurred, but only in isolated cases.[178] Charges and denials continued into 1971. No less a witness than Wiliams F. Buckley, Jr., expressed alarm in February 1971. He reported from Rio de Janeiro, on the word of an "apolitical" businessman, that the government was torturing. Indeed, lamented Buckley, "the fear is that in Brazil it is becoming endemic," as opposed to the Greek military dictatorship, where it was only "episodic."[179]

But with the decline of the guerrilla threat, government repression got fewer headlines abroad. The Médici government also benefitted, ironically, from increasing torture in other countries, whose notoriety eclipsed Brazil's. Meanwhile the government simply defied all criticism. It showed no sign of doubt or shame. On the contrary, Médici spokesmen accused their critics of being directly or indirectly manipulated by communists or Marxists. São Paulo Governor Abreu Sodré, for example, excoriated Dom Helder Camara, the outspoken critic who lectured widely in Europe and the U.S., as "this Fidel Castro in a cassock," who belonged to "the Communist Party's propaganda machine."[180]

U.S. critics had long argued that by its large-scale aid to Brazil the U.S. government was implicated in the Brazilian repression. In May 1971 Senator Frank Church, Democrat from Idaho and a leading critic of U.S. policy toward Brazil, conducted hearings on "U.S. Policies and Programs in Brazil." They provided a comprehensive look at all official U.S. programs, especially since 1964. The detailed information on the Office of Public Safety's (a USAID program to advise and assist security forces in recipient countries) operation in Brazil, for example, gave the critics new ammunition for arguing that U.S. tax dollars had gone into training and equipping possible torturers. There were charges that U.S. police advisers had participated in interrogation and even torture of prisoners.[181] In October 1971 Senator Fred Harris called for a cut in U.S. aid to Brazil, citing the Brazilian government's record of repression.[182] But there was no support for his proposal.

The Brazilian government simply waited out the unfavorable publicity, and its patience was rewarded. The Nixon government soon became a solid supporter of the Médici regime, both for its economic success and for its anticommunist credentials. President Médici visited Washington in December 1971 and was given a state dinner at the White House. Across Pennsylvania Avenue in Lafayette Park, a small band of protesters was hardly visible.[183] Whatever its reservations about human rights violations in Brazil, the Nixon administration had decided to give the Médici government its public support. The following month Secretary of the Treasury John Connally visited Brazil and announced his satisfaction with Delfim Neto's policies.[184] In July Arthur Burns, Chairman of the Federal Reserve and the most influential central banker in the western world, returned from a trip to Brazil full of praise for Delfim's "miraculous" work.[185]

U.S. opinion grew troubled, however, over the deepening authoritarianism which accompanied Brazil's burst of economic growth. A few days after Mr. Burns's visit to Brazil a *New York Times* editorial asked whether Brazil needed repression in order to achieve economic success.[186] Senator John Tunney, Democrat of California, proposed that all U.S. military aid to Brazil be suspended until the charges of systematic torture by Brazilian authorities had been satisfactorily answered.[187] Senator Frank Church joined Tunney in criticizing the Médici regime. U.S. academic and religious spokesmen continued their attacks on the "Brazilian model," charging that its repression allowed gross social injustices to continue uncontested. Interestingly enough, the USAID Public Safety Program was phased out in 1972.

Notwithstanding these attacks, the Nixon administration found Brazil's developmental direction more and more to its liking. Secretary of State William Rogers visited Brazil in May 1973, indicating continued U.S. support for the Médici government.[188] His visit was the prelude to an announcement in June that the U.S. had agreed to sell supersonic fighter planes to Brazil, a decision reached after sharp debate within the White House.[189] Virtually the only dissent came from the State Department. The U.S. military felt strongly that U.S. refusal to supply such weaponry would only alienate an important ally. The decision did further arouse the U.S. congressional critics of Brazilian policy, however, who were upset at arming a military government so implicated in repressing its own people. The critics were also worried that supplying these planes to Brazil might stimulate neighboring countries to escalate their arms purchases. In January 1974 the *Times* repeated its question about the link between authoritarian policies and economic development: Was it necessary to have a repressive government in order to achieve economic growth? Had the U.S. jeopardized its future relations with Brazil by identifying so closely with the Brazilian military?[190]

Taking Stock: What Kind of Regime?

Brazil's government at the end of the military's first decade of rule was an "authoritarian situation," in the words of political sociologist Juan Linz.[191] By that he meant Brazil had not carried out the political institutionalization typical of Franco's Spain. Even the Médici regime's use of political controls after 1968 stopped short of being as total as in most of postwar Eastern Europe, Castro's Cuba, or Salazar's Portugal. For millions of Brazilians, in fact, the Médici years probably seemed little different from previous eras. The relatively low degree of previous political participation, even before Goulart's overthrow in 1964, meant that many (perhaps most) middle-sector Brazilians were not greatly disturbed at their loss of political options.

Opinion surveys taken in 1972–73 (and in which the responses were remarkably frank) showed that ". . . for the poor, politics take a back seat to poverty and, for the rich, to industrial growth and the amenities that accompany it. Nowhere, regardless of social position, does political participation rise from the bottom of mass priorities."[192] A great majority of a sample of urban workers in central and southeast Brazil, for example, said that "a strong government is more important than an elected one."[193] This confirmed what many politicians, journalists, and diplomats said at the time: Médici had achieved a significant following.

The skillful PR campaign undoubtedly helped. So did the extraordinary economic growth. What elected president wouldn't like to have a growth rate of 11 percent per year in his record? Important also was winning soccer's World Cup, on which the president had gambled his prestige. If Médici had not been popular, would he have risked regular attendance at soccer matches, where spontaneous booing was always a danger for unwary politicians? His government exploited that popularity to divert attention from the repression and from the hugely unequal distribution of benefits from growth.[194]

If the hard-line military held the initiative throughout this era, and if they had been so determined to restrict political conflict to conform to their conception of the limits of dissent, why did they keep up the pretense of an eventual return to liberal democracy? Why did they fail to promote the creation of a totally new political system, perhaps along the lines of the Partido Revolucionario Institucional (PRI) in Mexico? In short, why did they fail to remove the ambiguities as Vargas did in 1937? By creating a one-party system, for example, the government might have resolved social conflicts outside the public eye more effectively than by using the emasculated legislatures of the early 1970s.

To abolish parties and legislatures altogether, as the military government later did in Chile, would probably had made their administrative task easier. Furthermore, there was readily at hand an ideological rationale for such solutions: corporatism. As we have seen, a small group of high Médici government officials tried to sell the president and the higher military on corporatism. Their task was eased by the fact that some corporatist elements had already entered Brazil's legal structure in the 1930s, and especially in Getúlio Vargas's Estado Nôvo. There was, furthermore, strong support for corporatism among the elite, as 1972–73 opinion surveys showed.[195]

Yet the corporatists' campaign was cut short when Ernesto Geisel's supporters won control of the presidential succession. Neither a one-party nor a non-party course was adopted. Why? One explanation may lie in the persistent, if ill-founded, belief that the malfunctioning of the representative system was only temporary, that if just one *more* set of corrupt or subversive or irresponsible politicians could be purged then all would go well in the political system. This attitude—which seems naive in retrospect—prevailed during the Castelo Branco era, and Ernesto Geisel and his supporters were loyal castelistas.

Another explanation for the attitude of the civilian revolutionaries may have been their attitude toward Vargas and what he symbolized for them. For the former UDN leaders prominent in the Castelo Branco government, such as Juracy Magalhães, Milton Campos, Eduardo Gomes, Juarez Távora, and Luiz Vianna Filho, the 1964 coup offered a chance at federal power that they had seldom been able to win against the populist politicians. Now they could reverse history and undo the damage done by their archopponent, Getúlio. Yet what were they attempting to reverse? Was it the democratically elected politician of 1951–54 or the dictator of the Estado Nôvo? Their doctrinaire antipopulism did not allow them to distinguish. One might suspect that their memories of the Estado Nôvo inhibited them from considering how to create a new structure for the Revolution of 1964. Tancredo Neves, a veteran politician and opposition leader, taunted them by calling the 1964 Revolution "the Estado Nôvo of the UDN."[196] It is likely that many civilian moderates feared Getúlio's political ghost too much to emulate the authoritarian institution-building efforts of his Estado Nôvo.

Such naiveté could not be attributed to the hardliners, however. The latter had never had illusions about the viability of representative democracy in Brazil over the short run or even the medium run. Yet they avoided publicly repudiating the Brazilian political elite's faith in the liberal idea. Why?

Ironically, it may be that the military extremists lacked confidence in their own ability to proclaim and direct a straightforwardly authoritarian regime because they feared the disapproval of international opinion. Influenced in a major way by their contacts with the American military, they wished to maintain a close alliance with the United States. They prized American support not only for its military and economic significance, but also for its symbolic importance. They saw America as the bastion of anticommunism, an ideology that furnished the justification for their unrelenting hold on the levers of power in Brazil. America's enormous investment in Vietnam was proof to them of her commitment to the battle against subversion they waged at home.

At the same time America preached the doctrine of liberal democracy. Thus the dependence of these authoritarian officers on America reinforced their contadictory position in domestic politics. On the one hand, they demanded emergency powers to fight the counterinsurgency war that United States foreign policy would seem to promote. On the other hand, they sought the approval of United States public opinion, which preferred democratic government and guaranteed civil liberties. The technocrats may also have shied away from embracing authoritarianism more openly because they feared the impact on world opinion. Educated in the ideals of political liberalism, they admired the technical and economic advancement achieved by the United States and the European democracies. Most apparently preferred to believe that Brazil need not opt for a long-term authoritarian solution.

How long could this alliance of hardliners and technocrats last? Would 1945 repeat itself? Would the oft-spoken commitment to liberal democracy finally come back to haunt the revolutionaries? The answer appeared to depend on two variables: the world context and the economic record. With respect to the former, it is worth remembering that Vargas's Estado Nôvo ran aground when the defeat of the Axis doomed fascist governments all over Europe—except in the Iberian peninsula. The coup of 1964 coincided with a swing toward "pragmatism" in United States policy toward Latin America. The anticommunist, private enterprise theme was resuscitated after its lull during the Kennedy presidency. That emphasis continued in United States Latin American policy, and the Rockefeller Report (1969) could be seen as a basic document in that policy. Had that policy changed, the Brazilian authoritarian regime would have found the international climate much less supportive.

The regime's economic success was important because failure to maintain the growth rate could alienate much of its support by the middle sector, which had never accepted the hardliner justification for authoritarianism. With continued expansion in the world economy, there was no a priori reason why an intelligently managed Brazilian economy could not continue to average high growth. Yet continuous economic success was a rare commodity in history, especially in Latin America. Perhaps it would have been prudent to assume that at some point the growth rate would falter, that the contradictions in the Brazilian model would become more evident, and that the failure to institutionalize the 1964 Revolution would appear more costly. But there is no evidence that any significant government insider was thinking along these lines in 1974.

The Brazilian military government as of 1974 can be defined as an "authoritarian situation" in part because it had not produced a Franco. The Médici government stuck by the timetable for the presidential succession in 1974 despite the fact that some hard-line military and their civilian allies were agitating to prolong Médici's rule. If successful, they would have led Brazil in the direction later taken by Pinochet's Chile. How was it avoided in Brazil? It was avoided because most of the military had agreed that they must allow no caudillo to emerge, no strongman who would fasten one-man rule on Brazil. Médici honored this principle. He was about to pass power to another general, but one with a different past, different allies, and a different agenda. Although this rotation of power could not guarantee change, at least it precluded the caudillo, whose tenure is limited only by God and the number of his enemies' guns.

VI

GEISEL: TOWARD *ABERTURA*

Ernesto Geisel reached the presidency as the climax to a carefully orchestrated campaign. The castelistas, having lost control of the Planalto in 1967 and having suffered through the presidencies of Costa e Silva and Médici, had fought their way back into power. They had done their homework; the military consensus behind the new general-president, once nominated, was solid.[1] The presidential succession came off more smoothly than any since 1964.

The Return of the Castelistas

The new President was yet another from Rio Grande do Sul.[2] Geisel's father was a staunch German Lutheran who had emigrated to Brazil in 1890 and become a school teacher. He inculcated in his children the importance of education. Ernesto attended military school and then officer training. He was first in his class both times. He then followed an orthodox army career, with interesting political interludes. In 1934, for example, he was briefly the state secretary of Finance and Public Works in the state of Paraíba, which the federal government had intervened. In 1945 he attended the Army Command and General Staff College in Fort Leavenworth, Kansas—the kind of U.S. experience standard among the castelistas. In 1946–47 he was a key staff member in the Dutra government when it purged communists and leftists from labor unions. Later he was on the permanent staff of the Higher War College, another castelista redoubt. Soon thereafter he became an administrator in Petrobrás, the huge state oil monopoly. There he had the chance to sharpen his skills as a military technocrat.

Between 1961 and 1967 Geisel was deeply involved in national politics, always as an active-duty officer. He was a top staff aide to War Minister Odílio Denis in August 1961, when President Jânio Quadros suddenly resigned. When the presidency passed temporarily to Chamber of Deputies president Ranieri Mazzilli, because Vice Presdient João Goulart was then travelling in the People's Republic of China, Mazzilli named Geisel to head his Presidential Military Staff. Geisel subsequently played a key role in arranging the political compromise by which Goulart, whom the military ministers tried to bar from the presidency, was allowed to assume office at the cost of greatly reduced powers under a parliamentary system.

Immediately after the 1964 coup, Geisel helped organize officer pressure on the Congress (which did the electing) to elect Castelo Branco president. Once elected, Castelo named Geisel head of his Military Presidential Staff. There he helped ward off the *linha dura* while also increasing presidential powers, as in AI–2. Geisel strongly opposed Costa e Silva's presidential candidacy and along withh Golbery fought it to the end.

Geisel left the Planalto in 1967 to become a minister of the Supreme Military Tribunal. There he was known for his tough interpretation of the security laws in judging such defendants as the student leaders arrested in October 1968. After two years on the Tribunal Geisel left for the presidency of Petrobrás, a prized position for a military technocrat. While there (1969–73) he successfully opposed efforts to extend the state monopoly from oil production into petrochemicals and the distribution of petroleum products. In that decision Geisel was following the castelista view that the state's economic role should be reduced in favor of private enterprise. At Petrobrás Geisel continued the policy of only modest oil exploration in Brazil, sensible at a time when cheap oil was plentiful on the world market.

In sum, Geisel brought to the Planalto a range of experience unusually broad for a top army officer. Especially important was his time at Petrobrás, Brazil's largest and one of the 25 largest non-U.S. corporations in the world. There he was exposed to economic analysis and decision-making on a macroeconomic level, particularly unusual for a general. Equally important was his earlier service on the Supreme Military Tribunal, where he came face to face with the human cost of the repression that intensified after December 1968. And as a Lutheran, he was Brazil's first non-Catholic president.

Geisel was known to have a relatively closed personality. His managerial style was autocratic, and had little of the charm and personal warmth so charcteristic of Brazilians in public life. Geisel's style quickly became evident when he downgraded the AERP, the high-powered public relations office that had so effectively promoted President Médici's image.[3] Like his mentor, Castelo Branco, Geisel wanted no part of a personalistic propaganda campaign. The official media shots now pictured a president whose austere style was the very opposite of his predecessor's slick identification with soccer champions. Geisel was also known as a perfectionist who immersed himself in administrative details. Subordinates called him a glutton for paperwork. In short, he was a tough administrator who called all his own shots. In this presidency there would be no doubt where the buck stopped.

Geisel's cabinet contained no surprises. Delfim Neto, the most powerful civilian minister in the outgoing Médici government, was replaced by

Mario Henrique Simonsen, another economics professor whose policies figured to be more orthodox than those of Delfim. The latter was sent off as ambassador to France, one of Brazil's most prestigious diplomatic posts. Clearly the new government wanted Delfim and his formidable political skills and ambitions far from Brazil. The Planning Ministry, on the other hand, remained in the hands of João Paulo Reis Velloso, the Northeast-born economist who was now the principal link in economic poilcy with the Médici government. The ministries of Health (Paulo de Almeida Machado), Communications (Commander Euclides Quandt de Oliveira), Mines and Energy (Shigeaki Ueki), Agriculture (Alysson Paulinelli), and Interior (Rangel Reis) went to technicians well-established in their respective fields. None represented any political weight.

Among the more interesting political appointees were Armando Falcão (Justice), who had held the same ministry in Juscelino Kubitschek's government, and Ney Braga (Education), a Christian Democrat (PDC) and former governor of Paraná, which made him one of only two ministers (the other being Falcão) who had ever won major electoral office. The new Minister of Labor and Social Security, Arnaldo da Costa Prieto, had been a relatively minor figure in the Riograndense ARENA. Severo Gomes, the new Minister of Industry and Trade, was a São Paulo businessman who had begun his political career in ARENA and had been Castelo Branco's agriculture minister; he had since earned the reputation of an economic nationalist. Foreign Affairs went to Antonio Francisco Azeredo da Silveira, a career diplomat, and most recently ambassador to Argentina. Transport and Public Works went to General Dirceu Nogueira, a Riograndense with training as an engineer.

The man who wielded greatest political weight in this cabinet was General Golbery, who now became head of the Civilian Presidential Staff. After leaving the Planalto in 1967 Golbery worked for Dow Chemical, first as a consultant and then as its president for Brazil. Holding that highly-paid post with a multinational firm opened Golbery to constant attack from Brazilian nationalists and military hardliners (although the censors kept such criticism out of the media).[4] The directorship of the SNI went to General João Batista de Oliveira Figueiredo, who had been head of the Military Presidential Staff under Médici, but who was also considered a castelista. The new holder of his former post was General Dilermando do Gomes Monteiro, also a loyal castelista.[5]

Several characteristics of this new cabinet were noteworthy. First, there were no "superministers," such as Médici had created in Delfim and Orlando Geisel. This was a cabinet led by the president. Second, there were no figures of prominent independent political stature.

The Geisel government—i.e., the president and his castelista collaborators—had four principal goals. The first was to maintain majority support within the military while eventually reducing the power of the hard line and restoring the military's more purely professional role. Solid military support was the sine qua non; without it no president could carry out any significant political changes. Although the castelistas had won out in the presidential succession, the three services were full of duristas deeply suspicious of the castelistas' desire to move toward political liberalization. Many of these officers were directly involved in the torture network which functioned under army command. Geisel would have to keep the duristas on the defensive while hoping to reduce their number by shrewd use (working through the military ministers) of promotions and military assignments. None of this intra-military politics could be discussed publicly. The public would continue to hear only banalities (with nuances lost on all but the cognoscenti) from military officers at their regular public ceremonies.

Returning to a more "professional" role for the military meant convincing officers that the long-run interest of the military services and of Brazil lay in shedding the role of a repressive national police and instead concentrating on updating equipment, organization, and planning of the three services. This approach appealed especially to officers who were neither duristas nor castelistas but who wanted to get the military "out of politics." It appealed also to those who worried about the corruption that had already penetrated military ranks as the officers settled into power.[6]

The new government's second goal was to control the "subversives." Almost none of the armed guerrillas had survived the Médici government's repression (except for a dying remnant in Amazonia). Yet the security forces—led by the duristas—continued to find dangerous enemies in every corner of Brazilian society. Geisel and Golbery agreed that Brazil still had subversives, but they knew the security forces were a hotbed of opposition to liberalization, and believed that some were overestimating the subversive threat to further their political aims. They would have to proceed slowly, so that the government wouldn't be left disarmed vis-à-vis the subversives. They did not want to hand the duristas an opportunity to accuse the Geisel government of being "soft" on the left.

Pursuing the first two goals—maintaining military support and controlling the subversives—required a delicate balancing act. To gain the legitimacy in military eyes to fight the duristas, Geisel would have to act tough against not only the subversives but the entire center-left.

The new government's third goal was an eventual return to democracy, albeit of an undefined variety. Here Geisel was true to Castelo Branco's vision: the Revolution of 1964 should, after a limited period of emergency government, lead to a prompt return to representative democracy. Geisel's hints of redemocratization had generated intense speculation among government opponents in the Church, the MDB, the Bar Association, and the press.

What was the Geisel–Golbery idea of redemocratization? Lacking detailed pre-1974 statements from the principals, we can still identify several points. First, the castelistas had ruled out the corporatist ideas certain Médici advisers had pushed in 1970–71. The castelistas had also decided against turning ARENA into a Mexican-style one-party system.[7] Addressing his first cabinet meeting in March 1974, Geisel promised "sincere efforts toward a gradual but sure democratic improvement." He suggested that "creative political imagination" might make it possible to replace the government's "exceptional powers" with "effective safeguards" compatible with a "constitutional framework."[8] Notwithstanding these assurances, Geisel and his team had no intention of letting the opposition win power. They envisioned a democracy in which the pro-government party (or parties) would continue to enjoy unquestioned sway. It was that emphasis that led some observers to believe that Geisel, despite his denials, really had in mind a PRI-style party. The Geisel government also knew that it could never move far toward even this kind of liberalization unless it could at the same time carry out the delicate balancing act with the military.

The fourth goal was to maintain high economic growth. The castelistas knew how high the stakes were here. They knew that the Médici government had depended on its high economic growth rate to give it legitimacy. Geisel made it clear to his technocrat policymakers that high growth was essential.

The new government was also concerned about the increasingly unequal distribution of benefits from economic growth. Although Geisel's government did not regard correcting this as an overriding goal, they nonetheless thought more equal distribution ought to accompany political liberalization. A first step was the creation of a new Ministry of Social Welfare to bring together the ill-coordinated welfare programs created by past governments. Its first minister was Luiz Gonzaga do Nascimento e Silva, a lawyer and technocrat who had headed the National Housing Bank in the Castelo Branco government.

Measures to distribute better the benefits from the economic "miracle" would be far easier to enact if high growth continued. With an increasing pie, relative shares could be altered without anyone losing in absolute terms. That was a further reason to maintain high growth.

Liberalization from Within?

Geisel and Golbery wanted to liberalize the authoritarian regime they had inherited. But so did many other Brazilians. Numerous intellectuals, journalists, and politicians, from both the ARENA and the MDB, had ideas about how to phase out Brazil's repressive military regime. They all faced one great psychological barrier: how to move gradually from absolute authoritarianism (as expressed in such documents as AI–5 and the National Security Law) to a more open, semi-rule-of-law, semi-democratic nation? The term "semi" illustrates the problem. Could there be a "semi" *habeas corpus*? Wasn't the rule of *habeas corpus* either observed or not observed? How could a regime "semi" censor? How could a government "semi" resort to the decree that permitted secret decrees? Golbery was fond of saying "out of power there is no solution." Now he had the chance to shape the castelista solutions.

These issues had begun to be debated even before the end of Médici's term.[9] Leitão de Abreu, head of the Civilian Presidential Staff under Médici, in mid-1972 took the initiative in discussing how the repression might be phased out in favor of a more open system. Also involved was Professor Candido Mendes de Almeida, a leading lay Catholic and political scientist. Mendes de Almeida arranged for Professor Samuel Huntington, a Harvard political scientist who specialized in the politics of developing countries and on the politics of the military, to visit Brazil in October 1972 for extensive talks with Leitão de Abreu annd Delfim Neto. Huntington later described both as having "recognized the need for an end to the extreme forms of repression that had existed and for an opening of the political system." Leitão posed some difficult questions to his visitor: "How can decompression occur in authoritarian political systems?" and "What is the best model for Brazil to follow in this regard?"

At Leitão's request, Huntington wrote in 1973 a paper entitled "Approaches to Political Decompression," giving his answers to Leitão's queries. He argued that "the relaxation of controls in any authoritarian political system can often have an explosive effect in which the process gets out of the control of those who initiated it. . . ." He further argued that such regimes should give first priority to institutionalization, and he suggested that the Brazilian government study carefully the Mexican one-party system of managing an orderly presidential succession. Huntington stressed also the weakness of Brazilian political parties, pointing to Mexico's PRI as the model of an effective party. And he concluded by recommending Mexico and Turkey as examples of comparable Third World countries that had successfully institutionalized their political systems.[10]

Huntington's document stimulated immediate debate among Brazilian intellectuals and academics. Wanderley Guilherme dos Santos, a Stanford-trained political scientist based in Rio de Janeiro, gave the most complete response in his "Strategies of Political Decompression," a paper presented at a September 1973 seminar sponsored by a non-partisan congressional research institute in Brasília.[11] Wanderley gave a sophisticated rationale for a gradual and highly controlled political liberalization. Unlike Huntington, who played down the reintroduction of classic liberal rights, Wanderley saw Brazil's goal as the restoration of six principles, in descending order of importance: independence of the judiciary; freedom of speech and the press; *habeas corpus* and other individual rights; freedom to organize in support of political views; orderly rules governing competition for political power; clear-cut legal procedures for the use of coercion.[12]

Wanderly laid out a piecemeal strategy for achieving this goal. The policy had to be "incrementlist," taking only small steps in order to avoid "the risks of recompression." The latter could, after all, return Brazil to an even deeper state of authoritarianism. The secret was to avoid "simultaneous pressure" on different fronts, as well as avoiding "an accumulation of challenges," both of which could overload the authoritarian regime's capacity to "absorb" discrete moves toward liberalization. Wanderley further argued the need for agreement on which steps would be carried out in which order. He suggested that the first step ought to be the phasing out of censorship and the reinstitution of free speech. Other steps should come later, along with reorganization of political party structures.

Wanderley's document was important on several counts. First, the author argued that liberalization could be achieved *only* if the opposition chose to collaborate with the government on a gradualistic process. Such advice flew in the face of those militant oppositionists, such as MDB leader Ulysses Guimarães, who demanded a complete and immediate return to democracy and the rule of law. Second, Wanderley never mentioned the military. His reference to the danger of a "recompression" obviously meant the hard-line military, but the reader had to make that link. His omission was hardly surprising. It reflected a tactic common to the moderate opposition who sought to preserve the fiction of military neutrality in politics. Their objective was to maintain room for the military to leave power with decorum. By avoiding direct attacks on the military, the moderates hoped to use the military's self-image of political neutrality to convince them to withdraw, assume their more traditional (*poder moderador*) role, and allow liberalization to proceed.

In subsequent discussion at the congressional seminar Pernambuco Senator Marcos Freire, a centrist MDB critic of the government, attacked the Wanderley strategy for "helping royally those who justify political authoritarianism."[13] Freire thought a far better strategy was the one followed in the redemocratization of 1945–46, when President Getúlio Vargas was deposed and a Constituent Assembly elected, which then wrote the constitution for a new republic. For Freire it was now a matter of "those in power being really ready to accept the will of the people alone."[14] This was the all-or-nothing mentality that Wanderley had been at pains to reject. The other MDB speaker was Deputy Lisaneas Maciel, a Methodist preacher and an unrelenting leftist critic of the military regime. He pointed to the military as "the only group that has decision-making power in the country," and he asked pointedly if they were not subject to "foreign pressures," especially from the U.S.[15] In his reply Wanderley sidestepped that issue, arguing that any consideration of it should be subsequent to the gradual steps toward liberalization.

Much elite expectation about the new government centered on the hope that Geisel would bring the repressive apparatus, especially the torturers, under control. The non-elite, by contrast, could hardly share that hope, since they suffered from repressive police practices under *both* democratic and authoritarian regimes. In late February Geisel, as President-elect, nourished those hopes by conferring with Cardinal Arns of São Paulo, an outspoken critic of the government for its frequent violation of human rights. Emissaries of the National Conference of Brazilian Bishops (CNBB) met with General Golbery and were encouraged by what they heard. Pressed by religious and secular critics for a commitment to return to the rule of law, Golbery showed genuine reponsiveness, although invariably speaking off the record. Optimism grew when in mid-March Geisel promised "sincere efforts toward a gradual but sure democratic improve-ment," although he also pointedly warned that "security" was indispens-able to ensure development.[16] It was, after all, still a military government.

There was one clue as to where the new government might be headed. In February 1974 Golbery had invited Samuel Huntington to Brazil again, where he had intensive talks with Golbery, who had studied his 1973 paper, and with others on the new team. Golbery was anxious to think through the process by which a gradual but steady broadening of participation in the political system could be achieved. He was focusing on what he termed "intermediary bodies," such as the Church, the press, universities, and labor. He thought the government had to establish channels of consultation with these groups, bringing them into the political system one at a time. Golbery also had a list of more specific questions, such as how the Congress and the political parties could be strengthened, how big money could be limited in elections, and how to expand the suffrage.[17]

One thing was clear. Geisel and Golbery did not plan a simple return to 1964. Yet, what kind of opposition would they allow to be legalized? The Communist Party? Which one? What of the other parties on the frag-mented left? What of the populists, a prime target of the Revolution of 1964?

Did the castelista desire to liberalize stem from a faith in the political institutions as they expected to overhaul them? If so, what features of the authoritarian structure would be retained? AI–5? The National Security Law? The 1969 amendments to the Constitution? Not surprisingly, the new government had not even hinted at their answers to any of the weighty questions they raised about the medium- and long-run political future. Only one thing was certain. Geisel and Golbery envisioned a gradual and highly controlled opening.[18]

For now, much elite opinion wanted to give the new President the bene-fit of the doubt. After all, redemocratization could come *only* under mili-tary leadership, and the military could hardly be expected to risk sudden large-scale changes. After his first few weeks in office, Geisel enjoyed an exceptionally favorable press. By late March *The New York Times,* ever an important foreign bellwether, was praising Geisel for his efforts.[19] But— the army officer corps held less favorable, if less public, views. In February a vicious anti-Golbery manifesto began circulating among army officers. By mid-April two more had appeared. Golbery minimized their importance, noting that such views had always existed.

The Geisel regime's first six months saw continuous maneuvering by government and civilian critics over possible redemocratization. It was clear from the outset that the Geisel-Golbery goal of liberalization would lead them into a confrontation with the torturers and the SNI. Geisel's military objective was to return power to the four-star generals, who had lost authority in the jungle of DOI-CODI, the SNI, and the welter of right-wing paramilitary terrorist groups. Of those observers who perceived the looming battle, few thought Geisel and Golbery had a chance.

Geisel chose to begin his administration with a drive to leash the DOI-CODI units. Some progress was made by General Reinaldo Mello de Almedia (a liberal, and son of the renowned writer-politician José Américo de Almeida), commander of the First Army (based in Rio). Less was made elsewhere around the country. One feature in this struggle much impressed the Geisel forces: military hierarchy had often been flouted as the security forces (DOI-CODI) were able to routinely ignore the chain of command. That meant the torture teams could proceed without danger of being reined in by higher command. Geisel and the castelistas saw this "subversion of military hierarchy" as highly dangerous and made it a prime target for their offensive against the torturers.[20]

In the early months of Geisel's presidency there were signs that the duristas still controlled that apparatus and were using it to undermine the move toward liberalization. An incident in the Northeast illustrated the problem. Just two days before Geisel's inauguration, the Fourth Army command, headquartered in Recife, arrested Carlos Garcia, a well-respected journalist who headed the Recife bureau of O Estado de São Paulo. After interrogation and torture, Garcia was released. The owners of O Estado, who had been archenemies and stubborn critics of military rule, vigorously protested the mistreatment of their reporter, against whom no public charges were ever brought. The incident seemed well chosen to give Geisel's new government the worst possible publicity.[21]

The hard line was on the offensive elsewhere as well. In early April a prominent São Paulo lawyer, Washington Rocha Cantral, was arrested and tortured, Upon release he sued CODI for illegal detention and mistreatment. The Bar Association strongly protested their colleague's "physical and moral torture." The fact that he could be hauled in and tortured showed how little government behavior had changed from the Médici era. But the fact that he dared to sue the army and that the Bar Association so vociferously supported him showed how much the public mood had changed. Fear of the security forces had begun to ebb, and one elite institution was ready to challenge them.[22]

As one of Rocha's colleagues said, the repression is "as bad as ever. But now we have hopes that the Government will do something about it and that's why we're pushing the issue."[23] April also saw an attack on CEBRAP, the internationally known social science research center organized with Ford Foundation funding by faculty purged from the University of São Paulo in 1969. Two senior researchers were arrested and one was badly tortured. Here again the security forces (apparently DOI-CODI and CIEX) chose an internationally visible target, guaranteeing the Geisel government embarrassment abroad.

What made these events so painful was that they collided with the hope the Geisel team had aroused. Foreign journalists had reported in detail the off-the-record promises made by the new government.[24] Censorship was going to be eased, the security forces would be brought under control, and the government would welcome an increase in the constructive input by Brazil's civil society.

Late May brought further signs that the hard line might be prevailing. The federal censors cracked down on the media, including the leading newsweekly *Veja,* which now faced stricter prior censhorship of copy.[25] They were reacting to more aggressive criticism from the opposition. The Brazilian Bar Association expressed concern over the government's failure to account for missing persons believed to have been apprehended by security forces. Even under the Médici repression the vast majority of detainees were known to be held at some police or military facility. That localization (even though often abruptly changed) made it possible for human rights groups in Brazil and abroad to trace prisoners and attempt to intervene on their behalf. In the case of "disappearances," however, the security forces could (and did) disclaim knowledge of the "disappeared" and thereby frustrate legal inquiry.[26] In July the MDB formally requested Justice Minister Armando Falcão to comment on the whereabouts of persons believed held by the government.[27] Cardinal Arns led a delegation that presented General Golbery with a list of 22 "missing persons," complete with extensive documentation from those who had last seen them, many in prison. Of the 22 missing, 21 had "disappeared" since Geisel took office. The implied question was obvious: was the government not in control of the security apparatus? Golbery promised to investigate all the cases and to reply promptly.[28] In August the National Bar Association (OAB) devoted its national convention in Rio entirely to "The Lawyer and the Rights of Man." In a stirring closing speech the OAB President, João Ribeiro de Castro Filho, proclaimed that "the technocrats will continue working like machines while we shall be the defenders of man."[29]

In October came further evidence that liberalization was far from imminent. The first was the arrest and torture in Recife of a former Methodist missionary, an American who had left church service and settled in Brazil, where he was a part-time correspondent for *Time* and the Associated Press. His interrogators apparently thought he was responsible for foreign news stories favorable to Dom Helder Camara, a leading critic of the military regime. It was even more likely that the notably hard-line Fourth Army command was deliberately challenging the Geisel government. Fred Morris became the first full U.S. citizen, i.e., not of dual citizenship, to have been tortured.[30] The incident provoked a major crisis in U.S.–Brazilian relations. At first the Fourth Army command in Recife denied that they were holding Morris. On that basis Brasília told the U.S. embassy there was no Morris case. Soon thereafter, to Brasília's embarrassment, the Fourth Army admitted they had Morris. The U.S. consul then visited Morris at the military quarters and confirmed that he had been tortured. This news shocked the embassy. It also made clear that the security forces had chosen a victim, an American, whose detention would create acute embarrassment for the Geisel government.

Once the consul had been able to see Morris, his torture stopped, but Morris was not released for several weeks, presumably so any physical evidence of torture would fade. Morris was then expelled by presidential decree. This case dramatized the U.S. government's interest in "liberalization." It also led to a (government-inspired) press campaign against U.S. Ambassador John Crimmins, who had vigorously protested to the Brazilian government about Morris's treatment. In late November Crimmins returned to Washington for home leave, and the campaign died down. Once back in Brasília, however, Crimmins discovered that the incident had reduced his effectiveness with army sectors of the Geisel regime. But the State Department backed him, and he remained in Brazil.[31]

The second incident in October revolved around Francisco Pinto, a firebrand MDB federal deputy. Back in mid-March, when foreign heads of state assembled in Brasília for Geisel's inauguration, Pinto spoke in the Chamber of Deputies denouncing Chilean President Pinochet (who had seized power only months earlier in the coup against Salvador Allende) as a "fascist" and "the oppressor of the Chilean people." The hardliners were incensed that a fellow army officer from Spanish America—and a leading anticommunist—could be so freely abused by a Brazilian Congressman. The justice minister immediately moved against Pinto under the powers of the National Security Law.[32] With that cloud still over his head, Pinto repeated his attack on Pinochet on a radio broadcast from the interior of Bahia, the Congressman's home state. The Geisel government must have worried that Pinto's outbursts might become a rerun of the 1968 Márcio Moreira Alves case which furnished the pretext for the takeover by the hard line. Pinto was charged with insulting a head of state of a friendly nation, a crime under the National Security Law. His prosecution dragged on. In October he was finally deprived of his congressional seat and stripped of his political rights. It was done under authority of the National Security Law, rather than Institutional Act No. 5, a distinction that encouraged those optimists who hoped Geisel might let the latter "arbitrary" instrument lapse into disuse.

Notwithstanding the periodic eruptions from the *linha dura*-oriented security forces, animated talk about liberalization continued. In August Harvard Professor Samuel Huntington, the ever-willing consultant to Brazilian reformers, returned to Rio for a seminar on "Legislatures and Development." The mere fact that the seminar could be held was notable, given the fact that the repressive security apparatus was still in place.[33] *O Estado de São Paulo* gave high marks to the Geisel government for encouraging debate over questions of basic political organization.[34] More to the point, President Geisel shortly thereafter reiterated his commitment to liberalization. But he also warned the opposition against attempting to manipulate public opinion in order to pressure the government. Creating such pressures, Geisel warned, "would only generate counterpressures of equal or greater weight, thereby reversing the slow, gradual, and secure *distensão* [liberalization] . . . and ending up in a climate of deepening polarization and rigid radicalization, with calls to emotional irrationality and destructive violence. And this, I assure you, the government will not permit."[35]

Geisel's "counterpressures" were the hard line and its ragtag band of civilian allies, including Justice Minister Falcão, who acted as a government contact with them. By the implicit rules of current political discussion no one could say openly the military was the object of their worry. In the press coverage of the contemporary debates over liberalization the reader will find only veiled references to divergent opinion within the military.

One could, however, read between the lines. In mid-August, for example, Carlos Castello Branco found the prospects for liberalization improved because "conditions on the flank are being systematically bolstered (*saneadas*) by the current President of the Republic." The use of the military term "flank" was not coincidental. But the next day Castello Branco informed his readers that the Geisel government had decided they could not depend on rapid economic growth to give them legitimacy. That would not offer sufficient long-term stability. The only way out was political liberalization. But that was a dangerous game, since it would inevitably provoke destabilization efforts from the duristas, or from "fanaticism," in Castello Branco's euphemism.[36] One thing was certain. The Geisel government would not be pressured into any rigid schedule of political change. The pace would be set by the Planalto, not the opposition.[37]

Hoping to accelerate liberalization, the politicians and constitutional lawyers began using the "creative imagination" called for by the President. Flavio Marcílio, ARENA pillar and President of the Chamber of Deputies, suggested that AI-5, the sine qua non of the arbitrary regime, should be incorporated in the Constitution. He was immediately attacked by MDB Deputy Marcos Freire, who found it "absurd" to consider incorporating into the constitution an extra-constitutional act.[38] Obviously, it would not be easy to find legal formulae to fit any new political realities.

November 1974: An MDB Victory

All these struggles between government and critics were but a minor prelude to the congressional elections of November 1974, Brazil's most important electoral test at the federal level since 1964. The Geisel government had received a contradictory electoral legacy from its predecessor. On the one hand, the Médici government had blocked the MDB from controlling any state government by making the election of governors, scheduled for October 1974, indirect. The state legislatures, easily manipulated by Brasília, would do the electing. On the other hand, the November congressional elections were to be direct. The Médici regime had its own way of meeting such political challenges. In the congressional elections of 1970, for example, Brasília resorted to massive intimidation of the electorate and harassment of the opposition. But what if the elections were relatively free?

ARENA swept the indirect election of governors in October 1974. This should not have been surprising in light of ARENA's control of all the legislatures that did the electing, yet the Planalto's political strategists may have misconstrued the victory's meaning. Time and again moderate revolutionaries had underestimated the depth of electoral opposition to their military governments. Perhaps they were once more lulled into a false sense of security by the ARENA leaders, who exuded confidence about the upcoming Congressional elections. As late as early October few informed political observers would have bet against an ARENA sweep.

The President's attitude was decisive here. His approach to elections was much like that of Castelo Branco, including a highly moralistic view of candidates and voters. Like Castelo, Geisel believed that Brazilian voters would vote for good candidates, if given the chance. That chance would be provided by ARENA.

Geisel also believed in the ARENA leaders, especially Senate President Petronio Portella, who was ARENA's leading campaign strategist, and thought they could lead the party and the government to victory at the polls. What he failed to understand was the state of political opinion in 1974. Most basic was the fact that under the Brazilian authoritarian regime any two-party race at this time inevitably turned into a plebiscite on the government. As the latter's repression and policy of highly unequal economic rewards tended to alienate the ordinary voter, especially in the cities, the plebiscite was almost bound to go against ARENA in the cities.

This was especially true in November 1974, ironically enough, because the government had made every effort to keep the elections clean. There was special attention to guaranteeing the sanctity of polling places and to neutralizing any "unfair" advantage ARENA might have as the incumbent party in most regions.[39]

As November began, the political climate that so favored ARENA had changed rapidly. To everyone's surprise, the government decided to allow all candidates relatively free access to television.[40] Suddenly the electorate began to wonder if their votes *could* make a difference. Perhaps the MDB *did* represent a real alternative, perhaps the President *was* prepared to cooperate with the opposition. This realization was no accident. The MDB had for some months been arguing that *it* was more in tune with the President's liberalization plans than the government party. The fortnight before the election brought a rush of enthusiasm for the opposition. Even many militants on the left who previously scorned elections (and urged blank balloting) decided that they could send a "message" to the government by voting MDB.

The election results were stunning.[41] The MDB almost doubled its representation in the lower house (the number of seats had been increased from 310 to 364), jumping from 87 to 165; ARENA dropped from 223 to 199. Although ARENA prevailed in the total vote for federal deputies by 11.87 million to 10.95 million, that margin paled in comparison with the 1970 congressional elections, which ARENA won by a margin of 10.9 million to 4.8 million. The results in the Senate were equally dramatic. The MDB delegation leapt from 7 to 20; ARENA dropped from 59 to 46. In the vote for senators (the best indicator of national opinion because senators, being elected statewide, had the largest constituency of any elected officials) the MDB won 14.6 million votes to ARENA's 10 million. The size of the MDB sweep surprised even the most optimistic of the MDB strategists.

The government's defeat did not stop at the congressional level. The elections for state legislatures also brought striking reversals for ARENA and the government. The MDB won control of the legislatures in São Paulo, Rio Grande do Sul, Rio de Janeiro (including the city of Rio), Paraná, Acre, and Amazonas. Previously they had controlled only the state legislature in greater Rio de Janeiro city (then still the state of Guanabara). Now the opposition had won in key states where the urban electorate was crucial.

What did the MDB victory mean? The party had focused its campaign on three issues: social justice (denouncing the trend toward a more unequal income distribution), civil liberties (the human rights violations which so worried elite critics), and denationalization (denouncing foreign penetration in the Brazilian economy).[42] MDB leaders argued that their victory showed they had developed appeal as a genuine opposition party.[43] At a minimum, everyone agreed the elections showed wide lack of support for the "Revolution." In the Northeast state of Maranhão, for example, the MDB did not even present a senatorial candidate, and the victorious ARENA candidate got less than the total of the abstentions plus the blank and mutilated ballots.[44] In São Paulo the MDB ran a political unknown, Orestes Quércia, who won by three million votes over a highly respected ARENA candidate, Carvalho Pinto, who had already been governor, senator, and minister. The economic slowdown of 1974 had certainly played a role. Even so, the Planalto could no longer harbor any illusions about ARENA's ability to win relatively free elections. From the government's standpoint, there was one heartening fact. The hugely successful MDB campaign had been against Médici, not Geisel, a point MDB Senator Franco Montoro later acknowledged.[45]

"Decompression" Under Fire

By December President Geisel faced a political landscape under much less control than the one he had inherited in March. The results of the November elections were to becloud the rest of his presidency. First, the MDB had won more than a third of Congress. That meant the government had lost the two-thirds majority necessary for amending the constitution. Now any constitutinal amendment opposed by the MDB could become law only through use of AI–5, which Geisel had hoped to avoid.

Second, the elections had cast doubt on ARENA's ability to serve as an effective government party. Geisel was counting on a strong ARENA to control the civilian political scene during a gradual liberalization. But with ARENA so inept and unpopular, what was to stop the MDB, if free elections continued, from gaining power far faster than the *linha dura* would tolerate? And what was to stop the MDB's left from gaining control of the party as it rose to power?

Third, the elections had shown that electoral liberalization, i.e., allowing all candidates ready access to TV and stopping intimidation and harassment of the opposition, could produce very unpredictable results. And surprises did not figure in the Geisel–Golbery scenario. A surprise from the left (in *linha dura* logic) might lead to the "recompression" Wanderley had warned of—a regression comparable to 1965 or 1968.

The Geisel strategists found themselves in a corner. Were they prepared to pass real power to the opposition? In São Paulo and Rio Grande do Sul, for example, the MDB controlled the legislatures that would elect the next governors. Was the Planalto prepared to accept opposition governors in such key states?

President Geisel moved quickly to give assurance that the election results would be respected. He was strengthened by the fact that the MDB had won only legislative positions and the Congress had long since been stripped of the power to take any initiative. Presidential advisers also argued, strictly in private, that the electoral defeat had been a plus for liberalization. Now the government had proof that they must adapt quickly to the much more politicized and self-aware public that had emerged during Médici's rule.[46]

In January the Geisel government made a conciliatory move. It lifted prior censorship of *O Estado de São Paulo* just in time for the paper's centennial.[47] This concession ended, at least for the moment, a bitter battle between the paper's owners (the Mesquita family) and the military government. None of the other publications subject to prior censorship—*Veja, O São Paulo, Pasquim, Opinião,* and *Tribuna da Imprensa,*—was removed from the list. The government had made a limited gesture, typical of Geisel's style. Meanwhile, all other publications remained subject to seizure by the Federal Police on order of the censors. This threat forced editors to continue self-censorship (which the *O Estado de São Paulo* had always refused to do but now acquiesced in). Finally, the censors maintained the power to order editors not to print specific news items. Meanwhile, the *Folha de São Paulo,* a generally pro-government paper that avoided controversy, now emerged as a forceful opposition voice. Led by Claudio Abramo and Alberto Dines, the *Folha* opened its editorial and op-ed pages to leading critics of the military regime. For the succeeding decade the *Folha* remained the most important forum for the national debate over the need for fundamental political, economic, and social changes.[48]

By February 1975 the opposition was again demanding action on political prisoners. The MDB and the Roman Catholic Church activists who had in mid-1974 wanted an accounting of the 22 "disappeared" were calling for the answer Golbery had promised. But March brought only a new wave of arrests, centered in São Paulo. Golbery never gave an accounting. Instead, there was only Justice Minister Falcão's February radio-TV speech in which he obfuscated the issue by dragging in extraneous cases and giving no satisfactory accounting of the 22. The conclusion was inevitable: the Geisel government did not control its security forces. Golbery's failure was not lost on the opposition. Many now wrote off the Geisel regime as no better than Médici.[49]

At this point the Geisel government began to act on its fundamental distrust of the opposition. In January 1975, Justice Minister Armando Falcão led a crackdown in São Paulo on the Communist Party (the PCB, or Moscow-line party), claiming it was behind the MDB election victory in November 1974. He was supported (or prodded?) by the hard-line military, who were circulating a secret memo claiming that São Paulo state Congressman Alberto Goldman was a communist agent assigned to manipulate the MDB.

The security forces had for some time been hunting down the PCB leadership. Since the end of 1973, four members of the PCB's Central Committee had been among 21 "missing" militant oppositionists. The others, and all were presumed dead, came from the remnants of the guerrilla movement (VPR, ALN, and splinter groups). This technique of "disappearing" suspects was an ominous innovation, in that previously the police and military had usually taken prisoners through military channels. Sweeping the PCB into the net was bitter irony, for the PCB had steadfastly refused to take up arms. But they were an easy target, and Falcão wanted evidence to satisfy the paranoid military. It did not matter for the moment that the Planalto was far from buying Falcão's conspiracy theory.[50] Arrests followed, as did torture of detainees, including the son of General Pedro Celestino da Silva Pereira, a prominent general.[51] By their treatment of a prisoner so militarily well connected, the security forces again demonstrated their autonomy. They were also testing the new government. Other arrestees included 10 Rio labor leaders accused of subversive crimes committed before 1964. They were so obscure that not even the U.S. labor attaché at the Rio consulate had heard of them. In May Rio was buzzing with rumors of a virtual hard-line coup attempt against Geisel.[52] Church, Bar Association, and MDB critics replied with continued protests against torture and arbitrary police action. The Commander of the always-important Third Army, General Oscar Luís da Silva, responded by citing Portugal, where, he argued, protest had led directly to the threat of communist control.

In July 1975 Geisel decided he again had to use his arbitrary power, this time to discipline an ARENA Senator from Pernambuco who had allegedly been caught (and tape recorded) in an act of political extortion. Senator Wilson Campos and two other minor political figures were deprived of their mandates. These cassations, made for moralistic reasons, i.e., corruption, not subversion, resembled many made by Castelo Branco. Heavy-handed censorship continued, stimulating more protests from artists and intellectuals.

In early August 1975 Geisel gave an important speech defining his government's attitude toward liberalization. He argued that any such change had to be slow and sure. "What we desire for the country . . . is an integrated and humanistic development which combines—organically and homogeneously—all sectors of the national community—political, social, and economic. With that development we will achieve *distensão,* i.e., the attenuation, if not the elimination, of those multiple and ever-present tensions that obstruct our national progress and the well-being of our people." He announced that the government had no intention of surrendering the powers in Institutional Act No. 5.[53] His meaning was clear: government policy could only emerge from a compromise between vying military viewpoints. Only if the military felt confident about national security, as *they* defined it, could the opposition hope to see a return to the rule of law. At the same time, Geisel unleashed rhetoric worthy of the best duristas. He attacked alleged communist infiltration of the media, the bureaucracy, and especially educational institutions.[54]

Thus the Geisel government was delicately balanced: arrests and torture continued, but prior censorship had been lifted from *O Estado de São Paulo,* and the much-increased MDB congressional delegations were seated in Brasília. This "balance" was about to be rudely upset.

Church and Bar Association officials were among the few who could effectively contest the government's continuing denials of torture and arbitrary behavior. By mid-September they were again on the attack, citing government mistreatment of the Indians and torture of political prisoners.

Suddenly the protesters were presented with the most sensational death of a political prisoner since Geisel took office. The victim was Vladimir Herzog, widely respected director of the news department of São Paulo's noncommercial television channel.[55] Herzog was a 38-year-old, Yugoslav-born Jew who had emigrated with his family to Brazil. He held a degree from the University of São Paulo and taught in its School of Communications. He subsequently rose to the top rank of journalists in São Paulo. He was also known for his three years of work on the Brazilian Service of the BBC, and he had other extensive professional contacts abroad. In October 1975 Herzog learned from friends that the Second Army security forces were looking for him. In an ingenuous effort to cooperate, he voluntarily reported to the Second Army barracks. He had no notion that that unit's intelligence considered him a communist plotter.

The next day the Second Army command announced Herozg had committed suicide in his prison cell after having signed a confession of Communist Party membership. São Paulo was stunned; no one believed the suicide explanation.[56] Here was a prominent member of the media elite suddenly dead, surely from torture. The fact that Herzog was Jewish added to the frightened reaction of the Paulista elite, because there had been hints of anti-Semitism in past hardline behavior. Students and faculty went on strike for three days at the University of São Paulo, and the Journalists' Union went into permanent session to demand an inquiry. The national Bar Association made the same demand. Forty-two São Paulo bishops signed a statement denouncing the government's violence.

Fear gripped Herzog's family and much of São Paulo's intellectual and cultural elite. Opposition leaders decided they had to show resolve by holding a public funeral ceremony to honor Herzog, but his mother and several rabbi friends were against it. The Mayor warned that if a public ceremony were held he could not guarantee police protection.

Cardinal Arns, an increasingly important opposition figure in São Paulo and Brazil, then took matters into his own hands. He organized and presided over a dramatic ecumenical funeral service for Herzog, including two rabbis and a protestant clergyman, in São Paulo's cathedral. In Medici's time the security forces would have used whatever force necessary to prevent such an event. At this point, however, the police resorted only to petty harassment to frighten away participants. They ran lengthy "safety checks" on all cars coming into the central city, greatly reducing the attendance. Yet the service was held—a minor triumph in a community gripped by fear.

The shock over Herzog's death was all the greater because many in and out of government had hoped that President Geisel was bringing the military security apparatus under control.[57] Following routine procedure, Geisel ordered an immediate investigation (by an all-military panel) into the incident. Observers skeptical about the impartiality of the panel saw their doubts justified in late December when the military panel simply confirmed the death as a suicide. A military court confirmed that ruling in early March of the following year.

The sense of shock lingered in São Paulo and in the country.[58] Attention focused on the Second Army commander, General Ednardo d'Avila Melo, who had long given a virtual free hand to the local DOI-CODI. Local observers recalled with bitterness how at the time he assumed his command (January 1974) General Ednardo was hailed by many as being far more enlightened than his hardliner predecessor, General Humberto de Souza Mello, an outspoken apologist for repression.[59] As 1975 ended, many in the opposition thought "decompression" was doomed. The President, they feared, was too weak for the military extremists. Or perhaps he had never been committed to real liberalization. At any rate, there remained little grounds for optimism.

The Second Army security men now obviously thought they had nothing to fear from higher authority. In early January 1976 they were interrogating Manoel Fiel Filho, an activist in the metalworkers union, long one of the best organized and most militant unions.[60] Suddenly the news leaked out, through a hospital employee, that he was dead. Officially it was ruled another suicide. But could anyone doubt he had been killed under torture? The Second Army's (and General Ednardo's) challenge to Geisel could hardly be more blatant.

President Geisel was livid. He now looked ridiculous for his defense of General Ednardo d'Avila in the Herzog case. Indeed, back then Geisel had made clear to Ednardo that he would not tolerate any more such incidents. After satisfying himself of the facts, he summarily dismissed Ednardo d'Avila and replaced him with General Dilermando Gomes Monteiro, a known moderate and a close Geisel associate.[61] More significant than the dismissal was the fact that Geisel acted without convening the army High Command, normally essential in changing such a high-level commander.[62]

Being able to act on his own showed Geisel's great power within the army officer corps. It was a power that up to now he had not had to demonstrate. By firing General Ednardo, Geisel sent a shock wave through the officer ranks. A few more such firings and the balance between hardliners and moderates might change dramatically. The hardliners were shaken. Their colleagues in the security forces could no longer assume the higher command would cover for them in public uproars over violence against political suspects.[63]

Geisel's show of power within the military, as indicated by his ability to remove General Ednardo, had its price. To maintain officer support he now had to show toughness on the civilian political scene against corruption and subversion, as the castelistas defined them. That definition could only emerge from the government's behavior.

New Economic Problems

The Geisel government began with high hopes for the economy. Its *II National Development Plan: 1975–1979*, dated September 1974, set a target growth rate of 10 percent per year, to be achieved by shifting from consumer durables to intermediate industrial products and capital goods. The high growth was to improve income distribution and would require a continued high level of capital inflow, as well as an increase in domestic savings. In presenting the plan President Geisel admitted "there is no room for exaggerated optimism." But he pointed to the "creative energy of leadership" in both the public and private sectors and to how "we confronted the internal difficulties of the beginning of the decade of the 1960s with energy, conviction, and a capacity to plan and act."[64]

These hopes soon dimmed, however, because the international economic climate had worsened. OPEC succeeded in tripling the world price of oil. Brazil, dependent on imports for 80 percent of its oil consumption, suddenly faced a massive increase in its import bill. How had it become so vulnerable?

The explanation involved no mystery. In the late 1950s the Kubitschek government had decided to commit the expansion of Brazil's transportation future to highways rather than railways (although upgrading of existing rail lines was a priority). The reason was simple: in so vast a country the initial cost per mile was far lower for highway construction than railway building. In opting for truck transport, the federal and state governments could proceed to build an extensive network of relatively inexpensive unpaved feeder roads. Once the traffic justified the expense, such roads could be paved. By contrast, the locomotive, highly efficient once on the rails, could cover Brazil only after a large initial investment in railway-bed construction.

The Kutitschek decision seemed eminently sensible at the time. Soon

Brazilian-built Mercedes-Benz trucks were lumbering across the country, usually over unpaved roads. They ran on diesel fuel, readily available at a cheap price on the world market. Petrobrás, the state oil enterprise, concentrated on refining and distributing imported oil. Its exploration of Brazilian reserves was modest, in keeping with the availability of cheap oil abroad and the general view that mainland Brazil was geologically unpromising for exploration. By coincidence President Geisel had been director of Petrobrás from 1969 to 1973, precisely when Petrobrás solidified its reliance on imported oil.

When the OPEC price shock hit, the Geisel government played for time. Understandably, policymakers hoped the OPEC cartel would not last. Perhaps Brazil could negotiate, on a bilateral basis, a better price for oil imports. If the OPEC price rise was irreversible, then Brazil would have to alter radically its energy strategy. It might also want to rethink its Middle East foreign policy, which had traditionally been moderately pro-Israeli.[65]

The Geisel policymakers responded to the need for a long-term strategy in several ways. First, Petrobrás expanded its program of offshore exploration—a more promising target than mainland Brazil, where finds had been disappointingly meager. Even with rapid large-scale investments, though, significant returns would take years. Next, an immediate search was begun for other sources of energy in Brazil. The most heralded alternative in the industrial world was nuclear power. But Brazil's nuclear capacity was rudimentary (one Westinghouse reactor being installed, dependent on U.S. fuel supply) and would require heavy capital imports to become significant. The second alternative was alcohol, which would require distilling ethanol from biomass (primarily sugarcane) to power specially designed engines.[66] Neither alternative could help Brazil's balance of payments in the short run. Indeed, both would require heavy investment before their eventual payoff. Finally, there was hydro-electric power. Even before the OPEC shock the Brazilian government had embarked on an ambitious dam-building program. The most famous site was Itaipú, on the Paraná River between Brazil and Paraguay, which when finished would be the world's largest hydro-electric dam site. Yet none of this electricity could fuel Brazil's trucks, buses or cars.[67]

What made Brazil's adjustment to this balance of payments squeeze so difficult was that its rapid growth since 1967 had been import intensive. From 1970 through 1973 Brazilian imports grew at an annual rate of 24 percent. In rough terms that meant that every one percent of GDP growth required a two percent growth in import volume.

Given the huge increase in the price for imported oil, how could Brazil manage the squeeze on the balance of payments? In the short run there were only three options: reduce its non-oil imports, draw down the foreign exchange reserves, or borrow abroad.

To cut non-oil imports would have slowed growth—a price the Geisel government refused to pay. To increase export earnings was difficult in the face of the world recession created by OPEC's price shock. The obvious solutions were to draw down the exchange reserves and borrow abroad. Geisel's Brazil did both. In 1974 alone Brazil almost doubled its net external debt, from $6.2 billion to $11.9 billion.[68]

In order to attract badly needed foreign loans, the government abolished the 40 percent compulsory deposit Brazilian borrowers had to make against new loans. It also reduced the minimum loan period from ten to five years. A final measure was to reduce from 25 percent to 5 percent the tax on remittances of interest abroad. These regulations all dated from the early 1970s when Brazil had to reduce capital inflow (because of its frequently inflationary effect). Now Brazil's need was the opposite. The net effect of the new measures was to reduce Brazil's control over the movement of foreign capital.

The Geisel economic team was able to maintain rapid growth in 1974. The economic record for that year bears closer examination, because it indicated what was in store for the Brazilian economy in the second half of the 1970s. The growth rate hit 9.5 percent, but inflation shot up from 15.7 percent to 34.5 percent. That differential is suspect due to government manipulation of the index in 1973 and early 1974. In fact, the inflation rates for 1973 and 1974 probably would have been relatively close if government statistical offices had been left free of political interference in compiling the 1973 data.

The 9.5 percent overall growth rate in 1974 was composed of a 9.9 percent increase in industrial output, down slightly from the 1968–73 average of 13.1 percent, and an 8.5 percent increase in agriculture, which was higher than all but one year since 1968. This growth record would have been ample grounds for satisfaction had it not been for the news on the balance of payments.

Although exports increased by 28.2 percent in 1974, imports leapt ahead by 104 percent, in part reflecting the fourfold increase in oil prices extracted by OPEC. In the single year of 1974 Brazil's imports doubled from $6.2 billion to $12.6 billion. The trade balance (goods imports as against goods exports), which had almost come into balance in 1973, suddenly ballooned to a deficit of $4.7 billion. The deficit on the services account added another $2.4 billion. The resulting deficit of $7.3 billion on current account was covered by a $6.8 billion net inflow of capital (a 56.5 percent increase over 1973) and the use of $1.2 billion in foreign exchange reserves. In 1974 Brazil had survived the initial impact of OPEC's economic blackmail. But how long could the ad hoc response succeed?

Voices from Civil Society

The security forces under the Médici dictatorship had counted on fear to help them track down and eliminate Brazil's "internal enemies." Repression hit especially hard those groups trying to organize the working classes. Trade unions, for example, were under draconian controls. Church members attempting to organize any potentially political activities were under surveillance, harassment, or worse. The security forces also watched closely the grass-roots organizing among shantytown dwellers or rural workers. It was as if the military government believed the guerrillas' propaganda—that the Brazilian masses were ready to rise in revolt against their rulers. By 1973 even the few remaining guerrillas had given up that belief.

The Médici regime had also struck fear among the elite.[69] The families of political prisoners could seldom find any lawyer willing to take their case. Lawyers were frightened of challenging the security forces on behalf of a politically marked client. The press was another elite institution intimidated by the repression.[70] Arrest and torture of journalists, economic pressure on (or inducements to) owners, along with direct censorship, had reduced almost all the media, except a few low-circulation weeklies, to the role of cheerleaders for the government, or, at the least, innocuous purveyors of government-generated information.

Finally, there were the businessmen. They were profiting from the economic boom, and in the mid- and late 1970s Brazilian executive salaries were among the world's highest.[71] Yet these businessmen were irritated at the maze of incentives and controls created by Delfim and his technocrats. They also worried that the rapidly growing state sector might combine, de facto, with the foreign-owned sector to crowd out Brazilian business. The Médici government had no need of arrests to keep businessmen in line. It needed only use its many instruments (interest rates, government contracts, tax incentives, etc.) as reward and punishment.[72] (There is further discussion of businessmen's opposition to the government below.)

In sum, Brazilian authoritarianism had rendered both the non-elite and elite institutions of civil society incapable of significant autonomous action. Their fear and immobility reflected the kind of Brazil the hardliners had worked to create.

Onto this scene had come a new President talking of a new dialogue with the leaders of civil society. Geisel and Golbery wanted to ease the repression they had inherited.[73] But any experienced dictator could have told them that attempting to reduce repression gradually is dangerous. It is dangerous because fear, so important for inhibiting the opposition, can disappear overnight if the government apears to be losing both its authority and its power.

Relations with the Church were a crucial case for Geisel's decompression strategy.[74] During the Médici years there had been a long succession of ugly clashes between the government and Catholic activists. A number of the latter had been arrested and tortured. In the few months before Geisel's inauguration more than 40 Catholic activists in greater São Paulo were arrested, most of them journalists or labor organizers.[75] In February the Médici government had attempted to assert a veto over all Catholic missionaries working with the Indians.[76] This move stemmed from government worry over bitter conflicts breaking out over land claims and Indian rights. Catholic missionaries had often aggressively defended both Indians and small farmers, who were menaced by the land speculators, the large land owners, and their gunmen. The arrest of activists in São Paulo and the move against the missionaries were part of the hardliner strategy to strengthen the new government's hand, and at the same time demonstrate a de facto commitment to toughness toward the Church.

Those who wanted better church–state relations looked all the more eagerly to the new governnment for relief. Such signs were given when in January and February President-elect Geisel's representatives met confidentially with six leading prelates.[77] In July came a signal from the Church that relations had already improved. Cardinal Agnello Rossi, the former archbishop of São Paulo (until 1971) and now president of the Vatican's Sacred Congregation for the Evangelization of People, announced in Brazil that church-state relations were completely harmonious. Archbishop Dom Paulo Evaristo Arns of São Paulo was also optimistic, saying in late August the dialogue had begun.

In order to understand the Church's strengths and weaknesses as decompression began, we must first look at two of the Church's important internal changes during the Médici years. One was the emergence of the CNBB as the institutional spokesman for the Church. The Conference had been founded in 1952, under the guidance of Dom Helder Camara, who skillfully led it into progressive political and theological positions many prelates did not share. But Dom Helder's transfer to Recife in 1964, and the bishops' endorsement of the 1964 coup, set the CNBB on a relatively passive political course until 1968. The subsequent repression, however, provoked the bishops into aggressive opposition, as noted earlier. By 1974 the CNBB had consolidated its role as the key Church body in relations with the Brazilian government. Its staff had the trust of most bishops, partly because the government's repressive policies had pushed "moderate" bishops into endorsing an aggressively anti-government stance.

The Church's second internal change was the rapid growth of the ecclesiastical base communities (*comunidades eclesiais de base,* or CEBs).[78] These were the lay study cells whose creation had been encouraged by the Brazilian Church hierarchy since the 1960s. They had no set structure. The pastoral agent, or organizer, was usually a priest or nun. The communities averaged 15–25 although they could reach a 100 or 200 in the countryside. They began as Bible-study groups, meeting weekly to discuss current issues in reference to the Bible. One of the hierarchy's reasons for launching the CEBs was the desperate shortage of priests and religious. CEBs were designed to operate on their own, thus increasing lay involvement without requiring additional clerical personnel. The hierarchy was also worried over the rapid spread of Protestantism, as well as Spiritism and Afro-Brazilian religion (primarily *umbanda*). In no sense did the hierarchy intend the CEBs to become any form of "parallel" church. In the early 1970s the Church, through its pastoral plan, gave a high priority to the CEBs. By 1974 they were said to number approximately 40,000, scattered throughout Brazil. All observers agreed that the growth of the communities had greatly increased lay involvement in the Church.

Notwithstanding the hierarchy's original intentions, the CEBs soon took on a life of their own. Many became a force in the "popular church," a movement emphasizing the Church's base by integrating elements of folk catholicism and by propagating the quasi-revolutionary liberation theology, represented in Brazil by such theologians as Leonardo Boff. CEBs of this kind also gave the Church a network of dedicated parishioners who might be mobilized for social action. Many members were mobilized in the "Cost of Living Movement" (*Movimento do custo de vida*), a grass-roots protest movement that began in 1973 and reached its peak in 1977–78. Among its accomplishments was helping to regain the streets for public protest.[79]

It is worth noting that the rapid growth of the CEBs disquieted many in the military regime. The latter liked to think that Church opposition came from isolated "opportunists" such as Dom Helder Camara, whom the hard-line military and their civilian hangers-on cordially hated. They dismissed him as an egomaniac capitalizing on social tensions to pave the way for a communist takeover. These military and civilian allies could not bear the thought that Dom Helder (or his views) might have mass support in the church. If he did, then a deeper repression would be needed to root them out.

The Church therefore began the Geisel years with both tighter coordination at the top (CNBB) and broadening participation at the bottom (the CEBs). Given the repressive political climate, the Church was concentrating on its enormous internal, essentially pastoral needs. But Geisel had not been able to deliver on "decompression." The hard line and the security forces had been sabotaging the policy from the start. Their most spectacular move to date was the October 1975 death of Vladimir Herzog in Second Army headquarters in São Paulo. Cardinal Arns's ecumenical funeral service in the cathedral was a direct challenge to the government. The São Paulo security forces, commanded by the ultra-reactionary Colonel Erasmo and accompanied by their German Shepherd attack dogs, soon answered. While Cardinal Arns was on a trip to Rome, they raided São Paulo's Catholic University, destroying furnishings and research materials and beating those students and faculty unable to escape in time. More than 700 students were arrested. It was one of the most violent attacks on an academic institution in Brazil since 1964.

The year 1976 brought a rash of direct violence against the clergy. In July Father Rodolfo Lunkenbein, a German missionary to the Indians in Amazonia, was murdered by ranchers. In October Amazonia police murdered Father João Bosco Penido Burnier, who had been protesting their torture of local women. The violence was by no means limited to the country's least-settled frontier. Back in September there was a shocking incident in the heart of Brazil's modernizing Center-South. Unidentified thugs kidnapped Dom Adriano Hypolito, the bishop of Nova Iguaçú (on the outskirts of Rio de Janeiro), beat him, stripped off his clothes, and dumped him on the roadside.[80] To underline their message the kidnappers drove his car to the CNBB headquarters, where they blew it up. Church spokesmen bitterly protested this attack on a bishop, but never received satisfaction from any level of authority.

This violence against the clergy showed that the Geisel government could not control the police and right-wing vigilantes (undoubtedly linked to the security forces). More important from a political standpoint, it helped unite the bishops in support of a tough anti-government stand. Without such constant outrages against the clergy, the "moderate" prelates might never have endorsed manifestos that only the "progressive" prelates would sign in the early 1970s. The hardliners had helped propel the Church into becoming a powerful and aggressive voice of civil society.

The weight of opinion within the hierarchy had also moved toward the "progressives" as the prelates looked closely at the socio-economic policies of the successive military governments. The 1970 census had shown increased income inequality, and there were innumerable studies—many produced by the government itself—showing the country's desperate need for more investment in health, education, sanitation, and housing. While Brazilian managers earned salaries among the world's highest, São Paulo shantytown children faced an increasing risk of illness or death.[81]

Because the Church had been carrying out its "option for the poor," i.e., a deliberate orientation toward those at the bottom, more clergy and laity became aware of the squalid living conditions and grim life choices that many Brazilians had to face.[82] Church people became identified with the cry for social justice that had been endorsed by the Latin American Bishops Conference at Medellin in 1968.

The Brazilian Church had thus gone through a twofold radicalization. First, it was forced into a defiant stand on human rights, as clergy and laity (as well as citizens unaffiliated with the Church) fell victim to government violence. Second, by turning toward pastoral work with the destitute, it acted on a radical critique of the brand of Brazilian capitalism being shaped by the technocrats and their military mentors.

The most conspicuous figure in this radicalized Brazilian Catholic Church was no longer Dom Helder Camara, about whom the censors allowed not a word to reach the public. Even without that handicap, Dom Helder would have been eclipsed by Cardinal Arns of São Paulo.[83] Archbishop of the largest Catholic parish in the world, Cardinal Arns had proved since his appointment in 1971 to be an aggressive and effective activist. Under his wing São Paulo's CEBs and lay-clergy pastorals (*pastorais*) multiplied, creating a network of activists in Brazil's largest and most industrialized urban center.

From this panorama it should be clear that in the era of the attempted decompression the Church was the only national institution capable of speaking out strongly against the military regime and also of having a national network of members who could be mobilized. It was also generally regarded as the most progressive church in the Catholic world, having earned that reputation both as a defender of human rights and as an advocate of radical change to help the poor. Spokespersons for the latter sought a "popular church," and enjoyed influence in the Brazilian Church through the Geisel and early Figueiredo years. The Church conservatives were biding their time, while the moderates were unreliable long-term allies of any extreme position, including that of the "popular church."[84]

The Brazilian Bar Association (*Ordem dos Advogados do Brasil or, OAB*) was another traditional elite institution that became an aggressive opponent of the military government.[85] Law had long been Brazil's most prestigious profession, and it was the preferred path to public power. Although Brazilians drew heavily on European and North American liberalism, and although Brazilian lawyers had written the democratic constitutions of 1824, 1891, 1934, and 1946, they were no strangers to authoritarian rule. Every revolution or coup in Brazil had succeeded in finding lawyers who would produce a juridical rationale for the seizure of power. The year 1964 was no exception. The Institutional Act of April 1964, which legalized the purges by the revolutionary government, was written by Francisco Campos, the *mineiro* lawyer who had also written the authoritarian constitution Getúlio Vargas used to legitimize his dictatorship.

Many UDN supporters of Goulart's overthrow were also eminent lawyers, such as Adauto Lúcio Cardoso, Prado Kelly, Afonso Arinos de Melo Franco, Bilac Pinto, and Milton Campos. They had no difficulty reconciling their belief in the rule of law with the ouster of a sitting president. They justified their stand as necessary to protect lawful government, which Goulart, they charged, was subverting.

Yet many of these same UDN lawyers grew worried about the authoritarian rule imposed by the hard-line military after 1964. One by one they abandoned the regime. At the peak of Médici's power few UDN lawyers of top caliber were to be found among active government supporters. The "classic" UDN-style legal defense of military government was gone.[86]

After 1968 the Revolution had assumed a radically different legal dimension. Widespread and blatant violations of human rights, a wholesale bypassing of the civil judiciary, and a blizzard of arbitrary actions had all produced a legal situation that was unprecedented since the end of the Vargas dictatorship in 1945.

The most telling evidence of this state of illegality was the record of human rights violations. The torturers had gotten their way, and, despite censorship, news of their carnage spread quickly. The real test of Brazil's tradition of respect for the law was Brazilian lawyers' reaction to the gross violation of human rights.

Since 1968, when Sérgio Fleury and his brand of torturers won a free hand, the reaction had not been impressive. Scarcely any lawyers had answered the desperate pleas of families and friends of political prisoners.

The few who did, probably no more than 30 in all, were mostly criminal lawyers. They pressured the military courts to report on the location and condition of prisoners. These lawyers were swamped with cases, sometimes 50 or 100 at once. Often they could make no more than a gesture. Yet at other times they would provoke a response from the military court, thus at least confirming where a prisoner was held. The total effect of these lawyers' efforts did not threaten the Brazilian leviathan, but it did finally prod the conscience of the legal profession.[87]

Although lawyers had a special reason to be shocked by what they heard of torture—their government had simply declared itself above the rule of law—many lawyers, like most citizens, preferred to doubt the torture, mutilation, and death really were common. By 1972, however, few doubters were left. In the final Médici years the sentiment of revolt grew among lawyers. Those who insisted that torture was an aberration were shaken, for example, when they talked to torture victims brought by their lawyers to the Bar Association.

In 1972 the officers of the Bar issued a manifesto proclaiming that "the most important cause for our country is the primacy of law. They warned the technocrats and the generals, "If it is true that peace and security are indispensable for development, it is no less true that tranquility and peace cannot exist where there is neither liberty nor justice."[88]

When the OAB's August 1974 national convention met in Rio de Janeiro, its leadership was committed to an aggressive advocacy of the rights of political prisoners, including safety from arbitrary arrest and torture. The convention's motto was "The Lawyer and the Rights of Man."[89] The OAB now launched a campaign to educate the public on the importance for every citizen of fundamental legal and political rights. The OAB's eventual goal was for the government to restore *habeas corpus,* revoke AI–5, and issue an amnesty. In the short run the most they could hope was to convince the public that the post-1964 military governments were illegitimate because their constitution was not the product of a popularly elected Constituent Assembly, as had been the constitutions adopted after coups in 1889, 1930, and 1945.

Here was one of Brazil's most (arguably *the* most) elite institutions organizing to undermine the foundations of the authoritarian regime. Like the Church, it was a national institution (its national conventions rotated around the country), in cooperation with each state's Bar Association. The Bar's anti-government offensive at the outset of the Geisel presidency, often coordinated with the ABI (Brazilian Press Association), reverberated across Brazil. The Bar's campaign was certain to reach an important cross-section of the elite, especially politicians, both inside and outside the government.[90]

The Geisel government was angered by the Bar's offensive. At the 1974 national convention Minister of Justice Armando Falcão, was scheduled to appear at the closing ceremony. He did not. It was hardly surprising, given the fusillades the lawyers had been firing at the government all week. In 1976 the Geisel government aimed its own fusillade at the OAB—proposing, as part of a general reform of the judiciary, to revoke the OAB's unique status as the only secular organization not subject to direct governmental control. The OAB would become an ordinary professional association, subject to the control and oversight of the Ministry of Labor.[91] This heavy-handed threat to the OAB's legal status, and therefore to all lawyers, galvanized them into a militant stand, much as the government's complicity in violence against the clergy had galvanized the church "moderates."

They inveighed against the "illegitimate juridical order," which they contrasted to the "legitimate juridical order." The former, they argued, had been created by use of arbitrary acts, above all AI–5. These acts and decrees constituted a "state of exception." The "state of law" could only be restored by revoking AI–5 and by reinstating *habeas corpus.* The subsequent step, in OAB thinking, was to call a Constitutent Assembly that could write a new, legitimate, constitutional order for Brazil.[92]

The OAB was thus another institution of civil society that, starting in 1974, chose to contest the military government's legitimacy. It challenged the "revolutionary" structure the hard-line military and their lawyers had erected since 1968. It also supported efforts to defend prisoners who suffered the brutalities of the torturers. As with the Church, the OAB was traditionally a conservative body whose members had become more radical after their confrontation with the authoritarian state. So both Church and Bar were at the heart of the civil society that gained its voice just as the Geisel government chose to apply its ill-defined blueprint for liberalization.

No opposition, especially under a highly authoritarian regime, can organize if it has no way to communicate internally and with the public. The Church and the OAB had their own networks of communication, based on their long-standing national organizations. But how could they bring more of the civil society into the opposition?

The media had been hit especially hard by the repression.[93] Censors could easily control radio and television because the owners could be threatened with loss of their (government-granted)license or with pressure on advertisers. Thus radio and TV were unable to assume any opposition role in the early Geisel years.

The print media were another matter. Brazil had a long and distinguished journalistic tradition, although in the aftermath of AI–5 the censors put the heat on newspapers and magazines. The major dailies were Rio's *Jornal do Brasil* and São Paulo's *O Estado de São Paulo* and *Jornal da Tarde,* the latter two both owned by the Mesquita family. These were the most respected papers, read all over the country (if in small numbers outside Rio and São Paulo), and had the most impact on elite opinion. Since 1972 the sensationalistic *Tribuna da Imprensa* and the two Mesquita-owned papers had been subject to prior censorship (*censura prévia*).

The Geisel government was well aware of the press's key role. In January 1975 the government, as we have seen, removed prior censorship from *O Estado de São Paulo* and *O Jornal da Tarde.* Even in the rest of the press there was a margin for covering controversial events or people in such a way that the intelligent reader could glean the facts.

Ironically, heavy press censorship had stimulated creation of a new genre of publication, the political weekly. Best-known of this genre were *Opinião* and *Movimento*. Both were published out of strong political conviction, *Opinião* being of a center-left viewpoint and *Movimento* on the radical left. Both suffered heavy censorship causing them large financial losses, as the copy had to be paid for before the censor's review. Approximately half of *Opinião*'s initial copy was censored, requiring the substitution of new material at additional cost. The mere fact that these two weeklies survived in the early Geisel years showed that some space had remained for the opposition. However mangled by the censors, *Opinião* and *Movimento* remained opposition rallying points, especially for the intellectuals.

The 1975 removal of prior censorship on *O Estado de São Paulo* and the creation of a climate of liberalization had unforeseen consequences. The torture and other human rights abuses by the security forces had far from ceased, so the press was bound to report on them. Vladimir Herzog's death in October 1975, for example, was covered extensively in the major papers, as was the ecumenical funeral service for him. By creating a slightly less rigid atmosphere for the press, the Geisel regime made possible a better-informed and more easily mobilized public opinion. And that opinion was moving massively, especially in the cities, toward the opposition, as the 1974 elections had shown. Geisel was helping to reawaken civil society, but he was unprepared to hear what society's voice would say.

Planalto Problem: How to Win Elections

In early 1975 the Geisel government faced a delicate political situation. In his early days in office the new President had seemed receptive to the opposition idea that the Fifth Institutional Act (AI–5) could be phased out, thus speeding a return to the rule of law. Some ARENA congressional leaders even suggested it could be "incorporated" into the Constitution. That solution was quickly denounced by the MDB. Either the government would be limited by an agreed set of constitutional rules, argued the MDB, or else it rested on arbitrary power. There could be no mixture of the two.

Yet a few months after taking office, Geisel was warning Congressmen of both parties that the government would not relinquish the extraordinary powers granted in AI–5. The President promptly demonstrated what he meant. Before 1975 had ended, the President resorted to AI–5 in dismissing three judges for alleged corruption and in settling a political squabble over the mayorship of Rio Branco, in the distant state of Acre. These cases were so minor that the MDB optimists still hoped the Act might fade for lack of significant use. But the Geisel government's determination to purge any remaining "subversives" made further use of AI–5 inevitable.

Throughout 1975, as we saw earlier, Armando Falcão, the federal Justice Minister, had waged a hunt for the Communists he and the security forces thought had played a key role in the MDB's November 1974 congressional election victories. In March 1975 he staged trials in which defendants were convicted of attempting to rebuild the shattered Communist Party and others were convicted of having belonged to Carlos Marighela's once active ALN. In October military spokesmen announced they had arrested another 76 alleged communists, of whom 63 were said to be military police.

In January 1976 Geisel used AI-5 to strip two Paulista state legislators of their mandates. They were accused of having welcomed communist support in previous elections. At the end of March Geisel took the same step against two federal deputies who had used violent rhetoric in attacking the government and the military. As the order was about to be signed at the Planalto, Congressman Lysaneas Maciel, the fieriest of the MDB spokesmen, was giving a speech in defense of the two deputies about to lose their mandates. Only force, he charged, had kept the government in power. Word of his attack reached the Planalto in time for the President to add Lysaneas to the purge list. News of the order hit the Congress floor when Lysaneas was still at the podium. Wild insults were traded, as ARENA deputies vented their fury at the MDB militant. It was an ugly scene of ARENA–MDB recriminations that had been brewing for some time. The MDB leadership, deeply frustrated at this reversal of "decompression," attacked the government's resort to "violence."

Few politicians were surprised when the ax fell on these young MDB deputies, notorious for skating near the edge of military tolerance. Yet the President's use of AI–5 against minor federal Congressmen who had no large following suggested that hardliner influence in the Planalto was still significant. Other signs of the government's ill-coordinated nervousness surfaced. In early 1976 the federal censor banned a television broadcast of the Bolshoi Ballet. Since censorship had recently eased, the government now looked ridiculous, as the humor mills churned out jokes about possible "contamination" from communist dancers on TV.

In late June the government took a far more serious step to control the media. Geisel requested and got from Congress a law (known as the "Falcão law," after the justice minister) forbidding campaign use of radio or television, except time for a few still spots (made available, it should be noted, to all candidates). This was a heavy-handed reaction to the 1974 elections, when the MDB candidates used television to attract winning votes in the closing weeks. All these measures seemed to add up to an assault on the MDB. Geisel now openly referred to the MDB as the "enemy."

If the MDB were to observe the rules of the political game, as altered since 1974, they held high cards.[94] The MDB was very strong in several major states—São Paulo, Rio de Janeiro, and Rio Grande do Sul—where governors were to be elected in 1978. The MDB was likely to win any direct gubernatorial election in those economically important states. Resort to indirect elections was not a possible solution for the government, since that would require a constitutional amendment, and ARENA lacked the necessary two-thirds majority in Congress. Nor did the state legislatures offer any way out for the government, because all three legislatures had MDB majorities. The Geisel government therefore found itself in a political cul-de-sac. The commitment to "decompression" had been overshadowed by the fear of electoral defeats that might undermine the military's ability to decide how soon and how far it might want to loosen its control. In the meantime, the MDB leadership had decided to look moderate and wait to collect the fruits of victory in the 1978 elections, still three years away.

The final months of 1976 saw politics complicated by the eruption of a force that many Brazilians had long feared—rightist terrorism. It was feared because it could so easily become the pretext for more tightly closing the system. And an apparent terrorist carte blanche implied hardliner influence in the military command. In September a bomb exploded at the Rio de Jaeniro headquarters of the Brazilian Press Association, and in early October there were firebombs and telephone threats aimed at notable clerical critics of the government. A bishop was kidnapped and beaten. A group calling itself the "Brazilian Anti-Communist Alliance," sounding ominously like the Argentine terrorist group, claimed credit for the attack on the bishop. This terrorism was a direct response to the awakening of civil society encouraged by Geisel's "decompression." But these rightist incidents did not develop into a larger campaign, nor did the Geisel government change course, and those responsible (undoubtedly linked to the police and the military) were either restrained by their superiors or decided themselves to lie low.

The most important political developments of late 1976 were the municipal elections of November 15, 1976. ARENA, as expected, did well in the less developed regions, where running against ARENA on the local level was often political suicide. But in the larger cities the MDB ran strongly, winning control of the muncipal councils in Rio de Janeiro, São Paulo, Belo Horizonte, Pôrto Alegre, Salvador, Campinas, and Santos. The opposition victory in so many important cities boded ill for ARENA's electoral future. In Rio some 150,000 voters cast their ballots for "black beans," the staple of the working class that had disappeared from stores (suppliers were holding out for a price increase) a month earlier, touching off riots. It was another danger sign for the regime.[95]

Government Response: The "April Package"

In early 1977 the Geisel government finally moved to deal with the political consequences of the 1974 congressional election results. Those elections had created both a long-term and a short-term problem. The long-term problem was how to prevent the MDB from winning significant power by the ballot box. The short-term problem was finding a legal way to block that threat in the next election. The Planalto was most worried about the 1978 gubernatorial elections, which the Constitution stipulated were to be direct.

A government defeat—which seemed very likely in several key states—could only be prevented in two ways. One would be to intimidate the electorate on an even greater scale than in 1970, when the Médici government arrested thousands on the eve of the election. But such a mass operation would contradict the Geisel government's style and would give the hard line too much power. The other way out, and a favorite since 1965, was to make the gubernatorial elections indirect. But that would require a constitutional amendment, and ARENA lacked the necessary two-thirds majority in the Congress. The government could turn to AI–5, but that could only be used, according to the act itself, if Congress were not in session.

Geisel chose to go the route of a constitutional amendment via AI–5, and on April 1, 1977, he closed the Congress. The issue he chose was an ambitious judicial reform bill opposed by the MDB, who had argued that no judicial reform made sense until the arbitrary laws such as AI–5 and the National Security Law were first revoked. Invoking the arbitrary powers of AI–5, Geisel announced a series of major constitutional changes (dubbed the "April package," or *pacote de abril*), all aimed directly or indirectly at making ARENA unbeatable in future elections. Constitutional amendments would henceforth need only a congressional majority; all state governors and a third of the federal senators would be selected indirectly in 1978 by state electoral colleges (which would include municipal councilors, thus assuring ARENA control);[96] federal deputies would be allocated on the basis of population rather than registered voters (as it had been for the elections of 1970 and 1974); and election candidates were strictly limited in their access to radio or television by the *lei Falcão,* already approved by Congress in 1976.[97]

The MDB reacted bitterly to this new manipulation of the political rules. The press was rife with commentary on Geisel's apparent betrayal of his commitment to decompression.[98] The President responded by calling for the Congress to reconvene on April 15. He was anxious to resume the game under the new rules.

One of the first issues to be taken up in Congress was the legalization of divorce. (There had been a decades-long campaign to legalize divorce, headed by Rio de Janeiro MDB Senator Nelson Carneiro.) As divorce was barred by the Constitution, only an amendment could legalize it. The "April package" had reduced the congressional vote needed for an amendment from two-thirds to a majority. A majority (but less than two-thirds) of the 1975 Congress had voted for the amendment. Now, in June 1977, the Geisel government encouraged amendment backers by announcing that it would not enforce party discipline, thereby freeing ARENA Congressmen to vote their conscience. The amendment now passed (permitting each Brazilian only one divorce), to animated celebrations from the congressional galleries. The vote, which undoubtedly had the support of a majority in the country, had suddenly relegitimized the Congress. It was, at least for the moment, the decision-making center on an issue of wide social significance. The episode helped to blunt the anger that many, in both the government and the opposition, had felt over the "April package."

The vote had another significance. It was a highly visible defeat for the Church, which might be outspoken on human rights and social justice but was absolutely opposed to legalizing divorce. The Geisel government (headed by a Lutheran) could not have failed to draw some satisfaction from the defeat of the clerics who had become such a thorn in its side.

The rest of 1977 provided no shortage of evidence for those who doubted the Geisel government's commitment to liberalization. In May 1977 Justice Minister Falcão announced that censorship would be extended to all imported printed matter. Following an earlier anti-censorship manifesto signed by 1,000 intellectuals in January, 2,750 journalists issued a nationwide protest. (That these protests could be staged, it must be noted, showed the degree to which politics had already opened.)[99] In June Geisel purged the MDB leader in the Chamber, Alencar Furtado, and stripped him of his political rights for ten years. Geisel acted in response to Furtado's denunciation of the President in a television broadcast (under the law the opposition got one hour a year) earlier in June.[100]

Earlier in 1977 there had been signs of opposition to the Revolution from another, more familiar source—students. Student protests in March expanded into anti-government demonstrations in May at several universities.[101] Although repression occurred in most cases, the police often showed initial hesitation. Justice Minister Falcão banned all further demonstrations, but that did not stop strike attempts at the University of Brasília and a "national" student meeting in Belo Horizonte, calling for the restoration of democracy. For the first time since 1968, activist students felt that they could defy the security apparatus. Of course, most of these students were too young to remember the bloody repression of their predecessors in 1968. Even so, their enthusiastic demonstrations were a sign that Geisel's promise of liberalization had struck a sympathetic chord among a key elite sector. They were also a sign that patience with the government strategy—and its frequent concessions to the *linha dura*—was wearing thin.

A U.S.–Brazil Rift: Nuclear Technology and Human Rights

The military and civilian revolutionaries of 1964 had seen the United States as Brazil's indispensable ally. Through the 1960s the U.S. remained Brazil's leading investor, trading partner, and military ally, although the authoritarian turn of 1968–69 had led the U.S. to distance itself somewhat from Brazil. But the Geisel government brought a new tone to relations with the U.S. The president was less inclined than his predecessors to accept the idea of the U.S. as Brazil's "indispensable ally." He wanted more room for maneuver, a less "automatic" following of the American lead. That view was warmly shared by Foreign Minister Azeredo Silveira.

This alliance was not without points of discord. The most important from the Brazilian side was economic relations, especially restrictions on access to the U.S. market and the U.S. unwillingness to support a fundamental overhaul of the world trading and financial system. The latter issue had been a principal element in Goulart's foreign policy. The Castelo Branco government foreswore that approach, as did its successors. But the arguments persisted in a more pragmatic form, as Delfim Neto fought to improve Brazil's access to markets, capital, and technology.

Yet it was not economics that caused a rift between the U.S. and Brazil in the Geisel years. It was nuclear technology and human rights. The first stemmed from Brazil's need to seek alternative energy sorces, for the country was poorly endowed with fossil fuels, and imported oil had quadrupled in price since 1973. One alternative was hydro-electric power, but Brazilian experts had already calculated that at the country's historic rate of economic growth its hydro-electric potential would be exhausted by the end of the century, if not before.[102] The next logical alternative, based on the experience of the industrial countries, was nuclear power. But nuclear technology could, if it included the complete fuel cycle, also be used to produce nuclear weapons, and that was an issue on which the U.S. had strong views.[103]

Since 1945 the U.S. had campaigned, in the end unsuccessfully, to prevent the proliferation of nuclear weapons technology. Obviously, the U.S. could not stop the Soviets, and did not try to stop the British or French from becoming self-sufficient in all phases of nuclear technology, including weapons production. But it was a different story with smaller countries (at least in technological capacity) that wanted to develop atomic power as an energy source.

In the short run such countries had little choice but to seek nuclear technology from a major power, which in Brazil's case meant the U.S. The U.S. encouraged such requests, hoping thereby to reduce the spread of the nuclear technology which could also be used for weapons construction. But the latter goal could only be achieved if the recipient country did not acquire the ability to produce enriched uranium, a technology necessary both for maintaining a supply of reactor fuel and for producing explosive devices.

Westinghouse Electric had won a contract in 1972 to build Brazil's first nuclear power plant. It did so on the basis of a U.S. government guarantee that it would supply Brazil with the enriched fuel from its huge plant at Oak Ridge, Tennessee. After 1973 the Brazilians pressed Westinghouse to come up with a contract that would provide them with the entire fuel cycle. Instead, Westinghouse, operating under U.S. government guidelines, offered more reactors on the basis of continued dependence on the U.S. for enriched fuel.

Two events in 1974 ended the Brazilian government's willingness to accept that relationship. The first was India's explosion of a nuclear device in May. The Indians had gained the necessary technology from the Canadians and were the first Third World country to get the bomb. Their success stimulated the military in both Brazil and Argentina to demand faster progress toward accuring their own nuclear capacity (with the implication that it would be the full fuel cycle).

The second event in 1974 was the U.S. Atomic Energy Commission's announcement that due to limited processing capacity it could no longer guarantee to meet Brazil's (and other countries') full needs for enriched uranium.[104] This news came in the midst of negotiations for a mammoth Brazilian contract with Westinghouse, which was to supply Brazil with up to 12 reactors, at a value of $10 billion. When the U.S. withdrew the fuel guarantee, the Westinghouse negotiations collapsed.

The apparent ease with which the U.S. had revoked its commitment seemed to confirm the direst predictions of Brazilian nationalists (on both the right and the left), who had long criticized their government policy of indefinite dependence on a foreign source for the crucial element in the nuclear fuel cycle. This critique well suited the purposes of the Geisel government, which sought to follow a nationalist course. It also served the purposes of those within the Geisel government who had already begun negotiations to buy reactors from West Germany.

West Germany was the most logical source because of its advanced nuclear technology and its eagerness to find new customers. Furthermore, Geisel looked to Germany as one of the poles, along with Iran, of the structure of Brazil's new geopolitical relations. In June 1975 the Brazilian government and a consortium of West German suppliers signed an agreement calling for Brazil to purchase two to eight giant reactors, with the cost of eight reactors at $10 billion.

If the Brazilians had bought all eight reactors it would have been a record transfer of nuclear technology to a developing country. It also promised to be a giant boost for the West German atomic generator industry, which had run out of orders. (The industrial countries built their own.) The Germans were delighted to have beaten Westinghouse in such a key Third World country but from the political standpoint there was an even more important consideration. The technology to be supplied included the capacity to produce nuclear weapons (either by enriching uranium or by separation of plutonium by reprocessing spent fuel).

While the West German–Brazilian contract was still under negotiation, the U.S. administration of President Gerald Ford decided that the West Germans were not making a sufficient effort to prevent the Brazilians from acquiring nuclear weapons technology. Brazil's refusal to sign the 1970 Nuclear Nonproliferation Treaty had only reinforced U.S. worries. Washington pressured Bonn not to sign the contract. When that ploy failed, the U.S. tried to persuade West Germany to obtain an agreement with safeguards against the use of the technology for nonpeaceful purposes. The two nations did so, although the implementation procedures were far from ironclad, especially once Brazil had acquired the complete fuel cycle technology.[105]

The Brazilians had tacitly declared their right to engage in nuclear proliferation, a sin against which the U.S. had crusaded since its own monopoly was first threatened. The U.S. government had prevented any U.S. firms from offering Brazil nuclear technology adaptable to military use. But now, thanks to the deal with West Germany, Brazil could move toward joining the exclusive club of nations (Argentina was ahead) that possessed the complete atomic fuel cycle.

The Brazilian negotiators of the contract had worked largely in secret. The military and the Foreign Office had taken charge, never consulting with Brazil's experienced energy specialists (Petrobrás and Electrobrás) nor with Brazil's nuclear scientists. It was an operation typical of Geisel's autocratic style. When finally presented with the contract, the Brazilian Congress approved it unanimously. Geisel himself kept a low profile on the West German deal. The official volumes of his speeches for 1975 and 1976, for example, include nothing on the subject. Finally, in March 1977, Brazil published a white paper explaining its nuclear program. It included a two-paragraph introduction by Geisel emphasizing that Brazil's nuclear program "has the unanimous support of national opinion, is based on our own efforts, along with cooperation from abroad, and accepts safeguards, which guarantee its strictly peaceful application."[106]

On the domestic scene, the Geisel government needed to make no apologies for its nuclear deal with West Germany. The overwhelming majority of the political elite were delighted with Brazil's enhanced image as a sovereign nation. After all, Brazil had successfully pursued a policy the U.S. heatedly opposed (U.S. pressure had been focussed on the West Germans as the source of the technology). Geisel's government had successfully asserted Brazil's right to decide for itself how far it would try to go in developing its nuclear capacity, although it had accepted safeguards in the agreement and would remain dependent on West Germany. Of great importance for the Geisel regime, many hard-line military officers were pleased with this coup by a government they otherwise distrusted or detested. Meanwhile, key voices of the opposition, such as *O Estado de São Paulo,* vigorously supported the nuclear accord. There could be no doubt: the Geisel government had found an issue which struck a deep nationalist chord among the elite.

On another level, the Brazilian government took a step toward increased U.S.–Brazilian cooperation. Foreign Minister Azeredo da Silveira capitalized on a personal friendship with Secretary of State Kissinger to formulate a joint memorandum (signed February 21, 1976, while Kissinger was visiting Brasília) that provided for regular bilateral consultative meetings on a wide range of levels.[107] The idea was to create a mechanism to insure that vital (and not so vital) questions could be discussed routinely, before misunderstandings could grow. By signing this memorandum, the U.S. was acknowledging Brazil's emergence in Latin America as the preeminent economic power. Brazil, in turn, was reaffirming "the solidarity of the Western World," as the text had it.

The memorandum, which Silveira had been urging on the U.S. government for some time, provided a convenient means for the government to reassure its highly anticommunist military critics (and some civilians, such as those represented by *O Estado de São Paulo*) who would be pleased by an apparent re-emphasis on the U.S. alliance. They regarded the latter as a lodestar of the 1964 Revolution especially in moments of geopolitical preoccupation such as those recently provoked by the radicalization of Portugal, now safely in moderate hands, and Angola, where Brazil had been the first major country to recognize the pro-Soviet MPLA.[108]

In 1976 President Gerald Ford's loss of the presidency to Jimmy Carter portended changes in U.S. foreign policy. Once in office, the new president put a high priority on preventing nuclear proliferation, the very issue on which the West Germans and indirectly the Brazilians had been pressed by the U.S. at the time of their June 1975 contract.[109]

Carter, who had once been a navy officer specializing in nuclear engineering, chose to make a major issue of Brazil's defiance of the U.S. stand on nuclear proliferation. In early 1977 the Carter administration, as one of its first initiatives, mounted an offensive aimed at both West Germany and Brazil, arguing forcefully for a repeal of the two-year-old agreement for Brazil to receive West German nuclear techology. Deputy Secretary of State Warren Christopher took the U.S. plea to Brazil, but the Brazilians remained adamant. In the short term, at least, U.S. pressure only stiffened the resolve of the Geisel government.[110]

Nor did the U.S. make any more headway in West Germany. It had now been rebuffed by the two countries that had been its most reliable post-1945 allies in their respective regions. By late 1977 the Carter administration had given up head on tactics. Its fervent campaign had only made Bonn and Brasília more determined. Both capitals encouraged the speculation that Carter's zeal had more to do with Westinghouse's lost business than U.S. desires to save the world from nuclear proliferation.

The fight over nuclear policy produced some political benefits for the Geisel government. Most important, it capitalized on the support of military officers who had long worried about Argentina's nuclear lead. Some of these officers wanted Brazil to develop its own nuclear weapons. Not a few of these officers were also indignant about U.S. pressure on Brazil over human rights.[111] No less important, the nuclear deal offered an equal opportunity to outflank the Brazilian left, still a discernable if muffled voice. Finally, the nuclear imbroglio gave Geisel the opportunity to be nationalistic in a manner that many middle-class civilians could understand.

The Carter administration, arriving in power in January 1977, inadvertently helped consolidate military support for Geisel on another issue: human rights. In fact, the initiative had come from the U.S. Congress before Jimmy Carter even took office. In its 1976 foreign aid bill the Congress required the State Department (in a clause known as the Harkin amendment) to issue an annual report on the state of human rights in any country receiving U.S. military assistance. Brazil was such a recipient, and the first report prepared by the State Department appeared in early 1977, although preparation of the report predated the change of government. It strongly criticized Brazil along the lines of such earlier documents as those of Amnesty International.[112]

The Geisel government reacted with calculated fury. Foreign Minister Silveira, well known for his personal antagonism to the U.S., denounced the intolerable interference in Brazil's internal affairs. Even some MDB leaders closed ranks publicly behind the government; others remained silent. By pursuing the cause of human rights through bilateral aid, the U.S. Congress had aroused Brazilian nationalism. President Geisel fully shared the nationalist reaction, not least because he feared this outside pressure might disrupt his plan for a gradual and highly controlled liberalization.[113] Within days the Brazilian government announced cancelation of a U.S.–Brazil military aid agreement begun in 1952. In September four more military agreements were cancelled, including one for U.S. participation in the aerial mapping of Brazil. U.S. Ambassador John Crimmins noted that the Brazilian government's actions had ended "all formal structure of military cooperation between the two countries."[114] By rejecting all military aid, the Geisel government eliminated for the moment any occasion for future State Department reports on human rights in Brazil.

President Carter scheduled a visit to Brazil for late November, in the hope that he could repair the damage done to U.S.–Brazilian relations. By early November he canceled, in part because Brasília reacted lukewarmly. The trip was rescheduled for late March of 1978.

Instead, it was the U.S. First Lady who made an official tour, in June of 1977. In Brazil Mrs. Rosalyn Carter was immediately swept into the human rights controversy. She was given a letter by a Brazilian student representative denouncing his government's human rights violations. During a stop in the Northeastern port city of Recife, Mrs. Carter met with two U.S. missionaries, who gave a hair-raising account of their mistreatment by police only a few days earlier. She promised to raise the matter with her husband. The effect of Mrs. Carter's trip was to dramatize anew the U.S. role in trying to influence Brazilian government policies. Hard-line military played upon the reaction to this foreign criticism in an attempt to exploit nationalist sentiments among their more moderate colleagues. Even though criticism by both the Carter administration and the U.S. Congress of human rights violations raised resentment in Brazil—inside and outside the government— those who worked for a democratic Brazil thought the U.S. pressure had been helpful. U.S. diplomats reported frequent conversations with Brazilians who expressed gratitude for the U.S. stand. Nevertheless, no one thought the effect was more than marginal.

Geisel Subdues the Hard Line

Meanwhile, within the Geisel government the struggle had intensified between the hardliners and the moderates (although the positions had become more complex than that dichotomy suggests). Army Minister General Sylvio Frota was now the hard line's leader. He certainly had the credentials. Back in 1955 Frota, as a junior officer, joined the other officers opposed to War Minister Henrique Lott's "preventive coup" guaranteeing the inauguration of president-elect Juscelino Kubitschek. Both Lott and Kubitschek were anathema to the hard line. Frota had also been an active conspirator against President Goulart and in December 1968 was a key officer guiding the much stepped-up repression. In 1972 he assumed command of the First Army, where, interestingly enough, he was an indefatigable opponent of torture, an unusual stance for a commander in that period. Frota then became army minister in May 1974, replacing Geisel's original appointee, General Dale Coutinho, a notorious hardliner who died only two months after taking office.

Frota believed Brazil was in imminent danger of communist subversion. He considered liberalization a ruse that would only ease the path of the subversives, many of whom had already, in Frota's view, infiltrated the MDB, the Church, and every other key institution. Frota made no secret of his views, which he enunciated on every available public occasion. Most important, Frota considered himself presidential material and was already organizing his military support. He was using the Army Intelligence Service (*Centro de Informações do Exército,* or CIEX) as a means of confidential contact with fellow officers. Frota knew CIEX well, having helped create it in 1967. But the army minister did not control the SNI, the top-level intelligence agency, headed by General João Batista Figueiredo, Geisel's choice in the presidential succession. Thanks to the SNI, the Planalto remained fully informed of Frota's moves.

Frota's behavior angered the Planalto on several counts. First, Geisel had made clear that he wanted no discussion of the presidential succession before January 1978.[115] Yet Frota's campaign was in full swing, with a "Frotista" wing of Congressmen now banging the drums for the army minister's candidacy. Second, Frota was explicitly attacking liberalization. By May of 1977 Frota had begun courting congressional support. By July he was publicly criticizing the Geisel government's strategy, especially toward the subversives. In September General Jayme Portella, former head of Costa e Silva's military staff, joined the Frota forces to help coordinate military support. Some 90 Congressmen were now reported to support Frota's candidacy. Journalists speculated over how much longer Geisel would tolerate this blatant challenge to his authority.

They did not have to wonder long. On October 10 the President told his closest staff he was going to dismiss Frota on October 12, a holiday. With the Congress and government offices closed, it would be difficult for the soon-to-be-ex-Army Minister to rally his forces. Geisel also alerted the top regional army commanders, telling them of Frota's impending dismissal and replacement by General Fernando Belfort Bethlem. When Geisel delivered the coup de grace in person on October 12, Frota marched off to issue a fiery manifesto, accusing the government of "criminal complacency" over "communist infiltration" at high levels of government. He attacked Brazil's 1974 recognition of the People's Republic of China and the 1975 recognition of the Marxist government in Angola. Frota ordered his manifesto sent to every barracks in the country, evidently not knowing that Geisel had already communicated his dismissal to the army commands. The manifesto was never transmitted.[116]

Frota tried another last-minute gambit. He called a meeting in Brasília of the army High Command (the key members were the commanders of the four regional armies) where he would present his case. Again Geisel outmaneuvered him. Each member of the High Command had also received orders from Geisel to come to Brasília but to come directly to the Planalto. As each general arrived at the Brasília airport, he found waiting for him two cars (each with officer and driver)—one from Frota and one from the President. Every one chose the presidential car, knowing full well that Frota had already been dismissed. Back at the Planalto, General Hugo Abreu held a press conference to announce Frota's firing and replacement by Bethlem. The statement denied that the change had any connection with the presidential succession, but added, in apparent contradiction, that any discussion of that subject before January 1978 would be "prejudicial for the country."[117]

Frota had undoutedly foreseen his firing, and thought he could still rally hardliner support and thereby force the President to accept a previously unacceptable presidential candidate. Frota apparently thought he could force the President to accede to a reverse, as with Castelo Branco in October 1965, or with Costa e Silva in December 1968. But times had changed. There had been no dramatic event to fire up the hardliners, such as the 1965 gubernatorial elections or the congressional vote against lifting Márcio Moreira Alves's parliamentary immunity in December 1968. The hardliners, however sympathetic they might be to Frota's perfervid anti-communist rhetoric, chose not to challenge Geisel. The three years of liberalization had undoubtedly taken their toll on the hard line. They had shrunk in number and they faced a public mood overtly hostile to their methods. Civil society had become more difficult to intimidate.

Frota's salvo did find support from several prominent rightist officers. But they were retired men—such as Marshal Odílio Denis, Air Force General Marcio de Sousa Melo, and Admirals Augusto Rademaker and Silvio Heck—who were discounted as long-time anti-castelista critics and who had little current influence in either military or civilian circles. The active-duty army officers knew that if they opted for a losing cause (as Frota already seemed to be), their military careers would be sidetracked or finished. Geisel's decisiveness had made that clear.

Frota's dismissal demonstrated that Geisel had accumulated more personal power than any previous president. He had taken the unprecedented step of firing the Army Minister without consulting the High Command. Previous military presidents had all experienced a drop in their power *within* the army, once they became President. Geisel had not only retained that power, he had increased it with the dismissals and/or resignations of Second Army Commander General Ednardo, and Army Minister Frota, and General Hugo Abreu (see below). Geisel was now using his augmented power within the army to promote liberalization.[118]

The key political question, as always, was the presidential succession. Who would be the official nominee for the 1978 election? Would it be a candidate pledged to carry out the Geisel—Golbery political strategy?[119] From the day he entered office Geisel had made clear to his closest advisers that he wanted General João Baptista Figueiredo, now the SNI director, as his successor. In late December 1977 Geisel made his choice public (which was tantamount to nomination by the party). For the vice-presidential candidate Geisel selected a civilian: Aureliano Chaves, an electrical engineer, energy specialist, and former governor of Minas Gerais.

Although Figueiredo seemed a shoo-in, there was an awkward problem with his military rank. Whereas all previous presidents had had four stars, he had only three. There was time to promote him, but he would have to be jumped over four generals with greater seniority. Geisel prevailed; his new Army Minister, Belfort Bethlem, an apparent moderate, stage-managed Figueiredo's promotion in time.[120] In April at the national convention ARENA endorsed Figueiredo and Chaves in a manner that again underlined how little initiative this "governmental" party was allowed.[121]

Although Geisel had firm control over the succession, there was continuing military dissent. General Hugo Abreu, chief of the presidential military staff and the paratroop commander who had liquidated the guerrillas in the Amazon, resigned in protest over the choice of Figueiredo.[122] He was replaced by General Moraes Rego, a well-known Geisel loyalist. Geisel maintained his mastery among the officers, at least on the succession. Elsewhere the battle against the hardliners was far from over, although Amnesty International reported that the number of arrests of suspected subversives had declined since early 1976.[123]

On the other side of the political spectrum, the voices from civil society, especially the Church and the Bar, continued to demand a rapid transition to the rule of law, aided by a de facto relaxation in censorship. In August 1977, on the occasion of the sesquicentenary of law teaching in Brazil, a prominent professor of the São Paulo law school issued a "Letter to Brazilians," calling for immediate redemocratization and a return to the rule of law. A crowd of 3,000 demonstrators then marched through downtown São Paulo, without police interference.[124] In May 1978 the Bar Association's national convention in Curitiba was entirely devoted to the rule of law and its implications. The meeting ended with a "Declaration of Brazilian Lawyers," calling for a return to the rule of law but also for the writing of a new constitution, the granting of amnesty, and the complete revision of existing labor legislation. Under President Raymundo Faoro, the OAB had become highly aggressive in spreading its message, building on its activism of the earlier 1970s. Even so, pro-liberalization leaders within the government wanted more public pressure in order to show why change "had" to come. Justice Minister Petronio Portella asked Faoro if he could increase the pro-amnesty publicity. Faoro and the OAB did so, and changes favoring eventual amnesty were made.[125]

Meanwhile, a new voice from civil society was making itself heard—the business community. Previously there had been individual criticisms of government policies, especially over such issues as credit policy, import controls, and price controls. But the more independent-minded businessmen had been hoping for more from the Geisel government because they had a voice within the cabinet: Severo Gomes, Minister of Industry and Commerce. Gomes, earlier Minister of Agriculture in the Castelo Branco government, was an authentic representative of one sector of São Paulo business, where he had worked for the textile companies his family owned. He was on record as favoring a more nationalist economic policy, strengthening domestic producers, and focusing on the internal market. In 1976 he became outspoken on the need for political liberalization, arguing it was essential if the private economic sector were to flourish.

Gomes reflected and also stimulated opinion in the business community, especially that sector oriented primarily to the home market. Businessmen were by nature cautious, given the fear that most had of a threat from the left. They had eagerly supported the coup of 1964. Some had even helped finance the São Paulo Death Squad until the guerrillas' demise removed the need.[126] Businessmen were also cautious because they depended on government at every turn—credit, import licenses, price controls, wage setting, tax assessments, government purchases, to name but a few. While the economy boomed (according to a 1976 study, Brazilian business executives had the highest salaries in the world), the business sector's principal complaint was the enormous presence of the state in the economy.[127] Now, however, with censorship eased and the air alive with salvos from the Church, the Bar Association, and the press, many from business found their voice. In November 1977 the Fourth National Congress of the Productive Classes called for increased dialogue, wherein they could better defend their interests. In closing, the Congress called for a new program of economic and social development, which could only be achieved "with a desirable degree of political freedom, and in a pluralistic, multiple society, one in which economic power had been decentralized . . ."[128]

The latter referred to businessmen's ongoing campaign to reduce the state's role in the economy. They charged that government had invaded too many sectors, at the cost of private business. Their rallying cry was "denationalize!" (*desestatizar*). Their support for democratization, which surprised some observers, had several sources. One was a general belief in the desirability of representative government and the rule of law. Another was a belief that under such a regime business would have a better chance to influence policy, especially against the bureaucrats and the foreign business interests, which the authoritarian regime had favored. Many businessmen were equally upset about the expansion of foreign firms, arguing that government should do more to help Brazilian businesses.

As Brazilian businessmen found their political voice, they became another force in the political game. One business sector had a spokesman within the government, Severo Gomes, who, as we have noted, argued that government policies had unduly favored foreign investors. The Planalto did not appreciate his new visibility, his growing outspokenness on the need for political reform, or his semi-public attacks on the hard line. He was asked for his resignation in early February 1977.[129] But there was no ignoring the fact that a key socio-economic sector, once in the government's pocket, had gotten other ideas. In 1979 eight prominent São Paulo industrialists issued a manifesto calling for a rapid return to democracy. Among the signers were Gomes, José Mindlin, Antonio Emírio de Moraes, and Laerte Setubal. This was the strongest statement to come from the business community, and it signalled a split in their ranks. The more conservative wing was represented by Teobaldo de Nigrís, the long-time president of the São Paulo Federation of Industries (*Federação das Industrias do Estado de São Paulo,* or FIESP), who had been a virtual yes-man for the military governments and took a tough stance on relations with labor. The liberals were represented by the eight signatories of the manifesto and by such younger figures as industrialist Luiz Eulálio Bueno Vidigal, who led a two-year campaign to defeat Nigrís in 1980 for the presidency of FIESP. This new generation did not hesitate to criticize the government nor to stake out its own positions in labor relations and economic policy. Although business was not an institution with the nationwide presence of the Bar or the Church, its criticism was a significant factor in eroding the legitimacy of a regime that claimed to be promoting capitalism.[130]

The presidential election campaign proved more interesting than at first promised. The MDB decided to field its own entire slate, though they knew their electoral chances were zero. For president they nominated General Euler Bentes Monteiro, the former director of SUDENE (the Northeast development agency), whose finances he unsuccessfully fought to protect during the Médici regime. The MDB convention endorsed Euler, along with *gaúcho* MDB Senator Paulo Brossard, an eloquent advocate of a return to the rule of law, as his vice-presidential running mate. The ticket was supported by *A Folha de São Paulo,* now a principal opposition voice. Some within the MDB thought the party should have no part of the election, arguing that participation would lend legitimacy to an illegitimate order. But these dissenters lost to the majority view that the election offered a good opportunity to wage a "symbolic" campaign that could educate the public on the key issues.

There was a campaign, with speeches and rallies. Figueiredo promised to carry forward a gradual democratization. Euler called for a constituent assembly to write a new constitution. The MDB also called for a new economic policy to correct the glaring economic inequities. To no one's surprise, the ARENA-dominated electoral college chose Figueiredo and Chaves on October 14, 1978. The vote was 355–266, following party lines.

A month later came the congressional elections.[131] The electoral law changes in Geisel's 1977 "April package" had succeeded in guaranteeing ARENA a congressional majority. A new provision made a third of the Senate elected indirectly (which assured the government enough Senators to veto any constitutional amendment—in September 1978 irreverent Brazilians christened these Senators the "bionics"), and a revision of the formula on representation in the Chamber of Deputies gave ARENA continued control of both houses. But the trend in direct voting was obvious: the national vote totals in the direct elections for Senator in November 1978, were 52 percent for MDB, 34 percent for ARENA, 14 percent spoiled or blank ballots.

In late 1978 Geisel fulfilled his promise to phase out key elements of the authoritarian structure. In October the Congress approved a set of extensive reforms in the form of Constitutional Amendment No. 11. The MDB boycotted the final vote, arguing that the government proposals did not go far enough and therefore to vote at all would be to legitimize a sham. The most important change was abolition of AI–5, thereby ending the President's authority to declare a congressional recess, remove Congressmen, or strip citizens of their political rights. In addition, *habeas corpus* was reinstituted for political detainees, prior censorship was lifted from radio and television, and the death sentence and life imprisonment were abolished. Independence of the judiciary was restored by the guarantee of job tenure and the depoliticization of decisions over judges' salaries and court assignments. At the same time, however, articles 155–158 of the amendment gave vast new powers to the executive to proclaim "emergency measures," a "state of siege," or a "state of emergency," all of which could be renewed for at least 120 days without congressional approval. Executive powers under this authority were vast, from suspension of legal guarantees to appointment of governors to censorship. The Bar Association and the opposition attacked this provision as a thinly disguised resuscitation of AI–5.[132]

The government also proposed a revised version of the National Security Law, which many constitutional law specialists considered as important a source of arbitrary power as AI–5. The number of possible crimes against state security was reduced and the penalties softened. But the law still allowed for political prisoners to be held incommunicado for eight days (instead of ten). Because torture was most likely to occur in the days immediately following arrest, human rights advocates rejected the proposed revisions in the law as a fraud. In fact, the Congress never voted on the bill. It was promulgated (as Law 6,620/78) in December under the *decurso de prazo* clause, which provided automatic approval of any presidential bill not acted on by the Congress within 40 days.[133]

At the very end of 1978 Geisel took another step to promote political reconciliation. He revoked the banishment orders on more than 120 political exiles, most of whom had left Brazil in 1969–70 in exchange for foreign diplomats kidnapped by the guerrillas. Eight of the more famous exiles were excluded, however. Among them were Leonel Brizola, the former governor of Rio Grande do Sul who had called for an insurrection in 1964, and Luis Carlos Prestes, the long-time secretary general of the Brazilian Communist Party. Both were *bêtes noires* to the hard line.

The "New Unionism" in Action

Not only on the political front did 1978 prove to be an eventful year. While Geisel was quashing the hard line and stage-managing the nomination of General Figueiredo, he was suddenly reminded of another voice from civil society: organized labor.

In the decade after the 1968 wildcat strikes at Contagem (Minas Gerais) and Osasco (São Paulo) workers were successfully demobilized. The best they could manage were "work-to-rule" slowdowns in which there was no direct challenge to the security forces.[134] The military regime's repressive presence, through both the Labor Ministry and the police and military, finally put an end to any attempt to rebuild the labor movement along the ambitious lines envisioned in the late 1950s and early 1960s, with a CGT, etc. The union leadership had no alternative but to work within the given structure.

But forcing them to work within the official structure had an unexpected result in São Paulo and a few other urban areas. It directed activity toward bread-and-butter issues on the shop floor. Some ably led unions won concessions on fringe benefits and on such issues as equal pay for new hires. They also won demands on work rules, such as special clauses for pregnant workers. Much of this was done through the labor courts, a central instrument of the corporatist labor relations structure. In granting some union demands, the courts were functioning in the paternalistic manner their creators in the 1930s had intended—the demands were won not from the employer but from a government-appointed body. Nonetheless, the union activity created a focus that had often been missing in Brazilian labor relations: the shop-floor link between worker and union representative. The lack of such a link was no accident. The corporatist structure had defined union locals geographically, i.e., by *município* (approximately an American county or township), which fragmented the union horizontally. There were, for example, four metalworkers unions in greater São Paulo city—in the *municípios* of Santo André, São Bernardo, São Caetano, and São Paulo. Forcing union activities inward stimulated the emergence of a new generation of leaders, principally in São Paulo, who began to denounce the corporatist labor relations structure and wanted to build a new independent union movement (*novo sindicalismo,* or new unionism) by throwing out the old pro-government union bosses (*pelegos*).[135] The most prominent of those new leaders was Luis Inácio da Silva, known by his nickname of "Lula," who was president of the Metalworkers Union of São Bernardo, a São Paulo industrial suburb that housed key industries, especially in motor vehicles.[136]

It was inevitable that these new union leaders, long faced with repression, would join other spokesmen for civil society in demanding change. An issue that had especially angered workers was the government's frequent failure to compensate fully for inflation when setting new minimum wage rates. This had been repeated on and off since 1964, and the systematic distortion had been documented (using a more complete cost-of-living index) by DIEESE, an independent labor union statistical office inn São Paulo. MDB orators, as well as critics from the Church and the universities, had harshly attacked this wage policy.[137]

The minimum wage adjustment for 1973 was an especially flagrant distortion. It was the last full year of the Médici government, and Delfim Neto was apparently determined to record an inflation rate close to what the President had predicted (13 percent) at the year's outset. Delfim set it at 15 percent, whereas non-government sources put it at 20–25 percent.

There was little that workers, unions, or anyone else could do at the time, given the repressive atmosphere. But the World Bank was to give the issue an unexpected twist. The World Bank obviously needs to have accurate data on its borrowers. The discrepancy in Brazil's official 1973 inflation figure was so large as to distort all of Brazil's official post-1972 data. So several World Bank economists produced their own inflation estimate for 1973, a figure of 22.5 percent.[138] São Paulo union leaders seized on the World Bank study as proof they had been cheated in all post-1973 wage adjustments.

The first large-scale worker action in the Geisel presidency began in May 1978 with a sit-down movement.[139] Twenty-five hundred of Lula's metalworkers at the Saab-Scania truck and bus factory in the São Paulo industrial suburb of São Bernardo do Campo punched their time clocks, assumed their work positions, crossed their arms, and sat down, refusing to start their machines. This sit-down action was a shrewd tactic. The workers did not begin with pickets outside the plant, where the police could (as in the past) readily attack and arrest them. A sit-down action was new in the recent history of labor activism. Plant management was unprepared to drag the immobile workers away from their machines.

The mood at the Saab-Scania became contagious. Within ten days the strike action had spread to 90 firms in greater São Paulo, evetually involving 500,000 workers. Given the "liberal" stance of the government, the workers were in a favorable position. The employers decided to bargain directly. By bargaining, the metalworkers got an extra 11 percent one-time pay increase (they had demanded 34 percent) to adjust their base pay for the past understatement of inflation. Future calculations of inflation would start from this base. This 12-day strike against the auto industry, and especially the subsequent direct bargaining, was heavily reported by the press, much of which depicted the movement as the workers' response to President Geisel's promised liberalization.[140]

The strike effort was less successful in other sectors. Neither the bank workers (traditionally a militant union) nor the cigarette factory workers had the success of the metalworkers. And by October 1978 another group of the latter found the going much tougher. The statewide São Paulo Federation of Metalworkers, whose work agreement expired in November, came up short. Its president, Joaquim dos Santos Andrade, stage-managed an agreement that ended the strike with few gains for the workers. The contrast was thus stark, between the "new unionist" Lula and the pro-government collaborator "Joaquimzão."

The Metalworkers Union and Lula gained surprising visibility, with much of the press (aided in some cases by suggestions from the Planalto, i.e., Golbery) and Church progressives picturing Lula as a legitimate, that is, noncommunist spokesman for a small but strategic part of the working class. Lula had suddenly become Brazil's best-known labor leader since 1945. The argument in much of the press was that inasmuch as the government itself was moving toward redemocratization, a move toward direct negotiation between labor and capital was highly appropriate. The political opening was therefore used to justify union activism, and the government response became a test of its real intentions.

The Economic Record Since 1974 and Geisel's Legacy

As the Geisel government reached the end of 1978, its last full year in power, economic commentators began to draw up their balance sheets on its record. How had the economy performed since 1973? Had the government's economic strategy changed? Had the OPEC challenge put an end to the economic "miracle?"[141]

Judged by the basic marcoeconomic indicators, the Geisel team's economic performance was good. Between 1974 and 1978 GDP grew at an average annual rate of 7 percent, although the last two years had brought a slowdown—5.4 percent in 1977 and 4.8 percent in 1978. By Brazil's past standards the 7 percent average was a strong showing, though it was less than the 10.8 percent rate of the 1968–73 "miracle" period.

As for inflation, the trend was similar. For 1974–78 the inflation rate averaged 37.9 percent. But it worsened toward the end, with the 1977 rate at 38.8 percent and the 1978 rate at 40.8 percent. The 37.9 percent average for the 1974–78 was almost exactly double the 1968–73 average of 19.3 percent. This increase in inflation worried many inside and outside the Geisel government. But by using indexation and mini-devaluations, the government was able to prevent the higher inflation rates from seriously distorting relative prices. When faced with a choice between lowering inflation and maintaining growth, Geisel's policymakers opted for growth.

The final major indicator of economic health was the balance of payments. We saw earlier how from 1967 to 1973 Brazil's economy was propelled by rapid industrial growth, which in turn was import intensive, especially in capital goods. OPEC's 1973 oil price shock imperilled this growth strategy by doubling Brazil's oil bill suddenly and threatening to crowd out imports needed by industry.

In 1974 Brazil survived its balance of payments crisis by eating into its foreign exchange reserves and by doubling its external debt. In the following years the government severely restricted imports, which hovered between $12.0 billion and $12.6 billion from 1974 through 1977. In 1978 imports increased to $13.6 billion, a modest rise given the Brazilian economy's growth over the previous four years. Exports rose from $7.8 billion in 1974 to $12.5 billion in 1978. The rise of industrial exports within that total was even more impressive. In 1978, for the first time ever, more than half of Brazil's exports were industrial products. The figures were 50.2 percent industrial goods, 48.4 percent commodities (the residual was "other products"). As recently as 1973 commodities had accounted for 66 percent of exports. But export growth, impressive as it was, failed to pay for imports, much less cover the payments on repatriated profits and the service on foreign loans, which by 1978 had reached $4.2 billion.

What saved Brazil was the continued heavy inflow of foreign capital, primarily loans. In 1978, for example, there was a net inflow of $7.0 billion. By the end of 1978 Brazil had incurred a total external debt of $43.5 billion, more than double the level of only three years earlier.

Brazilian policymakers, their creditors, and their critics now began closely watching the size of the foreign debt. The standard indicator was the debt burden, i.e., the cost of debt servicing (payment of interest plus amortization) as a percentage of current export earnings. By 1978 the debt burden had risen to 58.8 percent, the highest figure for the 1970s and very high by Brazil's past experience. Brazil, thanks in part to its relatively high growth, attracted U.S., European, and Japanese commercial bank loans. True, Brazil was paying interest rates higher than those charged to domestic customers in the industrial economies, but that difference was negligible in view of the fact that the U.S. rate of inflation was rendering the loan rates negative.

There were, nonetheless, obvious problems with "debt-led growth." If the heavy lending should slow down or stop, Brazil's economic growth would follow. Second, most of the commercial bank loans carried an interest rate linked to the prime interest rate in the London or New York Eurodollar market. That made the future debt burden impossible to predict, especially worrisome at a time when interest rates were notoriously volatile. Third, the borrowing spree had made the Brazilian private sector especially vulnerable. Most of the foreign debt (70 percent according to an ECLA estimate) had been incurred by the private sector, which found Eurodollar interest rates lower than Brazilian rates. The government kept the latter high so as to push Brazilian borrowers toward the Eurodollar market. They thereby brought in more foreign capital to help cover the balance of payments deficit. As a result, Brazil's private sector was tied to two potentially volatile factors: (1) Eurodollar interest rates and (2) Brazilian exchange rate policy. The danger in the former is obvious. The latter could create serious problems for private sector borrowers if the Brazilian government accelerated its mini-devaluation schedule or went for a maxidevaluation.

These threats to the debt-led economic strategy materialized in varying measure during Geisel's presidency. Capital inflow, at least, had continued at a rate sufficient to finance the import-intensive growth. The availability of the loans was hardly coincidental, since they came primarily from commercial banks anxious to recycle the petrodollars the Brazilians and other oil importers had to pay their oil suppliers.

Another danger in the debt-led strategy was the private sector's vulnerability to interest rate increases abroad and devaluations at home. Here the impact was already major in the Geisel period. Rising Eurodollar interest rates pushed many Brazilian firms to the wall. They found themselves much disadvantaged vis-à-vis the multinationals (MNCs) in Brazil, which had access to capital from the U.S. or European home firms. Brazilian businessmen complained bitterly about this advantage of the MNCs. The Geisel government tried to compensate by increasing the credit available for Brazilian firms. But insofar as that suceeded, it worked against the need to maximize foreign capital inflow (for balance of payments purposes) through private borrowing.

Finally, there was a danger of the crowding out of non-oil imports. This did occur with the import of capital goods. From 1975 to 1978, the annual rate of capital imports fluctuated between $3.1 and $4 billion. Given inflation, this meant a relative decline in the real value of capital goods imports. The Geisel government recognized this problem and created new incentives to expand Brazil's import substituting capacity, especially in capital goods.

Another hallmark of development policy in these years was commitment to large-scale public investment projects, such as the Itaipú hydro-electric complex on the Brazil–Paraguay border, the Açominas steel project in Minas Gerais, the nuclear energy program, and the Steel Railroad (Ferrovia do Aço). The goal was both to increase energy self-sufficiency and to increase exports. Yet all these projects would require years of investment before any significant payoff.

They would also increase the state sector of the economy, a trend Brazilian businessmen were attacking. The Geisel government had promised to strengthen the private sector, yet the President typified the military mentality that prized rapid growth even at the cost of a larger state sector. That commitment was all the stronger when it came to strategic sectors such as energy and transportation.[142]

The Geisel government thought the energy crisis so severe that it violated a long-standing nationalist taboo by granting "risk contracts" to international oil firms to explore for oil in Brazil. In late 1976 contracts were signed with British Petroleum and Shell. A later contract was granted to a consortium of smaller foreign firms. Nationalist critics howled over this breach of what had been a nationalist monopoly since the creation of Petrobrás in 1953–54. The last laugh was on the foreign companies, who found no oil. The cynics suggested that the most promising zones had been reserved for Petrobrás all along.[143]

On balance, the debt-led growth strategy remained viable during the Geisel presidency. The Geisel policymakers had played for time and won. But Brazil's long-term prospects were another matter.[144]

What political legacy was Geisel about to deliver to his hand-picked successor?[145] There could be no doubt that Geisel and Golbery had pursued liberalization farther than most observers would have thought possible in 1974. *Habeas corpus* restored, AI–5 revoked, most of the political refugees back in Brazil, censorship ended—these were impressive accomplishments for a military government. But significant arbitrary powers remained, especially in the new national security law.[146]

It was also worth remembering that since 1964 the federal executive had been sharply increasing its legal and economic powers. The federal Congress, for example, was deprived in 1965 of what democratic countries have long considered a primary legislative power, control over appropriations. Furthermore, the huge security apparatus remained untouched: each military service's intelligence arm, the Army's DOI-CODI, and the SNI with its agents inside every government ministry. Given the remaining legal authority of the executive and the omnipresence of the SNI, any opposition politician had ample reason for still considering politics a dangerous occupation.

Only at the end of Geisel's presidency could one see clearly the contrast between his public manner and the net effect of his rule. In public Geisel was the stereotype of a German in Brazil—stiff, rigid in expression, and quite alien to the informal give-and-take of Brazilian politics.[147] Yet his rigidity was an asset in his relations with the military. His insistence on fulfilling orders and missions, combined with his fearless assertion of authority, made him a figure fellow officers had to respect. The most autocratic president since 1964 had mastered the challenge of the *linha dura*.

VII

FIGUEIREDO: THE TWILIGHT OF MILITARY GOVERNMENT

The new president came from a military family. His father, General Euclides Figueiredo, had commanded a contingent of troops in the 1932 São Paulo rebellion against President Getúlio Vargas's government.[1] Three of his sons, João Batista and two brothers, joined the army and made general. João graduated first in his class at the Colegio Militar in Pôrto Alegre and first in his class at the *Escola Militar* (*Arma de Cavalaria*). He later repeated that standing at the *Escola de Aperfeiçoamento de Oficiais* (*Cavalaria*) and at the *Escola de Estado-Maior*. In 1960 he spent a year at the Higher War College (*Escola Superior de Guerra*), which brought together for a year-long course leading representatives of the military and civilian elites. During Jânio Quadros's seven-month presidency in 1961 Figueiredo worked under General Golbery in the National Security Council (*Conselho de Segurança Nacional*). He was an early conspirator against João Goulart and returned after the coup of 1964 to work under Golbery in the SNI (*Serviço Nacional de Informações*), the powerful new intelligence agency which had both domestic and foreign jurisdiction. Golbery was its creator and head, and he put Figueiredo in charge of the Rio office. In 1969 Figueiredo moved into the Planalto when President Médici named him head of the Military Presidential Staff. In the Geisel government Figueiredo became head of the SNI, thus gaining entrée to all top-level decision-making.

It is easy to see why many in the military saw Figueiredo as a "bridge" between the castelistas and the Médici camp. He had served in highly sensitive positions under both Geisel and Médici, and his links to Golbery went back to 1961. Figueiredo had another quality which his supporters in the Geisel government thought important: an amiable personality. That could prove, they thought, an asset in the more open political system that was emerging. The human touch in dealing with the press and the public had been conspicuously absent in Geisel. It would be all the more essential with the president now depending less on coercion and more on the conventional political skills.

Complexion of the New Government

The new cabinet showed more continuity than change. The key minister was Mario Simonsen, previously the Minister of Finance, now Minister of Planning in a new "superministry" for economic policy. Delfim Neto returned from his ambassadorship in Paris to become the Agriculture Minister. Few observers thought Delfim would be patient in that post, despite the new president's claim that agriculture was to gain new emphasis.

The new Finance Minister was Karlos Rischbieter, who had headed the Bank of Brazil for four years and earlier was a top-level state enterprise administrator in Paraná. The Interior Minister was Mário Andreazza, a former army officer who had been Minister of Transport from 1967 to 1974. He was a genial politician and often mentioned as a possible presidential candidate. His involvement in huge public works (such as the Rio-Niteroi bridge and the Transamazon Highway) inevitably made him the target of corruption rumors. Funding those public works had enabled Andreazza to build up a formidable array of political contacts throughout Brazil. Not least among them were the construction contractors, who lived or died by government contracts.

The Labor Minister was Murilo Macedo, a São Paulo banker who had been São Paulo Finance Secretary. Macedo had ideas for reforming the archaic labor relations system and was also prepared to argue for modest increases in the real minimum wage. The new Education Minister was Eduardo Portella, a highly respected literary critic, who also had reformist ideas. Many centrists hoped his appointment meant the new government would overhaul an educational structure that was badly outdated and underfinanced.

The Army Minister was General Walter Pires, who had worked closely with both Figueiredo and Golbery in the early 1960s. Pires was a key conspirator against Goulart in 1964 and headed the Federal Police from 1969 to 1971—a period of extreme repression. Pires had strongly supported Figueiredo for president and was now a key figure in facilitating military support for further liberalization.

The only politically interesting figure was Petrônio Portella, an ARENA senator from the Northeastern state of Piauí who had gained wide respect for his leadership and conciliatory skills.[2] The most influential political figure inside the government was General Golbery, who retained his position as head of the Civilian Presidential Staff. His strong hand in the Planalto seemed to guarantee that the Geisel-Golbery liberalization plan would continue, presumably along gradual and tightly controlled lines.[3] At the same time, however, conspicuously hard-line generals were appointed to key commands, such as General Milton Tavares de Souza at the Second Army, and similarly-minded colleagues at the First and Third Armies.[4] The new president had the reputation of being highly effective with his fellow officers. That skill would certainly be tested.

The new president's work habits could not have been more different from his predecessor's. Where Geisel had intervened in a wide range of decision processes, redrafting bills and memoranda, Figueiredo reminded the U.S. ambassador of President Eisenhower's style: he delegated liberally and expected the cabinet officers to run things in their areas. Figueiredo had no stomach for the paperwork Geisel savored.[5]

Figueiredo's cabinet resembled Geisel's in several respects. First, no member had significant independent political appeal. Having such stature almost seemed a disqualification. Second, the cabinet had a mildly reformist bent, presumably part of a strategy to combine political liberalization with small doses of socio-economic reform. Third this cabinet included few military. The question was whether their relative absence in the cabinet would mean less military influence in government.

In his inauguration speech President Figueiredo committed himself to continuing liberalization (*abertura*): "I reaffirm the commitments of the 1964 Revolution to assuring a free and democratic society." He waxed emphatic: "I reaffirm my unshakable intention . . . to make of this country a democracy." He went on to make wildly optimistic projections, such as "guaranteeing every worker a just wage," and "ourselves financing the cost of our development."[6] For the moment the press and public reaction was favorable—based on the hope that Figueiredo could continue the liberalization which had accelerated in Geisel's final year.[7]

The 1979 Strikes

In 1979 the key word in Brazilian politics was "negotiation." It was the logical counterpart to *abertura,* for those who wanted a genuinely pluralist Brazil. The trend toward negotiation, however, went beyond the political arena. Much of the press argued, for example, that negotiation should be extended to relations between labor and capital.[8] The aggressive "new unionists" in São Paulo heartily agreed. They then exploited the political opening to step up union activism. The government's response would be an indicator of its intentions—a test that was not long in coming.

The experience of the 1978 strikes had led Lula and other independent union leaders to plan for a different strategy when their annual working agreement expired in March 1979, which by coincidence was the month the Figueiredo government took office.[9] The era of the sit-down actions, so successful in 1978, was over, all the more since both the federal government (through a new decree banning strikes affecting "national security") and the employers (through new security procedures) were much better prepared than in 1978. Furthermore, nothing had changed in the legal structure of labor relations. In 1978 the government had simply decided to be less rigorous in enforcing the labor code (CLT).

The metalworkers leadership in the "ABC" region (the three major São Paulo industrial suburbs of Santo André, São Bernardo, and São Caetano), were determined to test the water again. Led by Lula, they called a strike of their 160,000 members in mid-March 1979 after the employers had rejected their demands. Their principal demand was a wage increase of 78 percent, well above the previous year's official inflation of about 45 percent. They also demanded legal recognition of the nonofficial union representatives who had emerged in competition with the official pro-government hacks (*pelegos*).

The 1979 strike proved more complicated than the sit-down action of May 1978. This time the São Bernardo metalworkers were in the lead, but they had to reduce their demands in order to win support from the statewide Federation of Metalworkers, whose leadership included virtually no independent leaders.

The employers were determined to take a tough line this time and believed the government would back them up. They refused to bargain until the strikers returned to work.[10] The strikers met in a local soccer stadium, where, swept along by Lula's oratory, they responded with a thundering "no." Brazil's auto industry, largest in the Third World and promising to become a major export earner, now lay paralyzed by a strike clearly illegal under the corporatist labor laws. The challenge to the government was obvious to all.

The day following the strikers' no vote the Ministry of Labor "intervened" the São Bernardo union, removing Lula and other elected officers. After waiting a fortnight, the São Paulo police cracked down on the strikers, arresting at least 200 people. It was an early test for the independent movement. Could it survive the loss of its leaders just as it faced the combined power of the employers and the government? Most observers, especially those in the government, expected a rapid surrender.

They did not get it. The strikers stood firm, demanding immediate negotiation. Strike funds were nonexistent, so the strikers had to depend on relatives and friends. They also had a new source of support: a sympathetic public, especially among the Catholic clergy and laymen, who donated money, food, and time to keep the strike alive. Here was a direct link between the "new unionism" and radical Catholics—two of the most important expressions of civil society to emerge in the late 1970s. In the prolonged struggle that followed, the Church, led by Cardinal Arns, provided meeting space (the strikers reasoned that they could reduce the risk of police raids if they operated from a church) and moral support—which the strikers welcomed in light of their employers' threatened reprisals against the strike leaders.[11]

As the strike dragged on, the workers' position grew weaker. In late April the employers offered a 63 percent raise but no pay for the strike days. In response to Church mediation, Lula decided it was the best offer possible under the circumstances and convinced a tumultuous mass meeting of 90,000 workers to accept it. If it fell short of their demands, at least the settlement had come from direct bargaining. Furthermore, Lula and the other purged leaders were now allowed to return to office, as the Ministry of Labor assumed that they would be compromised in the eyes of their rank and file. The assumption was false. The annual May Day rally at Vila Euclides soccer stadium brought an overwhelming show of support for Lula, now a major Brazilian political figure.

Several precedents had been set by the 1979 metalworkers strike. First, new union leaders had continued to emerge, contemptuous of the government endorsed *pelegos* who had since 1964 collaborated with the repressive labor regulations and facilitated work agreements against the workers' interests. As could be seen in both the 1978 and 1979 metalworkers' strikes, the new leaders showed themselves to be well disciplined, in constant contact with union members, and skilled at evading police surveillance. For example, they rotated command posts and avoided using proper names. Union members were drilled to avoid giving names of any leaders. Such tactics could hardly succeed against a truly repressive regime (which could readily extract names), but that was just the point. The government was now trying to avoid repression. After all, it had been the torture death of the metalworker Fiel Filho at the hands of DOI-CODI and the Second Army in 1976 that brought down Geisel's wrath and in the end strengthened the hand of the castelistas.

A second precedent set by the strike was the willingness of some employers to negotiate directly with the workers. The parent firms of Volkswagen and General Motors, for example, were accustomed to collective bargaining in their home countries. Yet the legal structure of Brazilian labor relations tended to undermine direct negotiations, because either the employers or the unions could stop negotiating and go to the labor court, which would then impose a settlement. The court was more likely to favor the employers than the workers. Thus the growth of direct bargaining—for those who wanted it (which excluded a number of employers *and* union leaders)—was inhibited by the existing legal framework of labor relations. Nonetheless, in the period 1979–82 there was rapid growth in the number of directly negotiated agreements, which created a set of mutual obligations parallel to the official system of legal norms and procedures. This pattern of direct negotiation developed because the "new" union leaders and management saw this partial bypassing of the corporatist system to be in their immediate interest.[12]

The third precedent was the solidarity shown the workers by other elements of the public, such as the Church and its lay groups, along with middle-class professionals. Was mobilization from below under way? Any overconfidence dissipated when memories turned to the leftist boasts about popular mobilization supposedly under way in the final months of the Goulart government in 1964.

Although the São Paulo metalworkers got the most publicity, they were not alone on the picket line in 1979. The atmosphere of abertura and the successful strike precedents in São Paulo, along with the rising inflation (41 percent in 1978, then 77 percent in 1979), led many workers to act. Between January and October of 1979 there were more than 400 strikes. Bus drivers and schoolteachers in the state of Rio struck in March, as did the garbage collectors in the city of Rio. Construction workers staged a riot in Belo Horizonte, sending a shudder of fear through that traditionally conservative city. Other sectors hit by strikes were steel, ports, trucking, banking, and telecommunications. All São Paulo state civil servants walked out, as did their counterparts in the state of Rio Grande do Sul. These public employee strikes, although often failing in their wage demands, helped transform the labor relations (and therefore the political) atmosphere. Many of these workers (teachers, civil servants) were middle class, and their strike actions gave economic protest a multi-class legitimacy.

Delfim Neto Again

Labor strife was not the only problem on the economic front. Storm signals were also building in the world economy. Brazil had maintained high economic growth since the 1973 oil shock only by rapidly increasing its borrowing abroad. Planning Minister Mario Simonsen, Figueiredo's chief economic policymaker, argued that now the increasing balance of payments pressure gave Brazil no choice but to throttle down its economy. One clear symptom of the problem was the inflation rate, accelerating upward from its 1978 rate of 40 percent.[13]

Simonsen began to spell out his diagnosis as the new government drafted its five-year economic plan. Forced to explain the need for a slowdown, Simonsen suddenly became the target of wrath from every quarter. The MDB had long argued that the government's economic strategy was deeply flawed and saw Simonsen's diagnosis as confirming their view. Political strategists within the new government were no more favorably disposed. They had not entered office only to discover the "miracle" was over. How could political liberalization continue if the economy were to falter?

The business community was upset for more immediate reasons. Only a buoyant economy could keep their factories and businesses operating at a high rate of capacity and thus earn them profits. Any significant recession would wipe out the many Brazilian firms that operated with perilously little working capital.

Nor was the Brazilian public ready for Simonsen's message. Brazilians had lived through 11 years of uninterrupted economic growth. Few, especially among the elite, were prepared to believe it couldn't continue. They rejected the premises of Simonsen's diagnosis, arguing (or hoping) that Brazil could somehow isolate itself from the world economy and maintain high growth.

Simonsen was inept at bureaucratic intrigue, nor did he have the political touch to be highly effective in public. These personality features detracted from his effectiveness as he delivered the bad news that Brazil had to slow down if runaway inflation and a severe foreign exchange crisis were to be avoided.

In different circumstances Simonsen might have been able to sell his message—perhaps if it had been in the second half of a presidential term, and perhaps if the father of the "miracle" had not been looking over his shoulder. But as Simonsen's credibility faded, Delfim Neto loomed larger. Delfim made no secret of his belief that Simonsen's economic diagnosis was wrong. He had always been less orthodox than Simonsen on inflation. Delfim offered the public the hope they wanted: that he could work another miracle and keep the growth going. Equally important, Figueiredo's political advisers shared that hope.

Under pressure from every side and exuding indecision, Simonsen finally resigned in August 1979, only five months into the Figueiredo presidency. Figueiredo immediately named Delfim as his successor.[14] The São Paulo business community was jubilant. Hundreds of them flocked to Brasília for Delfim's swearing-in ceremony. After all, Roberto Campos in 1966–67 had sounded much like Simonsen now. And Delfim had found a way then.

Delfim began by assuring the public, the business community, and the new government that growth could continue. From August to December he pursued a rapid growth policy. What was the thinking behind this policy? The official version was the *III National Development Plan: 1980– 1986,* drafted in the second half of 1979 and approved by Congress in May 1980.[15]

Plan III was a curious document. It contained virtually no numbers. The opening chapter described the plan as "above all a qualitative document," that would avoid "fixing rigid targets."[16] Current problems were duly noted, such as the energy crisis, the balance of payments constraint, the rising cost of the foreign debt, and increasing inflationary pressure.

Despite these problems, the plan's authors grandly announced, "a developing country with as many potentialities and problems as Brazil cannot give up growth, both because of its citizens' legitimate aspirations for greater prosperity and because of the high social cost of stagnation or decline."[17] It was typical Delfim language. What is striking is the assumption that Brazil could choose to accept or reject a slowdown, perhaps even a recession. In laying out the plan's "strategy," the optimism recurred, as in the argument that "continued growth can be consistent with containing inflation and controlling the external disequilibrium."[18]

Delfim was hoping to repeat his earlier performance. The Plan noted that from 1968 to 1974 (Delfim's previous years in power) Brazil had combined high growth with declining inflation. So expanding investment, output, and employment could be combined with reducing inflationary expectations. "This is the basic lesson which will guide the Government's anti-inflation policy."[19] The inflation target was the level achieved in the early 1970s, namely, 15–20 percent.

The rest of the plan emphasized greater agricultural production as a key to reducing inflation and expanding exports. Industry, on the other hand, was given only two pages and few specifics. Other priorities were to be energy (expand domestic non-oil sources) and social needs, such as education, health, and housing. Investment in the latter areas would accompany "a progressive change in the income distribution profile to benefit the poor."[20] There was also much rhetoric about reducing the great regional inequities, especially by helping the Northeast.

Could Delfim repeat his earlier success? Or had the deteriorating world economy ruled out a high growth strategy in Brazil? The end of 1979 brought a partial answer. The economic indicators were mixed. GDP had grown at 6.8 percent, the best rate since 1976. But inflation roared up to 77 percent, almost double the rate of 1978 and the highest of any year since 1964. The news from the external sector was also ominous. The deficit on current account rose from $7.0 billion in 1978 to $10.5 billion in 1979, and the foreign capital inflow dropped from $10.1 billion in 1978 to only $6.5 billion in 1979. To cover its balance of payments deficit Brazil would have to reduce its foreign exchange reserves by $2.9 billion.

Simonsen's earlier diagnosis seemed vindicated. The Brazilian economy was being hit by the two problems so familiar since 1945—accelerating inflation and a growing foreign exchange squeeze—that Delfim had not had to worry about in his economic czardom of 1967–74. Now he did. No longer able to pursue the unambiguous high growth policy he had announced in August, Delfim decided to gamble. He went for a maxi-devaluation of 30 percent in December 1979 and then in January announced the schedule for devaluations and indexation adjustments for all of 1980. The goal was to reduce inflationary expectations and thereby reverse the inflationary momentum. But if inflation exceeded the preset schedule, the overvalued cruzeiro would encourage imports, discourage exports, and stimulate investors to avoid financial instruments paying negative real interest rates. The odds did not favor Delfim's gamble, in that the forces behind inflation and the balance of payments deficit lay deep in the structure of the Brazilian economy and its relationship with the world economy.[21]

The Amnesty Issue

Although economic problems were pressing, one of the Figueiredo government's most important early decisions was political. It concerned anmesty, a vital question if Brazil was to leave behind authoritarian rule and reintegrate into Brazilian society and politics the thousands of political exiles who had fled or been pursued abroad since 1964.[22] This was an issue on which the opposition had been able to mobilize wide support. Amnesty enthusiasts showed up wherever there was a crowd. At the soccer matches their banners (*Anistia ampla, geral e irrestrita*) were hung where the TV cameras would catch them. Wives, mothers, daughters, and sisters were especially active, which made it more difficult for hard-line military to discredit the movement. Cardinal Arns later called the amnesty struggle "our greatest battle."[23]

Geisel's December 1978 reversal of most of the earlier banishment orders was now followed by Justice Minister Petrônio Portella's amnesty bill, approved by Congress in August 1979. Given amnesty were all those imprisoned or exiled for political crimes since September 2, 1961 (the date of the last amnesty—there had been 47 in Brazilian history.) Excluded were those guilty of "acts of terrorism" and of armed resistance to the government, who turned out to be few, as the law was applied. The law also restored political rights to politicians who had lost them under the institutional acts.[24]

The new law brought back a flood of exiles, including Leonel Brizola and Luis Carlos Prestes, who had been excluded under Geisel's earlier order. Back in Brazil now were also such additional *bêtes noires* of the military as Miguel Arraes, Márcio Moreira Alves, and Francisco Julião, along with key figures in the PCB and the PC do B (neither was legal).[25] The amnesty was a powerful tonic in the political atmosphere, giving an immediate boost to the President's popularity. It also showed that Figueiredo was confident he could withstand hardliner objections to having so many "subversives" back in politics. With the old-line Communists and Trotskyists now back in Brazil, and with the press virtually uncensored (although subject to pressures, threats, and even occasional violence), Brazil was looking more like an open political system than at any time since 1968.[26]

The amnesty movement was not content with the new law, however. It demanded also an accounting for the 197 Brazilians believed to have died at the hands of the security forces since 1964. For many there were detailed dossiers, including eyewitness accounts by other prisoners. Here the opposition was pressing on a very sensitive nerve—the military fear that a judicial investigation might someday attempt to fix responsibility for the torture and murder of prisoners. A good example of the hardliner reaction (perhaps shared by "moderates" whose records might not turn out to be so clean) came in March 1979 when the military took steps to close *Veja* magazine because it had published an exposé on alleged torture camps, complete with photographs.[27] Police also seized copies of *Em Tempo*, a leftist biweekly that in mid-March published a list of 442 alleged torturers.[28]

No torturer was more infamous than Sérgio Fleury, the São Paulo detective who had planned Marighela's ambush, killed Joaquim Camara Ferreira, and carried out the interrogation-torture of countless political prisoners.[29] How could an amnesty possibly extend to him? Events on May 1 rendered that question moot. Fleury had recently purchased a yacht and was anxious to try it out at Ilha Bela, a fashionable boating haven on São Paulo's Atlantic coast. He went on board in the evening and, in attempting to step across to an adjoining yacht, slipped and fell into the water. He was pulled out and given resuscitation, but suffered a heart attack and died on the spot. There was no autopsy.[30]

The air was soon full of rumors that the accident was "planned" by those (presumably prominent military and civilian figures) who feared that Fleury might tell his many secrets from the repressive era. But this explanation faded as observers looked more carefully at the circumstances. On the night of his death Fleury had been drinking. Furthermore, he was reportedly a drug addict and was certainly overweight, a combination increasing the

chances of such an accident. From the political standpoint the precise explanation did not matter. What counted was that Fleury had been removed as a
prime target for the opposition. As he was highly arrogant and revelled in
defending himself against torture charges (he had already survived many
indictments in São Paulo), he would never have gone to a low profile. There
could be no doubt: Fleury's death fit very conveniently into Figueiredo's
plan for a continuing *abertura.*

The issue of possible action against the torturers had in fact been settled
by inclusion in the amnesty law of a definition that included perpetrators of
both "political crimes" and "connected crimes." The latter euphemism was
generally understood to cover the torturers.[31] It was a political trade-off.
The opposition leaders knew that they could move toward an open regime
only with the cooperation of the military. There might well be future
attempts to reopen the question, especially by those close to the torture
victims. But for the moment the Brazilian politicians had been given a
lesson, for better or worse, in the art of "conciliation." There were numerous precedents in Brazilian history. The *Estado Nôvo,* for example, had
ended in 1945 without any official investigation of its repressive excesses.[32]

Reformulating the Parties

The Figueiredo government had a fundamental political problem with
ARENA, which had grave problems in trying to shake its identification
with the post-1964 repressive policies and with the weak electoral appeal of
the UDN, its true forerunner. The rapidly accelerating inflation created an
additional liability. Given recent Brazilian history, the "opposition" had a
natural advantage in a one-on-one party battle with the government, especially in the cities and in the more economically developed Center-South.

Figueiredo's political strategists, led by General Golbery, came up with a
partial solution: dissolve the two-party system and promote the creation of
multiple parties among the opposition, while retaining government forces
within a single party (presumably under a new name). The government
might thereby maintain its hold, either by splitting the opposition vote or
by forming a coalition with the more conservative elements of the opposition.[33] Above all, the government had to break up the united opposition.

A bill to accomplish this end was sent to the Congress and passed in
November.[34] By the end of 1979 the new parties had been formed. ARENA
had regrouped as the Partido Democratico Social (PDS), while most of the
MDB had coalesced in the PMDB (Partido Movimento Democrático
Brasileiro); this verbal sleight of hand both met the new rules (forbidding
use of any previous party label) and irritated the government, because the
opposition had preserved its name recognition and its use of the terms
"democrático" and "brasileiro."

Golbery's strategy was vindicated, at least in the short run, however,
when other opposition parties emerged. Most publicized was the struggle
for the PTB party label, which Leonel Brizola coveted and for which he

had good credentials. He was, after all, a political product of Rio Grande do Sul, the birthplace of Getúlio Vargas and of the PTB. Brizola had been PTB Governor of Rio Grande do Sul and then was elected PTB Congressman from Guanabara (Rio de Janeiro city) in 1962 with the largest vote (269,000) ever received by a federal deputy. But the electoral authorities, probably on government cue, awarded it to Ivete Vargas, a minor political figure who was a grand niece of Getúlio Vargas, but who also had links with General Golbery. Her PTB was a pale copy of its pre-1964 namesake and appeared to have little prospect for long-term survival, although it enjoyed scattered pockets of support. Brizola then founded his own Partido Democrático Trabalhista (PDT). To the left of both those parties was the Partido dos Trabalhadores (PT), led by Lula.[35] Rounding out the field was the Partido Popular (PP). This was the most ironic label of all, in that it was led by establishment figures such as Magalhães Pinto (a prominent banker) and political veteran Tancredo Neves.

The PT is worth a more detailed look, for it was the first serious attempt in 30 years to organize a genuine working-class party. By May 1978, after just a year of the new worker militancy, Lula and his leaders had begun to think that workplace activism might not be enough. Although they had just carried out a successful strike, they were highly suspicious of the employers, who had responded in a more unified way than the union leaders had expected. Over the next year Lula and his group (which included a few intellectuals) debated whether they ought to enter politics. Under the repressive military regime of the earlier 1970s that could only be done by voting for the broad front MDB (Movimento Democrático Brasileiro), the only legal opposition party. In the 1974 congressional elections, for example, the MDB leaders had launched a blistering attack on the military government's labor policies and won a massive working-class vote in the industrial centers of São Paulo. Notwithstanding these MDB efforts, some union militants thought the time had come to create their own party.

Why not continue working through the MDB, which was growing stronger by the day, especially in São Paulo? Partly because these union militants (not all of whom favored a new party) deeply distrusted the MDB, not least because it was supported by the Brazilian Communist Party (PCB), the breakaway Maoist Communists (PC do B), and the *pelegos,* all enemies of the independents in the battle for union control. The PCB strongly opposed the creation of the PT, arguing that Lula and his lieutenants should stick to union organizing. But Lula replied that the workers could never gain political influence until they had a party that spoke *exclusively* for them. Whatever its virtues, the argument went, the MDB represented widely contradictory interests, of which only one was workers. As in any coalition, the workers might find *their* interests sacrificed at key moments. As for the PCB, the independents regarded it as a discredited and tiresome bureaucracy whose rigid dogma rendered it unable to speak for workers.

The debate over the PT followed predictable lines. Lula and his allies argued that because the structure of labor relations was created and enforced by the government, only those in control of the government could change it. That logic aroused angry opposition from some of Lula's lieutenants and fellow leaders in other unions. These dissenters argued that priority *must* go to strengthening the still highly fragile structure of new independent union leadership.[36] The *pelegos* and the communists remained strong and could only be ousted by systematic and patient organizing. What point was there in a Worker's Party if the independents did not even control the industrial unions?

Some of the nay-sayers suspected that Lula's national fame had gone to his head. He fascinated the public, this man who challenged the giant auto companies, the old labor bosses, the communists, and the government. The new PT would have to ride on Lula's name, at least at the outset, and that reinforced his personal role. Thus the PT's creation opened a rift between the PT organizers and those who opted to concentrate on union organizing.

Disregarding the many warnings, Lula and his allies founded the PT (*Partido dos Trabalhadores,* or Workers' Party) in October 1979. It created a new pole of leadership in labor relations, especially in São Paulo. In the short run it diverted some valuable PT manpower from the union scene. That would necessarily weaken the PT in their battles to win control of key unions. On the other hand, it offered an alternative outlet for action by leaders such as Lula whom the government had purged from their union positions. Furthermore, it jibed nicely with the government's strategy of dividing the opposition. The Planalto was therefore quick to facilitate—not ostentatiously—the emergence of the PT.

In the short run the new party could not hope to have a major electoral impact, except perhaps in São Paulo state. This reflected the fact that the greatest PT support would come from the strongholds of the industrial unions in that state. The chance to influence national politics anytime soon was remote. But the PT enthusiasts optimistically plunged into the formidable task of registering the party *município* by *município*.

The PT's natural base was the industrial heartland—above all São Paulo, but also urban areas in Rio de Janeiro, Minas Gerais, Paraná, and Rio Grande do Sul. A new electoral regulation required every party to run a gubernatorial candidate in every state. The PT complied, but this forced the fledgling party to spread its resources throughout Brazil, most of which was far from ready for a workers' party.

No sooner was the new party alignment clear when maneuvering began for the 1982 elections. Few thought the Planalto had finished tinkering with the electoral machinery. It became a cat and mouse game, with government and opposition trying to guess each other's next move, especially the possible campaign coalitions. The PDS leadership suffered a heavy loss when Justice Minister Petrônio Portella, a key figure in building a network of party strength around the country, died of a heart attack in early January 1980. He had no adequate successor, either in the Justice Ministry or in the PDS leadership.[37]

Despite the Figueiredo government's frequently repeated commitments to further *abertura,* many Brazilians had remained skeptical. In May 1980 the government only strengthened their doubts by cancelling the nation-wide municipal elections scheduled for the end of the year. The vast major-ity of mayors and municipal councilors were PDS, and the government feared big losses if the elections were held as scheduled. Ironically, the PMDB leaders had also favored postponement because they feared they could not organize quickly enough under the 1979 party law. In September 1980 the Congress passed a law postponing the elections until 1982, when direct elections were to be held for state governors (for the first time since 1965), a third of the Senate, the entire Chamber of Deputies, and all state legislatures. The government was gambling that the PDS, not the opposi-tion, would benefit by piling so many elections on one day. But when push came to shove, would the government really put all those elected positions on the block in 1982? In mid-July 1981 the President vehemently reiterated his commitment to the elections.[38]

Another government action apparently contrary to liberalization was the tough new law (August 1980) regulating the entry and residence of foreign-ers in Brazil. The law gave the government greater authority to bar or expel foreigners, which included a number of refugees from elsewhere in Latin America (ironically enough, the military government, with its high eco-nomic growth rates, had welcomed such refugees, especially if skilled), as well as the large fraction of Brazil's Catholic religious who were foreign.[39] Some foreign clergy had angered local and state authorities by leading popular protests, such as the resistance to land takeovers on the agricul-tural frontier in the West and Northwest and in the Amazon. The CNBB and human rights activists fought to revise the government bill on foreign-ers, arguing that it was a radical change in Brazil's long-standing, relatively open door to foreigners.

The government remained firm, however, as the PMDB and even some PDS Congressmen fought the bill. The opponents were able to delay action past the 40-day limit, after which the government, in early August, de-clared the bill to be law by *decurso de prazo.*[40] Here was a clear example of how limited were the legislators' powers. The government's aggressiveness carried again in October, when it deported an Italian priest for actions allegedly contrary to the national interest.[41]

Another Challenge from Labor

The new Figueiredo government had cast a wary eye on the labor turmoil it faced when it took office in 1979. After the 1979 strike experience, the new Labor Minister, Murillo Macedo, decided the conflict might be turned to the government's benefit. He convinced the new President that major changes had to be made in the government formula for annual minimum wage adjustments.[42] All analysts agreed that the real value of the minimum wage had dropped since 1964. The minimal estimate was a loss of 25 percent, and DIEESE, the independent labor union research institute, placed it much higher.[43] Macedo, an articulate reformist, proposed two significant changes, which Congress adopted in Law 6,708. First, wage adjustments would now be semiannual, a move of crucial importance as inflation raced toward 100 percent annually. Second, the percentage wage increase would vary by wage categories. Workers receiving the equivalent of less than three minimum wages per month (about 70 percent of the workforce) would be given the full inflation adjustment, plus 10 percent. Those earning the equivalent of three to ten minimum wages would get only the full inflation adjustment and productivity adjustments. Those earning above the equivalent of ten were to receive 80 percent. This was a deliberate attempt to redistribute wage income. It was also an attempt to undercut the growing worker mobilization and the public sympathy for the workers' cause so evident in the 1978 and 1979 strikes. *Abertura* could succeed only if labor were kept under control, according to both the Geisel and the Figueiredo strategists. Macedo was now trying to regain that control over São Paulo's most militant labor unions.

The metalworkers' leadership was not impressed with Macedo's new wage formula. They were all too familiar with the government's ability to distort any formula in practice. Furthermore, the independent leaders wanted to make up for the unfavorable settlement forced on them in 1979. Now, in March 1980, they demanded a real wage increase of 15 percent, plus recognition of shop stewards and 12-month job security (which would have been de facto indefinite tenure, as the contracts were for one year). The latter demand was to stop employers from using high labor turnover as a way to minimize the number of long-time, and therefore more highly paid, workers.[44]

The employers offered 3.6 percent (later raised to 5.9 percent) and nothing on job security, so the workers struck on April 1, 1980. The strike was centered in the ABC region, under Lula's general leadership. This time the Ministry of Labor was determined to maintain control of the São Paulo labor scene. The Ministry immediately appealed to the labor court, which ruled in favor of the employers. The court set the real wage increase at 6–7 percent and threw out the demands for 12-month job security and recognition of shop stewards; but it did not declare the strike illegal—itself a minor victory for the workers.[45] The strikers, again packed into the Vila Euclides soccer stadium, debated the court finding amid much shouting and anger. With public support still strong, especially from the Church, the workers defied the court and their employers and voted to continue the strike.

The stakes had now risen for the government. President Figueiredo, only a year in office, was struggling to regain control over events in São Paulo. After a week Labor Minister Macedo declared the strike illegal and launched a massive crackdown. The strike area swarmed with police, army intelligence, and security agents. Pickets were attacked and hundreds arrested. The Ministry "intervened" the unions and removed their officers, including Lula, who were jailed for a month. The government then forbade the companies from bargaining directly. When the employ-

ers had bargained in 1978 and 1979 the Ministry had winked at the practice. Now it was time to rein in the employers also, and they readily
complied.

The strike wore on. Once again community sympathizers raised money
and furnished food to the strikers. Politicians and activists on the left and
even some from the center spoke out to support the strikers. The jailing of
Lula and other union leaders only spread their fame. The heavy-handed
security forces, using police dogs, riot squads, and omnipresent army secret
security officers (DOI-CODI), brought to mind the worst of the Médici
years.

In early May, after 41 days on strike, the workers returned to work with
their demands unmet. Why had they failed? One reason was the lack of
strike funds. Another was the threat that the employers might start hiring
anew, always possible in a labor-surplus economy such as Brazil. The strike
had proved costly for the workers. Government repression was back, despite *abertura* talk and the new pay formula. The limits of the tactics
established by the "new unionism" were now clear. How could the workers
ever reach direct negotiations with the employers if the government always
took the employers off the hook? The 1979 wage law's automatic indexation for inflation had robbed the militant union leaders of one of their key
issues. In fact, the number of strikes had declined from 429 in 1979, to 42 in
1980, and to 34 in 1981.[46]

But the 1979 wage law lasted only two years. Conservative economists,
starting in mid-1980, began a campaign against wage indexation and the
wage law, arguing it was a major stimulus to inflation because of the 110
percent adjustment at the lower levels. Ironically, their efforts helped lead
to passage of a new law in December 1980 (Law 6,886) which left untouched the 110 percent rate at the bottom, but which further slashed the
adjustment for those in the top brackets.

The next year, 1981, brought a change from the strike pattern of recent
years. São Paulo metalworkers found the going even tougher than in 1980.
In February 1981 a military court convicted Lula and 10 other union leaders
of violating the national security law. Lula had already been removed from
his union post by the Minister of Labor. Furthermore, many leaders of
previous strike actions had been fired, because the existing laws provided
little protection against employer retaliation. When the time for annual
wage adjustment came in March 1981, the metalworkers did not strike.
They were weakened by the loss of leadership, but also by a severe recession that brought huge layoffs in the São Paulo firms which had been prime
targets in the earlier strikes. Meanwhile, the mills of Brazilian justice
ground fine, and in September a higher military tribunal overturned the
national security conviction of Lula and his 10 comrades. There were
retrials, and Lula won every case except his second removal from the São
Paulo union presidency. Even the latter was a punishment in name only,
for Lula continued to participate in his union's deliberations (although not
appearing formally).

Working in favor of the militant union leaders was the interest and support they had aroused in Brazil and abroad. The strikes had created a network of sympathizers, led in São Paulo by Cardinal Arns and his well-organized laymen. The new unionists also attracted interest and support from foreign governments, unions, and foundations in Western Europe, especially West Germany. The U.S. labor attachés across Brazil were in close touch with Brazilian union leaders and had sponsored study trips to the U.S. for many of them. All this foreign involvement also meant that a government crackdown on labor union leaders (more extreme than in 1980) would alienate U.S. and Western European opinion—a consequence the Figueiredo government preferred to avoid.

There was no need for the Figueiredo government to worry about labor union demands in 1982 or 1983. In both years, as we shall see, the deep recession undercut the unions' bargaining strength. As a result, they were mostly forced to accept the wage adjustment laid down by the government.[47]

Some pockets managed to escape this trend. Enterprises linked to the export trade did well, some even showing growth, as the government continued to pay high export subsidies. The agricultural crops which benefitted were soybeans, sugar, coffee, and oranges; the industrial products were shoes, vehicles, and a range of intermediate goods.

Union activity in these prosperous export pockets became more frequent than in the recession-hit sectors, and collective agreements became more complex and sophisticated. In addition, new mechanisms for conflict resolution at the plant level began to be created in the export sector. This meant a decentralization away from the *município*-wide union activity mandated in the labor code. Although these changes did not transform the labor relations system, especially the heavy state role, they represented a new frontier of labor relations in Brazil.

One sector deserving mention is the program to produce alcohol from sugarcane. Forced to substitute for oil, 75 percent of which in the late 1970s was imported, Brazil had increased annual alcohol production from 900 million liters in 1979 to 9 billion liters in 1984, with the product going largely to supply alcohol-fueled automobiles (now 90 percent of Brazilian auto production). This huge increase, based on an equally huge increase in sugarcane cultivation, had greatly affected labor relations in those areas. Workers involved in alcohol production became aggressive, both sugarcane cutters (*bóias-frias* was the general term for itinerant rural wage labor) as well as millworkers. In rural regions where both workers and managers lacked the experience with unions that urbanites had, this increased open labor conflict, in turn pushing the system toward more organization and innovation.[48] In regions where rural unions had a long history, such as the northeastern state of Pernambuco, the recurrent strikes proved more manageable.

Meanwhile, the Figueiredo government and the Congress (when in session) were displaying dazzling inconsistency in wage legislation. The critics had continued their attack on the 110 percent adjustment at the 1–3 times the minimum wage levels, which included about 70 percent of the labor force (although only 30 percent of the total wage bill).[49] In January 1983— when Congress was in recess—President Figueiredo issued Decree-Law 2012, which reduced the 110 percent adjustment to 100 percent and reduced the adjustment for 3–7 times the minimum wage to 95 percent and for 7–15 to 80 percent. The rest were unchanged. This was the most severe cut to the upper wage categories yet seen, as well as an abandonment of the bonus for the lowest paid. In May 1983 the government had to backtrack under pressure from Congress, and issued Decree-Law 2024, which established the 100 percent adjustment for 1–7 times the minimum wage, thereby restoring the full cost of living adjustment for those in the 3–7 times the minimum wage category. In July 1983 the government reversed its field again, as it gave in to IMF pressure to reduce the wage bill. Decree-Law 2045 now established an 80 percent adjustment for all brackets and declared illegal any negotiated settlement above that level. It was the first time since 1979 that the adjustment formula did not favor the lowest paid. This move was highly unpopular. The government had to declare a state of emergency in Brasília during congressional debate over the bill in order to prevent massive demonstrations by the opposition.

Decree-Law 2045, like all the other recent wage laws, had a short life. In October 1983, only three months later—in a calmer political atmosphere— the Congress passed Decree-Law 2065, re-establishing a 100 percent adjustment for 1–3 times the minimum wage, and fixing the adjustment at 80 percent for 3–7 times and 50 percent for 7–15 times the minimum wage. The law also provided that automatic indexation would apply only until mid-1985; for the rest of 1985 the indexation adjustment would fall to 70 percent, then 60 percent for 1986, and 50 percent for 1987. The parties would be free to bargain for anything beyond the indexation adjustment until mid-1988, after which wage increases would be left completely to bargaining.

This law marked the first time in 50 years that the government had explicitly promoted collective bargaining as a way to settle wage disputes. But the new posture did not last long. After six months Decree-Law 2,065 was under attack, not surprisingly, for having reduced the wages of the middle class. In October 1984 the Congress passed a new law restoring the 100 percent indexation adjustment for the 1–7 times the minimum wage. The adjustment was to be 80 percent for all higher brackets, with bargaining permitted only up to 100 percent of the indexation formula. This new law eliminated the plan to move gradually toward bargaining. In short, Brazil went back to a simple indexation adjustment for 90 percent of the labor force.

The dizzying changes in the indexation formulae had only served to arouse new bargaining demands. None of the formulae had succeeded in pleasing everyone. The net effect of all these wage bills (except Law 2,045) was to shift significantly the distribution of wage and salary income, to the benefit of the lowest-paid two-thirds of workers and to the detriment of the top 1.6 percent, with varying shifts in between. The Figueiredo government received little credit from the unions for this income redistribution, while middle and upper income earners were indignant over their relative losses. In part this was due to the workers' understandable focus on the declining purchasing power of their absolute wages.[50] Meanwhile, the IMF continued to demand wage austerity, stipulating that total wages should increase at a rate no greater than 80 percent of the official cost of living.

The impact of the world economic crisis and the national recession on Brazilian labor relations after 1980 was therefore mixed. In the depressed sectors, the short-run effect was to strengthen both the bargaining hand of employers and the government's control over unions and over the entire labor relations system. In the export and energy sector, workers won more space and bargaining power. This variation in labor's bargaining power was a reminder that as the economy became more complex so did the pattern of labor relations.

On the political front liberalization had remained on course. In November 1980 the Congress passed a government-sponsored constitutional amendment to reintroduce direct elections for state governors and all senators. This was a partial undoing of Geisel's 1977 "April package," which had allowed ARENA to come out of the 1978 elections with continued majorities in both houses of the federal Congress. The Figueiredo government thought it could still count on those majorities, so it decided to push on with *abertura*.

Explosion on the Right

But not everyone wanted to play the liberalization game. The clandestine opponents of *abertura* were preparing their campaign of violence.[51] During 1980 and the early months of 1981 Brazil was wracked by explosions. Newsstand vendors had been sent notes ordering them to stop selling leftist publications. Some who refused had their stands firebombed in the night. Suddenly scores of newsstand proprietors stopped selling these publications, whose circulation (which came primarily from newsstand sales) plummeted. Many publications never recovered from the financial blow and soon disappeared. Anonymous terror (by the SNI or military intelligence, most journalists agreed) accomplished what censorship had not. Not all the violence was bloodless. A letter bomb sent to the Brazilian Bar Association Headquarters killed the woman who had the misfortune to open it. In light of the Bar Association's lead in the redemocratization fight, few doubted the attack had come from the right.[52]

Then on April 30, 1981, came an even bigger explosion. The incident began when an army captain and sergeant of the DOI-CODI (in plainclothes) drove into the parking lot of a Rio theater (RioCentro) where a concert to benefit leftist causes was under way. A few minutes later a bomb exploded in the car, killing the sergeant and gravely wounding the captain. Although army authorities later released stories with elaborate disclaimers, all evidence indicated that the duo were bringing the bomb to disrupt the concert, perhaps even to create mass panic. This suspicion was reinforced by the fact that another bomb had exploded harmlessly inside the building near a power generator.[53] This was apparently a desperate move by rightest military who felt the political process had gotten out of hand, i.e., the *abertura* was approaching a point of no return. The army immediately asserted jurisdiction over the investigation and carried out a clumsy cover-up, made more difficult by the fact that the civil authorities had already issued a medical report on the dead sergeant which contradicted the army version of his death.[54] Congressional leaders condemned the terro₎ism and many worried that the cover-up was evidence the hardliners might yet be able to sabotage the *abertura*.

No one had a greater stake in *abertura* than Golbery. He immediately pressed (behind the scenes, where he always worked) for a no-holds-barred inquiry into the RioCentro incident. As the whitewash became obvious, Golbery found himself increasingly isolated in the presidential palace. He resigned in August 1981.[55]

Golbery's departure generated major waves on the political scene. He had been a key strategist, doing battle on several fronts. The first was the fight to continue gradual redemocratization. Golbery had helped launch this policy when he was head of the Civilian Presidential Staff in the Geisel presidency (1974–79). He continued to be its most articulate advocate among Figueiredo's advisers. He regarded redemocratization, if of a limited kind, as both right and necessary. He recognized that the two-party system, created in 1965, had put the government party (PDS) on the defensive, so he formulated the 1979 party reorganization as a preparatory step for the 1982 elections.

Golbery's political strategy had been to proceed steadily with *abertura*, while at the same time juggling the electoral rules and using all the traditional weapons of an incumbent government (patronage, etc.). He played from an intuition that the government, if skillful, could keep winning the necessary electoral margin. He was planning strategy for the 1982 elections when he resigned.

The prime opposition to Golbery's strategy came from the military hardliners. Their most effective leader was General Octavio Aguiar de Medeiros, chief of the powerful SNI, which Golbery had helped create and had once headed.[56] These officers feared any open electoral system. They preferred the authoritarian path laid out by the generals in Argentina, Chile, and Uruguay. Threatened by *abertura*, their more militant colleagues were prepared to engage in (or cover for) terrorism. For them a cover-up of the RioCentro incident was essential to protect the clandestine network. For the same reason, Golbery wanted a thorough investigation, with well publicized punishment for the responsible officers. The hardliners won.[57]

Another of Golbery's battle fronts was economic policy. He had been pushing for mildly "populist" measures to strengthen the PDS in the 1982 elections—loosening up on wage increases, channeling public funds to pro-government gubernatorial candidates, delaying any increase in employer and employee contributions to the financially strapped social security system, and, most important, relaxing the recessionary policy that was reducing industrial production and increasing unemployment. All these measures were bound to be expensive. They would swell the federal deficit and thereby add to inflation, which was by mid-1981 running at an annual rate of 111 percent. Planning Minister Delfim Neto opposed all such measures. By the time Golbery resigned, Delfim had already won on the issue of increased payroll deductions for social security. There were those who predicted that he would soon win on wage policy, thereby probably provoking the departure of Labor Minister Murilo Macedo, one of the few remaining ministers of a liberal hue.

Golbery was immediately replaced as head of the Civilian Presidential Staff by João Leitão de Abreu, who had held the same post under Médici. Leitão de Abreu was a lawyer from Rio Grande do Sul and was said to have links to the rightist military, with whom he had worked closely in the Médici presidency. That might have boded ill for *abertura,* which required a very different set of political skills. Yet the momentum behind the redemocratization remained great. Most important, there was no significant social base, especially among the urban middle class, for a return to the repression of the early 1970s. Nonetheless, Golbery's departure had removed the most powerful pro-*abertura* voice around the President.

The immediate effect of Golbery's departure was to give Delfim Neto a freer hand to pursue the economic slowdown on which he had embarked after the failure of his December 1979 policy of pre-announced devaluations and indexing adjustments. Now economic prudence (as defined by balance of payments considerations) would prevail, at least in 1981. Golbery's departure also meant that the rightist military would probably enjoy more direct access to the President. This major shift suggested that Figueiredo was a weak, or at best, an indecisive President. Golbery quit because his influence was ebbing, not because Figueiredo decided to change course. The President was left with his strenuously proclaimed commitment to elections but with a cabinet visibly weakened in its commitment to that goal. The trend in Figueiredo's recent appointments had been toward men closely identified with Médici, the authoritarian par excellence.

The RioCentro bomb blast had thrown the rightist military on the defensive. Although they and their repressive security apparatus remained in place, they had been neutralized. Terrorism now stopped, as if to confirm that the rightist military had decided to lie low. Finally, the pro-*abertura* military were prompted to reaffirm their "faith in democracy," thereby reinforcing the momentum toward democratization.

An event in September 1981 might well have stopped *abertura*—a presidential stroke. On September 18 a stricken President Figueiredo entered the hospital, and his military ministers met within a day to announce that Vice President Aureliano Chaves would assume the presidency. Opposition fears that the military might shunt aside the Vice President, as happened with Pedro Aleixo after Costa e Silva's stroke in 1969, were allayed when Army Minister Walter Pires de Albuquerque declared his support for Chaves, the first civilian to hold the presidency since 1964. Chaves exercised the presidential duties for almost eight weeks, until Figueiredo resumed his post in early November. The President's doctors seemed certain he would have no trouble resuming a full load. During his absence the government had continued to function (although Chaves was excluded from decision-making on military or security matters) and there had been no major shifts in policy. The experience had proved very different from 1969, when Costa e Silva fell seriously ill. Why?

The first factor was Figueiredo's medical condition. From the outset the doctors said that the President had suffered only a mild stroke, nothing comparable to Costa e Silva's paralysis 12 years earlier. Figueiredo was expected to recover in a matter of weeks. Second, there was no guerrilla threat on the horizon, unlike 1969. Third, the hardliners were on the defensive, unable to capitalize on events. In sum, liberalization, such as it was, had enough momentum to survive this scare.

The Balance of Payments: A New Vulnerability

The economy, however, was again causing grave concern. To understand how Brazil's economic fortunes had deteriorated, we must return to 1980. As that year wore on, the public grew restive over the effects of the economic strategy Delfim Neto had launched in December 1979. The policy of prefixed indexation and devaluation schedules was intended to reduce inflationary expectations. But inflation raced ahead of schedule, leading to negative real interest rates and an overvalued cruzeiro. In 1980 inflation jumped to 110 percent, then a record for this century. Government policy had created a disincentive to save (with negative real interest rates) and an incentive to import (with an overvalued cruzeiro). Not surprisingly, the balance of payments worsened in 1980. The $3.5 billion overall deficit had to be covered, as in 1979, by drawing on foreign exchange reserves. GDP grew by 7.2 percent, but at that rate the reserves could not last long.

In late 1980 Delfim accepted the inevitable. He scrapped the pre-fixing of devaluation and indexation adjustments, and he unceremoniously dumped the high-growth strategy, so confidently laid out in the *III Plan Nacional*. The first move was toward a more realistic exchange rate. Unfortunately for Brazil, the international economic climate had turned hostile. Interest rate were rising, Brazil's terms of trade were declining, and the industrial countries were heading for recession.

The year 1981 turned out to be one of reckoning. For the first time since 1942 Brazil's GDP showed a decline, of 1.6 percent. Even in the crisis-wracked year of 1963 the GDP had managed a 1.1 percent rate of growth. To make matters worse, Brazil's high population growth rate meant that per capita GDP for 1981 was a negative 4.3 percent. The only bright spot was agriculture, which grew at 6.4 percent. The other sectors were down:

–5.5 percent in industry,—2.8 percent in commerce, and—0.2 percent in transportation and communication.

Inflation eased slightly in 1981, coming down to 95.2 percent after 1980's record of 110.2 percent. As for the balance of payments, the $11.7 billion deficit on current account was almost completely covered by the $11.5 billion inflow of long-term capital. Although a godsend in the short run, this capital added to Brazil's heavy foreign debt. By the end of 1981 that debt had risen to $61.4 billion, and its servicing that year totalled a startling $7 billion, or 65.6 percent of the value of exports. In only three years Brazil's payments on interest had more than tripled (from $2.7 billion in 1978 to $9.2 billion in 1981). It was obvious that this rate of growth of the foreign debt could not long continue.[58]

A closer look at the 1981 balance of payments revealed the problem on the import side. Imports, at $27.2 billion, had been kept slightly below their 1980 level of $27.8 billion. But owing to a rise in import prices by 11 percent in 1981, Brazil was paying more for a smaller quantity of imports. Given the import-intensive nature of Brazilian industry, this import squeeze helped contribute to the 5.4 percent drop in industrial production.

The only viable short-run response to this crisis was either to cut imports sharply or to gamble on raising even more foreign loans to finance the current account deficit. Not surprisingly, Delfim opted for more loans.

It had been a successful tactic in the past. During the 1970s Brazil as a borrower had earned high marks among New York, European, and Japanese bankers. Brazil had cashed in on that credit rating as the current account deficits grew after 1973. They aggressively solicited loans for Brazilian state enterprises, such as Petrobrás (oil) and Electrobrás (electricity). Each loan was geared to a specific investment program, but balance of payments considerations soon led policymakers to push marginal projects. Furthermore, these investments would yield a cruzeiro return, not the hard currency needed to service the loan. The pressure to raise such loans increased with the second oil price shock in 1979. Fighting for time, Delfim had run up the foreign debt rapidly in 1980 and 1981. By then the phalanx of negative factors facing Brazil was clear: deteriorating terms of trade, rising interest rates, and depressed foreign demand for Brazil's exports. All the foreign loans were based on a faith in Brazil's ability to earn the foreign exchange necessary to repay the loans. What if Brazil couldn't? It would have to default (unthinkable for this kind of military government) or turn to the IMF, a move highly unpopular at home.

That question seemed secondary to Brazilian economists and businessmen in 1981. Their immediate worry was the declining economy. The elite had long believed that Brazil couldn't "afford" a recession. The belief was accurately mirrored in Delfim's Third Economic Plan. Such talk assumed Brazil could control its economic fate. In 1981 that was shown to be an illusion. For the first six months industrial production fell 3.3 percent. Total sales (including exports) by the motor vehicle industry in the first seven months fell by 23.2 percent compared to the same period in 1980. In

August Mercedes-Benz dismissed one quarter of its 20,000 workers and closed its production line for a month and a half. Unemployment in greater São Paulo was estimated at 320,000 (although trade union researchers put it at double that figure). Despite all the government's rhetoric and all its manipulation of the economic levers, Brazil had plunged into its most serious recession in 30 years.

What now made economic policymaking even more difficult was election-year politics. President Figueiredo was keeping his promise to hold the November 1982 elections, the most important since 1974. Delfim, a thoroughly political animal, maneuvered to maximize his government's campaign advantage. Given some play still in the economy, Delfim tried to ease up enough to show economic improvement (or at least no further deterioration) by election time in November. He succeeded to a remarkable degree. For calendar 1982 GDP growth turned positive, at 1.4 percent, with agriculture at—2.5 percent, industry at 1.2 percent, commerce at precisely no growth, and transportation and communication at 4.0 percent. Inflation was 99.7 percent, only slightly above the 1981 rate of 95.2 percent.

The external sector was the crucial test. The world banking community had been rocked by Mexico's August 1982 announcement that it could no longer service its foreign debt. Nervous bankers now cast a suspicious eye on Brazil, whose debt surpassed even Mexico's. New loans and rollovers from the creditor commercial banks suddenly became scarce. Brazil resorted to extreme measures to balance its external account. Until election day (November 15), Delfim Neto and his technocrats denied any intention of going to the IMF—always a red flag to Brazilian nationalists. Immediately after the election, Delfim and his team announced that Brazil had opened formal negotiations with the IMF.

Brazil's 1982 balance of payments proved even worse than the critics had predicted. The current account deficit had shot up to $16.3 billion, compared to $11.7 billion in 1981. The overall balance was a negative $9.0 billion. This unprecedented figure resulted from two principal factors: (1) the increase in the current account deficit; and (2) the sharp drop in the net inflow of foreign capital, which in 1982 totalled only $7.9 billion, as against $12.8 billion in 1981.

The overall deficit was covered by a quickly thrown-together patchwork of loans. All had to be negotiated under extreme pressure in late November and December. Brazil was so desperate that Delfim was said to have ordered Petrobrás tankers headed for Brazil to divert to Rotterdam, where they were to sell their cargo on the free market for hard currency in order to increase export earnings. Brazil had no fewer than 1,114 credit banks abroad, and each had to agree to a rollover, a new loan, altered interest rates, or any other change in existing commitments. Although there was a group of 40 major banks coordinating the effort, procedures were cumbersome.[59] It took the Brazilian Central Bank's telex more than two days of non-stop operation to send to its creditor banks details of its proposed refinancing. Major help from the IMF would take longer, for Brazil would have to submit

an acceptable stabilization plan. Just to survive 1982, Brazil had to spend
$3.5 billion of her foreign exchange reserves. She also got a $2.3 billion
"bridge loan" from foreign banks, $1.5 billion from the U.S. Treasury, $500
million from the IMF, and $500 million from the Bank of International
Settlements in Switzerland. These frantically negotiated loans permitted
Brazil to get through 1982 without defaulting on interest payments. Since
mid-1982 Brazil had not even attempted to pay amortization.

Delfim Neto, João Figueiredo, and the sixth revolutionary government
now found themselves in the worst of all possible worlds. Economic growth,
the consensus goal of the elite, had vanished. Brazil was just another suppli-
cant at the IMF. One of the military governments' advantages since 1967 had
been their relative autonomy in economic decision-making. For 15 years
they had no need of the IMF. The debt crisis had ended that.

The 1982 Elections

On the political front 1982 had been dominated by the prospect of the
November elections. For the first time since 1965 governors were to be
elected directly. Because local elections had been postponed from 1980
until 1982, the voter was now being asked to choose at every level except
the presidential. Both the PDS and the PMDB mounted sophisticated
media efforts; the smaller parties, such as the PT, PDT, and PTB, had to
rely on volunteer canvassing and street corner bullhorns. In many locales
this election, like every federal election since 1974, turned into a plebiscite
on federal government policies, except where the PDS could capitalize
effectively on voter interest in some local or state issue.

What did the opposition propose to do if they won power? Some clues can
be found in the manifesto issued by the leaders of the four major parties (all
but Brizola of the PDT), who met in mid-July to discuss collaborative election strategies.[60] They proposed to enfranchise illiterates, increase trade
union autonomy, legalize strikes, and adopt a "just policy" of income distribution. They also advocated an end to the "privileges granted to huge firms,
multinationals, and finance capital," and proposed to "strengthen" the internal market. The politicians behind this manifesto were hardly radical figures. PMDB leaders such as Tancredo Neves, Franco Montoro, and Ulysses
Guimarães were familiar and moderate faces from the pre-1964 era. On the
other hand, the Chamber of Deputies now contained 36 members who had
previously had their political rights or mandates cancelled. This indicated
that the *abertura* was beginning to incorporate previously excluded political
elements into the system.[61]

Despite hardliner attempts at sabotage, and despite the public's understandable cynicism, the elections proved to be an impressive civic exercise:
over 45 million voters went to the polls, the largest electorate ever to vote
in Latin America. There were relatively few charges of vote fraud, and
Brazil could congratulate itself on having given a lesson in electoral democracy all too rare in the Third World.

The electoral results largely vindicated Golbery's original strategy. Although the opposition won 59 percent of the total popular vote, it failed to gain a majority in the Congress (considering the two houses together) or in the electoral college, which was to choose Figueiredo's successor. In the Chamber of Deputies the opposition (combining all four parties—PMDB, PDT, PTB, and PT) now outnumbered the PDS by 240 to 235, but in the Senate the PDS enjoyed an advantage of 46 to the opposition's 23. In the electoral college (consisting of both houses of Congress plus six representatives from the majority party of each state) the PDS enjoyed a majority of 356 to a combined total of 330 for all other parties.

Several features of these results deserve note. First, the government party had lost its absolute majority in the lower house of Congress. If the opposition voted together, it could block any government proposed legislation (although the government could use the *decurso de prazo* if no vote was forthcoming). Second, even to retain its relative strength in Congress and the electoral college, the government had to rely heavily on the less populous and less developed states, where the government's incumbent political machines could produce PDS votes.

The government's problems were equally evident in the governorships. The PDS was supposed to be the government party, yet it was disadvantaged by its lack of input into executive decision-making, even when the party was directly concerned. As a result, the PDS leaders were identified with policies they did not help to make. They were "of" the government, but not "in" it, making PDS candidates highly vulnerable at the polls. Voting against the PDS candidates was as close as the ordinary voter could get to voting against the military government in Brasília.

The opposition won the governorships of nine states, including São Paulo, Rio de Janeiro, Minas Gerais, and Paraná.[62] Leonel Brizola, long an anathema to the military, won the governorship of the state of Rio, carrying in as his vice governor Darcy Ribeiro, who, as a Goulart adviser, called for the public to take to the streets in defiance of the 1964 coup.[63] In fact, both Brizola (who now proclaimed himself a Social Democrat in the Western European sense) and Darcy had moderated while in exile. Brizola proceeded to carry out a mildly populist program, including the construction of pre-fabricated schools (*Centros Integrados de Educação Popular,* or CIEPs, better known as "Brizolões," for their maker) that were also to serve as community centers. Elsewhere the opposition gubernatorial winners were PMDB centrist politicians, such as Franco Montoro in São Paulo and Tancredo Neves in Minas Gerais.

A closer look at the election results revealed that the opposition (PDT and PMDB) won governorships in the more developed Center-South, while the PDS won primarily in the Northeast and lightly settled far west, except for PDS victories in Santa Catarina and Rio Grande do Sul. The PDS held an overall edge of 14 in the Congress, and 38 in the electoral college. Given past unreliability of government party votes, it was not at all unlikely the Planalto might face trouble on future votes in the Congress or even in the electoral college.

The most interesting new development in party politics was the PT. Although it won fewer votes than its enthusiasts had expected, the PT did represent an important new political force. It achieved registration in every Brazilian state, building a network of local volunteers who could be valuable in future electoral battles. The PT's independence of ideology was shown by the fact that the Communist party (PCB) scorned it and continued to support the PMDB, as did the Maoist PC do B. The real question about the PT was whether it could grow quickly enough to survive under the electoral rules. Since the government wanted to divide the opposition as much as possible, it might give the PT the benefit of the doubt in applying the rules. There was also the larger question of the PT's ability to attract the huge urban vote that would be decisive in any democratic (one person/one vote) system.

Its best performance in 1982 was, not surprisingly, in São Paulo, not only in the capital but across the state. The PT elected six federal deputies from São Paulo and one each from Minas Gerais and Rio de Janeiro. Lula ran for governor of São Paulo and lost to Franco Montoro, the highly popular Senator of the PMDB. In fact, Lula ran fourth, behind Jânio Quadros (PTB), the enigmatic and unpredictable former president, and PDS candidate Reynaldo de Barros. The party did manage to elect scattered state deputies, mayors, and city councilmen, largely in the state of São Paulo.[64]

As for the PMDB, it proved stronger and more cohesive than the skeptics had predicted.[65] Many had predicted the party would split, with the right forming a centrist Partido Liberal, and the left forming a Partido Socialista. The two major governorships that had been predicted to vote PMDB, and did not—Rio Grande do Sul and Pernambuco—were lost for differing reasons. In Rio Grande do Sul Leonel Brizola, who still had influence in his home state, split the opposition by endorsing his own (PDT) candidate, who won with a plurality. In Pernambuco, on the other hand, the winning PDS candidate benefitted from old-fashioned clientelistic control of votes in the interior and from a skillful smear campaign against Marcos Freire, the PMDB candidate who faced divisions in his own ranks.

The opposition had now gained control of key states. At the same time, however, the government retained the federal executive. The opposition governors, Franco Montoro of São Paulo, Leonel Brizola of Rio de Janeiro, Tancredo Neves of Minas Gerais, and José Richa of Paraná, were in no position to undertake radical experiments. Entering office in the midst of Brazil's worst recession since the 1930s, they badly needed financial and other help from Brasília. But the Figueiredo government was in no position to be generous. It had already been forced to subordinate domestic goals to servicing the foreign debt. For the first time since 1966, Brazil was modifying its aggressive growth objectives to please foreign creditors.

The resulting austerity policies meant that the opposition governors, highly dependent on the federal government in finances, found themselves without enough money to meet urgent needs. The opposition, thanks to *abertura,* was coming to power just as the economy was failing. Would that discredit them? Was the voter as interested in redemocratization as in prosperity? Did he/she see a trade-off between the two?

A dramatic and early case was in São Paulo. In early April 1983 a protest march of the unemployed was organized by a small, far-left political group. They intended to flex their muscle within the São Paulo left, but they lost control of the demonstrators, who ran wild in the city streets, looting stores. A group marched on the Governor's Palace (*Palácio Bandeirantes*), where they trampled down an iron fence (largely decorative) around the palace and peered up at a large window where a very worried Governor Montoro was peering down. The palace incident ended peacefully and might have been quickly forgotten but for the widely publicized photograph of the visibly shaken governor at the window, peering down at the demonstrators and the fallen fence. That picture disturbed many who thought Montoro too weak to lead, and gave ammunition to those who said Brazil was not ready for democracy.

The Economy in Deep Recession

The total collapse of the growth strategy outlined in Delfim's Plan III was confirmed in 1982. It was no longer up to Brazil to "choose" or "reject" a recession. By late 1982 the need to stave off external default overshadowed every other economic goal. GDP, industrial production, employment, social welfare, all were subordinated to finding dollars to pay interest on the foreign debt.

A series of external events had landed Brazil in its plight. First came the oil price shocks of 1974 and 1979. Then there was the upward spiral of Eurodollar interest rates from 8.7 percent in 1978 to 17 percent in 1981, a climb that had been touched off by the radical change in U.S. monetary policy in 1979. The latter helped to trigger a severe world recession, which reduced demand for Brazilian exports and therefore reduced export earnings. Then there was the fall in Brazil's terms of trade, which declined by 46 percent between 1977 and 1982. The combination of blows was formidable, capped off by the financial scare resulting from Mexico's de facto default in August 1982.

Brazil was not alone in its plight. Argentina and Mexico also plunged into a payments crisis, as did much of Latin America and the Third World. But Brazilian economic policymakers had thought they were different. They considered themselves superior in their handling of the external accounts. Brazil's sustained export drive, including a steadily rising share of industrial products, had given her high standing among Eurodollar market bankers and analysts. But that made little difference when the storm hit.

All the Brazilian economic policymakers were now discredited in the eyes of the public, notwithstanding the fact that uncontrollable external forces had played a large role. After all, Delfim and his team had never hesitated to claim credit for the "miracle." Why should they now be denied credit for the disaster? Whatever targets the government announced, and there had been many, the public reacted with scorn. The rotund Delfim, the undisputed czar of economic policymaking, was a favorite subject for cartoonists. Many of his critics were irritated even more to learn he enjoyed the cartoons and kept a large framed collection of them at home. But it was no longer a question of Delfim's wisdom or popularity. Now it was a matter of Brazil's following the dictates of her creditors.

After intense negotiation, the Figueiredo government signed a "letter of intent" with the IMF in January 1983. The letter committed Brazil to meet detailed targets in fiscal and monetary policy, as well as foreign exchange policy and tariff policy. To receive continued installments of its IMF loan ("drawing," in IMF parlance), Brazil would have to reach the agreed targets on the agreed schedule or convince the IMF to grant a waiver.

The nature of the IMF's medicine for Brazil's economic ills was hardly a surprise. It followed the IMF's classic paradigm of why the would-be borrower has gotten into a foreign exchange squeeze and how it can get out. The IMF simply applied its orthodox formula: reduce the rate of growth of the money supply, tighten credit, reduce the public sector deficit, devalue faster, eliminate subsidies, and restrict wage increases.

The Figueiredo government's recourse to the IMF plan touched off a wave of angry protest among opposition economists. The best known was Celso Furtado, one of the most frequent and systematic critics of the military government's economic policy since the coup of 1964. He published a rousing manifesto, *No to Recession and Unemployment* in which he argued that "we must break away from the guardianship of the IMF and, secondly, as a sovereign country, decide to what extent Brazil will honor its foreign financial commitments in the context of the international crisis." Many other nationalist voices arose to condemn Brazil's agreement with the IMF. But they had no effect on Delfim or his colleagues, who knew the fusillades they would provoke and the replies they would hurl back.[66]

Satisfactory relations with the IMF were essential because the commercial banks, which held most of Brazil's debt, now looked to the IMF for signals on further lending to Brazil. Before the IMF entered the picture in late 1982, the commercial banks had made their own evaluation of Brazil's economic health whenever they rolled over old loans or made new ones. Since no single bank or group of banks could produce as experienced and qualified a team as the IMF, when Brazil dealt only with the banks it had more room for maneuver. That privilege ended when the threat of Mexican financial collapse in August 1982 frightened the bankers into stopping new commitments and deferring to the IMF's judgment on Brazil's creditworthiness.[67]

The consortium of creditor banks was now cautious, for some of their stockholders ferociously opposed any further lending (even extensions or rollovers) to Latin American customers. The IMF, the commercial banks, and the U.S. and European governments were all determined to keep Brazil on a short leash. Delfim Neto and his colleagues spent all of 1983 struggling to come up with the dollar loans that would allow Brazil to stay current on interest payments (payment on the principal was still out of the question).

Meanwhile, the economy sank deeper and deeper into recession. GDP declined by 5.0 percent in 1983, the worst record since national income accounts had been kept. Industry was hit hardest, declining 7.9 percent, while commerce dropped by 4.4 percent. Countering this trend was agriculture, where output grew by 2.1 percent, due primarily to coffee and other export crops. The overall GDP drop of 5 percent translated into a 7.3 percent decline per capita.

The capital goods industry was a prime victim of the slump. Its output dropped 23 percent in 1983, the fourth consecutive yearly decline. These firms' best customers, the state enterprises, were slashing their budgets as part of the stabilization program stipulated by the IMF. Payments due from state firms for previous purchases went unpaid and when paid were not corrected for inflation. By late 1983 many firms were facing bankruptcy, and idle capacity was estimated at 50 percent. These alarming trends were part of what the government's critics were calling the "deindustrialization" of Brazil.

By December 1983 employment in the greater metropolitan regions of São Paulo and Rio de Janeiro had both fallen by 15 percent compared to their August 1978 averages. Industry was hit especially hard. By February 1984 industrial production had dropped by 14 percent from its average level during 1980. Industrial employment was hit even harder. Compared to the August 1978 average, December 1983 industrial employment was down by 26 percent in greater São Paulo and 30 percent in greater Rio. Real wages in São Paulo manufacturing held up through 1982 but fell sharply in 1983 and early 1984. These data on average wages in fact understate the decline, in that during a recession the lower paid workers were laid off first. Those earning only the minimum wage in Rio or São Paulo suffered even greater losses.

Along with the slump went *accelerating* inflation (thereby giving a new meaning to "stagflation"), which hit another Brazilian record of 211 percent for 1983, more than double the 1982 rate. Inflation at this rate played havoc with the economy, notwithstanding indexation. Wages, for example, were now losing their real value five times as fast as in 1978, the year immediately preceding the Figueiredo government's move to adjust wage rates semi-annually instead of once a year. (By that logic, given the 200 percent annual inflation, the wage adjustments ought now to have been made at least quarterly.)

Brazilian authorities continued to reduce imports by every imaginable device. The severe industrial recession helped on that score, because industry normally generated much of the import demand. But those foregone imports meant delayed maintenance, as well as the loss of new technology Brazil needed to compete in export markets. Both trends boded ill for Brazilian industry's medium- and long-term prospects.

The large public sector deficit was another item on which the IMF was demanding tough action. By slashing the budgets of the state enterprises, as well as squeezing hard the expenditure side of the fiscal budget during 1983, Delfim was able to move the entire public sector budget toward balance. The cost was high. The federal university system, for example, lost at least 30 percent of its real appropriations from 1982 to early 1984. And the construction, communications, and transportation industries, heavily dependent on orders from state enterprises, dropped to 50 percent capacity and below.

Another key policy area was interest rates. We have seen earlier how by the late 1970s the government forced Brazilian interest rates above Eurodollar rates in order to maximize private borrowing abroad and thus maximize capital inflow. That policy helped keep capital flight at a minimum, but it also raised the cost of business, thereby feeding inflation.

Similar logic applied to the financing of Brazil's public sector deficit and national debt. To help assure an attractive rate of return on ORTNs, the indexed government bonds, the government tied their redemption value to the change in the dollar exchange rate, plus the set interest rate. If devaluation exceeded the rate of inflation (or indexation rates on other investments), then the investor was ahead. Such was the case in 1983, when the dollar rose in cruzeiro value by 289 percent or 78 percent higher than the official inflation rate. Such a phenomenal real rate of return gave investors an incentive to engage in "financial speculation," rather than investment in productive enterprises. In fact, firms with idle cash often found it more profitable to buy ORTNs than to reinvest in their own businesses.

All the other orthodox measures—tight monetary policy and wage "discipline" (which in practice meant reducing real wages)—reinforced the immediate economic downturn. By 1984 Brazil was into its fourth successive year of per capita economic decline. Her GNP, in per capita terms, had fallen by 10 percent between 1980 and 1983. Years of hard-won economic progress had slipped away.[68]

Nationalist voices, which seldom got a hearing in the days of the "miracle," now began to sound more relevant. PMDB National President Ulysses Guimarães rejected the IMF formulae as "extremely harmful." Since Brazil needed more money, "the only way out is a three-year moratorium, paying neither interest nor principal."[69]

Such sentiments worried the military, who soon after the 1964 coup had purged both the Congress and the armed forces of most of the nationalist voices. But the military had more immediate worries. Their almost two decades in power had taken a toll on their public prestige and internal morale. Financial scandals involving military officers were exploding regularly on newspaper front pages. Resentment was growing at the number of highly paid executive positions in the state enterprises reserved for retired officers. The long campaign against torture had deepened the association in the public's mind between the military and repression. There was another indicator that for some officers indicated a decline in military prestige, the increasing percentage of lower-middle and lower-class cadets at the military academies.[70]

And the higher military were deeply worried about their outmoded equipment. Saddled with largely out-of-date U.S. gear, the armed services were reacting to their relative budgetary neglect at the hands of successive military governments. From 1970 to 1981, the defense share of federal expenditures declined from 9.36 percent to 3.43 percent and as a share of GDP from 1.63 percent to 0.67 percent. Army Minister Pires saw that the military needed to concentrate on strengthening itself as an institution. That meant pulling back from the many (often lucrative) personal distractions and "returning to the barracks," monitoring politics, but concentrating primarily on the urgent need to reorganize and re-equip. Paradoxically, the Brazilian military were using the civilian politicians' desire to see them out of politics in order to bargain for increased budgets.[71]

The Campaign for Direct Presidential Elections

As the economy deteriorated, the Planalto also had to face a deteriorating political situation. The 1982 election results had further eroded the control of key political posts held by preceding military governments. The PDS not only lost majority control of the Chamber of Deputies, it also lost the governorships of Minas Gerais, Rio de Janeiro, and São Paulo. Furthermore, President Figueiredo was in a weaker position because most of the arbitrary powers enjoyed by the last three presidents, especially AI–5, had been jettisoned by Geisel.

Figueiredo had yet another liability—his precarious health. He had already suffered a heart attack in September 1981, and in July 1983 he flew to Cleveland, Ohio, for bypass surgery. Vice President Chaves again (as in 1981) served as acting president for six weeks. Figueiredo was thereafter ordered to reduce his work load, as well as to stop smoking and reduce his weight. Because the presidential system (military or not) in Brazil's increasingly open political climate demanded the constant presence and intervention of the president, Figueiredo's reduced schedule meant reduced effectiveness at the center of government. His ill health reinforced another trait, often typical of military officers in politics: a dislike of negotiation. He had neither the patience nor the temperament for political bargaining. Even in the best of cases he held a difficult hand. How could he hold off the opposition in favor of a PDS that consumed itself in ineffectual or divisive maneuvers? Figueiredo had been shocked by the PMDB's electoral gains in 1982. Why had the public voted down so many PDS candidates? How could the PDS leaders have been so wrong when they assured him about the government's electoral appeal? Given the events of 1982, how could a military regime win a popular majority in an open election? That question had bedeviled every government since 1964. Figueiredo's was the first to face that challenge in a relatively open political forum. One feature of the system continued to favor the Planalto: the presidential election was still indirect.

And Figueiredo had another asset. He still had the strong support of the military. This had been demonstrated anew in late 1982 when his supporters in the army High Command chose not to promote to four-star rank General Coelho Neto, the leading hardliner. By military regulation Coelho Neto then had to retire, thus removing him from what was shaping up to be a key position in the presidential succession.

The legitimacy of indirect elections, however, had now come under frontal attack. A campaign was under way in favor of direct election of the president in 1985;[72] a constitutional amendment to that effect had been proposed by PMDB deputy Dante de Oliveira in March 1983. Although it drew relatively little attention at the time, PMDB leaders sensed strong public support for the amendment. In April 1983 Cardinal Arns and Dom Ivo Lorscheiter (general-secretary of the CNBB) both endorsed direct election of the president. By June the PMDB's national board (direção) had launched a national campaign, to begin in Goiania, where a rally of 5,000 cheered the manifesto.

Many prominent opposition figures now began to join the campaign. Lula was a fixture at most rallies, as were Governors Leonel Brizola, Franco Montoro, and Tancredo Neves. But the two politicians who commanded greatest respect were Teotônio Vilela and Ulysses Guimarães. Teotônio was a Senator from the Northeastern state of Alagoas who had left the PDS for the PMDB in April 1979.[73] With his drooping mustache, black hair down over his ears, and leathery face, he looked the caricature of the Latin politician. He had a deep, riveting voice and the florid rhetoric for which the Northeast was famous. Everyone knew he was dying of cancer, which made his political appeal all the more immediate. Teotônio thundered against the military government for its embrace of arbitrary powers and its neglect of burning social needs, thereby summing up the opposition case since 1964. His style was perfect for the rallies in the interior cities, the organizers were saving the bigger cities for a later phase of the campaign.

Ulysses Guimarães had weathered well the years of repression. He had consistently opposed the military governments, excoriating them for violating human rights and subverting representative government. Yet he was never purged from Congress nor deprived of his political rights. The military seemed to view him as a figure whose removal would be too costly. Ulysses, like Teotônio, was a master at traditional political oratory— sweeping gestures, a penetrating voice, total courage, and the ability to command respect. These two veteran politicians, whose political roots went back to before 1964, symbolized political continuity, as they fought to return Brazil to an open political system.

The campaign for direct presidential election (diretas) generated a momentum of its own. In city after city the public responded enthusiastically as the local opposition leadership, usually including PMDB, PDT (Brizola's party), and PT mobilized support. Others joined in, including the bar associations and leading media, such as the *Folha de São Paulo*. Most important, however, were the national artists and show business personalities who helped turn the rallies into major cultural happenings. The biggest star was Fafá da Belem, a well-known young singer who became a total convert to the campaign and its embodiment. Others were Chico Buarque de Hollanda, the wildly popular samba composer and performer; Elba Ramalho, a highly popular songstress; and Socrates, the soccer star. The vocal trademark of the rallies belonged to Osmar Santos, Brazil's leading soccer announcer-commentator. At the end of each rally he led the audience in singing the national anthem—the opposition's ritual to demonstrate its patriotism.

The Geisel government had opened up more space for public participation. The *diretas* campaigners were exploiting this change, as the campaign tapped into a swelling civic spirit in Brazil. By giving the show business personalities a prominent role, the organizers muted the campaign's partisan character (the PDS and the Planalto stood united against the *diretas* amendment when the campaign began).

At this point an interesting shift occurred in the media coverage. When the campaign began, the TV, above all TV-Globo, ignored the rallies, per government instructions. But as the public enthusiasm grew, the networks decided they were missing a major story, as well as an important political event. They began to cover the rallies from beginning to end. Suddenly this powerful medium, which the government had exploited so skillfully, was aiding the opposition. And it was led by TV-Globo, which had risen to great power and profit under military regimes. It was a dramatic demonstration that the government's power was on the decline.

The campaign now took on a festive air. Supporters of *diretas* sported yellow T-shirts (yellow being one of the two colors of the Brazilian flag) emblazoned with "I want to vote for president!" The rallies were always orderly, showing a discipline that surprised observers, both foreign and Brazilian. This festive, popular, orderly quality made the campaign difficult for its opponents to discredit, but, nonetheless, such efforts were made. Army intelligence photographed rallies and circulated the results in the Planalto, pointing to the banners demanding legalization of the Communist Party. In fact, the time was past when such gambits by the intelligence community could scuttle organizing and mobilization by the opposition. The blast at RioCentro had been the last hurrah of military-sponsored rightist disruption.

The *diretas* campaign now focused on the congressional vote on the amendment, scheduled for late April. As a constitutional amendment, it needed a two-thirds vote of both the Chamber of Deputies and the Senate. That seemed impossible. After all, the PDS controlled almost half the seats in the Chamber of Deputies (235 of 479) and well over half (46 of 69) in the

Senate. But the PDS ranks were beginning to break. Individual PDS governors and deputies were endorsing the amendment, heartening the campaigners. Suddenly every Congressman faced a barrage of questions about where he stood on the Dante de Oliveira amendment.

As the vote approached, the size of the rallies grew. In early April over 500,000 Brazilians assembled in downtown Rio de Janeiro, cheering speakers who demanded their right to elect the president directly. Once again sports and arts celebrities were featured, along with opposition governors and party leaders. It was Rio's largest political rally ever, exceeding even the record-setters on the eve of the 1964 Revolution. Next came rallies of 200,000 in Goiania and 200,000 in Porto Alegre. On April 16 the scene shifted to São Paulo, where a crowd of one million, the largest of all, brought the campaign to a climax.

The final stage for the campaigners was to monitor the congressional vote. In one state capital after another huge tally boards were erected with the names of the state congressional delegation. Each Congressman's vote would be recorded for every citizen to see. The amendment supporters next demanded that the voting session be televised live. They knew some wavering Congressmen would lack the courage to vote "no" if their constituents were watching on live TV. As a compromise the government allowed live radio coverage.

From its beginning the *diretas* campaign had been suspect in the eyes of many military. They distrusted the organizers' motives—the mere participation of Leonel Brizola or Lula, for example, was a red flag to many. They looked askance at the mass rallies, remembering the leftist-inspired rallies in the final weeks of President João Goulart's presidency in 1964. Yet these worried military had no way to translate their fears into action. The hardline leaders had been routed by Geisel and discredited once again in the RioCentro affair. They were therefore on the defensive, an increasingly familiar posture for them.

The hard line still had one public voice, that of General Newton Cruz, a former high-level SNI officer who was now the army commander for the Planalto (Brasília). General Cruz was a belligerent, heavy-handed martinet who had clashed with the press repeatedly, once (in December 1983) grabbing a reporter by the throat—a scene immediately captured for the national TV audience. A silver-haired man often given to intimidating his interlocutors, General Cruz was a political gift for the opposition. Although he could denounce demonstrators and threaten them with imprisonment, General Cruz could not carry out his threats because his superiors, who had adopted a lower profile, would not back him up. He thus symbolized arbitrary but impotent power, a disastrous combination in this political climate.[74]

As the congressional vote neared, the Figueiredo government feared that the *diretas* campaigners might try to coerce the Congress by massive demonstrations. Citing this danger, it imposed a state of emergency in Brasília. The campaigners responded with a call to converge on the capitol—not inside the congressional chambers, but in an automobile parade around the Congress buildings, honking horns to show support for the amendment.

General Cruz, as the commander for Brasília, was responsible for enforcing the emergency order. On April 25, the day of the vote, the car horns began to blare. General Cruz rushed out to stop them. When they did not heed his shouts, he began rapping on the car hoods with his riding crop, like a latter-day George Patton. Once again the media captured his gestures. The symbolic level was unmistakable: an extremist military figure appeared as both powerless and ridiculous.

When the vote finally came, the amendment fell short of the required two-thirds in the Chamber by only 22 votes. It needed 320 out of the total membership of 479, and got 298. The latter included 55 PDS deputies who voted "yes" despite heavy pressure from the party leadership and the Planalto. The campaign had come closer to victory than anyone would have dared predict a year, or even six months, earlier. No less important, its supporters had with impunity staged the largest political rallies ever seen in Brazil.[75]

The President, the Planalto, the PDS leadership, and the military had all been caught off guard. They could neither stop nor ignore the mounting national campaign. Some elements were familiar—the emotional appeal and the call to put direct pressure on the Congress. But the campaign also had its unique aspect. It was a surge of civic spirit of unprecedented size, and no candidate was asking for votes for himself. Rather, the objective was to restore the *right* to have such a vote. It was a dramatic message from a civil society steadily regaining its voice.

PDS Presidential Aspirants

The campaign for the *diretas* put the Planalto in a difficult position. The President obviously wanted to keep the election indirect, because the electoral college votes were stacked in favor of the government party, thus protecting the military from any surprises in the presidential succession. Figueiredo also favored the indirect route because it would maximize his influence. His problem was how to defend this position in the face of growing public demand for direct election. Figueiredo and his advisers thought they were playing from strength, in that the PDS enjoyed a majority in the electoral college. This in mid-1983 they, and almost everyone else, thought the only meaningful question was, Who would the PDS convention nominate? In that process Figueiredo expected to indicate his preference, and the PDS-controlled electoral college would then elect the PDS nominee. The pattern of the last four presidential successions would thus be followed.

There were three leading candidates within the PDS.[76] The first was Aureliano Chaves, Figueiredo's vice president. Chaves, 55, was a *mineiro,* a civilian, and trained as an engineer—a rare breed, as few Brazilian politicians had technical backgrounds. He used that training in the early 1960s in high positions with Electrobrás and CEMIG, the state energy authority. He began his political career as a UDN state deputy, rising to become government leader in the Minas Gerais legislature. He later served in the state cabinet of Governor Magalhães Pinto, one of the fathers of the 1964 Revolution. He next served as federal deputy and was one of the few ARENA deputies voting in 1968 against the government's demand to lift the parliamentary immunity of Márcio Moreira Alves. That put Chaves on the blacklist of many military, but he survived as federal deputy, specializing in energy policy. In that capacity he caught the eye of Ernesto Geisel, then President of Petrobrás. With Geisel's backing Chaves was (indirectly) elected Governor of Minas Gerais, serving from 1975 to 1978, when he resigned to run for vice president on Figueiredo's ticket.

On first glance Chaves might have appeared an unlikely candidate, inasmuch as no civilian vice president since 1964 had gone on to higher things. Owing their positions to the military, they were mere token figures. The military's veto of Pedro Aleixo's succession to the presidency after Costa e Silva's stroke in October 1969 demonstrated that fact.

Yet Chaves had real assets. He had shown good judgment and restraint when thrust into the role of acting president in 1981 and 1983. Military officers thought he had shown the moral stature to be president. He also had the credentials of a loyal ex-UDN and ARENA leader. And his *mineiro* origins were an asset, because *mineiros* had a highly effective political network (channeled by party identity) across the country.

Chaves also had his liabilities. During his stints as acting president the press had depicted him as energetic and efficient, thereby arousing resentment in presidential circles. That effectively ended Chaves's chances of getting Figueiredo's support. He had other problems as well. As Vice President he was gradually losing his political base. In Minas Gerais the governor was Tancredo Neves (PMDB), who, as leader of the pre-1965 PSD, was a long-time opponent of the UDN, Aureliano's former party. As Vice President he could not diverge significantly from presidential views, for fear of weakening the Planalto and discrediting himself as disloyal. This hurt him especially on economic issues, since the public blamed the Figueiredo government for the deep recession. Finally, Chaves was an impulsive man, known for his short temper.[77] That could impair his ability to negotiate, a quality that was much in need as the military were backing out of power.

Interior Minister Mario Andreazza, 65, was a second "inside" candidate for president. He attended military school in Rio de Janeiro and entered the army, opting for the infantry. He worked his way up to lieutenant colonel and in 1964 joined the staff of War Minister Costa e Silva. The next year he made colonel, his highest military rank. Andreazza helped legitimize Costa e Silva's succession to the presidency with a PR campaign selling his general as a good-hearted liberal. Andreazza then served as Minister of Transportation in both the Costa e Silva and Médici governments. That put him at the center of both the Transamazon Highway project and the Rio-Niteroi bridge project to span Guanabara bay. Both projects were criticized as too expensive for their probable payoff. As Minister of the Interior under Figueiredo, Andreazza once again presided over extensive public works projects, especially in housing, safe water systems, and electrification. Through the years Andreazza had built a formidable network of personal and political contacts throughout Brazil. With his budget (in 1984 the World Bank was scheduled to finance roughly a billion dollars worth of projects through the Interior Ministry), Andreazza wielded obvious political power. His ministry's projects were in the economically less developed regions, which were also the centers of PDS electoral strength. That increased his leverage in campaigning for votes in the PDS nominating convention.

Andreazza had the further advantage (to the PDS electors) of being a familiar face, someone who had held ministerial responsibility in three military governments. For PDS politicians who disliked surprises, Andreazza was an obvious choice. Yet those years of experience had also made him a frequent target for charges of corruption. Rumors of payoffs for awarding the Rio-Niteroi bridge contracts refused to die. These suspicions of corruption hurt him among the more moralistic military. They also bothered many politicians and opinion-makers. Andreazza had thus acquired a shopworn flavor—not what progressive PDS leaders wanted for the changing times.

The third principal PDS presidential aspirant was Paulo Maluf, 52. Unlike Chaves or Andreazza, he had held no post in the Figueiredo government. Yet he was working furiously to win the president's favor or at least insure the president's neutrality in the nominating process.

Every politically informed person in Brazil had a strong opinion about Maluf. He came from a wealthy São Paulo clan (Lebanese in origin) which owned Eucatex, a huge building materials firm. His wife, Silvia Lutfalla, came from another wealthy family. Maluf thus pursued politics with more family wealth than any other Brazilian politician. His first political breakthrough came from his friendship with President Costa e Silva (they met because both were eager horsemen), who got Maluf appointed to the presidency of *Caixa Econômica Federal* (Federal Savings Bank) in 1967 in São Paulo. The president helped a second time by arranging Maluf's appointment as Mayor of São Paulo in 1969. As mayor, Maluf awarded each member of Brazil's championship soccer team an automobile. It was characteristic of Maluf's political style. It also told much about key symbols in authoritarian Brazil.

Costa e Silva's death ended Maluf's support from Brasília, but it did not end Maluf's political ambitions. His eye was next set on the São Paulo governorship. The contest was to be decided in the 1978 ARENA convention, for ARENA had a comfortable majority in the electoral college. Laudo Natel, a previous governor, was strongly endorsed by both President Geisel and President-elect Figueiredo. His nomination seemed a foregone conclusion. But to the surprise of many, Maluf carried the convention, defeating Natel. He won because he campaigned indefatigably among the convention members, offering lavish promises of what his administration would bring. He benefitted also from the mood of political independence in the air. Wasn't a defiance of Brasília's instructions consistent with *abertura*?

As governor, Maluf was a whirlwind activist on such traditional public works as schools, health posts, and roads. There were also quixotic ventures, such as a proposal to move the capital to the interior,[78] and the creation of a São Paulo oil exploration company (Paulipetro). Neither idea outlived Maluf's governorship. He used his governorship of Brazil's wealthiest state to promote his presidential candidacy. One of his most publicized ploys was to donate ambulances to poor cities of the Northeastern interior. Another gambit was to fly Brazilians from across the country to São Paulo (on VASP, the São Paulo state airline) to receive medals from the Governor. The charge most often levelled against Maluf's governorship was corruption. Yet the evidence proved lacking. Both *O Estado de São Paulo* and *A Folha de São Paulo* opposed Maluf and presumably sent their reporters to find the dirt, but without success. The next government (Franco Montoro) spent months in an unsuccessful search for the proof. It was reduced to arguing that Maluf had covered his tracks too carefully (an argument that by its nature can never be disproved) and to attacking the unwisdom of such ventures as Paulipetro and unneeded new hydro-electric projects. As for his ideology, Maluf was clearly a conservative, as shown by his hostility to the metalworkers' strike in April 1980, and his government's heavy-handed repression of street protests in June 1980.[79] Maluf had a powerful champion in General Golbery, who termed him a "successful, progressive, dynamic, and intelligent businessman" who has the "best qualities for facing the difficult period ahead."[80]

Maluf resigned his governorship in May 1982 so that he could run for federal deputy in the November election. He was elected with 673,000 votes, a Brazilian record. From Brasília he pressed his presidential candidacy even harder. The heart of his support was in the PDS of the Northeast, which he had courted so avidly. As the campaign was for electoral college votes and not public opinion, Maluf concentrated on those 686 deputies, senators, and state delegates. His opponents soon accused him of buying votes.

Yet Maluf had a following across Brazil. His supporters praised his legendary organizing ability and his phenomenal memory, especially for names and faces. Maluf promoted the image of a strong leader, someone who could organize the (some said) eternally disorganized citizenry. He appealed especially to conservatives who feared the power of the left under a more open system. His tough stance as governor against unions, students, and street protestors promised what the conservatives wanted to see more of on the federal level.

Maluf generated near apoplexy on the left, much of the center, and even some of the PDS. These critics saw him as a menace to the slowly emerging democracy. Former Bahia Governor Antonio Carlos Magalhães, for example, declared in August 1984 that Maluf was the most hated man in Brazil and couldn't walk a city block without endangering his life. Maluf immediately sued for libel. Such hyperbole was the rule in discussing Maluf. The longer he campaigned, the more divisive he became within the PDS.

Several other PDS presidential aspirants were merely long shots. The best known was Marco Maciel, who, as an ARENA federal deputy from his home state of Pernambuco in the 1970s, had risen to become president of the Chamber of Deputies. He was appointed Governor of Pernambuco and then elected Senator in 1982. Maciel was a workaholic and a serious young politician who had helped articulate the rationale for a redemocratized Brazil.[81] He was also somewhat shy and likely to win the nod only if there were a deadlock among the front-runners.

José Costa Cavalcanti was another oft-discussed candidate. He began as a career military officer, but retired to become a federal deputy in the 1960s. He had been a minister in both the Costa e Silva and Médici governments. In 1983 he was the president of Itaipú Binacional, the authority constructing the huge dam on the Paraná River between Brazil and Paraguay. He had a reputation as a superb administrator, but he lacked any significant political following.

Helio Beltrão, Minister for Social Welfare and Debureaucratization in Figueiredo's cabinet, was another long shot. His post, which was unprecedented, was as a super-ombudsman. He invited every Brazilian to contact him directly about any problem they encountered in dealing with the federal bureaucracy. He promised to pursue every complaint personally. Although Beltrão undoubtedly helped many individuals, the novelty faded, the task proved gargantuan, and Beltrão's electoral appeal dimmed. His principal support came from the business community, which liked his background in Rio commerce and his commitment to reducing the public sector while improving the economic climate for the private sector.

Other candidates included Bahia Governor Magalhães and Education Minister Rubem Ludwig. Both were skilled political operators in their own way, but neither had more than a very outside chance for the nomination.

In the ensuing succession struggle journalists frequently reported that Figueiredo preferred Andreazza. Time after time the press announced a date on which the President would announce his choice.[82] As each date passed without an announcement, Andreazza looked weaker. He had geared his campaign to the presidential blessing, which he (and many others) assumed would be forthcoming, just as it had been from Geisel in Figueiredo's case. Maluf feared such an endorsement of Andreazza and worked frantically to head it off.

As of June 1984 most members of the electoral college were uncommitted, with Andreazza and Maluf having a roughly equal number of supporters among those delegates willing to declare a preference. Aureliano Chaves was at a particular disadvantage in this fight. Although ministers, such as Andreazza, had to mute their criticisms of the incumbent government, Chaves as Vice President had even more difficulty distancing himself from the government. For Chaves to support, as he did, the constitutional amendment for direct election of the president only destroyed the support from Figueiredo which would be crucial in the PDS convention.

The President's own political position grew weaker as the succession struggle heated up. Figueiredo had been saying for some months he would not attempt to dictate his successor. Rather, he promised to leave the choice up to the PDS convention. Other post-1964 presidents had said the same and nonetheless tried to impose their choice. Geisel had succeeded in imposing Figueiredo as the PDS nominee and the new President. Would Figueiredo now stage-manage his own succession?

The scene was complicated by the fact that Figueiredo showed clear signs of wanting to extend his term. Two of his ministers, Mines and Energy Minister César Cals and SNI Director Octávio Medeiros, openly urged the president to stay on, perhaps for two more years, until a new constitution was adopted. Such an ambition directly contradicted the post-1964 military consensus that no general-president should succeed himself (Castelo Branco's extended term being a one-time exception). Figueiredo could easily have stopped these trial balloons, but he did not. By encouraging such speculation, the president was dividing the government forces which ought to have had an interest in selecting a strong candidate behind whom the military and their civilian allies could unify.[83]

The President argued that leaving the choice up to the convention would be the democratic procedure. It fit in with *abertura* by moving in the direction of giving the public a greater say in choosing its leaders—a goal the entire political elite endorsed. Furthermore, it helped enhance the prestige and power of the PDS—a goal endorsed by outside observers who thought Brazil needed to strengthen its parties. Along with these reasons, there were personal factors at work as well. Given his temperament and his health problems, Figueiredo wanted to stay out of the succession fight.

Figueiredo could afford to take this stance in part because control over the next presidential election seemed firmly in PDS hands. The electoral college that would elect the president had a PDS majority (356 out of 686). That should ensure that for another presidential term power would be held by a president chosen under the aegis of the military government. Brazil would thus continue to be governed by an *in*directly elected president into a third decade since the 1964 Revolution.

Was this system viable for the future? All post-1964 military governments had steered with ad hoc plans. Despite repeated attempts to produce a new constitutional structure (1967, 1969, and 1977, to mention only the major examples), the question was always how to retain power now with a semblance of electoral legitimacy. That meant making the elections indirect, while overrepresenting the rural regions and the Northeast.

Neither the Figueiredo team nor the PDS party leadership seemed to have formulated any viable strategy for the longer run. Their goal was to keep control of the 1985 presidential election. Even that proved elusive, as the President first encouraged talk of his staying on and then refused to choose a candidate who could prevail within the PDS. They also faced the larger question of how to make the PDS into a party able to win elections in an increasingly urbanized Brazil.

The Victory of the Democratic Alliance

Maluf's aggressive strategy had put the PDS on edge. By early 1984 he was gaining ground. His campaign team was better equipped and better funded than Andreazza's, while Chaves was inhibited from campaigning by his link to the Planalto. In late June the anti-Maluf forces in the PDS proposed to the party's National Committee that state primary elections be held—a move bound to hurt Maluf, who lacked grass roots popularity. Maluf's lieutenants answered by packing the next committee meeting; they became so disruptive that committee president José Sarney (a veteran Senator from Maranahão) and other anti-Maluf members walked out of the meeting in protest and promptly resigned from the committee. Divisions within the PDS were deepening. July brought another surprise to PDS leaders and voters. Vice President Chaves withdrew from the race. He joined Marco Maciel, who had also withdrawn, in forming a PDS breakaway, the *Frente Liberal*. They then cut off all contact with the Maluf-dominated PDS National Committee.

The move touched off a mass defection of formerly pro-government political elite. The succession of UDN and PSD politicians who had collaborated with the generals since 1964 was now broken. Just as the military were attempting to begin the last stage of the transition, the once "responsible" civilian politicians decided they had had enough. And they had the incentive of possibly winning power.

Maluf was proving to be the divisive force his critics had predicted. Attacks on Maluf, however, only increased his determination. In August he gained his reward when the PDS national convention nominated him for president. It was a victory produced by intensive lobbying with every convention delegate, aided by generous promises of positions in a future Maluf government. But the PDS was now badly divided, with the anti-Maluf PDS forces in open revolt.

The PMDB was proving more unified. By mid-1984 the opposition name on everyone's lips was Governor Tancredo Neves of Minas Gerais.[84] Tancredo had been a federal deputy in the 1950s, '60s and '70s, and he was Senator from 1978 to 1982. He had held three key posts—Justice (1953–54) under President Getúlio Vargas, a Banco do Brasil executive position (1956–58) under President Juscelino Kubitschek, and the prime ministry during the 1962 parliamentary interlude under President João Goulart (1961–64). He was 74, but that was an asset for the many who saw in him a father figure who, as the first elected civilian president since 1964, could unite the country. Never a man of extreme opinions or aggressive behavior, Tancredo was the consummate politician.

His politics were moderately left of center, as could be seen in his argument that Brazil should not sacrifice its economic development to pay its foreign debt. In fact, Tancredo's moderate views appealed to a public ranging from center-right to center-left. That would help make him an ideal candidate against Maluf. In August the PMDB convention nominated Tancredo.

Within a month Tancredo faced a public challenge from a crucial quarter: the military. Army Minister Walter Pires, known in the past as a hardliner, bitterly criticized the Liberal Front politicians who "had deserted their commitments" in favor of a "future that looks more attractive."[85] It was an ominous judgment from the only source of power that now stood between Tancredo and the presidency. Brasília was alive with rumors that a coup was in the making. Walls suddenly blossomed with posters showing Tancredo giving the victory sign, flanked by a hammer and sickle, the letters PCB (*Partido Comunista Brasileiro*), and the words *Chegaremos la!* (we'll get there). Brasília police caught several boys putting up the posters and took them to the station, where they were released on the orders of a man identifying himself as a lieutenant colonel in the Army. Army intelligence (CIEX), or free lancers linked to it, was clumsily covering its tracks in the wake of a "disinformation" operation.[86]

There were also other signals that a military coup might be in the making. In late July the army High Command had given orders to increase the stocks of arms, fuel, and food. General Newton Cruz, the theatrically hardline commander of the Planalto, planned to seal off Brasília for election day to prevent any public demonstrations or any live TV or radio coverage of the vote.[87] Such an operation would have been the most logical prelude to a coup, with the army taking over all government buildings—a simple task in Brasília with its concentration of power in a small area. In response to these rumors, Tancredo and his staff had formulated an escape scenario, by which he would flee to Minas Gerais or Paraná (depending on the local army commanders), where he would organize a fight against the *golpistas*.

Tancredo was not even fazed. He had already reassured key military that he had no intention of turning the clock back to pre-1964 Brazil. Equally important, he publicly opposed any attempt to try military or police accused of torture and other human rights violations. Tancredo thus calmed military worries by tapping his wide network of military contacts, including several generals who had supported Aureliano Chaves and several close collaborators with Geisel. Even better, Tancredo made direct contact with Geisel, who had mostly kept aloof from politics in his retirement. In late August they had a much-publicized meeting, at which Geisel gave Tancredo his discreet support. This was a great boost for Tancredo among the military, where Geisel still commanded great respect.[88] The higher military agreed on a low profile role in the presidential succession, based on accepting the electoral college's choice. An important sign of the shift in military opinion came when the army High Command relieved General Newton Cruz of his Brasília command, transferring him to a bureaucratic post.[89]

Maluf was meanwhile continuing to achieve what the opposition could never have done: sundering the PDS. The dissident faction, the *Partido da Frente Liberal,* or PFL (the Liberal Front Party), joined with the PMDB to create the *Aliança Democratica* (Democratic Alliance). Their presidential candidate was Tancredo Neves, and for vice president it was José Sarney, a long-time UDN and later PDS stalwart. It was understood that if their coalition ticket won, there would be a sharing of the spoils in the new government.

Senator Sarney's political background was long and varied. At first glance he seemed the prototype of an old-style Brazilian politician. He came from Maranhão, in the heart of the poverty-stricken Northeast. He had studied law, then entered state politics bearing the colors of the UDN. He survived that feud-ridden arena to enter the national stage as a federal deputy in 1958. Sarney soon joined the UDN's "Bossa Nova" faction, a nationalist and reformist faction on the UDN left.[90] In 1961 Sarney was elected national vice president of the UDN. He used his post to push "Bossa Nova" positions, such as land reform and support for President Goulart's three-year economic stabilization program (*Plano Trienal*). Those positions were vigorously attacked by conservative UDN leaders, such as Carlos Lacerda. When Jânio Quadros (who had been the UDN candidate) resigned the presidency in 1961 the gap between the "Bossa Nova" and the conservatives (known as the *banda da música*) deepened. Goulart's overthrow in 1964 divided the UDN further. Several "Bossa Nova" leaders, such as José Aparecido and Seixas Doria, were stripped of their political rights for 10 years. Sarney, on the other hand, joined the 1964 Revolution and escaped the subsequent purges. In 1965 he was elected governor of Maranhão and greatly strengthened his political base there by carrying out many public works projects.

In 1970 he returned to Brasília as Senator and soon became an articulate defender of government policies. He welcomed Geisel's initiative on liberalization and in 1977–78 played a key role in drafting the legislation to reform the judiciary and the electoral system. He fought to retain the two-party system but lost to Golbery's plan to encourage additional parties. As a national PDS leader, Sarney worked to give the party a "modern" reformist program within clear capitalist limits. It was the "Bossa Nova" message with a new label.

Sarney had reached the top of the PDS congressional delegation by hard work, forceful prose, and a low-key manner. With his secure electoral base in Maranhão he could afford to concentrate on national politics. He was chosen as Tancredo's running mate in 1984 because he was a respected and nonabrasive PDS dissident leader, but also because as a Northeasterner he could draw votes away from Maluf. In sum, Sarney was the kind of solid politician one might expect to find running for vice president.

The creation of the Democratic Alliance immediately changed the electoral outlook. Maluf, who assumed that he had the PDS in hand, now lacked the solid PDS electoral college vote which was supposed to follow from his nomination. Instead, he faced a widening PDS defection. As his

PDS support eroded, Maluf made a desperate move. He had the PDS announce that it would purge from the party any PDS electoral college member who did not vote for the party's official nominee. Maluf's leverage here was future patronage, but that weapon lost its meaning as his victory chances faded.

In early September Air Force Minister Délio Jardim de Mattos had the bad judgment to brand former Bahia Governor Antônio Carlos Magalhães a "traitor" for supporting Tancredo. Antfonio Carlos lashed back: "the traitor is he who supports a corrupt man." *Veja* magazine later noted that "it was the first time in 20 years that anyone used that tone with a military minister."[91]

The Tancredo-Sarney campaign picked up momentum, largely on the strength of vast enthusiasm for Tancredo. His personality and his image were exactly what the Brazilian public wanted. In October one poll showed Tancredo with 69.5 percent support and Maluf with only 18.7 percent.[92] The media, especially TV-Globo, were overwhelmingly pro-Tancredo. As the campaign continued, Tancredo achieved virtually mythic proportions for most Brazilians. Meanwhile Maluf, whose sense for PR was often startlingly maladroit, came across both on TV and in the print media as a heavy-handed and somewhat sinister figure. Tancredo's campaign, even though for an indirect election, built up increasing momentum. One effect was to put pressure on the wavering voters in the electoral college, under a glare of TV coverage, to vote against Maluf.

On January 15, 1985, the electoral college elected Tancredo Neves and José Sarney by 480 votes out of 686. Maluf received only 180 votes. There were 17 abstentions and 9 absent members (both categories included politicians who had opted out of the bruising struggle or who—on the left—claimed the election was meaningless). The composition of the vote was revealing. Tancredo won all but five of the 280 PMDB votes; he also won 166 PDS votes, almost as many as Maluf's 174. It was an authentic coalition victory.

How had it been possible? After all, in the early 1980s the higher military had made no secret of their view that the opposition must not be allowed to assume the presidency before 1991.[93] How could the government have lost? Only by a highly unlikely combination of circumstances, as Alfred Stepan has argued. First, the government candidate so alienated many government party delegates that they defected from the PDS and openly supported Tancredo.[94] Tancredo then united the opposition and skillfully incorporated the PDS defectors into his camp. Figueiredo by this point had decided to maintain a neutral role—another crucial contribution making possible Tancredo's growing strength. Finally, the military decided, despite Maluf's certain defeat, to allow the election to take place, as long as the rules were observed.[95]

Now the question was whether Tancredo's winning coalition could govern.

Economic Turnaround

The winning coalition was given an initial boost by the improving climate in the economy in 1984. The savage recession of 1981–83 had been Brazil's worst since the Great Depression.[96] Along with the rest of Latin America, Brazil saw her per capita living standards decline while she exported capital to her North Atlantic and Japanese creditors. The recession had also led to a precipitous drop in the Figueiredo government's popularity.[97] The President, once lauded for his amnesty law (1979), understood little of economics and grew weary of aggressive questioning about how the government was going to ease the economic disaster. Delfim became a favorite target of critics; he defended government policies by attributing Brazil's economic woes to adverse shocks from abroad.[98] The recession-linked unpopularity had hurt the PDS in the 1982 elections and threatened a similar result in future elections.

In 1983 the recession bottomed out. The upturn began in 1984, as capacity utilization increased and unemployment dropped.[99] GDP growth recovered to a respectable 4.5 percent for 1984. Inflation, however, had also increased: from 99.7 percent in 1981 to 211 percent in 1982 and up to 223.8 percent in 1983. Brazilian inflation clearly differed from inflation in the industrial economies, where a sharp recession normally reduces inflation. Many thought inflation had gone beyond a level where indexation and mini-devaluations could neutralize it.

Indexation, for example, had become an incentive for financial speculation. Because government debt instruments were indexed in addition to their interest rate, investors often bought government bonds rather than invest in a business enterprise, where risks were far higher. Yet the government had to maintain a high rate of real interest in order to finance the public sector deficit. All agreed that investment incentives needed an overhaul.

There was at least good news on the balance of payments front. The trade balance went from a $1.6 billion surplus in 1981 to a $6.5 billion surplus in 1983, then to an unprecedented surplus of $13.1 billion in 1984. This extraordinary swing was largely due to a sharp drop in imports. Between 1981 and 1983 exports fell from $23.7 billion to $21.9 billion (accounted for by falling demand and prices abroad) while imports dropped much more sharply, from $22.1 billion in 1981 to $15.4 billion in 1983. Only in 1984 did exports spurt, reaching $27.0 billion. Thus the story of Brazil's trade balance here was her ability to cut imports (greatly helped by the recession) while maintaining a strong export performance in the face of an adverse world economy.

That trade surplus came none too soon. The credit crisis triggered by Mexico's de facto bankruptcy in mid-1982 led Eurodollar bankers to reduce sharply their loans to Latin America. In 1981 Brazil received $15.6 billion in new loans, which more than covered the $11.7 billion deficit on current account. In 1982 that lending dropped to $12.5 billion, which fell short of covering the current account deficit of $16.3 billion. In 1983 loans dropped further to $8.2 billion, but they exceeded the much lower current account deficit of $6.8 billion. Lending rose only slightly in 1984, to $8.5 billion, but by then the current account deficit had turned into a small surplus ($166 million).

This strong performance in the external sector had several interesting features. First, Brazil's export drive was continuing to pay off. Exports were increasingly diversified, strengthening Brazil's ability to penetrate world markets. Second, the Brazilian economy was continuing the import-substituting industrialization that some had said was over. The incentive for industrial expansion was great because the government, facing the debt crisis, barred many imports. Third, the favorable balance of payments performance as of 1984 gave the government more maneuvering room vis-à-vis the IMF. The foreign exchange reserves at the end of 1984 stood at $12.0 billion. The civilian government that took power on March 15, 1985, would not have to seek a new agreement with the IMF. At least, not immediately.

VIII

THE NEW REPUBLIC: PROSPECTS FOR DEMOCRACY

With the election of Tancredo Neves, Brazil would have its first civilian president since 1964. He was, moreover, an opposition candidate, elected by defecting government party delegates. During his campaign Tancredo had aroused an astounding show of support. Brazilians came to see this diminutive, cautious, soft-spoken, conciliatory, and thoroughly traditional politician as a political savior, ready to lead their nation out of the wilderness into a new Canaan. Every dissatisfied Brazilian saw in Tancredo what he wanted to see. That gave him more political legitimacy than any Brazilian president-elect in living memory.[1]

In the three months before his inauguration Tancredo traveled to the United States, Europe, and elsewhere in Latin America. In Washington he built contacts with the U. S. Congress, the White House, and the multilateral lending agencies. He talked also with U.S. religious and academic groups which had long criticized U.S. support for the Brazilian military regimes. In Western Europe, Tancredo conferred with governments and political parties. He also made the compulsory pilgrimage to the Vatican.

Tancredo, now seventy-four, was eager to prove his physical resiliency. He insisted on a demanding agenda and on pursuing every political contact to the end. His regimen would have exhausted even a far younger man. In fact, Tancredo was concealing a serious health problem.[2] For months he had been battling an intestinal ailment, relying on antibiotics prescribed by his family doctor in São João del Rey but refusing the doctor's urgent request for a complete physical examination. Tancredo feared that if he were not well enough to be inaugurated, the Figueiredo government—aided by opportunists and hardliners—might use it as a pretext to not pass power to the elected vice president, José Sarney. "Do whatever you want with me," Tancredo told his doctors, "but after the inauguration." He was determined to make it through the day of March 15. By then he would have been inaugurated, power would have been passed to the Democratic Alliance, and the "New Republic" would have been born.[3]

It was not to be. On the eve of being sworn in, Tancredo could no longer

bear the pain. He was admitted to Brasília's *Hospital de Base* and prepared
for surgery.

How Much Did Democratization
Depend on the Person of Tancredo?

The Democratic Alliance was now in a quandary. Tancredo had failed to
become president, if only by hours. The constitution specified that the
succession went from the president to the vice president, thence to the
president of the Congress. PMDB congressmen on the left argued that
since Tancredo had never been inaugurated, Congress President Ulysses
Guimarães was now the legal successor. Ulysses had long hoped to become
president, but not under these circumstances. To the relief of almost everyone, Ulysses insisted that Sarney should be sworn in as "Acting President."
Tancredo's doctors predicted that in two weeks he would be ready to
assume his duties. In the meantime, Sarney would govern as a caretaker.
The first constitutional crisis of the New Republic had been surmounted.

Sarney's awkward status was underlined when President Figueiredo
refused to participate in Sarney's swearing-in. Figueiredo was deeply angry at Sarney, whom he considered a traitor for having deserted the
government party to run with the opposition candidate. He had helped
destroy Figueiredo's mission, which had been to carry out *abertura* but
also to elect another PDS president. Ironically, Figueiredo would have
stayed to pass the presidential sash to Ulysses, a far more radical opponent than either Tancredo or Sarney. Figueiredo saw in Ulysses a worthy
antagonist, whose politics had never changed. But passing the sash to
Sarney he could not stomach. He left the Planalto by a side entrance, just
as the new president stepped forward to take his oath of office.[4]

Figueiredo was sick of public life. The presidency had proved far more
difficult and thankless than he had ever dreamed. He had the bad luck to
assume the presidency shortly before Brazil entered its worst economic
downturn in fifty years, and soon suffered the enormous unpopularity such
an economic disaster made inevitable.[5] To make matters worse, he had
fallen into a psychological depression in recent months, rendering him
angry and hostile. When a journalist asked for his final words to the country in a January farewell television interview, Figueiredo replied causti-
cally, "Forget me."[6] He simply wanted out. But his personal pique compounded the fragile symbolism of the occasion. Power was passing from an
absentee general to a stand-in civilian.

The country had gone into a state of shock at the news of Tancredo's
hospitalization. Public expectations had been so high, aroused not only by
Tancredo's campaign but also by the waves of mobilization the opposition
had recently mounted. Sarney's caretaker government was in no position to
meet these expectations. Only months earlier Sarney had been a leader of
the pro-government party against which the opposition had long fought.
Now he led a political coalition (PMDB-PFL), and coalitions seldom make

for strong governments. Furthermore, there was ample suspicion between the two parties. PMDB leader Ulysses Guimarães regarded the PFL as latecomers to the campaign to restore democracy and the rule of law. Sarney and the PFL were, in militant PMDB eyes, trimmers whose move across the political spectrum had been dictated by self-interest, not principle. The PFL, which was almost as heterogeneous as the PMDB, was suspicious of the PMDB left, which included a handful of communist deputies.

As if this were not enough, the Sarney government also faced uncertainty about its powers. Everyone expected the authoritarian Constitution of 1969 (with its many amendments) to be replaced.[7] But when? There were two choices. The first was to elect a Constituent Assembly, perhaps separate from the existing Congress, as soon as possible, even as early as 1985. The other choice was to delay such an election, perhaps combining it with the congressional and gubernatorial elections scheduled for November 1986. The former course was favored by those (the PMDB left, most of the PDT, PT, and other leftist parties) who wanted to dismantle the authoritarian remains as quickly as possible. The second option was favored by the PMDB center and right, along with the PFL and PDS.

Sarney opted for a later date, i.e., November 1986, specifying that the Congress elected then (along with the senatorial carryovers) would also be the Constituent Assembly. To satisfy demands on the left for immediate action, he appointed a fifty-member "Commission of Notables" to prepare a draft constitution, from which the Assembly could presumably start its work in 1987. The Commission chair was Professor Afonso Arinos de Melo Franco, a distinguished constitutional lawyer, member of one of Brazil's best-known political clans, and onetime UDN leader. Sarney had deflected onto the Arinos Commission some of the demand for action on the remaining authoritarian laws. But he left unresolved the many questions about how his government would proceed.

Sarney soon answered some of those questions. He announced that his government would not use such authoritarian devices as the *decurso de prazo* rule, whereby the president sent a bill to Congress with a time limit (30 or 45 days) within which the Congress had to act or the bill was automatically passed. He also pledged not to use the power of presidential decree, which the post-1964 governments had relied on as a way of bypassing Congress.[8] Yet these promises, made during Tancredo's illness, were mere expressions of good will. There was nothing to stop Sarney from using such convenient devices if times became difficult. The Congress thus remained greatly weakened—compared with pre-1964—by the authoritarian constitutional changes carried over from the military era.

Sarney had no choice but to govern with the cabinet Tancredo had chosen. The most important civilian member was Finance Minister Francisco Neves Dornelles, a nephew of Tancredo. He was a tested technocrat who had run the federal tax service with distinction and was known to have highly orthodox economic views. Although the rest of the cabinet was a mix of PMDB and PFL leaders, the latter got only four ministries, which

included Marco Maciel (Education), Olavo Setubal (Foreign Affairs), and
Aureliano Chaves (Mines and Energy). Most of the remaining cabinet
appointments went to PMDB politicians, such as Fernando Lyra (Justice),
José Aparecido (Culture), Pedro Simon (Agriculture), Waldir Pires (Social
Welfare), and Almir Pazzianotto (Labor). The last had been Secretary for
Labor in Franco Montoro's São Paulo government in office since 1983.
João Sayad (Planning) was a university economist who had held the same
post in the Montoro regime. His Keynesian views differed sharply from the
orthodoxy of Dornelles.

The new cabinet illustrated important features of the political landscape.
First, the PMDB had a 9–4 majority of the ministries (counting only those
ministers with a clear party affiliation). This reflected the PMDB's dominant role in the democratic transition, but it could become awkward if
Sarney should remain in the presidency for long and try to increase the PFL
role.

Second, no fewer than five of the new ministers (José Aparecido,
Renato Archer, Aluísio Alves, Waldir Pires, and Roberto Gusmão) had
once seen the military government strip them of their elective office or
their political rights or both. The fact that the military would tolerate their
return was further proof that they had revised their estimate of the Brazilian electorate or their assessment of these once dangerous figures. The
military had earlier given that signal in 1982 when, despite the wishes of
some hardliners, they did not try to block the election to the Rio de Janeiro
governorship of Leonel Brizola, long their greatest nemesis on the left.

Third, both the army minister and the head of the SNI were strongly
committted to a successful transition to civilian government. Finally, the
cabinet included contradictory views, as between Finance Minister Dornelles's monetarist economics and Agrarian Reform Minister Nelson Ribeiro's radical land-reform views. Tancredo epitomized the ambiguity inherent in the new government. Although a centrist politician, in the 1984
campaign he had called for bold action in attacking Brazil's enormous
social problems and in dealing with the foreign debt. Yet Tancredo had
chosen a finance minister who was a conservative on both issues. Where
would the government come down?

Tancredo's illness dragged on, and the Brazilian public grew steadily
more worried. The doctors' initial confidence now rang hollow. Complica-
tions set in. Either the doctors' initial diagnosis had been wrong or it had
been deliberately misleading. Or perhaps it was merely a case of medical
incompetence.[9] The doctors, now under enormous pressure, grew ever
more evasive.

There had been ugly rumors about the past record of infections at the
Brasília hospital, which had long been the butt of macabre jokes among the
press. Given the growing doubts about the quality of Tancredo's medical
care, he was moved by air to São Paulo's Heart Institute, Brazil's best
hospital. The trip had its bizarre moments, as when sheets were drawn over
his face to conceal his identity from onlookers as he was taken from the

plane in São Paulo. The public prayers of ordinary citizens became desperate. Operation followed upon operation. A month went by. Tancredo was now in Intensive Care, kept alive by life-support machines. He had passed the point of no return, yet the doctors would not admit it.

Meanwhile, the new government was virtually paralyzed, able to take only a few major actions. Justice Minister Fernando Lyra announced an end to political censorship (always dependent on how the minister applied the existing laws)[10] and Labor Minister Pazzianotto amnestied all union leaders dismissed from their posts since 1964. Both steps were important in creating the freer atmosphere promised for the New Republic.

The only other area of an initiative was economic policy. The Sarney government inherited a public sector deficit even worse than expected. Finance Minister Dornelles ordered a 10 percent cut in public spending, a two-month suspension of all government bank lending, and a one-year freeze on all public-sector hiring. This was not happy news for politicians who had been barred from national power for two decades and had heavy political debts to pay. The austerity policy also worried Planning Minister Sayad, who feared it might cause an economic slowdown or even a recession.

The lack of policy initiative in other areas had one ready explanation. The higher bureaucracy was peppered with vacancies, greatly weakening its efficiency. Tancredo was notorious for playing his political cards close to his chest, and he had kept to himself the identity of those to whom he had promised appointments in the new government. Tancredo had used those promises (and half promises) as a key tactic in his campaign. As a result there was now a gaggle of competing claimants for jobs. Sarney and his aides struggled to reconcile their choices with those of Tancredo, when known.

PMDB-PFL rivalry, which suddenly became visible in early April, further complicated the awarding of patronage. The conflict stemmed in part from the fact that Sarney's assumption of the presidency on March 15 had met initial resistance from Ulysses, who then quickly endorsed it. That conflict had been more than procedural. Behind it lay PMDB worries that their victory—based on years of solitary battle against military governments—would be purloined by politicians who only months earlier were happily serving a general-president. Both Ulysses and Sarney saw the dangers in this rivalry. Tapping their vast political experience (going back to the 1950s for both), they struck an informal agreement. It quickly bore fruit in increased cooperation between the Congress and the executive.

But attention was still riveted on the daily medical bulletins relayed by Tancredo's press secretary. Could a late-inning miracle somehow save the man meant to lead Brazil into a new democratic age? That miracle was not to be. Tancredo died on April 27, after seven operations and thirty-nine days in the hospital. The public, although increasingly skeptical of the many "successful" surgeries, was stunned by the news. In life Tancredo had loomed as a political savior. In death he assumed saintly proportions. All the stored-up hopes, centered on the man who had not lived to fulfill them, came spilling out.

Tancredo's last journey began on a fire engine in São Paulo, where two million paulistas jammed the elevated superhighway to mourn and accompany his departure. His body traveled first to Brasília, where 300,000 grief-stricken onlookers watched his coffin ascend the ramp of the presidential palace, a climb he never got to make in life. Tancredo's next stop was Belo Horizonte, his state capital, where a million grieving *mineiros* surged forward to pay their last respects. His final stop was São João del Rey, where he was buried in his native soil.[11]

Tancredo shared his birthplace with Brazil's most famous independence hero—"Tiradentes" (Joaquim José da Silva Xavier), leader of an unsuccessful 1789 plot against the Portuguese colonial masters. By a further coincidence, Tancredo had died within one week of the April date of Tiradentes's execution in 1792. For many Brazilians these were not merely coincidences. They were busily elevating Tancredo to the secular sainthood once reserved for Tiradentes.[12]

The outpouring of grief exceeded anything Brazilians could remember. The older generation agreed it surpassed the trauma following President Getúlio Vargas's suicide in 1954. The massive surge of emotion showed the extraordinary bond Tancredo had developed with the public. PMDB politicians were asking themselves the obvious question: Could the New Republic survive without him?

José Sarney was sworn in as full-fledged president on April 22, after the doctors had declared Tancredo's illness terminal. Now laboring in Tancredo's lengthening shadow, Sarney faced formidable odds. As Sarney later wrote, "I, without wishing it, without having any time to prepare myself for it, became the holder of the largest foreign debt on the face of the earth, as well as the greatest internal debt. My inheritance included the deepest recession in our history, the highest rate of unemployment, an unprecedented climate of violence, potential political disintegration and the highest rate of inflation ever recorded in our country's history—250 percent a year, with the prospect of reaching 1,000 percent."[13]

Many openly questioned his ability to assume the presidential reins. He had always been a genial, low-key politician. He frankly admitted that he was neither the "protest candidate" nor the "President of Hope," titles Tancredo earned during his campaign. Sarney was not without his strengths, however. He had been at the center of national politics for more than two decades. He knew the Congress intimately, an advantage at a time when restoring the legislature's powers was a key objective in the redemocratization drive. Further, Sarney had a reformist streak, from his pre-1964 days in the UDN's "bossa nova," which gave him some affinity for tackling the many reforms on the New Republic's agenda.

The Sarney government enjoyed another advantage generated by the political atmosphere. There was a consensus, with which neither the extreme left nor extreme right disagreed, that Brazil needed to continue its transition to democracy. Indeed, all social sectors were focusing on how to make their claims through the democratic process. This pro-democracy consensus had been aided by the creation of the PT, which recruited many on the left who might otherwise have been less committed to the "bourgeois" political process.[14] Both the PCB and the PC do B were also committed to electoral politics.

There was also evidence that Brazilians were regaining confidence in their ability to achieve bread and butter gains by direct collective action, an indispensable ingredient in any democracy. Many of the thousands of mortgage holders (*mutuários*) in arrears with the National Housing Bank, for example, withheld mortgage payments to protest the indexing rates the Bank applied to such payments. The employees of two Riograndense banks that went bankrupt in 1985 gave another example: a caravan of angry employees invaded Brasília in March and persuaded the Congress and the government to rescue the banks (and their employees).[15] Similar activism could be found in the *Movimento de Defesa dos Contribuintes* (Movement in Defense of Taxpayers), which was founded in mid-1985 and soon became a platform for small businessmen who felt hard hit by the Sarney government's tax changes. There was also a more broadly based political fund-raising effort led by businessmen from Rio Grande do Sul and São Paulo. The labor unions were not far behind. About 230 of them had joined to create DIAP (*Departamento Intersindical de Assessoria Parlamentar,* or Inter-Union Office for Congressional Information), headed by an experienced Brasília lobbyist. This office geared up to lobby on the many issues sure to arise as changes were proposed in the archaic labor law.[16] Ironically, Brazilians had reacted to the final years of authoritarian rule by learning how to protect their interests through political mobilization. The point about these "single interest" efforts was their obvious faith in the political process, however one might evaluate their particular claims.

In his first major speech after Tancredo's death, Sarney moved cautiously. He promised to convene a Constituent Assembly "as soon as possible." That body would decide the many pressing constitutional questions, such as the length of the presidential mandate (Sarney had six years by the present constitution). Sarney, echoing an earlier argument of Tancredo, promised Brazil would meet its foreign debt commitments, but not at the cost of hunger at home. Fiscal and monetary austerity would prevail, along with an emergency program to feed and employ the nation's poorest. The latter was part of a 15-year program to raise living standards, especially in the Northeast. Finance Minister Dornelles had earlier forced its deferral, arguing the government could ill afford it. Sarney's subsequent endorsement of the program showed that Dornelles's influence was already ebbing. Some said that Sarney was emerging as more progressive than Tancredo would have been, the argument being that Tancredo's immense popularity would have allowed him to defer PMDB demands for costly socio-economic programs. In short, Sarney was beginning to stake out his own ground.

In early May the Congress passed and the president signed a series of laws aimed at restoring democratic political institutions. One brought back direct presidential elections, thereby eliminating the electoral college (variously defined) the military had used to control every presidential election since 1964. Left unspecified was the date of the next presidential election. Also approved were enfranchisement of illiterates (disenfranchised since 1882) and the legalization of all political parties that met minimal registration requirements. Both measures had been bitterly opposed by conservatives before 1964.[17] Now, however, they passed with relative ease, standing as another indication of the New Republic's broad interpretation of democratization. The new law led to the speedy legalization of the Moscow-line Communist Party (*Partido Comunista Brasileiro,* or PCB) and the (originally Maoist) dissident Communist Party (*Partido Comunista do Brasil,* or PC do B), as well as splinter parties on the left. These parties had previously operated under the PMDB umbrella, where their participation was always the subject of much argument and negotiation. As the party's secretary-general noted, with the legalization of the communists the PMDB would now be "a party of the center looking to the left. Just like the Brazilian people."[18]

Many conservative and centrist politicians agreed that legalizing the leftist parties would reduce their influence. Being forced to campaign on their own (even if supporting another party), the argument ran, would expose their lack of voter support and thereby disarm the rightists who forever used the specter of the left to discredit the center or center-left. Finally, the Congress restored direct election for mayor of all cities in which the military had made the office appointive, which had included all state and territorial capitals and other cities designated to be in national security zones. The mayoral elections were set for November 15, 1985, with the new mayors to take office on January 1, 1986. It would be the New Republic's first electoral test.

On one electoral fact of life in the New Republic virtually everyone agreed: the political parties were weak, undisciplined, and often manipulated by strong personalities. Furthermore, charged the critics, too many politicians put their own interest above that of the public. The politicians had certainly provided much ammunition for such criticism. The Congress, for example, had a practice of paying a per diem (*jeton*) to Congressmen when in Brasília, but the congressional leadership had gotten into the habit of paying the *jeton* whether the Congressmen were there or not. The Congressmen saw this payment as an automatic supplement to an inadequate salary. But the press attacked it as a case of deliberate fraud.[19]

Another questionable practice was a Congressman's voting for an absent colleague by reaching across (labeled a *pianissimo*) his bench to press, along with his own, his colleague's button during an electronic role call vote. The press published photos of Congressmen stretching to vote twice. Accompanying editorials soundly condemned the practice. Other examples were plain for all to see. Both state and federal legislators had excelled in appointing their relatives and cronies to lucrative sinecures. In December 1985, for example, Federal Senate President Moacyr Dalla appointed 1,554 new employees in the Senate Printing Office, including Senator Dalla's son, along with at least nine other sons or daughters of Senators and Deputies.[20]

There were more important disappointments, however. The federal Congress in its 1985 session failed to act on legislation vital to its own future, such as measures to regain fundamental legislative powers, especially budgetary, usurped by the military governments. Furthermore, nothing had been done about key authoritarian laws such as the Press Law, the National Security Law, or Decree No. 1,077 (authorizing *censura previa,* or prior censorship).[21]

The criticisms were all well founded, but hardly surprising. The military governments had, after all, repressed the fundamental principle of democratic politics: that elected representatives seek to adjudicate and solve, in a public forum, their society's basic conflicts. Only at their worst do politicians in an open system resort to the backdoor decision-making which was the rule in military-technocratic regimes such as post-1964 Brazil. Was it therefore reasonable to expect that the politicians emerging from twenty years of military government would act like Athenian statesmen?

The public reaction to the sins of "unprincipled" politicians of the New Republic came partly from its shock at witnessing anew the political process at work. Such an explanation does not change the fact that political behavior pursued for personal (or family) interest could greatly damage the public interest. But it does remind us that an open system lets the public see the essential (and often petty) transactions that in an authoritarian regime are veiled.

As for the political parties, they were still working through the effects of the government's creation of a multi-party system in 1979. In the 1982 elections the PDS and the PMDB still predominated, with the PDT and the PT the more successful new parties. In early 1984 it looked as if the PDS-PMDB dominance would continue. But that assumption was shattered when the PDS split over Paulo Maluf's growing strength within the party. The PDS breakaways, now bearing the PFL label, had a doubtful future as a separate party. Created to vote for Tancredo in the electoral college, the PFL had at best an uncertain future.

How did the voter regard this New Republic? The November 1985 mayoral elections were the first indicator. At stake were the mayorships of 201 cities, including 25 state and territorial capitals. The pressure was on the PMDB because it had won a steadily increasing share of the vote since the early 1970s and was now the majority party in the government. With the departure of the military government it would presumably do even better.

The PMDB won 19 of the 25 capitals and 110 of the 201 other cities. At first glance that appeared impressive. But the PMDB also lost four key capitals: São Paulo (where the maverick ex-President Jânio Quadros defeated PMDB Senator Fernando Henrique Cardoso), Rio de Janeiro (where the Leonel Brizola-endorsed candidate, Roberto Saturnino Braga, won) Pôrto Alegre (where another Brizola-endorsed candidate, Alceu Collares, won) and Recife (where a leftist coalition elected Jarbas Vasconcelos).

What could one conclude from these urban elections?[22] First, the majority of the electorate had voted center to center-left. The PDS and PFL did poorly. Where the PMDB lost it was primarily not to rightist candidates, except in São Paulo, but to candidates on the left. That trend was clear in the strong showing of the PT, which won the mayorship of Fortaleza, capital of the important Northeastern state of Ceará, and finished second or third in numerous mayoralty races across the country. Considering that the PT refused to run in coalition with other parties, its drawing power was notable.[23] The PDS was the biggest loser, thereby continuing a steady decline in the nationwide (as opposed to mayoral) conservative (ARENA, PDS) vote over the last two decades: in 1966 that vote was 50.5 percent, in 1970 48.7 percent, in 1974 40.9 percent, in 1978 40 percent, and in 1982 36.7 percent.

Second, populism had apparently reappeared in the form of two pre-1964 politicians, Leonel Brizola and Jânio Quadros. Brizola had earlier won the Rio de Janeiro state governorship in November 1982. That was not surprising, since in 1962 he had been elected federal deputy from Rio de Janeiro city (when it was the state of Guanabara) with the biggest vote ever given to a Brazilian federal deputy. Brizola's eyes were clearly set on the presidency. Other governors had similar ambitions but the difference was that Brizola had electoral charisma—or so journalists and fellow politicians believed. Of all the pre-1964 politicians he had best adapted to television. He also had an instinctive feeling for fundamental socio-economic issues and how to package his message on them skillfully. He still fit the category of "populist" as it had been used in Brazil before 1964. Now he had gotten his candidates elected mayor in Rio and Pôrto Alegre, cities where he had a strong political following. Where did that leave Brizola and his PDT?

First, it seemed to confirm Brizola's drawing power even in campaigns where he was not running. Yet the winning candidates—Alceu Collares in Pôrto Alegre and Roberto Saturnino Braga in Rio—were older politicians well known to their respective electorates, and electable in their own right. Even so, neither got much more than a third of the vote (Collares 34 percent and Saturnino Braga 39 percent). Third, Brizola's PDT continued as his personal vehicle, as could be seen by its electoral fate elsewhere in the country. None of the PDT candidates in the other 21 state capitals approached a victory. Fourth, Brizola continued his long-shot quest for the presidency, which had to be based on a PMDB decline. The PMDB defeats in Rio and São Paulo gave Brizola much publicity as the coming figure on the left. That prospect worried some higher military, whose antipathy toward Brizola went back two decades.[24]

Jânio Quadros was a different case. He was a highly eccentric politician whom many in the political establishment thought could never win office again. In the campaign he displayed his delphic political style, abusing the

press and ignoring the existence of his opponents. Despite, or perhaps because of, his eccentricities, Jânio worked his electoral magic among enough
voters to win by a plurality. He won votes by attacking Governor Montoro's
PMDB government, unpopular during the recession and burdened by inept
public relations. He also enlisted much support on the right, which had no
candidate of its own, receiving endorsements from such diverse figures as
Delfim Neto, Aureliano Chaves, Olavo Setubal, and Paulo Maluf. Their
only common denominator was a desire to defeat the PMDB.[25] Jânio won
with 37 percent of the vote, as Fernando Henrique Cardoso, the pre-election
favorite, got only 33 percent and Eduardo Suplicy, the PT candidate, 20
percent. With the electorate so fragmented, the PMDB's once mighty São
Paulo vote shrank. The PT vote was high because of the large union membership within the city.

These elections had demonstrated how having more than two candidates
in the field could undermine PMDB strength. If an election were to be
decided by plurality, then the centrist candidate—often from the PMDB—
could be defeated by a candidate from either extreme. That, of course, had
been one of General Golbery's objectives in his 1979 revision of the party
legislation. Not surprisingly, PMDB stalwarts were now calling for the
introduction of runoff elections.

What other implications did these elections hold for the future? First, the
party lines seemed likely to change significantly. The right, for example, still
had no adequate party. The *Partido Popular,* organized in 1979 by longtime
UDN leader Magalhães Pinto and ex-MDB moderate Tancredo Neves, had
looked as if it might become a strong center-right party. But the PP merged
with the PMDB, in response to electoral changes in 1981. One impetus from
the right came from the *União Democrática Ruralista* (UDR), an alliance of
landowners provoked into organizing by the land invasions and other activities of agrarian reform proponents (discussed below). One of their objectives was to put pressure on Brasília, and they were collecting the money
necessary to make a major impact in the November 1986 elections.[26]

A second likely development was voting on increasingly polarized and
ideological lines. The vast economic and social chasms reinforced by military rule seemed obvious targets for politicians seeking a mass following.
The "new unionism" and the PT were evidence of that trend.

Third, the growth of well-organized non-party groups, such as the CEBs,
the independent unions, and some professional groups, could overshadow
political parties, which might thereby be deprived of their representative-
ness and flexibility.[27]

Fourth, Brazil was crying out for new political leadership. It was no accident that in 1985 the civilian political elite should have chosen as President
and Vice President two men whose political personalities were formed long
before 1964. Of the many major pre-1964 personalities in the headlines one
need only point to Jânio Quadros, once elected president in 1960, and
Leonel Brizola, a populist carryover from pre-1964. Where were the new
leaders, those who had entered politics after 1964? Names that came to mind

were (among others) José Richa, Nelson Marchezan, Fernando Lyra, Paulo Maluf, Orestes Quércia, Aureliano Chaves, and Marco Maciel. Yet such names failed to arouse much enthusiasm, among either political observers or the voters.

Brazil was paying the price for its years of authoritarian rule. Those brave enough—or cynical enough—to enter politics in those two decades got a distorted apprenticeship in democratic governance. Legislatures with truncated powers, elections with changing rules, surveillance by multiple intelligence agencies, media censorship, and military intervention in virtually every institution—these were hardly designed to nurture a new generation of politicians skilled in the arts of identifying and representing citizen opinion. Rather, those years favored two types of politicians: the opportunists who could prosper in, or alongside, the government party; and the orators who eloquently excoriated the government for its subversion of human rights, democracy, and national sovereignty. Democracy was not starting anew in Brazil, but it nonetheless faced important obstacles. Brazilians were learning that to abolish the authoritarian constraints (not all were gone) had no magical effect, either on the politicians or on the public.

Despite all these reservations, Brazil was not doing badly under its substitute president. By December 1985, José Sarney had established a solid record as a highly competent politician thrown into the impossible role of replacing Tancredo Neves. Sarney had asserted himself and shown he was prepared to eliminate policy contradictions left by Tancredo, such as in the Dornelles-Sayad battle. It was clear: there was democracy after Tancredo.

But what kind of democracy? How durable? How effective? As the New Republic is only fifteen months old as this is written, its history is still in the making. Certain important questions are already clear, however, and the next sections of this chapter look selectively at preliminary evidence on those questions. (I end with a postscript added in June 1987.)

How Did the Military React to Democratization?

Tancredo's choice for army minister, always the key figure in military politics, was General Leônidas Pires Gonçalves, who enjoyed the great respect of his colleagues. As Third Army commander, Leônidas had played a key role in isolating coup-minded military during the presidential campaign. Tancredo's other key military appointment was General Ivan de Souza Mendes as head of the SNI. Mendes had two important credentials: he was clearly a castelista, and he had never held a post within the intelligence community. These were favorable signs for those, including many military, who wanted to reduce the SNI's power. When Sarney stepped into the presidency he developed good personal rapport with both Leônidas and Mendes. In January 1986 Air Minister Brig. Octávio Moreira Lima could announce that President Sarney was more popular with the armed forces than any civilian leader of the last four decades.[28]

One of the more critical issues for the military under civilian rule was possible accountability for past human rights violations. Would any military or police be made to answer for their deeds of torture (it was known as the "Nuremberg syndrome")? The Brazilian military and police were understandably worried about that possibility, for the press had published names of torturers and details of their grisly work. President Figueiredo had apparently settled the question of trying torturers with his 1979 amnesty law, which granted amnesty to torturers as well as to the scores of past "political" offenders for whom it was initially intended. The military and the political elite had breathed a sigh of relief at the time. Virtually no one in the political elite, even on the left, thought it politically viable to try the torturers.

But some victims and their champions would not let the issue rest there. They wanted their day in the court of public opinion; they wanted Brazilians to face up to the human cost of their repressive government. In May 1985 the Catholic Church's leading publishing house, Editora Vozes, produced a volume that unnerved many in the military. *Brasil: Nunca Mais* (Brazil: Never Again) was a report by a group of São Paulo Church activists on the torture underworld from 1964 to 1979.[29] The sources consisted entirely of Military Justice records. The cases included names of both victims and torturers, along with time and place of torture. The descriptions were horrifying. They matched accounts already in circulation, but with the added force of coming from official military records. The same São Paulo group subsequently published a list of 444 police and military officers involved in torture.[30]

Public concern in Brazil was further stimulated in April 1985 when nine of the members of the 1976–82 Argentine military juntas, including former Presidents Videla, Viola, and Galtieri, went on trial for the barbarities committed under their commands. In 1984 a presidentially appointed National Commission on the Disappeared in Argentina had issued a report based on depositions from victims and their families and other witnesses. They documented a full range of crimes—torture, theft of personal property—and were able to establish the disappearance of 8,960 persons.[31] The Argentine military's torture of prisoners did not differ in kind from the barbarities practiced by the DOI-CODI, Sergio Fleury, and CENIMAR. Brazil's ex-torturers watched the Argentine events with apprehension.

Such documentation (which no one contested) as in *Brasil: Nunca Mais* was potential dynamite in the political climate of the New Republic. Nor was it the only evidence of past military torture to surface after March 1985. In August, Bete Mendes—a federal deputy accompanying President Sarney on an official visit to Uruguay—recognized a Brazilian army attaché in Montevideo as her torturer after her arrest as a guerrilla in 1970. Because Military Justice had eventually absolved Mendes, thus leaving her free of any criminal charges, she demanded that President Sarney recall the officer. But Army Minister Leônidas Pires Gonçalves intervened to defend his colleague. Leônidas also told the president that he would defend any other such officers in the future. His objective? Maintain "military morale." The incident ended with both army minister and deputy issuing conciliatory statements. He acknowledged "lamentable excesses," and she said how much she admired the army.[32]

The army minister need not have worried about any attempt to call former torturers to account. Although some activists in the press and the church wanted investigations, if not trials, the political consensus of 1979 still held. This pragmatic agreement was in part feasible because the Brazilian military regime, notwithstanding its horrors, had caused far fewer deaths than the Argentine and (probably) Chilean military governments. The Brazilian death toll from government torture, assassination, and "disappearance" for 1964–81 was, by the most authoritative count, 333, which included 67 killed in the Araguaia guerrilla front in 1972–74. The official Argentine investigative commission verified 8,960 deaths and disappearances, and many well-informed observers estimate the real total to approach 20,000. Even taking the lower total, Argentina turned out to have had a per capita death toll over 100 times as high as Brazil's—Argentina lost one citizen for every 2,647 of her population, while Brazil's loss was one for every 279,279. Although a single death was one too many in either country, Brazil's less murderous repression created a smaller backlash and made it easier for the politicians of the New Republic to live with the 1979 amnesty. It also relieved them of the endless questions of whom to try and how long to extend the statute of limitations.[33]

Acceptance of the amnesty had another source: the "conciliatory" strain in Brazilian political culture, as reflected in the incident of Deputy Mendes. Brazilian elites over the last century have believed their people have a unique ability to resolve social crises peacefully. True or not, the belief itself has powerfully influenced politicians and other opinion-makers. In this case it contributed to the rationale underlying the 1979 amnesty law.

The rationale was captured in the introduction to *Brasil: Nunca Mais:* "It is not the intention of our Project to assemble a body of evidence to be presented at some Brazilian Nuremberg. We are not motivated by any sense of vengeance. In their quest for justice, the Brazilian people have never been motivated by sentiments of revenge."[34] What the authors wanted was maximum publicity for the documentation they had unearthed, so that torture would never again be practiced in Brazil. The military could live with this kind of exposé, if not happily.[35] Thus future revelations about torturers seemed unlikely to cause severe problems for either the military or the Sarney government. For better or for worse, the military and police "excesses" had apparently been put beyond the reach of justice.[36]

If a reaction to the disposition of torturers was unlikely to destabilize military-civilian relations, would the military try other forms of political disruption? The SNI, along with the three services' intelligence units, remained a worry to most politicians.[37] The SNI had become the repository for an enormous amount of information, and even more raw data, ready to be used by anyone in power. Its huge budget and vast authority gave it further clout. And its archives included extensive data on the SNI's own operations, revelation of which could acutely embarrass more than a few military and civilians.[38]

The key question about all the intelligence agencies was whether their activities went beyond information-gathering to operations. The latter was true of the SNI during the Figueiredo presidency, when its power within the government increased markedly. If it continued in such a role it could threaten democratic politics, especially if the SNI directorship were in unfriendly hands. It could resort to "dirty tricks," or "disinformation." By its surveillance activities it could also unnerve politicians and undermine the democratic process.[39]

The potential for such disruption, which had been practiced as recently as the 1984 presidential nomination campaigns, depended on who controlled the intelligence agencies.[40] In practice, the SNI and military intelligence had become accountable only to the three military ministers. The military ministers were in turn theoretically accountable to the president. But now, for the first time in twenty-one years, the president was a civilian. How much control over the SNI or the military could he develop?[41]

The SNI Sarney inherited was already weakened. In late 1984 some SNI staff were said to be burning records. They apparently had enough to hide. They were embarrassed, for example, by the accusation that they were responsible for murdering Alexander von Baumgarten, a journalist who died of gunshot wounds in what was supposed to look like a boating accident in 1982.[42] Baumgarten, on the SNI payroll before his murder, had left a letter explaining why the SNI was likely to kill him. The government stonewalled the charge brought by the victim's family, but the SNI earned another black mark in the minds of the many military officers who had long distrusted it.[43] The SNI or one of the military service intelligence agencies was also believed to be behind the murder of Mario Eugenio, a journalist with the Brasília newspaper *Correio Brasiliense*. He had apparently been investigating an earlier suspicious murder.[44]

Evidence of the SNI's self-perceived need to improve their image was its new director's efforts with the press. In April 1985, General Ivan took the unprecedented step—for an SNI director—of holding a press conference. He also made himself available to the press on a "background" basis, a practice unknown in previous SNI administrations.[45]

Military pressure in the early New Republic proved strongest where it might be most expected: measures directly affecting the armed forces. A prime example was the bill Congress passed in October 1985 giving amnesty to 2,600 military officers who had been fired (either cassated or administratively dismissed) between 1964 and 1979. The bill would have granted them all their back pay and restored them to the active duty position they would have reached through subsequent promotions. If all these ex-servicemen had been able to claim their posts, chaos would have resulted. The higher military vigorously opposed the measure and got the president and the congressional leadership to kill it.[46] The higher military also weighed in on such issues as agrarian reform and strike law reform. In both cases they were on the conservative side.

On other issues the military could be overruled. One was the new law on political party registration. The immediate beneficiaries were the Moscow-line PCB and the dissident PC do B, both anathema to most military. Yet the bill became law. A second example was the resumption of diplomatic relations with Cuba. Brazil had broken relations soon after the 1964 coup, as part of the Castelo Branco government's anticommunist line. In 1985 the Foreign Ministry recommended resuming relations. The military opposed this step, yet it was taken in July 1986.[47]

One particularly important area to the military was national security, as shown by their actions as the Afonso Arinos commission prepared its preliminary constitutional draft for the Constituent Assembly of 1987. An early issue was the constitutional clause on the role of the armed forces. The Constitution of 1969 (article 91) had given them a broad mandate in saying, "the armed forces, which are essential to carrying out national security policy, are charged with defending the country and with guaranteeing the constitutional powers and the preservation of law and order." The 1946 and 1967 Constitutions had given a similar mandate in similar wording. The Afonso Arinos commission now proposed to omit the phrase "and the preservation of law and order," arguing that involving the armed forces in maintaining internal order had been a disaster for both the armed forces and the country. It pitted the military against the populace, discrediting the men in uniform and displacing the civilian authorities who should be responsible for law and order. These critics therefore wanted to revoke the constitutional clause making them national policemen. The preservation of order would instead become the responsibility of a greatly beefed-up *Polícia Civil* (civilian police).[48]

The higher military issued a document announcing that it would be "a dangerous omission" for the Constitution "to ignore the wide range of problems related to national security. . . ." It noted with frankness that "the allegedly excessive use of this wide range in recent decades can and should be corrected, but that does not justify an omission, which would prejudice the security of the nation and its entire structure, including democratic government." Off the record, some top military were more outspoken. One remarked "legalized or not, the Communists want power," while two generals described the constitutional commission as wanting "to transform the Constitution into an instrument for preventing coups. As if anyone would overthrow a government while carrying the Constitution under his arm."[49]

The military wanted, in effect, a mandate to continue their role as the "moderating power," a phrase first used to describe the emperor's role in the imperial political system (1822–89). In that era, the emperor could intervene whenever the political parties reached an impasse. After 1889 the military assumed the "moderating power." Over the next forty years the army intervened in politics repeatedly on both the state and federal level, although the 1891 Constitution had no clause making the military responsible for maintaining law and order.[50]

If the military had intervened so readily in 1889–1930 when they had no clause, why did they bother to argue about it now? Because they knew how their prestige with the public had suffered since 1964.[51] The constitutional commission, in fact, refused their request to include explicit reference to their moderating power in their preliminary draft. And the military made it clear that they would feel free to intervene, as they had under previous constitutions, if they felt it necessary for the public good.

What, then, was the military's own conception of its role as of mid-1986? As Alfred Stepan has explained in detail, there had been two conflicting conceptions.[52] The "old professionalism," which was geared to the external threat, held that the military should concentrate on technical expertise, internal discipline, and a nonpolitical stance. The military would thereby preserve their professional integrity,[53] all-important if they were called upon to summon civilian support in defense of the nation. The Brazilian military never completely adopted this orientation, but it had prevailed during and after World War II.

In the late 1950s the "old professionalism" was challenged by the "new professionalism of internal security and national development." We have seen how this doctrine, oriented toward internal problems ranging from guerrilla threats to gross economic inequities, prevailed after the early 1960s. In the Médici years Brazil became a textbook case of a "national security state," as the military imposed their new doctrine by force. It emerged in such statutes as the SNI law, the National Security Law, AI–5, and the 1969 Constitution.

Yet the succeeding military government began the move toward liberalization, toward the rule of law. What had happened to the "new professional" dogma of "internal security and national development?" Were the higher military reverting to the "old professionalism?"

The answer is that the Brazilian military were schizophrenic about their mission. They embraced both the "professional" and the "internal warfare" models. The relative commitment to each depended upon how endangered they thought their professionalism had become, how serious they considered the internal threat, and, always of prime importance, how to protect their own unity. The weight of officer opinion had recently tipped toward the "old professional" model.

This shift was reinforced as officers contemplated the many recent scandals to have tarnished the military's image. Many personnel were directly involved, such as in the Capemi scandal (involving a military officers' pension fund and a deforestation scheme in the Amazon valley), the Rio Centro terrorist attempt, and the Baumgarten case. President Figueiredo's frequent junketing abroad and his abusive attitude toward the press further damaged the military image.[54]

What was the military's role fifteen months into the New Republic? Was there any political development that would provoke even the moderate military to intervene? To put it in military terms, could the internal threat to national security lead a majority of military to believe that they had no choice but to repeat the 1964 pattern? The crucial question was how future officers would interpret both the laws and the political realities around them.[55]

On the one hand, the military were still a large presence. Retired officers occupied an estimated 8,000–10,000 top posts in government and the state enterprises. And there was still the lavishly funded SNI, operating in the shadows and heavily staffed with military officers. On the other hand, however, their primary concern now appeared to be, not with any potential political threat, but with their largely antiquated equipment. Unlike their Argentine, Chilean, and Peruvian counterparts, the Brazilian military had not used their time in power to boost military appropriations. Brazilian officers apparently thought Brazil did not face an external threat that would justify expensive re-equipping of its forces. In part this reflected Brazil's successful pursuit by skillful diplomacy of its border interests (hydro-electric projects, trade, etc.) with Paraguay, Uruguay, and Bolivia, three neighbors of traditional concern. But military self-confidence received a rude jolt when the Argentines and the British went to war over the Falklands/Malvinas. Brazilian officers watched as the Argentine military seized the Falklands, only to be humiliated by the British counterattack. That drama led the Brazilian military to rethink the defense of their thousands of miles of unguarded Atlantic shoreline. They looked anew at the limited mobility of their ground troops. And they thought again about their lack of modern armor—of the kind Brazil was now selling in great quantities to other countries. They remembered also the more than two years they had taken to defeat 69 communist guerrillas in the Amazon Valley (Araguaia) in 1972–75.

The Brazilian military decided to push for the long-postponed upgrading and expansion of their forces. In its last year the Figueiredo administration approved their requests and in 1985 the army got the go-ahead for a far-reaching reorganization and re-equipping program. The "FT-90" plan (*Força Terrestre 1990*) was to increase the army's authorized size from 183,000 to 296,000 men. New armored cars, tanks, missile launchers, cannon, radar, and helicopters were to be purchased, primarily from Brazilian suppliers.[56] Military officers now had an incentive to cultivate congressmen who would have to vote on the appropriations as the program continued.

How Did the Democratic Government Deal with the Hard Economic Choices?

Running an economy involves inherent trade-offs: inflation vs. growth, growth vs. stability, income increase vs. income distribution. In running the economy a democracy is at a disadvantage in one major respect: its continued existence depends on the acceptability of its policies to the voters. This imparts a bias to decision-making with respect to the trade-offs, in favor of decisions that are politically popular in the relatively short run. As I have already noted, fifteen months into the new regime is hardly a vantage point for definitive analysis. However, a selective look can begin to shed light on the possibilities. My discussion runs through the same chronology several times to give the context for each economic issue as it is discussed. The reader's indulgence is requested for the inevitable repetition.[57]

THE FOREIGN DEBT: TEMPORARY BREATHING ROOM. The foreign debt was one of the most severe economic problems facing the Sarney government as it took office.[58] It was the largest foreign debt in the world (approximately $95 billion in the early 1980s). Could Brazil service this debt without crippling its own economy? Should the goal be "a general rescheduling of the foreign debt on conditions that protect our people from unbearable sacrifices and which preserve our national sovereignty," as the August 1984 manifesto of the Democratic Alliance had argued?[59] The U.S. and European press constantly warned that a Mexican or Brazilian default might trigger a collapse of the world banking system. In late 1982 the world recession, the soaring interest rates, the declining terms of trade and the sudden refusal of commercial banks to lend "new" money forced Brazil, along with many other debtor countries, to seek IMF help. The left and much of the center had bitterly criticized Figueiredo and Delfim Neto for this step, predicting that the IMF conditions would further depress Brazil's economy.

The Figueiredo government knew the dangers in applying the IMF formulae. But Delfim Neto and colleagues saw no alternative and so negotiated with the Fund a series of agreements (known as "letters of intent") which specified policy targets for the rate of expansion of the money supply, the size of the public sector deficit, level of minimum wage settlements, etc. Brazil had to meet these targets in order to continue receiving IMF loans. Between early 1983 and late 1984 Brazil signed six such letters and met the targets of not a single one.

Why, then, did they continue to be signed? The only explanation is that both sides had their reasons for wanting to sign, even though both were skeptical that the targets would be met. Brazil, on the one hand, wanted IMF approval so it could continue receiving IMF funds, but also because other creditors, especially the commercial banks, required an IMF imprimatur before they would negotiate. The Fund, on the other hand, recognized Brazil's pivotal position among Third World debtors and wanted to push Brazilian policymakers in the right direction. Negotiations for a seventh letter of intent stretched into early January 1985, but in February the IMF rejected the outgoing Figueiredo government's proposed plan and broke off negotiations. The Fund also suspended further payments, citing Brazil's failure to meet agreed-to 1984 fourth-quarter targets. The IMF was obviously preparing to take an equally tough line with the new government.

The Figueiredo government had also failed to reschedule the heavy principal payments falling due over the next five years to the commercial banks, which held almost 70 percent of Brazil's foreign debt. Finally, the Paris Club (creditor nations that had earlier given Brazil bilateral aid) had put negotiations with Brazil on the back burner. All of Brazil's creditors were waiting to see the new government's line. Sarney had promised in his May 7 speech, echoing Tancredo's earlier warning, that Brazil's foreign debt would not be paid with the hunger of the poor. Was this bravura meant only for home consumption?

As they entered office in the shadow of Tancredo's illness and death, the new economic policymakers cast a wary eye at the foreign debt problem. Finance Minister Dornelles might have welcomed (under his breath) the creditors' pressure, on the assumption that it would help make the case for the orthodox stabilization measures he favored. Unfortunately for Dornelles's bargaining position, Brazil's balance of payments outlook was surprisingly favorable. In 1984 the trade balance (exports minus imports) reached a record total of $13.1 billion, almost double 1983's total of $6.5 billion. The increase resulted from a $5.1 billion growth in exports and a $1.5 billion drop in imports. The growth was due to a long-term export drive, especially in manufactured goods (now including almost half of all exports). The import drop reflected partly continuing import substitution, not only in industrial goods, but also in some raw materials (oil, potash). The price of imported oil, although still a significant burden, was dropping rapidly. The current trade surplus was roughly equivalent to the interest on Brazil's foreign debt. This foreign trade strength was complemented by a strong foreign exchange reserve position, about $9 billion at the end of 1984. The new government thus had room for maneuver in negotiations with the IMF, the Paris Club, and the commercial banks.[60]

Prospects for 1985 looked equally favorable. The early 1985 monthly figures indicated a probable 1985 trade surplus of $11–12 billion. The current trade surplus and the hefty foreign exchange reserves meant there was no short-term problem in servicing the debt. For the moment Brazil did not need IMF dollars and therefore would be spared the political abuse at home that came with any agreement with the Fund.

Given this room for maneuver, the Sarney government could select the creditors on whom it wished to concentrate. It chose the commercial banks, which held $35 billion of Brazilian loans falling due between 1985 and 1989. The bankers were impressed with Brazi's trade and domestic growth performance, but the Sarney government's problem was to convince the banks to reschedule these loans despite the lack of IMF approval of Brazil's policies. In late July 1986 it succeeded, signing an agreement to roll over $15.5 billion in principal due in 1985 and 1986, and to renew $15.5 billion in trade credits.[61] If the trade surplus continued, the Sarney government would have the relative autonomy of decision-making so essential to its ambitious agenda of national needs. If it did not, the July agreement would come back to haunt them.

This short-term maneuverability in no way changed the fact that Brazil continued to face a staggering load in servicing its foreign debt. For 1985 Brazil would pay foreign creditors 5 percent of its GDP. That 5 percent had to come from domestic savings, reducing the amount for investment at home. To continue paying at this rate would mean exporting capital on a scale never seen in the Third World. By mid-1986, however, Brazil was paying the interest on its foreign debt and enjoying an economic boom at the same time. For the moment, the hard choices on handling the debt could be avoided.[62]

"Hardheaded" economists of both right and left have long argued that democracy in developing countries leads to "unsound" economic policies. One reason, they say, is that politicians respond to short-run popular opinion, which favors consumption over investment, thus crippling future growth. A similar dilemma often arises over inflation, they argue. Politicians tailor their policy (on exchange rates, real interest rates, real wage rates, public utility rates, etc.) to please the most powerful pressure groups, rather than to maintain prices, wages, and interest rates in the optimal relationship for the desired growth rates.[63]

Many of the New Republic's economists vigorously rejected this logic, which had often been invoked to justify Brazil's authoritarian regime. José Serra, for example, has argued that none of the economic "accomplishments" of the 1968–74 "miracle" could be attributed to the military government's authoritarian power.[64] No area of economic policymaking could be more relevant for this question than inflation, long a bane in Latin America.[65]

PLANO CRUZADO: A NEW RESPONSE TO INFLATION. Brazil had experienced a long series of failed anti-inflation programs before 1964. In every case the government found the political costs of economic stabilization too high and abandoned the attempt. Until the early 1960s the economy had been able to survive each failed stabilization one way or another. But João Goulart found no exit from his financial and foreign debt crises. Not only were Brazil's foreign exchange reserves approaching zero, but inflation by March 1964 had reached the unprecedented annual rate of 125 percent. That inflationary explosion was a key factor in Goulart's fall. In the military regime's "miracle" years, inflation was contained between 14 percent and 34 percent. It then began to accelerate, reaching triple digits in the early 1980s. In 1984, the last full year of military government, inflation hit the alarming historic record of 222 percent. In the inaugural speech Tancredo Neves was never able to deliver, he called inflation "the clearest evidence of disorder in our national economy," and added, "we must face up to it from our first day."[66]

Brazil was a country that had supposedly learned to live with inflation, thanks to indexation and mini-devaluations. It suffered an average annual inflation of 32 percent for the years 1968 through 1979, yet it also achieved an average annual real growth rate of 9 percent. Brazil seemed a lesson in how to neutralize inflation while promoting growth. In 1979, however inflation hit 77 percent, and by the early 1980s virtually all economists agreed that Brazil's inflation, notwithstanding indexation, had gotten out of hand. The triple-digit rate was causing severe distortions in the economy. The six-month interval between minimum-wage adjustments, for example, hit workers with a large loss in real income between adjustments (some firms, after de facto bargaining with their workers, and independently of the ministry of labor, adjusted annual wage rates every three months, thereby easing but not solving the problem). Small discrepancies in indexing rates (as between wages and public housing mortgage payments) were magnified when inflation went over 200 percent. The capital market offered another example. The government's need to finance a large public-sector deficit and to keep capital at home while also attracting capital from abroad led the treasury to issue bonds (ORTNs) that guaranteed the highest return of any financial instrument.[67] More and more private savings went into these and other government bonds, reducing capital available for productive investment, as financial speculation became Brazil's most profitable activity.

These inflationary distortions—and many more—would have worried any government. Tancredo Neves and Finance Minister Dornelles had already identified inflation as Brazil's number one problem. But how it should be attacked depended on whom one tried to please. As long as the IMF set the targets, Brazilian policy had to follow orthodox lines. That was Dornelles's approach—no doubt one reason Tancredo had picked him. During Sarney's first (caretaker) phase as president, Dornelles pushed through, as we saw earlier, an across-the-board 10 percent budget cut and a hiring and lending freeze. The aim was to cut government borrowing needs and thereby reduce a continuing inflationary source—the government's issuing money (largely via the Banco do Brasil) to cover its cash deficit.

The pressure behind this policy came from the assumption that Brazil had to negotiate a new IMF agreement in order to restore IMF lending. If for any reason that agreement were no longer necessary, Dornelles would lose his strongest card. And he would find virtually no political support in the government. He already faced strong opposition from Planning Minister Sayad, who warned that a heavy-handed anti-inflation program might push the economy back into recession.

For four months Dornelles and Sayad battled. Dornelles prevailed at the outset but soon began losing ground. Rumors of his resignation ran rampant. When would he acknowledge the inevitable? It had become evident that Brazil's balance of payments and foreign exchange reserves were healthy enough to save it from needing any immediate IMF agreement. Dornelles was thus deprived of his most important ally. In late August he resigned. The monetarist Central Bank president Antonio Carlos Lemgruber resigned with him.[68]

The new finance minister was Dilson Funaro, a São Paulo industrialist who was president of the National Development Bank (BNDES) in the Sarney government. He had been especially active in the São Paulo Federation of Industries, a focus of opposition to the Figueiredo government.

Funaro was a growth-oriented Keynesian, close to Sayad's views. In February 1985 Funaro had said that "Brazil can't go through another recession. If there is any risk of it then we should renegotiate the foreign debt." Funaro was also the Brazilian government's first authentic São Paulo business representative since 1964. He brought in (either full-time or as consultants) a bevy of young economists (with views roughly similar to Sayad's) from the University of São Paulo-Campinas and the Catholic University of Rio de Janeiro.[69] The Sarney government could now speak with one voice on economic policy.

As a PFL member, the president might have been expected to lean to the orthodox school. Instead, Sarney chose to strengthen the PMDB side of his government. Judging by where public opinion lay, he had acted wisely in opting for Sayad in the battle with Dornelles. Whether he showed economic wisdom was a different question.

Funaro and Sayad now set about reformulating the government's macroeconomic strategy. Pressure was mounting to do more about inflation. Virtually every newspaper, TV station, and special-interest group was on the warpath about inflation. They wanted immediate action—though not, of course, at their own expense. The government initially relied on such well-worn devices as limited price controls and jawboning. Neither offered the prospect of any long-term relief.

More substantive was an effort to stimulate the credit side of the market. The government put priority on measures (credit, for one) that would increase food production for domestic consumption. But such steps would take time to show results. Meanwhile, every eye was fixed on the constantly changing price tags at the corner store.

Could something be amiss in the government's diagnosis of the problem? Several younger Brazilian economists thought so.[70] They pointed out that the inflation rate had remained almost unchanged during the 1981–83 recession, when the country lost 10 percent of its per capita GDP, and unemployment soared. Yet in the advanced industrial economies (from which most economic analysis had been borrowed), recessions, with their increased unemployment, normally reduced inflation (the trade-off known as the Phillips Curve). Why didn't it happen in Brazil?[71]

The explanation began with the role of indexation. In an indexed economy, such as Brazil's, past inflation became built in as "inertial inflation." The latter never declined, becoming the base to which new inflation was added. The only way to reduce inflation, these economists argued, was to de-index the economy. But how? Most important, as always in dealing with inflation, was any effect on expectations. Policymakers debated these questions during 1985, but did not change their cautious, pragmatic course.

It should be noted that analyzing the inflation data was not as easy as it might have seemed because the measuring stick had been changed. The government's basis for calculating both inflation and indexation had been the General Price Index (IGP) prepared by the Getúlio Vargas Foundation. In November 1985 the IGP was replaced by a consumer index (IPCA) calculated by the Brazilian Institute of Geography and Statistics (IBGE). The change, not surprisingly, led to charges that the government was manipulating the data for its own purposes.[72]

One optimistic sign was that, along with the inflation, the Sarney government had inherited a rapidly growing economy. GDP for 1985 rose 8.3 percent, making Brazil the world's fastest growing country that year. It was, however, a boom dependent on consumer durable goods. The resulting growth benefited first the industrial sector, only then trickling down to the lower-paid workers, urban and rural. It was the kind of economic growth that had been criticized by most of the economists now ensconced in Brasília.

The boom was also bound to feed inflation. Increased demand might be satisfied in the short run by using the excess capacity left over from the long recession. But if the boom continued into 1986, the economy would hit full capacity in some sectors, creating supply problems. At that point the "inertial" inflation might merge with demand inflation to ignite a price explosion big enough to shake the foundations of the New Republic.

Although the economy had shown remarkable growth (8.3 percent) in 1985, the Sarney policymakers were preoccupied with the inflation rate of 222 percent. Having side-stepped the IMF and its orthodox formulae, they were determined to develop their own plan to reverse the inflation that threatened to roar out of control.

The inflation rate for January 1986 confirmed their worst fears. At 16.2 percent for the month, the rate combined with those of the two preceding months for a 360 percent annual rate. If measured by the old (IGP) index, the November–December–January rate translated into a 454 percent annual rate. This difference in the indices, much discussed in the media, again aroused public distrust of government data. The inflation surge was caused partly by a severe drought that sent food prices up, but no one was ready to accept such explanations. The press was now in full cry, demanding tougher action against inflation. Sarney's popularity had dropped steadily in the polls, and his government, despite a recent cabinet shake-up, came across as ineffectual.[73]

In the midst of these darkening fortunes, Finance Minister Funaro offered Sarney a bold gamble. It would be a "heterodox shock" approach to stopping inflation. The idea owed its inspiration in Brazil to economist Francisco Lopes, along with economists Persio Arida and André Lara-Resende. They were close to the Argentine economists who had formulated the "heterodox shock" applied by the Alfonsín government in June 1985. Brazil would announce a radical monetary reform, with the following principal features: It would replace the cruzeiro (at 1,000 to 1) with the cruzado, a new currency. Indexation would be abolished.[74] There would be a one-year freeze on mortgage rates and rents, and an indefinite freeze on prices. The minimum wage would be adjusted to its average value over the previous six months, plus a bonus of 8 percent. Thereafter a sliding scale would automatically compensate workers whenever inflation reached 20 percent a year. Workers would also be free to bargain with employers for further wage increases. Finally, an unemployment benefit was established. Recipients would have to have a minimum employment record and be a contributor to the social security system. This program was aimed at the formal labor market, which was concentrated in the more developed Southeast and South. Even though the benefits would be low and its start-up would be slow, Labor Minister Pazzianotto was proud to have gotten the unprecedented program proposed.[75] Exchange-rate policy would also be altered. The government, thanks to a drastic fall in inflation, would no longer need to devalue almost daily, as was necessary with three-digit inflation. Now the Central Bank would decide when and how much to devalue.

Sarney took the gamble. He announced the "Cruzado Plan" (enacted by presidential decree) to the nation on February 28, 1986. The President described inflation as "public enemy number one" and called on all Brazilians to join in a "war of life and death" against it. He invited his fellow citizens to make themselves price inspectors at their local stores, confronting any shopkeepers who raised their prices in violation of the price freeze.[76]

The plan was an instant success with the public, and overnight Sarney and Funaro became national heroes. The government switchboards were jammed with favorable calls.[77] Brazilians streamed out to stores (wearing newly printed buttons proclaiming "Sou fiscal de Sarney!"—"I'm one of Sarney's inspectors!") and inspected price labels, badgering managers when they found illegal increases. The food price control agency (SUNAB) was swamped with complaints. Some citizen "inspectors" took the law into their own hands, smashing windows of shops they found marking up prices.

The reasons for this enthusiasm were not difficult to find. Average citizens were fed up with having to invent new defenses against inflation. They had watched financial speculators win all the prizes in the triple-digit inflationary economy. Now they were more than ready for a credible promise of monetary stability.

By June 1986 most observers were calling the plan a qualified success. The inflation rate for March-April-May was a reassuring 3.38 percent. Business was enthusiastic, partly in the hope that the plan would reduce the previously sky-high interest rates. Consumers were enthusiastic, believing their buying power would be increased.[78] Bankers were smarting, having suddenly lost the easy profits they had enjoyed under high inflation. Was the notorious financial speculation finally abating? Everyone agreed the banking system had been vastly overexpanded. Faced now with leaner profit margins, the banks immediately retrenched, closing branches and increasing service charges.[79]

What did the decision to adopt this bold anti-inflation program tell us about the transition to democracy? José Serra, the PMDB economist who has written on the relationship between government types (democratic vs.

authoritarian) and economic performance, had no doubts. Weeks after its announcement he declared the Plano Cruzado victorious, arguing that "democracy" was "a necessary condition" for its implementation. He contrasted it with the Roberto Campos-directed 1964–67 stabilization program carried out in "an authoritarian regime, which alone made it viable."[80] Edmar Bacha, a PMDB economist who headed the IBGE, also made Roberto Campos his point of reference in defending the Plano Cruzado. In June, Bacha cited a recent Campos warning that since every anti-inflation program produces a stabilization crisis, Brazil could not hope to be original on this score. Bacha fired back: "fortunately Brazil is more original than Roberto Campos. We have succeeded in maintaining economic growth while carrying out a radical stabilization program."[81]

The PMDB economists' comparison with 1964 was not entirely fair. Nor would it have been if they had chosen any of the aborted stabilization attempts of 1953–54, 1955, 1958–59, 1961, and 1962–63. In every case, as well as in 1964, Brazil faced a severe balance of payments crisis. In fact, every one of these anti-inflation programs was adopted in part to appease foreign creditors, above all the IMF. That meant adopting an orthodox stabilization program, which until 1964 was invariably dropped as each government faced the political fallout that such programs provoked.

The New Republic, in contrast, inherited one of the most favorable trade surpluses Brazil had seen since 1945. The Sarney government was thus able to bypass the IMF and negotiate directly with its commercial bank creditors. In announcing the Plano Cruzado Sarney could honestly say "these measures are not copied from any program carried out by any other country."[82]

The Plano Cruzado had its problems, however. Most important, it had been launched in the face of rapid economic growth. Having hit an 8.3 percent rate in 1985, the economy roared ahead in early 1986. The announcement of the Plano Cruzado in fact had a perverse effect. Hearing that prices were frozen, consumers now fortified with real wage increases (especially in the developed Center-South) went on a spending spree. Indicators of excess demand surfaced almost immediately. Car buyers faced delays of several months, unless they found one of the growing number of dealers willing to take an under the table "premium" (agio). Prices for recent-model used cars, another indicator of new car demand, shot up. Other consumer durables sold briskly. Foreign travel became so popular that Brazilian airlines had to lease foreign planes. There was a noticeable shortage of meat, and the agio began to spread to the butcher shops. Brazilian consumers were not behaving as the Cruzado Plan's architects had hoped. Funaro's economists hoped that Brazilians would believe in the new currency and in the return of price stability. But by their actions Brazilians believed the opposite: that price controls couldn't last, and one should buy now before prices went up. Obviously the Brazilian public's deep-seated inflationary expectations would not easily be uprooted.

Brazil was thus facing not just inertial inflation but also demand-induced inflation. How long before the beneath-the-counter practices of new car dealers and butcher shops extended to other products? Funaro charged the cattlemen and slaughterhouses with producing an artificial meat shortage and he ordered meat imports from the U.S. and the EEC. Milk also disappeared from the shops as dairy suppliers complained that the frozen retail price was too low. Given the strength of overall demand, the varying effect that frozen prices had on profits, and the limits on capacity, inflationary pressure seemed certain to increase.[83]

Yet another problem had surfaced by June. Despite the government's early success with the inflation rate, long-term lending had not yet resumed.[84] The problem was investor uncertainty. Under inflation, the longer the loan period the greater the risk. Brazil had handled that problem after 1964 by indexing virtually all loans. With indexation gone, the lender was no longer protected, leaving all long-term financial decisions up in the air and slowing the business borrowing needed to finance investment and therefore economic growth.

A final symptom of uncertainty in the financial market was the high premium the dollar commanded on the "parallel" (black) market. By the end of June the dollar sold at a 52 percent premium over the official rate. Ordinarily, that high a premium indicated speculation over a devaluation (there had been none since the Plano Cruzado). The causes were undoubtedly multiple, but it was another sign of public worry over the cruzado's stability.

In July 1986 the government acted to reduce the inflationary pressure. Sarney announced a package of measures designed to deal with the problems evident since the February launching of the Plano Cruzado.[85] The primary objective was to reduce consumption and increase investment. The government chose to concentrate on spending in two areas close to middle- and upper-class hearts: cars and foreign travel. Sales of new and used cars (up to four years old) and of gasoline and alcohol would now be subject to a 20–25 percent compulsory loan refundable in three years.[86] International air tickets would likewise carry a 25 percent compulsory loan, also refundable after three years. Any purchase of dollars would now carry a *nonrefundable* surcharge of 25 percent.

These steps were bound to cost the Sarney government some of the popularity it had enjoyed when it launched Plano Cruzado. Governor Leonel Brizola and the PT, for example, had opened fire on the plan from the outset. The right, such as represented by *Visão*, had also attacked.[87] Centrist opinion had remained solid, although the shortages and demands for *agios* were raising doubts.

The automobile-owning and foreign-traveling public was bound to take the new measures hard. Even military governments had shied away from the compulsory-loan scheme approach to controlling gasoline consumption. In early 1977 the Geisel government, reeling from another OPEC oil price increase, was about to impose a compulsory loan of 2 cruzeiros per liter of gasoline. At the last minute President Geisel vetoed it.[88] Geisel undoubtedly thought the political price he would have to pay with the upper middle and upper classes was not justified by the economic gain expected.

Other measures in the July package were designed to promote investment, in part through channeling the forced savings generated by the refundable surcharges into a new National Development Fund (*Fundo Nacional de Desenvolvimento*). Both state enterprises and private enterprises were to be given new forms of debentures and commercial paper in an attempt to revive the long-term investment market. The law governing foreign purchases of shares in national enterprises was eased. Along with the measures to damp down consumer demand and stimulate investment, the government also announced a Target Plan (*Plano de Metas*—language reminiscent of Kubitschek's *Programa de Metas*) aimed at promoting social change and improving the Brazilian quality of life, another installment in the Sarney government's attempt to promote greater economic equity.

CONCLUSION. What did the Sarney government's first fifteen months tell us about a democratic government's ability to make the hard economic choices? First, we should note the Sarney government inherited highly favorable trends in two spheres: economic growth and the balance of payments. The latter enabled Sarney's policymakers to start without the albatross of another IMF agreement because of Brazil's favorable trade balance and foreign exchange reserves position. Economic growth, on the other hand, was a mixed blessing. It generated public support but it also fed the inflationary pressure that threatened to explode in early 1986. Sarney's economic policymakers came up with an ingenious anti-inflation plan that won immediate public acceptance. Within months it required corrective measures, however, and whether it could work for the full year its designers intended was increasingly in doubt.

We should also remember that the president's power to govern by decree-law was still intact, and was used both to implement the Plano Cruzado, and to decide on spending. Economic policy could still be made without conferring with key congressional forces. An important test of public attitudes toward economic policy would come in the November 1986 elections, in which a new Chamber of Deputies, a third of the Senate, and all the governors, would be chosen. Few democratic governments can resist the temptation to help their candidates in a vital election.

Did Democratization Include Efforts to Create a More Equal Society?

What can we tell from the Sarney government's first fifteen months in power about trends in economic equity? The PMDB had long attacked the military governments for policies that allegedly increased Brazil's vast economic and social inequalities. The PMDB's 1982 manifesto had given the principles and the priorities by which it intended to govern, calling Brazil "one of the world champions at concentrating income and wealth," despite the fact it ranked as one of the largest industrial powers "among market economies." It described Brazil's "enormous pockets of absolute poverty" as a "national disgrace."[89]

Data published by the World Bank concurred on the income distribution issue, showing that Brazil had one of the most unequal income distributions in the world.[90] The highest 20 percent of Brazilian households received more than 60 percent of total household income. None of the other countries above 60 percent (Panama, Zambia, Peru, and Kenya) were "newly industrializing countries," which offered the most relevant comparison for Brazil. Appalling deficiencies in the health of Brazilians were also documented. In 1983, for example, 47 percent of all eighteen-year-old boys failed the physical exam in preparation for compulsory military service. The causes varied from malnutrition and being underweight to congenital deformities of the limbs and spinal column.[91] To put these income and health statistics into perspective, however, we must review the record over the previous twenty years.

TRENDS IN SOCIAL AND ECONOMIC INDICATORS UNDER THE AUTHORITARIAN REGIME. Data on key social indicators in three census years (1960, 1970, and 1980) are shown in Table 1. Steady improvement throughout the period is obvious for all of them. The rise in life expectancy and the decline in infant mortality resulted from improvements in nutrition, health care, sanitation, and housing. The rising literacy rate[92] indicated a more educated work force (although "literacy" was often defined minimally), and the improvements in housing (piped water, sewer facilities, and electricity) showed that a steadily

TABLE 1   Change in Brazil's Social Indicators, 1960–1980

	1960	1970	1980
Life Expectancy at Birth (years)[a]	51.6	53.5	60.1
Mortality Before One Year (per 1,000 live births)[a]	121.1	113.8	87.9
Private Dwellings with Piped Water (%, all Brazil)[a]	24.3	33.3	55.1
Private Dwellings on Sewerage Network or Septic Tank (%, all Brazil)[a]	23.8	26.6	39.6
Private Dwellings with Electricity (%, all Brazil)[a]	38.5	47.5	68.5
Literacy Rate (15 years or older, (all Brazil)[a]	60.5	66.9	74.6
Private Dwellings with TV (%, all Brazil)[b]	NA	24.1	56.1

Source: a) Hélio Jaguaribe, et al., *Brasil, 2000: para um novo pacto social* (Rio de Janeiro: Paz e Terra, 1986), 138, 140, 142; b) Edmar Bacha & Herbert Klein, eds., *A Transição incompleta: Brasil desde 1945* (Rio de Janeiro: Paz e Terra, 1986), Vol. II, 89.

increasing percentage of Brazilians were enjoying living standards associated with modern, industrializing societies. These improvements resulted from both market forces and government action. High rates of growth created more and better jobs, thus helping to absorb the rapidly growing labor force. Governments on the *município,* state, and federal level financed the infrastructure required to improve living standards.

The question was not, therefore, whether there had been improvement, but how rapid it had been and how equitably it had been distributed. The opposition emphasized the shortfall, while the government pointed to the progress.

How does the relatively consistent pattern of improvement in living standards for Brazil as a whole between 1960 and 1980 indicated by the social indicators in Table 1 compare with the record indicated by income and wage trends? The answer has been an issue of lively controversy and is complicated both by data comparability problems and by arguments about which measure of economic well-being to use.

The three obvious candidates are minimum wage levels, individual or family income levels, and the degree of income inequality. All three measures are subject to comparability problems over time. Even conceptually, however, minimum wage levels are problematic as a measure of economic well-being for at least three reasons. First, major groups of the economically active population are not covered by the minimum wage— the self-employed, the unintegrated sector of the urban economy, and most of the rural sector. Second, the long-term trends in the real value of the minimum wage have not been consistent across the country: while its real value fell in the major industrial areas over the 1960–1980 period, it rose in some of the more backward areas. Finally, and most fundamentally, the legal minimum wage bears no necessary relationship to actual wage levels (and, therefore income received), which are determined at least in part by market forces.

Even when attention is restricted to income, data inadequacies (and the methodological problems involved in adjusting for the inadequacies) preclude calculation of any single income series as the one correct description of income change in Brazil over time. This is true to a degree for any country. It is true to a much greater degree for Brazil, for which analysts have constructed a wide range of plausible cost-of-living adjustments (to which income comparisons are extremely sensitive), which has undergone a rapid movement of workers from the non-money to the money economy; and where coding and other technical changes from one census to another further complicate the interpretation of income changes.

Fortunately, careful analysts have developed appropriate adjustments. Several recent analyses of income trends in Brazil since 1960 reveal substantial consensus, at least in qualitative terms.[93]

There is little doubt that the income distribution in Brazil is extremely unequal. The degree of income inequality, as noted, is probably the highest of any of the newly industrializing countries. There is also relatively little

TABLE 2   Distribution of Income in Brazil, by Decile (1960–1980, percent)

	Household Income		Individual Income	
	1960	1970	1970	1980
Bottom 10 Percent	1.4	1.2	1.2	1.2
2nd Decile	2.4	2.4	2.1	2.0
3rd Decile	3.6	3.2	3.0	3.0
4th Decile	4.6	4.1	3.8	3.6
5th Decile	5.6	4.9	5.0	4.4
6th Decile	7.2	6.0	6.2	5.6
7th Decile	8.1	7.7	7.2	7.2
8th Decile	13.1	10.8	10.0	10.0
9th Decile	14.6	16.6	15.2	15.4
Top 10 Percent	39.4	43.1	46.5	48.0

Source: Columns (1) and (2) M. Louise Fox, "Income Distribution in Post-1964 Brazil: New Results," *The Journal of Economic History*, Vol. 43, no. 1 (March 1983), Table 1, p. 264; Columns (3) and (4) individual data on the Economically Active Population, David Denslow, Jr., and William Tyler, "Perspectives on Poverty and Income Inequality in Brazil," *World Development*, Vol. 12, no. 10 (1984), Table 5, p. 1023.

doubt that the inequality grew substantially between 1960 and 1970. There is less agreement about the trend from 1970 to 1980, but most estimates suggest that income concentration probably continued though at a much slower rate. Table 2 shows two sets of estimates of changes in the size distribution of income (i.e., the percentage of income held by each decile of the population). I have chosen these estimates because both authors show comparisons by decile, both use census data, and both make adjustments for missing and noncomparable data. One limitation of the table is that the 1960–1970 comparison is for household income (more conceptually appropriate), whereas the 1970–1980 comparison is for individual income. The two distributions for 1970 are reassuringly similar, however; such similarity is plausible in Brazil, where the degree of social stratification keeps most individuals in roughly the same income class as that of their family.

Even allowing for data uncertainty, the picture is relatively stark. Throughout the period, the bottom two deciles together had less than one-twentieth of the income; the top two deciles had between one-half and two-thirds of the income. Between 1960 and 1970 only the top two deciles improved their relative position; all the others except one lost ground. Between 1970 and 1980 the top two deciles made further slight gains; four of the other eight deciles held their position.

What about absolute income levels? (See Table 3.) It is possible that everyone became better off and that the rich simply became better off more quickly. Here the weight of the evidence suggests that the 1960–1970 period saw relatively little change in the overall income levels (some analysts estimate a slight decline), but a change in the relative positions of different

TABLE 3   Changes in Mean Monthly Income, by Decile and Region, 1970–1980
*(August 1980 Cruzeiros)

	1970	1980	Percent Change
Decile			
Bottom 10 Percent	933	1,404	50
2nd Decile	1,650	2,422	47
3rd Decile	2,415	3,519	46
4th Decile	3,064	4,260	39
5th Decile	4,037	5,264	30
6th Decile	4,959	6,658	34
7th Decile	5,798	8,555	48
8th Decile	8,003	11,794	47
9th Decile	12,178	18,447	51
Top 10 Percent	37,366	57,183	53
Region			
Southeast	9,746	13,925	45
Rural	4,907	8,589	66
Urban	11,967	16,593	39
Northeast	4,486	7,062	55
Rural	2,681	4,141	52
Urban	4,569	9,533	34
Frontier	6,678	10,808	56
Rural	4,569	8,459	73
Urban	9,276	13,323	44
All Brazil	8,040	11,940	49

Source: Data are for members of the economically active population with positive incomes as reported to census takers. David Denslow, Jr., and William Tyler, "Perspectives on Poverty and Income Inequality in Brazil," Table 5, p. 1023.

groups. The major factor seems to have been a relative increase in urban poverty.[94] Although the proportion in poverty remained very similar overall, the percentage of the total poverty population in *urban* areas increased from about one-third to about one-half. The migrants to the city seem to have brought their poverty with them, which is consistent with the increase in infant mortality (from a much lower initial level than characterized Brazil as a whole) that occurred for Rio de Janeiro and São Paulo over at least part of the period.[95] Analysis by José Pastore et al. also indicates that extreme poverty in the rural sector eased substantially less than it did in the urban sector.

What has happened in the last years of the authoritarian regime, in response to the recession and to changes in the minimum wage law intended expressly to reduce inequality? Data from the 1981 and 1982 National Household Surveys (PNADs) indicate that income levels have dropped substantially. The effect on income inequality is not yet determined. Ralph Hakkert quotes some observers who suggest that income dropped across the spectrum and that, in his words, "the Brazilian economy is more equitable in spreading the burdens of recession than it has been in distributing the benefits of development."[96]

RECORD OF THE NEW REGIME. The PMDB, along with critics from academia, the press, the church, and the left and center-left, had argued for years that the post-1964 economic policies were bound to prolong and even worsen socio-economic inequalities.[97] Delfim Neto always answered his critics by saying Brazil first had to create a bigger cake so there would be something to distribute. Otherwise, he charged, they would merely "redistribute misery."[98] More than two decades of a free hand for the technocrats had certainly increased the cake. Redistribution, argued the PMDB and its economists, was long overdue.

Tancredo was no stranger to these criticisms, which he had repeated in his campaign speeches. Improving economic equity was one of the topics he instructed his *Comissão do Plano de Ação do Governo* (COPAG) to study. This ad hoc economic planning commission, appointed in early 1985 and chaired by José Serra, then Secretary for Economic Planning in Franco Montoro's São Paulo state government, was asked to identify the most important economic problems awaiting the new government. Among COPAG's recommendations was an emergency program to help the poorest. It included distribution of subsidized milk to children of low-income families, along with public job programs, emergency housing, and a crash health program for the most backward areas. These were only emergency measures. For the future, Brazil needed far more investment and overall economic planning.[99]

Even the proposal for an emergency program did not sit well with Finance Minister Dornelles and his fellow monetarists. Where would the money for this laudable program come from, given the federal budget cut of 10 percent? Which ministries or agencies were going to cede funds to aid the neediest? And beyond the budget problem lay the fact that the poor wielded no weight in the political system, although the newly enfranchised illiterates might eventually change that. The Sarney government was, after all, peopled mainly by members of the same political elite that had governed Brazil for untold decades. Were they prepared to compromise the interests of their constituents for the sake of the dispossessed?

The emergency program was soon relegated to the back burner, as the Sarney government scrambled to manage the more urgent short-term problems. Dornelles did find modest emergency funding. By January 1986 milk distribution was under way, but on a much smaller scale than its advocates had hoped.[100]

Yet the President was not giving up on efforts to correct Brazil's appalling inequities. Since the early 1970s Brazil had been the target of extensive social science research, much of it financed by the military governments.[101] The 1970 and 1980 censuses and the national household surveys, along with myriad other studies, provided extensive data. The Sarney government lost no time in tapping them. In August 1985 the President commissioned Professor Hélio Jaguaribe to head a study team to prepare a report "on Brazil's grave social problems and the urgent need to create, through a New Social Pact, a broad national consensus favoring measures and policies that will lead the country, as fast as possible, toward a substantially more egalitarian social structure." Presented in early May 1986,[102] the team's report painted a by-now familiar picture of Brazil: although boasting the eighth largest economy in the Western world, Brazil fell into the same category as the less developed African or Asian countries when it came to social welfare indices. The framing of the problem was meant to make the Brazilian elite take notice. Fancying themselves a powerful Third World leader, the elite were now told their masses lived an existence many preferred to believe Brazil had long left behind.

The report then proposed a fifteen-year strategy to lift Brazilian living standards to the level of Spain or Greece. It would require significantly increased spending for social welfare programs, including agrarian reform, along with an average economic growth rate of 6 percent. The report spelled out a strategy by area within a Multi-year Plan of Social Development (*Plano Plurianual de Desenvolvimento Social*). President Sarney accepted the report and immediately pledged 12 percent of GNP for social welfare programs. Could such a commitment be kept? At least the full dimensions of Brazil's "internal social debt" had now been laid out.

URBAN LABOR. The debate over social welfare policy and the Sarney government's policies is well illustrated by the area of urban labor. (Agrarian reform and police treatment of prisoners will be discussed below.) The PMDB had made labor policy a key issue in its 1982 manifesto, calling for "a new strategy of social development" that would achieve "a more just distribution of income." This would come "only with democracy."

The first area targeted for reform was labor legislation. The goal should be "union autonomy," which meant liquidating "the remains of corporatism in the labor law." They "facilitate the authoritarian manipulation of the unions through financial links, the power of intervention, and other mechanisms of dependence." These "vices must be rooted out of the legislation once and for all" so that "workers can organize freely to defend their interests." This required "full restoration of the right to strike" and the "possibility of a central workers' organization with the constitution of a *Central Unica,* as was resolved last year in CONCLAT I."[103] The latter stood for *Coordenação Nacional da Classe Trabalhadora,* and was a confederation of unions led by such different groups as the PMDB, PC, PC do B, MR-8, the AIFLD (AFL-CIO linked) unions, and assorted *pelegos.* CONCLAT's rival was the CUT (*Central Única dos Trabalhadores*), dominated by the PT and markedly more militant.

During his 1984 presidential campaign, Tancredo had reaffirmed the goal of revising labor legislation, especially by freeing unions from government intervention and expanding the latitude for legal strikes. In his undelivered inaugural speech Tancredo had "a special word for workers." He called them "the majority of our people" and promised that he would "dedicate all his energy to seeing that their rights were increased and respected." How far did the Sarney government go by July 1986 toward fulfilling these promises?[104]

The Sarney government achieved at least one first in its labor policy by appointing as its labor minister a former union employee. Almir Pazzianotto had for ten years been the lawyer for a leading São Paulo metalworkers union. He had strong views on how the new government should treat workers and unions. As he knew, the Sarney government could take a number of steps to better the economic lot and bargaining power of urban workers.[105]

The most obvious was to increase the real minimum wage, a figure set by the government.[106] For decades this had been a bitterly debated policy area. Getúlio Vargas's doubling of the minimum wage in 1954 had provoked employers to align against him. Juscelino Kubitschek earned labor support by setting the minimum wage at a historic high in 1957. João Goulart struggled unsuccessfully to protect wages from rapidly accelerating inflation.[107] The military governments reversed these populist policies. The real minimum wage rate declined significantly during the Castelo Branco regime. Thereafter the intermittent real minimum-wage rate increases were quickly eroded by inflation. The Figueiredo government and Congress produced a bewildering series of minimum wage rate changes so close together that the effects could hardly be measured. That experience showed that wage policy could quickly become chaotic if the Planalto and Congress were at loggerheads.

The 1982 PMDB manifesto had left no doubt about the party's wage policy. It called for "the gradual recovery of the minimum wage's buying power. Recovery should be achieved by keeping adjustments above inflation, with the aim of doubling its real value as soon as possible, within what is economically viable for the country."[108]

In addition to promising a higher real minimum wage rate, the PDMB had vowed to overhaul the legal structure of labor relations, as established in the 1943 labor code (CLT) and subsequently amended. A key provision defined legal strikes so narrowly as to render them nearly impossible. Should the government wish to enforce that law to the hilt, it could declare virtually any strike illegal—and leave the rest to the police. Invoking other labor code powers, the government could remove union officers who led a strike. In the decade after Costa e Silva had amply used these powers for the Osasco and Contagem strikes in 1968, there were virtually no strikes.

In 1977, however, a new generation of union leaders was ready to defy the repression. The Figueiredo government reacted cautiously to strikes, avoiding early use of force. Labor Minister Murillo Macedo discussed a possible labor code reform, but the Ministry never reached consensus within its own ranks. As strikes increased, Labor Minister Macedo cracked down on some unions (such as the Petroleum Workers) by purging their officers. The Macedo Ministry's relative tolerance of intense union strike activity—compared with previous military governments—raised both expectations and fears about labor's future role.

A second labor code element that reformers attacked was the compulsory payroll deduction (formerly the *impôsto sindical* and now called the *contribuição sindical*), collected by the employer and sent on to the Labor Ministry. The latter then controlled distribution of these funds (minus a portion retained by the Ministry) to the unions, the federations, and the confederations. Dropping this compulsory deduction, which would free unions from government financial control, would also mean, at least initially, a drastic drop in funds. Although most unions had some form of voluntary dues, probably fewer than 10 percent of the country's unions would survive the loss of the *contribuição sindical*. The likely survivors included the largest São Paulo unions, along with other scattered unions such as the Rio commercial workers and the Blumenau textile workers. The "independent" unionists, such as Lula, endorsed in principle the abolition of the *contribuição sindical,* notwithstanding its probable short-run effect. The communist-led unions, however, loudly opposed its outright abolition. The stakes were obvious. Making the unions depend on voluntary dues would force the leaders to become more responsive to their members.

Union pluralism was another sensitive question. Under the labor code only one union (*sindicato único*) represented all the workers in one category in a given *município*. The labor ministry then certified each union, which was thus protected from any rival organizing within its *município*. The members elected their officers, often on very low turnouts. The labor ministry had to approve the elections and it could at any time replace the officers with its own appointees. This system of the *sindicato único* greatly favored incumbent union leadership. Those who wanted a freer union system argued that allowing competing unions within the same trade in the same *município,* would be more democratic. On the other hand, it might produce more and smaller unions, with less bargaining power. It might also greatly reduce their potential political power.

The recognition of shop stewards and/or factory commissions, on the other hand, was a reform that could strengthen unions. Under the labor code the only legal union representatives were the union officers for the entire *município*. That meant many workers—normally the majority—had no plant-level representative to pursue grievances and other worksite-specific issues. In the late 1970s de facto shop stewards had begun to emerge in São Paulo, as had factory commissions (*commisões de fabrica*). Even where management decided to work with them, as at Ford, they had no legal standing.

Job security was another issue on which the PMDB had called for reform. As we saw earlier, until 1967 the labor code had guaranteed workers job security (*estabilidade*) after ten years with the same employer. As we also saw earlier, Roberto Campos and his technocrats replaced that labor code provision with a worker's severance pay fund (FGTS) that indemnified laid-off workers in proportion to their years of employment. It also made easier the dismissal of workers without cause. Employers used this new instrument to increase their labor turnover and thereby lower their labor costs, a move made possible because the wage increases were given in proportion to the amount of time workers had been on the job since the last wage increase. Firms routinely fired workers shortly before wage adjustment time, hiring new workers who would qualify for only a fraction of the increase. Employers also took advantage of the opportunity to fire more highly paid workers, replacing them with lower-paid workers already on the job. Employers could therefore selectively use dismissals (some continuity had to be maintained in their work force) to reduce their wage bill below what it would have been under the *estabilidade* system. The 1982 PMDB manifesto declared that "this perverse and highly unjust mechanism should be eliminated immediately and job security should be reestablished."[109] The objective was to retain the severance fund (FGTS) while eliminating the incentive it gave to dismiss workers without cause.

These were the principal options in urban labor policy that the Sarney government faced. In its first several months, as noted, the government was preoccupied with the need to reduce inflation. With the cabinet split between the Dornelles and Sayad factions, Labor Minister Pazzianotto had to pick his issues carefully. He could not now afford a wholesale attack on the archaic legal structure of labor relations.

Although many Brazilians, including many workers, expected the Sarney government to bring fundamental change, the independent union leaders and the PT saw it as a potential threat. They reasoned that any reforms might lull Brazilians into forgetting their real need: revolutionary (but nonviolent) change in the country's economic and political structure. The independent union leaders vowed to pull no punches with the new government. The PT-oriented metalworkers unions of greater São Paulo, for example, formulated ambitious demands to present when the semi-annual wage adjustments came due in March 1985.[110] At the same time, these leaders were tactically cautious. They had a stake in not giving the conservatives within (or without) the Sarney government a pretext to push the New Republic to the right. They also knew that any action taken while Tancredo had a chance to recover would incur the public's wrath. They therefore waited until Tancredo's return was ruled out to launch their strike on April 10.

The union demands were a 40-hour week, automatic monthly wage adjustments for inflation, and a 6 percent real wage increase each quarter. When the employers rejected these demands, the metalworkers struck. They were challenging the Sarney government just as it emerged from the limbo created by Tancredo's illness. The ABC metalworkers, headed by PT-linked leaders, wanted to show their independence of the PMDB-PFL regime. It was their counterpart to the PT's boycott of the electoral college's presidential vote in January 1985.

The metalworkers' strike dragged on for weeks. The employers, including the multinational auto companies, were determined not to yield in the

New Republic's first major strike test. There were more than a few ugly moments. The General Motors plant in São José dos Campos fired 93 workers, including many strike leaders. Reaction among the GM workers led to a takeover of union (*Metalúrgicos de São José*) leadership by radical dissidents, including (*Convergência Socialista*) (Socialist Convergence), a Trotskyist group. The radical-led workers then took hostage 370 administrative workers who had refused to join the strike and kept them without food or sleep for two days. The incarceration (but not the strike) ended only after the labor minister's direct appeal. This "hostage" spectacle damaged the union image among the public, which had often sympathized with past strikes.[111]

As tension over the strike arose, all eyes were fixed on Labor Minister Pazzianotto. Would the former union lawyer intervene on the strikers' behalf? Or would he act like labor ministers before him, unleashing the police when the government decided the strike had to end? Minister of Industry and Commerce Roberto Gusmão, a hardliner, argued for the latter. But Pazzianotto did neither, deciding instead to wait out the strike. Since he could count on both the São Paulo and the federal governments to avoid repression, the ball was back in the court of the workers and employers. The latter were in no mood for concessions now, although they had offered some before the strike began. Pressure therefore shifted to the strikers. When the police and security forces did not attack their pickets, they lacked the public sympathy such repression generated in earlier strikes.

The metalworkers' strike—the longest on record—did not end. It simply petered out after 54 days, failing to gain its demands overall, though individual firms granted some. In fact, the strikers' motivation was as much political as economic. The "independent" unions and the PT wanted to test their strength against the new government. But the government won in that it preserved its independence by neither aiding nor repressing the strikers.

The outcome was significant on several other counts. First, it showed that if the government avoided repression the workers might find they enjoyed less public sympathy. This could force the militant unions to reassess their strike strategy. Second, the result was a political success for the Sarney government because it preserved a centrist position, independent from both the left and the right. Third, the strike and its outcome drove home the point that strikes are normal in a democratic system with open bargaining. Finally, numerous strike leaders were fired (the union officers were legally protected). Since major firms maintained blacklists of workers dismissed for union activism, many victims found themselves with no job prospects.

The metalworkers had not been alone in striking: a long line of other unions joined in. Many were public employees, such as the São Paulo railroad workers, who had seen their real salaries decline and their working conditions deteriorate.[112] Many health workers in INAMPS, the national social welfare system, for example, worked in appalling conditions in a grossly overloaded system with inadequate funding. Given the federal government's austerity budget, the public agencies had no resources from which to pay for better wages or working conditions. Most of these strikes failed. It should be noted that the government was quite prepared to live with wage settlements in the private sector which it refused to match when it came to its own workers. That inconsistency escaped the attention of neither the leaders nor the members of the public sector unions.

This strike action during the second half of 1985 and early 1986 showed a number of factors at work. First, the metalworkers were not the only well-organized and skillfully led union. The São Paulo bank workers, long known as militants, staged a two-day strike and won a significant real wage rate increase, but not the quarterly adjustment which was their principal demand. Especially interesting here was the fact that the settlement handed down by the regional labor court was more generous than what Funaro and Sayad had wanted.

Second, well-timed government concessions could and did reduce worker militancy. In early November the Sarney government announced a semi-annual minimum wage increase of 5.6 percent more than the inflation rate of the past six months. This was an effort to regain part of the loss in the minimum wage's real value under the military governments. It was also keeping a long-standing PMDB promise to raise wages. In São Paulo, where a huge strike backed by a coalition of unions had been called for November, the workers went back to work after two days, with most having received real wage increases of 8 percent to 20 percent, de facto quarterly wage adjustments, and a work-week reduction from 48 to 45 hours.[113] The employers could afford to make these concessions in part because the São Paulo economy was booming. The employers were also anxious to avoid a lengthy strike. The settlement confirmed that the São Paulo industrial unions had impressive bargaining power.

Finally, strike action in the second half of 1985 highlighted the ideological and political differences between the CUT and the CONCLAT, as the more militant, PT-oriented CUT gained ground among individual unions. Although the unions halted their strike, it was clear that both the CUT and the CONCLAT (having now changed its name to the CGT (*Central Geral dos Trabalhadores*)) were planning even bigger mobilizations for the future. In the short run, however, their rivalry might well weaken labor's bargaining power.

The cycle of government—union confrontation was broken by the Plano Cruzado at the end of February 1986. The context of bargaining was suddenly disrupted by a totally new approach to inflation. Two items in the plan, the price freeze and unemployment compensation, had long been urged by the PT and the CUT. Labor was also granted an 8 percent bonus on top of an inflation adjustment. This was the government's second increase in the real minimum wage, and was again intended to compensate for past losses, as well as win worker support for the government program.

The PT and DIEESE initially attacked the government's formula for calculating wage adjustments under the Plano Cruzado, arguing that it did not use the correct base.[114] Nonetheless, the public enthusiastically welcomed the plan and thereby put the militant union leaders on the defensive. In response, Lula and the other CUT and PT leaders soon began planning a national general strike with the aim of defeating the Plano Cruzado wage policy. Any truly general strike is virtually impossible to carry out in Brazil because of its size, regional variations, and the weakness of most unions. Yet the government took the strike threat seriously, preparing especially for strikes against "essential" public services. No general strike had occurred by July, although there had been major strikes by the Rio railroad workers and the Brasília civil servants. Since these were public employees, the government was their employer and was perforce in the negotiations. Pazzianotto and his colleagues took a hard line in these cases, since any government concessions would have become an immediate precedent for union militants in other sectors.

What was the verdict on the Sarney government's fifteen-month record on the labor negotiation front? First, it had delivered, if modestly, on the PMDB's commitment to increase the real minimum wage. Second, it had largely avoided government intervention in labor disputes. It was a start toward the objective—endorsed by Funaro, Sayad, and Pazzianotto—of more autonomy for labor-management relations.

This was not the first time since 1964 that a government had decided to increase the real minimum wage. It happened in 1967 when the newly installed Costa e Silva government upped the real wage as part of its attempt to "humanize the Revolution," in a bid for public support at a time when voting, although curtailed, was still important. The second case was in 1979, when the Figueiredo government got through Congress a wage law giving the lower-paid workers a 10 percent bonus over the cost-of-living adjustment. Here, too, the government in question was looking for political support in a much loosened authoritarian structure.[115] In sum, these two earlier cases came either before 1969 or after 1979, i.e., not in the decade of the greatest repression.

Another key issue in labor relations was the strike law. The government labored mightily to produce a new strike law proposal. Labor Minister Pazzianotto's draft began its way through intra-government channels in mid-1985 and finally emerged in June 1986.[116] The president and his minister won only a shaky government consensus on how far they could go in legalizing strikes. The higher military, for example, had long cast a wary eye on unions and opposed any weakening of government power over strikers.[117] The São Paulo industrialists also spoke out against making strikes easier. They liked the existing law, which gave employers a permanent advantage, assuming strict application of the law. Both the higher military and the São Paulo industrialists argued aggressively against what they charged was excessive liberalization in Pazzianotto's draft bill.[118] The labor minister was pressured also by the hundreds of union leaders and union members he had consulted. They wanted the government's heavy hand out, so that unions could exercise the same right to strike long held in the industrialized countries.[119]

The Sarney government's proposal for a new strike law was finally sent to Congress in July 1986.[120] It was to replace a July 1964 law which the Castelo Branco government promulgated to crack down on unions. The proposed law, a product of elaborate intra-government compromises, would reduce the number of essential sectors whose workers were prohibited from striking.[121] A wide range of workers, such as civil servants, hospital workers and dockworkers, would still be on the forbidden list. Second, strikes could henceforth be authorized only by a secret ballot, in contrast to the voice vote many unions practiced. Third, workers and employers would now be offered a new option: recourse to an outside arbitrator who could be asked to recommend a settlement. Fourth, the proposal would reduce the bureaucratic obstacles to calling a strike. Fifth, employer lockouts would still be prohibited (though employers had lobbied hard to legalize them). Finally, the proposal would maintain the government's authority over strikes and strike actions.

The proposal drew immediate fire from militant unionists, such as Gilmar Carneiro, a member of the CUT's national directorate, who saw it as nothing but a "more flexible law for repressing strikes." A key issue was bound to be the requirement for a minimum secret vote to call a strike. Pazzianotto argued that the new law would "make certain that strikes are not decreed by minorities." Many observers believed that the higher the minimum vote required, the less likely a strike. In other words, more democratic procedures might, in the short run, slow down the radical union leadership.

The strike law proposal was undeniably an anticlimax. The government had labored for fifteen months to produce a very cautious document. Its fate would depend on a complex play of forces in the Congress and the country. And would the law be obeyed even if passed? It was worth remembering that much of the change in labor relations since the late 1970s had been either against or around existing law. As union leader Gilmar Carneiro said, "if this law is passed it will be disobeyed, just like the present one." Enforcement would then be the key, and past governments had sometimes chosen to enforce the labor laws selectively.

Two other important labor law changes were said to be in the works.[122] The first was abolition of the compulsory dues (*contribuição sindical*). The second would abolish the requirement that only one union could represent workers in one trade (*categoria*) in each *município*. In other words, competing unions would be able to represent workers in different worksites within a *município*.

Both changes were being urged in the name of greater union democracy. The metalworkers union in the São Paulo satellite city of Osasco already had a system whereby the employers deducted separate dues from workers' paychecks and gave them to the unions. These dues were parallel to the *contribuição sindical,* which continued being collected but which the union refused to accept. Yet there were few unions prepared to take such bold action. Introducing union pluralism would presumably also stimulate union democracy because leaders would need to cultivate member loyalty in order to hold off rival organizers.

These two reforms—abolishing the *contribuição sindical* and exclusive representation—were favored by the independent union leaders and by the PT and the CUT. They believed they would win increasing support in a more competitive climate, which they had been doing since 1978 by a strategy based on grassroots activism. Many other leaders lacked that confidence, however. The PCB, PC do B, MR-8, and the old-line *pelegos* opposed both reforms. One thing was certain: enacting these reforms would greatly weaken union bargaining power in the short run. That would in turn make it easier for the Sarney government to pursue its anti-inflation program.

This trade-off was especially stark for Labor Minister Pazzianotto, who had conflicting loyalties. He wanted systematic reform of the labor laws but he was also committed to the success of Plano Cruzado. Would pursuit of the latter jeopardize achievement of the former? Pazzianotto threatened further labor law revisions in order to keep off balance the union opponents of the anti-inflation program. Obviously this tactic was more effective with the CGT unions than with the CUT.[123] Thus labor policy was intertwined with the government's larger economic goals. Democratizing union structures, just as democratizing political structures, was proving far from simple.

Union democratization was also being prompted from another direction. Although the massive strikes had gotten the labor headlines since the late 1970s, there were less publicized but no less important changes under way. Many larger private firms and their unions, for example, had developed de facto collective bargaining in limited areas.[124] In July 1985, 80 percent of 180 foreign-owned firms responding to a survey said they were already paying cost-of-living raises on a quarterly basis—this at a time when the government vehemently opposed quarterly adjustments.[125] Employers were making agreements with their workers while ignoring government guidelines. Another example was provided by the rapidly spreading *comissões de fábrica,* or factory commissions.[126] These worker-organized commissions arose to defend workers' interests on the shop floor, precisely where the *município-*based unions were often weakest. In some cases the commissions gained recognition from the employers who incorporated them into joint management-worker committees (sometimes also called *comissões de fábrica*). These committees were then given limited authority over such questions as work rule interpretations, safety regulations, allocation of overtime work, dismissals, and other plant-level concerns. Workers in these joint committees varied from "bread and butter" activists to those who saw the committees as a base for future political action. Although these factory joint committees had totaled only about twenty in 1984, there were 220 by mid-1986.[127]

Another democratizing influence was at work within the unions: the offensive by aggressive leftist organizers. Many were the "independent" unionists now linked to the CUT and the PT. Others came from left groups such as the Trotskyist *Convergência Socialista* and the Catholic-Church-sponsored *Pastoral do Trabalho*. All these organizers worked from the bottom up, proselytizing union members who had never bothered to be active in their union. Many of these unions were led by *pelegos,* whose position depended on their being passively accepted by their members. The independents were skilled, well informed, and zealous. They found fertile ground among the inactive rank-and-file. As these organizers spread their gospel, the targeted unions suffered an upsurge of participation. Whether or not the organizers succeeded in toppling the union leadership, and whether or not the leftist organizers' ideology took hold, the unions were shaken out of their lethargy. Democratization, defined as greater member participation, was clearly furthered.

The most basic question in urban labor relations by mid-1986 was whether Brazil would adjust its official labor relations system to the new realities of the 1980s. Easing the strike law would strengthen labor's hand, but by no means would it make unions invincible. They would still have to deal with such variables as the reserve army of unemployed ready to take their jobs, the demand for their employers' products, the size of strike funds or outside aid, and the militancy of their members. Making strikes easier would shift the focus from police repression (or its threat) to the real issues at stake between employers and unions. They could then concentrate on bargaining, long accepted in the industrial West as the democratic approach to labor relations.

AGRARIAN REFORM. The PMDB's 1982 manifesto had selected the agrarian sector as another area urgently needing change. Brazil's rural poor were at the bottom of the bottom by every social indicator—mortality, morbidity, housing, sanitation, literacy. Yet Brazil was a vast country with still unexploited land. What had gone wrong? Hadn't there been frontier agricultural booms through the centuries, including the twentieth? Yes, but too often the landless could not get to the frontier, or once there they found the land in the hands of speculators or large holders. As a leading government economist noted, "We're all aware we're living in a country that has the world's highest income concentration, and, to be specific, one of the highest land concentrations."[118] In this century rapid population growth combined with Brazil's brand of capitalist development to produce large pockets of impoverished rural dwellers. Between 1978 and 1984 the government policies favoring large, capital-intensive land holdings had helped increase the number of farm laborers with little or no land from 6.7 to 10.6 million.[129]

One key to improving the lot of those laborers lay in access to land. But how? In 1964 the Castelo Branco government had made agrarian reform a top priority. Its 1964 *Estatuto da Terra* (land law) created the legal basis for land redistribution. Land redistribution was to be promoted by a progressive land tax, which was to penalize owners of unutilized or underutilized land. If aggressively applied, the tax scheme could have led to a significant shift in land ownership. But landowners got ample safeguards, such as limits on the expropriation powers. Most important, neither the Castelo Branco government nor its successors in the 1960s and 1970s were prepared to allocate the enormous government funds that such a compensation plan would have required.[130]

In fact, government policy since the 1950s had placed its highest priority on industrialization. Agricultural policy favored not land redistribution but increased production, which usually meant large, capital-intensive units.[131] Meanwhile, since the 1970s an increasingly large fraction of agricultural production was going for export. The 7 percent increase in the 1985 harvest, for example, was attributed primarily to soybeans, cotton, and wheat (the first two being export crops), while rice and beans, staples of the popular diet, fell 3 percent and stagnated, respectively. "It makes no sense for Brazil to be one of the world's major food exporters," observed Agriculture Minister Pedro Simon, "while 30 million of us are starving."[132]

How had the rural dweller fared during these changes? As Brazil industrialized and urbanized, the city dwellers saw their nutritional, health, and other social indicators improve. They left the rural poor, who saw less such improvement, far behind.[133]

What could the rural dwellers do about their lot? In the early 1960s a few had begun to organize when the Goulart government and the Congress extended the right of unionization to the rural sector. Organizers of every political persuasion, especially on the left, poured into the countryside. The peasant leagues, primarily in the Northeast, had made front-page news by their demands for radical change in the wage laborers' working conditions. The 1964 military coup stopped this mobilization in its tracks. The repression was especially ruthless in the Northeast, where the Fourth Army hunted down (and in some cases killed) rural organizers.[134]

After 1964 the landowners worked hand in glove with the police and the military, giving the rural poor little chance to organize. By the early 1980's, however, the situation had begun to change. The political opening on the national level emboldened some landless peasants and their leaders to organize and demand land redistribution. These groups were often linked to radical Catholic clergy, who in the late 1970s and early 1980s were especially active in the Amazon basin, the Center-West, and the Northeast. Since, as we have seen, other institutions of civil society were either absent or unable to function effectively, the church offered the only recourse for many of the landless and their would-be organizers. The military governments reacted angrily to the involvement of clergy in land conflicts, and several foreign clerics were expelled from the country. Meanwhile the CNBB continued to push for an aggressive policy of land expropriation and redistribution.[135]

Along with increasing land conflicts had gone escalating violence. One study showed assassinations of rural organizers rising from 58 in 1982 to 191 in 1985. The first five months of 1986 brought 100 more deaths.[136] Landowners were openly claiming their right to arm themselves in defense of their property. Others relied on hired gunmen to rid them of protestors and land invaders.

The Sarney government early on committed itself to a major land redistribution. In May 1985 Sarney announced to 4,000 cheering delegates at the fourth national congress of rural workers (*Confederação Nacional dos Trabalhadores na Agricultura,* or CONTAG) an ambitious land-reform plan which was sent to Congress shortly thereafter. The proposal took as its starting point the 1964 *Estatuto da Terra* and aimed by the year 2000 to settle 7.1 million landless families on 480 million hectares of land.[137] *Latifúndios*—vast, privately held tracts—were to be the source of 85 percent of the land. Selection of these lands was to be made by INCRA (*Instituto Nacional de Colonização e Reforma Agrária,* or National Institute for Colonization and Agrarian Reform), with priority given to areas of conflict over ownership. Compensation was to be by 20-year government bonds, redeemable in 20 years and paying 6 percent plus inflation adjustment. Minister of Land Reform and Agrarian Development Nelson Ribeiro, whose selection had been strongly supported by the CNBB, then presented a first-stage plan calling for 100,000 families a year to receive land in 1985 and 1986. Part of the logic behind the proposal was that increased access to land could create a more productive, more prosperous, and healthier rural population. It was also hoped that such reforms could help slow the migrant flow to the swollen cities.[138]

Implementing this plan would involve many difficult decisions. INCRA was to select the lands for expropriation. That would require measuring the productivity of many holdings, since relative productivity was to be the chief criterion in selection. Next came calculating compensation to the owner, based on the tax assessment and INCRA's estimate of worth. Once expropriated land was distributed to the new owners, the government would have to decide expenditures on vital services, such as credit, transportation, technology, and storage facilities. Availability of these services has proved crucial and unexpectedly expensive in land reform projects in other countries. Finally, there was the question of how much money the Sarney government would commit to the program.

Agrarian reform is a particularly complex matter in a country as vast as Brazil, with its widely varying regions and subregions. In socialist countries such as the U.S.S.R. and Cuba, where state planners have enjoyed decades of uncontested control, agricultural productivity has often proved disappointing. The same could be said of nonsocialist cases such as Mexico and Bolivia. Although productivity and production were separable from land redistribution, no Brazilian government could afford to ignore their relationship, especially given the country's rising demand for food crops.[139]

The Sarney government's agrarian reforms had several objectives. The first was to create more landowners. That would presumably help defuse the tense, sometimes violent, rural scene. It would also help increase the number of small farmers, who in turn could be a source of political stability in the countryside. If the small farmers stayed on the land, they would at least reduce the exodus to the choked cities, another government objective. And it was hoped that increasing the smallholder contingent would improve income distribution. In sum, this was an effort to promote healthier and more equitable capitalist relations in the countryside.[140]

The Sarney government proposal provoked a series of fierce battles in Congress. Conservatives, such as Flavio Teles de Menezes of the *Sociedade Ruralista Brasileira* (Brazilian Rural Society), rallied in defense of private property. They charged that dangerous radicals (communists or fellow travelers) were behind the proposal. The higher military added its disapproval of the plan. The Church hierarchy supported it, though many of its more radical members criticized it as overly cautious. Those from the Church's *Pastoral da Terra* (Pastoral Land Commission) and *Os sem Terra* (The Landless) were well informed and had first-hand knowledge of the areas in conflict. They argued that a widespread agrarian reform was a moral necessity. The bill also had the support of CONTAG, the organization of rural workers unions. These were Brazil's fastest growing unions, although their poor organization and inexperienced leadership sapped their political effectiveness.

In response to this storm from all sides, in October 1985 the government produced another plan, very different from the original. The new plan called for the expropriation primarily of public lands, with no cultivated private land, regardless of size, to be touched. The expropriations would be largely in Brazil's far north, and almost half of the recipients were to come from the misery-stricken Northeast. About 150,000 peasant families would receive land in 1986, and a total of 43 million hectares was to be distributed to 1,400,000 families by the end of 1989. The advocates of radical agrarian reform, including church militants and rural workers' groups, denounced the plan as a sellout. José Gomes da Silva, INCRA director, agreed, and resigned in protest.[141]

Meanwhile, fierce land conflicts continued, with peasants staging land invasions, sometimes with the encouragement of Catholic clergy.[142] The Sarney government had grown impatient over clerics' role in land invasions, expecially in the Amazon valley. Justice Minister Paulo Brossard, who as a PMDB Senator had once attacked government repression, now struck out at the Church radicals. He warned that clergy engaged in such political activities as organizing land invasions would be subject to the same laws as every other citizen. In short, the Sarney government was asserting its secular authority against the Church radicals' moral claims. The radicals pointed to the frequent deaths among their number as proof that state power protected the landowners' gunmen. For weeks Brossard and the clergy traded angry charges. In June 1986 President Sarney, in a gesture typical of his political style, sought to defuse the religious aspect of the crisis by visiting Rome to discuss with the Pope the seriousness of the Brazilian Church radicals' involvement in this volatile issue. It was dramatic confirmation of the Brazilian

Church's importance in national politics, at least in agrarian matters.[143] But would that influence, achieved when the Church stood alone against the repressive governments, continue?

In June 1986 President Sarney signed 37 decrees authorizing the first land expropriations, which totalled 257,135 hectares in 12 states. The largest single expropriation was of the Citusa *fazenda* of 43,820 hectares in Maranhão. It was notable as the home of the 150 workers who had hacked to death with scythes a *pistoleiro* (professional gunman) suspected of having killed activist rural workers. Early in June, Sarney had reiterated his pledge to carry out the rest of the program on schedule.[144] There were many skeptics. Some pointed to the president's own status as a landholder (albeit modest) in Maranhão, a state riddled with gross inequalities in land ownership and living standards.

Whatever the Sarney government accomplished in agrarian reform, the issue was bound to remain hot. Any expropriation and resettlement would keep the pot boiling in the countryside. And if the steps were seen as grossly inadequate by the landless and their organizers, then activism was likely to grow. The escalating number of assassinations had shown that the police presence—under landowner control or else nil in most of the interior—could not cope with the level of conflict. The rural social crisis so often predicted by Brazilian and foreign observers seemed closer than ever before.

Even if the government's agrarian reform went well, there were clear dangers. In the long run, i.e., beyond 1986, this plan would be a heavy burden on the Treasury. If production fell (as has so often happened with agrarian reform elsewhere) and food prices rose, then agrarian reform could rapidly lose its popularity with the politicians of the New Republic. It was, of course, possible that distributing unutilized land to landless families might increase total production over the longer run. Much would depend on the services made available to the new owners.[145]

TREATMENT OF PRISONERS. The successful campaign to end torture of political prisoners generated a campaign to end torture of ordinary criminal suspects, detainees, and prisoners.[146] We have seen how the Brazilian police had, over the last century, developed a reputation for violence against suspects and prisoners.[147] This tradition of police brutality (found in many countries) was dramatized when the police and military were unleashed against political suspects after the 1964 coup.

The pre-1964 criminal laws had exempted from incarceration in ordinary jail a host of Brazilians, from ministers of state to clergymen to any holder of a higher degree from a Brazilian faculty. In effect, no member of the elite—given good legal counsel—needed to fear relegation to a common jail cell. Once the repression hit, however, that privileged status suddenly disappeared.[148] Elite suspects now suffered the abuse normally aimed at ordinary suspects, which was for many only the first step toward the horror of systematic torture. Their abuse was news, whereas that of ordinary criminal suspects had seldom been.

The campaign to liberalize the military regime centered initially on the restoration of civil liberties, including above all *habeas corpus*. But many political prisoners knew that political liberalization would not bring an end to abuse of ordinary criminal suspects. How could this concern be kept alive after the (primarily elite) political prisoners' relief at escaping the Brazilian gulag?

The leaders of the campaign against police torture of ordinary suspects came from the Church, the Bar, and the academic world—with the São Paulo Pastoral Commission on Human Rights and the Marginalized, strongly endorsed by Cardinal Arns, in the lead.[149] They found little support. The public, including most who had fought against the repression, was less interested in the fate of ordinary victims. They were nameless. A second reason the campaign lacked wide support was public anger over an increase in street crime. Robberies and assaults were on the rise during the early 1980s—or so the media and public believed. Public anger exploded in street "lynchings," where a fleeing suspect would be cornered by a crowd and then beaten or kicked to death. Sometimes the police would intervene; but sometimes they would stand by, letting the crowd vent its fury.[150] This anger was hardly the attitude needed to back a campaign against police violence. On the contrary, the public reacted by demanding tougher police actions against suspects.[151]

Nonetheless, President Sarney took several steps that were important, at least symbolically. One was to sign the Inter-American Convention for the Prevention and Punishment of Torture, which was part of a larger convention against torture and cruel, inhuman, or degrading punishment.[152] Ratification of these conventions would not bring the end of abuse and torture. Even the current constitution—a product of military government—required "all authorities to respect the moral and physical integrity of anyone detained or imprisoned" (article 153). Yet symbols and laws can be powerful in politics, especially when supported by a consensus. But even the most zealous reformers realized they were struggling against powerful social attitudes. An instructive case in point was provided by São Paulo, where PMDB Governor Franco Montoro's secretary of justice, José Carlos Dias, attempted to reform the state police and penal system by enforcing regulations against physical abuse. He soon encountered strong resistance among prison administrators and judges over his attempt to discipline guards guilty of torturing suspects or prisoners. In the end, Dias, one of the handful of criminal lawyers defending political prisoners at the height of the repression, lost. He was forced to resign, in the state that had probably the strongest campaign against police violence.[153]

Postscript: Economic Realities and Political Fallout

The eleven months since the conclusion of this chapter in July 1986 saw two key events: the November 1986 elections and the February 1987 suspension of interest payments on $68 billion of the foreign debt. The two were closely connected.

The PMDB scored a landslide in the November elections, winning 22 of the 23 governorships and gaining enough congressional seats to achieve an absolute majority in both houses. President Sarney's party, the PFL, did poorly, leaving the governing coalition even more unbalanced. The president's shaky political legitimacy was highlighted by the fact that the new Congress and governors had been elected directly, whereas he had been the choice of an electoral college for a term whose length was not even certain.

The PMDB's victory could be attributed in part to its continuing image as the party that had fought military government and to the fact that it had been able to sink roots at the local level, while the PDS grew steadily weaker. But the victory also reflected the public's approval of the Plano Cruzado, which they associated with Finance Minister Funaro, the PMDB, and the president, but not with the president's party.

Few voters could have known how deeply the Cruzado Plan was in trouble. With prices frozen and most wage income up, the Brazilian consumer had gone on a buying spree after February 1986. The government's "midcourse adjustments" in July failed to cool the overheated economy. Some policymakers urged the president to take tougher action. One needed step was devaluation of the overvalued cruzado. But the frozen cruzado exchange rate was a key symbol of the new economy for Sarney, who was basking in his post-Plano Cruzado popularity. The PMDB leaders were equally happy to draw political profit from the boom.

As we saw earlier, the New Republic had inherited a highly favorable balance of payments. For 1984 and 1985 Brazil had run unprecedentedly high trade surpluses of $13 billion and $12.4 billion, which covered the interest due on the foreign debt. By September, however, the trade surplus had begun shrinking, in part due to the boom. Soaring domestic demand diverted some export-designated production to home buyers. Exporters were also hit by shortages (auto parts being a prime example). At the same time, some imports rose, especially raw materials for industry. Brazil's foreign exchange reserves began to fall. Finally, the increasingly overvalued cruzado was hurting exports. It was suddenly clear that however much Sarney and Funaro wanted rapid growth, pressure from the balance of payments was going to slow it down.

The desire to win the November election led the government to delay most of the badly needed corrective measures. Foreign exchange reserves had already fallen from $8 billion to $5 billion. Less than a week after the election the government announced a package of tough measures, including greatly increased taxes on cigarettes and alcoholic beverages and sharply higher electricity, telephone, and postal rates. The intent was to cut $12 billion from consumer buying power. The public reaction was angry and Sarney's popularity plummeted in the polls.

The November economic measures would undoubtedly slow the economy and halt the slide in the balance of payments. But was it enough? In her 1982 balance of payments crisis Brazil, like most of debt-wracked Latin America, accepted IMF intervention as the price of getting the new loans necessary to service the old. Figueiredo and Delfim Neto were violently criticized then for having agreed to IMF tutelage.

Finance Minister Funaro was determined to avoid that path. He succeeded, but at a cost yet to be determined. In February 1987 President Sarney announced Brazil's suspension of interest payments on $68 billion of its foreign debt—the medium and long-term debt with U.S., Western European, and Japanese commercial banks. Payments on short-term commercial bank loans and on government and international agency loans (World Bank, Inter-American Development Bank, etc.) were to continue. Although Sarney's announcement included an emotional plea for national support, the Planalto tried to play down the gravity of the situation. Follow-up comments suggested the suspension might last only 90 days, yet no timetable was announced.

Funaro then upped the ante by announcing that Brazil would no longer negotiate with its commercial bank creditors. Henceforth it would negotiate only with governments. He quickly visited the U.S. and Western Europe, where he got polite but noncommittal responses from the principal governments (except the British, who made clear their displeasure).

The Brazilian public's response to the suspension was subdued. There was no burst of nationalist fervor, as there had been in 1959 when President Kubitschek broke off negotiations with the IMF. The public, preoccupied by the return of inflation (16.8 percent in January 1987), had heard so many warnings about the debt burden that Sarney's melodramatic announcement was an anticlimax.

Funaro had not had complete support within the government for his actions. Planning Minister Jõao Sayad was a permanent critic. He had favored more drastic measures in July 1986 and continued to argue for further steps as the balance of payments trouble emerged. In March 1987, soon after the debt payment suspension, Sayad was forced out, provoking an exchange of recriminations between his champions and those of Funaro. Sayad's departure, and the downgrading of the Planning Ministry, left the government perilously short of policy ideas. One month after the debt-payment suspension the government still had no clear plan either for directing the economy or managing the debt crisis. Annual interest rates were 600 percent, as inflationary expectations had returned with a vengeance. By late March, rumors of Funaro's impending resignation swirled through Brasília, as Sarney solicited leading businessmen for suggestions of economic policy changes.

In March, foreign creditor banks began to write down their Brazilian loans. Should the banks call in their short-term commercial credits, Brazil's foreign trade could be jeopardized. Even the World Bank, one of Brazil's most constant lenders, decided to delay disbursing $2 billion in loans until it saw evidence of a coherent policy. The longer the debt-payment suspension lasted, the greater the danger to Brazil's ability to borrow.

Management of the foreign debt was not the only problem area in Brazil's relations with the foreign sector. Direct foreign investment was another. The 1964 revolutionaries had considered increased foreign investment to be crucial, both to help in the balance of payments and to introduce new technology. In 1986, however, net foreign investment had turned negative, with profit remittance and capital remissions exceeding by $1.4 billion new investment entering Brazil.

The crisis over the debt and the negative flow of direct foreign investment threw into question the entire role of the foreign sector in Brazil's economy. It gave ammunition to the strong nationalists in the Constituent Assembly, which would soon be voting on constitutional provisions affecting foreign investment.

As the Sarney government struggled in June to formulate yet another economic plan, numerous other problems remained, including two of the social policy areas analyzed earlier in this chapter. Efforts at reform of the corporatist labor relations system faded, as Labor Minister Pazzianotto was absorbed in trying to fend off or help negotiate strikes. Most serious were the walkout by the dockworkers and a threat of similar action by petroleum workers in early March 1987. The paralysis on the docks was another source of danger for Brazil's exports. The navy intervened, sending its marines to occupy the docks. The petroleum workers' threatened walkout was equally serious, because so much of the nation's transportation was oil-powered. The army intervened there, occupying the refineries. In the midst of such pressures, neither the labor ministry, the unions, nor the politicians saw any immediate advantage in pushing to overhaul the labor relations framework that all had learned to manipulate.

The military's intervention in the strikes reawakened questions about the military's role in the New Republic. Army Minister Leônidas Pires Gonçalves blunted those fears by continuing his strong support for the Sarney government. The president in turn continued cultivating the higher military. Strong military backing would have been essential for any president at this stage, but it was even more important for Sarney, who lacked a powerful party or constituency support.

Progress on agrarian reform also lagged. Rural violence had subsided, or at least faded from the front page. And the equivalent of the many billions of dollars necessary to carry out the land distribution program adopted in 1986 would be very difficult to find, especially in view of the constant pressure from foreign creditors to reduce public expenditure.

Political attention in early 1987 was fixed on the Constituent Assembly (it was also the new Congress) elected the previous November. The need to write a constitution diverted attention of key party leadership from the Congress. It also underlined the incompleteness of Brazil's transition to a democratic regime. It had been fourteen years since newly inaugurated

President Geisel launched the liberalization process. That length of time could be seen as proof of the Brazilian political elite's skill at maneuvering around the shoals toward electoral democracy and the rule of law. But it also showed the same elite's unrivaled capacity for avoiding fundamental questions about socio-economic equity.

As the New Republic moved into its third year, it had neither fulfilled the hopes of its enthusiasts nor confirmed the fears of its critics. It was not a fully functioning democracy nor a launching pad for "subversives." It was another transition. The new constitution would offer clues about where Brazil was headed. But on that, political reality would be more important than juridical ideas. In the meantime, the Sarney government had its hands full in trying to deal with the economy, especially the balance of payments.

The fact is that the New Republic had been presented with the bill for the military government's second decade. Brazil had maintained high growth (until 1981) but only by running up a staggering foreign debt. In 1982 the seemingly endless new loans to pay interest on previous loans ran out. The resulting recession stripped the military government's economic record of its "miracle" status.

The bill to be paid was of a level to make any prudent banker shudder. Merely paying interest on its debt in 1985 caused Brazil to export capital at the rate of 5 percent of GDP. Few economists believe any developing country can long continue exporting capital at such a rate. Such "foreign aid" to the advanced industrial economies is bound to stir a reaction at home.

Two decades ago I ended a similar book on Brazilian politics by noting that Brazil's "growing foreign indebtedness" had been "a growing political liability for successive governments." From 1951 to 1964, I suggested, Brazil was "caught in a deepening 'credit crisis.' " I concluded that Brazil had been "unable to find a new method of financing her development once she had incurred a level of indebtedness that reached the maximum tolerance for her foreign creditors."

For a decade after 1964 the military governments seemed to have solved Brazil's credit crisis. The Castelo Branco government renegotiated the debt repayment schedule which had steadily worsened since the mid 1950s. The Costa e Silva and Médici regimes then benefited from successful export promotion and from the return of direct foreign investment. The 1973–74 oil shock hit Brazil hard, but a sharply increased capital inflow, primarily loans, paid the oil bill and permitted the country to maintain high growth. Even the 1979 oil shock did not immediately cripple Brazil. But the 1982 lending halt did. It plunged Brazil into a credit crisis from which it is yet to emerge.

One feature, however, was different from 1964. In the early 1960s coffee was still Brazil's prime export. By 1982 the majority of Brazil's exports were manufactures, whose prices and markets were more reliable. Rapid export growth helped to lift Brazil out of the 1982–83 recession but the resulting trade surpluses of 1984 and 1985 also misled Sarney's policymakers into thinking that Brazil's credit crisis was no longer immediate. They were disabused of that illusion in late 1986 when Brazil's foreign exchange reserves sank so low that zealous staff actually falsified the published trade data. When the Sarney government unilaterally suspended interest payments on commercial bank debt in February 1987 it took a step not even the left-lending Goulart had dared to take.

Given this grim scenario, what are the prospects for Brazil's continued economic development? In attempting to answer that question in 1967 I suggested that mobilizing resources requires three steps: (1) a sound technical assessment of the situation; (2) the selection of a strategy for action; (3) the construction of a reliable political base for the strategy adopted. Let us apply these steps to mid-1987 Brazil.

As for technical assessments, there can be few Third World countries whose economic development alternatives have been as well studied as Brazil's. The wealth of studies prepared by the Planning Ministry and by the relevant ministries and agencies are complemented by the detailed evaluations from multilateral agencies such as the World Bank and the Inter-American Development Bank. For the poverty-stricken Northeast, for example, any Brazilian government can turn to the detailed World Bank surveys of how better to meet basic human needs by government action. Furthermore, Brazil now (in contrast to 1964) has the institutions plus the skilled and experienced personnel to pursue economic development and to target its beneficiaries. To take another example, the sophisticated financial system is greatly more responsive than the rudimentary structure (which lacked even a central bank) the military inherited in 1964.

The second step involves selecting a development strategy. The military governments gave their technocratic policymakers virtual free rein. Their development strategy was neo-liberal. It continued the preceding emphasis on industrialization but with greater export promotion. Massive public investment was directed to infrastructure. Indexation was applied throughout the economy to neutralize the effects of inflation. This strategy also aimed at strongly encouraging foreign investment, which came primarily to the capital-intensive industrial sector. One result of this strategy was rapid industrial growth, especially in consumer durables. Another result was a widening in income inequality to the relative neglect of the poorest third of the population.

The MDB and the PMDB had, as we have seen, consistently attacked this strategy as short-sighted, discriminatory, undemocratic, and unjust. When the opposition reached power in 1985, however, their own strategy was far from clear. Tancredo formulated an eclectic strategy, which he did not survive to define in practice. While sounding nationalistic on the foreign debt, he chose a neo-liberal finance minister. That minister did not manage to remain in office through 1985. His successor unveiled the dramatic Plano Cruzado, a distinctly populist measure, with its sharp increase in urban wages and a freeze on prices. The debacle of the Plano Cruzado led Sarney to swing back toward orthodoxy, replacing Funaro with Luiz Carlos Bresser Pereira. Yet none of the New Republic's three finance ministers succeeded in establishing a coherent strategy for medium and long-term development.

This was hardly surprising. Tancredo and Sarney won the 1985 election on a coalition ticket, whose heterogeneity became obvious when the president turned out to be, not from the PMDB—the true opposition party— but from the PDS (via the PFL)—which could never have won a direct presidential election in 1985.

The Sarney government has been torn between neo-liberal and populist voices in attempting to formulate a development strategy. Given the divisions between the PFL and the PMDB, no easy resolution is likely. And the difficulty is compounded by the severe divisions within the PMDB itself. During the first half of 1987 the party repeatedly failed to agree on such a basic issue as the length of President Sarney's mandate (once the new constitution is adopted—presumably by the end of 1987), not to speak of key policy areas such as labor relations, agrarian reform, and foreign investment.

If a development strategy were to be adopted, there would remain the third step: building a political base to carry it out. The key is the PMDB, but its divisions over strategy reflect real divisions among leaders and their electorate. If the warring wings of the PMDB should split off to form new parties, as has been oft predicted, the basic problem would remain: how to articulate a centrist political force capable of governing effectively.

Unlike 1964, Brazil has little hope of soon receiving any net inflow of foreign capital. On the contrary, it must struggle to reduce the net outflow. If Brazil wishes to grow rapidly and also service its foreign debt, it will have to mobilize domestic savings on an unprecedented scale. How are the burdens of reduced consumption to be allocated?

Is there a political force in the center and center-left (which comprise the great majority of the electorate) ready and able to undertake the mobilization that such a policy will require? Can such mobilization be achieved in a democracy?

Brazil's only experience with mass-scale electoral democracy was from 1946 to 1964. That regime succumbed to an overthrow made possible by economic crisis, deepening political polarization, and a severe deficiency of political leadership. Twenty-three years later, can a new, stable, mass democracy be institutionalized? Can its leaders develop policies that will promote rapid economic growth and also raise the standard of living for Brazil's poorest? Can they find a way to live with Brazil's foreign lenders and investors?

The Brazil of 1987 is far from the "national security state" the military labored to implant. The older parties of the left—the PCB and the PC do B—are now legal, along with the PT, a larger and potentially far more powerful force. The radical nationalist arguments, which the military tried to extirpate, once again dominate much of university student politics and parts of the press. Student demonstrations and labor strikes—prime targets for military suppression after 1964—are once again commonplace.

Was the New Republic therefore a return to pre-1964? Clearly not. The Brazilians of 1987 have survived a traumatic passage. The physical and mental scars inflicted by the repression will not soon disappear, and the non-elite still face the threat of police abuse. That experience gave public life a sobriety that had often been missing in the politics of the early 1960s.

There is also a difference in attitudes toward electoral democracy. Many on the left, who before 1964 had contemptuously dismissed "bourgeois democracy," now praise it as an indispensable precondition for the recovery from authoritarianism. The higher military share this commitment, despite rumblings from dissenters whose future number will depend on the political stability of the New Republic. Virtually all those who in 1964 had thought democracy little more than an obstacle to higher goals now agree on the need to consolidate a new democratic order.

Brazil had been the first Latin American democracy to suffer a military coup in the 1960s, and it was one of the last to shed its authoritarian trappings. With an electorate larger than that of any country in Western Europe and a foreign debt larger than any in the Third World, the stakes are high in its new experiment with democracy.

NOTES

Chapter I: The Origins of the 1964 Revolution

1. Alberto Dines, et al., *Os idos de março e a queda em abril* (Rio de Janeiro: José Alvaro, 1964), 144.
2. The role of the U.S. government in the overthrow of João Goulart has been the subject of much speculation and debate. The radical nationalists argued that the U.S., using public and clandestine means, contributed significantly to the victory of Goulart's enemies. That is the view in Edmar Morel, *O golpe começou em Washington* (Rio de Janeiro: Editora Brasiliense, 1965). In an appendix to *Politics in Brazil, 1930–1964: An Experiment in Democracy* (New York: Oxford University Press, 1967), I discussed the evidence on the U.S. role as of January 1967. Subsequent publications have not caused me to revise significantly that interpretation. Subsequent research has shown how closely the U.S. government followed events and how important President Johnson and his aides considered Brazil to be. The best documented account of the U.S. role is Phyllis R. Parker, *Brazil and the Quiet Intervention, 1964* (Austin: University of Texas Press, 1979). For a Brazilian revelation of relevant documents from the Lyndon B. Johnson presidential library, see Marcos Sá Correa, *1964: Visto e comentado pela Casa Branca* (Pôrto Alegre: L & PM, 1977). For an attempt at broader interpretation of U.S. influence in Brazil, see Jan Knippers Black, *United States Penetration of Brazil* (Philadelphia: University of Pennsylvania Press, 1977).
3. In *Politics in Brazil,* I analyzed in detail the origins of the 1964 revolution, with extensive references to printed sources. There has since emerged a vast literature on the subject. The additional works cited in this chapter are merely examples of this literature on specific topics.
4. It is perhaps fitting that Castelo Branco's first biographer was an American. For an assiduous if unimaginative work, see John W.F. Dulles, *Castello Branco: The Making of a Brazilian President* (College Station: Texas A&M University Press, 1978), which is devoted to Castelo's life before be became president. His presidency is covered in Dulles, *President Castello Branco: Brazilian Reformer* (College Station: Texas A&M University Press, 1980).
5. The changing political views of the Brazilian military are analyzed skillfully in

311

Alfred Stepan, *The Military in Politics: Changing in Patterns in Brazil* (Princeton: Princeton University Press, 1971). John Markoff and Silvio R. Duncan Baretta, "Professional Ideology and Military Activism in Brazil: Critique of a Thesis of Alfred Stepan," *Comparative Politics,* XVII, No. 2 (January 1985), 175–91, make a convincing critique of the overall logic of Stepan's analysis, but for purposes of this exposition Stepan's description of the patterns of officer behavior remains valid.

6. For an analysis of 20th century Brazilian history which puts the 1964 coup into context, see Peter Flynn, *Brazil: A Political Analysis* (Boulder: Westview Press, 1978).

7. The era begun by the Revolution of 1930 is gaining rich documentation from the archive and publications of the Centro de Pesquisa e Documentação de História Contemporânea do Brasil (CPDOC) in Rio de Janiero. The Center is the depository of a growing body of personal archives and oral histories from principal figures of the post-1930 era. Among its publications on Getúlio are: Valentina de Rocha Lima, ed., *Getúlio: uma história oral* (Rio de Janeiro: Editora Record, 1986); Ana Ligia Silva Medeiros and Maria Celina Soares D'Araújo, eds., *Vargas e os anos cinqüenta: bibliografia* (Rio de Janeiro: Fundação Getúlio Vargas, 1983); and Adelina Maria Alves Novaes e Cruz, et al., eds., *Impasse na democracia brasileira, 1951–1955: coletânea de documentos* (Rio de Janeiro: Fundação Getúlio Vargas, 1983). For one of the most widely read interpretations of the half-century following the 1930 Revolution, see Luiz Bresser Pereira, *Development and Crisis in Brazil, 1930–1983* (Boulder: Westview Press, 1984).

8. *O Estado de São Paulo,* January 12, 1954.

9. For an excellent study of the UDN, see Maria Victoria de Mesquita Benevides, *A UDN e o udenismo: ambigüidades do liberalismo brasileiro, 1945–1965* (Rio de Janeiro: Paz e Terra, 1981). There is also a good study of the PSD in Lucia Hippolito, *De raposas e reformistas: o PSD e a experiência democrática brasileira, 1945–64* (Rio de Janeiro: Paz e Terra, 1985).

10. The manifesto is reprinted in Bento Munhoz da Rocha Netto, *Radiografia de Novembro,* 2nd ed. (Rio de Janeiro: Civilização Brasileira, 1961), 118–19.

11. The text of the letter is reprinted in Afonso César, *Política, cifrão e sangue: documentário do 24 de Agosto,* 2nd ed. (Rio de Janeiro: Editorial Andes, 1956), 219–20.

12. This relatively unstudied chapter in labor history is analyzed in José Alvaro Moisés, *Greve de massa e crise política* (São Paulo: Editora Polis, 1978).

13. Cesar, *Política, cifrão e sangue,* 121–24.

14. The manifesto is reprinted in Mário Victor, *Cinco anos que abalaram o Brasil* (Rio de Janeiro: Civilização Brasileira, 1965), 347–48.

15. *Brasil 1960: Situação, recursos, possibilidades* (Guanabara: Ministério da Relações Exteriores, 1960), 725.

16. Franz-Wilhelm Heimer, "Education and Politics in Brazil," *Comparative Education Review,* XIX, No. 1 (February 1975), 51–67.

17. For a clear explanation of the origins of Brazil's labor relations system, see Kenneth Paul Erickson, *The Brazilian Corporative State and Working-Class Politics* (Berkeley: University of California Press, 1977). Data on the real minimum wage in Guanabara from 1952 to 1964 are given in *Programa de ação econômica do governo: 1964–1966* (Rio de Janeiro: Ministério de Planeja-

mento e Coordenação Econômica, 1964), 86; and in São Paulo in Paulo Renato Souza, *O que são empregos e salários* (São Paulo: Brasiliense, 1981), 57.

18. Donald E. Syvrud, *Foundations of Brazilian Economic Growth* (Stanford: Hoover Institution Press, 1974), 183.

19. The most complete analysis of the Goulart presidency is Moniz Bandeira, *O governo João Goulart: as lutas sociais no Brasil: 1961–1964* (Rio de Janeiro: Civilização Brasileira, 1977), which draws on unpublished materials in private archives, as well as interviews with principal actors. The author is sympathetic to Goulart and emphasizes the role of foreign, i.e. U.S., pressure, both economic and political, against Goulart's government. The latter is also analyzed in my *Politics in Brazil*. For a detailed analysis of the economic problems facing Goulart and how his inability to meet them contributed to his fall, see Michael Wallerstein, "The Collapse of Democracy in Brazil: Its Economic Determinants," *Latin American Research Review*, XV, No. 3 (1980), 3–40, and the accompanying comment by Werner Baer.

20. Articles 88 and 89 provided for the impeachment (by the Chamber of Deputies) and trial (before the Federal Supreme Court or the Federal Senate, depending on the nature of the charges). For an edition of all Brazil's national constitutions from 1824 to the Constitution of 1967 (with its 25 amendments as of November 28, 1985), see Senado Federal, Subsecretaria de Edições Técnicas, *Constituições do Brasil* (Brasília: Senado Federal, 1986), 2 vols. The second volume is a highly useful index by topic to all the constitutions (and amendments).

21. The most exhaustive inquiry into the role of IPES in Goulart's overthrow is René Armand Dreifuss, *1964: a conquista do estado* (Petrópolis: Vozes, 1981). The author's interesting analysis is at times overshadowed by rigid theorizing and excessive detail. Helosia Maria Murgel Starling, *Os senhores das Gerais: os novos inconfidentes e o golpe de 1964* (Petrópolis: Vozes, 1986), which studies the Minas Gerais conspirators, and Solange de Deus Simões, *Deus, patria e familia: as mulheres no golpe de 1964* (Petrópolis: Vozes, 1985), on the role of women marchers in the anti-Goulart demonstrations, both follow Dreifuss's approach.

22. In fact, the Brazilian political system had deteriorated into paralysis, as is shown clearly in Wanderley Guilherme dos Santos, *Sessenta e quatro: anatomia da crise* (Sao Paulo: Editora Vertice, 1986).

23. This fragmentation of the left is described in greater detail in Skidmore, *Politics in Brazil*, 276–84.

Chapter II: Castelo Branco: Cleaning House—April 1964–March 1965

1. These phrases are from the manifesto sent out on March 30 by Army Chief of Staff Castelo Branco to start the military rebellion against the Goulart government; Luis Viana Filho, *O governo Castelo Branco* (Rio de Janeiro: José Olympio, 1975), 3.

2. These events are described in Auro Moura Andrade, *Um congreso contra o arbítrio: diários e memórias, 1961–1967* (Rio de Janeiro: Nova Fronteira, 1985), 240–47.

3. This dimension of the Brazilian military's role in politics is analyzed in Stepan,

The Military in Politics. For a historiographical review of research on the military, see Edmundo Campos Coelho, "A instituição militar no Brasil," *BIB,* No. 19 (1st semester, 1985), 5–19. Sources on the hard line are difficult to come by. One of the best examples of their anticommunist thinking is Pedro Brasil (pseud.), *Livro branco sôbre a guerra revolucionário no Brasil* (Pôrto Alegre: O Globo, 1964), a pamphlet written in the format of a military staff paper and published just before the coup of 1964. Transcripts of the innumerable trials before military tribunals after 1964 would be an excellent source, although they are, to my knowledge, unavailable to the public. Examples of the thinking behind such trials may be found in Inquérito Policial Militar 709, *O comunismo no Brasil,* 4 vols. (Rio de Janeiro: Biblioteca do Exército, 1966–67). One of the most stimulating analyses of the Brazilian military's new role was Guillermo A. O'Donnell, *Modernization and Bureaucratic–Authoritarianism:* Studies in South American Politics (Berkeley: Institute of International Studies, 1973), which compares Brazil with Argentina's 1966 coup. For a comprehensive review of O'Donnell's ideas, as seen in the light of later Latin American development, see David Collier, ed., *The New Authoritarianism in Latin America* (Princeton: Princeton University Press, 1979).

4. The text of the Act is reprinted in Alberto Dines, et al., *Os idos de março e a queda em abril* (Rio de Janeiro: José Alvaro, 1964), 401–3, and its provisions are analyzed in Ronald M. Schneider, *The Political System of Brazil: Emergence of a "Modernizing" Authoritarian Regime, 1964–1970* (New York: Columbia University Press, 1971), 127. For an attempt to fit the "institutional acts" into the Brazilian legal system, see Jessé Torres Pereira Júnior, "Os atos institucionais em face do direito administrativo," *Revista Brasileira de Estudos Políticos,* No. 47 (July 1978), 77–114.

5. The best "inside" portrait of the Castelo Branco government is Viana Filho, *O Governo Castelo Branco.* Viana Filho was a close collaborator of the president as the head of the Civilian Presidential Staff. A valuable ongoing commentary on events in this period may be found in Carlos Castello Branco (a very distant relation), *Os militares no poder* (Rio de Janeiro: Editora Nova Fronteira, 1976), which is a collection of Castello Branco's widely esteemed daily political columns in the *Jornal do Brasil.* For the acerbic views of an army general who had been a leader of the anti-Goulart revolt in Minas Gerais but who later had little good to say about either Castelo Branco or Costa e Silva, see Olympio Mourão Filho, *Memórias: a verdade de um revolucionário* (Pôrto Alegre: L & PM, 1978). Among the earlier general accounts of Brazil since 1964, the most useful are Schneider, *The Political System of Brazil,* which emphasizes the political narrative and gives much detail on political alignments among the military, and Georges-André Fiechter, *Le Régime modernisateur du Brésil, 1964–1972* (Geneva: Institut Universitaire de Hautes Etudes Internationales, 1972), which has been translated into both English and Portuguese. Fiechter attempts to include more socio-economic analysis in his survey. The similarity of titles reveals an interesting convergence of foreign thinking about Brazil. Carlos Chagas, *A guerra das estrelas, 1964–1984: os bastidores das sucessões presidenciais* (Porto Alegre: L & PM, 1985) is a leading journalist's memoir-cum-narrative of presidential politics from Castelo Branco to Figueiredo. For a sympathetic portrait of the Castelo Branco presidency by a U.S. historian, see John W.F. Dulles, *President Castello Branco: Brazilian Reformer* (College Station: Texas A&M Press, 1980). One of the most original attempts by a

Brazilian social scientist to come to grips with the new government was Candido Mendes, "Sistema política e modelos de poder no Brasil," *Dados,* No. 1 (1966), 7–41. Also useful is the chronology in Luisa Maria Gaspar Gomes, "Cronologia de govêrno Castelo Branco," *Dados,* Nos. 2/3 (1967), 112–32. A very careful political analysis of the Castelo Branco presidency can be found in James Rowe, "The "Revolution" and the "System": Notes on Brazilian Politics," American Universities Field Staff Reports, East Coast South American Series, XII, Nos. 3–5 (1966); and his "Brazil Stops the Clock: Part I: "Democratic Formalism' Before 1964 and in the Elections of 1966," *ibid.,* XIII No. 1 (1967); and his "Brazil Stops the Clock: Part II: The New Constitution and the New Model," *ibid.,* XIII, No. 2 (1967). For a useful chronicle of the 1964–67 period see José Wamberto, *Castelo Branco, revolução e democracia* (Rio de Janeiro, 1970). The author was Castelo Branco's press secretary. Very valuable also is Peter Flynn, *Brazil: A Political Analysis* (Boulder: Westview Press, 1978), chap. 9, which covers the years 1964–67. The present chapter expands on my earlier analysis of the 1964–65 period in Skidmore, *Politics in Brazil, 1930–1964* (New York, 1967), 303–21; and Skidmore, "Politics and Economic Policy Making in Authoritarian Brazil, 1937–71," in Alfred Stepan, ed., *Authoritarian Brazil* (New Haven: Yale University Press, 1973), 3–46.

6. Castelo Branco's career before becoming president is the subject of a volume by John W.F. Dulles, *Castello Branco: The Making of a Brazilian President.*

7. We owe our understanding of these alignments within the military to Stepan, *The Military in Politics,* 229–48.

8. Dulles, *President Castello Branco,* 19.

9. Here and in subsequent chapters I discuss the membership of presidential cabinets not because of the political and policymaking importance of all cabinet members, but because their having been selected can give valuable clues to a government's political and policymaking intentions. The reader should also note that not all cabinet changes will be mentioned.

10. The thinking of Bulhões is spelled out in Octávio Gouvéia de Bulhões, *Dois conceitos de lucro* (Rio de Janeiro: APEC Editora, 1969).

11. Campos was not shy about replying to his critics. Speeches given while he was Planning Minister are included in Roberto de Oliveira Campos, *Política econômica e mitos políticos* (Rio de Janeiro, 1965). Articles published after he left office, often commenting on his policies and those of his successors, were collected in *Do outro lado da cêrca* (Rio de Janeiro, 1967); *Ensaios contra a maré* (Rio de Janeiro, 1969); with Mária Henrique Simonsen, *A nova economia brasileira* (Rio de Janeiro, 1974); with Mário Henrique Simonsen, *Formas criativas no desenvolvimento brasileiro* (Rio de Janeiro, 1975); *O mundo que vejo e não desejo* (Rio de Janeiro, 1976), and other volumes.

12. Cordeiro de Farias's long career has been explored in the form of an oral history: Aspásia Camargo and Walder de Goes, *Meio século de combate: diálogo com Cordeiro de Farias* (Rio de Janeiro: Nova Fronteira, 1981).

13. Only one chapter of Dreifuss, *1964: A conquista do estado,* is devoted to IPES/IBAD influence in the Castelo Branco government.

14. The best brief overview of this repression is given in Maria Helena Moreira Alves, *State and Opposition in Military Brazil* (Austin: University of Texas Press, 1985), 34–38. This book systematically analyzes the "natural security state" created in law and in practice after 1964. It is indispensable for any study of this period. The most complete inventory of denunciations of torture in

1964–65 is found in Márcio Moreira Alves, *Torturas e torturados* (Rio de Janeiro: Idade Nova, 1966), and in Alves, *A Grain of Mustard Seed: The Awakening of the Brazilian Revolution* (Garden City, New York: Anchor Books, 1973), 78–87. For an account of the aftermath of the coup in Recife, see Paulo Cavalcanti, *O caso eu conto, como o caso foi* (São Paulo: Alfa–Omega, 1978), 337–72. Cavalcanti was a longtime leftist political activist and literary historian. Alves's reporting laid greatest stress on the Northeast. We await a comprehensive survey of immediate post-coup repression across Brazil. For a highly useful inventory of the left in the 1960s, including those that chose the armed path after 1964, see Daniel Aarão Reis Filho and Jair Ferreira de Sá, *Imagens da revolução: documentos políticos das organizações clandestinas de esquerda dos anos 1961–1971* (Rio de Janeiro: Marco Zero, 1985). One widely read student of the 1964 revolution and its aftermath notes that "the repression was less violent than was feared in view of the conditions ruling at the time. It was violent enough partially to satisfy the hard-line officers and must have brought at least some of them to the notice of Brazilians throughout the country," Georges-André Fiechter, *Brazil Since 1964: Modernization Under a Military Regime* (New York: John Wiley & Sons, 1975), 44. Fiechter leaves the reader to guess at what "was feared," as well what "brought to the notice of" might mean. Several authors who have written at length on 1964 make no mention of the mass arrests and abuse of detainees in the weeks after the 1964 coup. Such is the case with Peter Flynn, *Brazil: A Political Analysis,* and John W.F. Dulles, *President Castello Branco.*

15. The continuing accounts of torture in the *Correio da Manhã* and *Ultima Hora* had concerned the Castelo Branco government, but not enough to prompt any action. That changed in mid-September when word came of the death of an army sergeant, Manuel Alves de Oliveira. He died in early May in an army hospital in the state of Rio de Janeiro. He was said to have died from tortures inflicted while he·was a prisoner in his own unit. Numerous officers who had been indifferent to the abuse of civilian prisoners were now worried that torture might have infected their institution, which would signal a dangerous breakdown in military discipline. President Castelo Branco immediately ordered General Ernesto Geisel, head of the Military Presidential Staff and one of Castelo's most trusted collaborators, to investigate these charges on the spot in Recife, Salvador, Rio de Janeiro, Sáo Paulo, and Fernando de Noronha (an island off the Northeast coast where prisoners were held). Geisel reported back that the charges were groundless, except in Recife. Because Geisel did not begin his inquiry until mid-September, he reached Recife months after the height of the repression. Furthermore, the reader might justifiably doubt that any such inquiry entrusted to a military subordinate would produce findings likely to embarrass higher authority. Luís Viana Filho vigorously defends the Geisel report (never published), noting that it found no torture, except in Recife, which Viana Filho called "lamentable incidents in a disorganized period, which was soon restored to legality," Viana Filho, *O ğoverno Castelo Branco,* 139–41. The President used similar language in his October 30 press conference, saying that most reports were exaggerated or deceptive and that the few confirmed cases "almost all dated from the first days of the Revolution," Humberto de Alencar Castelo Branco, *Entrevistas: 1964–1965* (Rio de Janeiro: Departamento de Imprensa Nacional, 1966), 31. A civilian commission, appointed by the Fourth Army Commander to investigate charges of

mistreatment of political prisoners in Recife, reported in early October that they could confirm four cases of prisoners having suffered physical violence. Their report was published in Moreira Alves, *Torturas,* 65–80. None of the military and police involved were ever tried or punished.

16. In its early months the Castelo Branco government had promised to issue a "white paper" documenting the corruption and subversion against which the Revolution had been waged. President Castelo Branco referred to it in an interview on May 14, 1964. Castelo Branco, *Entrevistas: 1964–1965,* 23. As the months passed, the government saw increasing difficulties in compiling such a document, as the sins of corruption and (to a lesser extent) cooperating with subversion were not unknown among some luminaries of the Revolution. Soon the white paper became a dead letter.

17. There has been considerable confusion over how many Brazilians were hit by punitive actions of the military governments. The total of 441 for the 60-day period under the Institutional Act is taken from Edmar Morel, *O golpe começou em Washington* (Rio de Janeiro: Civilização Brasileira, 1965), 248–59. Morel was one of those hit. A total of 378 was given in a feature story in *Correio da Manhã,* April 1, 1965. The most detailed analysis of the use of punitive powers is Marcus Faria Figueiredo, *Política de coerção no sistema político brasileiro* (Rio de Janeiro: Comissão Nacional de Justiça e Paz, 1978). By including forced retirements and dismissals not carried out under explicit authority of the Institutional Act, Figueiredo finds a total of 2,985 punished in 1964. Another researcher, drawing on unpublished data in the air force ministry, lists the civil service dismissals as 1,408 in 1964 and the purge of military officers as totaling 1,200 in 1964. Maria Helena Moreira Alves, *Estado e oposição no Brasil, 1964–1984* (Petrópolis: Vozes, 1984), 63–65. Dulles gives a total of 4,454 forced retirements during the six-month life of Article 7 of the Institutional Act, i.e., up to October 9, 1964, comprised of 1,697 civilians and 2,757 members of the military (*President Castello Branco,* 79).

18. The military governments after 1964 never gave any official justification for the individuals who were hit by the successive Institutional Acts. All analysis, including mine, is speculative. The blow to the FNP is noted in Schneider, *The Political System of Brazil,* 127–28. The targeting of the FNP is spelled out in unmistakable terms in Glaucio Ary Dillon Soares, "La cancelación de los mandatos de parlamentarios en Brasil," *Revista Mexicana de Sociologia,* XLII, No. 1 (January–March 1980), 267–86.

19. Castelo Branco told U.S. Ambassador Lincoln Gordon at the time that suspending Kubitschek's rights was, as Gordon recalled, "both a political necessity and an act fully justified by the record, but he said that it would 'embarrass the nation' to publish that record in full." Letter of Lincoln Gordon to Luiz Viana Filho, July 27, 1972, in the Arquivo Humberto de Alencar Castelo Branco (Centro de Pesquisa e Documentação de História Contemporanea do Brasil–Fundação Getúlio Vargas, Rio de Janeiro). Speaking to the Higher War College in late 1966, Castelo argued that starting in 1956 (when Kubitschek began his presidential term) there had been "a policy of gradual internal destruction along with an external demoralization of the country, which was completely contrary to the interests of the people." Castelo Branco, *Discursos: 1966,* 80. Despite the frequent charges of corruption against former President Kubitschek, no post-1964 government produced any evidence to substantiate such charges.

20. Kubitschek's version of the events leading up to his cassation is given in a September 1964 interview in Madrid, reprinted in Osvaldo Orico, *Confissões do exílio–JK* (Rio de Janeiro: F. Alves, 1977).

21. Planning Minister Roberto Campos, once a high official in the Kubitschek government, was the only dissenter from the National Security Council decision to deprive Kubitschek of his political rights. Campos offered his resignation, which was not accepted. He retained his post. Dulles, *President Castello Branco*, 38.

22. Dulles, *President Castello Branco*, 32–44; Viana Filho, *O Governo Castelo Branco*, 94–96.

23. The logic behind these military purges is explained in Stepan, *The Military in Politics*, chap. 10. Figueiredo, *Política de coerção*, gives data by principal governmental phase. The 1964 data are given in greatest detail in Morel, *O golpe*, 248–59.

24. For an analysis of these newspapers, see Stepan, *The Military in Politics*, 57–121. The arbitrary actions–purges, tortures–of the military junta and then of the Castelo Branco government quickly aroused criticism in the press. A collection of such criticisms has been published in Thereza Cesario Alvim, ed., *O golpe de 64: a imprensa disse não* (Rio de Janeiro: Civilização Brasileira, 1979).

25. Alberto Venancio Filho, *Notícia histórica da Ordem dos Advogados do Brasil: 1930–1980* (Rio do Janeiro: OAB, 1982), 132. It should be noted that as early as October 1964 the Bar's Federal Council had begun to discuss what it considered illegal actions by the new government (*ibid.*, 133).

26. The bishops' document is reprinted in Luiz Gonzaga de Souza Lima, *Evolução política dos católicos e da igreja no brasil* (Petrópolis: Vozes, 1979), 147–49. For a discussion of its context, see Thomas C. Bruneau, *The Political Transformation of the Brazilian Catholic Church* (Cambridge: Cambridge University Press, 1974), 120–22. The activists being defended were from *Ação Católica* and *Movimento de Educação de Base* (MEB). The reaction of the younger Catholic activists was described to me by Father Tibor Sulik, interview in Rio de Janeiro, June 9, 1983, and by Frei Betto, interview in São Paulo, June 30, 1983.

27. The *Revista Civilização Brasileira* first appeared in March 1965. Its principal editor was Ênio Silveira, director of the publishing house Editoria Civilização Brasileira. The *Revista*'s first issue announced that the journal's focus was to be on Brazil's national interests, "but it will not be limited by a sentimentalistic and narrow nationalism, nor will it slip into the geopolitical schema or the continental strategic planning which the State Department and the Pentagon promote and which some of our national politicians put into action." The relative moderation of this statement suggests that the left still felt cautious even a year after Goulart's overthrow. The article on "cultural terrorism" was published on pages 239–97 and the statement of the magazine's principles was on pages 3–4, both in *Revista Civilização Brasileira*, I (March 1965).

28. Cony's columns were published in Carlos Heitor Cony, *O ato e o fato: crônicos políticos* (Rio de Janeiro: 1964), and Alves's in Márcio Moreira Alves, *A velha classe* (Rio de Janeiro: Editora Arte Nova, 1964). For a collection of articles by these and other critics, see Alvim, ed., *O golpe de 64*.

29. Alceu Amoroso Lima, *Revolução, reação ou reforma?* (Rio de Janeiro: Tempo Brasileiro: 1964), 224; 232. For a multi-authored volume evaluating Amoroso Lima's important role in Brazilian culture, including the repressive era of the

1960s and 1970s, see Francisco de Assis Barbosa, ed., *Alceu Amoroso Lima, memorando dos 90* (Rio: Nova Fronteira, 1984).

30. This was the theme of Morel, *O golpe.*

31. The U.S. involvement in the coup has been given its most complete documentation and analysis in Phyllis R. Parker, *Brazil and the Quiet Intervention, 1964* (Austin: University of Texas Press, 1979). My quotations of Johnson are taken from page 85. The author mined official documents in the Kennedy and Johnson presidential libraries, as well as gaining interviews with such key U.S. participants as former Ambassador Lincoln Gordon and former U.S. Military Attaché General Vernon Walters. Important documents from the Johnson Library have been published in Portuguese in Marcos Sá Corrêa, *1964 visto e comentado pela casa branca* (Pôrto Alegre: L & PM. Editores, 1977). U.S. support for the new Brazilian government is placed in the context of post-1945 U.S.–Brazilian relations in Robert Wesson, *The United States and Brazil: Limits of Influence* (New York: Praeger, 1981).

32. This is my translation of a passage form the Portuguese text published in *O Estado de São Paulo,* May 4, 1964.

33. Dulles, *President Castello Branco,* 19; Lincoln Gordon later said he was so shocked by the (first) Institutional Act that he almost withdrew to Washington but didn't because of his confidence that Castelo Branco (the consensus candidate about to be elected) "would use his arbitrary powers with restraint and guide the nation back to constitutional legitimacy within a few months." Gordon letter (July 27, 1972) to Viana Filho, Castelo Branco Archive.

34. Humberto de Alencar Castelo Branco, *Discursos: 1964* (Rio de Janeiro: Secretaria da Imprensa, n.d.), 14.

35. The literature on Brazil's post-1964 stabilization policies is extensive. Among the studies favorable to government efforts are: Alexandre Kafka, "The Brazilian Stabilization Program, 1964–66," *Journal of Political Economy,* 75 (August 1967), 596–631; the chapters by Howard S. Ellis, Mário Henrique Simonsen, and Octávio de Gouvéia Bulhões in Howard S. Ellis, ed., *The Economy of Brazil* (Berkeley: University of California Press, 1969). The most detailed analysis sympathetic to the Castelo Branco government is Mário Henrique Simonsen, *Inflação: gradualismo x tratamento de choque* (Rio de Janeiro: APEC, 1970). The most penetrating critical analysis of the 1964–67 policies is Albert Fishlow, "Some Reflections on Post-1964 Brazilian Economic Policy." Fishlow emphasizes the relatively rigid orthodox monetarist assumptions of the Campos-Bulhões approach. For an excellent overview that puts the Castelo Branco policies in a larger context, see Werner Baer and Isaac Kerstenetzky. "The Brazilian Economy in the Sixties," in Riordan Roett, ed., *Brazil in the Sixties* (Nashville: Vanderbilt University Press, 1972). A representative left-wing criticism of government economic policy during the Castelo Branco presidency was Cibilis da Rocha Viana, *Estratégia do desenvolvimento brasileiro: uma política nacionalista para vencer a atual crise económica* (Rio de Janeiro: Civilização Brasileira, 1967). A milder critique, which appeared in the press during the 1964–66 period, was published in book form: Antonio Dias Leite, *Caminhos do desenvolvimento* (Rio de Janeiro: Zahar Editores, 1966). Dias Leite was the best-known of the "moderate" critics and later became minister of mines in the Costa e Silva government. For a view that paralleled the thinking of the economic policymakers who came to power with the Costa e Silva government (and who disputed the economic diagnosis of the Castelo

Branco policymakers), see Samuel A. Morley, "Inflation and Stagnation in Brazil," *Economic Development and Cultural Change*, XIX, No. 2 (January 1971), 184–203. Many of the ideas and personnel for economic policymaking in the Castelo Branco period came from the Instituto de Pesquisas Estudos Sociais-Guanabara (IPES-GB), a business-sponsored pressure group in Rio de Janeiro. Campos had been closely associated with the group before taking office. Norman Blume, "Pressure Groups and Decision-Making in Brazil," *Studies in Comparative International Development*, III, No. 11 (1967–68). Blume stresses the differences between the IPES groups in Rio and São Paulo. The latter had virtually no influence in the government. IPES influence was also confirmed by Stepan, *The Military in Politics*, 186–87. The most ambitious claim for the influence of IPES (and a similarly minded political group, IBAD) is Dreifuss, *1964: a conquista do estado*, which is primarily on the period before the 1964 coup.

36. Ministério de Planejamento e Coordenação Econômica, *Programa de ação econômica do govêrno, 1964–66* (Rio de Janeiro, 1964).

37. Ministério de Planejamento, *Programa*, 35. There was an implication that the "residual" rate might remain at 10 percent. The 1963 and 1964 figures are from Fishlow, "Some Reflections on Economic Policy," 72. For a detailed analysis of monetary policy in the Castelo Branco period, see Syvrud, *Foundations of Brazilian Economic Growth*, which includes a wealth of data. Syvrud was a treasury department representative in the U.S. embassy in Rio from 1965 to 1969. His evaluation is favorable to the relatively orthodox approach of the Campos-Bulhões stabilization policy. For an excellent analysis of Brazilian monetary policy from a comparative viewpoint, see Alejandro Foxley, "Stabilization Policies and Stagflation: The Cases of Brazil and Chile," in *World Development*, VIII, No. 11 (November 1980), 887–921.

38. This figure is taken from Fishlow, "Some Reflections on Post-1964 Brazilian Economic Policy," 72.

39. For a favorable account of the institutional reforms carried out by the Castelo Branco government, see Mário Henrique Simonsen's "A imaginação reformistia," chapter 6 in Simonsen and Roberto de Oliveria Campos, *A nova economia brasileira* (Rio de Janeiro, 1974).

40. Syvrud, *Foundations of Brazilian Economic Growth*, 59–81.

41. To discuss this question is to step onto the always treacherous soil of "historical inevitables." All five anti-inflation programs attempted in Brazil over the preceding decade had been abandoned by the president. One of the key reasons was the high political cost the governments would have had to pay if they continued the programs. Roberto Campos, obviously not an impartial judge in this matter, argued in 1969 that no elected government could have carried out the PAEG. Roberto Campos, *Temas e sistemas* (Rio de Janeiro: APEC, 1969), 282–87. It would certainly be fair to conclude that given the layout of political forces in 1964, there was no potential government that could have met this test. The Dantas-Furtado plan of 1962–63 had been the last such hope. Recent research has cast doubt on the argument that democratic regimes have been unable to carry out stabilization programs. In "The Politics of Economic Stabilization: IMF Standby Programs in Latin America, 1954–1985," *Comparative Politics*, XIX, No. 1 (October 1986), 1–24, Karen Remmer argues from a comparison of nine countries over 31 years that the democracies were (slightly) more likely to fulfill IMF standby agreements. Her argument does not apply to

my foregoing analysis, since several of Brazil's failed stabilization attempts did not involve an IMF standby agreement.

42. Keith Rosenn, "Adaptations of the Brazilian Income Tax to Inflation," *Stanford Law Review*, XXI, No. 1 (November 1968), 58–105.

43. Werner Baer, *The Brazilian Economy: Growth and Development* (New York: Praeger, 1983), 244.

44. For a historical account of the introduction of indexation, see Simonsen, *Inflação*, 183–88. For an account that carries the story up to 1973, see Werner Baer and Paul Beckerman, "Indexing in Brazil," *World Development*, II, Nos. 1–12 (October–December 1974), 35–47. For another account of that period, which stresses how much of the indexation system could be and was manipulated by the government, see Albert Fishlow, "Indexing Brazilian Style: Inflation Without Tears?" *Brookings Papers on Economic Activity* (1974, 1), 261–82. Ten years later Roberto Campos reflected on the Castelo Branco government's resort to indexation: "Given that chronic inflation had created the strong belief that prices would go up forever, monetary correction was a way of controlling that expectation and preventing a disruptive impact on other sectors of the economy." Mário Henrique Simonsen and Roberto de Oliveira Campos, *Formas criativas no desenvolvimento brasileiro* (Rio de Janeiro: APEC, 1975), 68. For an account of how indexation developed during subsequent military governments, see Peter T. Knight, "Brazil: Deindexation and Economic Stabilization" (paper prepared at the World Bank: December 2, 1983).

45. Based on the author's interviews with officials of the International Monetary Fund and the World Bank in October 1971 and September 1977. In Brazil's protracted negotiations with the IMF in early 1983 the question of indexation's role in propagating inflation was hotly debated. For a comparative analysis of the function of indexation in Brazil, Chile, Argentina, and Colombia, see Gustav Donald Jud, *Inflation and the Use of Indexing in the Developing Countries* (New York: Praeger, 1978).

46. Syvrud, *Foundations of Brazilian Economic Growth*, 130.

47. Fishlow, "Some Reflections on Economic Policy," 72.

48. After its first year in office the Castelo Branco government took great pride in the relative success of the stabilization program and the extensive reorganization of the public sector. The president and Planning Minister Campos had constantly called for a return to "rational" policies. They saw themselves as guiding Brazil back to a "realistic" understanding of her own potential and of the rate at which it could be developed. (See, for example, Campos's stern lectures to businessmen in late 1964 and early 1965. Campos, *Politica econômica e mitos politicos.*) One observer, in summing up the Castelo Branco "model of development," noted that it emphasized the increased ties to the United States and the other capitalist nations and that it expressed a lower level of expectations regarding primarily Brazilian solutions to certain key problems." Rowe, "Brazil Stops the Clock: Part II," p. 8. The targets for the government's attack were the populist politicians who had allegedly misled the country by promising more than the economy could produce, while managing government policy incompetently. Furthermore, it was alleged, these politicians had threatened the basis of the market economy—private property and foreign investment. Goulart and his government were the most immediate symbol of this "irresponsibility." Attacks on the deposed president were a

constant refrain in the Castelo Branco government's claim to legitimacy. (See, for example, the president's speech of December 22, 1965, Castelo Branco, *Discursos: 1965,* 109–23.)

49. One leading Brazilian economist, later to be finance minister in the Geisel government, argued that the failure of the Kubitschek stabilization attempt was crucial: "It was in 1959 that Brazilian inflation really broke into a gallop, the proximate cause being the government's abandonment of a promising program for monetary stabilization." Mário Henrique Simonsen, "Brazilian Inflation: Postwar Experience and Outcome of the 1964 Reforms," in *Economic Development Issues: Latin America* [Committee for Economic Development Supplementary Paper No. 21] (New York, August 1967), 267.

50. Syvrud, *Foundations,* 95–107.

51. For analyses of the distortions in resource allocation introduced by inflation, see Werner Baer, "Brazil: Inflation and Economic Efficiency," *Economic Development and Cultural Change,* XI, No. 4 (July 1963), 395–406; Werner Baer and Mário Henrique Simonsen, "Profit Illusion and Policy Making in an Inflationary Economy," *Oxford Economic Papers,* XVII, No. 2 (July 1965), 279–90; and Werner Baer, Isaac Kerstenetsky, and Mário Henrique Simonsen, "Transportation and Inflation: A Study of Irrational Policy Making in Brazil," *Economic Development and Cultural Change,* XIII, No. 2 (January 1965), 188–202.

52. For brief description of the legal framework of the Brazilian labor relations system, see Octávio Bueno Magano, *Organização sindical brasileira* (São Paulo: Editora Revista dos Tribunais, 1982). The classical historical analysis of the system is Evaristo de Moraes Filho, *O problema do sindicato unico no Brasil* (Rio de Janeiro: Editora A Noite, 1952). The most careful description of the system as it operated in the early 1960s is Kenneth Paul Erickson, *The Brazilian Corporative State and Working Class Politics* (Berkeley: University of California Press, 1977). The system's evolution in the 1960s is given close analysis in Kenneth S. Mericle, "Conflict Regulation in the Brazilian Industrial Relations System" (Ph.D. dissertation, University of Wisconsin–Madison, 1974), which is partially summarized in Mericle, "Corporatist Control of the Working Class: Authoritarian Brazil Since 1964." in James Malloy, ed., *Authoritarianism and Corporatism in Latin America* (Pittsburgh: University of Pittsburgh Press, 1977), 303–38. A very useful history of the structure of labor relations, including changes after 1964, is given in Heloisa Helena Teixeira de Souza Martins, *O estado e a burocratização do sindicato no Brasil* (São Paulo: Editora Hucitec, 1979). The author spent some years working for DIEESE, the non-governmental, inter-union research office which after 1964 became virtually the only independent source of data on the cost of living and real wage levels. For highly useful surveys of the literature, see Leôncio Martins Rodrigues and Fábio Munhoz, "Bibliografia sobre trabalhadores e sindicatos no Brasil," *Estudos CEBRAP* (São Paulo, 1974), and two studies by Luiz Werneck Vianna: "Estudos sobre sindicalismo e movimento operário: resenha de algumas tendências," *BIB (Boletim informativo e bibliográfico ciências sociais),* No. 3 (1978), 9–24, and "Atualizando uma bibliográfia: 'novo sindicalismo,' cidadania e fábrica," *BIB,* No. 17 (1984), 53–68. In subsequent chapters there will be reference to the large literature on the Brazilian industrial relations system and the labor movement since the mid-1970s.

53. This trend in labor union activity is well described in Erickson, *The Brazilian*

Corporative State. Analysis of the CGT, a much-discussed (and technically extralegal) institution active in this period, is given in Lucfília de Almedia Neves, *O Comando Geral dos Trabalhadores no Brasil, 1961–64* (Belo Horizonte: Editora VEGA, 1981).

54. Departamento Intersindical de Estatística e Estudos Socio-Econômicos (DIEESE), "Dez anos de política salarial," in *Estudos Socioeconômicos,* I, No. 3 (August 1975).

55. Mário Victor, *Cinco anos que abalaram o Brasil* (Rio de Janeiro: Civilização Brasileira, 1965), 550.

56. Argelina Maria Cheibub Figueiredo, *Política governmental e funções sindicais* (Tese de mestrado apresentada ao Departamento de Ciências Sociais da Faculdade de Filosofia, Letras e Ciências Humanas da Universidade de São Paulo, October 1975), 67. This work includes a detailed analysis of government interventions in unions from 1964 to 1970.

57. The formula is explained in Ministério de Planejamento, *Programa,* 83–85. A more detailed analysis, using geometry, is given in Simonsen, *Inflação,* 26–28. The calculation of the formula and its application in practice generated bitter controversy. For a representative critical overview of the system from a left viewpoint, see Fernando Lopes de Almeida, *Política salarial, emprego, e sindicalismo, 1964–81* (Petrópolis: Vozes, 1982). The relationship between wage policy and social equity in post-1964 Brazil has been given a searching investigation in Samuel A. Morley, *Labor Markets and Inequitable Growth: The Case of Authoritarian Capitalism in Brazil* (Cambridge: Cambridge University Press, 1982). For a history of the application of the wage law, see Lívio de Carvalho, "Brazilian Wage Policies, 1964–81," *Brazilian Economic Studies,* No. 8 (1984), 109–41.

58. DIEESE, "Dez anos de política salarial," 12–13.

59. Roberto de Oliveira Campos, *A moeda, o govêrno e o tempo* (Rio de Janeiro, 1964), 184. Nationalism—of a kind he found misleading or pernicious—was a favorite target for Campos's rhetoric.

60. For a study of the operation of the 1964 profit remittance law, see Jan Hoffman French, "Brazil's Profit Remittance Law: Reconciling Goals in Foreign Investments," *Law and Policy in International Business, XIV* (1982), 399–451. Brazilian policy toward multinationals up to 1976 is reviewed in Stefan H. Robock, "Controlling Multinational Enterprises: The Brazilian Experience," *Journal of Contemporary Business,* VI, No. 4 (1977), 53–71.

61. In a speech in July 1964, Castelo Branco announced that the anti-inflationary policy would not be paid for with stagnation. Growth would come from, among other things, a "restoration of the inflow of foreign capital" and a "return to serious understandings with the international financial organizations, including the Alliance for Progress." Humberto de Alencar Castelo Branco, *Discursos: 1964,* 66.

62. Roberto Campos, interview with the author, London, July 3, 1978. Unless otherwise indicated, the source for data and information in the rest of this section is Syvrud, *Foundations of Brazilian Economic Growth,* chap. VIII.

63. *Ibid.,* 182–87; 206–11. Valuable also on the history of Brazil's foreign debt from 1947 to 1966 is Jon Donnelly, "External Debt and Long-Term Servicing Capacity," in H. John Rosenbaum and William G. Tyler, eds., *Contemporary Brazil: Issues in Economic and Political Development* (New York: Praeger, 1972), 95–123.

64. Lincoln Gordon letter (July 27, 1972) to Viana Filho, Castelo Branco Archive.
65. A useful summary of changes in Brazil's official exchange rates is given in Syvrud, *Foundations of Brazilian Economic Growth,* 194–95.
66. *New York Times,* August 10, 1965.
67. Syvrud, *Foundations,* 206. The official source on U.S. assistance to Brazil is Agency for International Development, Bureau for Program and Policy Coordination, Office of Statistics and Reports, *U.S. Overseas Loans and Grants and Assistance from International Organizations: Obligations and Loan Authorizations, July 1, 1945–June 30, 1971* (Washington, 1972), 38.
68. "United States Policies and Programs in Brazil," *Hearings Before the Subcommittee on Western Hemisphere Affairs of the Committee on Foreign Relations, United States Senate, Ninety-second Congress,* First Session: May 4, 5, and 11, 1971 (Washington: U.S. Government Printing Office, 1971), 218–29.
69. The ambassador, John Tuthill, launched a highly publicized plan to reduce the size of the mission, although not the scale of economic assistance. He described it with wit in Tuthill, "Operation Topsy," *Foreign Policy,* No. 8 (Fall 1972), 62–85.
70. Castelo Branco, *Discursos: 1964,* 20. I have not attempted a comprehensive analysis of economic policymaking from 1964 to 1967. A number of areas, including agriculture, education, housing, and social welfare, have been omitted. These topics were covered in two volumes of the early 1970s on Brazil: Rosenbaum and Tyler, eds., *Contemporary Brazil,* and Roett, ed., *Brazil in the Sixties.* Each policy has been the subject of monographic research. An excellent source on this research can be found in the bibliographies regularly published in *BIB: boletim informativo e bibliográfico de ciências sociais.* The first issue was published as part of *Dados,* No. 15 (1977), although it soon began separate publication and in 1985 was being published by the Associação Nacional de Pós-Graduação e Pesquisa em Ciências Sociais (Rio).
71. Castelo Branco, *Discursos: 1964,* 40.
72. *Ibid.,* 13.
73. The links of the UDN to the military government and the subsequent fate of the party are lucidly described in Maria Victória de Mesquita Benevides, *A UDN e udenismo: ambigüidades do liberalismo brasileiro, 1945–1965* (Rio de Janeiro: Paz e Terra, 1981), 125–43. The UDN argument in favor of an absolute majority is recapitulated in Prado Kelly's interview in Lourenço Dantas Mota, ed., *A história vivida,* Vol. 1 (São Paulo: O Estado de São Paulo, 1981), 158–60.
74. Dulles, *President Castello Branco,* 53.
75. A lengthy memoir by Lacerda, the product of marathon collective interviews by journalists recorded only a month before his death in 1977, was published in Carlos Lacerda, *Depoimento* (Rio de Janeiro: Nova Fronteira, 1977). It includes his account of his relationship with the Castelo Branco government. For a valuable analysis of Lacerda's political following, based on an analysis of voting patterns and survey data from greater Rio de Janeiro, see Gláucio Ary Dillon Soares, "As bases ideológicas do Lacerdismo, "*Revista Civilização Brasileira,* No. 4 (September 1965), 49–70.
76. For a lurid account by an anti-Borges local journalist, see Lisita Junior, *Goiás, novembro 26* (Goiaia: Liv. Figueiroa, 1965).
77. Dulles, *President Castello Branco,* 123–26.

78. For an overview of the elections, see Schneider, *The Political System of Brazil*, 162–69.
79. The test of the electoral law changes in 1965 is given in Senado Federal: Subsecretaria de Edições Técnicas, *Legislação eleitoral e partidária: Instruções do TSE para as eleições de 1982*, 4th ed. (Brasília: Senado Federal, 1982), 5–107. For a succinct explanation of how the electoral reform fits within the political evolution since 1945, see Robert Wesson and David V. Fleischer, *Brazil in Transition* (New York: praeger, 1983), chaps. 3 and 4. The most systematic analysis of the party system in the 1945–64 era is Olavo Brasil de Lima Junior, *Os partidos políticos brasileiros: a experiência federal e regional: 1945–64* (Rio de Janeiro: Graal, 1983).
80. Schneider, *The Political System of Brazil*, 167–68. It should be noted that Castelo Branco's personal position was more complicated than this account suggests. He was a good friend of Negrão de Lima and probably would have preferred his victory to that of Flexa Ribeiro, who, as a Lacerda protégée, represented as serious (perhaps more) a threat to the federal government as did the opposition candidate. But this was not, of course, how the general public and Castelo's fellow military saw it.
81. Fernando Pedreira, *Brasil política* (São Paulo: DIFEL, 1975), 162; Dulles, *President Castello Branco*, 202; Carlos Chagas, *Resistir é preciso* (Rio de Janeiro: Paz e Terra, 1975), 50.
82. Campos later explained that before 1964 the Congress had been an "engine of inflation" with its profligate spending and a "distorting factor" in investment because of its "hypersensitivity to regionalist pressures that can destroy the coherence and balance of plans and programs." The decision to take away its power to initiate spending bills and its power to increase any presidential money request "stemmed from the useful lessons of experience and not from the futile capriciousness of the technocrats." Roberto de Oliveira Campos, "O poder legislativo e o desenvolvimento," in Candido Mendes, ed., *O legislativo e a tecnocracia* (Rio de Janeiro: Imago Ed., 1975), 31–41.
83. Syvrud, *Foundations*, 130.
84. *Ibid.*, 50.
85. Details on the coffee account transactions by the federal government may be found in Edmar L. Bacha, *Os mitos de uma década* (Rio de Janeiro, 1976), 137–75, and in Syvrud, *Foundations*, chap. X.
86. Fishlow, "Some Reflections on Post-1964 Brazilian Economic Policy," 72.
87. On the eve of the gubernatorial elections of October 1965 Castelo Branco noted that it was Brazil's commitment to civil liberties and democratic procedures that explained "the growing respect of other free peoples and the continuous influx of foreign resources," Castelo Branco, *Discursos: 1965*, 285.
88. The bitter arguments over this new recourse to arbitrary power are described in Rowe, "The 'Revolution' and the 'System,' " 24–26; and Stepan, *The Military in Politics*, 254–57. Stepan based his analysis on extensive interviews with participants and observers. The Planalto's intense efforts to get congressional approval are related in Viana Filho, *O governo Castelo Branco*, 340–55. Viana Filho neatly summarized the Planalto viewpoint in noting, "the dilemma was not whether or not to preserve legality, but whether or not to permit the country to waiver between a rightist fascist dictatorship and a return of the forces deposed in 1964" (*ibid.*, 353).

Chapter III: Castelo Branco: The Attempt to Institutionalize

1. Typical was the president's speech of December 11, 1965, in which he predicted that Brazil would "gradually and uninterruptedly resume the normal life
   of a democracy." Castelo Branco, *Discursos: 1965,* 289–91.
2. When the court-packing scheme was being formulated, Ribeiro da Costa attacked the military intervention as "something never seen in truly civilized
   nations." The statement prompted a blistering reply from War Minister Costa e
   Silva, who called it "without doubt the greatest injustice ever practiced against
   the Brazilian soldier." Castelo Branco's top military aide, General Ernesto
   Geisel, who lost no love on Costa e Silva, was incensed at what he saw as the
   war minister's intrusion into such a delicate area and strongly recommended to
   Castelo that he fire Costa e Silva. Castelo did not. Dulles, *President Castello
   Branco,* 182–84.
3. For a useful analysis of AI–2's provisions and how they related to the political
   context, see Maria Helena Moreira Alves, *State and Opposition,* 54–66.
4. In *Minhas memórias provisórias* (Rio de Janeiro: Civilzação Brasileira, 1982),
   189–96, Juracy Magalhães gives his account of being offered the ministry and
   his subsequent role in drafting the Second Institutional Act.
5. Castelo Branco, *Discursos: 1965,* 35.
6. Costa e Silva was, as always, disarmingly frank: "Castelo, even though you
   don't intend to stay in power, don't signal your intention in the Act. With you
   out, the succession problem will open up sooner than it should. All the candidates will jump into the fray, including me"; quoted in Daniel Krieger, *Desde
   as missões . . . saudades, lutas, esperanças* (Rio de Janeiro: José Olympio,
   1976), 200.
7. Dulles, *President Castello Branco,* 157–58; the text of the letter is given (in
   English) on 499–500.
8. *Ibid.,* 321–22.
9. Alfred C. Stepan, *Os militares: da abertura à nova república* (Rio de Janeiro:
   Paz e Terra, 1986), 98; Viana Filho, *O governo Castelo Branco,* 207; and
   Wilfred A. Bacchus, "Long-Term Military Rulership in Brazil: Ideologic Consensus and Dissensus, 1963–1983," *Journal of Political and Military Sociology,*
   XIII (Spring 1985), 100.
10. One widely read and ultra-conservative economist, Eugenio Gudin, an-
    nounced in his column in *O Globo* that Brazil ought to adopt Mexico's single-
    party system, "that has given and is giving such good results," quoted in Dulles,
    President Castello Branco, 195–96. There were persistent rumors that Castelo
    Branco himself was considering the one-party model, based on the Mexican
    PRI, but I have found no evidence of it. For an analysis of the operation of the
    two-party system, see David Fleischer, "A evolução do bipartidarismo no Bra-
    sil, 1966–79," *Revista Brasileira de Estudos Políticos,* No. 51 (July 1980), 154–
    85. The electoral system for the 1964–79 period is analyzed in depth in
    Christiano Germano, *Brasilien: Autoritarismus und Wahlen* (München: Welt-
    forum Verlag, 1983).
11. Fiechter, *Brazil Since 1964,* 88. For an account of Planalto thinking on party
    reformulation, see Viana Filho, *O governo Castelo Branco,* 369–73.
12. Fiechter, *Brazil Since 1964,* 87–88; Viana Filho, *O governo Castelo Branco,*
    356–64.

13. João Batista Berardo, *Guerrilhas e guerrilheiros no drama da América Latina* (São Paulo: Edições Populares, 1981), 251. *A repressão militar-policial no Brasil* (1975), 97–98. The latter source is a 267-page documentation by former guerrillas and victims of government repression. Because it was compiled when censorship and repression were still omnipresent, no authors are listed.

14. Dulles, *President Castello Branco,* 296–300.

15. Costa e Silva's style is described in Vernon A. Walters, *Silent Missions* (Garden City, New York: Doubleday, 1978), 405.

16. Viana Filho, *O governo Castelo Branco,* 341; there is a very interesting account of the struggle over the presidential succession in Krieger, *Desde as missões,* 221–37. The most penetrating analysis of these events is Stepan, *The Military in Politics,* 248–52, who thought the Costa e Silva group should be called "authoritarian nationalists" rather than "hardliners."

17. The direct quotes come from a January 27, 1966, confidential memorandum on the succession which Castelo Branco sent to the principal army commanders. Viana Filho, *O governo Castelo Branco,* 380–83.

18. The struggle to choose Castelo's successor is treated at length in Dulles, *President Castello Branco,* 237–76; Viana Filho, *O governo Castelo Branco,* 377–90; and Daniel Krieger, *Desde as missões* 221–37. Krieger had been a UDN leader from Rio Grande do Sul and was now a key figure in ARENA. Castelo unsuccessfully pushed Krieger's presidential candidacy during the succession fight.

19. Castelo Branco, *Discursos: 1966,* 372.

20. For an analysis of the 1966 elections, see *Revista Brasileira de Estudos Políticos,* Nos. 23/24 (July 1967/January 1968), which includes articles analyzing the returns on a national scale, as well as in selected states.

21. There is a detailed account of the emergence of the *Frente Ampla* in Dulles, *President Castello Branco,* 318–70. Lacerda gave his version in his *Depoimento,* 379–97.

22. There was a small pocket of U.S. critics who opposed aid to Brazil. Senator Wayne Morse, a perennial congressional maverick, proposed in October 1965 the suspension of all aid because of the authoritarian turn signaled by the Second Institutional Act. In USAID and the State Department a minority of officials shared Morse's reaction. They had little impact, however, and the U.S. government remained a vigorous supporter and oft-time apologist for the Castelo Branco regime. Details on the debate within the U.S. government may be found in Jerome Levinson and Juan de Onís, *The Alliance That Lost Its Way* (Chicago: Quadrangle Books, 1970), 194–200. Levinson, who worked in USAID in that era, was a spokesman for the losing dissenters.

23. Syvrud, *Foundations of Brazilian Economic Growth,* 252. Coffee policy deserves further research, especially its political aspects. A good source for the economic context is Edmar Lisboa Bacha, "An Econometric Model for the World Coffee Market: The Impact of Brazilian Price Policy" (Ph.D. dissertation, Yale University, 1968). A translation of chapter 1 appeared in *Dados,* No. 5 (1968), 144–61. The failure of the production control program up to 1968 is described in Kenneth D. Frederick, "Production Controls Under the International Coffee Agreements," *Journal of Inter-American Studies and World Affairs* XII, No. 2 (April 1970): 255–70; and Stahis Panagides, "Erradicação do café e diversificação da agricultura brasileira," *Revista Brasileira de Economia,* XXIII, No. 1 (January–March 1969). Source material may be found in *Instru-*

mentos da Política Cafeeira, 2 vols. (Rio de Janeiro: Escola Interamericana de Administração Pública, 1967), published under the sponsorship of the Fundação Getúlio Vargas and the Banco Interamericano de Desenvolvimento. Only after 1967 did the market incentives (if the "market" is defined to include government purchase of surpluses!) turn against investment in coffee for many farmers, as Frederick explains. Leff's claim that coffee growers were powerless to gain government support before 1964 is therefore unsupported by the evidence. Nathaniel Leff, *Economic Policy Making and Development, in Brazil 1947–1964* (New York: Wiley, 1968), especially pp. 19–33. The Castelo Branco government continued the surplus policy in 1965 and 1966, thereby undermining the anti-inflation program.

24. The following data are drawn from Fishlow, "Some Reflections on Economic Policy," 72; and Syvrud, *Foundations of Brazilian Economic Growth*, 50.

25. The castelista worries over continuity are reported in *Visão*, July 29, 1966, p. 11; August 12, 1966, p. 11; August 5, 1966, pp. 22–26; March 3, 1967, p. 11. After mid-1966 there was constant speculation that Castelo Branco might try to continue in power. *Visão*, August 19, 1966, p. 13.

26. For analyses of the Constitution of 1967 and its adoption, see Maria Helena Moreira Alves, *State and Opposition*, 70–79; Feichter, *Brazil Since 1964*, 112–18; Schneider, *The Political System of Brazil*, 195–202; and Dulles, *President Castello Branco*, 381–420.

27. There is a detailed comparison of the 1967 law with the later National Security Laws of 1969 and 1978 in Ana Valderez A.N. de Alencar, *Segurança nacional: Lei No. 6,620/78—antecedentes, comparações, anotações, histórico* (Brasília: Senado Federal, 1982).

28. For an enlightening case study of government policymaking in the Castelo Branco and (part of) the Costa e Silva governments in the areas of wages, education, and *favela* removal, see Barry Ames, *Rhetoric and Reality in a Militarized Regime: Brazil Since 1964* (Beverly Hills: Sage Publications, 1973).

29. Ministério do Planejamento e Coordenação Econômica, *Plano Decenal de Desenvolvimento Econômico e Social*, 7 vols. (Rio de Janeiro: March 1967). The seven volumes were divided into as many as 10 subvolumes, evidence of the enormous staff work consumed in their preparation.

30. DIEESE, *Dez anos da política salarial*, 64–65. Albert Fishlow estimated the decline in the real minimum wage from 1964 to 1967 to be 20 percent, Fishlow, "Some Reflections on Economic Policy," 85. The president tenaciously defended his government's wage and labor policies. He argued that the government wanted to raise real wages, not simply nominal wages. In none of his speeches did he deal with the criticism that the real minimum wage was falling. Catelo Branco, *Discursos: 1965*, 317–22; Castelo Branco, *Discursos: 1966*, 1–16; 31–41.

31. Albert Fishlow in oral comments at the Yale University conference on "Authoritarian Brazil" in April 1971.

32. Details on Brazil's export policies may be found in William G. Tyler, *Manufactured Export Expansion and Industrialization in Brazil* (Tübingen, 1976) [Kieler Studien: Institut für Weltwirtschaft an der Universitat Kiel: 134], who cites the Brazilian literature, especially the studies done by IPEA. For a striking example of the "export pessimism" predominant among critics of the

Castelo Branco economic policies, see Antonio Dias Leite, *Caminhos do desenvolvimento* (Rio de Janeiro, 1966), 127–41. Dias Leite offered a dispiriting survey of the export potential, dismissing the possibility of significant sugar exports and never mentioning soybeans. The burden of his argument is that Brazil must concentrate on import-substituting industrialization, while large-scale expansion of export earnings is written off. In all fairness, it should be noted that before 1968 virtually no one had foreseen the huge increases that were about to occur in Brazilian exports. Interview with World Bank officials, September 1977.

33. For an excellent analysis of the political context of policymaking in Brazilian foreign trade, see Steven Arnold, "The Politics of Export Promotion: Economic Problem-Solving in Brazil, 1956–69" (Ph.D. dissertation, School of Advanced International Studies, Johns Hopkins University, Washington, 1972). I am grateful to Dr. Arnold for making available a copy of his dissertation. For a careful survey of Brazil's external economic relations up to 1966, see Joel Bergsman, *Brazil: Industrialization and Trade Policies* (London: Oxford University Press, 1970). Economists differed sharply over the role that "import constraints" played in the economic slowdown of the early 1960s. Nataniel Leff has analyzed what he saw as an "import bottleneck" in two articles: "Export Stagnation and Autarkic Development," *Quarterly Journal of Economics* 81 (1967): 286–301; and "Import Constraints and Development: Causes of the Recent Decline of Brazilian Economic Growth," *Review of Economics and Statistics* 49 (1967): 494–501. The latter article provoked a critical commentary by Joel Bergsman and Samuel A. Morley in *Review of Economics and Statistics* 51 (1969): 101–2.

34. Arnold, "The Politics of Export Promotion."

35. The case is analyzed in Raymond F. Mikesell, "Iron Ore in Brazil: The Experience of the Hanna Mining Company," in Mikesell, et al., *Foreign Investment in the Petroleum and Mineral Industries: Case Studies of Investor–Host Country Relations* (Baltimore: Johns Hopkins University Press, 1971), 345–64.

36. The "basic identity of views" between the Castelo Branco government and the international financial authorities and U.S. government is stressed in Teresa Hayter, *Aid as Imperialism* (London: Penguin Books, 1971), 135–42. One indicator of how seriously the U.S. treated Brazil was the fact that the USAID mission in Brazil was the largest of any country in the world except for India and Vietnam. Stepan, *The Military in Politics,* 232. By early 1967 the U.S. embassy was reporting to Washington that the Castelo Branco government's "all-out public support for United States policies has served rather to increase anti-Americanism than to lessen it," quoted in Dulles, *President Castello Branco,* 442.

37. A history of this institutional change may be found in Wanderly J.M. de Almeida and José Luiz Chautard, *FGTS: uma política de bem-estar social* (Rio de Janeiro, 1976). For a streamlined explanation of the FGTS system, see Celso Barroso Leite, *O que todo trabalhador deve saber sobre FGTS* (Rio de Janeiro: Edições de Ouro, 1980). The context of the shift to FGTS is succinctly explained in Erickson, *The Brazilian Corporative State,* 165–67. The FGTS funds were channeled into financing housing programs of the *Banco Nacional de Habitação.* For one evaluation which stresses how the funds did *not* go for low-income housing, see Gabriel Bolaffi, *A casa das ilusões perdidas: aspectos*

sócio-econômicos do Plano Nacional de Habitação [CEBRAP Caderno 27] (São Paulo, 1977).

38. The effort and its limitations are very clearly analyzed in David M. Trubek, "Law, Planning, and the Development of the Brazilian Capital Market," *The Bulletin* of the Institute of Finance, Graduate School of Business Administration, New York University, Nos. 72–73 (April 1971).

39. Campos was speaking to a group of Rio businessmen in December 1964; Campos, *Política econômica e mitos políticos*, 29.

40. For an evaluation by a key IPES leader and a prominent supporter of the 1964 coup, see Glycon Paiva, article in *O Estado de São Paulo*, March 29, 1969, which was one of a series.

41. This "denationalization" of Brazilian business was one of the most vigorously debated results of government policy. One of the best-known critics was Fernando Gasparian, whose articles and speeches are collected in *Em defesa da economia nacional* (Rio de Janeiro: Editora Saga, 1966). The problem became serious enough to become the subject of a congressional inquiry (although there were few illusions in the purged Congress about the possibility of any "action"). The text of the congressional commission's published report may be found in Rubem Medina, *Desnacionalização: crime contra o Brasil?* (Rio de Janeiro: Editora Saga, 1970). Celso Furtado appeared as an expert witness before the commission (returning only briefly to Brazil for the testimony). His testimony was later published in Celso Furtado, *Um projeto para o Brasil* (Rio de Janeiro: Editora Saga, 1968). An English translation is included in his *Obstacles to Development in Latin America* (Garden City, New York: Anchor Books, 1970). Furtado saw post-1964 Brazil as a prime example of what is essentially a new "structuralist" interpretation of the technologically imposed "dependence." The advantageous credit position enjoyed by foreign-owned firms is discussed also in Samuel A. Morley and Gordon W. Smith, "Import Substitution and Foreign Investment in Brazil," *Oxford Economic Papers*, XXIII, No. 1 (March 1971), 134.

42. One of the ablest defenders of the Campos policies during the Castelo Branco era never tired of baiting leftists over the fact that it was a supposedly right-wing government that was rescuing the state sector of the economy: Gilberto Paim, "Realidade econômica," in Mário Pedrosa, et al., *Introdução à realidade brasileira* (Rio de Janeiro: Editora Cadernos Brasileiros, 1968), 35–71. Paim published widely in the Rio press in 1967–68. See, for example, his "Aliança com a modernização," *Jornal do Brasil*, July 7, 1968. Paim also wrote the preface to Campos, *Do outro lado de cêrca*.

43. Some of these questions are discussed in William G. Tyler, "Brazilian Industrialization and Industrial Policies: A Survey," *World Development*, IV (1976); Nos. 10/11, 863–82.

44. Flynn put this well when he referred to Castelo's "Cromwellian conviction in his own righteousness and a deep contempt for playing the demagogue." Peter Flynn, "Sambas, Soccer and Nationalism," *New Society*, No. 463 (August 12, 1971), 327. For a content analysis of a sample of Castelo Branco's presidential speeches, see Eurico de Lima Figueiredo, *Os militares e a democracia: análise estrutural da ideologia do Pres. Castelo Branco* (Rio: Graal, 1980). The ideology Lima Figueiredo analyzes here was an important element in what became the castelista current of military thought.

45. Castelo Branco, *Discursos: 1966*, 61.

Chapter IV: Costa e Silva: The Military Tighten Their Grip

1. Nelson Dimas Filho, *Costa e Silva: o homen e o líder* (Rio de Janeiro: Edições o Cruzeiro, 1966) is a journalist's campaign biography written to improve the then war minister's image. For useful chronologies on the Costa e Silva presidential years, see Lúcia Maria Gaspar Gomes, "Cronologia do 1° ano do govêrno Costa e Silva," *Dados*, No. 4 (1968), 199–220; and Irene Maria Magalhães, et al., "Segundo e terceiro ano do Govêrno Costa e Silva," *Dados*, No. 8 (1971), 152–233. An invaluable source is Jayme Portella de Mello, *A revolução e o governo Costa e Silva* (Rio de Janeiro: Guavira Editores, 1979). The author was head of the Military Presidential Staff. He had also been Costa e Silva's chief of staff when the latter was war minister under Castelo Branco. Portella de Mello's thousand-page book is a day-by-day account of presidential activities and includes the texts of numerous documents and presidential speeches. Portella's interpretation is especially interesting on military politics. The most penetrating interpretation of the Costa e Silva years in Flynn, *Brazil: A Political Analysis,* 366–440. Helpful also are Schneider, *The Political System of Brazil,* 203–311, and Fiechter, *Brazil Since 1964,* 123–77.

2. His code name in the 1964 conspiracy against Goulart was "the old uncle" (*Tio Velho*), a clue to his personality. Portella de Mello, *A revolução e o governo Costa e Silva,* 646.

3. Viana Filho, *O governo Castelo Branco,* 351.

4. This contrast is brought out clearly in Stepan, *The Military in Politics,* 248–52.

5. Celso Furtado, "Brasil: da república oligárquica ao estado militar," in Furtado, ed., *Brasil: tempos modernos* (Rio de Janeiro: Paz e Terra, 1968), 16–19. Furtado was referring to the infamous Morgenthau Plan, a working document in the U.S. Treasury that never became U.S. policy. Furtado was writing from exile, after the "High Command of the Revolution" (the military junta that ruled in the first weeks after the coup) had dismissed him from the directorship of SUDENE and stripped him of his political rights.

6. These export promotion efforts did not begin to pay off until 1968–69. Carlos von Doellinger, et al., *A política brasileira de comercio exterior e seus efeitos: 1967–73* (Rio de Janeiro: IPEA/IPES, 1974), 8–13.

7. When Helio Beltrão was sworn in as Roberto Campos's successor in March 1967, Campos could hardly have been more explicit: "Everyone would like to achieve a maximum of development with a minimum of inflation. But those who think it is possible to ease up in the fight against inflation in order to stimulate development will end up having much more inflation than development . . ." *Revista de Finanças Públicas,* XXVII, No. 257 (March 1967), 9. Delfim's thinking was captured in a 1969 comment to his monetarist critics: ". . . We are not going to sacrifice the goal of economic development just so we can go down in history as the man who finished off inflation at all costs." *O Estado de São Paulo,* November 30, 1969.

8. This account of Delfim Neto's career draws on articles in *O Estado de São Paulo,* January 1, 1967, and *Jornal da Tarde,* May 17, 1971.

9. Delfim's speech, given to a seminar at the University of São Paulo, was reprinted in *Revista de Finanças Públicas,* XXVIII, No. 275 (Sept. 1968).

10. Delfim Neto sketched out these ideas in a speech given on the eve of beginning his ministry, *O Estado de São Paulo,* March 12, 1967. The new diagnosis was offered in May 1967 by a group of government economists, who contended that

Brazil had experienced a "profound" change in the nature of the inflationary process. Since 1966, they argued, the process had become "cost–push," whereas the Campos policy had continued to suppress demand. The Castelo Branco government was criticized for pursuing a monetary and fiscal policy that lacked any "great continuity" in 1964 and 1965 and then adopting a "rather inflexible [monetary] policy" in 1966. Ministério do Planejamento e Coordenação Geral, *Diretrizes de govêrno: programa estratégico de desenvolvimento* (1967), 145–62. An influential critique of Campos's failures (as well as accomplishments) in monetary policy was given in articles in the annual volumes published by APEC [Análise e Perspectiva Econômica]: *A economia brasileira e suas perspectivas*. Mário Henrique Simonsen's summary assessment of the 1964–69 period is included in his *Inflação: gradualismo x tratamento de choque,* chap. 2. A convincing analysis of the way in which credit policy had inadvertently promoted both inflation and stagnation between 1962 and 1967 is given in Morley, "Inflation and Stagnation in Brazil." Morley was in Brazil in 1966–68 and worked with the EPEA group of economists who authored the critical diagnosis cited above. Clues to the thinking of Delfim and his University of São Paulo colleagues can also be found in Antonio Delfim Neto, et al., *Alguns aspectos da inflação brasileira* (São Paulo: Editora Piratininga, 1965).

11. These citations are drawn from Delfim's speeches, as reported in *O Estado de São Paulo,* March 12, 1967; and *Revista das Finanças Públicas,* XXVII, No. 257 (March 1967).

12. Fishlow, "Some Reflections on Economic Policy," 72. Fishlow's article examines in detail the underlying assumptions of the Campos-Bulhões policies. Fishlow argues that the availability of excess capacity in 1967 greatly facilitated growth. He also notes the low savings rate—something that would limit investment and, therefore, future growth. Early on Delfim had signalled that zero inflation was not his primary goal. In his first speech as Minister he noted, "Economic development and severe inflation are incompatible, but it is perfectly possible to accelerate development with a controlled inflation of about 15 percent." *O Estado de São Paulo,* March 30, 1967. Such talk angered Roberto Campos. In February 1969 he wrote an article explaining the post-1967 growth surge and again warning against dangerously lax monetary policies (although avoiding a direct attack on the Costa e Silva policymakers). He did attack "our mania to believe that 'Brazilian inflation is different,' despite the lessons of history and the example of our neighbors." Roberto de Oliveira Campos, *Temas e sistemas* (Rio de Janeiro: APEC, 1969), 112–14.

13. A detailed history of the price control system is given in Fernando Rezende, et al., *Aspectos da Participação do governo na economia* (Rio de Janeiro: IPEA/ INPES, 1976). Price control, often used before 1964, was maintained in one form or another throughout the post-1964 era. Its use, apparently in conflict with the post-1964 governments' commitment to the free market, merits a careful study.

14. An excellent analysis of the political dimensions of the price control system can be found in Celso Lafer, *O sistema político brasileiro* (São Paulo: Perspectiva, 1975), 89–100.

15. See footnotes for the preceeding chapter for sources on Brazilian wage policy. A history of wage law changes from 1964 to 1974 is given in Departamento Intersindical de Estatística e Estudos Sócio-Econômicos (DIEESE), *Dez anos*

da política salarial; one of the earliest analyses of the income distribution effects of post-1964 wage policy is found in Edmar Lisboa Bacha, *Política econômica e distribuição de renda* (Rio de Janeiro: Paz e Terra, 1978), 25–52. In *Labor Markets and Inequitable Growth,* Samuel Morley raises important questions about the interpretation of wage data and stresses the need to use a broad range of indicators in judging changes in personal welfare.

16. The citations are from a speech given by Delfim at the University of São Paulo and reprinted in the *Revista da Finanças Públicas,* XXVIII, No. 275 (September 1968).

17. As cited in Fiechter, *Brazil Since 1964,* 131.

18. Lacerda has given his version of these events in his *Depoimento,* 379–97. As Kubitschek was undoubtedly still the most popular politician in Brazil, Lacerda badly needed his support. Pedreira, *O Brasil político,* 277.

19. For a non-Brazilian perspective on these attacks, see the *New York Times,* December 28, 1967.

20. *New York Times,* March 6 and 12, 1968.

21. A history of student politics through 1967 may be found in Arthur José Poerner, *O poder jovem* (Rio de Janeiro: Civilização Brasileira, 1968). The author unabashedly favors the student protesters. For a succinct analysis of student politics from 1964 to 1971, see Robert O. Myhr, "Student Activism and Development," in H. Jon Rosenbaum and William G. Tyler, eds., *Contemporary Brazil: Issues in Economic and Political Development* (New York: Praeger, 1972), 349–69. For the flavor of the student protests, see Luiz Henrique Romagnoli and Tania Gonçalves, *A volta da UNE: de Ibiúna a Savador* (São Paulo: Alfa-Omega, 1979).

22. Data are from Fay Haussman and Jerry Haar, *Education in Brazil* (Hamden, Conn: Archon Books, 1978), chap. 6. For an overview of Brazilian higher education up to the early 1970s, see Douglas Hume Graham, "The Growth, Change and Reform of Higher Education in Brazil: A Review and Commentary on Selected Problems and Issues," in Riordan Roett, ed., *Brazil in the Sixties* (Nashville: Vanderbilt University Press, 1972), 275–324.

23. Typical of the debate were the eight articles in the "Caderno Especial" of *Jornal do Brasil,* June 10, 1968. On July 14 the same newspaper ran a feature story with the heading "The Ministry of Education and Culture has hundreds of bureaus, even a spaghetti factory, but it still doesn't work."

24. Seminário da União Nacional dos Estudantes, *Infiltração imperialista no ensino brasileiro* (UNE, 1967). The texts of a number of the MEC-USAID agreements are reprinted in Márcio Moreira Alves, *Beabá dos MEC-USAID* (Rio de Janeiro: Edições Gernasa, 1968), along with the author's scathing commentary. Another useful contract-by-contract analysis is José Oliveira Arapiraca, *A USAID e a educação brasileira* (São Paulo: Cortez, 1982).

25. The Meira Mattos reort was published in full in a special supplement of *O Estado de São Paulo,* August 31, 1968. The Commission arrived at one "basic and fundamental conclusion: the conception of Brazilian education must be totally reformulated. It must be revamped and revitalized."

26. The ideas, tactics, and moods of the militant student leaders were well captured in "Eles querem derrubar o govêrno," *Realidade,* July 1968; and "Eis o que pensa um novo líder da esquerda" and "A faculdade está ocupada," both in *Realidade,* August 1968.

27. The presidential bill became Law 5,540 (1968). Under this reorganization Bra-

zilian universities moved from the French model (on which they had been based since the 1920s and 1930s) toward the U.S. model. The 1968 reform law called for the introduction of departments and the phasing out of the previously all-powerful *professores catedráticos* (holders of chairs), as well as transition to the course credit system. Haussman and Haar, *Education in Brazil*, 80–88. Many of the reforms had been goals of the MEC-USAID project on higher education. It was easier for the Costa e Silva government—still worrying about public opinion—to push for the reforms after that MEC-USAID project expired at the end of June 1968. The 1968 reforms included many changes favored by IPES, the businessmen's study and pressure group. Maria Inêz Salgado de Souza, *Os empresários e a educação: o IPES e a política educacional após 1964* (Petrópolis: Vozes, 1981), 193–205. A number of Brazilians on the MEC-USAID projects or linked to IPES were instrumental in formulating or laying the groundwork for the 1968 reform.

28. The planning and execution of the takeover is described by one of its leaders in José Ibrahim, *O que todo cidadão precisa saber sobre comissões de fábrica* (São Paulo: Global, 1986), 51–71; and in Antonio Caso, ed., *A esquerda armada no Brasil 1967–1971* (Lisbon: Moraes, 1976), 62–66. The latter volume was first published in Spanish by the Casa de Las Américas in Havana under the title *Los Subversivos*.

29. The principal source on the Contagem and Osasco strikes is Francisco C. Weffort, "Participação e conflito industrial: Contagem e Osasco, 1968," *Caderno 5* (São Paulo: CEBRAP, 1972), which skillfully depicts the differing political and institutional contexts of the strikes. Further detail on the strikes is given by José Ibrahim in Caso, *A esquerda armada*, 50–81.

30. For an extended discussion of the National Security Doctrine and its importance in the post-1964 context, see Moreira Alves, *State and Opposition*, 3–28. The doctrine's relevance for the Church is explained in Bruneau, *The Church in Brazil*, 58–60. The Belgian theologian José Comblin, who lived and taught in Brazil until his expulsion in 1972, wrote extensively on the National Security Doctrine, as in José Comblin, *The Church and the National Security State* (Maryknoll, New York: Orbis Books, 1979). The Bishops' paper was published in the *Correio da Manhã*, July 21, 1968. The paper compared Brazil's situation to that of Nazi Germany, where Christians "accepted government doctrines without recognizing that they contradicted the true demands of Christianity. . . ." The bishops warned that Brazil faced the same threat. That was strong language for the military, who prided themselves on having fought the *Wehrmacht* in Italy in 1944–45.

31. Stepan, *Military in Politics*, 258–59; Bruneau, *The Political Transformation of the Brazilian Catholic Church*, 200–202.

32. João Quartim, *Dictatorship and Armed Struggle in Brazil* (New York: Monthly Review Press, 1971), 146–47; Flavio Deckes, *Radiografia do terrorismo no Brasil, 1966–1980* (São Paulo: Icone, 1985), 49–67.

33. While interviewing military officers from July to October 1968, Stepan noted a growing "anti-political" sentiment, Stepan, *The Military in Politics*, 259. For the flavor of hardliner rhetoric in the midst of the 1968 political crises, see "Críticas sérias de jovens oficiais," *Visão*, November 22, 1968. The manifesto of officers from the Escola de Aperfeiçoamento de Oficiais was reprinted in *Jornal do Brasil*, November 7, 1968.

34. As a journalist and federal deputy, Alves had spoken out and published books

on the hottest issues, such as government torture in *Torturas e torturados* (1966), radical Catholics and their persecution by the government in *O Cristo do povo* (1968), and the U.S. attempt to transform the Brazilian educational system in his *Beabá dos MEC-USAID* (1968). Alves has given his account of the events leading up to the December 12 vote in *A Grain of Mustard Seed: The Awakening of the Brazilian Revolution* (Garden City, New York: Anchor Books, 1973), 4–25.

35. Alves, *A Grain of Mustard Seed,* 17.

36. In mid-September Justice Minister Gama e Silva asked Senator Daniel Krieger, national president of ARENA, for his help in getting the Chamber of Deputies to allow the minister to try Federal Deputies Israel Dias Novais, Luiz Sabiá, and Davi Lerer for having slandered him. Nothing came of that bravado. Krieger, *Desde as missões,* 327. By early December General Portello de Mello, the president's top military aide, ordered police surveillance of Lerer and Sabiá, plus Márcio Alves, Mário Covas, Mata Machado, Hermano Alves, "and other leftwingers so they could be arrested at any moment, but only on orders." Portella, *A revolução e o governo Costa e Silva,* 648. The deputies mentioned were all prime targets for hardliner wrath.

37. Castello Branco, *Os militares no poder,* vol. 2, p. 519.

38. At the height of the crisis Krieger told Labor Minister Passarinho that he would never "cooperate in the castration of the Congress and the rape of the 1967 Constitution," Krieger, *Desde as missões,* 335. Marinho thought the issue was "whether we can follow the Constitution while adopting totalitarian controls that suffocate free speech . . . ," *ibid.,* 339. A leading political journalist observed ironically that Marinho, while handling the issue, had succeeded in spreading the "dangerous germ of ethical considerations," Castello Branco, *Os militares no poder,* vol.2, p. 545.

39. Schneider, *The Political System of Brazil,* 265–72. The growing tension between the ARENA-controlled legislature and the Planalto is shown clearly in Sérgio Henrique Hudson de Abranches and Gláucio Ary Dillon Soares, "As funções do legislativo," *Revista de Administração Pública,* Vll, No. 1 (January/March 1973), 73–98.

40. Details on the Council's meetings are given in Portella, *A revolução e o governo Costa e Silva,* 651–57. The most systematic analysis of the wide range of authoritarian measure is Klein and Figueriedo, *Legitimidade e coação no Brasil pós-64.* The context of military politics is given in Stepan, *The Military in Politics,* 259–66.

41. Portella, *A revolução e o governo Costa e Silva,* 668.

42. Maria Helena Moreira Alves states it differently: "Perhaps the most serious consequence of the Institutional Act was that it opened the way for an unbridled use of the repressive apparatus of the national security state' (*State and Opposition,* 96).

43. Dalmo Abreu Dallari, "The Forca Pública of São Paulo in State and National Politics" (unpublished manuscript).

44. Information on censorship, rather chaotically organized, can be found in Paolo Marconi, *A censura política na imprensa brasileira:1968–1978* (São Paulo: Global, 1980). Because of censorship of the Brazilian press after December 1968, I have frequently used reports by foreign correspondents as a source. The operation and effects of censorship will be discussed in more detail in the following chapter.

45. *New York Times*, May 6, 1969; *Christian Science Monitor*, May 9, 1969. The purges of academics is given a well-informed analysis in Philippe C. Schmitter, "The Persecution of Political and Social Scientists in Brazil, *PS*, lll, No. 2 (Spring 1970), 123–28.

46. Luiz Antonio Cunha and Moacyr de Góes, *O golpe na educação* (Rio: Zahar, 1985), 74–75.

47. The passages in the bill are cited from Maria Inez Salgado de Souza, *Os empresários e a educação: o IPES e a política educacional após 1964* (Petrópolis: Vozes, 1981), 176–78. For a highly critical look at the program and some of its approved textbooks, see "Moral e cívica: deformações e violamões de uça disciplina," *Journal do Brasil,* August 24, 1974.

48. Portella de Mello, *A revolução e o governo Costa e Silva*, 669; Magalhães, et al., "Segundo e terceiro ano do governo Costa e Silva," *Dados*, No. 8 (1971), 171.

49. *New York Times*, August 27, 1969.

50. One close student of Brazilian political history described AI–5 and the accompanying authoritarian swing as Brazil's first purely military coup, "without the support or stimulus of any civilian political sector," Pedreira, *Brasil político*, 163, 278.

51. The complete story of armed resistance to the post-1964 governments can never be told, for many key guerrillas were killed and members of the security forces had obvious reasons not to document their work. A highly useful overview of the armed opposition movements in Brazil can be found in João Batista Berardo, *Guerrilhas e guerrilheiros no drama da América Latina* (São Paulo: Edições Populares, 1981). An analysis of the Brazilian case as of 1973 is given in James Kohl and John Litt, *Urban Guerrilla Warfare in Latin America* (Cambridge, Mass: MIT Press, 1974), 29–170. An invaluable collection of manifestoes and programs of the clandestine left up to 1971 is provided in Daniel Aarão Reis Filho and Jair Ferreira de Sá, *Imagens da revolução*. A first-hand account covering October 1967 to May 1971 by a Rio high-school boy who became a full-fledged guerrilla is told with wit in Alfredo Syrkis, *Os carbonários: memórias da guerrilha perdida* (São Paulo: Global, 1980). For a collection of testimonies and documents of guerrillas, see Caso, *A esquerda armada no Brasil*. Another revolutionary guerrilla perspective is given in Quartim, *Dictatorship and Armed Struggle in Brazil*. For an interesting journalistic portrail based on interviews with exiled Brazilian guerrillas in Algeria, see Sanche de Gramont, "How One Pleasant, Scholarly Young Man from Brazil Became a Kidnapping, Gun-Toting, Bombing Revolutionary," *New York Times Magazine*, November 15, 1970.

52. For an excellent recent survey of the history of guerrilla movements in Latin America, see the edition of Che Guevara's *Guerrilla Warfare* (Lincoln: University of Nebraska Press, 1985) as edited with an introduction and case studies by Brian Loveman and Thomas M. Davies, Jr. It is significant (and probably justified) that the book contains not a single reference to Brazil.

53. This discussion makes no pretense at exploring in depth the fortunes of the left after 1964; the focus here is on the origins of the guerrilla movements. Leads on the larger topic can be found in such overviews as John W.F. Dulles, "La Izquierda Brasileña: Esfuerzos de Recuperación," *Problemas Internacionales*, XX (July–August 1973), 1–39, which covers 1964–70. For an example of the

rethinking by the PCB, see Assis Tavares, "Causas da derrocada de 1° de abril de 1964," *Revista Civilização Brasileira*, No. 8 (July 1966), 9–33.

54. The Latin American context of these debates is sketched in Richard Gott, *Guerrilla Movements in Latin America* (Garden City, New York: Doubleday, 1971); William E. Ratliff, *Castroism and Communism in Latin America, 1959–1976* (Stanford: Hoover Institution, 1976); and Donald C. Hodges, *The Latin American Revolution: Politics and Strategy from Apro-Marxism to Guevarism* (New York: William Morrow, 1974), although none of these works gives significant attention to Brazil.

55. The indispensable source on the history of the PCB is Ronald H. Chilcote, *The Brazilian Communist Party: Conflict and Integration, 1922–1972* (New York: Oxford University Press, 1974). A valuable document collection is *PCB: vinte anos de política, 1958–1979: documentos* (São Paulo: Livraria Editora Ciências Humanas, 1980), which has interesting detail on how the PCB lost members to the new guerrilla groups. See also Edgar Carone, *O P.C.B.: 1964–1982* (São Paulo: DIFEL, 1982), and Moisés Vinhas, *O partidão: a luta por um partido de massas, 1922–1974* (São Paulo: Hucitec, 1982). An account of the intra-party struggles after 1964 is given by Luís Carlos Prestes, the long-time PCB secretry-general, in his interviews as published by Dênis de Moraes and Francisco Viana, *Prestes: lutas e autocríticas* (Petrópolis: Vozes, 1982), 177–96. Pro-Maoist dissidents in the PCB were expelled in 1961 and formed their own party, the *Partido Comunista do Brasil* (PC do B). There is a collection of their documents and manifestos in Partido Comunista do Brasil, *Cinquenta anos de luta* (Lisboa: Edições Maria da Fonte, 1975). For other collections of documents, see two publications of the Partido Comunista do Brasil: *Política e revolucionarização* (Lisboa: Ed. Maria da Fonte, 1977) and *Guerra popular: caminho da luta armado no Brasil* (Lisboa: Ed. Maria da Fonte, 1974). The hold of the PCB over university-age radicals is poetically described in Álvaro Caldas, *Tirando o capuz* (Rio de Janeiro: CODECRI, 1981), 144–45.

56. For the sake of simplicity, the group affiliation of these terrorist (in the parlance of the authorities) or guerrilla (in the parlance of the perpetrators and their supporters) actions have not been distinguished. Later in this chapter the principal groups will be discussed.

57. The story of this guerrilla action is documented and analyzed in Gilson Rebello, *A guerrilha de Caparaó* (São Paulo: Alfa-Omega, 1980).

58. *New York Times*, August 2 and September 26, 1967.

59. One of the most detailed sources on Marighela is Frei Betto, *Batismo de sangue: os dominicanos e a morte de Carlos Marighela* (Rio de Janeiro: Civilização Brasileira, 1982). The author was a strong admirer of Marighela. Marighela became the best-known figure on the Brazilian revolutionary left, in part because of his writings. An important collection of the latter is in Carlos Marighela, *For the Liberation of Brazil* (London: Penguin Books, 1971), which includes the famous "Mini-Manual of the Urban Guerrilla."

60. *Ibid.*, 81.

61. Interview with Antonio Carlos Fon, São Paulo, June 27, 1983.

62. José and Miranda, *Lamarca*, 42–43.

63. The assassination of Chandler is described by one of his killers in Caso, *A esquerda armada no Brasil*, 159–71. They had planned to assassinate him on October 8, the first anniversary of Che Guevara's death. They staked out his

house, but Chandler never left home that day, so they had to reschedule the action for October 12. For a major story on Chandler's assassination and the "tribunal" that preceded it, see *O Estado de São Paulo*, April 10, 1980. A brief account of the U.S. embassy's inquiry into Chandler's death is given in "United States Policies and Programs in Brazil," *Hearings Before the Subcommittee on Western Hemisphere Affairs of the Committee on Foreign Relations, United States Senate, Ninety-Second Congress, First Session*, May 4, 5, and 11, 1979 (Washington: U.S. Government Printing Office, 1971), 41–42.

64. Lamarca's story is told in Emiliano José and Oldack Miranda, *Lamarca, o capitão da guerrilha* (São Paulo: Global, 1980). The authors cite no sources, although they say they used published material, especially from *Pasquim*, *Em Tempo*, and *Coojornal*, and they conducted interviews with survivors.

65. José and Miranda, *Lamarca*, 59–60; Alex Polari, *Em busca do tesouro* (Rio de Janeiro: CODECRI, 1982), 93–94.

66. Charges of torture were more frequently leveled against Brazil's military government after the imposition of Institutional Act No. 5 in December 1968. The government denied all such charges of torture by its security forces, at whatever level. One of the first documented and well-publicized accusations from abroad was the "Livre noir: terreur et torture au Brésil," a collection of firsthand accounts of government torture and persecution of priests, peasant leaders, and students, published in the December 1969 issue of *Croissance des Jeunes Nations* (Paris). This dossier was delivered to Pope Paul VI at the end of 1969, stimulating one of the many Vatican representations to the Brazilian government. On December 31, 1969, *The Wall Street Journal,* hardly in the vanguard of foreign criticism, ran a feature story describing government torture as an established fact. Reports of torture increased in 1970 and 1971, leading to even more accusations from abroad. One of the most effective was Ralph della Cava, "Torture in Brazil," *Commonweal*, XCII, No. 6 (April 24, 1970). *"Pau de arara": la violencia militar en el Brasil* (México: Siglo XXI Editores, 1972) included personal testimonies of torture victims, with details on the time, place, and identity of torturers. Amnesty International's *Report on Allegations of Torture in Brazil* (London: Amnesty International, 1972) listed by name 1,076 torture victims as of September 1972. This dossier was especially important because of Amnesty International's well-known care in cross-checking all charges. This documentation of systematic torture by Brazilian government units (police and military) had convinced most of the outside world by 1971. Because of the censorship, much of the evidence published abroad was not available to Brazilians. For those prepared to listen, however, there was no shortage of chilling stories told by relatives, friends, and acquaintances. One of the most tragic cases was Frei Tito de Alencar Lima, a young Dominican monk who was savagely tortured, later exiled, and who finally committed suicide in France. His story is told in Pedro Celso Uchoa Cavalcanti, et al., *Memórias do exílio: Brasil, 1964–19??* (Lisbon: Editora Arcádia, 1976). 347–69.

67. The "parrot's perch" was a horizontal pole onto which the victim was tied with the ankles and wrists bound together. The victim could then be beaten with paddles and given electric shocks. One survivor said his OBAN torturers played samba music while he was on the parrot's perch. Interview with Paulo de Tarso Wenceslau, São Paulo, June 30, 1983. The "dragon's chair" was a facsimile of a dentist's chair where the strapped-down victim could be

given electric shocks and subjected to a dental drill. The "refrigerator" was a box so small the victim could neither stand up nor lie down. Once inside the victim was subjected to great and rapid variations in heat and light, as well as bombarded by high-intensity sound. Victims who had experienced all three forms of torture often said the "refrigerator" was the worst. I was told by several sources that the idea of this machine was picked up from the British.

68. In Portuguese the title was *Operação Bandeirantes*, shortened to "OBAN" by police and journalists. The *bandeirantes* were the famous São Paulo-based explorers of the colonial era. A police reporter picked up and tortured by OBAN in September 1969 said, "If Hell exists, Operação Bandeirantes is worse." Antonio Carlos Fon, *Tortura: a história da repressão política no Brasil* (São Paulo: Global, 1979), 11. Fon earned the reputation of being the best-informed journalist on the repressive apparatus in São Paulo. That cost him more than a few threats on his life.

69. The economic data cited here and in subsequent chapters are, unless otherwise indicated, from the annual *Economic Survey of Latin America* published by the Economic Commission for Latin America. These data typically differ some-what from the standard series published by Brazilian official sources such as the Fundação Getúlio Vargas and the Banco Central. The orders of magnitude are, however, similar, and the trends over time are consistent. The data form the annual *Economic Survey of Latin America* have the advantage for the historian that they reflect the estimates that policymakers had to work with at the time.

70. *Programa estratégico de desenvolvimento: 1968–70*(Brasília: Ministerio do Planejamento e Coordenação Geral, 1968), 2 vols. In his introduction, Plan-ning Minister Helio Beltrão stressed the importance of the national market and the need to strengthen national firms. Beltrão, at least in his rhetoric, was more nationalistic than Delfim. Owing to Delfim's successful monopoly on economic policymaking, Beltrão had little opportunity to implement proposals that Del-fim might oppose.

71. Syvrud, *Foundations of Brazilian Economic Growth*, 136–39; Interview with Luiz Fernando Correia de Araújo (director of planning for SUDENE), Recife, May 23, 1975. Mario Simonsen applauded the change in allocations of tax revenues. He accused the *municípios* of having often wasted their funds on "illuminated fountains, useless town squares, and other non-essential proj-ects." Mario Simonsen, *Ensaios sobre economia e politica econômica* (Rio de Janeiro: APEC Editora, 1971), 39. The same eagerness to capitalize on the authoritarian procedures was shown by Glycon Paiva, an engineer and a key figure behind the Revolution of 1964, who thought the "efficient legal instru-ment in AI–5" offered an ideal opportunity to "eliminate once and for all the inflationary residual over the next two years without stopping develop-ment . . . ," *O Estado de São Paulo*, April 6, 1969. Back in November 1968, shortly before the crisis that produced AI–5, Delfim had urged Costa e Silva to press for the amendment that would reduce the federal revenue share going to states and municipalities. The president replied, "Drop that idea. Come up with another approach, because we need to learn to work with the constitution we've got." Quoted in Carlos Castello Branco, *Os militares no poder,* vol. 2. (Rio: Editora Nova Fronteira, 1977), 532–33. Once he had AI–5, the president lost no time in using it to decree precisely that amendment.

72. Syvrud, *Foundations of Brazilian Economic Growth*, 1981. Footnotes 32 and 33 in the preceding chapter contain further references on the making of Brazil's commercial policy.

73. The speech was reprinted in the *Revista de Finanças Públicas*, XXXVIII, No. 269 (March 1968). Costa e Silva gave a hint of future presidental rhetoric when he predicted that "there is nothing and there is no one who can prevent Brazil from reaching its radiant destiny."

74. The balance of payments data for the first half of 1968 convinced policymakers that they had to revise their exchange rate policy. Carlos von Doellinger, et al., *A política brasileira de comércio exterior e seus efeitos: 1967–73* (Rio: IPEA), 14.

75. The best analysis of the background leading up to the decision to go to the flexible rate is given in Donald E. Syvrud, *Foundations of Brazilian Growth*, 167–215. Delfim Neto's preoccupation with capital movements as a primary factor in leading him to introduce the flexible exchange rate was stressed by officials of the World Bank whom I interviewed in December 1971. For a defense of the newly introduced flexible rate policy, see Antonio Delfim Neto, "Verdade cambial e inflação," *O Estado de São Paulo*, October 13, 1968.

76. The exchange rate on the free market was not the only factor to determine the profitability of exports. Other factors were prior deposit requiements, multiple official rates, tax credits, and capital movements. At least the administration of the crawling peg seemed to have prevented any potential disincentive from the exchange rate. One analyst found that from August 1968 (when the crawling peg began) through 1972 Brazilian devaluations just about matched the differential between Brazil's inflation rate and that of her major trading partners. Syvrud, *Foundations of Brazilian Economic Growth*, 196.

77. Data are drawn from Syvrud, *Foundations*, 107–8; 157. The proliferation of tables of different official formulae for monetary correction can be seen in Acir Diniz Chara, *Compêndio de índices de correção monetária* (Rio: APEC, 1971). The discretionary character of the application of indexation in Brazil is stressed in Gustav Donald Jud, *Inflation and the Use of Indexing in Developing Countries* (New York: Praeger, 1978), 68.

78. There is a large body of literature on Brazilian agricultural policy and performance. An extensive review of data and principal interpretations is given in Fernando B. Homem de Melo, "Políticas de Desenvolvimento agrícola no Brasil," Universidade de São Paulo, Instituto de Pesquisas Econômicas, Trabalho Para Discussão No. 29 (January 1979). For analyses of government policymaking on agriculture in the decade and a half before the Costa e Silva government, see Gordon W. Smith, "Brazilian Agricultural Policy, 1950–1967," in Howard S. Ellis, ed., *The Economy of Brazil*, 213–65; and William H. Nicholls, "The Brazilian Agricultural Economy: Recent Performances and Policy," in Roett, ed., *Brazil in the Sixties*, 147–84. For another valuable overview which goes through 1976, see Fernando B. Homem de Melo, "Economic Policy and the Agricultural Sector During the Postwar Period," *Brazilian Economic Studies*, No. 6 (1982) (published by the Instituto de Planejamento Econômico e Social, Rio de Janeiro), 191–223.

79. The magnitude of the expansion in agricultural credit was striking. From 1968 through 1974 agricultural credit amounted to an average of 26 percent of total credit, whereas from 1960 through 1967 it had averaged only 13 percent of total

credit. Homem de Melo, "Economic Policy and the Agricultural Sector During the Postwar Period," 214.

80. The evolution of agricultural policy from 1967 to 1973 is given a useful review in "Economia teve impulso decisivo na gestão Delfim," *O Estado de São Paulo*, March 14, 1974. My brief discussion of agricultural policy is meant only to illustrate certain features of economic policymaking in the Costa e Silva presidency. The range of agricultural issues was much larger than can be suggested here.

81. There is much useful data and analysis of the balance of payments scene in Syvrud, *Foundations of Brazilian Economic Growth*, chap. VIII.

82. Portella de Mello, *A revolução e o governo costa e Silva*, 653.

83. Costa e Silva had an army minister (General Lyra Tavares) unable to discipline higher army officers who criticized government policies. The army minister's inability to head off challenges was notable in the case of General Moniz Aragão, who charged Costa e Silva with obtaining government favors for his relatives. Exasperation with Lyra Tavares's ineffectiveness runs through out (*ibid.*). For the army minister's statements through 1967, see Gen. A. de Lyra Tavares, *O exército brasileiro visto pelo seu ministro* (Recife: Universidade Federal de Pernambuco, Imprensa Universitaria, 1968). His difficult time as army minister is included in his memoirs: A. de Lyra Tavares, *O Brasil de minha geração*, 2 vols. (Rio de Janeiro: Biblioteca do Exército, 1976). The author, unfortunately, does not reveal much of himself or of the continuous battles in the military politics of that period.

84. Carlos Chagas, *113 dias de angústia: impedimento e morte de um presidente* (Pôrto Alegre: L & PM, 1979), 27–28; Portella de Mello, *A Revolução e o governo Costa e Silva*, 760.

85. Chagas, *113 dias de angústia,* 41. Looking back five years later, the dean of Brazilian political commentators, Carlos Castello Branco, described Costa e Silva as having become "imbued with an unexpected and tenacious consciousness of his civilian responsibilities." *Jornal do Brasil*, September 5, 1974.

86. Chagas, *113 dias de angústia* is a firsthand account of the political crisis created by Costa e Silva's stroke. Chagas was the presidential press secretary. The first edition of this book (Rio de Janeiro: Agência Jornalística Image, 1970) was confiscated by the Federal Police on the grounds it infringed on "national security." The second edition (1979) includes a number of new documents. The other principal published "inside" source on the 1969 crisis is Portella, *A revolução e o governo Costa e Silva*. Although Chagas and Portella were hardly mutual admirers, their accounts substantially agree. Unless otherwise indicated, they are the source for the account in the remainder of this chapter. For an incisive account of the succession crisis, see Flynn, *Brazil: A Political Analysis*, 425–40. A Brazilian analysis that stresses the interaction of civilian opposition groups and the military is Eliézer R. de Oliveira, *As Forças armadas: política e ideologia no Brasil, 1964–1969* (Petrópolis: Vozes, 1976). See also Schneider, "The Brazilian Military in Politics," in Robert Wesson, ed., *New Military Politics in Latin America* (New York: Praeger, 1982), 51–77. Clues to military thinking in this period can be found in the collected newspaper columns of Carlos Castello Branco, *Os militares no poder*, vol 2: O Ato 5 (Rio de Janeiro: Nova Fronteira, 1978); and Fernando Pedreira, *Brasil política* (São Paulo: DIFEL, 1975).

87. Portella de Mello, *A revolução e o governo de Costa e Silva,* 827.
88. *Ibid.,* 831. General Portella de Mello later wrote: "Barring the Vice President would be a revolutionary act, as revolutionary as AI–5 or recessing Congress" (*ibid.,* 818).
89. Hélio Silva and Maria Ribas Carneiro, *Os governos militares: 1969–1974* (São Paulo: Editora Três, 1975), 102. The authors give no source for the quotation from Aleixo. In any case, the tone of the remarks is similar to others by Aleixo at the time.
90. Portella de Mello, *A revolução e o governo de Costa se Silva,* 831.
91. Pedro Aleixo made no attempt to capitalize politically on his being blocked from succession to the presidency. In a 1975 magazine interview he noted that he had had to "recognize the impracticality of any reaction, given the responsibility assumed by the three military chiefs who took over the government and ended up distributing the power." José Carlos Brandi Aleixo and Carlos Chagas, ed., *Pedro Alexio: testemunhos e lições* (Brasilia: Centro Grafico do Senado Federal, 1976), 289.
92. The following sentence in the Act showed how the military wished to appear: "The nation can trust the patriotism of its military leaders who now, as always, know how to honor the historical legacy of their predecessors. while, at times of political crisis, remaining loyal to the national spirit, to the orderly and Christian evloution of their people, and oppose to extremist ideologies and violent solutions." The Act is published in Chagas, *113 dias de angústia,* 231–33. Later the junta issued a document pledging to continue the previous policy even as concerned "the reestablishment of democratic normality." Carlos Castello Branco, *Os militares no poder,* vol. 3: *O baile das solteironas* (Rio de Janeiro: Nova Fronteira, 1979), 335.
93. One analyst of Brazilian military politics suggests that there was an unoffical "electoral college" of 104 generals (which she lists by position) "responsible for collecting suggestions from armed forces officers." Maria Helena Moreira Alves, *State and Opposition,* 105–6.
94. *New York Times,* September 18, 1969.
95. This mentality of the senior officers was eloquently expressed by General Muricy at the ceremony when Army Minister Lyra Tavares left the army ministry to become ambassador to France: "In the Brazilian Revolution fortunately there does not exist and never has existed the charismatic leader, who is blindly followed by fanatics and who always leads his country into the most extreme dictatorships and therefore to chaos. The highest Brazilian military leaders do not have a militaristic spirit, much less the detestable figure of the human messiah who has a cure for everything and who is for himself and his followers the lord of all truth and the only savior of his country." Chagas, *113 dias de angústia,* 288.
96. Both letters are in Portella de Mello, *A revolução e o governo Costa e Silva,* 887–91.
97. *Ibid.,* 926.
98. Margaret S. Jenks, "Political Parties in Authoritarian Brazil" (Ph.D. dissertation, Duke University, 1979), 178. Because the constitutional text that Costa e Silva had ready to promulgate is unpublished, it is not possible to compare it with the final version. Carlos Chagas thought the changes more important than did General Portella de Mello. Chagas, *113 dias de angústia,* 175; Portella de Mello, *A revolução e o governo Costa e Silva,* 947.

99. Institutional Acts Nos. 12–17 are reprinted in Chagas, *113 dias de angústia*, 231–38.

100. Emílio Garrastazú Médici, *O jôgo da verdade* (1970), 10.

101. Much colorful detail on the Elbrick kidnapping has been given by Fernando Gabeira, one of Elbrick's kidnappers and later famous for a widely read memoir about his guerrilla days and his years in exile. Fernando Gabeira, *Carta sobre a anistia* (Rio de Janeiro: CODERCRI, 1979), 41–57; and Gabeira, *O que é isso, companheiro?* (Rio de Janeiro: CODECRI, 1980), 107–30. Gabeira was caught by the police and tortured. In June 1970 he was one of forty political prisoners ransomed for the West German ambassador, whom other guerrillas had kidnapped. On the Elbrick affair, see also A. J. Langguth, *Hidden Terrors* (New York: Pantheon Books, 1978), 167–96. Langguth, a former *New York Times* reporter, interviewed both Elbrick and Gabeira. I gained valuable information on the Elbrick kidnapping from an interview (June 30, 1983, in São Paulo) with Paulo de Tarso Wenceslau, a former guerrilla who was based in São Paulo and was sent to Rio to help on the logistics of the operation.

102. Interview with J. Ribeiro de Castro Filho, Rio de Janeiro, June 10, 1983.

103. *New York Times*, September 6, 1969. One of the manifesto's authors later explained that in it they were trying to escape from the usual "tedious prose of the left." Gabeira, *O que é isso*, 114.

104. Fernando Gabeira, *Carta sobre a anistia* (Rio de Janeiro: CODECRI, 1979), 50, 54; Langguth, *Hidden Terrors*, 186. One surviving guerrilla involved in the Elbrick kidnapping doubts that the government security forces had identified the house. Interview with Paulo de Tarso Wenceslau. But Gabeira's testimony seems convincing.

105. *New York Times*, September 7 and 10, 1969.

106. The Elbrick kidnapping apparently had little influence on the intra-military power struggles that emerged after Costa e Silva's stroke. The detailed accounts of those events in neither Carlos Chagas nor Jayme Portella de Mello give much weight to the military reaction to the kidnapping. Chagas, *113 dias*; Mello, *A revolução e o governo Costa e Silva*. When I interviewed one of the surviving Elbrick kidnappers, I asked if they had chosen September 4 because Costa e Silva's stroke made the government look more vulnerable. He looked surprised and said, "Not at all, we wanted to get as close as possible to September 7" (Brazil's Independence Day). Paulo de Tarso Wenceslau, interview.

107. It took more than a decade for the government version to be questioned with new documentation. The most important new source was Frei Betto, *Batismo de sangue: Os dominicanos e a morte de Carlos Marighella* (Rio de Janeiro: Civilização Brasileira, 1983). Betto concedes that the Dominicans, under torture, gave Sergio Fleury information on Marighela. But he argues convincingly that Fleury and his men mush have had information from other sources, probably informants. Betto also analyzes the ambush scene in detail, revealing many inconsistencies in the official version of the ambush. The purpose of the latter was of course to divide the left and the militant Christians. An earlier source claimed that captured ANL memebers, not Dominicans, provided the information. Quartim, *Dictatorship and Armed Struggle*, 215.

108. Gabeira, *O que é isso.*, 135. One widely read student of terrorism described Marighela as "predominantly interested in military (i. e., terrorist) action: the

more radical and destructive, the better." He further argues that "For this anti-intellectual and even irrational attitude there were perhaps mitigating circumstances: the sterile and unending ideological debates of the Latin American left, usually a rehash of ideas imported from France." Walter Laqueur, *Terrorism* (Boston: Little, Brown, 1977), 185. For the December memorial service for his onetime fellow PCB member, Jorge Amado sent a tribute to that "incorruptible Brazilian, that Bahian native son of the jovial laugh and the impassioned heart . . . ." Batista Bernardo, *Guerrilhas e guerril-heiros*, 259.

109. On U.S.–Brazil relations, see Jerome Levinson and Juan de Onis, *The Alliance That Lost Its Way* (Chicago: Quadrangle, 1970) and Peter Bell, "Brazilian–American Relations," in Roett, ed., *Brazil in the Sixties*, 77–102.

110. *New York Times*, December 18, 1968.

111. These data are drawn from a table in "United States Policies and Programs in Brazil," *Hearings Before the Subcommittee on Western Hemisphere Affairs of the Committee on Foreign Relations, United States Senate, Ninety-second Congress, First Session, May 4, 5, and 11, 1971* (Washington: U.S. Government Printing Office, 1971), 162.

112. For examples of the debate, see *New York Times*, December 22, 1968, and April 28, 1969.

113. *Christian Science Monitor*, July 11, 1969.

114. Extensive coverage was given to the Rockefeller visit in the *New York Times, June 9 and 16–18, 1969.*

115. *The Rockefeller Report on the Americas* (Chicago: Quadrangle, 1969), 34, 63.

Chapter V: Médici: The Authoritarian Face

1. In his first speech after being selected by the military, Médici himself said he had been chosen by the High Command because he was "capable of keeping the Armed Forces of the Nation united and working together in pursuit of the ideals of the Revolution of March 1964," Emílio Garrastazú Médici, *O Jôgo da Verdade* (Brasília: Secretaria de Imprensa da Presidência de República, 1971), 9. There is a useful chronology of Médici's first year as president in Fernando José Leite Costa e Lucia Gomes Klein, "Um ano de Govérno Médici," *Dados*, No. 9 (1972), 156–221. A valuable source on Médici's first sixteen months is the collection of daily newspaper columns by Carlos Castello Branco, *Os militares no poder*, vol. 3: *O baile das solteironas* (Rio de Janeiro: Nova Fronteira, 1979). Médici apparently intended to write no memoirs. He granted no interviews until one appeared in *Veja*, May 16, 1984. In it Médici discussed his policies and governing techniques. A more elaborate version of the interview appeared in book form in A.C. Scartezini, *Segredos de Médici* (São Paulo: Editora Marco Zero, 1985). Médici revealed himself to be proud of his government's accomplishments (inflation under control, the foreign debt under control, government projects finished on time, etc.) but resentful of the image promoted by his critics as the president who tortured and kept down wages. Some of the material in this chapter was published in an earlier form in Thomas E. Skidmore, "The Political Economy of Policy-Making in Authoritarian Brazil, 1967–70," in Philip O'Brien and Paul Cammack, eds., *Generals in Retreat:*

The Crisis of Military Rule in Latin America (Manchester: Manchester University Press, 1985), 115–43.

2. Carlos Castello Branco, *Os militares no poder*, vol. 3, 336–37. Castello Branco was paraphrasing the testimonies of civilian politicians who described Médici as "discreet and serene of manner." The latter was a phrase few observers would have associated with the SNI.

3. Médici, *Jôgo*, 23.

4. *Ibid.*, 23–24.

5. He was also the brother of Ernesto Geisel, destined to succeed Médici in the presidency.

6. Fernando Pedreira was one of the few who were more positive, He thought hope was as high when Médici assumed power as it had been for Costa e Silva in 1967. Pedreira, *Brasil política*, 152. Within months Pedreira had become disillusioned with the new government (*ibid.*, 166–67).

7. In the words of the always well-informed columnist Carlos Castello Branco, the military believed that "by rigid control of the country the Armed Forces can at the same time crush subversion and produce development," Castello Branco, *Os militares*, vol. 3, 345.

8. There were, however, spontaneous protests and riots. The notoriously bad commuter train service between the greater Rio suburbs and the city prompted several spontaneous passenger riots starting in 1974. They are analyzed in Jośe Alvaro Moises, et al., *Contradições urbanas e movimentos sociais* (Rio de Janeiro: CEDEC, 1977). A similar riot, over greatly increased bus fares, in Brasília in 1974 is described in Peter Evans, *Dependent Development* (Princeton: Princeton University Press, 1978), 3.

9. The questions of the wage pattern and labor mobility are discussed in more detail in Chapter VIII, below. Income distribution is discussed in the section on "The Economic Boom and its Critics" later in this chapter.

10. In retrospect Médici insisted that "the decisions of my government were always mine." As for his ministers, they "had the power to choose their subordinates but they were forbidden to decide anything I didn't want." *Veja*, May 16, 1986, p. 15. The obvious question was how many important decisions were never run past him. Other evidence would indicate there were many.

11. The National Security Council consisted of the president, all ministers of state, all members of the Armed Forces High Command and the Head of the Civilian Presidential Staff. Maria Helena Moreira Alves, *State and Opposition*, 77. Fernando Pedreira grew steadily more alarmed over the Council's role as the Médici presidency wore on. Pedreira, *Brasil política*, 166–67, 190, and 214.

12. Decision-making within the military is clearly explained in Stepan, *The Military in Politics*.

13. Medeiros, for example, had rejected direct presidential elections for Brazil, explaining that they caused too much "agitation" and thus would make the country ungovernable. "Medeiros responsabiliza eleições diretas pelas crises," *Jornal do Brasil*, June 23, 1968.

14. For greater detail, see Maria Helena Moreira Alves, *State and Opposition*, 118.

15. Sérgio Caparelli, *Televisão e capitalismo no Brasil* (Pôrto Alegre: L & PM, 1982), 156; Muniz Sodré, *O monopólio da fala* (Petrópolis: Vozes, 1977), 91, 99.

16. Neuma Aguiar, "Papéis sexuais na propaganda governmental," in Maria Isabel Mendes de Almeida and Margareth de Almeida Gonçalves, eds., *Sociologia do*

cotidiano (forthcoming), 1. One communications researcher found the AERP's TV and movie spots to be far superior to the traditional commercial spots because they more skillfully played on "the unconscious associations of the individual." Luiz Fernando Santoro, "Tendências populistas na TV brasileira ou as escasas possibilidades de acesso às antenas," in José Marques de Melo, coord.,*Populismo e comunicação* (São Paulo: Cortez, 1981), 140.

17. Quoted in Caparelli, *Televisão e capitalismo*, 160.

18. Departamento de Estudos e Indicadores Sociais: Superintendência de Estudos Geográficos e Sócio-econômicos, *Indicadores sociais: tabelas selecionadas* (Rio de Janeiro: IBGE, 1979), 100.

19. Carlos Rodolfo Améndola Avila, *A teleinvasão: a participação estrangeira na televisão do Brasil* (São Paulo: Cortez Editora, 1982), 109; Sérgio Mattos, "Advertising and Government Influences: The Case of Brazilian Television," *Communication Research*, XI, No. 2 (April 1984); Mattos, "The Impact of the 1964 Revolution on Brazilian Television," (San Antonio: Klingesmith, 1982), 67; Caparelli, *Televisão e capitalismo*, 165, 178.

20. It is worth nothing that President Castelo Branco had indignantly rejected any idea of a PR campaign to improve his image. Dulles, *President Castello Branco*, 286.

21. Janet Lever, *Soccer Madness* (Chicago: University of Chicago Press, 1983), 67–68.

22. This government strategy is well described in Flynn, "Sambas, Soccer, and Nationalism," 327–30. The social function of soccer in Brazil in these years is well analyzed in Lever, *Soccer Madness*, 63–69. For a critique of Lever on the grounds that she does not satisfactorily relate Brazilian soccer to its social and political context, see John Humphrey and Alan Tomlinson, "Reflections on Brazilian Football: a Review and Critique of Janet Lever's *Soccer Madness*," *Bulletin of Latin American Research*, V, No. 1 (1986), 101–8. Ulysses Guimarães, the MDB leader, acknowledged that the government was shrewdly exploiting Brazilian (male!) psychology: "Enquanto houver cachaça, samba, carnaval, mulata, e campenonato de futebol, nao haverá rebelião no Brasil. O Corintians [São Paulo team] segura mais o povo do que a Lei de Segurança Nacional." Ulysses Guimarães, *Rompendo o cerco* (Rio de Janeiro: Paz e Terra, 1978), 24. The Médici government's attempt to exploit soccer for political purposes began to sour as the years went on, as shown in Robert M. Levine, "The Burden of Success: *Futebol* and Brazilian Society through the 1970s," *Journal of Popular Culture*, XIV, No. 3 (Winter 1980), 453–64.

23. The authoritarian stance in the executive found its echo among the pro-government legislators, such as Petrônio Portella, a prominent ARENA senator who in early November 1969 attributed Brazil's political problems to the politicians who meddle in disputes "that benefit only the radicals, those destroyers of the constitutional democratic order. There was no choice but the heroic remedy of the Fifth Institutional Act." Petrônio Portella, *Tempo de Congresso* (Brasília: Senado Federal, 1973), vol. 1, 137.

24. There is a discussion of Médici's selection in each state in Schneider, *The Political System of Brazil*, 320–22.

25. Fernando Pedreira thought President Médici had chosen politically inept figures, an arrangement Pedreira generously attributed to the new president's tendency to govern by military command. Pedreira, *Brasil política*, 169–72.

26. There is an excellent analysis of the political rise of Chagas Freitas in Eli Diniz, *Voto e máquina política: patronagem e clientelismo no Rio de Janeiro* (Rio de Janeiro: Paz e Terra, 1982).

27. The following analysis draws extensively on the account in Margaret S. Jenks, "Political Parties in Authoritarian Brazil" (Ph. D. dissertation, Duke University, 1979).

28. A detailed study of the congressional debates (both houses) in the Médici presidency can be found in Lidice A. Pontes Maduro, et al., "O congresso nacional no atual sistema político brasileiro: sétima legislatura (71–74)," *Revista de Ciência Política*, XXI (número especial, December, 1978). Unfortunately the debates—analyzed by party position—are cited almost entirely in paraphrases and do not give the original speaker or date. For a discussion of the government's relationship with the Congress, see Castello Branco, *Os militares*, vol. 3, 330–37.

29. David V. Fleischer, "Constitutional and Electoral Engineering in Brazil: A Double-Edged Sword: 1964–1982," in D. Nohlen, ed., *Wahlen und Wahlpolitik in Lateinamerika* (Heidelberg: Esprint Verlag, 1983).

30. Censorship effectively limited what Brazilians could know about the crackdown. The *New York Times*, November 7 and 16, 1970, and *Newsweek*, November 23, 1970, reported the story. The latter noted that "there seemed no rhyme or reason to the arrests. Nuns, politicians, journalists, musicians, slum-dwellers, clerks, maids and even housewives were carted away." It cited Brazilian speculation that "hard-line generals, who constitute the backbone of the present Brazilian regime, wanted to remind everyone—including Médici—that they were really in charge, and that Brazilians would be well advised to keep on going to soccer matches with the President and forget all the talk about democracy."

31. Emílio Garrastazú Médici, *A verdadeira paz* (Brasília: Departamento de Imprensa, 1973), 176.

32. Schneider, *The Political System of Brazil*, 323.

33. A case study of politics on this level can be found in Geert A. Banck, "The War of Reputations: The Dynamics of the Local Political System in the State of Espírito Santo, Brazil," *Boletín de Estudios Latinoamericanos y del Caribe*, No. 17 (December 1974), 69–77.

34. In the 1974 elections, which were far more competitive than those in 1970, the incidence of blank ballots was only 9 percent. Ruy Santos, "A Eleição de 1974," *Revista Brasileira de Estudos Políticos*, No. 43 (July 1976), 8.

35. A careful analysis of the Senate races showed the closer the race, the lower was the percentage of blank ballots, which tends to confirm that more blank ballots were cast when the opposition had little chance of winning.

36. MDB deputies and senators could speak in Congress but their legislative function was sharply reduced after AI–5. A look at what happened to bills will demonstrate the point. In 1967–68, some 83 percent of bills introduced by legislators were eventually approved, and 98 percent of those introduced by the executives were approved. For 1970–73 only 8 percent of the legislator-initiated bills were approved, while 98 percent of the bills from executive became law. Gláucio Ary Dillon Soares, "Military Authoritarianism and Executive Absolutism in Brazil," *Studies in Comparative International Development*, XIV, Nos. 3–4 (Fall–Winter 1979), 104–26.

37. Alencar Furtado, *Salgando a terra* (Rio de Janeiro: Paz e Terra, 1977), 29.

38. It was Decree-law No. 69,534, issued on November 11, 1971. Its text was, of course, secret. For details, see Maria Helena Moreira Alves, *State and Opposition*, 119.
39. Carlos Chagas, *Resistir é preciso* (Rio de Janeiro: Paz e Terra, 1975), 32.
40. *Ibid.*, 23–24; Jenks, "Political Parties," 211–12.
41. Chagas, *Resistir é preciso*, 19–21.
42. I am not arguing that the guerrillas wanted this outcome. The point is only that, in retrospect, such an outcome might have better served their very short-term goals.
43. The Mitrione case is analyzed at length in Langguth, *Hidden Terrors*. Before being posted to Montevideo, Mitrione spent several years as a police adviser in Belo Horizonte and Rio de Janeiro.
44. The would-be kidnappers were members of the VPR in Rio Grande do Sul, who had feared they wouldn't be able to bring off the action. They had been pushed into it by emissaries from the Rio VPR. The Riograndenses agreed to go ahead because they desperately wanted to ransom some comrades who were in prison and facing (or undergoing) torture. Indio Vargas, *Guerra é guerra. dizia o torturador* (Rio de Janeiro: CODECRI, 1981), 96–101.
45. Alfredo Syrkis, *"Os carbonários": memórias da guerrilha perdida* (São Paulo: Global, 1980), 176–95. Syrkis was one of the kidnappers.
46. Emiliano José and Oldack Miranda, *Lamarca: o capitão da guerrilha* (São Paulo: Global, 1980), 99–101.
47. José and Miranda, *Lamarca*, 101.
48. The best source on the von Holleben kidnapping is Syrkis, *Os carbonários*. There is information also in José and Miranda, *Lamarca*. Unless otherwise stated, my subsequent analysis draws on these sources.
49. The best linguist among the kidnappers told Bucher in English that "Yankee imperialism bought fifteen prisoners, Japan five and Germany forty. Now it's time for the Swiss banks to buy the lives of some of our tortured comrades." Syrkis, *Os carbonários*, 237.
50. To get some idea of the severity of government censorship, one need only note that the Brazilian representative of the Associated Press was jailed for breaking the story on Bucher's kidnapping. When follow-up stories were filed by Agence France-Presse, its correspondent was deported. Marvin Alisky, *Latin American Media: Guidance and Censorship* (Ames: Iowa State University Press, 1981), 111.
51. Syrkis, *Os carbonários*, 243–44; *A repressão militar-policial no Brasil* (n. p.: Photo offset, 1975), 106.
52. José and Miranda, *Lamarca*, 104.
53. Syrkis, *Os carbonários*, 289–94.
54. A fuller account of government repression, including treatment of prisoners, is given in the next section of this chapter.
55. Caldas, *Tirando o capuz*, 186. Caldas was paraphrasing Debray, still the Bible for many on the left.
56. After the guerrilla war finished in Brazil, Anselmo had plastic surgery and took the precaution of living abroad. He has given several long interviews in which he related fragments of his past but never the whole story. Opinion is divided on when he started working for military intelligence. He claimed it was after his guerrilla training in Cuba, where he became disillusioned with communism. Some journalists and former guerrillas think he had been working for the

military even before 1964—that he had been planted in the navy by Brazilian intelligence—perhaps working with the CIA. Henrique Lago, "Cabo Anselmo, um agente secreto," *Folha de São Paulo*, October 14, 1979; Marco Aurélio Borba, *Cabo Anselmo* (São Paulo: Global, 1981); and Octavio Ribeiro, *Por que eu traí: confissões de Cabo Anselmo*(São Paulo: Global, 1984).

57. The following account is drawn primarily from José and Miranda, *Lamarca*.

58. Jones subsequently died under torture. He was tied to the back of a car with his mouth over the exhaust pipe and dragged around the prison courtyard. His fate was described by Alex Polari, a fellow guerrilla imprisoned with him, in *Em busca do tesouro*, 163–98. Jones had an American father and a Brazilian mother. The latter, a well-known fashion designer with the professional name of Zuzu Angel, never got any official explanation of her son's death. A woman of enormous persistence, she protested the government's silence to everyone in earshot, and because she was known in U.S. and European fashion circles, that included the foreign press. When Secretary of State Henry Kissinger visited Brazil in February 1976 she bypassed the heavy security and thrust into his hand documents about her son's death, much to the embarrassment and fury of foreign ministry officials. She became convinced that the government planned to kill her (she left a statement to this effect) and in fact she died on April 14, 1976, in an automobile accident similar to the one that killed Karen Silkwood. *Folha de São Paulo*, July 26, 1976; Silva, *Governos militares*, 132–36. Friends in the U.S. consulate in Rio informed me that their vigorous investigation into the accident left them convinced the chance of its having been foul play was at least 50–50. Four months later another automobile accident took the life of former President Juscelino Kubitschek. Although the circumstances appeared much less suspicious, some immediately raised doubts about this "accident," too. Juscelino's widow, Dona Sarah, said later, "the suspicion is great that this was no accident." "Entrevista: D. Sarah Kubitschek: a suspeita morte de JK," *Jornal do Brasil*, October 19, 1986. Whatever the truth about the two deaths, the fact that many in the opposition could believe in such government-orchestrated murders says much about the political atmosphere during Geisel's third year in office.

59. See, for example, *Diário de São Paulo* for September 19, *O Globo* for September 20, *Manchete* for October 2, and *O Estado de São Paulo* for September 19, 1971.

60. Marighela, *For the Liberation of Brazil*, 98–101; a similar line of argument is developed in "Algumas questões sobre as guerrilhas no Brasil," first published in the *Jornal do Brasil*, September 5, 1968, and reprinted in *Escritos de Carlos Marighela* (São Paulo: Editoral Livramento, 1979), 117–30.

61. João Batista Berardo, *Guerrilhas e guerrilheiros no drama da América Latina* (São Paulo: Edições Populares, 1981), 259.

62. I have drawn here on the useful overview of the Araguaia front in Maria Helena Moreira Alves, *State and Opposition*; 121–23.

63. Marighela wrote that guerrillas "should avoid a confrontation with the overwhelming superiority of the enemy along the Atlantic coast, where he has concentrated his forces." In the interior, Marighela argued, the military would be on unfamiliar ground and urban guerrillas could cut their supply lines from the coast, *Escritos de Carlos Marighela*, 121.

64. The fullest account of the Araguaia guerrilla front is Fernando Portela, *Guerra de guerrilhas no Brasil* (São Paulo: Global Editora, 1979), which is an ex-

panded version of a series of articles by Portela in the *Jornal da Tarde* in January 1979. A useful collection of documents and interviews can be found in Palmério Dória, et al., *Guerrilha do Araguaia* (São Paulo: Alfa-Omega, 1978). The most complete source from the guerrilla side is Clóvis Moura, ed., *Diário da guerrilha do Araguaia* (São Paulo: Alfa-Omega, 1979). The latter appears to be a composite of several documents. My account draws primarily on Portela, *Guerra de guerrilhas.*

65. Interview with Técio Lins e Silva, Rio de Janeiro, July 7, 1983.

66. In consulting the Associated Press office files in Rio in May 1975 I found a copy of a mimeographed declaration from the "Araguaia Guerrilla Forces Command" dated October 21, 1972. There was also a May 1974 communiqué (No. 44) from the "União da Juventude Patriotica," an Amazon guerrilla group. The accompanying AP story of June 27 (presumably not published in Brazil) identified the authors as a "pro-Cuban clandestine splinter group of the outlawed PCB." The AP author was well informed, for the story said the guerrillas had held out against a heavy government attack, including air sorties.

67. In a conversation with Indio Vargas in Uruguay, Leonel Brizola once dismissed Régis Debray and his "foco" theory thus: "Don't swallow that one. Brazil is no Cuba: our country is a continent and we would need thousands of guerrilla focos." Indio Vargas, *Guerra é guerra, dizia o torturador* (Rio de Janeiro: CODECRI, 1981), 27.

68. One militant leftist who carried out a postmortem on the left's failure in Brazil argued that in Argentina, Chile, and Uruguay the working class was already organized as a class. Not, however, in Brazil. Quartim, *Dictatorship and Armed Struggle,* 123.

69. There is a huge literature on this subject. Two useful works on Latin America are Loveman and Davids, eds., *Guerrilla Warfare,* and Georges Fauriol, ed., *Latin American Insurgencies* (Washington: National Defense University Press, 1985).

70. Syrkis, *Os carbonários,* 280.

71. The Director of *Isto É* was unequivocal on this point, arguing that the guerrilla violence had been used to "justify the severe control [the government] achieved over civil society . . ." Antonio Fernando de Franceschi in Paulo Sérgio Pinheiro, ed., *Crime, violência e poder* (São Paulo: Brasiliense, 1983), 175. Another leading journalist was equally adamant, arguing that it was the guerrillas and especially their kidnappings that had helped achieve "a reconciliation between the military establishment and public opinion." Pedreira, *Brasil política,* 279. The effect on the left was profound. In the words of one survivor of torture: "The Brazilian left experienced in ten years what it had not experienced in 40, and it paid a cost, high in painful human suffering." Alvaro Caldas, *Tirando o capuz* (Rio de Janeiro: CODECRI, 1981), 140.

72. Alves, *Torturas e torturados.*

73. Amnesty International, *Report on Allegations of Torture in Brazil.*

74. Obviously, such generalizations about the administration of Brazilian justice are dangerous. Yet we must somehow deal with an argument that has been made repeatedly by Brazilian scholars and victims of the repressive era. Some guidance is given by Brazilian police reporters. The journalists have done their best to open the Brazilian public's (meaning the elite's) eyes to the routine police resort to violence when handling common criminals or criminal suspects.

Examples of such works (which usually originate as magazine or newspaper stories) are Percival de Souza, Marcos Faerman, and Fernando Portela, *Violência e repressão* (São Paulo: Edições Símbolo, 1978); and Octávio Ribeiro, *Barra pesada* (Rio de Janeiro: CODECRI, 1977). The horrors of life in the overcrowded prisons are graphically described in Percival de Souza, *A prisão: histórias dos homens que vivem no maior presídio do mundo* (São Paulo: Alfa-Omega, n.d.); and André Torres, *Ilha grande* (Petrópolis: Vozes, 1979). No area of police maltreatment has been more shocking than that towards minors, as documented in Carlos Alberto Luppi, *Agora e na hora de nossa morte: o massacre do menor no Brasil* (São Paulo: Ed. Brasil Debates, 1982).

75. Paulo Sérgio Pinheiro, "Violência e cultura," in Bolivar Lamounier, Francisco C. Weffort, and Maria Victoria Benevides, eds., *Direito, cidadania e participação* (São Paulo: T.A. Queiroz, 1981), 31, 33–49; Pinheiro, "Polícia e crise política: o caso das polícias militares," in Roberto da Matta, et al., *Violência brasileira* (São Paulo: Brasiliense, 1982), 71. A scholar who has researched the São Paulo criminal records for 1880–1924 found frequent references in the press to physical mistreatment of prisoners: Boris Fausto, *Crime e cotidiano: a criminalidade em São Paulo, 1880–1924* (São Paulo: Brasiliense, 1984), 163. I am not discussing here the extent to which police violence (in the form of torture) was used as a general means of social control. That much larger question is explored in a general way in Alberto Passos Guimarães, *As classes perigosas* (Rio: Graal, 1982).

76. Gilberto Freyre, "O escravo nos anúncios de jornal do tempo do imperio," *Lanterna Verde*, No. 2 (1935), 7–32.

77. Aderito Lopes, *O Esquadrão da morte* (Lisboa: Prelo, 1973), 29; Pinheiro, "Violência e cultura," 51–54.

78. Lopes, *O esquadrão da morte*, 30; Maria Victoria Benevides, *Violência, povo e polícia* (São Paulo: Brasiliense, 1983), 77.

79. Fernando Gabeira, *Carta sobre a anistia; a entrevista do Pasquim; conversação sobre 1968* (Rio de Janeiro: CODECRI, 1979), 27. Gabeira was one of the many political prisoners who had their eyes opened while imprisoned: "In jail you get to know Brazil's other side." Gabeira was worried that with the end of violence against political prisoners (which included many from the elite), the elite would forget about the violence routinely practiced on the poor (*ibid.*, 30). Another political prisoner who had the same revelation when watching the treatment of common prisoners was Indio Vargas, *Guerra é guerra*, 84–87.

80. The history of torture since Greek and Roman times is discussed in Edward Peters, *Torture* (New York: Basil Blackwell, 1985) and Peter Singer, "Unspeakable Acts," *The New York Review of Books*, February 27, 1986, 27–30. The philosopher was Michael Levin, "The Case for Torture," *Newsweek*, June 7, 1982, p. 13.

81. Fon, *Tortura*, 27–32. The background to this line of military thinking is well analyzed in Stepan, *The Military in Politics*.

82. Fon, *Tortura*, 15–16.

83. *Ibid.*, 55–58; Moniz Bandeira, *Carteis e desnacionalização* (Rio de Janeiro: Editora Civilização Brasileira, 1979), 204–5; *Veja*, January 15, 1986, p. 27. Interview with Kurt Mirow. Interviews with Antonio Carlos Fon, São Paulo, June 27 and 29, 1983. Boilesen had access to OBAN's torture rooms, where he often taunted prisoners. In April 1971 guerrillas machine-gunned Boilesen to

death in an act of calculated revenge. It was costly. Within a week the entire assassination team had been captured. Syrkis, *Os carbonários*, 295; Langguth, *Hidden Terrors*, 122–23.

84. Fon, *Tortura*, 18. One of General Carvalho Lisboa's successors, General Humberto de Souza Mello, who commanded the Second Army from January 1971 to January 1974, was noted for his enthusiastic support of the repressive apparatus in São Paulo. Samples of his thinking can be found in Humberto de Souza Mello, *Idéia e ação: pronunciamentos* (São Paulo: Secretaria de Cultura, Esportes e Turismo do Estado de São Paulo, 1974).

85. Emílio Garrastazú Médici, *Nova consciência do Brasil* (Brasília: Departamento de Imprensa Nacional, 1973), 29, 91.

86. Petrônio Portella, *Tempo de Congresso* (Brasília: Centro Gráfico do Senado Federal, 1973), 140, 144.

87. For a careful description of this security network, see Maria Helena Moreira Alves, *State and Opposition*, 121–32.

88. Pinheiro, "Polícia e crise política," 59, 64.

89. The best single source on Sérgio Fleury is Helio Pereira Bicudo, *Meu depoimento sobre o esquadrão da morte* (São Paulo: Pontifícia Comissão de Justiça e Paz de São Paulo, 1977). Bicudo is the São Paulo prosecutor who courageously attempted for years to bring action against Fleury and his fellow São Paulo police in the Death Squad. Also useful is Lopes, *O esquadrão da morte*. Several times Bicudo won indictments against Fleury, but higher authorities— judicial or executive—always blocked conviction. On one occasion the federal government amended the penal code (thereafter known as the *lei Fleury*) to allow the defendant to avoid jail while awaiting a jury decision. As usual, the latter cleared him of all charges. The best analysis of the historical context in which the "death squad" emerged is Deborah L. Jakubs, "Police Violence in Times of Political Tension: The Case of Brazil, 1968–1971," in David H. Bayley, ed., *Police and Society* (Beverly Hills: Sage, 1977), 85–106.

90. A good overview of the right-wing groups is Delcio Monteiro de Lima, *Os senhores da direita* (Belo Horizonte: Antares, 1980).

91. Fon, *Tortura*, 51–53. The prisoner in question was Shizuo Ozawa, who was a link to Carlos Lamarca, the government's number one target. Fleury was disciplined for this incident with exile for six months to an outlying police station. From there he was saved in August 1970 by CENIMAR, which got him reinstated at DOPS in order to interrogate a prize guerrilla commander, Eduardo Leite (with the nom de guerre of Bacurí), whom CENIMAR had just captured.

92. Helio Bicudo, *Meu depoimento*, 51. One imprisoned guerrilla who saw Fleury at work said he was clearly adulated by all the military, Polari, *Em busca do tesouro*, 237.

93. A typical example is described in Gabeira, *O que é isso?*, 160–61. The doctors were also asked how close the prisoner was to death.

94. A moving account of his torture and nine years in prison is given by Alípio de Freitas, *Resistir é preciso: memória do tempo da morte civil do Brasil* (Rio de Janeiro: Editora Record, 1981). The author was Portuguese-born and a former priest. He had been active in organizing peasants in the Northeast before 1964 and in the later 1960s joined the guerrillas. Imprisonment and torture breathed a powerful creative urge into some victims. One of the best known was Alex Polari (de Alverga), whose prison poems are published in *Inventário de cicatrizes* (São Paulo: Global, 1979) and *Camarim de prisioneiro* (São Paulo: Global,

1980). Latin American authoritarian governments of the 1960s and 1970s so often resorted to torture of political prisoners that scholars of these countries have started to study systematically the impact of "the culture of fear," not only on the political system, but on the society at large. For details of one project, see Joan Dassin, "The Culture of Fear," *Social Science Research Council Items*, XL, No. 1 (March 1986), 7–12.

95. Details on the Paiva case are given in Hélio Silva and Maria Cecília Ribas Carneiro, *Emílio de Médici: o combate às guerrilhas, 1969–1974* (São Paulo: Grupo de Comunicação Tres, 1983), 103–29; the Paiva case was often cited by the opposition, as in Marcos Freire, *Oposição no Brasil, hoje* (Rio de Janeiro: Paz e Terra, 1974), 88–100; some educated guesses about why Paiva was a target for the security forces are given in Marco Antonio Tavares Coelho in Carlos Rangel, *1978: a hora de enterrar os ossos* (Rio de Janeiro: Tipo Editor, 1979).

96. In September 1986 new information came to light, demolishing the claim Paiva had been kidnapped. Dr. Amilcar Lobo, an army officer and psychiatrist who worked in the Rio DOI-CODI operations in January 1971, described having seen Paiva there in shock from massive hemorrhaging over his entire body, about to die and able only to murmur his name. *Veja,* September 10, 1986, pp. 36–41.

97. One of the most eloquent and penetrating analyses of the social impact of torture and the repressive apparatus is the document sent by political prisoners to the Brazilian Bar Association in November 1976, which is reprinted in Luzimar Nogueira Dias, ed., *Esquerda armada: testemunho dos presos políticos do presídio Milton Dias Moreira, no Rio de Janeiro* (Vitória: Edições do Leitor, 1979), 85–110. One longtime observer noted in early 1973, "What is significant is that the Brazilian army has institutionalized and protected torture and brutality as instruments of social control and that such methods have, and are intended to have, far-reaching consequences of intimidation," Brady Tyson, "Brazil: Nine Years of Military Tutelage," *Worldview,* XVI, No. 7 (July 1973), 29–34.

98. For an explanation of the structure of military justice, see Joan Dassin, ed., *Torture in Brazil* (New York: Random House, 1986), 141–60.

99. This description of how lawyers for the prisoners struggled to penetrate the labyrinth is based on interviews with Técio Lins e Silva (Rio de Janeiro, July 7, 1983), José Carlos Dias (São Paulo, June 29, 1983), and J. Ribeiro de Castro Filho (Rio de Janeiro, June 10, 1983).

100. "Quem tem medo da Justiça Militar?" in Rangel, *A hora de enterrar os ossos,* 83–90.

101. *O Globo,* April 17, 1978, p. 6.

102. Dassin, ed., *Torture in Brazil,* 77–80.

103. *Veja,* December 21, 1977, p. 23.

104. The tribunal's opinion was published in *Revista Trimestral de Jurisprudência,* LIX, 247–59. I am indebted to Professor Keith Rosenn of the University of Miami Law School for this reference.

105. Frei Betto, *Batismo de sangue,* 153.

106. The political prisoners who in 1976 analyzed the functioning of military justice saw it as little more than "a logical continuation of torture" and as a "cover" for torture; Nogueira Dias, ed., *Esquerda armada,* 93–110. If they knew of any acquittals they did not find them relevant.

107. F.A. Miranda Rosa, *Justiça e autoritarismo* (Rio de Janeiro: Zahar, 1985), 34–37.
108. *Veja*, December 21, 1977, p. 23.
109. Fiechter, *Brazil Since 1964*, 149. It was rumored at the time that some of the dismissed officers had also been guilty of corruption (in connection with the building of the giant Rio–Niteroi bridge), which gave the High Command a further motive for the purge. *A repressão militar-policial no Brasil*, (n.p.: Photo offset, 1975), 64.
110. Rivaldo Chinem and Tim Lopes, *Terror policial* (São Paulo: Global, 1980), 17; it was alleged that men of the Second Army Command gave Fleury a reward of 50,000 cruzeiros for killing Joaquim Camara Ferreira, the successor to Marighela in the command of the ALN, *A Repressão militar-policial no Brasil*, 131. São Paulo Governor Abreu Sodré gave Fleury a public commendation for his "act of bravery" in killing Marighela; Chinem and Lopes, *Terror policial*, 15–16.
111. Covering up deaths, especially from torture, was the gravest involvement for a commander. A general with experience in the security network later commented that "to secretly dispose of a body the order would have to come from someone with at least four stars (or the equivalent in the other two services)," Rangel, *A hora de enterrar os ossos*, 14. The most publicized missing body was Rubens Paiva, who was probably disposed of by the PARA-SAR, the elite air force rescue service.
112. Joan R. Dassin has provided an excellent account of this subject in "Press Censorship—How and Why," *Index on Censorship*, VIII, No. 4 (July–August 1979), 13–19, and "Press Censorship and the Military State in Brazil," in Jane L. Curry and Joan R. Dassin, eds., *Press Control Around the World* (New York: Praeger, 1982), 149–86. The period of self-censorship is omitted in Dassin's account. Argemiro Ferreira, "Informação sub controle," *Revista Arquivos*, No. 165, pp. 94–110. I am indebted to Alberto Dines for details on how censorship was applied. For foreign reports on Brazilian censorship, see the *New York Times*, December 28, 1970, and February 17, 1973. For a firsthand account of how censorship worked at *O Estado de São Paulo*, see the interview with the paper's editor-in-chief, Oliveiros Ferreira, in Rangel, *A hora de enterrar os ossos*, 92–99.
113. Robert N. Pierce, *Keeping the Flame: Media and Government in Latin America* (New York: Hastings House, 1979), 45.
114. A reflection of the buildup to this decision can be seen in the articles of *O Estado de São Paulo* by Carlos Chagas. From mid-April to mid-August his columns were full of fables, a sure indication that names could not be named; Chagas, *Resistir é preciso*, 31–40.
115. Pierce, *Keeping the Flame*, 44; Marvin Alisky, *Latin American Media: Guidance and Censorship* (Ames: Iowa State University Press, 1981), 110–11.
116. Gerald Thomas, "Closely Watched TV," *Index on Censorship*, VIII, No. 4 (July–August 1979), 43–46.
117. Krane, "Opposition Strategy," 55.
118. As one Church activist later put it, the government couldn't name a bishop the way they could name the rector of the University of Brasília. Interview with Frei Betto, São Paulo, June 30, 1983. In the 1970s the Brazilian Catholic Church emerged as one of the most innovative and controversial in the world. For background on that process, see Ralph della Cava, "Catholicism and

Society in Twentieth-Century Brazil," *Latin American Research Review,* XI (No. 2, 1976), 7–50, and Thomas Bruneau, *The Political Transformation of the Brazilian Catholic Church* (Cambridge: Cambridge University Press, 1974). Bruneau has continued the story to 1978 in *The Church in Brazil: The Politics of Religion* (Austin: University of Texas Press, 1982), which includes studies of a number of ecclesiastical base communities. The most successful attempt to place the contemporary Brazilian Church in perspective is Scott Mainwaring, *The Catholic Church and Politics in Brazil, 1916–1985* (Stanford: Stanford University Press, 1986), which gives a wealth of detail on both the Church–government conflicts and the process of change within the Church. See also Ralph della Cava, "The 'People's Church,' the Vatican, and the Abertura," to appear in Alfred Stepan, ed., *Democratizing Brazil* (forthcoming, Oxford University Press), which is primarily on post-1970. Della Cava is especially interesting on the European influences on both the progressive and the conservative elements in the church. There is a series of interviews with bishops in Helena Salem, ed., *A igreja dos oprimidos* (São Paulo: Ed. Brasil Debates, 1981). Researchers on the church can consult an extremely useful annotated index to a Paris-based press archive on the Brazilian Church: Ralph della Cava, ed., *A igreja em flagrante: catolicismo e sociedade na imprensa brasileira, 1964–1980* (Rio de Janeiro: Editora Marco Zero, 1985). For a major story in the foreign press on Church criticism of the government, see the *New York Times,* July 27, 1972. See also the important study by Marcio Moreira Alves, *L'Église et la politique au Brésil* (Paris: Les Éditions du CERF, 1974) which has much valuable institutional analysis of the Church.

119. For an excellent summary and chronology of government attacks on the Church, see Centro Ecumenico de Documentação e Informação, *Repressão na igreja no Brasil: reflexo de uma situação de opressão 1968–1978* (São Paulo: Comissão Arquidiocesana de Pastoral dos Direitos Humanos e Marginalizados da Arquidiocese de São Paulo, 1978). For a primary source on the police and military repression against the clergy, see Frei Fernando de Brito, Frei Ivo Lesbaupin, and Frei Carlos Alberto Libanio Christo, *O canto na fogueira* (Petrópolis: Vozes, 1977), which consists of their letters and diaries during their imprisonment from 1969 to 1973. Frei Fernando and Frei Ivo were accused of involvement with Carlos Marighela and were portrayed as informants by Detective Sérgio Fleury in Marighela's highly publicized ambush in São Paulo. Frei Betto (Carlos Alberto Libanio Christo) was arrested shortly after the ambush and accused of involvement, as was Frei Tito, a Dominican brother who became deranged from torture and committed suicide in France shortly after release from prison.

120. The *New York Times* reporter in Brazil estimated in February 1974 that of 240 prelates, approximately fifty were "conservatives" who supported the military government, and approximately forty were "left-wing radicals." The other 150 were "moderates." *New York Times,* February 24, 1974. This estimate is roughly similar to a survey of bishops' opinion published by the *Jornal do Brasil,* July 29, 1980, which counted 39 conservatives, 62 progressives, and 159 moderates. Cited in Marcos de Castro, *A igreja e o autoritarismo* (Rio de Janeiro: Jorge Zahar, 1985), 54.

121. For a study highly sympathetic to Dom Helder, see Marcos de Castro, *Dom Helder* (Rio de Janeiro: Gral, 1978).

122. At an Anti-Communist Congress held in Rio in January 1974 Dom Geraldo Sigaud gave an impassioned speech, attacking "subversives" left and right. He drew a rebuke from Rio's Archbishop Araujo Sales, who said Dom Geraldo did not speak for the church. The latter barked back a rebuke of the Rio archbishop. The exchange was a good indication of the political divisions in the church. *New York Times*, January 23, 26–27, 1974. Gustavo Corção was one of the best-known conservative lay Catholics. For an example of his many newspaper columns attacking church progressives, see *O Globo*, September 16, 1971.

123. Greater detail on foreign protests over human rights violations in Brazil is given in the section on "The Guerrilla Emerges" in the preceding chapter.

124. The principal source for data on macroeconomic trends in this section is the U.N. Economic Commission for Latin America's annual *Economic Survey of Latin America* for 1969–74. Unless otherwise indicated, data come from this source.

125. *O Estado de São Paulo*, January 7, 1970. When assuming the planning ministry in November 1969, Velloso had sounded the same note: "It is highly important to select for our Great Decisions areas that are strategically crucial and of high priority and then allocate massive resources to carry them out." *Desenvolvimento e planejamento: pronunciamentos dos Ministros João Paulo dos Reis Velloso e Helio Beltrão, na transmissão do cargo, em 3 de november de 1969* (n.p.: Ministério de Planejamento e Coordenação Geral, November 1969), 19.

126. Presidência da República, *Metas e bases para a ação de govêrno: síntese* (Brasília, September 1970). This document was only intended as an initial outline of goals. It was followed by the *I Plano Nacional de Desenvolvimento (PND)– 1972–74* (Brasília, 1971), which spelled out the targets by sector.

127. *Metas e bases*, 3.

128. A good example was the ebullient message of the journalist Murilo Melo Filho in three best-sellers in Brazil: *O desafio brasileiro* (Rio de Janeiro: Edições Bloch, 1970), *O milagre brasileiro* (Rio de Janeiro: Edições Bloch, 1972), and *O modelo brasileiro* (Rio: Edições Bloch, 1974). With each volume the author grew more confident that Brazil had adopted exactly the right political and economic options to assure future prosperity. He relied on official data, sometimes even improving on them.

129. The World Bank soon reacted to the manipulated official inflation figure for 1973 and made its own estimate of 22.5 percent, which became widely used in Brazil, although censorship prevented its public notice. *Folha de São Paulo*, July 31, 1977.

130. Celso Furtado, *Análise do "modelo" brasileiro* (Rio: Civilização Brasileira, 1972); Furtado, *O mito do desenvolvimento economico* (Rio de Janeiro: Paz e Terra, 1974); Maria da Conceição Tavares, *Da substituição de importações ao capitalismo financeiro: ensaios sobre economia brasileira* (Rio de Janeiro: Zahar, 1973).

131. Favorable U.S. attention to Brazil's exchange rate policy could be seen in such articles as "The 'Crawling Peg' Works in Brazil," *Business Week*, September 16, 1972.

132. *Folha de São Paulo*, September 14, 1971, p. 21. Delfim Neto replied characteristically by arguing that any anti-inflation policy "must attempt to accelerate development while simultaneously reducing inflation."

133. The successful use of credit and tax incentives is analyzed in Bela Balassa, "Incentive Policies in Brazil," *World Development,* VII, Nos. 11/12 (November/December 1979), 1023–42.

134. The capital inflow also released private savings for consumption and thus made it easier for Brazilians to avoid using more domestic savings for long-term investment. It financed a bias (by the Ministry of Industry and Commerce) toward the importation of capital goods, thus exacerbating the capital-intensive tendency of Brazilian industry. José Eduardo de Carvalho Pereira, *Financiamento externo e crescimento econômico no Brasil: 1966–73* (Rio: IPEA/INPES, 1974), 182–99. It should also be noted that by some indicators foreign investors were hurting, not helping, the balance of payments. For 1960–69, for example, remittances by U.S. firms narrowly exceeded their new investment, "U.S. Policies and Programs in Brazil," 215. For 1974 the net impact of 115 multinational firms on Brazil's balance of payments was a negative $1.73 billion, *Jornal do Brasil,* May 30, 1976.

135. Speeches by these MDB leaders may be found in Alencar Furtado, *Salgando a terra* (Rio de Janeiro: Paz e Terra, 1977); Franco Montoro, *Da "democracia" que temos para a democracia que queremos* (Rio de Janeiro: Paz e Terra, 1974); Ulysses Guimarães, *Rompendo o cerco* (Rio de Janeiro: Paz e Terra, 1978); and Freitas Nobre, *Debate sobre problemas brasileiros* (Brasília: Coordenada—Editora de Brasília, 1974).

136. The first analysis of income data from the 1970 census was Albert Fishlow, "Brazilian Size Distribution of Income," *American Economic Review,* LXII, No. 2 (May 1972), 391–402. Fishlow, who argued that government policies (such as the wage policy) had exacerbated the inequalities, got wide publicity in Brazil when the newsweekly *Veja* published a long feature article on the topic on June 7, 1972, including an interview with Fishlow. But *Veja* took care to surround Fishlow with a long interview with Delfim Neto and a report on a government-commissioned study by Carlos Langoni showing that income disparities could in large part be attributed to differences in educational level. The question of Brazil's income distribution became one of the premier controversies in the study of the Brazilian economy and of the policies of the military governments. The resulting bibliography is now vast. There is a useful collection of key articles up to 1975 in Ricardo Tolipan and Arthur Carlos Tinelli, eds., *A controvérsia sobre distribuição de renda e desenvolvimento* (Rio de Janeiro: Zahar, 1975). The crucial question of the trade-off between equity and growth in Brazil—to which the income distribution debate was usually reduced—is explored at length in Lance Taylor, Edmar L. Bacha, Eliana A. Cardoso, and Frank J. Lysy, *Models of Growth and Distribution for Brazil* (New York: Oxford University Press, 1980), which includes in chapter 10 a detailed reexamination of the 1960s' data and the principal interpretations of it. For a well documented challenge to the conventional wisdom on income distribution in Brazil, see Samuel A. Morley, *Labor Markets and Inequitable Growth* (Cambridge: Cambridge University Press, 1982). For more recent reanalyses and a discussion of trends in economic and social well-being in 1960–80, see Chapter VIII below.

137. Alencar Furtado, *Salgando a terra,* 55.

138. The quotations are from Delfim Neto's interview in *Veja,* June 7, 1972. Roberto Campos never tired of preaching the doctrine of growth before redistribution. See, for example, a 1969 newspaper article reprinted in Roberto de

Oliveira Campos, *Temas e sistemas* (Rio de Janeiro: APEC, 1969), 159. There is a detailed defense of Brazilian government policy with respect to income distribution and growth in Mário Henrique Simonsen, *Brasil 2002* (Rio de Janeiro, 1972) 47–64. The Médici government's first planning document had rejected "redistributive excesses," which would prevent "an acceleration in the rate of national growth," *Metas e bases para a ação de governo,* 6.

139. *Vega,* June 7, 1972. The Planalto had been well aware of the income distribution issue, as can be seen in Médici, *O Jôgo,* 34, 91; Médici, *Entrevista colectiva* (Brasília: Departamento de Imprensa Nacional, 1971), 27; *New York Times,* April 1, 1971. The military governments had launched a flurry of programs aimed at social needs. They included MOBRAL (a literacy program); PROTERRA, PIN, and PRORURAL (agrarian programs); and PIS and PISEP (profit-sharing funds). Details on post-1964 socio-economic trends (and how government funds and programs affected them) can be found in the chapter by Wanderley Guilherme dos Santos in Helio Jaguaribe, et al., *Brasil, sociedade democrática* (Rio de Janeiro: José Olympio, 1985), and in Edmar Bacha and Herbert S. Klein, eds., *A transição incompleta: Brasil desde 1945* (Rio de Janeiro: Paz e Terra, 1986), 2 vols.

140. A very useful overview of policy toward the Northeast as of the mid-1970s is Roberto Cavalcanti de Albuquerque, "Alguns aspectos da experiência recente de desenvolvimento do Nordeste," *Pesquisa e Planejamento,* VI, No. 2 (August 1976), 461–88. The papers from a 1975 conference at the University of Glasgow on development problems of the Northeast have been published in Simon Mitchell, ed., *The Logic of Poverty: The Case of the Brazilian Northeast* (London: Routledge & Kegan Paul, 1981).

141. The creation of the tax credit program (known as "article 34/18," after the 1961 regulation establishing it) is traced in Albert Hirschman, *Journeys Toward Progress* (New York: Twentieth Century Fund, 1963), 1–92. Hirschman wrote a follow-up study in "Industrial Development in the Brazilian Northeast and the Tax Credit Scheme of Article 34/18," in *A Bias for Hope* (New Haven: Yale University Press, 1971), 124–58, which was highly optimistic about the program's effectiveness. For a former U.S. government official's view of the failure to promote employment in the Northeast, see Harold T. Jorgenson, "Impending Disaster in Northeast Brazil," *Inter-American Economic Affairs,* XII, no. 1 (Summer 1968), 3–22. A 1975 SUDENE (the development agency for the Northeast) study showed that from 1968 to 1972 there had been no increase in industrial jobs in the Northeast. *O Estado de São Paulo,* April 8, 1975, reprinted in *Diário de Pernambuco,* April 17, 1975.

142. My account of Médici's trip to the Northeast at the time of the 1970 drought draws on Fernando H. Cardoso and G. Müller, *Amazônia: expansão do capitalismo* (São Paulo: Brasiliense, 1977), 167ff., and on his own account in *Veja,* May 16, 1984, p. 16.

143. Emílio Garrastazú Médici, *A verdadeira paz* (n.p.: Imprensa Nacional, 1970), 149; World Bank, *Brazil: An Interim Assessment of Rural Development Programs for the Northeast* (Washington: World Bank, 1983), 35.

144. *Metas e bases,* 60.

145. *Ibid.,* 29.

146. *Ibid.,* 80.

147. Médici interview in *Veja,* May 16, 1984. Northeasterners linked to SUDENE were especially indignant over this diversion of funds once designated for

SUDENE's exclusive use in Northeastern development. In the words of a former Cearense federal deputy, "The dream of the Transamazon was paid for, in the billions, by the Northeast." He castigated Brasília: "The government became a treacherous trustee, because it did not deliver what it had received for a designated purpose." J. Colombo e Sousa, *O Nordeste e a tecnocracia de revolução* (Brasília: Horizonte Editora, 1981), 173.

148. The Jarí concession, larger than the state of Connecticut, aroused the ire of Brazilian nationalists, as can be seen in Marcos Arruda, et al., *The Multinational Corporations and Brazil* (Toronto: Brazilian Studies/Latin American Research Unit, 1975), 131–207. One of the most careful investigations of the scientific issues surrounding Jarí was Philip M. Fearnside and Judy M. Rankin, "Jarí and Development in the Brazilian Amazon," *Interciencia*, V, No. 3 (May–June, 1980), 146–56. For an authoritative analysis of these problems for the Amazon valley, see Philip M. Fearnside, *Human Carrying Capacity of the Brazilian Rainforest* (New York: Columbia University Press, 1986).

149. Médici, *A verdadeira paz*, 147.

150. Fernando Morais, et al., *Transamazônica* (São Paulo: Brasiliense, 1970), 112ff.

151. Cardoso and Müller, *Amazônia*, 169.

152. Testimony of Delfim Neto in the federal Senate reprinted in *Revista de Finanças Públicas*, XXX, No. 298 (August 1970), 51–52. For highly optimistic projections of how many families could be settled in the newly opened Amazon region, see the interview with the president of INCRA (*Instituto Nacional de Colonização e Reforma Agrária*) in *Jornal do Brasil*, September 27, 1971.

153. The text of Delfim Neto's press conference was published in the *Revista de Finanças Públicas*, XXX, No. 300 (October 1970), 6.

154. Médici, *A verdadeira paz*, 148.

155. The statement is from Médici's speech on the third anniversary of his assuming the presidency, as published in *Revista de Finanças Públicas*, XXXII, No. 312 (November–December 1972), 1–5.

156. *Ibid.*, 147. For an example of a Brazilian scientist's angry attack on the crash programs to "develop" the Amazon, see Orlando Valverde, "Ecologia e desenvolvimento da Amazônia," *Revista Brasileira de Tecnologia*, XII (No. 4, October/December 1981), 3–16. He argues that inappropriate technology and insufficient study of the Amazon region have led to serious damage of the region's ecology. His view is shared by many scientists both inside Brazil and abroad.

157. The Transamazon colonization program proved a failure, as can be documented in several works by Emilio Moran: "Current Development Efforts in the Amazon Basin," in J. W. Hopkins, ed., *Caribbean Contemporary Record*, vol. 1 (New York: Holmes & Meier, 1983), 171–81; "Colonization in the Transamazon and Rondonia," in Marianne Schmink and Charles H. Wood, eds., *Frontier Expansion in Amazonia* (Gainesville: University of Florida Press, 1984), 285–303; and "An Assessment of a Decade of Colonisation in the Amazon Basin," in John Hemming, ed., *The Frontier After a Decade of Colonisation* (Manchester: University of Manchester Press, 1985), 91–102. The way the Brazilian bureaucracy's behavior contributed to the failure of the overblown government goals for Amazonian settlement is documented in Stephen G. Bunker, *Underdeveloping the Amazon* (Urbana: University of Illinois Press, 1985). Amazon policy has continued to be a topic of intense

debate, as in Sue Branford and Oriel Glock, *The Last Frontier: Fighting Over Land in the Amazon* (London: Zed Books, 1985). The Transamazon Highway also proved overly ambitious. The heavy rains washed much of it away, as is described in Valdir Sanches, "Transamazônica: A Travessia do Inferno," *Afinal,* May 20, 1986. The author describes in hair-raising terms how his car bogged down in the mud or in holes in the road. The most systematic analysis of the Amazon valley's potential for settlement and development is Philip M. Fearnside, *Human Carrying Capacity of the Brazilian Rainforest* (New York: Columbia University Press, 1986).

158. Emílio Garrastazú Médici, *O sinal do amanhã* (Brasília: Secretaria de Imprensa da Presidência da República, 1972), 33.

159. Robert N. Pierce, *Keeping the Flame,* 31; Dassin, "Press Censorship," 166.

160. Juan J. Linz, "The Future of an Authoritarian Situation or the Institutionalization of an Authoritarian Regime: The Case of Brazil," in Alfred Stepan, ed., *Authoritarian Brazil,* 233–54.

161. Hélio Silva and Maria Cecilia Ribas Carneiro, *Os governos militares: 1969–1974* (São Paulo: Editora Três, 1975), 149–50.

162. The hope, usually on the left, of some Brazilian intellectuals for the emergence of a "military populist" is clearly reflected in Flynn, "Sambas, Soccer, and Nationalism," 330.

163. Chagas, *Resistir é preciso,* 51–53; Oliveiros S. Ferreira, *A teoria da "coisa nossa" ou a visão do público como negócio particular* (São Paulo: Ed. GRD, 1986), 11–24. The author had close military contacts during these years. In any intra-military battles the army minister had a powerful weapon at his disposal: Institutional Act No. 17 (of October 1969), which made any officer acting "against the unity of the armed forces" subject to transfer to the reserve.

164. The corporatist effort is described in Pedreira, *Brasil política,* 279–82.

165. In the words of the well-informed journalist Carlos Chagas, the Médici administration had to "accept a candidate who did not share its institutional concepts," Chagas, *Resistir é preciso,* 16. Another political commentator thought Geisel's selection had been done quite smoothly in the face of a potentially very divisive lineup within the military. Pedreira, *Brasil política,* 286. Ferreira, *A teoria da "coisa nossa,"* 18.

166. Ulysses Guimarães, *Rompendo o cerco* (Rio de Janeiro: Paz e Terra, 1978), 46.

167. *Ibid.,* 44.

168. André Franco Montoro, *Da "democracia" que temos para a democracia que queremos* (Rio de Janeiro: Paz e Terra, 1974), 69–78.

169. Portella, *Tempo de congresso,* II, 51.

170. *Ibid.,* 59–60.

171. Moreira Alves, *State and Opposition,* 133–37.

172. The words were taken from a lyric by Brazilian singer-composer Caetano Veloso, who had borrowed from the Portuguese poet Fernando Pessoa.

173. Freire, *Oposição no Brasil,* 11–12.

174. In March 1973, Deputy Freitas Nobre, leader of the MDB, delivered a hard-hitting speech against censorship, pointing out the "absurdity" that "today the *Diário do congresso* is the most liberal of all publications, since, with rare exceptions, it publishes what is said in these sessions." Freitas Nobre, *Debate sobre problemas brasileiros* (Brasília: Coordenada Editora, n.d.), 16.

175. This shift in the bargaining power of the U.S. government was discussed in the

concluding section of the chapter on the presidency of General Costa e Silva. For further discussion of U.S.–Brazilian relations in the Médici presidency, see Skidmore, "Brazil's Changing Role in the International System: Implications for U.S. Policy," in Riordan Roett, ed., *Brazil in the Seventies* (Washington: American Enterprise Institute for Public Policy Research, 1976), 9–40.

176. Documentation of these charges is given in the preceding chapter.

177. *New York Times,* April 23, 1970.

178. *New York Times,* October 21, October 23, and December 4, 1970.

179. William F. Buckley, Jr., "Is Torture Becoming Characteristic of Brazil?" *Washington Evening Star,* February 20, 1971.

180. Lopes, *Esquadrão da morte,* 94–95. In early 1970 Delfim Neto gave a speech in New York in which he announced that "Brazilian society is in no way violating anyone's conscience or depriving anyone of their human rights." Speech reprinted in the *Revista de Financas Publicas,* XXX, No. 295 (May 1970), 4. For another example, see the 1970 speech of the government party's deputy leader in the Chamber of Deputies, Cantido Sampaio. He cited Cardinal Eugenio Sales, who had just returned from Europe and reported that the Europeans swallowed any and all torture charges because of the "skillful distortion of information being carried out by those who wish to discredit Brazil." *O Estado de São Paulo,* June 18, 1970.

181. "U.S. Policies and Programs in Brazil." Senator Church conducted the hearings in his capacity as chairman of the Senate Foreign Relations Subcommittee on Western Hemisphere Affairs. The most extensive look at the OPS's operations in Brazil is A. J. Langguth, *Hidden Terrors* (New York: Pantheon, 1978). Neither Langguth nor Senator Church produced any conclusive evidence that the OPS advisers taught their Brazilian counterparts how to torture (*ibid.,* 158). It should be remembered that many of the torture methods used on political prisoners, such as the palmatória, the parrot's perch, and near-drowning, had long been used by Brazilian police on common criminal suspects. The use of electric shock had begun during the *Estado Nôvo* dictatorship (1937–45). The newest torture instrument (the *geladeira* or "icebox") was allegedly picked up from the British, who were said to have used it against IRA (Irish Republican Army) suspects. Fon, *Tortura,* 72–74, describes the *geladeira* and its acquisition from the British, as does an anonymous general in "O caso Rubens Paiva: o general está falando sobre a tortura," in Rangel, *A hora de enterrar os ossos,* 12–14. I have found only one firsthand description of interrogation by U.S. officials: Frei Betto, *Batismo de sangue,* 219. The author confirmed this to me and added that in his interrogation by U.S. officials he was not tortured, though he was during his interrogation by Brazilian officials. Interview with Frei Betto in São Paulo, June 30, 1983. A lawyer who represented political prisoners told a journalist that he had seen a "North American give a torture demonstration on a live subject." Fon, *Tortura,* 60. Fon implies it was Mitrione.

182. *New York Times,* October 7, 1971.

183. Médici's visit received heavy coverage in the U.S. press. The *New York Times,* for example, ran a story every day between December 7 and 12.

184. *New York Times,* June 10, 1972.

185. *Ibid.,* July 5, 1972.

186. *Ibid.,* July 10, 1972.

187. *Ibid.,* July 5, 1972.

188. *Ibid.*, May 23, 1972.
189. *Ibid.*, June 6, 1973.
190. *Ibid.*, January 23, 1974.
191. The distinction between an "authoritarian situation" and an "authoritarian regime" is elaborated in Linz, "The Future of an Authoritarian Situation." The Brazilian military government was less stable than the Franco regime had been. Subsequent events amply confirmed Linz's analysis.
192. Peter McDonough, "Repression and Representation in Brazil," *Comparative Politics,* XV, No. 1 (October 1982), 85.
193. Youssef Cohen, " 'The Benevolent Leviathan': Political Consciousness among Urban Workers under State Corporatism," *American Political Science Review,* LXXVI, No. 1 (March 1982), 102–14. One of the best-known political commentators observed at the time that Médici was "widely respected and even popular," Pedreira, *Brasil politica,* 279. The reliability of the survey data compiled by McDonough and Cohen are subject to question because they were gathered at a time of sharp government repression. But both researchers make a convincing case for the reliability of the responses they analyze.
194. An extensive analysis of the Médici regime as of 1971 may be found in Philippe C. Schmitter, "The 'Portugalization' of Brazil?" in Stepan, ed., *Authoritarian Brazil,* 179–232. Although subsequent history was not kind to his title, Schmitter's assembling of data and intelligent probing for the systemic characteristics of Brazilian military rule up to 1971 make it the essential starting point for any analysis. For elite attitudes (military excepted) in the early 1970s—essential for understanding subsequent political developments—see McDonough, *Power and Ideology in Brazil.*
195. McDonough, "Repression and Representation," 77–78.
196. The quotation is from Krane, "Opposition Strategy," 54.

Chapter VI: Geisel: Toward *Abertura*

1. One of the most penetrating accounts of the larger political and social forces at work during the Geisel presidency is chapter 7 of Maria Helena Moreira Alves, *State and Opposition.* A valuable journalistic account of the political struggle of the 1974–80 period in Bernardo Kucinski, *Abertura, a história de uma crise* (São Paulo: Brasil Debates, 1982). A somewhat different version, published as *Brazil: State and Struggle* (London: Latin American Bureau, 1982), is an excellent overview of the Geisel and early Figueiredo periods. The author was skeptical of the castelistas' real motives. For a well-drawn portrait of Brazil as it emerged from the economic boom of the Médici years, see Norman Gall, "The Rise of Brazil," *Commentary,* LXIII, No. 1 (January 1977), 45–55. Gall's portrait also covers the first two years of the Geisel presidency.
2. There is useful information on Geisel's background and on his ministers in Fernando Jorge, *As diretrizes governamentais do President Ernesto Geisel* (São Paulo: Edição do Autor, 1976). A highly favorable review of Geisel's first two years in the presidency is given in Adirson de Barros, *Março: Geisel e a revolução brasileira* (Rio de Janeiro: Editora Artenova, 1976).
3. Sérgio Caparelli, *Televisão e capitalismo no Brasil* (Pôrto Alegre: L & PM, 1982), 160.
4. Press coverage of General Golbery was never extensive, because he made a

point of working strictly behind the scenes. For a rare cover story on Golbery, see "O fabricante de nuvens," *Veja*, March 19, 1980, pp. 20–31, by Élio Gaspari, a senior editor at *Veja* and the journalist said to be closest to Golbery.

5. Due to a serious leg injury (suffered in a bicycle accident), General Dilermando was unable to assume his post and was replaced by General Hugo de Andrade Abreu.

6. In mid-1973, for example, six army colonels had been dismissed for participating in a kick-back scandal, *New York Times*, July 18, 1973.

7. In mid-1974 Geisel made clear his opposition to letting the ARENA develop into a single-party system, which he thought would be "one of the most undisguised forms of political dictatorship," *O Estado de São Paulo*, August 18, 1974.

8. Geisel, *Discursos*, vol. 1 (Brasília: Assessoria de Imprensa da Presidência da República, 1974), 38.

9. For a highly useful index to key speeches, statements, and newspaper articles on the liberalization, see Marcus Faria Figueiredo and José Antônio Borges Cheibub, "A abertura política de 1973 a 1981: quem disse o que, quando— inventário de um debate," *Boletim informativo e bibliográfico de ciências sociais* [*BIB*] (pub. by the Associação Nacional de Pos-Graduação e Pesquisa em Ciências Sociais), No. 14 (1982), 29–61. After Médici's death his widow came forth to claim that her husband had wanted to start the *abertura* before the end of his term, but that Geisel threatened to renounce the succession if Médici started the *abertura*. Interview with Dona Scylla Médici in *Jornal do Brasil*, June 1, 1986. Her statement provoked a flurry of denials and recriminations. Geisel remained silent. The debate can be followed in *Veja*, June 11, 1986, p. 51; *Correio Brasiliense*, June 12 and 15, 1986; *Folha de São Paulo*, June 17 and 18, 1986. For discussion of a study that argues the *abertura* initiative *did* originate in the Médici presidency, see *Jornal do Brasil*, June 8, 1986, and *Fatos*, June 23, 1986, pp. 28–29.

10. I was first furnished a copy of this paper through the kindness of Professor Wanderley Guilherme dos Santos. I am indebted to Professor Huntington for a description of his role in the early stages of the political liberalization. Letter of May 21, 1986, from Samuel P. Huntington to the author.

11. His paper and testimony, including questions from congressmen, was published as Wanderley Guilherme dos Santos, *Estratégias de descompressão política* (Brasília: Instituto de Pesquisas, Estudos e Assessoria do Congresso, 1973). It was reprinted in Wanderley, *Poder e política: cronica do autoritarismo brasileiro* (Rio de Janeiro: Forense-Universitária, 1978), and a résumé was published in the *Jornal do Brasil* on September 30, 1973, sparking a national debate. *Poder e política* also includes a series of 17 newspaper articles published by Wanderley between July and December 1974. These articles helped stimulate discussion of possible redemocratization scenarios when that issue was hotly debated both within the Geisel government and among spokesmen for prominent groups in civil society. For an interesting blueprint for political liberalization which was stimulated by the Wanderley document, see Roberto Campos, "A opção política brasileira," in Mário Henrique Simonsen and Roberto de Oliveira Campos, *A nova economia brasileira* (Rio de Janeiro: Editora José Olympio, 1974), 223–57.

12. This and subsequent references are drawn from Wanderley, *Poder e política*, 153–60.

13. *Ibid.*, 182.
14. *Ibid.*, 185.
15. *Ibid.*, 202–5.
16. Geisel, *Discursos*, vol. 1 (1974), 38.
17. Huntington's February visit was reported in the *Journal do Brasil*, February 10, 1974. Huntington returned to Brazil in August 1974 for a conference on "The Role of Legislatures in Developing Countries," where political scientists from the U.S., Canada, and West Germany discussed a topic of intense interest to the new government, as well as to the opposition. After the conference Huntington, accompanied by fellow U.S. political scientist Austin Ranney, flew to Brasília to discuss the conference and its themes with Golbery. The seminar was analyzed in Carlos Castello Branco's column in *Jornal do Brasil* for August 13 and 15, 1974. The government's willingness to allow, and even encourage such events (Huntington called Goldbery "the silent patron" of the seminar), is analyzed in *O Estado de São Paulo*, August 25, 1974.
18. In a July 1985 interview with Alfred Stepan, Geisel explained that in 1974 his task was complicated by the fact that the military linked to the security organs were vehemently opposed to liberalization. Geisel was determined not to lose control of the government (as he believed had happened to both Castelo Branco and Costa e Silva) and thought that asserting strong leadership of the military was essential. He did not have any fixed timetable for liberalization, although he had intended to abolish the Fifth Institutional Act before the end of his term. In other interviews with Stepan, General Golbery gave details on how the Geisel government attempted to proceed, especially in relation to the Church. Stepan, *Os militares*, 44–49.
19. Editorial in the *New York Times*, March 23, 1974. For genuine doubt in the Brazilian press, see Carlos Castello Branco's column in *Jornal do Brasil*, September 5, 1974.
20. Fon, *Tortura*, 65–66.
21. My sources were Carlos Garcia, other Recife journalists, U.S. consular officials, and the *New York Times*, March 25, 1974.
22. *New York Times*, November 4, 1974.
23. *New York Times*, July 9, 1974.
24. Examples are the *New York Times* stories for May 30 and August 11, 1974.
25. *New York Times*, May 29, 1974. For a similar crisis over censorship in late March, see *New York Times*, March 25, 1974. A favorite target of the censors was the weekly *Opinião*, which routinely had more than half of its copy disallowed by the federal censors in Brasília. The publication survived, nonetheless, from 1972 to 1977, when the editors finally closed it in protest against government pressure. Documentation of the struggle is given in J.A. Pinheiro Machado, *Opinião x censura: momentos da luta de um jornal pela liberdade* (Pôrto Alegre: L & PM, 1978). General information on censorship, rather chaotically organized, can be found in Paolo Marconi, *A Censura política na imprensa brasileira: 1968–1978* (São Paulo: Global, 1980).
26. *New York Times*, May 30 and August 11, 1974; *Capital Times* (Madison, Wisconsin), for December 30, 1974, carried a story from the Los Angeles Times News Service on some who "disappeared" during 1974.
27. *New York Times*, July 10, 1974.
28. The Rev. Jaime Wright, whose brother Paulo was on the list, was a member of the delegation and reported that Golbery was visibly moved when he read the

documentation on each case. Interview with Jaime Wright, São Paulo, May 14, 1975. There is a list of 32 "victims of *abertura*" by name in Kucinski, *Abertura*, 45-46.

29. Conselho Federal da Ordem dos Advogados do Brasil, *Anais de V Conferência Nacional da Ordem dos Advogados do Brasil:* Rio de Janeiro: August 11-16, 1974 (Rio de Janeiro: Conselho Federal da OAB, 1974), 101. The *New York Times* published stories on the lawyers' convention on August 11 and 13, 1974.

30. Morris related his experiences in "In the Presence of Mine Enemies: Faith and Torture in Brazil," *Harper's Magazine* (October 1974), 57-70. For further details on the Morris case, see "Torture and Oppression in Brazil," *Hearing before the Subcommittee on International Organizations and Movements of the Committee on Foreign Affairs, House of Representatives; Ninety-third Congress, Second Session:* December 11, 1974 (Washington: U.S. Government Printing Office, 1975).

31. This account is based in part on interviews with officials in the U.S. embassy in Brasília and the U.S. consulate in Recife in 1975. See also *New York Times*, November 26, 1974. The vigor of the U.S. embassy's reaction could be explained in part by its knowledge that the security forces were watching Morris; the embassy had warned the Brazilian government that it would follow the case closely.

32. *New York Times,* April 5, 1974.

33. See the coverage in *O Jornal do Brasil,* August 13 and 15, 1974.

34. *O Estado de São Paulo,* August 25, 1974.

35. Geisel, *Discursos,* vol. 1 (1974), 122.

36. *O Jornal do Brasil,* August 15 and 16, 1974.

37. *O Estado de São Paulo,* August 29, 1974.

38. *O Globo,* August 26, 1974; *O Estado de São Paulo,* August 28 and August 30, 1974.

39. In August, Carlos Chagas reported that Geisel was sternly ordering all governors and ARENA regional headquarters not to engage in any voter intimidation or other questionable electoral practices. Geisel clearly assumed that ARENA would still win. *O Estado de São Paulo,* August 18, 1974.

40. One television specialist later commented that the 1974 elections were decided by television, thus signaling the breakdown of the traditional rural isolation of much of the electorate. Sodré, *O monopólio,* 29.

41. For a detailed analysis of the November 1974 elections, see Bolivar Lamounier and Fernando Henrique Cardoso, eds., *Os partidos e as eleições no Brasil* (Rio de Janeiro: Paz e Terra, 1975); Margaret J. Sarles, "Maintaining Political Control Through Parties: The Brazilian Strategy," *Comparative Politics,* XV, No. 1 (1982), 41-72; and *Revista Brasileira de Estudos Políticos,* 43 (July 1976), which was entirely devoted to the elections. My data are taken from the last. For an amusing and irreverent view of the elections, see Sebastião Nery, *As 167 derrotas que abalaram o Brasil* (Rio de Janeiro: Francisco Alves Editora, 1975).

42. The flavor of the MDB campaign can be found in collections of speeches by two of its leaders: Franco Montoro, *Da "democracia" que temos para a democracia que queremos* (Rio de Janeiro: Paz e Terra, 1974), and Marcos Freire, *Oposição no Brasil, hoje* (Rio de Janeiro: Paz e Terra, 1974). Montoro was an MDB senator from São Paulo, and Freire, an MDB senator from

Pernambuco. The political views of the Congress as of early 1975 were analyzed in an in-depth survey conducted by A.C. Guimarães and Luís Henrique
Nunes Bahia and published in *Jornal do Brasil*, April 14, 15, 16, and 17, 1975.
A majority of both ARENA and MDB congressmen favored reduced activity
by multinationals in Brazil, and a majority of both also wanted state intervention in the economy to continue at least at the current level.

43. This was the conclusion of Lamounier and Cardoso from their detailed analysis
of election returns, in *Os partidos e as eleições no Brasil*. A researcher who had
previously found strong worker support for Médici now had to explain why the
workers voted so heavily for the MDB in 1974. Cohen's answer was that the
MDB had shrewdly pushed economic issues and had educated the workers on
the difference between the two parties. Finally, argued Cohen, "they simply
wanted an incumbent government that could improve the economic situation . . . rather than a fundamental reorientation of the policy." Cohen, "The
Benevolent Leviathan," 56. For a penetrating analysis of how agricultural
laborers in the interior of São Paulo regarded the elections of 1974 as irrelevant
to their plight, see Verena Martinez-Alier and Armando Boito Júnior, "The
Hoe and the Vote: Rural Labourers and the National Election in Brazil in
1974," *The Journal of Peasant Studies*, IV, No. 3 (April 1977), 147–70.

44. Chagas, *Resistir é preciso*, 114. Chagas argued that the 1974 vote was more
against Médici than for the MDB.

45. Interview with Senator Franco Montoro, Brasília, May 7, 1975.

46. A veteran U.S. journalist visiting Brazil in February 1975 noted after long talks
with journalists and influential political figures that "the Brazilian military
dictatorship . . . may well be the only government in the world to be quietly
delighted over what amounts to a widespread defeat at the polls." Tad Szulc,
"Letter from Brasília," *The New Yorker*, March 10, 1975, p. 72. Much the
same point was made by Ulysses Guimarães, national president of the MDB,
and Celio Borja, government leader in the Chamber of Deputies, in interviews
in *Veja*, November 27, 1974, pp. 31–34. A Brazilian journalist explained his
country's paradoxical political situation by arguing, "in these circumstances,
who would bet on the success of the present political *abertura?* No one. Only,
perhaps, these incorrigible optimists, the Brazilians." Fernando Pedreira, "Decompression in Brazil?" *Foreign Affairs*, LIII, No. 3 (April 1975), 498–512.

47. *New York Times*, January 5, 1975. There was no announcement that censorship was gone, but the alert reader would have noted that the poetry of
Camões, normally used to fill the place of censored material, was missing for
the first time since August 1972. General Golbery had in late 1974 told a U.S.
scholar that restoring freedom of the press was crucial. Stepan, *Os militares*,
48.

48. For details on the emergence of *Folha* as the leading opposition paper, see
Carlos Guilherme Mota and Maria Helena Capelato, *História da Folha de São
Paulo: 1921–1981* (São Paulo: IMPRES, 1980), 204ff.

49. Kucinski, *Abertura*, 44–45.

50. *Ibid.*, 44–46; Fon, *Tortura*, 67–68. By mid-1976 Amnesty International (AI)
estimated that about 2,000 "suspected communist sympathizers" had been
detained, of whom AI had adopted 240 as "prisoners of conscience." AI took
its evidence of Brazil's human rights violations to the United Nations Commission on Human Rights in February 1976. *The Amnesty International Report: 1*

June 1975–31 May 1976 (London: Amnesty International Publications, 1976), 89–92.

51. *O Estado de São Paulo,* March 21, 1975. In early May 1975 I talked with an army colonel on the presidential staff who was unapologetic about the repressive excesses. When I cited the case of General Pedro Celestino's son, he replied, "and how many of our comrades have fallen?" He then referred to an officer colleague in the Planalto who had lost half a hand in the bomb attack at Guararapes airport in Recife in July 1966. "War is war," he said, adding that he had three cousins who were "in the subversion—one in Chile, one in Paris, and another in Algeria." His examples were further proof that the guerrillas were drawn primarily from dissident members of the elite. Interview in Brasília, May 9, 1975. The colonel was a staunch castelista.

52. Interview with James Shea, labor attaché, U.S. consulate in Rio, April 30, 1975. Shea's experience in Brazil went back to 1957.

53. Ernesto Geisel, *Discursos,* vol. 2 (Brasília: Assessoria de Imprensa da Presidência da República, 1976), 139–56.

54. *Ibid.,* 151, 175, 236. Prior censorship continued at a handful of newspapers and magazines. One was the leftist *Movimento,* which in late 1976 had an entire special number banned. It was on the "Death Squad" and its entire contents—word for word—had already been published elsewhere, primarily in *O Estado de São Paulo* and *Jornal da Tarde.* Censorship of this kind was simply harassment, designed to keep the left off balance and to cause financial loss to the paper. *Jornal da Tarde,* November 6, 1976.

55. One of the most complete accounts of Herzog's death and the protest it unleashed is Fernando Jordão, *Dossiê Herzog: prisão, tortura e morte no Brasil* (São Paulo: Global, 1979). The author had been a close colleague of Herzog, going back to the days they had worked together on the BBC. Useful also is Hamilton Almeida Filho, *A sanguequente: a morte do jornalista Vladimir Herzog* (São Paulo: Alfa–Omega, 1978), a book version of an issue of *EX* magazine in 1975. For a collection of first-person reactions to Herzog's death, see Paulo Markun, ed., *Vlado: retrato da morte de um homem e de um época* (São Paulo: Brasiliense, 1985).

56. The official explanation was that Herzog had hanged himself from a window bar. Yet in a government photograph the bar appeared to be too near the floor to have been used by someone of Herzog's height. The medical certificate listing suicide was signed by Dr. Harry Shibata, who later admitted he had neither seen the body nor carried out an autopsy. Amnesty International USA, *Matchbox,* November 1980.

57. MDB Senator Francisco Leite Chaves criticized the use of the army for purposes of repression such as in the Herzog case and noted that even Hitler created the SS to carry out "such ignominious crimes," thereby saving the honor of the army. Response from the army High Command was immediate and angry. But the MDB and ARENA found a formula to save face all around. Chaves gave a speech praising the army and copies of the *Diário do congresso* with his earlier speech were recalled and destroyed. Hugo Abreu, *O Outro lado do poder* (Rio de Janeiro: Nova Fronteira, 1979), 109–10. A "Comité de Solidariedade aos Revolucionários do Brasil" held secret annual meetings, beginning in early 1973. Their annual reports included lists of torture victims, torturers, and details on the current operations of the repressive apparatus. To

publish lists of torturers (even in the manner of these clandestinely circulated typescripts) was potentially explosive, since it was bound to set off alarms among the hard line. I obtained copies of the 1975, 1976, and 1977 reports through the kindness of a Brazilian journalist.

58. Shock was also registered abroad. Five U.S. specialists on Brazil (including the author) signed a statement denouncing Herzog's death and the possible U.S. involvement in Brazil's repressive apparatus. "Brazil: The Sealed Coffin," *The New York Review of Books,* November 27, 1975.

59. In an August 1974 public lecture to students and faculty of the Faculdades Metropolitanas Unidas, General Ednardo reviewed, inter alia, Brazilian history (small population, weak races), Brazil's place in South America (Brazil surrounded by an ocean of Spanish speakers), and the current threat (hidden forces ready to use students again). To an outsider, the tone sounded arrogant and highly reactionary, but friends in the U.S. consulate, as well as Brazilian friends, assured me that on these counts General Ednardo was far more moderate than his predecessor.

60. Much documentation on this case can be found in Carlos Alberto Luppi, *Manoel Fiel Filho: quem vai pagar por este crime?* (São Paulo: Escrita, 1980).

61. In an interview General Dilermando later explained that he asserted control over the DOI-CODI operation by requiring all arrests to be approved by him. He also claimed to have found no evidence of torture during his predecessor's command. *Veja,* March 14, 1979.

62. General Hugo Abreu, head of Geisel's military presidential staff, described an army High Command meeting three days after General Ednardo's sacking where, although no votes were taken, five of the eleven generals supported Geisel's action and three were against. They all ended by expressing complete support for the president. Abreu, *O outro lado do poder,* 112. Two days after firing Ednardo, Geisel told Severo Gomes that he had acted not because Ednardo was involved in torture, but because he had failed to maintain control over all activities under his command. Severo Gomes, "Gato e Fabiano," *Folha de São Paulo,* May 23, 1982.

63. General Abreu thought Geisel's success in getting the more radical officers to accept General Ednardo's dismissal owed much to the effective support given him by his army minister, General Frota, and Ednardo's interim substitute, General Ariel Pacca de Fonseca. Abreu, *O outro lado do poder,* 113.

64. The citations are from *II National Development Plan (1975–1979)* (Rio de Janeiro: IBGE, 1974). For an influential analysis of the plan, see Carlos Lessa, *A estratégia de desenvolvimento, 1974–1976: sonho e fracasso* (Rio de Janeiro: Tese apresentada à Faculdade de Economia e Administração da Universidade Federal do Rio de Janeiro para Concurso de Professor Titular em Economia Brasileira, 1978). See also Sebastião C. Velasco e Cruz, "Estado e planejamento no Brasil, 1974–1976," *Estudos CEBRAP,* No. 27 (1980), 103–26. An interim assessment of the plan's implementation was given by Roberto Cavalcanti de Albuquerque, "A execução do Planejamento: o que se obteve em dois anos com o II PND," *Política* (Fundação Milton Campos), No. 4 (April–July 1977), 51–59. For a more critical assessment as of mid-1976, see *Jornal do Brasil,* June 13, 1976. My basic source for this analysis of economic policy is, as in the earlier chapters, the annual *Economic Survey of Latin America* published by the Economic Commission for Latin

America from the New York headquarters of the United Nations. The volumes consulted were for 1974–79.

65. For an incisive analysis of the economic policies of both the Geisel and Figueiredo governments, see Albert Fishlow, "A Tale of Two Presidents: The Political Economy of Crisis Management," in Alfred Stepan, ed., *Democratizing Brazil?* (forthcoming). There is a highly enlightening comparison of Geisel and Figueiredo policies in five key areas in Barry Ames, *Political Survival: Politicians and Public Policy in Latin America* (Berkeley: University of California Press, forthcoming). The investment strategy of the Geisel government is favorably evaluated in Antonio Barros de Castro and Francisco Eduardo Pires de Souza, *A economia brasileira em marcha forçada* (Rio de Janeiro: Paz e Terra, 1985), 11–95. Albert Hirschman has suggested that perhaps "oil-poor" Brazil had "a blessing in disguise" in comparison to "oil-rich" Mexico because the Brazilian policymakers were forced to be more creative and so ended up with a superior growth record. Hirschman, "The Political Economy of Latin American Development: Seven Exercises in Retrospection" (paper for the XIII International Congress of the Latin American Studies Association, Boston, October 23–25, 1986).

66. The most complete study of the Brazilian alcohol program is Michael Barzelay, *The Politicized Market Economy: Alcohol in Brazil's Energy Strategy* (Berkeley: University of California Press, 1986). For a broader critique of Brazil's energy policy, see Peter Seaborn Smith, "Reaping the Whirlwind: Brazil's Energy Crisis in Historical Perspective," *Inter-American Economic Affairs,* XXXVII, No. 1 (Summer 1983), 3–20. The larger questions are faced also in J. Goldemberg, "Energy Issues and Policies in Brazil," *Annual Review of Energy,* VII (1982), 139–74. The alcohol program has continued to be a target of criticism, as the cost of the subsidy to domestic sugar producers has grown. See, for example, Alan Riding, "Oil Price Fall Perils Brazil Alcohol Fuel," *New York Times,* July 29, 1985. The left also took aim at the program, as in Ricardo Bueno, *Pró-álcool: rumo ao desastre* (Petrópolis: Vozes, 1980), which excoriated the government for neglecting the railway system.

67. For an analysis of the complex legal and administrative basis for the huge Itaipú project, see José Costa Cavalcanti, "A Itaipú binacional—um exemplo de cooperação internacional na América Latina," *Revista de Administração Pública,* X, No. 1 (January–March 1976), 19–68. Brazil carefully prepared the way for its borderland hydro-electric projects by getting prior agreements, in principle, to multi-country activities, as in the Treaty of the Prata Basin (1969) and the Asunción Declaration on the Use of International Rivers (1971), both of which were signed by Argentina, Bolivia, Brazil, Paraguay, and Uruguay.

68. Economic Commission for Latin America, *Economic Survey of Latin America: 1973,* 141–42. For a more detailed analysis of import elasticities for this period, see Richard Weisskoff, "Trade, Protection and Import Elasticities for Brazil," *The Review of Economics and Statistics,* LXI, No. 1 (1979), 58–66.

69. Based on his in-depth interviews with representative members of the Brazilian elites (except the military) in the early 1970s, Peter McDonough concluded that what led the elites to question the regime's legitimacy "was a sense that the regime had plunged the country into a deepening reign of terror and arbitrary lawlessness from which the elites themselves were not safe." Peter McDon-

ough, *Power and Ideology in Brazil* (Princeton: Princeton University Press, 1981), 232.

70. One newspaper publisher's reaction was well expressed by Ruy Mesquita, of the family that owned *O Estado de São Paulo* and *Jornal da Tarde*, who in 1975 referred to "the process of gangrene which has invaded Brazilian institutions thanks to the growing arbitrariness of the revolutionary power." Ruy Mesquita preface to Bicudo, *Meu depoimento*, 11.

71. For stories on Brazil's high executive salaries, see *New York Times*, September 2, 1974, and July 11, 1976. A story on January 25, 1976, described how much less well the workers had done in the economic boom. For an analysis of data on income distribution, made available from the National Household Survey (*Pesquisa Nacional por Amostra de Domicílios*, or PNAD), see Paul Singer, "Quem são os ricos no Brasil," *Opinião*, February 14, 1975.

72. For a penetrating analysis of businessmen's campaign against the spread of state influence in the economy, see Charles Freitas Pessanha, "Estado e economia no Brasil: a campanha contra a estatização: 1974–1976" (M.A. thesis, IUPERJ, 1981). A leading voice in this campaign was the weekly *Visão*. See, for example, its issue of May 26, 1975, half of which was devoted to documenting the allegedly excessive role of the state in the Brazilian economy. For a collection of 1976–77 newspaper articles calling for reducing the state role in the economy, see J. C. de Macedo Soares Guimarães, *Para onde vamos?* (Rio de Janeiro: Ed. Record, 1977). Minister of Commerce and Industry Severo Gomes offered a carefully reasoned defense of the historical role of the Brazilian state in a speech given to the *Escola Superior de Guerra* and reprinted in *Folha de São Paulo*, July 18, 1976.

73. There is an excellent account of the awakening of civil society in Sebastião C. Velasco e Cruz and Carlos Estevam Martins, "De Castello a Figueiredo: Uma Incursão na pré-História de 'Abertura,' " in Bernardo Sorj and Maria Hermínia Tavares de Almeida, eds., *Sociedade e política no Brasil pós-64* (São Paulo: Brasiliense, 1983), 13–61. For a collection of papers analyzing "popular" movements in São Paulo such as blacks, women, lay Catholics, and neighborhood associations (*movimentos de bairro*), see Paul Singer and Vinícius Caldeira Brant, eds., *São Paulo: o povo em movimento* (Petrópolis: Vozes, 1981). For similar studies emphasizing the increase in public participation these groups stimulated, see Cláudio de Moura Castro, ed., "Do Sebastianismo aos 'grassroots': novas estruturas e formas de organização no Brasil," mimeo (Brasília: IPEA/Instituto de Planejamento, September 1983); José Alvaro Moisés, et al., *Alternativas populares da democracia: Brasil, anos 80* (Petrópolis: Vozes, 1982); José Alvaro Moisés, et al., *Cidade, povo, e poder* (Rio de Janeiro: Paz e Terra, 1982); and Renato Raul Boschi, *Movimentos coletivos no Brasil urbano* (Rio de Janeiro: Zahar, 1982).

74. There is a wealth of writing and analysis on the recent Brazilian Catholic Church. It should be obvious that I can treat here only those aspects of the Church that bear directly on the main lines of Brazil's political and economic development in the Geisel presidency. I have relied especially on Bruneau, *The Church in Brazil*, and Mainwaring, *The Catholic Church and Politics in Brazil, 1916–1985* (Stanford: Stanford University Press, 1986). See also Ralph della Cava, "The 'People's Church,' the Vatican, and the Abertura," in Alfred C. Stepan, ed., *Democratizing Brazil?* (forthcoming), which is especially enlightening on the relationship between the Brazilian Church and the Vatican.

75. *New York Times,* January 31 and February 24, 1974.

76. *Ibid.,* February 18, 1974.

77. *Ibid.,* February 24, 1974.

78. For a detailed analysis of how CEBs have operated in several regions of Brazil, see Bruneau, *The Church in Brazil.* For the insights of a Dominican who served as an *agente pastoral* of a CEB and who had earlier been imprisoned by the military government, see Frei Betto, *O que é comunidade eclesial de base* (São Paulo: Brasiliense, 1981). For a CNBB statement on the rationale for the CEBs, see *Comunidades eclesiais de base no Brasil: experiências e perspectivas,* 2nd ed. (São Paulo: Edições Paulinas, 1981). A comparison of the CEBs with other popular religious innovations is given in Rowan Ireland, "Comunidades eclesiais de base, grupos espíritas, e a democratização no Brasil," in Paulo Krischke and Scott Mainwaring, eds., *A igreja nas bases em tempo de transição (1974–1985)* (Pôrto Alegre: L & PM, 1986), 151–83. A study placing the CEBs in the context of other grass-roots movements is Cândido Procópio Ferreira de Camargo, Beatriz Muniz de Souza, and Antônio Flávio de Oliveira Pierucci, "Communidades eclesiais de base," in Paul Singer and Vinicius Caldeira Brant, eds., *São Paulo: o povo em movimento* (Petrópolis: Vozes, 1980), 59–81. In "As CEB's na 'abertura': mediações entre a reforma da igreja e as transformações da sociedade," *ibid.,* 185–207, Paulo Krischke explores how structural changes within the Church related to democratization in Brazilian society.

79. Tilman Evers, "Síntesis interpretativa del 'Movimento do custo de vida,' un movimiento urbano brasileño," *Revista Mexicana de Sociologia,* XLIII, No. 4 (October–December 1981), 1371–93; Kucinski, *Abertura,* 103–5. This group's protest tactics resembled the anti-Goulart marches of early 1964 in that they were both led by housewives. The social origins were, however, very different—working-class women marched in 1977–78 whereas middle- and upper-class women had marched in 1964. For details on a series of marches in São Paulo, see "O protesto das panelas vazias," *Movimento,* November 6, 1978. The movement also included some from the Maoist left.

80. Dom Adriano was instrumental in helping organize the neighborhood associations in Nova Iguaçu, which undoubtedly was a factor in making him a target for abuse and intimidation. On the Nova Iguaçu background, see Scott Mainwaring, "Grass Roots Popular Movements and The Struggle for Democracy: Nova Iguaçu, 1974–1985," in Stepan, ed., *Democratizing Brazil?* (forthcoming).

81. One of the most influential of the studies on living standards was Cândido Procópio Ferreira de Camargo, et al., *São Paulo 1975: crescimento e pobreza* (São Paulo: Edições Loyola, 1976). The research was done by staff from CEBRAP, an independent social science center, at the request of the Pontifícia Comissão de Justiça e Paz da Arquidiocese de São Paulo.

82. This orientation can be seen in the "Pastoral Communication to God's People" issued by a commission of the CNBB in October 1976. It is reprinted in Luiz Gonzaga de Souza Lima, *Evolução política dos católicos e da igreja no Brasil* (Petrópolis: Vozes, 1979), 240–54.

83. For background on Cardinal Arns there is the highly favorable portrait in Getulio Bittencourt and Paulo Sergio Markum, *O cardeal do povo: D. Paulo Evaristo Arns* (São Paulo: Alfa–Omega, 1979). There is a collection of interviews with Cardinal Arns in D. Paulo Evaristo Arns, *Em defesa dos direitos humanos* (Rio de Janeiro: Ed. Brasília/Rio, 1978). Unfortunately, the individ-

ual interviews, given between 1970 and 1978, are not dated. See also the cover story in *Veja*, October 5, 1977, and the August 1986 interview (conducted by Joan Dassin) in *NACLA Report on the Americas*, XX, No. 5 (September–December 1986), 66–71.

84. A leading student of the Brazilian Church's contemporary role concluded that "The church has become the primary institutional focus of dissidence in the country. It is no exaggeration to state that the authoritarian and arbitrary actions of the regime have forced this role on the church." Bruneau, *The Church in Brazil*, 151.

85. A valuable source on the role of the Bar Association is Alberto Venancio Filho, *Notícia histórica da Ordem dos Advogados do Brasil, 1930–1980* (Rio de Janeiro: Ordem dos Advogados do Brasil, 1982). A useful account of the lawyers' movement for a return to the rule of law is given in James A. Gardner, *Legal Imperialism: American Lawyers and Foreign Aid in Latin America* (Madison: University of Wisconsin Press, 1980), 109–25. I also benefited greatly from interviews (all in Rio de Janeiro) with four former national presidents of the OAB: Seabra Fagundes (June 7, 1983), J. Ribeiro de Castro Filho (June 10, 1983), Bernardo Cabral (June 7, 1983), and Raymundo Faoro (July 2, 1983). The story of the battle over civil liberties is given a very human dimension in Patricia Weiss Fagen, "Civil Society and Civil Resistance in Chile and Brazil," *Human Rights Internet: Special Paper No. 1* (Washington: Human Rights Internet, 1982), which focuses on four courageous lawyers: Anina de Cavalho, Modesto da Silveira, Helio Bicudo, and Dalmo Dallari. As Fagen notes, "those opposing the military responded with two lines of action: they sought to protect victims of repression by means of legal defense and denunciations of human rights violations, and they worked to create organizations which would be capable of defending economic as well as political rights" (pp. 3–4).

86. This disillusionment of prominent UDN figures is the end of the story told very incisively in Benavides, *A UDN e o udenismo*, 125–36. See also "UDN: o poder aos 30 anos," *Opinião*, April 25, 1975. I do not mean to imply that only the UDN went through this disillusionment. But they are indicative simply because their legal rhetoric was such a clear example of the Bar Association's traditional thinking.

87. Interviews with José Ribeiro de Castro Filho (June 10, 1983), José Carlos Dias (June 29, 1983), and Tecio Lins e Silva (July 7, 1983). All three are attorneys who represented political prisoners.

88. Reprinted in Venancio Filho, *Notícia histórica*, 157–58.

89. The speeches and papers delivered at the Rio convention are reprinted in Conselho Federal da Ordem dos Advogados do Brasil, *Anais da V Conferência*.

90. Interview with Eduardo Seabra Fagundes, June 7, 1983.

91. In his address upon assuming the presidency of the Bar Association in April 1976, Eduardo Seabra Fagundes ended by underlining the importance of "the independence of the brave Bar Association," which he called "more important than the independence of judges," because "when lawyers defend the autonomy of the Bar they are not motivated by the interests of their class, but by the interests of the nation." *Discurso de posse do Dr. Eduardo Seabra Fagundes como Presidente do Instituto dos Advogados Brasileiros, pronunciado em 22 de abril 1976* (typescript). The lawyers successfully fought off the government attempt to eliminate their legal autonomy. Venancio Filho, *Notícia histórica*, 183–201.

92. OAB logic is well analyzed in Maria Helena Moreira Alves, *State and Opposition in Military Brazil,* 160–62.
93. The role of the press in this period is examined in Joan R. Dassin, "The Brazilian Press and the Politics of Abertura," *Journal of Interamerican Studies and World Affairs,* XXVI, No. 3 (August 1984), 385–414. Despite the censorship, there circulated a booklet-sized publication, *Notícias censuradas,* containing recently censored stories. I found issue No. 15 (September 1974) in the Associated Press files in Rio in May, 1975. Admittedly, the circulation must have been quite limited.
94. For a typical example of how the politicians of both ARENA and MDB speculated about possible changes in the party regulations, see "Questão de tática e tempo," *Visão,* July 26, 1976, pp. 37–38.
95. For an in-depth analysis of four municipal elections, see Fábio Wanderley Reis, ed., *Os partidos e o regime: a lógica do processo eleitoral brasileiro* (São Paulo: Edições Símbolo, 1978).
96. As these Senators no longer needed to be elected directly, press wags dubbed them the "bionic senators," after the seemingly life-like U.S. television hero and heroine who were in fact indestructible machines.
97. The "package" also included a measure of far-reaching significance in police administration. The PMs (*Polícia Militar*), or state police, which had traditionally been accountable as part of the civil arm of state government, was now granted its own system of internal justice. This would put the PMs, always in the front line of crowd control, beyond the reach of accountability in civil channels. Pinheiro, "Polícia," 61.
98. Many foreign observers were equally upset. One U.S. specialist on the Brazilian church concluded, "that this regime was not liberating or opening up, but rather the reverse, and that the self-styled democrat was a complete autocrat." Bruneau, *The Church in Brazil,* 74.
99. Maria Helena Moreira Alves, *State and Opposition,* 164–65.
100. The television speech, along with a selection of his other speeches, is reprinted in Alencar Furtado, *Salgando a terra* (Rio de Janeiro: Paz e Terra, 1977).
101. Kucinski, *Abertura,* 105–8.
102. For an example of a study placing nuclear power in the context of Brazil's other energy sources, see Antônio Aureliano Chaves de Mendonça, "O Brasil e o Problema da energia nuclear," *Boletim Geográfico,* No. 247 (October/December 1975), 28–50. The author became vice president in 1979. In fact, the government overestimated future energy needs, partly as a result of inadequate staff work. Interview with Ambassador Robert Sayre, Washington, D. C., May 16, 1983.
103. A convenient summary of U.S.–Brazilian friction over the nuclear question may be found in Wesson, *The United States and Brazil,* 75–89. An early analysis which remains highly valuable is Norman Gall, "Atoms for Brazil, Dangers for All," *Foreign Policy,* 23 (Summer 1976), 155–201. A more recent overview can be found in David J. Myers, "Brazil: Reluctant Pursuit of the Nuclear Option," *Orbis,* XXVII, No. 4 (Winter 1984), 881–911. For a useful background to Brazilian nuclear policy, see Wolf Grabendorff, "Bedingungsfaktoren und Strukturen der Nuklearpolitik Brasiliens" (Ebenhausen, West Germany: Stiftung Wissenschaft und Politik, December 1979, mimeo). For a critique of official policy by Brazil's leading nuclear physicist, see José Gol-

demberg, *Energia nuclear no Brasil* (São Paulo: Editora Hucitec, 1978). The most widely read domestic critic of Brazil's nuclear policy was Kurt Rudolf Mirow, *Loucura nuclear* (Rio de Janeiro: Civilização Brasileira, 1979). Mirow is a Brazilian industrialist of German background who was well informed about the West German aspect of the nuclear deal.

104. According to a former U.S. ambassador to Brasil in this period, the prediction that the U.S. could not guarantee future supplies of enriched uranium was based on an erroneous report. Nonetheless, it was immediately believed in Brazil. Interview with Ambassador Robert Sayre, Washington, D. C., May 16, 1983.

105. For U.S. worries over the impending contract, see the *New York Times,* June 4, 10, and 15, 1975. Worries about the pact as concluded are reported in the *Wall Street Journal,* July 2, 1975.

106. Ernesto Geisel, *Discursos,* vol. 4 (1977) (Brasília: Assessoria de Imprensa da Presidência da República, 1978), 39.

107. This analysis is based in part on interviews with U.S. State Department officials in March 1976 and with officials of the Brazilian Ministry of Foreign Relations in July 1976.

108. My analysis of the February 21st Memorandum has centered on its links to Brazilian domestic politics, our main concern here. There is much to be said also about the Memorandum's importance to Brazil's economic relations with the U.S., with Europe (Brazil already had similar consultative understandings with France, the United Kingdom, and West Germany), and with the Third World.

109. U.S.–Brazil relations during the Carter presidency are given a chapter in Robert Wesson, *The United States and Brazil: Limits of Influence* (New York: Praeger, 1981). The wider context of U.S. human rights policy toward Brazil is given in Lars Schoultz, *Human Rights and United States Policy Toward Latin America* (Princeton: Princeton University Press, 1981). Economic issues are stressed in two articles by Albert Fishlow: "Flying Down to Rio: U.S.–Brazil Relations," *Foreign Affairs* 57:2 (Winter 1978/79), 387–405; and "The United States and Brazil: The Case of the Missing Relationship," *Foreign Affairs,* LXI, No. 4 (Spring 1982), 904–23.

110. For the views of a Carter administration official who played a key role in trying to get the Brazilians to reconsider their nuclear deal with West Germany, see Joseph S. Nye, Jr., "The Diplomacy of Nuclear Non-Proliferation," in Alan K. Henrikson, ed., *Negotiating World Order: The Artisanship and Architecture of Global Diplomacy* (Wilmington, Delaware: Scholarly Resources, Inc., 1986), 79–94.

111. Muckraking columnist Jack Anderson reported in 1979 that Brazil was about to test a nuclear device "as a way of appeasing the military hardliners," "Washington Merry-Go-Round," [Boston] *Times Herald-Record,* November 14, 1979. There was no such test.

112. The history of the U.S. human rights legislation is well told in Schoultz, *Human Rights and United States Policy Toward Latin America,* 194–98. Amnesty International (AI) had continued to monitor the mistreatment of Brazilian political prisoners ("prisoners of conscience" is AI's term) since its 1972 *Report on Allegations of Torture in Brazil* listing more than a thousand victims. In its reports for 1972–73, 1973–74, 1974–75, and 1975–76, AI documented both the trends in justice procedures and the individual cases of

abuse. For a later analysis of the U.S. role, see the interview with former President Carter in *Veja,* October 3, 1984.

113. Stumpf and Pereira Filho, *A segunda guerra,* 23; Kucinski, *Abertura,* 67; Stepan, *Os militares,* 53.

114. Interview with Ambassador John Crimmins, Washington, D. C., May 16, 1983.

115. The president did not seem to honor his own injunction. In mid-1977 Humberto Barreto, Geisel's chief press aide and a close adviser, announced the presidential candidacy of General João Batista Figueiredo, then head of the SNI. Geisel undoubtedly was forced to speed up his timetable due to Frota's rapidly building support.

116. Frota's manifesto appeared in the daily press on October 13, 1977. Frota warned that if his fellow officers did not follow his advice about preserving "a democratic Brazil," then "when the heavy shackles of Marxist totalitarianism make the sweat of bitterness ooze out of the pallid brows of their wives, I don't want them in their cries of despair to accuse General Sylvio Frota of not having pointed out to them the imminent threat."

117. The statement is reprinted in Hugo Abreu, *O outro lado do poder* (Rio de Janeiro: Nova Fronteira, 1979), 144. Divisions among military officers over government policies could be brought to a head by a dramatic event, but then the issue tended to be resolved in a matter of days, not weeks. Moves made in the earliest moments were often the most crucial—such as Geisel's preempting Frota's ability to communicate with any commanders by having already named General Bethlem as his successor.

118. These struggles within the Geisel government are clearly chronicled in three informative journalistic accounts: André Gustavo Stumpf and Merval Pereira Filho, *A segunda guerra: sucessão de Geisel* (São Paulo: Brasiliense, 1979); Walder de Goes, *O Brasil do General Geisel* (Rio de Janeiro: Nova Fronteira, 1978); and Getúlio Bittencourt, *A quinta estrela: como se tenta fazer um presidente no Brasil* (São Paulo: Editora Ciências Humanas, 1978). One well-informed journalist described Geisel as "keeping his uniformed colleagues at a distance and playing masterfully on their individual weaknesses . . . ," Kucinski, *Abertura,* 42. In December 1977 Geisel, in addressing the ARENA leadership, referred to a "healthy [political] climate," which had been achieved "despite obstacles of every kind—from the rigidity of sincere but radical revolutionaries to the irresponsibility, if not bad faith, of impassioned opponents, in the form of obstinate subversives or obdurate hooligans. . . ." Geisel, *Discursos,* vol. 4, p. 345. In this description Geisel was more explicit about the hard-line military than he could have been in the early years of his presidency.

119. Speculation over the identity of the official presidential nominee became a favorite sport. A leading journalist and political commentator provided a delightful spoof on all this in Alberto Dines, *E por que não eu?* (Rio de Janeiro: CODECRI, 1979). The author awakes one day and decides to become president, taking a witty and fantastical journey through the cultural and political landscape of the late Geisel presidency.

120. It is worth remembering that in 1969 Albuquerque Lima had been vetoed by the senior military on the grounds that he had only three stars. In fact, that had to do with Albuquerque Lima's views and not his rank. In Figueiredo's case he had as mentor an incumbent president of unprecedented power within the army.

121. There was a dissident slate for the ARENA nomination, consisting of Senator Magalhães Pinto (for president), longtime *mineiro* UDN leader and one of the fathers of the 1964 Revolution, and Severo Gomes (for vice president), who had been minister of industry and commerce in the Geisel government until his resignation in February 1977. Seeing that their chances were nil at the convention, Magalhães Pinto and Gomes did not appear, alleging the choice had already been dictated by the president.

122. Abreu gave his angry version of how Figueiredo's candidacy was "imposed" in Hugo Abreu, *O outro lado do poder* (Rio de Janeiro: Nova Fronteira, 1979) and in the posthumously published *Tempo de crise* (Rio de Janeiro: Nova Fronteira, 1980). The latter volume included Abreu's recommendations for reorienting Brazil's political, economic, and social policies.

123. *Amnesty International Report: 1977* (London: Amnesty International Publications, 1977), 127–29. The government's thin skin was made evident in September 1977 when it pressured the *Folha de São Paulo* to drop Alberto Dines's weekly column ("Jornal dos jornais") an acid review of the press over the preceding week which zeroed in on the publications that had withstood government or other pressures on their reporting and commentary. For a typical Dines column, see "Frivolidade, viagens, dores grandes e pequenas," *Folha de São Paulo,* June 13, 1976.

124. The law professor was Goffredo da Silva Telles, who afterward said he had been inundated with messages of support from all over the country, including "two military areas, which discretion prevents me from identifying." *Isto É,* August 17, 1977. For an outsider's acerbic view of the continuing harassment of academics and researchers during the Geisel presidency, especially at the University of Brasília, see Jeremy J. Stone, "Brazilian Scientists and Students Resist Repression," *FAS Public Interest Report,* XXX, No. 9 (November 1977).

125. The "Declaration" and Faoro's presidential address, as well as a wealth of other papers, are in Conselho Federal da Ordem dos Advogados do Brasil, *Anais da VII Conferência Nacional da Ordem dos Advogados do Brasil: Curitiba: 7 a 12 de Maio de 1978* (Curitiba: Conselho Federal da OAB, 1978). Interview with Raymundo Faoro, Rio de Janeiro, July 2, 1983. For a sympathetic analysis of Faoro's thought and role in the *abertura,* see Mark J. Osiel, "The Dilemma of the Latin American Liberal: The Case of Raymundo Faoro," *Luso-Brazilian Review,* XXIII, No. 1 (Summer 1986), 37–59.

126. Fon, *Tortura,* 67.

127. *Negócios em EXAME,* June 16, 1976.

128. Kucinski, *Abertura,* 33–34; Maria Helena Moreira Alves, *State and Opposition,* 169–70. For highly informative analyses of the role of business leaders in the *abertura,* see Fernando Henrique Cardoso, "O papel dos empresários no processo de transição: o caso brasileiro," *Dados,* XXVI, No. 1 (1983), 9–27; and Eli Diniz, "Empresariado e transição política no Brasil: problemas e perspectivas" (Rio de Janeiro: Instituto Universitário de Pesquisas do Rio de Janeiro: Série Estudos, No. 22, February 1984). Luiz Carlos Bresser Pereira argued then and later that the rupture of the alliance between the bourgeoisie and the state (or the technobureaucracy) was the key to liberalization. See his *O colapso de uma aliança de classes* (São Paulo: Brasiliense, 1978), 125–31. Although the attack by business was very important, it was only one factor

among others. The aforementioned paper by Diniz is convincing on that score.

129. Soon after leaving office, Severo Gomes published *Tempo de mudar* (Pôrto Alegre: Editora Globo, 1977), a collection of speeches and interviews in which his nationalist views were clearly stated. He continued to state those views frequently, as in a lengthy interview in *Movimento,* November 6, 1978.

130. Interview with Luiz Eulálio Bueno Vidigal, June 27, 1983.

131. Data and analyses of the 1978 elections may be found in *As eleições nacionais de 1978,* 2 vols. (Brasília: Edições da Fundação Milton Campos, 1979); articles by Luiz Navarro de Britto, Aloízio G. de Andrade Araújo, and Carlos Alberto Penna Rodrigues de Carvalho in *Revista Brasileira de Estudos Políticos,* No. 51 (July 1980); and Bolivar Lamounier, ed., *Voto de desconfiança: eleições e mudança política no Brasil: 1970–1979* (Petrópolis: Vozes, 1980).

132. Maria Helena Moreira Alves, *State and Opposition,* 167–68.

133. For a careful study of the new law, including systematic comparisons with previous legislation on national security, see Ana Valderez A.N. de Alencar, *Segurança nacional: Lei no 6.6520/78—antecedentes, comparações, anotações, histórico,* 2nd ed. (Brasília: Senado Federal, Subsecretaria de Edições Técnicas, 1982).

134. For an excellent overview of this period, see José Alvaro Moises, "Problemas actuais do movimento operario no Brasil," *Revista de Cultura Contemporanea,* I, No. 1 (July 1978), 49–61. See also Maria Hermínia Tavares de Almeida, "O sindicato no Brasil: Novos problemas, velhas estruturas," *Debate e Crítica,* No. 6 (July 1975), 49–74; the same author's "Novas demandas, novos direitos; experiências do sindicalismo paulista na última década," *Dados,* XXVI, No. 3 (1983), 265–90; and Amaury de Souza, "The Nature of Corporative Representation: Leaders and Members of Organized Labor in Brazil" (Ph.D. dissertation, Massachusetts Institute of Technology, 1975).

135. The "new unionism" in Brazil stimulated an outpouring of analysis. Important articles by Amaury de Souza, Bolivar Lamounier, Maria Hermínia Tavares de Almeida, and Luiz Werneck Vianna appeared in *Dados,* XXIV (No. 2) 1981. A useful view from a long-time U.S. observer is Thomas G. Sanders, "Brazil's Labor Unions," *American Universities Field Staff Reports,* 1981/No. 48 (South America). The flavor of the intense interest within Brazil is evident in Ricardo Antunes, ed., *Cadernos de Debate 7: por um novo sindicalismo* (São Paulo: Brasiliense, 1980). One of the most important research contributions is John Humphrey, *Capitalist Control and Workers' Struggle in the Brazilian Auto Industry* (Princeton: Princeton University Press, 1982), which is based on a careful study of actual shop floor conditions. Humphrey also analyzes in detail the 1978 and 1979 autoworkers' strikes. It should be noted that this ferment among union leadership appeared above all in São Paulo, where it got the publicity befiting the industrial heartland of Brazil. At the same time, however, most Brazilian unions remained remote from the workers and had little shop floor support. The best single analysis is Margaret E. Keck, "The 'New Unionism' in the Brazilian Transition," in Alfred Stepan, *Democratizing Brazil?* (forthcoming).

136. Overnight Lula became one of Brazil's most famous personalities. Background on his career and views is given in Mario Morel, *Lula, o metalúrgico* (Rio de Janeiro: Nova Fronteira, 1981).

137. The government was accused of other manipulations that hurt the workers. A prime example was the calculation of productivity gains. Workers had been credited with virtually none of these gains, which instead went to the employers.
138. *Folha da São Paulo*, July 31,1977.
139. For a collection of interviews with workers and union leaders involved in the May–July 1978 work actions, see *A greve na voz dos trabalhadores da Scania a Itu* (São Paulo: Alfa–Omega, 1979), which is No. 2 in the series *História imediata*. A concise account, based on extensive interviews, is given by John Humphrey in *Capitalist Control and Workers' Struggle*, 160–175. Many important documents from the 1978 (and 1979) strike are reprinted in Luís Flávio Rainho and Osvaldo Martines Bargas, *As lutas operárias e sindicais do metalúrgicos em São Bernardo: 1977–1979* (São Bernardo: FG, 1983). Another detailed account based on extensive interviews with workers in 1978 is given in Amnéris Maroni, *A estratégia da recusa: análise das greves de maio/78* (São Paulo: Brasiliense, 1982).
140. Some employers had ferocious reactions to the upsurge of labor activism, as can be seen in Laís Wendel Abramo, "Empresários e trabalhadores: novas idéias e velhos fantasmas," *Cadernos do CEDEC,* No. 7 (São Paulo: CEDEC, 1985).
141. Planning Minister João Paulo dos Reis Velloso, the Geisel government's principal technocrat, later defended its record vigorously. The current account deficit remained virtually stable, he pointed out, registering $7.0 billion in 1978, as against $7.1 billion in 1974. The foreign debt had risen to $43.5 billion by the end of 1978, from $17.2 billion at the end of 1974. Yet, argued Reis Velloso, the large foreign exchange reserves of $11.9 billion at the end of 1978 made the net foreign debt only $31.6 billion. He thus argued that the Geisel government policies had left a highly favorable economic legacy for its successor. Interview with João Paulo dos Reis Velloso, Rio de Janeiro, June 8, 1983. The former planning minister made some of the same points in his *Brasil: a solução positiva* (São Paulo: Abril–Tec, 1978). For a leading opposition critique of the Geisel policies, see Roberto Saturnino Braga, "Um modelo economico de oposição,"*Folha de São Paulo*, June 26, 1977. One of the most widely read academic critics was the Yale-trained economist Edmar Bacha, whose *Os mitos de uma década: ensaios de economia brasileira* (Rio de Janeiro: Paz e Terra, 1976) and *Política econômica e distribuição de renda* (Rio de Janeiro: Paz e Terra, 1978) took government policies to task on such key questions as income distribution and increasing foreign takeovers of Brazilian industry. Bacha was a leader in the new generation of economists, of whom many but by no means all, were trained in the U.S. and Europe. They soon became an important force in public debate over economic policy, both through articles and interviews in the principal daily papers and through new publications they launched, such as *Economia: revista da ANPEC* (first number in November 1977). ANPEC was the national association of centers of postgraduate training in economics. A second new publication, begun in 1977, was *Boletim do IERP*, published by the *Instituto dos Economistas do Estado do Rio de Janeiro*. Like the ANPEC periodical, it sought to discuss key questions of economic policy in terms understandable to a wider public.
142. The Brazilian state sector of the economy has been slow to receive the analysis

it deserves. For an example of a U.S. journalist who was deeply impressed by the state's commanding position in the economy at the beginning of Geisel's term, see Graham Hovey's story in the *New York Times*, July 3, 1974. The most complete analysis of the state's role in the Brazilian economy is Thomas J. Trebat, *The State as Entrepreneur: The Case of Brazil* (Cambridge: Cambridge University Press, 1983). A highly influential work which places the state sector in a broader context is Peter Evans, *Dependent Development: The Alliance of Multinational, State, and Local Capital in Brazil* (Princeton: Princeton University Press, 1979). Luciano Martins, *Estado capitalista e burocracia no Brasil pós-64* (Rio de Janeiro: Paz e Terra, 1985) is an important study based on extensive interviews with state sector administrators during the Geisel presidency. Brazilian critics ridiculed the commitment to so many huge projects as "pharoesque" (*faraônicos*). For a list of the largest state investment projects midway through the Figueiredo presidency, see "O delírio das obras," *Isto É*, July 28, 1982.

143. The history of the government decision to open Brazil to exploration by foreign oil firms is laid out in Bernardo Kucinski, ed., *Petróleo: contratos de risco e dependência* (São Paulo: Brasiliense, 1977). For examples of the sharply conflicting opinions about the "risk contracts," see *Gazeta Mercantil*, May 16, 1975, and *Jornal do Brasil*, May 25, 1975. The nationalist case against the contracts is spelled out in *Opinião*, May 23, 1975.

144. The Geisel government also attempted to promote industrial expansion in the capital goods and petrochemical sectors, in an effort both to replace imports with Brazilian production and to generate high domestic growth. The mixed results are analyzed in Peter Evans, "Reinventing the Bourgeoisie: State Entrepreneurship and Class Formation in Dependent Capitalist Development," in Michal Burawoy and Theda Skocpol, eds., *Marxist Inquiries: Studies of Labor, Class, and States* (Chicago: University of Chicago Press, 1982), S210–S247.

145. In the late Geisel presidency there were a number of collaborative efforts at diagnosing Brazil's ills—coming primarily from the opposition. One of the most interesting is the collection of interviews with prominent scholars, scientists, and technocrats edited by Celcio Monteiro de Lima, *Brasil: o retrato sem retoque* (Rio de Janeiro: Francisco Alves Editora, 1978). In early December 1978 the opposition-oriented Centro Brasil Democrático held a three-day plenary meeting to discuss Brazil's political, economic, social, and constitutional plight. The proceedings were published in Centro Brasil Democrático, *Paineis da crise brasileira: Anais do Encontro Nacional pela Democracia* (Rio de Janeiro: Editora Avenir, 1979), 4 vols. A similar effort, on more sharply focused themes, was held in São Paulo in mid-1979, and the papers were published in Bolivar Lamounier, Francisco C. Weffort, and Maria Victoria Benevides, eds.,*Direito, cidadania e participação* (São Paulo: T.A. Queiroz, 1981).

146. For a review of "the Geisel years," see the cover story in *Veja*, March 14, 1979.

147. For an example of the negative reaction, if retrospective, to Geisel's autocratic manner, see Carlos Chagas, political columnist in *O Estado de São Paulo*, July 8, 1981. "Geisel never listened to anyone," said Chagas, because "he assumed in his omnipotence that he knew everything."

Chapter VII: Figueiredo: The Twilight of Military Government

1. Some observers tried to interpret the father's rebellion against a "revolutionary" government as a possible harbinger of a similar attitude of the son toward the hard line.
2. For a collection of his speeches, primarily those given in the Senate between 1973 and 1979, see Petrônio Portella, *Tempo de congresso, II* (Brasília: Senado Federal, 1980). The author of the "apresentação" of this posthumously published volume was, appropriately, General Golbery.
3. The key role Golbery had carved out in the Geisel government is described in Elmar Bones, "Golbery: silêncio e poder," *Tribuna da Imprensa*, October 2 and 3, 1978. Analyses of how that role was to continue in the Figueiredo government are given in Walder de Góes, "Golbery no alto do poder," *Jornal do Brasil*, February 18, 1979; and A. C. Scartezini, "O irremovível Golbery," *Folha de São Paulo*, March 12, 1979.
4. Robert M. Levine, "Brazil: Democracy Without Adjectives," *Current History*, LXXVIII, No. 454 (February 1980), 50.
5. Interview with Ambassador Robert M. Sayre, Washington, D. C., May 13, 1983.
6. The speech was published in *Jornal do Brasil*, March 16, 1979. It is to be found also in João Figueiredo, *Discursos* (Brasília: Presidência da República, Secretaria de Imprensa e Divulgação, 1981), vol. 1, pp. 1–8.
7. The start-up of the Figueiredo government furnished the occasion for evaluations of Brazil's transition to a more democratic regime. The Brazilian Bar Association (OAB) continued in the forefront of democratization, as can be seen in the interviews with Raymundo Faoro, the outgoing OAB President, and Seabra Fagundes, the incoming president, in *Jornal do Brasil*, March 21, 1979. A comparable effort could be seen in the June 1979 conference on "Law, Citizenship and Participation" organized by the São Paulo research centers CEDEC and CEBRAP and the OAB. "Pelo direito de maior participação," *Isto É*, July 4, 1979, pp. 82–85. The papers were published in Bolivar Lamounier, et al., *Direito, cidadania e participação* (São Paulo: T.A. Queiroz, 1981). A target for continuing attack by the opposition was the National Security Law (*Lei de Segurança Nacional,* or LSN). For typical arguments, see *Pela revogação da Lei de Segurança Nacional* (São Paulo: Comissão Justiça e Paz de São Paulo, 1982), which includes contributions by Helio Bicudo and José Carlos Dias; and "Sociedade civil condena a LSN por unanimidade," *Folha de São Paulo*, May 15, 1983, which reports a mock trial of the LSN in the "Tribunal Tiradentes." In late 1983 a revised LSN became law, reducing the number of crimes punishable under it. This did not satisfy the critics, who had wanted a complete revocation of the law.
8. After comparing several Latin American countries over the preceding twenty years, one researcher concluded at the outset of the 1980s that Brazil was the most backward country in the effective use of direct collective bargaining for conflict resolution. Erfren Cordova, ed., *Las relaciones colectivas de trabajo en America Latina* (Geneva: International Labour Organisation, 1981).
9. For a description of the basic arguments used by the metalworkers' leadership in the strikes of 1979–1980, see José Alvaro Moisés, *Lições de liberdade e de opressão: os trabalhadores e a luta pela democracia* (Rio de Janeiro: Paz e Terra, 1982).

10. For examples of the tough talk by employers, see Laís Wendel Abramo, "Empresários e trabalhadores: novas idéias e velhos fantasmas," *Cadernos do CEDEC*, No. 7 (São Paulo: CEDEC, 1985).

11. A key figure in this link between the Catholic left and the "new unionism" was Waldemar Rossi, a metalworker who was the national coordinator of the *Pastoral Operária* (a Church-sponsored workers organization) and who in 1974 had been arrested and tortured. "Entrevista: Waldemar Rossi, exclusivo: 'Fui demitido depois do discurso para a Papa,' " *Revista de Cultura Vozes*, LXXVII, No. 2 (March 1981), 44–61.

12. This pattern emerges clearly from a study of a national sample of collective labor agreements registered for 1979–82: Amaury Guimarães de Souza, *Os efeitos da nova política salarial na negociação coletiva* (São Paulo: Nobel, 1985).

13. The problem of inflation is stressed in "Panorama," the opening article in *Conjuntura Econômica*, February 1979, the issue with the retrospective survey of the Brazilian economy during 1978. For an excellent review of principal economic problems as of late 1979, see *Revista de ANPEC*, III, No. 4 (October 1980), which includes papers given at the annual convention of Brazilian graduate economics faculties. For a concise description of the economic problems facing the new government in 1979, see Werner Baer, *The Brazilian Economy: Growth and Development*, 2nd ed. (New York: Praeger, 1983), chap. 6. The highly conservative U.S. financial weekly *Barron's* had run an editorial on September 18, 1978, with the heading "Distant Early Warning: Brazil's 'Economic Miracle' has lost its lustre." The argument of the editorial boiled down to another attack on indexation. Especially valuable overviews of economic policy in the Figueiredo presidency can be found in Fishlow, "A Tale of Two Presidents," and Edmar L. Bacha and Pedro S. Malan, "Brazil's Debt: from the Miracle to the IMF" both in Alfred Stepan, ed., *Democratizing Brazil?* (forthcoming).

14. Finance Minister Karlos Rischbieter survived his battles with Delfim until January 1980, when he finally resigned, to be replaced by Ernane Galveas, a veteran of Delfim's pre-1974 technocratic team. Like Simonsen, Rischbieter disagreed sharply with what he considered Delfim's unrealistically optimistic prognosis.

15. *III Plano Nacional de Desenvolvimento: 1980–85* (Brasília: Presidência da República, Secretaria de Planejamento, March 1981). The plan had been approved by the Congress in May 1980. The delay in publication may have reflected Delfim's desire to downplay its importance. Work on the plan had begun when Simonsen was still planning minister. When Delfim took over, the evaluation of prospects for growth and inflation were altered to fit his more optimistic view.

16. *III Plano Nacional de Desenvolvimento*, 5–7.

17. *Ibid.*, 6.

18. *Ibid.*, 16–17.

19. *Ibid.*, 19.

20. *Ibid.*, 47.

21. For a detailed analysis of the maxi-devaluation, see the article by Edy Luiz Kogut and José Júlio Senna in *Jornal do Brasil*, December 19, 1979. The new measures were widely debated by economists. See, for example, the interview with José Serra, an economist from the University of Campinas, in *Folha de São*

Paulo, December 12, 1979. Serra attacked the new policy as a "shock treatment for a very weak patient." Changes in economic policy were one among other policy changes announced by President Figueiredo in a major speech on December 7, 1979. In adopting the strategy of pre-fixed devaluations and indexation adjustments, Delfim was following similar policies in Argentina and Chile. He evidently thought they had discovered a key to financial stability.

22. Part of the amnesty campaign was directed at reminding Brazilians (and the Brazilian military) that amnesties had been frequent in their history and had played a vital role in maintaining long-term national unity. This approach is evident in Roberto Ribeiro Martins, *Liberdade para os brasileiros: anistia ontem e hoje* (Rio: Civilização Brasileira, 1978). For a collection of portraits of and brief interviews with Brazilian exiles, see Cristina Pinheiro Machado, *Os exilados: 5 mil brasileiros a espera da anistia* (São Paulo: Alfa–Omega, 1979). Her objective was to generate support for amnesty by highlighting the injustice the exiles had suffered. For an overview of the human rights situation at the outset of the Figueiredo presidency, see Joan Dassin, "Human Rights in Brazil: A Report as of March 1979," *Latin American Studies Association Newsletter*, X, No. 3 (September 1979), 24–36, which is reprinted from *Universal Human Rights*, I, No. 3 (1979).

23. Interview with Paulo Evaristo Arns in *NACLA Report on the Americas*, XX, No. 5 (September/December 1986), 67.

24. For a discussion of the law, see Moreira Alves, *State and Opposition*, 211–12. The history of the amnesty bill can be followed through feature stories in *Veja*, June 27, August 29, and September 5, 1979. The Planalto gave a festive cocktail party when the president presented the amnesty bill he was sending to Congress. He wept freely, recalling that his own father had twice been amnestied after having joined anti-government revolts. *Jornal de Brasília*, June 28, 1979. By early October the military courts had freed 711 political prisoners. *O Globo*, October 3, 1979. The decree spelling out regulations for application of the amnesty law was published in *O Estado de São Paulo*, November 2, 1979.

25. The views of Miguel Arraes had not changed significantly from 1964, as could be seen in the extensive interview published in Cristina Tavares and Fernando Mendonça, *Conversações com Arraes* (Belo Horizonte: Vega, 1979).

26. For an updating on the political lives of the most famous amnesty beneficiaries, such as Luiz Carlos Prestes, Leonel Brizola, and Francisco Julião, see *Veja*, August 13, 1980, which concluded that "when the government feared them it was really afraid of its own shadow." The question of the government's political self-confidence arose in dramatic form in late 1979. President Figueiredo made an official visit to Florianópolis and was the object while speaking of catcalls and personal insults. Figueiredo became so angry that he dashed off the platform in pursuit of his tormentors, who included students and young bystanders. Several were arrested and later prosecuted under the National Security Law. The incident is related in detail in Robert Henry Srour, *A política dos anos 70 no Brasil: a lição de Florianópolis* (São Paulo: Econômica Ed., 1982). Figueiredo certainly showed the common touch, a virtue for which Geisel had reportedly favored him.

27. The article, "Descendo aos porões" by Antonio Carlos Fon, appeared in *Veja*, February 21, 1979. It is reprinted, in a different format, in Fon, *Tortura*.

28. The list of torturers had been assembled by the *Comitê de Solidariedade aos*

Revolucionários do Brasil and published in Portugal by the *Comitê Pró-Anistia Geral do Brasil*.

29. Detective Fleury was much in the news in March 1979 when Catholic Sister Maurina Borges da Silveira returned from banishment abroad and testified to a military court that after her arrest in 1969 she had been tortured by Fleury (he supervised her electric shock torture "laughing and ridiculing me as I jumped"). She had been charged with aiding a guerrilla group and in 1970 was ransomed along with other prisoners in return for the freedom of the Japanese consul whom the guerrillas had kidnapped. The 1979 military court unanimously absolved her of all charges. *Jornal do Brasil*, March 16, 1979, and *Folha de São Paulo*, March 30, 1979.

30. Hélio Bicudo, the São Paulo state's attorney who had attempted unsuccessfully to prosecute Fleury, was not convinced that the death was an accident, thinking it more likely a revenge slaying among drug traffickers; Rivaldo Chinem and Tim Lopes, *Terror policial* (São Paulo: Global Editora, 1980), 13–14. Fleury's demise was given extensive illustrated coverage in *Manchete* for May 19, 1979, and *Fatos e Fotos/Gente* for May 14, 1979. A leading leftist weekly concluded that "his friends and enemies agree: he didn't deserve the death he got," *Em Tempo*, May 3–9, 1979.

31. The text of the amnesty decree was published in *O Estado de São Paulo* for November 2, 1979.

32. Raymundo Faoro, who had just retired as OAB president, helped convince a group of mothers and wives of those killed by the repression that there was no real prospect of punishing the torturers. Interview with Faoro, July 2, 1983. Seabra Fagundes, Faoro's successor as OAB president, fought against amnesty for the torturers and, losing on that, fought to make the torturers liable for civil action. The latter had proved to be a largely unsuccessful effort. Interview with Seabra Fagundes, June 7, 1983.

33. In July 1980 General Golbery delivered a lecture to the Escola Superior de Guerra in which he analyzed the political scene and explained how the government could retain the initiative if it showed patience and negotiating skill. This lecture was Golbery's most complete public statement on the Geisel government's political strategy. Golbery do Couto e Silva, *Conjuntura política nacional, o poder executivo e geopolítica do Brasil* (Brasília: Editora Universidade do Brasília, 1981), 3–35. The political strategy of the Figueiredo government stimulated a flood of analysis of the political scene and the prospects for further liberalization. Among the collective works, all with several chapters on aspects of the liberalization, were Bernardo Sorj and Maria Hermínia Tavares de Almeida, eds., *Sociedade e política no Brasil pós-64* (São Paulo: Brasiliense, 1983); Helgio Trindade, ed., *Brasil em perspectiva: dilemas da abertura política* (Pôrto Alegre: Ed. Sulina, 1982); Paulo J. Krischke, ed., *Brasil: do 'milagre' à 'abertura'* (São Paulo: Cortez Editora, 1982); Bolivar Lamounier and José Eduardo Faria, eds., *O Futuro da abertura: um debate* (São Paulo: Cortez, 1981); Lamounier and Faria, eds., "O Brasil agora e depois," *Jornal da Tarde*, June 2 and 9, 1984. Lamounier has published a number of other important articles, including: "Apontamentos sobre a questão democrática brasileira," in Alain Rouquié, et al., eds., *Como renascem as democracias* (São Paulo: Brasiliense, 1985), 104–40; "Opening Through Elections: Will the Brazilian Case Become a Paradigm?" *Government and Opposition*, XIX, No. 2 (Spring 1984), 167–77; and "Authoritarian Brazil Revisited: The Impact of Elections

on the Abertura," to appear in Stepan, ed., *Democratizing Brazil?* (forthcoming). Among the many other Brazilian analyses are Eli Diniz, "A Transição política no Brasil: uma reavaliação da Dinámica da Abertura," *Dados*, XXVIII, No. 3 (1985), 329–46; Luciano Martins, "The 'Liberalization' of Authoritarian Rule in Brazil," in Guillermo O'Donnell, Philippe C. Schmitter, and Laurence Whitehead, eds., *Transitions from Authoritarian Rule: Latin America* (Baltimore: Johns Hopkins University Press, 1986), 72–94; and Luiz Gonzaga de Souza Lima, "A Transição no Brasil: comentários e reflexões," *Contexto Internacional*, I, No. 1 (January–June 1985), 27–59. Non-Brazilian scholars also produced valuable analyses, such as in Thomas C. Bruneau and Philippe Faucher, eds., *Authoritarian Capitalism: Brazil's Contemporary Economic and Political Development* (Boulder: Westview Press, 1981), and Wayne A. Selcher, ed., *Political Liberalization in Brazil* (Boulder: Westview Press, 1986). Another overview is offered in Riordan Roett, "The Transition to Democratic Government in Brazil," *World Politics*, XXXVIII, No. 2 (January 1986), 371–82.

34. For a thorough analysis of this legislation on parties, see the two articles by Alfredo Cedilio Lopes in *Problemas Brasileiros: Revista Mensal de Cultura*, XVII, No. 186 (April 1980), 4–22.

35. Useful information on the founding of the PT is given in Mário Pedrosa, *Sobre o PT* (São Paulo: CHED Editora, 1980).

36. For the views of an independent labor union organizer who chose not to go the PT route, see the interview with Waldemar Rossi in Bernardo Kucinski, *Brazil: State and Struggle* (London: Latin American Bureau, 1982).

37. The political significance of Portella's death was emphasized in the press, as in the full-page coverage of January 8, 1980, in *Jornal do Brasil*.

38. *O Estado de São Paulo*, July 10, 1981.

39. Conferência Nacional dos Bispos do Brasil, *Situação do clero no Brasil* (São Paulo: Edições Paulinas, 1981), 11.

40. For a text of the law, along with previous laws and decrees on the subject, see Juarez de Oliveira, *Série Legislação Brasileira: Estrangeiro* 2nd ed. (São Paulo: Editora Saraiva, 1982).

41. The priest was padre Vito Miracapillo, who had long angered authorities in Pernambuco with his radical political views. He earned a cover story in *Veja*, October 29, 1980.

42. For the labor minister's speeches spelling out his thinking from 1979 to 1981, see Murillo Macêdo, *Trabalho na democracia: a nova fisionomia do processo político brasileiro* (Brasília: Ministério do Trabalho, 1981). For an analysis of the rationales given for the frequent changes in wage legislation in the Figueiredo presidency, see Maria Valéria Junho Pena, "A política salarial do governo Figueiredo: um ensaio sobre sua sociologia," *Dados*, XXIX, No. 1 (1986), 39–59. Change in the labor relations system between 1979 and 1984, is the topic in José Pastore and Thomas E. Skidmore, "Brazilian Labor Relations: A New Era?," in Hervey Juris, Mark Thompson, and Wilbur Daniels, eds., *Industrial Relations in a Decade of Economic Change* (Madison, Wisconsin: Industrial Relations Research Association, 1985), 73–113, which also includes data on the effect on employment of the 1981–84 recession.

43. From the large literature on wage policy, I have relied on the following: Departamento Intersindical de Estatística e Estudos Socio-Económicos (DIEESE), *Dez anos da política salarial* (São Paulo, 1975); Edmar Lisboa Bacha, *Política*

económica e distribuição de renda (Rio de Janeiro: Paz e Terra, 1978), 25–52; and Lívio W.R. de Carvalho, "Brazilian Wage Policies, 1964–81," in *Brazilian Economic Studies*, No. 8 (1984), 109–41. The degree to which individual workers benefitted by rising through the wage scale is stressed in Samuel A. Morley, *Labor Markets and Inequitable Growth: The Case of Authoritarian Capitalism in Brazil* (Cambridge: Cambridge University Press, 1982). Morley quite rightly argues that the larger question of poverty in Brazil cannot be understood without analyzing the effects of rapid growth in a capitalist economy which has extensive surplus labor.

44. The unfavorable context for this strike is described in an article with the indicative title of "Lula sob fogo cerrado," in *Veja*, April 2, 1980.

45. For a detailed description of this strike from the standpoint of the labor ministry, see Macedo, *Trabalho na democracia*, 217–68.

46. Data furnished by the Ministry of Labor.

47. The 1982–83 period was marked by only a few strikes at the plant level, usually against firms in the export sector. In 1984 this trend reached the rural sector, most notably the sugar cane areas producing for the alcohol program.

48. In May 1974 *bóias-frias* rioted in protest over low pay and poor working conditions. They burned sugarcane fields, sacked a supermarket, and razed a government building. They were quickly given a pay increase and some improvements in their working conditions. *Veja*, May 23, 1984. The principal student of the *bóias-frias* has been Maria Conceição D'Incao e Mello, who was interviewed in *Exame*, May 30, 1984. See also her *Qual é a questão do bóia-fria* (São Paulo: Brasiliense, 1984).

49. Although the 1979 wage law (Law 6,708) was attacked as a central cause of inflation, most empirical studies found other causes (the public sector deficit, indexation in the financial sector, etc.) to be more important than the 110 percent adjustment for the bottom category of wage earners. See, for example, José Marcio Camargo, "Salário real e indexação no Brasil," *Pesquisa e Planejamento*, XIV, No. 1 (April 1984), 137–60, and Paulo Vieira da Cunha, "Reajustes salariais na indústria e a Lei Salarial de 1979: uma nota empírica, " *Dados*, XXIV, No. 3 (1983), 291–314.

50. The independent, interunion research institute DIEESE had for some years been publishing its own analysis of changes in the cost of living. The January 1983 issue of *Boletim do DIEESE* (the title varied), for example, gave the number of working hours (at the minimum wage) needed to buy the basic foodstuffs, as defined by the government. The DIEESE data almost always showed an inflation rate higher—measured by the basket of goods—than the official rate, which was used to calculate minimum wage adjustments. The middle class was no less attentive to the effects of wage policy on their take-home income, as shown in Renato Boschi, "A abertura e a nova classe média na política brasileira: 1977–1982," *Dados*, XXIX, No. 1 (1986), 5–24.

51. For a valuable chronology of violence during the Figueiredo presidency, see Paulo Sergio Pinheiro, *Escritos indignados* (São Paulo: Brasiliense, 1984), 256–268.

52. Seabra Fagundes, OAB president when the bomb arrived, thought DOI-CODI had sent it. Only days earlier he had asked DOI-CODI to arrange a police lineup of its agents so that São Paulo Professor Dalmo Dallari, a prominent opposition lawyer, could identify his recent kidnappers, whom the opposition were convinced had come from the security agencies. Interview with Seabra

Fagundes, Rio de Janeiro, June 7, 1983. The wave of political terrorism aimed at the left alarmed many in Congress. They created a *Comissão Parlamentar de Inquérito* (Congressional Investigating Committee), or CPI, to hold hearings. The latter produced wild charges and countercharges, but also information valuable to those trying to solve the labyrinth of terrorist activities on the right. For examples of press coverage of the hearings, see *O Estado do São Paulo*, April 9, *Folha de São Paulo*, April 19, *Jornal da Tarde*, September 11, and *Correio Brasiliense*, September 18, 1981.

53. A blow-by-blow account as seen through journalists' eyes is given in Belisa Ribeiro, *Bomba no Riocentro* (Rio de Janeiro: CODECRI, 1982).

54. The press had a field day exposing the contradictions in the official investigation. The press was briefed (no questions permitted) by Colonal Job Lorena de Sant'Anna, who had directed the official inquiry. Crucial parts of the official account were contradicted by the autopsy issued separately by the civil authorities. *Isto É*, July 8 and 22, 1981. The humor weekly *Pasquim* (July 9, 1981) lampooned the inconsistencies in the colonel's story. This embarrassment of the military was a product of the *abertura*, which itself was contradictory. Units such as DOI-CODI still existed, but censorship was gone and civilian authorities had regained stature. Before *abertura* a genuine cover-up of RioCentro would have been simple. The military would have simply confiscated the discredited autopsy and held no press briefing.

55. For evaluations of Golbery's resignation by two of Brazil's better-informed political journalists, see Mino Carta's column in *Folha de São Paulo*, August 12, 1981, and Elio Gaspari's in *Jornal do Brasil*, August 21, 1981. *Veja's* cover story of August 12, 1981, was appropriately entitled (given Golbery's image in Brazil) "O feiticeiro desistiu."

56. Golbery was struggling against Medeiros as part of his fight against the "Médici group," which he feared might regain the presidency. See the columns by Carlos Chagas in *O Estado de São Paulo*, December 6, 1981, and July 6, 1982. One well-placed journalist wrote in the early 1980s: "The difference between the Geisel and Figueiredo governments is that with Geisel the President of the Republic also commanded the *Serviço Nacional de Informações*, while with Figueiredo the operational autonomy and influence of the SNI is greater than that of all the military ministries." Oliveiros Ferreira, *A teoria da "coisa nossa"*, 12.

57. It should be added, however, that many officers were upset over the army's involvement in the attempted bombing or over the clumsy cover-up or both. The hard line won only on the immediate issue of preventing a genuine investigation. Officer opinion at the time is analyzed in Stepan, *Os militares*, 79. General Gentil M. Filho, the commander of the Rio-based First Army, had formal authority over the DOI-CODI. He was soon relieved of his command and failed to get the "golden parachute" of a well-paying state sector job, as commanders had come to expect in this era.

58. The foreign debt crisis stimulated an outpouring of analysis in the press and in book form. A useful summary of the history of Brazil's foreign debt is given in Sergio Goldenstein, *A dívida externa brasileira* (Rio de Janeiro: Guanabara, 1986). The debt was put into a larger economic perspective in Persio Arida, ed., *Dívida externa, recessão e ajuste estrutural: o Brasil diante da crise* (Rio de Janeiro: Paz e Terra, 1983), with contributions from 13 economists at the Catholic University of Rio de Janeiro. Paulo Nogueira Batista, Jr., *Mito e realidade na*

dívida externa brasileira (Rio de Janeiro: Paz e Terra, 1983) is an analysis which looks especially at the relationship between the debt and monetary and exchange rate policy. For an analysis that stresses the link between the debt and the domestic political context in Brazil, see Eul-Soo Pang, "Brazil's External Debt: Part I: The Outside View," and "Brazil's External Debt: Part II: The Inside View," *USFI Reports*, 1984/Nos. 37 & 38 (South America). For a quite optimistic early 1986 view of Brazil's balance of payments and foreign debt prospects, see Marcílio Marques Moreira, *The Brazilian Quandary* (New York: Priority Press, 1986), which gives an excellent analysis of the debt negotiations in the first half of the 1980s. The author was subsequently named Brazilian ambassador to the U.S. Other helpful analyses are: Edmar L. Bacha, "Vicissitudes of Recent Stabilization Attempts in Brazil and the IMF Alternative," in John Williamson, ed., *IMF Conditionality* (Cambridge: MIT Press, 1983), 323–40; Bacha, "Brazil and the IMF: Prologue to the Third Letter of Intent," *Industry and Development*, No. 12 (1984), 101–13; Bacha and Pedro S. Malan, "Brazil's Debt: From the Miracle to the IMF," in Stepan, ed., *Democratizing Brazil?* (forthcoming); Carlos F. Diaz-Alejandro, "Some Aspects of the 1982–83 Brazilian Payments Crisis,"*Brookings Papers on Economic Activity* (Washington, D. C.: Brookings Institutions, 1983), No. 2, 515–52; and Jeffrey A. Frieden, "The Brazilian Borrowing Experience: From Miracle to Debacle and Back," *Latin American Research Review*, XXII, No. 1 (1987), 95–131.

59. *Veja*, December 15 and 29, 1982.
60. The manifesto was published in *Jornal do Brasil*, July 16, 1981.
61. *Country Reports on Human Rights Practices for 1983: Report Submitted to the Committee on Foreign Affairs, U.S. House of Representatives and the Committee on Foreign Relations by the Department of State* (Washington, D. C.: U.S. Government Printing Office, 1984), 489.
62. For an evaluation by a veteran U.S. student of Brazilian elections, see Ronald M. Schneider, *1982 Brazilian Elections Project Final Report: Results and Ramifications* (Washington: Georgetown University Center for Strategic and International Studies, 1982). A very useful overview of elections and the party system from 1946 through the 1982 elections is given in chapter four of Robert Wesson and David Fleischer, *Brazil in Transition* (New York: Praeger, 1983). For a collection of detailed studies of the 1982 elections, see *Revista Brasileira de Estudos Políticos*, No. 57 (July 1983). The links between the 1982 elections and the 1985 presidential election are explored in David Fleischer, "Brazil at the Crossroads: The Elections of 1982 and 1985," in Paul W. Drake and Eduardo Silva, eds., *Elections and Democratization in Latin America, 1980–1985* (San Diego: University of California, San Diego: Center for Iberian and Latin American Studies, 1986), 299–327. Detail on the election in key Northeastern states is given in Joaquim de Arruda Falčao Neto, ed., *Nordeste: eleições* (Recife: Massangana, 1985). The lighter side of the campaign was provided by Carlos Eduardo Novaes, *Crônica de uma brisa eleitoral* (Rio de Janeiro: Nórdica, 1983). For a wealth of information on the deeper trends at work in the post-1964 elections, see Raimundo Pereira, Alvaro Caropreso, and José Carlos Ruy, *Eleições no Brasil pós-64* (São Paulo: Global, 1984) and Gláucio Ary Dillon Soares, *Colégio eleitoral, convenções partidárias, e eleições diretas* (Petrópolis: Vozes, 1984).
63. For an analysis of the racial composition of the vote for Brizola—as far as it can be known—see Gláucio Ary Dillon Soares and Nelson do Valle e Silva,

"O charme discreto do socialismo moreno," *Dados*, XXVIII, No. 2 (1985), 253–73.

64. For an analysis of the 1982 vote in São Paulo, see Bolivar Lamounier and Judith Muszynski, "São Paulo, 1982: a victória do (P)MDB," (São Paulo: IDESP Texto No. 2, 1983). The fact that Lula was eligible to run for governor of São Paulo but not for president of his union is an interesting example of the archaic nature of Brazilian labor law. Or perhaps the message was correctly conveyed: as a state governor he would endanger the status quo less than he would as president of a key union.

65. In mid-1981 the party began publishing a magazine, *Revista do PMDB*, containing party manifestoes and articles on principal economic and social problems.

66. Celso Furtado, *No to Recession and Unemployment: An Examination of the Brazilian Economic Crisis* (London: Third World Foundation, 1984), 3. The original version was *Não à recessão e ao desemprego* (Rio de Janeiro: Paz e Terra, 1983). A lucid analysis of Brazil's situation in light of IMF policy was Edmar Bacha, "Prólogo para terceira carta," *Revista de Economia Política*, III, No. 4 (October–December 1983), 5–19. For more radically nationalist attacks, see Argemiro Jacob Brum, *O Brasil no FMI* (Petrópolis: Vozes, 1984); Marco Antonio de Souza Aguiar, Marcos Arruda, and Parsifal Flores, *Ditadura econômica versus democracia* (Rio de Janeiro: CODECRI, 1983); and Nilson Araujo de Souza, *Sim: reconstrução nacional* (São Paulo: Global Editora, 1984). The last argues: "By their new 'deal' the IMF and the foreign bankers do not intend to attack inflation. Their objective is to use the economic devastation their measures will wreak to prepare the way for a deeper pentration by imperialist capital in our country" (p.110). For a spirited defense of the IMF against such charges, see Jahangir Amuzegar, "The IMF Under Fire," *Foreign Policy*, No. 64 (Fall 1986), 98–119. The author is a former executive director of the IMF.

67. For a journalistic inquiry into Brazil's ability to continue servicing its foreign debt, see "When the Music Stopped," *The Economist*, March 12, 1983. The author's conclusion, after much hedging, was optimistic: "to billionaire lenders, Brazil in 1991 still looks a good bet."

68. The data are from the Getúlio Vargas Foundation and were published in *Jornal do Brasil*, June 4, 1984. For 1980–85, Latin America as a whole suffered a per capita decline in GDP of 8.9 percent. Bela Balassa, et al., *Toward Renewed Economic Growth in Latin America* (Washington: Institute for International Economics, 1986), 151. For an interesting analysis of the link between politics and economic policy, including foreign debt policy, in the post-1973 era, see Bolivar Lamounier and Alkimar R. Moura, "Economic Policy and Political Opening in Brazil," in Jonathan Hartlyn and Samuel A. Morley, eds., *Latin American Political Economy* (Boulder: Westview Press, 1986), 165–96.

69. *Jornal do Brasil*, August 9, 1983.

70. There were many exposés on the military's penetrating the higher bureaucracy, such as Walder de Góes, "Militares ocupam 1/3 dos cargos federais," *O Estado de São Paulo*, November 25, 1979. Data on the increasing percentage of military academy cadets from lower middle and lower class backgrounds are analyzed in Frank D. McCann, "The Military Elite," in Michael Conniff and Frank D. McCann, eds., *Elites and Masses in Modern Brazil* (forthcoming). The comparison of class backgrounds is based on a comparison of cadets in 1985 with cadets for 1955–79. The statistical soundness of comparing one year and

24 may be questionable, but the officers' interpretation of it is the important point.

71. Data on defense expenditures kindly supplied by Mr. John Bowen, economic officer at the U.S. embassy in Brasília. The data are furnished to the IMF, then made available to the U.S. government. The rationale for the military's strategy is spelled out in André Gustavo Stumpf, "Volta aos quartéis," *Playboy*, August 1983. The military worries about outdated equipment, inadequate budgets, and declining prestige are also documented in Stepan, *Os militares*, 68–71 and 85–93. Such concerns were not new. In late 1971 the army chief of staff, General Souto Malan, proposed a "controlled disengagement of the armed forces" along with a "reorganization and re-equipping of the army." *O Estado de São Paulo*, December 15, 1971.

72. For an account of the campaign, see Ricardo Kotscho, *Explode um novo Brasil: diário da campanha das diretas* (São Paulo: Brasiliense, 1984). A briefer, poetic account is Júlio Cesar Monteiro Martins, *O livro das diretas* (Rio de Janeiro: Editora Anima, 1984).

73. Vilela was the subject of a detailed and sympathetic biography: Márcio Moreira Alves, *Teotônio, Guerreiro da Paz* (Petrópolis: Vozes, 1983).

74. The actions of General Newton Cruz at the time of the congressional vote on the *diretas* are recounted in *Veja*, May 2, 1984. The same article has information on his earlier career. For an analysis of the government measures aimed at the control of all communication about the vote on the direct election amendment, see Moacir Pereira, *O golpe do silêncio* (São Paulo: Global, 1984).

75. The *Veja* lead story on the rejection of the Dante de Oliveira amendment suggested that "the popular participation in the campaign for direct elections shifted the central axis of Brazilian politics." *Veja*, May 2, 1984.

76. Brief biographies of the leading presidential candidates are given in Villas-Bôas Corrêa, et al., *Os presidenciáveis: quem é quem na maratona do Planalto* (Rio de Janeiro: RETOUR, 1983). In early 1984 *Veja* did a cover story on each of the three front-runners: Maluf (January 25), Aureliano (February 8), and Andreazza (February 22).

77. Aureliano was also a weight lifter, which gave another dimension to his temper. Thales Ramalho, a veteran congressman, said, "Aureliano was the only deputy that I ever saw pick up an entire bench. He thought he'd been insulted by [MDB deputy] João Herculino and he went after him." *Veja*, February 8, 1984.

78. Maluf modeled himself on several of former President Kubitschek's appeals, which here was the precedent of Brasília. Maluf called his private plan "Esperança" (hope), a favorite word of Kubitschek, who dubbed Brasília the "capital of hope."

79. An account hostile to Maluf may be found in Fernando Morais, et al., *Freguesia do O: o inquérito que desmascarou as brigadas de Paulo Maluf* (São Paulo: Alfa–Omega, 1981).

80. Golbery's endorsement came in "Basta de trapaça," *Veja*, May 16, 1984, an interview in which he gave his view of the political scene, excoriating the "emotional intoxication" of the direct election rallies (after praising them as a "magnificent civil spectacle") and criticizing presidential aide Leitão de Abreu (Golbery's successor) for inviting the dissolution of the existing party system.

81. For a collection of Maciel's speeches, see Marco Maciel, *Vocação e compromisso* (Rio de Janeiro: José Olympio, 1982).

82. A story in *Veja* for January 25, 1984, was an early example. By June Figueiredo was supposedly sticking by his preference for Andreazza but felt he could not announce it for fear of alienating Maluf. See stories by Carlos Chagas in *O Estado de São Paulo*, June 3 and 9, 1984.

83. Stepan, *Os militares,* 79; Gilberto Dimenstein, et al., *O complô que elegeu Tancredo* (Rio de Janeiro: Editora JB, 1985), 28–36.

84. For a detailed account of the process leading to Tancredo's nomination, see Dimenstein, *O complô.*

85. "A historia secreta da sucessão,"*Veja,* January 16, 1985, 43.

86. The incident is reported in *Veja*, September 19, 1984.

87. "A história secreta da sucessão," 42.

88. *Veja*, September 5, 1984, and January 16, 1985.

89. Tancredo's contacts with Army Minister Walter Pires in November 1984 are described in *Veja*, November 28, 1984. A late-December 1984 meeting between Tancredo and Third Army Commander General Leônidas Pires Gonçalves has been described as the one which guaranteed military support for Tancredo's election in January. *Veja*, May 14, 1986. For a blow-by-blow account of Tancredo's nomination and election to the presidency, see *Veja*, January 16, 1986, which also includes the quotation from Pires.

90. The UDN faction was tagged with the same name as that of a new brand of popular music. The opposing faction was named "a banda de musica" because its members had the habit of sitting on the front rows in the Chamber of Deputies (near the musicians if it had been a dance floor) and opening sessions with aggressive attacks on their enemies.

91. "A história secreta da sucessão," 39.

92. *New York Times*, October 28, 1984.

93. Stepan, *Os militares*, 64.

94. The point was captured neatly in the opening sentence of a September magazine story: "Today there is only one person who is absolutely indispensable for Tancredo Neves's opposition victory in the January electoral college: the government candidate, Paulo Maluf."*Senhor*, September 5, 1984, p.30.

95. Stepan, *Os militares*, 73–74. For an analysis of the ineptitude of the government forces, including both the Planalto and the PDS, see Gláucio Ary Dillon Soares, "Elections and the Redemocratization of Brazil," in Paul W. Drake and Eduardo Silva, eds., *Elections and Democratization in Latin America, 1980–1985* (San Diego: University of California, San Diego Center for Iberian and Latin American Studies, 1986), 273–98. Soares includes a figure showing the steady decline of the combined congressional votes for conservative parties from a level above 80 percent in 1945 to barely 40 percent in 1978.

96. The human dimension of the recession is painted in *Folha de São Paulo*, May 28, 1984.

97. In February 1984 the Gallup poll reported that the president's popularity was the lowest ever, with 67 percent disapproving his government. *Veja*, March 14, 1984.

98. A city councilman in Salvador, Bahia, proposed the creation of a "Penitentiary for Technocrats," with Delfim Neto, Ernâne Galveas, and Carlos Langoni as its first inmates. *Jornal da Bahia*, May 31, 1984.

99. The upturn didn't come soon enough to stop a leading samba school from making Delfim Neto the butt of their satire in the 1984 carnival. One of their

floats was in the familiar shape of Delfim's massive head and neck protruding from a sack of coins. *Veja*, March 14, 1984.

Chapter VIII: The New Republic: Prospects for Democracy

1. The code word for this skill was *conciliação* (conciliation). In its highly favorable coverage of Tancredo's election, a leading illustrated weekly pronounced: "Como bom mineiro, Tancredo Neves conduziu sua campanha sob o signo da conciliação," *Manchete*, January 26, 1985, p.12. "Conciliation," which well described the Brazilian political elite's skill at muffling the class and sectoral conflicts, has long been the despair of those who want rapid social change. For a highly intelligent exploration of this theme, see *A "Conciliação" e outras estrategias* (São Paulo: Brasiliense, 1983) by Michel Debrun, a French-born philosopher and political scientist long resident in Brazil. The press, overwhelmingly pro-Tancredo, helped reinforce his image as the great conciliator. *Veja*'s cover story for September 19, 1984, for example, was titled "Doutor em alianças: Tancredo aperfeiçoou a arte de unir os contrários." The most important of the media—TV-Globo—was strongly in favor of Tancredo. All observers thought it had a crucial role in promoting Tancredo as Brazil's savior. The New Republic inspired further analyses of the state of Brazil's transition to democracy. One was Flavio Koutzii, ed., *Nova república: um balanço* (Pôrto Alegre: L & PM, 1986), which includes chapters on politics and on reform of the legal structure. A longer historical perspective was offered in Bolivar Lamounier and Rachel Meneguello, *Partidos políticos e consolidação democrática: o caso brasileiro* (São Paulo: Brasiliense, 1986). Two other assessments include discussion of Sarney's first year: Scott Mainwaring, "The Transition to Democracy in Brazil," *Journal of Inter-American Studies and World Affairs*, XXVIII, No. 1 (Spring 1986), 149–79; and William C. Smith, "The Political Transition in Brazil: From Authoritarian Liberalization and Elite Conciliation to Democratization," in Enrique A. Baloyra, ed., *Comparing New Democracies: Transition and Consolidation in Mediterranean Europe and the Southern Cone* (Boulder: Westview Press, forthcoming). Brazil's redemocratization has been of great interest to students of the transition from authoritarian regimes elsewhere. For an excellent overview of this question, see Samuel P. Huntington, "Will More Countries Become Democratic?" *Political Science Quarterly*, XCIX, No. 2 (Summer 1984), 193–218. Huntington regarded Brazil as one of the countries most likely to continue moving toward democracy. Between 1979 and 1981 the Woodrow Wilson International Center for Scholars in Washington sponsored a series of conferences and meetings on "Transitions from Authoritarian Rule: Prospects for Democracy in Latin America and Southern Europe." One of the four volumes resulting from the project is especially helpful in placing the Brazilian transition within a Latin American context: Guillermo O'Donnell, Philippe C. Schmitter, and Laurence Whitehead, eds., *Transitions from Authoritarian Rule: Comparative Perspectives* (Baltimore: Johns Hopkins University Press, 1986). In "Redemocratization and the Impact of Authoritarian Rule in Latin America," *Comparative Politics*, XVII, No.3 (April 1985), 253–75, Karen Remmer analyzes the effect of the authoritarian experience on efforts to redemocratize, although Brazil is not one of the princi-

pal countries included. A conference on "Reinforcing Democracy in the Americas" in November 1986 at the Carter Center of Emory University produced another bevy of interesting papers, including: Juan Linz and Alfred Stepan, "The Political Crafting of Democratic Consolidation or Democratic Destruction: European and South American Comparisons"; Guillermo O'Donnell, "Transitions to Democracy: Some Navigation Instruments"; and Samuel P. Huntington, "The Modest Meaning of Democracy." All three papers discussed or applied to the Brazilian case.

2. Tancredo's illness generated enormous press coverage. The president's press secretary-designate, who had the unenviable task of remaining calm in the eye of the journalistic storm, has given a gripping account: Antônio Britto (depoimento a Luís Claudio Cunha), *Assim morreu Tancredo* (Pôrto Alegre: L & PM, 1986).

3. Carlos Chagas, "Pais recorda hoje o drama de Tancredo," *O Estado de São Paulo*, April 21, 1986.

4. Figueiredo's attitude toward the inauguration was reported in *Veja*, March 20, 1985.

5. The economic and political calamities that bedeviled Figueiredo are chronicled, along with his ratings in the polls, in *Veja*, March 20, 1985. As of February 1985 the polls showed 69 percent of the public disapproving the Figueiredo government.

6. The interview was extensively reported in *Veja*, January 30, 1985. When asked for a candid shot of how he felt to be leaving behind the cares of office, Figueiredo made an obscene gesture to the camera. The president had lost none of his earthiness during six years in the Planalto.

7. For an insightful review of previous Brazilian constitution-writing, see Francisco Iglesias, *Constituintes e constituições brasileiras* (São Paulo: Brasiliense, 1986). For a collection of articles on the key constitutional questions to be faced by the new Constituent Assembly, see *Revista Brasileira de Estudos Politicos*, Nos. 60/61 (January/July 1985). A stimulating discussion of such issues as how the new government might be legitimized in a new constitution can be found in José Eduardo Faria, "Constituinte: seus riscos e seus muitos desafios," *Jornal da Tarde*, January 5, 12, and 19, 1985.

8. *New York Times*, April 23, 1985.

9. The quality of Tancredo's medical care became a topic of bitter controversy. Many observers thought he had become infected in the Hospital de Base in Brasília, which was reported as fact in *Veja*, April 3, 1985. The same story was repeated in *Newsweek*, August 5, 1985, which said that "nearly 50 people crowded into the operating room" to witness the first abdominal operation. Such conditions were one factor leading to Tancredo's transfer to São Paulo's Heart Institute. A year later the Regional Medical Council of Brasília released a report severely criticizing the medical care given Tancredo. The report charged that Tancredo was diagnosed as needing urgent surgery on the morning of March 13 but the operation did not take place until the early morning of March 15. *Isto É*, March 5, 1986. After Tancredo's death the Hospital de Base was closed for extensive cleaning.

10. Censorship proved more complicated than Justice Minister Lyra imagined in the early days of the Sarney government. The key question was how the government interpreted the existing legislation, which was always vague enough to allow great discretion. In January 1986 Lyra, under instructions from President

Sarney, prohibited the showing in Brazil of Jean-Luc Godard's film *Je Vous Salue, Marie*. Sarney's decision was part of a political trade-off with the Catholic Church leadership, whose support he wanted on other issues. *Jornal do Brasil*, June 18, 1986.

11. The public outpouring of grief is described in *Veja*, May 1, 1985. The title of the lead article conveyed the irony of the event: "Obra acabada no governo que não houve."

12. One of Brazil's leading political scientists explicitly compared Tancredo to Tiradentes, concluding that "one could say of Tancredo, as of Tiradentes, that he was a hero 'gone mad with hope.' " Bolivar Lamounier, *Afinal*, April 30, 1985.

13. José Sarney, "Brazil: A President's Story," *Foreign Affairs*, LXV, No. 1 (Fall 1986), 105–6. For a range of views on the nature of Brazil's ills in 1985, see Lourenço Dantas Mota, ed., *A Nova República: o nome e o coisa* (São Paulo: Brasiliense, 1985). Among the authors are Roberto Campos, Fernando Henrique Cardoso, Mario Henrique Simonsen, and Celso Furtado.

14. An eloquent exposition of PT logic on this point was given by one of the party's founders in Francisco C. Weffort, *Por que democracia?* (São Paulo: Brasiliense, 1984).

15. The "rescue" of the Banco Sulbrasileiro and the Banco Habitasul is described with irony in *Veja*, April 3, 1985.

16. "O lobby dos trabalhadores," *Senhor*, May 27, 1986, pp. 29–31; *Brazil Watch*, II, No. 13 (June 24–July 8, 1985), 2. For information on the taxpayer movement, see *Veja*, November 6, 1985, and for an interview with its leader, São Paulo Commercial Association President Guilherme Afif Domingos, see *Veja*, December 11, 1985.

17. The history of the Brazilian political elite's attitude toward enfranchising the illiterate is told cogently in José Honório Rodrigues, *Conciliação e reforma no Brasil: um desafio histórico-político* (Rio de Janeiro: Civilização Brasileira, 1965), 135–63.

18. Roberto Cardoso Alves, "Um PMDB sem comunistas," *Veja*, July 31, 1985, p. 122.

19. A cover story attacking the Congress for its anachronistic and self-serving ways is in *Veja*, August 21, 1985. The *jeton* was equal to more than double the regular salary of deputies and senators.

20. Senator Dalla's largesse, which had become common practice for Senate presidents at the end of their term, also rained down on Brasília-based journalists, such as social columnist Consuelo Badra (and her daughter) and longtime *Jornal do Brasil* political journalist Haroldo Hollanda (and two sons). *Isto É*, January 16, 1985. Such practices led *O Estado de São Paulo* to run a stinging editorial denouncing the New Republic as no better than the old, "A Novíssima veste roupa velha," *O Estado de São Paulo*, May 15, 1986.

21. The National Security Law was important because anyone accused of violating that law could be imprisoned for up to 15 days without right of *habeas corpus*. Furthermore, any court proceeding would fall under the jurisdiction of the military courts. Interview with Evaristo de Moraes in *Veja*, February 20, 1985. In June 1986 Carlos Chagas, a seasoned observer of the Brasília political scene, noted that the Congress had "not voted half of what it ought to have voted . . . in order to have allowed the Constituent Assembly time to deal with the really profound and important questions such as reexamination of the economic and

social order." *O Estado de São Paulo,* June 25, 1986. The chronic lack of a quorum in the Chamber of Deputies, despite appeals by the party leaders, was noted in the *Jornal do Brasil,* June 18, 1986. Scathing editorials against the Congress appeared in *O Globo,* June 4, 1986, and *Folha de São Paulo,* June 20, 1986.

22. There is a useful evaluation of the election returns in a panel discussion, "As Eleições Municipais de 85 e a Conjuntura Política," published as *Cadernos de Conjuntura,* No. 3 (December 1985) by the Instituto Universitário de Pesquisas do Rio de Janeiro (IUPERJ), Rio de Janeiro.

23. The rapid growth of the PT—in relative terms—was stressed in a cover story in *Veja,* December 25, 1985. PT strength showed up in several unexpected cities, such as Ceará, the capital of Fortaleza, where PT candidate Maria Luiza Fontenelle was elected mayor, and Goiânia, where the PT candidate got 40 percent of the vote although not a victory. Neither city was at all an industrial center, to which skeptics of the PT thought.the party would be limited. In its newspaper the PT proudly analyzed its 1985 electoral gains. Its share of the total national vote was 11 percent, almost as much as the PDS (4 percent) and the PFL (9 percent) together. The party claimed its 1985 vote had increased by 87 percent over its 1982 vote, but the comparison was questionable, since the 1982 election did not include mayors. *Brasil Extra,* No. 2 (December 1985).

24. Brizola's populist rhetoric and his history of extreme nationalism, along with his highly effective speaking style—both in person and on television—frightened many conservatives, including most military officers. Brizola's national vote-getting ability was questioned, however, in Glaucio Ary Dillon Soares, *Colégio eleitoral, convenções partidárias, e eleições diretas* (Petrópolis: Vozes, 1984), 65–73, in a chapter titled "O mito de Brizola e o medo das diretas," where Soares argued that in Brizola's 1982 election as governor he had won only 31 percent of vote, as compared with Franco Montoro's 45 percent in São Paulo and Tancredo Neves's 46 percent in Minas Gerais. Soares then argued convincingly that Brizola would not have a strong enough appeal to defeat a presidential candidate of either the PDS or the PMDB.

25. For a detailed report on the right's support for Jânio, see *Veja,* November 6, 1985. Jânio's Cold War-style appeal to the upper- and middle-class voters came out in such statements as (September 1985): "We face a conspiracy of communists and fellow travellers (*comunistóides*) who persist in discrediting military officers and civilians opposed to communism." *Veja,* November 20, 1985.

26. Founded in 1985 and led by a young doctor who is the nephew of a legendary "colonel" (political boss) of Goiás, the UDR received heavy national press coverage when rural conflict reached a high pitch in May–June 1986. Typical were the major stories in *Veja,* June 18, *Isto É,* June 10, and *Folha de São Paulo,* June 8. The movement, which auctioned donated cattle to raise funds, had spread rapidly, with strongholds in Pará, Maranhão, Goiás, São Paulo, Paraná, Mato Grosso do Sul, and Bahia. In 1986 the UDR was concentrating its efforts and financing on winning a maximum number of congressional seats in the November elections.

27. PMDB Senator Fernando Henrique Cardoso feared this might happen: "We are running aa grave risk in Brazil today because in some ways society has advanced further than the parties, and one can have the illusion that social movements have superseded parties." Cardoso argued that parties were indis-

pensable in resolving problems identified and publicized by social movements, and that communication was the key to better cooperation. Fernando Henrique Cardoso, "Primeiro limpar o entulho autoritário," in Lourenço Dantas Mota, ed., *A Nova República:*, 57–58. The fear that hyper-mobilization would crowd out the political parties was spelled out in Marcelo Pontes, "Nas ruas, os novos partidos," *Jornal do Brasil,* June 1, 1986.

28. Sarney's success (and its limitations) with the military is described in Alan Riding's "Brazil Chief Is Wooing the Army." *New York Times,* January 23, 1986.

29. *Brasil: Nunca Mais* (Petrópolis: Vozes, 1985). São Paulo's highly activist Dom Paulo Evaristo Cardinal Arns wrote the preface and was a key supporter in the project that produced the book. The authors were clergy and laymen long involved in human rights battles in São Paulo. Through sympathetic contacts in the military justice system the authors obtained more than a million pages of documentation, which they boiled down to the cases described in their book. The fact that such records were kept and could be obtained (surely some military or civilian employees must have been, anonymously, willing collaborators) shows how the repression was kept largely within the bureaucratic ken of regular army channels. The contrast with Argentina could hardly be more striking.

30. The São Paulo group had first planned to include the list of torturers in *Brasil: Nunca Mais,* due to be published in May 1985. But because the mayoral elections—the first elections under the New Republic—were scheduled for the following November, the authors decided to withhold publication of the list until after the elections so as to avoid being accused of disrupting the campaign with sensationalistic revelations. Such attention to political realities helps explain the project's great effectiveness in influencing public opinion. The list of 444 torturers was printed in the principal papers of November 22, 1985, such as *Folha de São Paulo* and *Jornal do Brasil.* There were also feature stories in *Veja* and *Isto É,* both for November 27, 1985.

31. The Argentine trials were a cover story in *Veja,* May 22, 1985. The cover depicted an Argentine army officer's hat on a human skull. The Argentine presidential commission's report was published as *Nunca Más* (Buenos Aires: Editorial Universitária de Buenos Aires, 1984) which has appeared in a U.S. edition: *Nunca Más: The Report of the Argentine National Commission on the Disappeared* (New York: Farrar, Straus and Giroux, 1986).

32. The army officer was Colonel Alberto Brilhante Ustra. The resolution came after tough initial positions by Deputy Mendes and Army Minister Leônidas. *Veja,* August 28 and September 4, 1985.

33. The list of 333 "dead and disappeared" was compiled by the *Comissão de Direitos Humanos e Assistência Judiciária da Ordem dos Advogados do Brasil (Seção do Estado do Rio de Janeiro)* and published in *Revista OAB: RJ,* No. 19 (1982), 2nd ed., 84–94. This list was built on earlier compilations such as Reinaldo Cabral and Ronaldo Lapa, eds., *Os desaparecidos políticos: prisões, sequestros, assassinatos* (Rio de Janeiro: Ed. Opção, 1979). Amnesty International estimated that 325 political activists had been killed or had "disappeared" between 1964 and 1979—a total very close to the Rio Bar Association's figure of 333. Power, *Amnesty International: The Human Rights Story,* 100. My per capita calculation is based on a 1970 population of 23 million for

Argentina and 93 million for Brazil. In *Os militares*, 82–83, Stepan makes a similar point about the sharply differing per capita rate in Brazil as compared with Argentina and Chile.

34. *Brasil: Nunca Mais*, 26. In May 1975 I talked with a Catholic cleric in São Paulo who was attached to the office of the cardinal and who had as a principal duty the monitoring of torture of political prisoners. He described the detailed documentation he and his colleagues were assembling, including names of torturers and their victims, and the locale of their deeds. He spoke with such passion and indignation that I asked, "Won't there be a great desire to try these men?" "Ah," he said, "aqui entra o espírito conciliador do brasileiro."

35. Some military tried to reply in kind. The army's Information Office circulated a list of victims of terrorismo (or guerrillas). It included 40 officers, soldiers, and police agents killed and another 212 wounded. *Veja*, September 4, 1985. In 1979 the army had given its count of 97 dead and 350 wounded as a result of guerrilla action. That included both military and civilians. *O Globo*, March 27, 1979. The army subsequently issued lists with differing totals, but the number of dead was always between 91 and 102. *Veja*, September 10, 1986. The counteroffensive was carried even further by federal deputy Sebastião Curió, a former army intelligence officer who played a key role in the liquidation of the PC do B guerrilla movement in Araguaia. In late August, Curió released a list of 21 names of Sarney government officials "linked to the international communist movement." Curió threatened to release 4,000 more if the charges against military officers did not cease. *Brazil Watch*, II, No. 18 (September 2–16, 1985), 12–13. His charges had little effect in the greatly liberalized atmosphere of the New Republic.

36. A separate question was whether confirmed ex-torturers should be penalized in their subsequent careers. The higher military tended to promote them, though there were occasions when civilian authorities managed to prevent it. One of the most publicized cases concerned Colonel Valter Jacarandá, identified in April 1985 as a torturer in the Rio DOI-CODI operation of the early 1970s. He was deputy chief of the Rio Fire Department when the identification was made. Jacarandá was stripped of his Fire Department rank but given no further punishment. *Veja*, April 24, 1985; *Latin America Weekly Report*, April 26, 1985; and *New York Times*, June 6, 1985. A more serious case surfaced in Ceará, where an ex-torturer was appointed superintendent of the Federal Police for the state. The newly elected PT mayor of Fortaleza protested the appointment and Justice Minister Fernando Lyra, who had jurisdiction over the appointment, had it reversed. *Veja*, January 15, 1986. It appears that torture by military personnel ended with the advent of the New Republic, while police torture continued, although now only on "ordinary" victims. The information is from Paulo Sergio Pinheiro, cited in Joan Dassin, "Time Up for Torturers? A Human Rights Dilemma for Brazil," *NACLA Report on the Americas*, XX, No. 2 (April–May 1986), 4–6.

37. For an interesting inventory of right-wing terrorism, including groups linked to the military, see Flavio Deckes, *Radiografia do terrorismo no Brasil: 1966/1980* (São Paulo: Icone Editora, 1985).

38. One journalist who was knowledgeable about the SNI doubted that its power was being reduced or made more accountable: Ana Lagoa, "O destino do SNI," *Lua Nova*, III, No. 1 (April–June 1986), 16–18.

39. In a feature story on SNI Chief General Ivan Mendes two months after the

New Republic began, *Veja* warned its readers not to be misled by Mendes's charm and openness. "The SNI of today," it declared, "is exactly the same as the SNI of yesterday." *Veja,* May 29, 1985, p. 17. One newsweekly claimed in June 1986 that the SNI was still wire-tapping at least 130 telephones of politicians and high officials. The charge was angrily denied by General Ivan, who said he would "kick out" anyone caught wire-tapping. *Isto É,* June 11, 1986; *Jornal de Brasília,* June 10, 1986.

40. Army intelligence (CIEX) involvement in a 1984 unsuccessful plot to discredit Tancredo (distributing posters implying he would be a Communist Party tool) had been reported in *Veja,* September 1984, and was confirmed by investigations that came to light a year later. *Veja,* October 30, 1985.

41. For an excellent overview of the military's role in the first year of the New Republic, with special attention to the intelligence agencies, see René Dreifuss, "Nova República, Novo Exército?" in Koutzii, ed., *Nova República,* 168–93. A sober assessment of the military's continuing presence throughout the state structure is given in Walder de Góes, "Os militares e a democracia," *Política e Estratégia,* III, No. 3 (July–September 1985), 444–54.

42. The first exposé of the Baumgarten case was in *Veja,* February 2, 1983. The case was still alive in 1985, as a São Paulo police chief continued to pursue the mystery of Baumgarten's death. A number of army officers, some already dead, were implicated in his inquiry. *Folha de São Paulo,* May 25, 1985; *Veja,* May 22 and 29, 1985.

43. In January 1985 it was reported that the SNI was considering the "demilitarization" of its staff, which included 460 colonels and lieutenant colonels, ninety of whom were on active service. *Veja,* January 30, 1985. Officers on SNI duty had the opportunity for higher pay and perquisites than their colleagues on regular army duty. The latter were understandably resentful and charged that this "elite" of SNI officers was creating serious discord in the army.

44. *Veja,* October 30, 1985, 42.

45. In reporting these apparently favorable developments, *Veja* concluded by noting that some politicians doubted the SNI had really changed. PMDB notables Ulysses Guimarães and Fernando Henrique Cardoso were said "to talk much less on the telephone today than in the days of the Figueiredo government." *Veja,* April 24, 1985.

46. The crisis provoked by the bill earned a cover story in *Veja,* October 30, 1985.

47. Brazil's Foreign Office had in August 1985 recommended resumption of relations with Cuba, but President Sarney decided to postpone action because of army opposition. *Veja,* August 21, 1985.

48. For an example of such thinking, see the article, "O poder civil dispensa tutela" by a lawyer and professor from Pará, in *Veja,* July 16, 1986, p. 154.

49. *Jornal da Tarde,* June 5, 1986. Details on the key role of Army Minister Leônidas, who was pressed by his ranks to speak out were given in *Correio Brasiliense,* June 10, 1986. The irrepressible General Newton Cruz, recently military commander of the Planalto, added his voice, warning that if the Constitutional Commission's version were adopted, "it would demolish the last barrier to the implantation of a state of anarchy." *Correio Brasiliense,* June 11, 1986.

50. For a discussion of these issues in the perspective of past Brazilian constitution-writing, see João Quartim de Moraes, "O Estatuto constitucional das Forças Armadas," *Política e Estrategia,* III, No. 3 (July–September, 1986), 379–90.

51. In 1986 a prominent Rio real estate developer published a long newspaper ad denouncing the low level of civilian pensions in comparison with military pensions. His meaning was unmistakable: "From 1966 to 1985 the military dictators have signed more than 18 decree-laws giving themselves financial benefits, thus alienating our military—most of whom come from middle class and poor families—from the civilian population, the victims of much suffering and injustice." Advertisement placed by Edgard Clare in *O Globo*, June 23, 1986.

52. These ideas have been spelled out in Stepan's chapter in Alfred Stepan, ed., *Authoritarian Brazil: Origins, Policies, and Future* (New Haven: Yale University Press, 1973), 47–65; and in Stepan, *Os militares: da abertura à Nova República* (Rio de Janeiro: Paz e Terra, 1986).

53. For the angry attack on what one army officer saw as endemic corruption during the military regime, see Coronel Dicksen M. Grael, *Aventura, corrupção, e terrorismo: a sombra da impunidade* (Petrópolis: Vozes, 1985). For two of the most widely read exposés, see José Carlos de Assis, *A Chave do tesouro: anatomia dos escândalos financeiros: Brasil 1974–1983* (Rio de Janeiro: Paz e Terra, 1983), and *Os mandarins da república: anatomia dos escândalos na administração pública: 1968–1984* (Rio de Janeiro: Paz e Terra, 1984).

54. Corruption of the military was vividly described in a magazine article touching on contraband: *Veja*, September 4, 1985, p. 60.

55. In early 1986 one of the most knowledgeable foreign correspondents in Brazil, Alan Riding, sounded sanguine: "In reality, the armed forces, relieved to be out of day-to-day government, appear to have reverted to their historical role of behind-the-scenes arbiters of Brazilian politics, a role they have exercised under every civilian administration since the monarchy was replaced by a republic in 1889." *New York Times*, January 23, 1986.

56. The program is described in José de Souza Fernandes, "FT-90: O novo exército brasileiro," *Defesa Latina*, Ano VI, No. 37, pp. 16–19, 31–32; and in *Latin America Regional Report: Brazil*, January 3, 1986.

57. For an analysis of the likely effects of the policy options open to the new government, see Kenneth Meyers and F. Desmond McCarthy, *Brazil: Medium-Term Policy Analysis* (Washington: World Bank, 1985), which warned that "the development strategy of the sixties and seventies and the concomitant technology is no longer adequate."

58. A congressional investigating commission (Comissão Parlamentar de Inquérito) held hearings in 1983–84 and produced a stinging report that held the technocrats responsible for the ill-considered recourse to massive foreign borrowing. The report was published as: Sebastião Nery and Alencar Furtado, *Crime e castigo da dívida externa* (Brasília: Dom Quixote Editora, 1986). It should be noted that Brazil's heavy borrowing was duplicated in virtually every Third World country that had even a mediocre credit rating. For an excellent overview of the foreign debt question on the eve of the New Republic, see Francisco Eduardo Pires de Souza, "Metamorfoses do endividamento externo," in Antonio Barros de Castro and Pires de Souza, *A economia brasileira em marcha forçada* (Rio de Janeiro: Paz e Terra, 1985), 97–189.

59. Dimenstein, *O complô*, 226.

60. The data are from *Brasil Econômico: Ajustamento Interno e Externo* (Brasília: Banco Central do Brasil, 1986), vol. 10 (February 1986). This source gives the

"position of international liquidity" (IMF definition) as $12 billion. The figure $9 billion seems a safer estimate of actual foreign exchange reserves.

61. The terms of the eventual agreement were described in the *Wall Street Journal*, July 25, 1986. The signing was confirmed in *Brazil Watch*, III, No. 16 (August 4–18, 1986).

62. For an inside look at Brazil's foreign debt strategy by a debt expert who worked in the planning ministry, see the interview with Paulo Nogueira Batista in *Senhor*, May 27, 1986. For an excellent overview, see Moreira, *The Brazilian Quandary*. For a view of the Latin American foreign-debt problem as of mid-1986, see Alejandro Foxley, "The External Debt Problem from a Latin American Viewpoint" (Notre Dame: Kellogg Institute Working Paper #72, July 1986).

63. One senior World Bank economist argued that "there need be no conflict between successfully completing the economic stabilization and achieving both faster economic growth and increased equity," Peter T. Knight, "Economic Stabilization and Medium Term Development in Brazil," in *Economic Policy and Planning* (Boston: Center for International Higher Education Documentation, Northeastern University, 1985), 30. Knight gives an excellent overview of the economic problems and prospects facing the new government in 1985. For another overview of the economic legacy bequeathed by the military governments, see Maria da Conceição Tavares and J. Carlos de Assis, *O grande salto para o caos: a economia política e a política econômica do regime autoritário* (Rio de Janeiro: Zahar, 1985). Maria Conceição had been one of the most effective and relentless critics of post-1964 economic policy.

64. José Serra, "Three Mistaken Theses Regarding the Connection between Industrialization and Authoritarian Regimes," in David Collier, ed., *The New Authoritarianism in Latin America* (Princeton: Princeton University Press, 1979), 99–163.

65. For a highly informative overview of Brazil's economic and political problems at the outset of the New Republic, see *Estudos Econômicos*, XV, No. 3 (September–December 1985). The entire issue, including a panel discussion, is devoted to "A Dívida externa e a recuperação econômica." For analyses of the Sarney government's economic policy in its first year, see Plínio de Arruda Sampaio Júnior and Rui Affonso, "A transição inconclusa," and Paul Singer, "Os impasses econômicos da Nova República," both in Koutzii, ed., *Nova República*.

66. Dimenstein, *O complô*, 244.

67. A Morgan Guaranty Trust study showed that Brazil had suffered far less capital flight than the other principal Latin American debtors. In 1976–85 Brazil suffered $10 billion in capital flight, while for Argentina it was $26 billion and Mexico $53 billion. Measured against the absolute size of each economy, Brazil's capital flight looks even smaller. This finding would corroborate the Brazilian government's claim that it put its borrowed dollars into productive investments. *The Latin American Times*, No. 73 (June 9, 1986). This view was shared by Professor Ingo Walter, a specialist in clandestine capital movements. Walter attributed Brazil's low capital flight to its attractive investment opportunities and to Brazilian optimism about the country's future. *Jornal do Brasil*, June 15, 1986. A study based on World Bank research concluded that Brazil's capital flight for 1974–82 was only $200 million, while for Mexico it was $32.7 billion,

for Argentina $15.3 billion, and for Venezuela $10.8 billion. The figure for Brazil seems implausibly low. Mohsin Kahn and Nadeem Ul Haque, "Foreign Borrowing and Capital Flight: A Formal Analysis," *IMF Staff Papers*, XXXII, No. 4 (December 1985), 606–28.

68. The divergences between Dornelles and Sayad were analyzed in "Uma longa briga sobre como cortar o deficit," *Folha de São Paulo*, August 27, 1985.

69. The quotation is from a lengthy interview with Funaro in *Senhor*, February 20, 1985. The younger economists are given a collective portrait in *Veja*, September 4, 1985.

70. The most influential of these younger economists was Francisco Lopes, whose ideas were spelled out in a collection of articles published as *O choque heterodoxo: combate a inflação e reforma monetária* (Rio: Ed. Campus, 1986). Two others who were influential in the formulation of the Plano Cruzado were Persio Arida and André Lara-Resende, whose views can be found in Persio Arida, ed., *Inflação zero: Brasil, Argentina e Israel* (Rio de Janeiro: Paz e Terra, 1986).

71. For an explanation of why the Phillips Curve did not hold for Brazil, see "Inflação inercial e a Curva de Phillips," in Luiz Bresser Pereira and Yoshiaki Nakano, *Inflação e recessão*, 2nd ed. (São Paulo: Brasiliense, 1986), 107–15. For a highly useful overview of Brazil's recent record, see Werner Baer, "The Resurgence of Inflation in Brazil, 1974–1985" (Paper prepared for the seminar "Inflation in Latin America" held April 4–5, 1986, at the University of Illinois at Urbana-Champaign).

72. There was another factor that led to false signals on the inflation rate. From April through July 1985 the government had imposed a partial price freeze, artificially reducing the inflation rate. By the IPCA measure the annual inflation rate from December 1984 through March 1985 had been 275 percent. For April through July it dropped to 156 percent. When the freeze was lifted at the end of July, inflation shot up to 305 percent annual rate for August 1985 through January 1986. Data from Luiz Bresser Pereira, "Inflação inercial e Plano Cruzado" (paper presented to the seminar on "The Resurgence of Inflation in Latin America").

73. Sharp criticisms of the Sarney government's anti-inflation policy were expressed in such leading newspapers as *Jornal do Brasil, Folha de São Paulo,* and *Estado de São Paulo,* as cited in *Latin America Regional Reports: Brazil Report,* February 7, 1986. The government's unsuccessful year-long struggle against the rising inflation rate is chronicled in the commentaries of Eduardo Modiano, *Da inflação ao cruzado: a política econômica no primeiro ano da Nova Republica* (Rio de Janeiro: Editora Campus, 1986).

74. In recent years there had been increasing debate about the virtues and liabilities of indexation. Virtually all agreed that indexation's effect in the 1980s differed greatly from its effect in the late 1960s and 1970s. For an overview of this issue, see Peter T. Knight, "Brazil: Deindexation and Economic Stabilization" (paper prepared at the World Bank: December 2, 1983).

75. The first recipients were to begin receiving benefits in July. Approximately 200,000 were expected to be eligible. *Jornal do Brasil*, June 4, 1986.

76. Labor Minister Pazzianotto argued the Plano Cruzado had two important innovations for labor: the unemployment pay and the automatic trigger that would increase the minimum wage when the inflation index hit 20 percent. To critics who said the plan should have been sent to Congress as a normal bill rather

than issued as a presidential decree, Pazzianotto said it had to be done quickly in order to foil the speculators. Pazzianotto interview in *Veja,* March 5, 1986. The text of President Sarney's address is reprinted in *Revista de Economia Política,* VI, No. 3 (July–September 1986), 112–14. For the play-by-play account of how the Plano Cruzado was formulated and sold to President Sarney, see Ricardo A. Setti, "O dia em que Sarney derrubou a inflação," *Playboy* (Brazilian edition), XI, No. 131 (June 1986), 57–58 and 136–52. *Conjuntura Econômica,* XL, No. 4 (April 1986) includes articles evaluating the Plano Cruzado from a wide range of viewpoints.

77. One private Rio de Janeiro survey research firm surveyed Rio and São Paulo heads of household on, inter alia, their opinion of President Sarney. In May 1985 in Rio 29 percent approved and in São Paulo 13 percent approved. By January 1986 Sarney's approval rating had dropped to a minus −22 percent in Rio and −36 percent in São Paulo. In March, just after the Plano Cruzado was launched, Sarney's approval rating had shot up to 71 percent in Rio and 68 percent in São Paulo. *Senhor,* June 24, 1986, p. 35.

78. Luis Eulalio de Bueno Vidigal Filho, president of the São Paulo Federation of Industries, praised the program for having put an end to "financial speculation," *Industria e Desenvolvimento,* April 1986, p. 4. Delfim Netto was also positive, saying "I believe the stabilization program is going to work," *Nordeste Econômico,* XVII, No. 4 (April 1986), 48; one economist viewing the Plano Cruzado favorably from abroad warned, "The challenge now is to prepare for the transition, when the economy will have to deliver price stability without pervasive controls. A first step is to give up the zero inflation fetishism. The cost of such an attachment would be overvaluation of the exchange rate and renewed crises," Eliana A. Cardoso, "What Policymakers Can Learn from Brazil and Mexico," *Challenge,* XXIX, No. 4 (September/October 1986), 25.

79. U.S. business people also expressed approval of Brazil's new economic course, as in "How Brazil Is Barreling into the Big Time," *Business Week,* August 11, 1986, and "Brazil: Beyond the Cruzado Plan," *World Financial Markets,* August 1986, pp. 1–11.

80. Interview with José Serra in *Veja,* March 19, 1986.

81. Interview with Edmar Bacha in *Veja,* June 18, 1986.

82. *Revista de Economia Política,* VI, No. 3 (July–September 1986), 112.

83. In the first 60 days after the Plano Cruzado began, meat consumption was up 30 percent and milk was up 15 percent, according to industry figures. Consumption of both soon dropped, however, when producers, as a protest against the level at which their prices were frozen, began refusing to supply the market. *O Globo,* June 16, 1986. One leading São Paulo travel agent noted his July bookings were up 40 percent over a year earlier. "A grande revoada," *Visão,* July 8, 1986, p. 31. Labor Minister Pazzianotto dismissed suggestions that the economy was overheating: "This is a poor country. People don't have the money to buy clothes or shoes. Looking at the country as a whole, the increased demand is healthy" (*Jornal do Brasil,* June 2, 1986).

84. The Banco Central's inability to sell anything longer than 90-day bonds is analyzed in Paulo Sérgio de Sousa, "Inflacão e taxa de juro," *Bolsa,* No. 748 (July 16, 1986).

85. The package was front-page news in the daily press, as in *O Globo,* July 23, 1986.

86. Gasoline consumption had leapt 13.6 percent for January–May as compared

with the same period in 1985. The comparable figure for alcohol was 24.8 percent. The increased gasoline consumption would have to be met almost entirely from imports, since Brazil was already consuming virtually all its domestic production. *Manchete,* July 5, 1986.

87. Within weeks the PT attacked the Plano Cruzado as anti-labor. See, for example, "Pacote arrocha salários," and related stories in *PT São Paulo,* VI, No. 38 (March 1986). *Visão* painted the "pacote da inflação zero" as a throwback to "populist demagoguery." *Visão,* June 25, 1986, pp. 16–19. For an interesting collection of debates in the press over the Plano Cruzado, and especially its effect on salaries, see *Revista de Economia Política,* VI, No. 3 (July–September 1986), 121–51.

88. Past experiences with compulsory loans levied on consumers were examined in the *Jornal do Brasil,* July 22, 1986.

89. The manifesto was entitled "Esperança e mudança: uma proposta de governo para o Brasil" and was published in *Revista do PMDB,* II, No. 4 (October/November 1982). The quotations are from p. ii.

90. The World Bank, *World Development Report: 1986* (New York: Oxford University Press, 1986), 226–27.

91. The data were cited in an interview with Air Force General Waldir de Vasconcelos in *Veja,* August 15, 1984.

92. The military governments had put great store in MOBRAL (Movimento Brasileiro de Alfabetização), a crash literacy program that began in 1968 and was to reduce illiteracy to 10 percent by 1975. When it became clear that that goal could not be reached, the newly inaugurated Geisel government committed itself to eliminating illiteracy completely by 1979. But by mid-1975 the campaign had bogged down from lack of funding and personnel. *O Estado de São Paulo,* August 22, 1974, and May 8, 1975. For later news stories spelling out the problems of MOBRAL and the persistence of illiteracy, see *Folha de São Paulo,* July 25, 1982, and June 5, 1983.

93. There is a large literature on income distribution in Brazil. The following sources were especially relevant for my analysis: David Denslow, Jr., and William Tyler, "Perspectives on Poverty and Income Inequality in Brazil," *World Development,* XII, No. 10 (1984), 1019–28; Guy Pfefferman and Richard Webb, "Poverty and Income Distribution in Brazil," *The Review of Income and Wealth,* Series 29, No. 2 (June 1983), 101–24; M. Louise Fox, "Income Distribution in Post-1964 Brazil: New Results," *The Journal of Economic History,* XLIII, No. 1 (March 1983), 261–71; Ralph Hakkert, "Who Benefits from Economic Development? The Brazilian Income Distribution Controversy Revisited," *Boletín de Estudios Latinoamericanos y del Caribe,* No. 36 (June 1984), 83–103; and José Pastore, Helio Zylberstajn, and Carmen S. Pagotto, "The Decline in the Incidence of Extreme Poverty in Brazil" (Madison: University of Wisconsin, Department of Rural Sociology, mimeo, February 1983).

94. See Fox, "Income Distribution in Post-1964."

95. See references quoted in Hakkert, "Who Benefits from Economic Development?," 85.

96. *Ibid.,* 100.

97. For two analyses (written on the eve of the New Republic) of the social consequences of economic policies during the military regimes, see Paul Singer, *Repartição da renda: pobres sob o regime militar* (Rio de Janeiro: Zahar, 1986) and Sérgio Henrique Abranches, *Os Despossuídos: crescimento e pobreza no*

pais do milagre (Rio de Janeiro: Zahar, 1985). Both authors are highly critical of the military governments for their failure to adopt economic policies that would do more for the Brazilians at the bottom.

98. Delfim's charge that any significant steps to improve distribution would necessarily reduce growth was refuted in the 1970s in William R. Cline, *Potential Effects of Income Redistribution on Economic Growth: Latin American Cases* (New York: Praeger, 1972); and Samuel A. Morley and Gordon W. Smith, "The Effect of Changes in the Distribution of Income on Labor, Foreign Investment, and Growth in Brazil," in Alfred Stepan, ed., *Authoritarian Brazil: Origins, Policies, and Future* (New Haven: Yale University Press, 1973).

99. *Brazil Watch*, April 29, 1985.

100. *Veja*, April 17, 1985, 85; *Latin America Weekly Report*, April 26, 1985; *Veja*, January 15, 1986, 72–74.

101. Among the most important outside studies was *Brazil: Human Resources Special Report* (Washington: World Bank, 1979), which was summarized in Peter T. Knight and Ricardo Moran, *Brazil: Poverty and Basic Needs Series* (Washington: World Bank, 1981). This careful study explored the probable costs of increased government effort in such vital areas as housing, water supply, sewerage, nutrition, and education. The 1970s had produced an intense discussion about the state of Brazil's social services. These problems and much of the literature are synthesized in Edmar Bacha and Herbert S. Klein, eds., *A transição incompleta*, which includes chapters on post-1945 trends in population, labor force composition, rural economy and society, urbanization, inequality and social mobility, wealth and poverty, social security, education, and health and medical care. In the monographic literature, especially helpful on the social security system are James M. Malloy, *The Politics of Social Security in Brazil* (Pittsburgh: University of Pittsburgh Press, 1979); Malloy, "Politics, Fiscal Crisis, and Social Security Reform in Brazil," *Latin American Issues*, II, No. 1 (Meadville, Pennsylvania: Allegheny College, 1985); Amélia Cohn, *Previdência social e processo político no Brasil* (São Paulo: Ed. Moderna, 1980). Valuable critiques of the health care delivery system can be found in *Saúde em Debate: Revista do Centro Brasileiro de Estudos de Saúde,* which began in late 1976. Another critical view can be found in *Saúde e trabalho no Brasil* (Petrópolis: Vozes, 1982), a collection of papers prepared by the *Instituto Brasileiro de Análises Sociais e Econômicas* (IBASE), a leading left-oriented think tank in Rio. For a typical news story on the inadequate public health service, see "A espera as vezes inútil em postos e centros de saude," *O Globo,* June 10, 1984. A more comprehensive critique appeared in "Um gigante combalido," *Senhor,* May 27, 1986. Malnutrition has been an important scourge, as is documented in *Ciência Hoje,* X, No. 5 (March–April, 1983), 56–79. Housing was an area where the military governments made a major effort, beginning with the Castelo Branco regime. Yet the system they created (based on a housing bank to administer funds from a compulsory workers' payroll deduction) failed to realize its goal of large-scale construction of low-income housing, as is clearly demonstrated in Gastón A. Fernandez, "The Role of the State in Latin America: A Case Study of the Brazilian National Housing Bank" (Ph.D. dissertation, University of Wisconsin-Madison, 1982). For a critical view of the program a decade after its founding, see *O Estado de São Paulo,* August 22, 1974. For an official view during the Figueiredo administration, see Roberto Cavalcanti de Albuquer-

que, "Habitação e desenvolvimento urbano no Brasil," *Revista do Serviço Público,* CX, No. 2 (April–June 1982), 41–51. The growth of the *favelas* was the most dramatic indicator of the housing problem, since they contrasted so sharply (especially in Rio de Janeiro) with the many luxury apartment buildings. The *favela* "removal" program in Rio attracted heavy criticism. Among the best-known critics were Janice E. Perlman, *The Myth of Marginality: Urban Poverty and Politics in Rio de Janeiro* (Berkeley: University of California Press, 1976); and Lícia do Prado Villadares, *Passa-se uma casa: análise do programa de remoção de favelas do Rio de Janeiro* (Rio de Janeiro· Zahar, 1978). For stories about the day-to-day struggles of shanty-town dwellers, see "Invasores, um perfil em mudança," *Folha de São Paulo,* July 3, 1983; and "Em São Paulo, 7.5 milhões moram de forma precária," *Folha de São Paulo,* June 8, 1986.

102. The Jaguaribe group's report was published the following year as Helio Jaguaribe, et al., *Brasil, 2000: para um novo pacto social* (Rio de Janeiro: Paz e Terra, 1986). There had been an earlier study, touching on many of the same topics, in Helio Jaguaribe, et al., *Brasil, sociedade democrática* (Rio de Janeiro: José Olympio, 1985), which included a highly enlightening chapter by Wanderley Guilherme dos Santos on Brazil's political and socio-economic change since 1964.

103. *Revista do PMDB,* No. 4, 21–22.

104. *Brazil Watch,* "Special Report: Brazil's Economic Crisis and the Transition to Democracy" (Washington: Orbis Publications, 1984), 42; the speech is reprinted in Dimenstein, *O complô,* 242–47, and in *Veja,* July 31, 1985, pp. 39–45.

105. Rural wage laborers began to be unionized in the 1970s and during the Figueiredo presidency were often able to bargain effectively. This is an important subject, but unfortunately cannot be treated here.

106. The relationship between government policy and wage behavior in Brazil is not as obvious as it might seem. In times of slack employment, and in the case of small firms, the minimum wage may well determine the actual wage. But in larger firms, especially in periods of high employment, the market pressures can produce both positive wage drift and job turnover as workers change jobs to enter a new job category and therefore get a wage increase. This pattern emerges clearly in Russell Edward Smith, "Wage Indexation and Money Wages in Brazilian Manufacturing: 1964–1978" (Ph.D. dissertation, University of Illinois at Urbana-Champaign, 1985). Job mobility is stressed also in Morley, *Labor Markets and Inequitable Growth.* For a careful analysis of wage policy up to the eve of the New Republic, see Domingo Zurron Oció, "Salários e política salarial," *Revista de Economia Política,* VI, No. 2 (April–June 1986), 5–33.

107. João Sabóia, *Qual é a questão da política salarial* (São Paulo: Brasiliense, 1985), 16–19. These minimum wage increases set by Vargas and Kubitschek were soon eroded by inflation.

108. *Revista do PMDB,* No. 4, p. 29. In May 1985 the labor ministry described the Sarney government's policy as having been to "reduce unemployment levels and recover the buying power of wages while at the same time attempting to reduce income inequality," Ministério do Trabalho, "Mercado de Trabalho: Evolução 1985 e l°Trimestre 1986."

109. *Revista do PMDB,* No. 4, p. 30. The most important study on this question is

Roberto Brás Matos Macedo and José Paulo Z. Chahad, *FGTS e a rotativi-dade* (São Paulo: Nobel, 1985), which was commissioned by the labor minis-try. The authors concluded, inter alia, that the FGTS system had given em-ployers excessive discretionary power to dismiss and the victimized workers inadequate protection. *Ibid.,* 164. There was a congressional attempt in June 1986 to outlaw dismissals made without due cause. The proposal died at the end of the congressional session. For details, see *Folha de São Paulo,* June 20, 1986; *Jornal da Tarde,* June 20, 1986; and *Exame,* June 11, 1986.

110. This account of strikes in 1985–86 is based on *Latin America Weekly Report, Latin America Regional Reports: Brazil,* and *Veja.* For a revealing analysis of the rigid reaction of the employers to the metalworkers' strike, see Eli Diniz, "O empresariado e o momento político: entre a nostalgia do passado e o temor do future," *Cadernos de Conjuntura* (Rio de Janeiro: IUPERJ), No. 1 (October 1985), 7–13.

111. The GM plant contretemps is reported in detail in *Veja,* May 8, 1985, pp. 38–39. A well-known economist sympathetic to the strikers argued that the GM workers had fallen into a "trap laid by management" designed to force the entry of police and thereby discredit the union. Paul Singer, "GM: a guerra de classes," *Lua Nova,* II, No. 3 (October/December 1985), 90–92.

112. Of the person days lost in 1985 strikes, 72 percent were by public employees. Ministério do Trabalho, "Mercado do Trabalho."

113. Labor ministry data indicate that in 1985 average real wage rates for industry rose 7.5 percent for Brazil and 15 percent for the state of São Paulo. *Ibid.*

114. A sampling of the debates on this and other features of the Plano Cruzado may be found in *Revista de Economia Política,* VI, No. 3 (July–September, 1986), 124–51. The average worker could not have found it easy to calculate how the new law would affect his or her wage. A dissident São Paulo metal-workers faction circulated a flyer attacking the union leadership's acceptance of an agreement with the employers. The flyer took the worker through no less than twelve arithmetical steps in showing how the new wage *should* have been calculated. On a national basis the impact of strikes was down in April 1986 over the same month in 1985. *Correio Braziliense,* June 15, 1986. The metalworkers, however, succeeded in gaining real wage increases. In some places, such as São Bernardo do Campo, they also suffered large-scale firings, undoubtedly meant to clean out union militants and also to reduce the number of employees eligible for the full cost of living increase when the next inflation adjustment came around. *O Estado de São Paulo,* June 13, 1986; *O Jornal do Brasil,* July 27, 1986.

115. For details on each case, see the earlier chapters on the Costa e Silva and Figueiredo presidencies.

116. The text of Pazzianotto's draft was published in the *Folha de São Paulo,* May 26, 1985. The final proposal was Projeto de Lei No. 8,059 (1986). The differ-ences in the two versions were analyzed in a leading São Paulo daily's edito-rial, which concluded that the new draft "is close to being the viable document on this subject," *Folha de São Paulo,* July 30, 1986.

117. The origins of this military animus toward unions is traced in Thomas E. Skidmore, "Workers and Soldiers: Urban Labor Movements and Elite Re-sponses in Twentieth-Century Latin America," in Virginia Bernhard, ed., *Elites, Masses, and Modernization in Latin America, 1850–1930* (Austin: Uni-versity of Texas Press, 1979), 79–126.

118. The often ferocious attacks by business spokesmen on the 1985 strike-law proposal are described in Diniz, "O empresariado e o momento politico," 13–30.

119. For a review of such objections, see Nair Heloisa Bicalho de Sousa, "Negociações coletivas e direito de greve: uma discussão sobre a mudança das relações trabalhistas no Brasil," paper presented at the IX Encontro Annual da ANPOCS: Grupo de Trabalho, Classe Operária e Sindicalismo (June 1985).

120. The government bill is analyzed in *Veja*, July 30, 1986, pp. 44–46, and *Senhor*, June 24, 1986, pp. 37–39. The reader should note that this was a complicated proposal, of which only a few aspects are discussed here.

121. Meanwhile, the Affonso Arinos Commission drafting the proposal for a new constitution decided to grant workers an unrestricted right to strike, i.e., including workers in the "essential sectors." *Folha de São Paulo*, June 11, 1986. The editorial writers of Rio's leading conservative daily quickly denounced the Commission's decision. *O Globo*, June 13, 1986.

122. *Veja*, July 30, 1986, pp. 45–46; *Isto É*, July 23, 1986, pp. 22–23.

123. *Folha de São Paulo*, June 16, 1986.

124. A University of São Paulo study (commissioned by the labor ministry) of labor-management agreements (*dissídios coletivos*) for the first half of 1985 showed that workers and management were turning increasingly away from the labor court system and to direct negotiation, especially on the plant level. During June in Minas Gerais, for example, 57 of 58 disputes were resolved by collective bargaining. Ministério de Trabalho/Fundação Instituto de Pesquisas Econômicas, *Boletim Bimensal de Acompanhamento dos Acordos, Convenções e Dissídios Coletivos de Trabalho nos Estados de São Paulo, Rio de Janeiro e Minas Gerais*, Ano 4, No. 4 (July–August, 1985).

125. The survey was conducted by the American Chamber of São Paulo and reported in *Latin American Daily Post*, September 7, 1985 (special supplement), 8.

126. For an overview of factory councils written during the Figueiredo presidency, see Ricardo C. Antunes and Arnalso Nogueira, *O que são comissões de fábrica* (São Paulo: Brasiliense, 1981). For the views of a longtime union activist who urged that the factory councils take a radical line, see José Ibrahim, *Comissões de fábrica* (São Paulo: Global, 1986).

127. Information supplied by Roque Aparecido da Silva of CEDEC in São Paulo, June 18, 1986. There was also a spread of professional "human relations" programs and staff on the part of management. For an example of their thinking, see Luiz Antônio Ciocchi, "Vamos subir o nivel?," in *Exame*, June 11, 1986, p. 82. A leading example of a joint labor–management committee—created after great pressure from the workers—is the Ford plant in São Paulo, described in José Carlos Aguiar Brito, *A Tomada da Ford: o nascimento de um sindicato livre* (Petrópolis: Vozes, 1983).

128. Interview with Edmar Bacha, *Jornal do Brasil*, June 8, 1986.

129. Special Report on agrarian reform in *Brazil Watch*, III, No. 12 (June 9–23, 1985), 10–17. For an excellent bibliographical overview of research on the Brazilian rural sector, see José Cesar Gnaccarini and Margarida Maria Moura, "Estrutura agrária brasileira: permanência e diversificação de um debate," *BIB: Boletim Informativo e Bibliográfico de Ciências Sociais* (Rio de Janeiro), No. 15 (1983), 5–52. For an example of recent debates on the transition from

small holders to wage laborers, see David Goodman, Bernardo Sorj, and John Wilkinson, "Agro-industry, State Policy, and Rural Social Structures: Recent Analyses of Proletarianisation in Brazilian Agriculture," in B. Munslow and H. Finch, eds., *Proletarianisation in the Third World* (London: Croom Helm, 1984), 189–215.

130. For an analysis of the land reform policy of Castelo Branco, as well as that of João Goulart and of all the military governments from 1964 to 1975, see Marta Cehelsky, *Land Reform in Brazil: The Management of Social Change* (Boulder: Westview Press, 1979). Cehelsky concluded: "The meager evidence of land reform available after fifteen years of a new agrarian policy in Brazil affirms the overwhelming capitalist/developmental bias of the effort and the limited benefits yielded to the nation's poor" (p. 223). The Figueiredo government, unlike its military predecessors, attempted an ambitious land redistribution. The government claimed to have delivered land titles to 800,000 persons, although critics scoffed at these figures. *Veja,* May 28, 1986, p. 20. A leading critic was Carlos Minc, *A reconquista da terra: lutas no campo e reforma agrária* (Rio de Janeiro: Zahara 1985), 7–12. From 1968 to 1981 the World Bank undertook ten rural development projects in Brazil, and found that political and bureaucratic pressures almost invariably frustrated the Bank's goals for land allocation and even for land titling. Robert L. Ayres, *Banking on the Poor: The World Bank and World Poverty* (Cambridge, Mass.: MIT Press, 1983), 116–18.

131. For an authoritative analysis of government policy, see *Brazil: A Review of Agricultural Policies* (Washington: World Bank, 1982).

132. *Veja,* September 18, 1985. There was no lack of penetrating research and writing on the subject of food policy. See, for example, Fernando Homem de Melo, "A agricultura nos anos 80: perspectiva e conflitos entre objetivos de política," *Estudos Econômicos,* X, No. 2 (1980), 57–101; and the same author's "A necessidade de uma política alimentar diferenciada no Brasil," *Estudos Econômicos,* XV, No. 3 (1985), 361–85. In the early 1980s the production per capita of rice, manioc, beans, and corn was either stagnant or declining. That meant food prices were rising faster than wages most of the time, with the obvious nutritional consequences. Jaguaribe, *Brasil, 2000,* 157. For a retrospective on how the Sarney government's 1985 policies affected agriculture, see Guilherme C. Delgado, "A política econômica e a questão agrícola," *Conjuntura Econômica,* XL, No. 2 (February 1986), 165–70. The author warned that a sizable repressed demand for foodstuffs would be released as the undernourished and unemployed began to benefit from the economic recovery and from more democratic government policies.

133. The rural sector's lag in improving on such basic indicators as education, safe water systems, housing, medical care, etc., is well documented in *Brazil: Human Resources Special Report* (Washington: World Bank, 1979).

134. For detail on the military's repression in the Northeast in 1964, see Chapter II.

135. For an overview of the Church's growing involvement in the agrarian question after 1964, and especially after 1970, see Mainwaring, *The Catholic Church and Politics in Brazil,* 84–94 and 158–64. For greater detail, see Vanilda Paiva, ed., *Igreja e questão agrária* (São Paulo: Edições Loyola, 1985). A typical attack from the right came from Armando Falcão, former justice minister in the Geisel government, who denounced INCRA as "a nest of Marxist bureaucrats." He accused the "Marxist minority within the Church"

of creating "an industry of conflict" in the countryside. *Folha de São Paulo,* June 1, 1986. The PT was also active in producing a rationale for radical change in the rural sector. See, for example, Amilton Sinatora, et al., *Política agrária* (Pôrto Alegre: Mercado Aberto/Fundação Wilson Pinheiro, 1985).

136. The 1982–85 data are from Movimento dos Trabalhadores Rurais sem Terra, *Assassinatos no campo: crime e impunidade, 1964–1985* (São Paulo: Movimento dos Trabalhadores Rurais sem Terra, 1986), 213. The data do not always make clear the role of those assassinated. The 1986 data are from *Isto É,* June 4, 1986, p. 21.

137. The *Estatuto da Terra* of 1964 established the legal basis for land reform. Subsequent governments had only to issue their plan of implementation. That greatly simplified the political job for the Sarney government.

138. *Veja,* May 29, 1985, pp. 114–17; *Veja,* June 19, 1985, pp. 20–26; *Latin America Weekly Report,* June 7, 1985; *Latin America Regional Reports Brazil,* July 5, 1985. Press accounts of the quantitative details of government land reform plans varied widely. This may in part have been due to confusion between long-term and short-term goals, both in terms of land to be expropriated and families to be settled. I am grateful to Steven E. Sanderson for access to his valuable unpublished paper (June 1986), "Brazilian Agrarian Reform Politics in the New Republic."

139. For an overview of evidence on productivity after land reforms in the non-socialist world, see Ian M.D. Little, *Economic Development: Theory, Policy, and International Relations* (New York: Basic Books, 1982), 171–75.

140. For a succinct overview of the factors behind the Sarney government's agrarian reform proposals, see Sanderson, "Brazilian Agrarian Reform Politics," 9. Several of these objectives can be traced back to the Castelo Branco government's agrarian policy. Increasing the rural middle class was emphasized in Castelo Branco, *Discursos: 1964,* p. 53, and increased productivity was stressed Castelo Branco, *Entrevistas: 1964–65,* p. 26.

141. *Brazil Watch,* III, No. 12, concluded on a pessimistic note: "Large landowners continue to wield an inordinate amount of power in Brazilian politics. Without an equally powerful base of political support in government or the legislature, and in the absence of a broad-based popular political consensus, it is unlikely that a comprehensive agrarian reform will occur in Brazil in the near future." Sanderson reaches a similar conclusion: "Given the current political climate and leadership, one cannot identify the mass political forces able to effectively demand a thoroughgoing reform," Sanderson, "Brazilian Agrarian Reform Politics," 37.

142. For examples of the extensive journalistic coverage of the Church's involvement in land conflicts, see "Agentes da CPT, os próximos a morrer," *O Estado de São Paulo,* June 1, 1986; "Igreja e fazendeiros, a guerra santa no Maranhão," *Jornal do Brasil,* June 1, 1986; "Por trás da luta do posseiro, a Pastoral da Terra," *O Globo,* June 15, 1986; "A terra assassina," *Afinal,* May 20, 1986; and "A vez de padre Josimo," *Veja,* May 21, 1986.

143. The trip received notable coverage in the U.S. press. See, for example, the stories in the *New York Times* for July 7 and 11, 1986.

144. The expropriations were reported in *Jornal do Brasil,* June 24, 1986. A *Jornal do Brasil* journalist explained that Agrarian Reform Minister Dante de Oliveira was pursuing the "possible," in contrast to his predecessor, Nelson Ribeiro, whose ambitious plans were vetoed at the Planalto: "The govern-

ment's commitment now is to carry out emergency settlements . . . from which it can gain the maximum political advantage." *Ibid.* Sarney's promise to meet the 1986 target of giving land to 150,000 families was given in an electoral primer distributed to all Democratic Alliance candidates in the November 1986 elections. *Jornal do Brasil,* June 13, 1986. For stories on alleged government ineptitude and hesitation in carrying out its program, see "O recuo no campo," *Veja,* May 28, 1986, and "Bagunça no campo," *Veja,* July 9, 1986.

145. For an example of an optimistic estimate seventeen years earlier on how land redistribution might have affected production, see William R. Cline, "Prediction of a Land Reform's Effect on Agricultural Production: The Brazilian Case" (Princeton: Woodrow Wilson School, Princeton University, Discussion Paper No. 9, May 1969).

146. We saw earlier in Chapter V on the Médici presidency how Brazilian scholars have documented the history of police abuse of ordinary suspects. In recent years the press had given wide coverage to allegations of such torture. The following are only a sample of many such stories: "O dossiê da tortura," *Contato* (Mato Grosso), March 5, 1986, which summarized press accounts about 80 cases in greater Cuiabá in 1984–85; "A escalada da violência policial no Brasil em 1974," *O Estado de São Paulo,* August 25, 1974, which listed 23 cases from around Brazil; "Cadeia gaúcha que era usada para tortura não acolherá mais menores," *Jornal do Brasil,* June 24, 1986; and frequent accounts of individual cases, such as in *Veja,* February 6 and April 3, 1985, and *Isto É,* March 12, 1986.

147. Mexican President Miguel de la Madrid, for example, announced in early 1986 a major effort to eliminate torture, which had become routine on the part of the attorney general's agents. William Stockton, "Mexico Trying to Halt Police Torture," *New York Times,* February 2, 1987.

148. This differential quality of Brazilian citizenship has been explored in Roberto da Matta, *A casa e a rua* (São Paulo: Brasiliense, 1985), 55–80; and *Carnavais, malandros, e heróis* (Rio de Janeiro: Zahar, 1979), 139–93. I am grateful to Professor da Matta for information on the labyrinthine spread of laws granting exemption from ordinary incarceration.

149. For an example of this commission's approach, see Arquidiocese de São Paulo (Comissão Arquidiocesana de Pastoral dos Direitos Humanos e Marginalizados de São Paulo), *Fraternidade vence a violência* (São Paulo, 1983), which is a handbook for study groups.

150. This gruesome practice has been studied in Maria Victória Benevides, "Linchamentos: violência e 'justiça' popular." For an interesting panel discussion of violence held in the 1970s, see "Reporteres do crime," *Folhetim (Folha de São Paulo),* December 11, 1977. For a later example, see "Violência mata mais de 600 por mês em São Paulo," *Folha de São Paulo,* June 5, 1983. These examples could be multiplied many times over.

151. This public anger reinforced the views of the more cynical police. One São Paulo police chief told a researcher in 1981: "The way we work (confession by beating) is used worldwide and there isn't any other way. We've already tried all the alternatives and they don't work." Maria Victória Benevides, *Violência, povo e polícia: violência urbana no noticiário de imprensa* (São Paulo: Brasiliense, 1983), 76. A like-minded São Paulo police chief told reporters in the late 1970s: "No one likes the police anywhere in the world, but we're

needed to guarantee society. We're like the garbagemen—nobody likes garbagemen but they need their services. Police are the garbagemen of society. And I like my work." He ended thus: "Look, if you're going to publish a list of torturers, don't leave out my name, because that could hurt my career." Fon, *Tortura*, 70.

152. *Folha de São Paulo,* June 3 and 14, 1986.
153. The São Paulo justice secretary's struggles with the penal system got extensive press coverage, as in *O Estado de São Paulo,* June 22 and 25, 1986, and *Folha de São Paulo,* June 23 and 24, 1986. For the account of a previous São Paulo secretary of justice's attempt to eliminate torture of ordinary suspects in São Paulo, see the interview with Octavio Gonzaga Júnior in *Veja,* August 29, 1979, pp. 3–6. State's Attorney Helio Bicudo, who had courageously prosecuted the notorious detective-torturer Sérgio Fleury, confessed that "in São Paulo an opposition government [of Franco Montoro] couldn't reduce police violence, which increased, and in 1984 more than four hundred persons were killed by police units," Helio Bicudo, "Violência, criminalidade e o nosso sistema de justiça criminal," *Revista OAB-RJ,* No. 22 (July 1985), 134. The state of Rio de Janeiro, on the other hand, saw a decline in the incidence of police violence in 1983–84, due to efforts of the Brizola government. *Country Reports on Human Rights Practices for 1985: Report Submitted to the Committee on Foreign Affairs, House of Representatives, and the Committee on Foreign Relations, U.S. Senate* (Washington: U.S. Government Printing Office, 1986), 440. The steady militarization of the police since 1968 also made more difficult any reforms, since the army was necessarily involved in policy changes. This issue is stressed in "O inimigo é o povo ou a polícia?" *Lua Nova,* II, No. 3 (October–December 1985), 38–45.

INDEX